PATRICK WHITE
LETTERS

SPOONER.

PATRICK WHITE
LETTERS

Edited by David Marr

The University of Chicago Press

Published by arrangement with Random House, Australia

The University of Chicago Press, Chicago 60637

Copyright © David Marr and the Estate of Patrick White 1994

All rights reserved. Originally published in Australia in 1994
University of Chicago Press Edition 1996
Printed in the United States of America
02 01 00 99 98 97 96   6 5 4 3 2 1
ISBN 0-226-89503-3 (pbk.)

Library of Congress Cataloging-in-Publication Data

White, Patrick, 1912–
    [Correspondence]
    Letters / Patrick White : edited by David Marr.
      p. cm.
    Includes bibliographical references and index.
    1. White, Patrick 1912–   —Correspondence. 2. Novelists,
Australian—20th century—Correspondence. I. Marr, David.
II. Title.
PR9619.3.W5Z48   1996
823—dc20
[B]   95-53185
                                            CIP

⊗ The paper used in this publication meets the minimum requirements of
the American National Standard for Information Sciences—Permanence of
Paper for Printed Library Materials, ANSI Z39.48-1984.

To
Peggy Garland
who showed me the first bundle
and said,
'You may be interested.'

SECOND LADY: Are there no letters? There's nothink I like better than a read of a good letter. Look and see, Mrs Goosgog, if you can't find me a letter. I'm inclined to feel melancholy at this hour of night.

The Ham Funeral

Contents

Note

THESE ARE the letters of a great artist speaking his mind, a wise man who could be stubbornly wrong. Occasionally I have given other versions of events, reported dissenting views and corrected facts, but I have not tried to adjudicate all the rows or balance every one of White's sharp but sometimes partial judgements. My aim in editing the letters is to allow the man to speak, as much as possible, for himself.

I have made no changes to White's grammar and punctuation and I have preserved most of his eccentricities, but I felt it necessary to standardise the often confusing ways he cites the names of books, ships, films, plays, and so on, just as I have reduced to order his erratic transliterations of Greek placenames.

For this book to sustain a narrative of White's life and opinions I have made cuts to most of the 600 or so letters here. So . . . indicates a cut made by me, and – – for White's own rare use of . . . If cuts have been made to the top of a letter there is no salutation, and if to the bottom there is no signature.

The number of White's correspondents is large and to help make sense of this crowd there is a guide beginning on p.632, 'The Cast of Correspondents'.

D.E.M.
6 August 1994

Finding his Feet

May 1912 – October 1939

ALMOST AS SOON AS he could hold a pencil Patrick White was writing letters. He scrawled them at his mother's direction to Whites and Withycombes in the bush and cousins far away in England. The habit of keeping in touch by letter, of asking and thanking in writing, was drummed into the little boy early and stayed with him for life. He was only six when he wrote,

LULWORTH, DECEMBER 1918
TO FATHER XMAS
Dear Father Xmas.
Will yoy please bring me
a pistol, a mouth organ
a violin
a butterfly net
Robinson Cruso
History of Australia
Some marbles.
a little mouse what runs
across the room
I hope you do not
think I am too greedy
but I want the
things badly
    your loving
    Paddy.

HE WAS THE CHILD of a famous family in Australia. For nearly a century, the Whites had amassed fine grazing land in New South Wales. They survived droughts, rode booms and prospered in busts. By the end of the First World War the family was at the height of its wealth and influence. The boy's father Victor – known to everyone as Dick – was one of four brothers in partnership at Belltrees, over 100,000 acres of gentle country on the upper reaches of the Hunter River. After twenty years in the valley

Dick left to marry his cousin Ruth Withycombe and they spent a long honeymoon in Europe. Their son, Patrick Victor Martindale White, was born in London in an apartment overlooking Hyde Park on 28 May 1912.

The family returned a few months later and settled in Sydney. It was Ruth's idea to stay in town for she was not cut to the pattern of plain White wives, happy to spend the rest of their days in the bush. Ruth was determined not to be bored. She set up an elegant house overlooking Rushcutters Bay. Here at Lulworth the boy's sister Suzanne was born in 1915. With her came a new nurse, Lizzie Clark, a tiny, no-nonsense woman not quite five feet tall, with sharp eyes and a tough Scots accent. She was determined her *bairns* would be good. The boy struggled all his life with the plain ideals Lizzie pitted against his mother's more opulent ambitions.

Ruth insisted Paddy aim high above the slovenly standards of Australia. He was forbidden to speak the larrikin drawl of the streets round Lulworth or the Dublin slang of his mother's kitchen. 'Nora Barnacle,' he later remarked, 'could have been one of the stream of Irish maids that flowed through our house.' He was taught the piano (a failure) and French conversation. He was drilled to lift his cap, shake hands and look adults in the eye. And at the age of four or five he was introduced to the art of writing letters. Ruth knew what weapons these could be in the social armoury of their class. Hers were good. Years later Manoly Lascaris read them as they arrived each week from London: 'She knew the language.'

The Whites' links with the bush were not severed. Dick disappeared every month to help his brothers for a few days at Belltrees. They all took for granted that Paddy would one day follow them onto the land, taking a share of their considerable acres. A great chunk of Belltrees was the boy's birthright and always part of his imagination.

EARLY 1919

TO THE FAIRIES

Dear Fairies would you give me a book I dont mind what kind it is can I have it on my birthday it is on the 28 of May. I hope you will have a nice danse to night. I expose you have tea on the toad stools at night. Do you live in the flowers. Would you please make it rain in the country soon it is very dry up there the sheep and cattle are dieing. And would make the influenza better I wish you would with love from

Paddy

AFTER FAMILY EXPEDITIONS TO Belltrees the boy wrote to thank his uncle Henry who for forty years ruled the place with a kind of genius. This remarkable man admired young Paddy who came to take after him in many ways, not least in choosing to deal with the world by post. Buried in the old man's immense correspondence with brothers and cousins, solicitors, bishops, aldermen, agents, trainers, book sellers, ornithologists and stamp collectors were scraps of praise for his clever nephew. 'A remarkably well written and expressed letter has come from Paddy . . .'

Asthma, the curse of both Whites and Withycombes, had been with the boy from birth. Mountain air was prescribed for his health when he was nine and the Whites bought a cottage at Mount Wilson, a hill station in wild country behind Sydney. Around a handful of English gardens on the summit of the mountain lay a wilderness of forests, deep ravines and waterfalls. This was paradise for the boy. His first piece published was a letter about the mountain written to 'The President of the League of Friendship' on the children's page of the Sydney *Sunday Times* in January 1922. White signed himself with the pseudonym 'Red Admiral' after his favourite butterfly. In spring he wrote again,

PUBLISHED 22.x.22
TO THE PRESIDENT OF THE LEAGUE OF FRIENDSHIP
This time I am going to tell you about a moonlight picnic at Mount Wilson. We started off at about 7 o'clock and walked for about a mile till we reached the picnicking spot. A fire was built and we cooked chops and sausages over the blaze. The waterfall nearby looked like silver in the moonlight, while the tree ferns made weird noises as they swayed to and fro in the breeze. The hanging vines glistened with the spray showered upon them from the waterfall, and the grass rustled as if a snake army was creeping along in its depths. We did not return from this beautiful picnic till quite late, and then I was very sorry to go.

RUTH WAVED THE RED Admiral letters like a flag above her boy's head. Here was evidence of genius: only ten and already published. However much he denied the truth in later life, cringing at the memory of his mother's enthusiasm, it was always Ruth's ambition that he would write.

For the sake of his lungs the boy was sent to school on the highlands south of Sydney. At Tudor House pupils were made to scratch a letter home every Sunday night. New boys were broken in by the headmaster who quizzed them gently on the doings of the week and drafted notes in pencil for them to copy in ink. The week was not over, not entirely lived, until some version of its small events had been written down: pony rides along the creek, eggs collected, rabbits trapped and cooked over fires in the bush. From Tudor House Paddy White wrote to both Ruth and Lizzie – 'my real mother,' he later called her – and continued writing for decades until senility claimed the women.

Ruth and Dick took the boy to England at the age of thirteen and left him there in boarding school. The next four years marked him for life. Cheltenham College fashioned his sexuality, set fast his grim view of the human race and made him, at least in his own eyes, a foreigner everywhere, part-English and part-Australian, never entirely at ease. Ruth's and Dick's last act before leaving London was to buy the boy a typewriter. Fifty years later he recalled, 'Somebody showed me roughly what to do behind the counter at Harrods.'[1] Now his letters home were a lifeline to the lost world of his childhood. With them he sent the sad, clever verse which Ruth had printed for the family in 1930, bound with a little silk ribbon and stamped *Thirteen Poems*.

In these lonely years, White found a few friends for life. Ronald Waterall was a flamboyant boy obsessed with the stage. Together they plotted revues, sent fan mail to actresses and haunted the West End on holidays. Later Waterall went into the theatre – taking the name Ronald Waters – but abandoned the stage after the war to become an actors' agent in London.

One holiday weekend in 1928 White met his three Withycombe cousins: Betty the bluestocking working at the Clarendon Press; Peggy the sculptor just back from Cape Town; and the youngest of the three sisters, Joyce the painter still training at the Slade. Of these Betty had the most immediate impact on White. She became both sister and mentor, the first person to take his intellectual education in hand. The boy became her protégé, almost her possession. From the start there were difficulties in this demanding relationship.

The young man returned to Australia in early 1930 for the next stage of his education. He was to work as a jackeroo, a kind of gentleman apprentice-grazier, to see if he was suited for life on the land. Once that was settled one way or another he would return to England to take a degree at Cambridge. He found himself in a bare valley on the edge of the Snowy Mountains. Here, by lamplight in a hut on the banks of the Murrumbidgee River he wrote his first (unpublished) novels. To help relieve the boredom of his existence in the bush Ronald Waters found

[1]PW to Frances Peck, 29.ix.74.

him a London pen friend: Jean Scott Rogers, another stagestruck young writer. They were to correspond for life.

BOLARO, 16.iii.31
TO JEAN SCOTT ROGERS
Dear Jean,
By your letter I feel sure that you are not the kind of person to object to my presumption in calling you by your Christian name. Even if you are – secretly – what's done can't be undone. But what kind of a person are you really? Are you a sport in a plaid skirt; or a Bohemian in spectacles and a Spanish hat; or a seductive siren with a willowy waist and magnetic eyes; or the taffeta ingénue; or the leafy nymph; or – but that could go on till the end of time. The next problem is: what are we going to talk about, for I'm sure you don't want to hear about sheep (neither do I, for that matter); and geographical situations bore you stiff; and weather charts finally exterminate. I suppose then, there's nothing left but your collaborator.[2] He's certainly an extraordinary person, the only one with whom I have ever been able to get on, and that, I think, because we are so rude to each other that we have to. Once in the dim and distant past, I collaborated with him myself. What a memory! It was a farcical comedy – always an apologetic appellation – and it rejoiced in the title of 'Amorous Wives.' Husbands, wives, friends, and lovers popped in and out of doors and hid behind curtains; you know the type? It generally has a four night run nowadays. Then there was 'The Madonna of the Forest' (by myself this time) a romantic comedy in four acts, though the fourth was never reached. The action took place in a castle in the forest with Isabel Jeans[3] traipsing up and down miles of staircase in search of true luv. I wonder if I shall ever finish a play, and have it produced, which is more to the point. Perhaps I shall be over to see the production of The play after all, as I may sail in August from this God-forsaken land, where everyone is gradually growing madder and madder. I am on the point of launching forth upon the subject of political science, but have no fear; I don't know enough about it, I'm much too unpractical for that. I like to plan highly impossible things and, well – if they don't come off there are always other highly impossible things to plan and think about. That there are so many new things to think about, so many new experiments to make, is the only thing which makes life possible. Sometimes I get fed up to the teeth here in the

[2]She was working with Waters on a still-born play called 'Snack Bar'.
[3](1892–1985), comedienne best remembered for her role in Vincente Minnelli's Gigi, 1958; PW was a fan for life.

country, where the type of Australian one encounters is the most uninspiring, unintelligent, deadening specimen to be found on earth. Although you will meet many charming people here, I detest the average Australian, who is little more than a cheap imitation of the American. There is quite a lot of amusement to be found in life in Sydney, but it is a rattling, jangling affair from morn till night. It makes one long for London, and the smooth, gliding feeling which it has. I haven't been to a show for ages, not a real show with professional West-End finish. The only serious work is done by amateur theatres where you can see O'Neill, Chekov, Strindberg, and other good stuff credibly acted. But they haven't the time, nor the money, nor the public, to do anything on a large scale. The professional stage is peopled by provincial companies in musical comedy and American farce, things which induce one to stay at home. And of course there are the talkies! Sumptuous cinemas of gilt and stucco; Spanish; Italian; Tudor; all nightmares of garishness and bad taste. I believe you read a lot, don't you? Lately I haven't had time as I am trying to scribble something myself, but usually I do nothing else. At odd moments during the week I have been struggling with the beginning of *The Fortunes of Richard Mahony* by Henry Handel Richardson. The dust-jacket is smothered in eulogies for which, so far, I can't find any reason. The descriptive passages are excellent but the characters and dialogue as crude as can be. You must read *Buddenbrooks* by Thomas Mann, if you haven't, and some Katherine Mansfield, about whom I can't say enough. Before I develop into a library list, pure and simple, I think I shall stop, and wish you all the usual salutary things. Hurry up and finish the play. If I can't see it, I shall itch to read the notices.

Yours sincerely,
Paddy White.

THE DEPRESSION HAD LEFT the Whites unexpectedly short of cash and the young man had to wait another year to make good his escape to Cambridge. After Bolaro he jackerooed briefly for his aunt and uncle, Clem and Mag Withycombe, at Walgett on the edge of the desert. Then he retreated to Mount Wilson to spend a hard winter writing a third novel, Finding Heaven, which was packed in his trunk when the *Niagara* sailed from Sydney with him on board in August 1932. He expected never to return.

At Cambridge he studied French and German, soon abandoning the lectures to read his own way through the syllabus. To perfect his German, he went often to Hannover where he found a home in the Holzgraben flat of the Oertel family. He was secretly writing poetry which again went home to his proud mother. Two poems, 'The Ploughman' and 'Meeting Again', he submitted to the *London Mercury*.

KING'S COLLEGE, 13.v.34
TO JEAN SCOTT ROGERS
May I accept the invitation? But I tell you both beforehand that I am very bad at parties, so that you must know what to expect if I venture to appear. At the moment I am suffering last-week tortures before my German exam, which starts on the 22nd and lasts two days. I go on revising and revising and as a result am about as bright as a shell-piece under a glass bell. But I expect, and hope that getting the exam over will clear the air. The other day I had a very reassuring surprise: in shape of the proof of two poems I had sent to the *London Mercury* and which I had long believed

PATRICK WHITE

to be in their waste-paper basket as I had heard nothing more. If they print them, I suppose they will appear in the next number, though I feel that something <u>must</u> go wrong in between and that they will decide to cut them out at the last moment. But at least I have never got so far as seeing the proof before – and it is very exciting.

THEIR PUBLICATION IN JUNE 1934 encouraged Ruth and Dick in an expensive scheme to promote their son's work in Sydney. They became principal shareholders in the local publishing house of P. R. (Inky) Stephensen. The deal seems to have been that Stephensen would publish a volume of Patrick White's poetry, and perhaps the novel Finding

Heaven which the author had tried and failed to have published in England, in return for the Whites' investment of £300.

KING'S COLLEGE, 21.x.34
TO P. R. STEPHENSEN

As regards Finding Heaven, I have not looked at it for some time and so could not say definitely whether it is possible to revise the book. Perhaps you could give me some idea of what you consider its greatest weaknesses. But I am really uncertain whether I could bring myself to revise it after all this time. I wrote it in a frame of mind with which I cannot altogether sympathise to-day.

To return to the poems: would it be possible to place a few copies somewhere in London after their publication? I might be able to get a sale for these. And a few cards for circulation might be a help.

Hoping the new poems may be included and that you will give me a more detailed opinion of Finding Heaven –

Yours faithfully,
Patrick White.

STEPHENSEN'S AFFAIRS WERE IN chaos. In early 1935 he went into liquidation; Ruth and Dick found a printer to finish the job and *The Ploughman and Other Poems* appeared a few months later. It was reviewed by the Sydney press with more goodwill than enthusiasm.

The Whites now gathered in London to settle the question of their son's career. Patrick – for he had decided he was no longer Paddy – wanted to stay in London rather than return to take up his Belltrees inheritance. Ruth and Dick acquiesced; Dick promised an allowance of £400 a year and their son settled down in a couple of rooms in Ebury Street to become a West End playwright.

After a barren year writing plays no managements wanted, White met the Australian painter Roy de Maistre who became his lover and mentor. The painter loathed the theatre and encouraged the young man to rework one of his jackaroo novels. This became *Happy Valley*, set in the harsh landscape of Bolaro where White had worked five years before. Escape is the common dream of most of the valley's inhabitants: adulterers, asthmatics, graziers (in the Furlows of Glen Marsh, White produced the first and perhaps best portrait of his parents), stockmen and Chinese. A murder brings the cast to its senses; some make an escape, but it is not to freedom. The prose was adventurous: 'I was still drunk with the techniques of writing . . . and had gone up that cul de sac the stream of consciousness.'[4]

In the summer of 1937 White took the manuscript to the resort of St Jean-de-Luz on the Atlantic coast of France. There he met and began an affair with a Spanish diplomat, José Ruiz de Arana y Bauer, Viscount Mamblas – known as Pepe Mamblas. The diplomat, a small man with perfect manners who was remembered for beautiful dinners and his devotion to the Ballet Russe, had served in London in the 1920s. He adored royalty. When Mamblas met White he was 44, living in Biarritz and making forays into Spain on business for Franco. White returned to London at the end of summer.

91 EBURY STREET, 2.xii.37
TO PEPE MAMBLAS
My dearest Pepe,
It was very sweet of you to send me the Rilke letters, which I shall enjoy reading again. For I did read them some time ago, in German – when I was beginning that language, and so I missed a great deal.

You sounded depressed, and I can understand it. But surely, the way things are turning, it can't go on for many more months?[5]

I have been in a state of turmoil myself the last couple of days. A cable came yesterday morning to say that my father had just died. Even though he has had a lot of illness lately one was not quite prepared for it. And since that I have been trying to readjust myself to this new situation and am feeling very tired and restless. I find I have the greatest difficulty in making myself sit down in one place for more than half-an-hour on end, which is an unusual state of affairs for me.

I think it would be much easier if I could feel what I ought to, and what other people are expecting me to feel. You are so lucky there, Pepe, with your own family. But now more than ever I realise what little connexion there always was between my father and me.

I am also faced with the problem of whether to go out to Australia or not. If my mother wants me I suppose I shall have to. And then there will also be business to attend to. But I do feel that to leave this side of the world just as I am getting my toe inside the door, would be to throw up all the progress made in the last two years. However, I shall not be able to receive a letter from my mother for another fortnight and needn't think about taking definite steps until I see how the land lies. Anyway, I

[4]To Keith Michell, 10.vii.57.
[5]The Civil War.

expect she and my sister will come over here soon for a trip, and perhaps to stay permanently.

I had a very good burst of literary energy at the beginning of the week, which I fear has waned before it should have, though I managed to finish a short story, with which I am still pleased before all this started to happen. It's a pity, because I had a couple of others planned out and was going to start on them right away. Now I don't know when I shall. One of them seems to have built itself round your descriptions of Percy – of course nothing like – these things never are – but he acts as a starting point. I want to make this a portrait of a rather awful old Edwardian who has spent his life beautifully (according to his own standards) and whose soul is Stopped and Bought in sordid circumstances in the middle of Brompton Road.[6]

I can't write you any more to-night. It seems such a long time since I saw you, and if I go out to Australia, when will it be again?!! That is too vast to bear thinking about.

Much love,

P.

91 EBURY STREET, 4.i.38

TO PEPE MAMBLAS

This New Year's Eve I decided to go off by myself and see some London Life. I fear it wasn't more than a depressing evening, but I suppose I asked for that by drinking too much draught beer in Charlotte Street. Everyone else appeared to be doing the same. There were bursting faces everywhere, and lots of mechanical music, and singing, and embracing. But I couldn't get rid of the impression that I was looking at it all through the wrong end of the telescope. In Shaftesbury Avenue an all-in wrestler tacked himself on and took a lot of getting rid of. Finally I lost him in a seething Piccadilly Circus, with everyone shouting, clambering on the roofs of taxis and buses, and even lifting up cars and carrying them along bodily. I got home intact and very sleepy but with my head in such a whirl that I might still have been in the thick of things.

The Spanish is going well and I can read with a lot of pleasure. At the moment I am reading the *Novelas Ejemplares* of Cervantes, and I manage to follow the general trend of things without any difficulty. But poetry needs a bit of working out – I should not have started *La Vida es Sueño*,[7] for instance, so soon. But you might suggest some modern prose

---

[6]If written, now lost.
[7]*Life is a Dream*, 1632, Pedro Calderón de la Barca.

some time. I am quite able to tackle that, and I find the only way I can get hold of a language is by reading and reading until it fills itself in.

Well, I have so many Christmas letters – you know the sort of thing – so I must leave you. You must be excited about the turning of the tables at Teruel.[8] Perhaps that is an omen for the year.

Much love,

P.

HE WAS ALSO WRITING revue sketches. 'Peter Plover's Party', a monologue for a chatterbox in the manner of Ronald Waters, was bought by the Shakespearian critic and director of revue Herbert Farjeon for his show *Nine Sharp* at the Little Theatre.

91 EBURY STREET, 27.i.38
TO PEPE MAMBLAS
My dear Pepe,
It was good to get your last letter and hear that you were well, but I don't like the idea of your plunging into all those air-raids. Is it Salamanca this time? I hope you'll let me know you're safe and sound again.

I am enclosing two cuttings about *Nine Sharp*! There are lots of others equally good – in fact, there have been no bad ones – but such is my vanity, I send the two in which my own sketch is mentioned. Though even here it is really attributed to Farjeon!

It was one of the most exciting evenings I have spent. A couple of nights before I had been to the dress rehearsals at which most things that could go wrong, did. My sketch was done so shockingly that I almost sank under the seat with shame and the thought of having to face it with an audience was almost too much. I spent a miserable couple of days, not helped at all by my developing a violent cold. On the night I arrived at the theatre with my nose hanging on by a couple of shreds of red flesh and feeling as if I had dressed for a wake. But the moment I entered the theatre I knew this was going to be an evening, and it was – everything went with a swing – it is the most elegant revue I have seen, and I am sure it will be the talk of the town.[9] (I feel I can speak like this because after all I only had a very small finger in the pie.) And even if it doesn't make me *Alguien*, or even *Quelqu'un*[10] I am a little bit farther on the way.

[8]Franco's forces had begun the bloody counter-attack that led to the reoccupation of the city after two months' fighting.
[9]The revue was a famous success: it made Hermione Baddeley's reputation and ran for over 400 performances.
[10]Someone, or even someone . . .

If only you'd been there. But I hope we shall be able to share some much more important triumphs later on.

I have just let myself be run into taking another flat. Some time ago, Roy de Maistre did up a house in Eccleston Street (just round the corner) and has been trying to let off the top part as flats. He has a studio himself on the ground floor at the back, the front ground floor has been let to a florist (very handy when visitors come), there is to be an office on the first floor, and now I propose to take the two top ones.

I shudder in the middle of the night when I think of the money I shall have to spend. But *tant pis*,[11] it is going to look nice even if it takes me into the bankruptcy court[12] . . .

I leave you now for the gas man. Until next time, my dear.

Love,

Patrick.

13 Eccleston Street, 16.ii.38

TO PEPE MAMBLAS

I moved in last Thursday or Friday; already I forget; anyway the workmen had not really finished – nor have they now, for that matter, one man comes and bangs in a nail, goes away, and twenty-four hours pass before I have persuaded another man to carry on with the good work. I still have a funny little woman, rather like George's Alice,[13] crouching on the stairs sewing at the carpets.

The sitting room is going to be charming. The brown-pink carpet and the bright yellow curtains are a great success. You will have to see them before they are dirty. I am afraid the coal stove, which nevertheless is a great joy, will very quickly do for them . . .

I have been doing sums in my head all the morning, for my going to St. Jean-de-Luz is going to depend on the state of my bank balance. I don't know that I could very well slip off with an overdraft unpaid and a large bill at one of the shops. All this may sound very unsophisticated, but it is the first time I have launched out in this particular way and I don't know what one does in the circumstances. Anyway, if you are going to disappear over the Spanish frontier and stay there for some time, I would have to make the effort to see you – somehow.

I went to the revue again the other night. They nearly always have

[11]No matter.

[12]Unlikely: Dick had left him £10,000.

[13]George was Mamblas' friend, the graphic artist George Plank, and Alice was Alice Smith of Philadelphia whom Plank liked to pretend was his sister.

a full house now, and lots of people go regularly and laugh before the joke comes – irritating though it will help to keep the show on. I am sending you a copy of *Punch* in which there is quite a good notice of the revue in general – and my sketch comes in for a little praise.[14] There is something in the air about a wireless revue – about which I believe I am going to be approached.

You finish up your letter with such a torrent of questions that I hardly know how to cope with them. Money has not yet come my way, except for the little weekly dribble from the revue. My inheritance seems to be disappearing in death duties. People who took no notice before are beginning to consider me, a state of affairs which makes me see how difficult it would be to recognise genuine friendship if one achieved success. But it does not look as if I shall have to worry seriously about that for some time.

I met a very pleasant pianist called Shepherd Munn a few weeks ago and have been seeing him on and off. Otherwise no new acquaintances – you know I don't make them easily.

I must go now and cook my lunch on my very handsome new black-and-white gas stove. I wish you were here to share my meal! But perhaps we shall be doing that soon somewhere in the south.

13 ECCLESTON STREET, 17.iii.38

TO PEPE MAMBLAS

My dear Pepe,

If there is any truth in the news one reads in the papers, the Spanish war looks as if it will soon be at an end. I sincerely hope for your sake that it is true. Otherwise the situation looks very black indeed. I fear <u>we</u> only begin where you are leaving off. One feels a wave of hysteria rising everywhere, as if people are going to <u>think</u> themselves into a European War even if there is a possibility of avoiding one. I am moving in a fog myself. For as you know, I have no head for international, or indeed any variety of politics – one is either born with it or one isn't. How do you think things will develop yourself?

Last week-end was particularly depressing. I went up to Trafalgar Square where of course there was a large meeting in progress, organised by

---

[14]16 Feb. 1938, p.189: Cyril Ritchard 'is an excellent all-rounder. His best individual turn is as a tight-waisted young man at a smart cocktail party where, alone on the stage, he conjures up the dreariness, the buzz and the insincerity with a touch as deft as Miss Draper's.'

Gollancz and his satellites.[15] People stretched right back to the edge of the National Gallery. What interested me was that by squeezing my way to within about twenty yards of the speaker on the plinth I could catch about one word in his twenty, so that of all those hundreds of people standing there, no more than 5% can have caught anything intelligible. All the same, the passive enjoyment of the crowd was immense and no doubt it went home feeling that it had taken part in something momentous.

Again I have no entertaining news for you. There is so much going on outside that one's own small activities seem to have been damped down. I have put in a lot of time at work. And one evening I went to see a production of *The Three Sisters*.[16] It was the fourth time I had seen the play, so I begin to feel I am familiar with it. I don't know if you like Chekov? To me, seeing one of his plays, especially *The Cherry Orchard* and *The Three Sisters*, is like having every emotion I have ever experienced played out before me in one evening. It is usually a wearing experience, but there is a polish about this present production that keeps it all very detached. A good thing at the moment really, for I don't think one should go out of one's way to accumulate this particular kind of *nostalgie*.

The weather continues to be very lovely – mild and occasionally sunny. This week-end I am going up to Oxford. I suppose I should look forward to a change of scene, air, and all those other things, but I don't. For I feel that I shall have a week-end of my cousin Betty in one of her Brontë-esque moods. Not that I am not very fond of her. But she is inclined to take up that 'myself-at-war-with-the-universe' attitude and to think that no one else can ever be affected in the same way. In the long run it is very trying.

Look after yourself, my dear. And let me know soon that you have some really satisfactory news of your country.

With much love,
Patrick.

13 Eccleston Street, 23.iii.38

TO PEPE MAMBLAS

I must say the bombardment of Barcelona was a horrible business, Pepe. I can't see that any end can justify such a means. For the first time in the

---

[15]Victor Gollancz (1893–1967), publisher and founder of the Left Book Club, a leading speaker at this rally of about 10,000 calling on Britain to support the League of Nations' efforts to end aggression in Europe.
[16]The famous production by Michel Saint-Denis with John Gielgud, Peggy Ashcroft, Angela Baddeley and Michael Redgrave.

whole war I think I have been really conscious of what it signifies – I suppose really the events of the last few weeks have brought us much closer to it – one sees what may be in store for all of us.[17]

They are starting to make appeals here for volunteers to train for the possibility of air-raids – people who will be ready to help the first-aid units, police, firemen etc. as a matter of course. I went along this afternoon and offered myself as a potential fireman! I have not yet heard what it will imply – whether the training will be merely theoretical, or whether one will have to run up ladders and uncoil hoses. Anyway, I am hoping there may be an opportunity for trying on that most decorative object: a fireman's helmet.[18]

I went up to Oxford for the week-end. It was very windy, but warm and sunny. We went for a couple of long walks and got quite burnt and red in the face. On one of the walks we discovered a lovely little Eighteenth Century parish church – very rare in England. This was a lovely little thing – Mozartian is the only word which can describe it – painted white with a blue and gilt clock face. Certainly not English. Near it there was a very peaceful red brick manor house with stone pilasters, which I must say I found myself coveting for a country seat.

This is a mixed, rather chaotic sort of letter, I'm afraid. But I can't help feeling mixed to-night – on the one hand this lovely gentle misty day, and coming home to tea and reading Cipion y Berganza,[19] which is so humane and balanced and civilised, and on the other hand, when one thinks, the other side of the wall just blackness.

IN APRIL WHITE RETURNED to St Jean-de-Luz and found to his distress that Mamblas considered their affair at an end. After a few miserable weeks travelling through the South of France, White returned to London. That summer the poet Geoffrey Grigson, a cousin by marriage, found a publisher for Happy Valley. The novel appeared to a great flurry of praise in early 1939. White decided to cross the Atlantic to seek a publisher in New York.

RMS AQUITANIA, 28.iii.39
TO JEAN SCOTT ROGERS
Dear Jean,
Thank you for your festive wire. It gave me quite a sense of importance

---

[17]The Germans had occupied Austria.
[18]For a time he was a fire-watcher, but the scare passed and he resigned out of boredom.
[19]From Cervantes' The Conversation of the Dogs.

in the face of such celebrities as Bunny Austin and Adrienne Allen. Bobbie Peel is also on board, with grandmother Lillie.[20] But most of these are in the First Class, while I prowl about our segregated end feeling decidedly Left.

The tourist is composed mainly of Jews – I should say quite 80% – off to their new Fatherland. But fortunately I am supported by two very charming people at my table, a New York girl, secretary to a lawyer, and a Connecticut engineer. We get together and decide we are misfits, which always helps build up a friendship . . .

Sorry you had to go early the evening of the party. I wanted you to meet my Australian journalist friend, Dorothy Jenner[21] (who, by the way, has given me a letter to Father Divine.)[22] The party developed quite well. The one misfortune was Hilda's getting drunk in the kitchen in the middle of it. I went down and told her to do something and she said: 'Shut up, you old cat'! Whereupon I had to sweep upstairs with my best Dinner-At-Eight technique.[23] I ended up at The Nest at 5 A.M. with Dorothy J., and John Willoughby.[24]

Only two more days of this Ghetto life and I shall be having to think up my impressions of the New York skyline. It is still an exciting and unbelievable thought.

AFTER A FEW FRUITLESS weeks in New York, White left to explore America by rail, heading south to New Orleans and through Texas to California. On his way east again he stopped in New Mexico where he met Spud Johnson. This ascetic figure mixed with the artists who had come to Taos in the wake of D. H. Lawrence. Johnson published a handset paper called the *Horsefly* and lived by literary odd jobs. A slim reputation as a poet rested on a single book, *Horizontal Yellow*, that appeared in 1935 in Santa Fe.

---

[20]Passengers: Henry (Bunny) Austin (1906–   ), tennis player and advocate of Moral Re-Armament; Adrienne Allen, actress and wife of Raymond Massey; Bobbie Peel was the son of the actress Beatrice Lillie (1898–1989) whom PW knew well for he had been having an affair with her pianist Sam Walsh. They planned to meet in America in late summer.

[21](1891–1985), later known as Andrea: nextdoor neighbour in childhood Sydney and companion for West End first nights, she gave PW useful publicity before they broke in the 1950s.

[22](c.1877–1965), born George Baker, short black founder of the Peace Mission Cult.

[23]To Hilda Richardson his servant he gave a copy of *Happy Valley* in February, 'with best wishes and thanks for many services admirably rendered'. The devoted Ruth Godbold in *Riders in the Chariot* owes most to Richardson.

[24]The Nest was a homosexuals' bar; Willoughby may have been a young diplomat.

White fell in love with Spud Johnson and New Mexico but, as so often happened in his life, he felt he must stick to his schedule: return to New York to push the novel, go up to Cape Cod to write for the rest of summer, then sail for London. Already he had in mind that he would return to America to live. So he left Johnson in Taos, spent a day in Santa Fe and caught the train for Chicago.

THE CALIFORNIA LTD, 26.vi.39
TO SPUD JOHNSON

To get away from literature, it is difficult not to be crude in words and say all the things I would like to say – to you and about you – but I think you have felt them as much as I have – so there is no need. The last few days have meant a great deal to me. I didn't realise how much till going away. We've got to see each other some more – I hope, some day. I'm sure we shall. Because I know I don't discover such a perfect complement at the end of the earth for nothing, just to throw it away again. I hope you are going to feel the same. If you don't, you can blame the plains of Kansas, which are going on ad infinitum!

HOTEL SUTTON, NEW YORK, 30.vi.39
TO JEAN SCOTT ROGERS

I spent ten of the most satisfactory days of my life in New Mexico. So satisfactory that I am thinking of dispersing all my worldly possessions and settling there in an adobe hovel. The desert has the most curious effect, though desert is hardly the right word. One immediately thinks of sand and the Sahara. Whereas New Mexico is all pink earth, grey sage-brush, blue mountains, some of them still streaked with snow.

I started off at Santa Fe, but was driven out of this after a couple of days by the arrival of Ronald Colman & Company, who took over the hotel, and settled down to film *The Light That Failed*, on the Rio Grande instead of the Nile. So I went on up to Taos, which is about seventy miles to the north, quite isolated (you have to reach it by stage), on a magnificent plateau surrounded by the Sangre de Cristos. Here I lapsed into a pair of blue jeans (which, when translated, means dungarees) and spent about a week riding the mesa on a hired horse, and talking to local celebrities. For I had a visit from Dorothy Brett,[25] who went out to Taos with the D. H. Lawrences, and she took me up to see Frieda, who still lives on the ranch

[25](1883–1977), painter and eccentric refugee from Bloomsbury.

that Mabel Dodge Luhan[26] gave to Lawrence, and all this led to various other interesting contacts, including a very charming poet, called Spud Johnson, who edits and prints the local weekly, and was for a time secretary to Lawrence ...

Perhaps my biggest excitement has been the Grand Canyon, which you just have to see – one can't give an impression in words. One day I spent wandering round the rim, and another riding to the bottom, altogether a fourteen mile trip, on a white mule, with an ex-cowpuncher called Slim Kite for guide. The guide would have made a very good stand-in for Gary Cooper – the same kind of figure, and also the same kind of humility. He was full of anecdotes, for as well as cow-punching, he has worked as a cook in a restaurant, a gold prospector in Arizona, and bouncer in a Nevada gambling saloon.

I seem to be getting deeper and deeper into a travelogue, and that won't do, except to mothers and aunts. But I <u>have</u> become very enthusiastic about the South-West, and it is difficult to avoid. California, apart from that seductive city San Francisco, is a great disappointment ... New Mexico, on the other hand, gets subtly under your skin and makes you part of itself.

DANIEL WEBSTER INN, SANDWICH, 24.vii.39
TO SPUD JOHNSON

Since arriving here four days ago I have been busy at work. It all suddenly came pouring out – a novel that has been fermenting for the last three years. So now I am going through all the misery and elation attached to the business, which you will understand if you have ever written a novel yourself – which I am sure you have. I realise now that one should never publish a novel until everything that has to be written is well out of the system. I am now as nervous as a cat about every word. So that I feel the result will be dead and self-conscious. If one could get over the period of waiting and working hopefully, it would be such a pleasant pastime for old age – watching one's complete works appearing all at once, or anyway, in quick succession.

I sent over for a copy of *Happy Valley* so that you could read it. Hope it arrived safely. It was posted from Boston before I left. My apologies for the War-and-Peace build-up on the jacket. This has only appeared with

---

[26](1879–1962), rich patron of writers and artists who invited Lawrence to Taos and then brawled with Frieda for possession of his soul. Her fourth husband, Tony Luhan, was an Indian from the Pueblo.

the second printing.[27] The first had a nice blue jacket, with white lettering, and not so much blurb ...

The Sage Holter week-end was a succession of social engagements.[28] I found a very rich environment – large white house, servants, swimming pools, and all that sort of thing. On the Saturday night we went to a dance, which I hated, at another large white house, owned by one of the publishers. And of course I didn't have one word with the publisher. Finally, I got into a corner with a bottle of champagne, and watched and listened to the gaggle of Long Island geese till I almost fell asleep.

The next day there was another large party, a luncheon, at the house of the second publisher, with whom I had possibly seven words. But on this occasion there was, at least, some conversation, supplied mostly by Dermid Russell, the son of 'Æ'[29] – a rugged, uncompromising person, who seemed to share my antipathy for large parties, and my interest in various topics.

(Is this becoming too much narrative? I can't help it.)

Sage Holter you would like. She has a lot of enthusiasm, and has made a surprising getaway from her environment. Altogether she is one of the people I have valued meeting in America.

Well, that about brings me to Boston, which was incredibly dull, English, provincial, and full of ugly people. I don't know why the Bostonians should be less attractive than other Americans. Low-Church views perhaps. These are always inclined to breed physical ugliness. I went, of course, to look at the conventional historic sights – Lexington, Concord, the houses of Longfellow, Emerson, Louisa Alcott – dutifully in a bus – , and also paid a visit on my own to the original Church of Christ Scientist. This is an excrescence in Bostonian romanesque, with St Peter's, Rome, growing miraculously out of one side. The interior smells predominantly of floor polish. Everything very clean. And the walls covered with texts from Mary Baker Eddy. I was shown round by two jaunty, uneasy women, whom I found increasingly sinister, like the whole atmosphere, in fact.

My life at Sandwich is as simple as could be. The place hasn't even the facilities of Taos! I was given letters of introduction to one or two people in the neighbourhood, but so far have been without the desire to do anything about it. No doubt that will come later on – when I am stuck for my next chapter! In the meantime, I occasionally sit on a stool in the

---

[27]Praise from Graham Greene, Elizabeth Bowen, Herbert Read, etc.

[28]Sage Holter of Mount Kisco and Santa Fe, wife of the lawyer Edwin O. Holter, had promised to introduce PW to two publishers if he came to stay.

[29]The Irish editor and poet George Russell (1867–1935).

English-looking, mahogany-coloured bar, and drink a glass of English-tasting beer, surrounded by uncommunicative natives playing cribbage. There is also a Wurlitzer Multi-Selector, which plays the 'Beer Barrel Polka', but unfortunately it hasn't got your theme tune – 'I Don't Worry, 'Cause It Doesn't Matter Now'.

Afternoons, I lie naked on the sand, in a line of dunes that remind me of the North coast of Norfolk. Or explore the lanes, which are full of blueberries and wood ticks and surprisingly green beetles. Occasionally I am driven places by my large landlord or his large wife, Al and Molly Govoni. The latter produced a remark yesterday worthy of joining the dicta of Mrs Burgmanus. I offered her my *New York Times*, and her reply was: 'No, thank you, I don't know any people in New York.'

This letter is so full of travelogue and anecdotes that I don't seem to have taken a breath to thank you for your really satisfying letter. I keep going back to it, trying to time myself away, to prolong the flavour. And I think that is only the fate of a letter from somebody one is very fond of, however good it may be as a letter. So I hope you are reassured as to the state of affairs. I am already wondering how soon I can decently get away from England in the New Year. This is also one of those lonely evenings, which only the right person can do anything about. What an absurd and maddening thing distance is! When I can feel you and know all about you and be quite unable at the same time to come close to you in fact.

Now I must go to bed, I suppose. It is one of those warm, sleepy evenings, with a scent of lindens that have stood all day in the sun. In the morning I lie in bed and work, and it is very delightful, with the trees just outside the window. There is nothing like that particular kind of golden light that comes through lindens. My room is also pleasing. Quite large, with rather ramshackle, ugly, but personal furniture, and a closet with a jug and basin inside.

I don't know why a jug and basin should remind me of Auden, but they do ... Never met him myself, though we have several common acquaintances, and I was told by one of them, John Macmurray,[30] to look him up in New York. I admire some of his work very much. Some of it not so much. And I have always disliked him, from what I have seen of him, as a public figure. He seems to me to try so hard, which only

---

[30] After first meeting the Scots philosopher (1891–1976), PW wrote to Mamblas, 10.xi.37: 'To look at, he is very much like D. H. Lawrence, but very grey and calm. I had expected something much more dynamic – alarming – then found myself sinking down into something reassuringly familiar. I don't know why one would ever expect more than simplicity from the great.'

accentuates that moon-calf look he has. But no doubt this is all stupid and unjust prejudice.

Here I am no farther towards bed, and the 'Beer-Barrel Polka' is playing so hard in the bar that I probably shan't sleep, anyway. But as I can't very well go on for ever, adding to this wad of literature, I'll leave you with my love – as much of it as I can possibly send on paper – Is that understood?

Patrick

P.S. I shall probably be here till mid-August, so write next time to General Delivery, Sandwich, Mass. I think that would be safer than the inn address.

HE BEGAN *THE LIVING AND THE DEAD* with the huge ambition of writing a novel that had London as its chief character. White imagined he was embarking on something of the scale of Joyce's *Ulysses*. The trouble was that since discovering America he was more than ever out of love with London. Elyot Standish, down from Cambridge and leading a literary life in Ebury Street, would wander through the Londons of Roy de Maistre, Pepe Mamblas and the pianist Sam Walsh. Though Standish was homosexual, that fact would be resolutely disguised from readers.

SANDWICH, 7.viii.39
TO SPUD JOHNSON

I blame myself a lot for leaving Taos when I did. I thought there was still a lot that I ought to see and do. And then I found, beside you, that nothing else was very important any more. But there we are, unfortunately. I've promised to go up to Maine on the 20th to stay with an old friend[31] for a couple of weeks. Then back to New York again, before I sail on 20th Sept.

All this is presupposing there is no <u>war</u>. To-day I don't like the look of things, even while feeling no one will be mad enough to start it. I can't, won't believe that everything is going to end in war. There's still some little nucleus of peace that's got to be made to spread. But if I'm all wrong, and I have to go back suddenly, I shall have to see you, Spud, for a couple of days. If it happened, could you meet me at, say, Albuquerque? I could get there in a day by air, and it would be worth it if all this is going to happen.

Supposing it isn't – and I refuse to let it – there's still so much that we're going to be able to do together in the future. Frankly you're the only

[31]Sam Walsh.

person I ever thought I might live with successfully. We might try – and I'd like to – if you're willing to wait a little and take the risk. But I've got to get back to London in the Fall, as I think my play is going to be done,[32] and then I have to do something about my apartment, which I have on my hands till February. Is all this too rushed? I hope you didn't return to a more sober frame of mind the morning after you posted your note! Because you've passed on the drunkenness.

If all goes well I could get out to Taos by March. It depends a little on my mother's plans. She will be going out to Australia about March or April, and I don't want her to feel I am washing my hands of her by rushing off before she leaves.

But I want to be with you Spud. I've never been so certain of anything in my life.

This won't be much more than a note either. I've been working most of the afternoon and am feeling rather exhausted. If this sounds as if I'm trying to make things too cut-and-dried, there's always the alternative of being somewhere within reach of each other. Though I think we could make the other a success. All these stupid words again, that don't convey anything much. Not like waking up together. That was one of the perfect moments that we've got to make again. Until then, I think of you a lot and I suppose the stupid words also have their merit. If you have any suggestions, any way for making things easier, let me know, Spud, and we'll see what's to be done.

Love,
Patrick.

Sandwich, 17.viii.39
TO SPUD JOHNSON
My dearest Spud,
One of those warm evenings, with nothing in particular to write about, when one shouldn't be writing at all, but it's the only possible means of approach, and so one takes it. Thank you for your letter, my dear. For all your letters. I can never thank you enough for these. I'm sure now that everything will eventually work out all right. Even Europe. It must. Because we've got to be able to dispense with letters.

Things seem to be piling up very quickly, and dangerously, according

---

[32]*Return to Abyssinia* was written after his breach with Mamblas: a young Englishwoman living near the Spanish border falls in love with a Spanish aristocrat on Franco's side, but her heart and her honour are saved by an ancient French actress who has a car crash at the bottom of the garden. The play is lost.

to the papers. And I go about the whole time waiting for something positive to happen – but it doesn't. Which may be a good sign. Don't you think that prolonged tension, with everyone having time to take in the situation, may be a sign that it will solve itself rationally in the end?

In Sandwich nobody thinks about anything but their tercentenary celebrations, which start tonight with a <u>Grand Ball</u>, and floor show from New York. I am faced with the possibility of having to escort my landlady while her husband keeps the bar here. But I don't want to. However depressing the dance that you don't go to, the music in the street, and the sound of the people coming home, it is never so depressing as the one you let yourself be persuaded into ...

I am working in fits and starts at what promises to be a <u>very</u> long novel. I keep discovering a fresh layer, and that leads to something else, with the probable result that nobody will ever find the thread. But on the whole, I am enjoying the process. And I also find I have become more tolerant. Perhaps <u>America</u> has done that!

Your idea of our writing autobiographies is an enticing one. But the difficult question would be: how comprehensive to make it? They might run away with themselves like my present novel. Actually, my autobiography, if a factual one, would be pretty uninteresting and bleak. I think vanity would compel me to explore its psychological possibilities, real or imagined! Just to eke out the comings and goings of fact. I do, of course, know a little of yours from the cover of *Horizontal Yellow*. And want to know more about Little Egypt. I hope you were born in Thebes.

But we've got to be able to talk this over some time, darling. Let it come in bits and pieces, in the natural way ...

Will you write next c/o American Express Co., 5th Avenue, New York, as I'm not sure of the Maine address? Do you know, the last couple of weeks, even on the days when there haven't been letters, you have been extraordinarily close. I could almost put out a hand. It's a dubious sort of comfort, but comfort of a kind.

Good-night, my dear.

Patrick.

SANDWICH, 20.viii.39

TO SPUD JOHNSON

Whenever I have been in love before, it has always seemed so one-sided, even when I have known that a certain amount was being returned. I had begun to believe that it was inevitable for two people to speak in two different languages. And both of those pretty limited. Why are people so afraid of <u>saying things</u>? I suppose it's due principally to their unwillingness to commit themselves definitely – because it might suggest permanency. Then this happens, and it feels as if everything is happening for the first time. That is why I am so happy, my dear. Incidentally, people have also been telling me that I look well.

AFTER A WEEK IN MAINE, White flew to Albuquerque on 3 September to meet Johnson. During the two nights and a day they had together the war began. White flew back to New York to find his passage to London cancelled.

HOTEL SUTTON, NEW YORK, 6.ix.39
TO SPUD JOHNSON
Dearest Spud,
This is just to show that I landed safely out of the air, and to say again that I'm so glad we did it. I feel that those two days will last me a long time, and I don't much mind now how soon I sail for England and whatever I shall have to do there.

This morning I went to the Cunard office to find out about boats for next week. But shipping arrangements a week ahead don't exist any more. However, I expect I shall get something when the time comes.

I had a great shock this morning – a cable from my mother to say my sister had got married. It must have been about the time we were talking of your sister's elopement on the mountain, though this wasn't necessarily an elopement. The man is a nice, dreary little man, to whom I can never find half-a-dozen words to say. I must admit I am very disappointed. I feel she should have done something much better – I hope that doesn't have a material sound, because it isn't meant to – , but someone who could have given her more in other ways.[33] This is another grudge I have against this damn war. I can see how this probably came about in a fit of heroics – the send-them-to-the-front-happy attitude which women always are inclined to adopt on the outbreak of war. But that is that, and I can't alter it.

My journey back was quite uneventful. I fell into a luxurious sleeper

[33]Geoffrey Peck (1908–56), a cheerful and charming former Army officer, was the English son of an Australian mother connected to half the grazing families of NSW. PW's rage at the match set a pattern for life: the engagement of each woman in his family provoked immediate anger and slow reconciliation. Diabetes ended Peck's brief Army career; from 1942 until his death he was a sports broadcaster and producer with the BBC.

at Kansas City, and slept very comfortably, till about 4.30 Mountain Time, when the hostess brought me a damp towel (!), with which I was supposed to wake myself thoroughly by wiping my face.

Since I got here I have been in a restless state of mind, unable to settle down to anything, or to think on the same subject for five consecutive minutes. I almost wish I could find myself in Europe at once and able to start doing something.

So you must forgive this drab letter. I received yours, the one that should have come last week, which acted as an epilogue to our two days . . .

I now have to dress and dine with some friends, who will, I am hoping, take me out of my gloom, and atone a little – but only a little – for the lack of Spud. Wish I was with you back in Taos, with your house, which I find myself wanting to see again.

Much love, my dear.

Patrick.

SOMEWHERE IN HIS LAST hectic week in America, White met Joe Rankin, a handsome doctor from the South, a man of his own age with ante-bellum manners and a Manhattan practice. All the certainties of summer were overthrown. White thought, once again, he had found the man who would share his life. For the moment he told Spud Johnson nothing.

TSS VANDYCK, 2.x.39

TO SPUD JOHNSON

My dear Spud,

This is the longest voyage made by anyone since the *Mayflower*. Spiritually, at any rate. Actually, it will be just about three weeks by the time we reach Liverpool. How we have got through it, I don't know, unless there has been some deadening of the mind and senses. Probably this has happened.

We spent five days of our three weeks merely kicking heels at Halifax, Nova Scotia, waiting for the convoy. Only the last day were we allowed on shore, in case we might give away information we hadn't got, or else post informative letters.

Allowed off in Halifax, I spent most of the evening in a kind of genteel brothel – very chastely, nevertheless – talking to a madam in flowered chiffon with a bust reaching to her knees. Her name was Margery, and her conversation stuck to the oh-my-yes-dear technique. Finally, I left, after she had suggested for the third time that she should send out for a girl, and was almost on the verge of suggesting herself.

Somehow or other the time has passed since we left Halifax. I have been driven back to work, in self-defence, in the mornings and the afternoons. At night I get drunk and walk the darkened decks in an Atlantic gale, not worrying about a thing. Unfortunately we have heard by radio there is going to be an enormous tax on liquor in England, so that even that consolation will be withdrawn. And as for the income tax – 7/6 in the pound, plus the additional Australian tax and exchange dues – well, I shall be left with a pittance.

Who cares? At the moment I don't a bit. I am drifting with about thirty other incongruous passengers in no particular direction. We may never arrive. I am quite cut off from the world, and from any kind of rational intercourse, and strange to say, I have got used to it. My chief sources of support are an Australian painter,[34] a South African Jewish scene designer, the pianist in the band, and one of the stewards! But nobody quite speaks the same language, or quite belongs to the same world.

I feel there are lots of questions in your last two letters that I ought to try to answer, but they are both at the bottom of one of my suitcases, and the only one I can remember is your suggestion for *Diddy Dumpkins*.[35] As a matter of fact, I did leave this with an agent in New York. So I can't say anything for the moment. I may also try it in London, if it fails in New York, provided any of the English publications are carrying on. But I have no idea yet what conditions are like over there.

And so it goes on. Complete vagueness. I envy you your nice, defined existence in your adobe house. Good-night, Spud. I think I am depressed tonight.

Much love,
Patrick
Arrived at last, after three weeks at sea. P.

---

[34]Peter Purves-Smith (1912–49), returning to enlist in the British Army.
[35]Prose piece now lost.

TWO

Love and War

February 1940 – January 1945

THERE WAS NO IMMEDIATE place for White in the war machine. 'Army and navy are not taking any more,' he told Spud Johnson in October, 'And all the civil defence services are full.'[1] He would be called up at some point but that was still many months away, so he went back to work on *The Living and the Dead* and plotted a return journey to New York to spend some time with Joe Rankin.

13 ECCLESTON STREET, 15.ii.40

TO PEPE MAMBLAS

I got back to a very changed London, which one now accepts as a matter of course, with the black-out and everything else. But wartime London also has its advantages – most of the rich, upholstered bores have fled into the fields, and altogether the secondary, mechanical relationships have disappeared out of one's life.

When I arrived I offered my linguistic services here and there, but as they weren't wanted – Whitehall and Bloomsbury were already packed to the roofs with those well-known sewn-up faces, all a bit afraid of someone else pushing in – , I settled down to my own work. I had begun a novel this summer while I was on Cape Cod, and finished it, as a matter of fact, this morning! Don't know when the final version will be ready, as it runs to roughly 150,000 words, and that will take a lot of revision.

A play of mine was supposed to be coming on in London last autumn. A comedy, set in a St Jean-de-Luz garden, (Putchutyia, no doubt),[2] about the first year of the Spanish war. As I say, the play was to have been done. Then the War broke instead. I shall never get over the disappointment of this. Especially as Françoise Rosay was coming over to play the lead – the part of a French actress of the Cécile Sorel type.[3] Now it is difficult to get

[1] 13.x.39.
[2] The house outside St Jean-de-Luz where they met in 1937.
[3] The great Rosay (1891–1974) would have made her London debut in PW's play; Cécile Sorel (1873–1966), later the Vicomtesse de Segur, Sociétaire of the Comédie-Française before her translation to music hall in the mid–1930s, ended her days as a Franciscan tertiary in Bayonne.

the right actress, and managers say the play wouldn't draw in wartime . . .

Those six months in the U.S.A. last year meant a great deal to me. For the first time in my life I remained continually alive, and for the first time I felt I was communicating continuously with other people. Then back to this – Living in a prosperous peaceful England after those six months would be like living with one's senses damped down to half their capacity.

I went a few weeks ago to drink with Nadal,[4] and Prieto,[5] who now shares his flat – since Nadal's mother went back to Spain. It was a strange gathering. Stephen Spender was also present – a great jangling creature, like an awkward provincial girl. He and Nadal sat at one end of the room and talked, while Prieto and I, at the other, indulged in his brand of Spanish-French conversation listened to by a rather unexplained friend of his. I'm afraid P.'s painting has reached the lowest depths of vulgarity. I can't do justice to the two canvases I saw – one a portrait of the Duke of Alba in a landscape, a gritty, choppy, scamped piece of work and the other a painting of Ram Gopal, the Indian dancer, in nothing but a few bangles and a Hindoo hat, which would do very well for the cover of a certain type of magazine. However, I hope this doesn't get back! He appears to be doing well, at the price of anything he had, and is now positively balloon-fat.

Have you any prophetic powers? Can you tell me when this war is going to end? What horrifies me almost more than anything, is the futile waste of time. There's so much I want to do and so short a time in which to do it. And even if one isn't killed, I feel there will always be that sense of time lost.

If the war had not broken out, I would have gone back to the United States permanently this year. Three months of the year in Europe and the rest over there, would be ideal as far as I'm concerned. I feel I could live a really creative life there – not this shadowy English existence – , and what's more, it may interest you to know I've met someone I want to live it with. Then all this had to go and happen.

I wish you were here, Pepe. There's such a lot I want to talk about, and it's such a long time since we talked at all. Anyway, we mustn't lose touch completely. Write to me and tell me more than the post-card had room for – how you are getting on and what you are doing . . .

---

[4]Rafael Martínez Nadal, senior lecturer in the Spanish Department of King's College in London and later the author of *El Público*, a study of the work of Lorca.

[5]Gregorio Prieto, Spanish painter and illustrator of skill and charm, working for some years in England.

Must stop now. I doubt if I could get another sheet into the envelope, and I'm still a bit feeble from my second attack of influenza within a few weeks.

I'm thinking of calling the novel *The Living and the Dead*. I'm more and more conscious, anyway in this country, of people being divided into two categories – the people who are aware and the people who are – well, just dead. That's something the political labellers will never take into account. To-night I could go out cheerfully and kill off all the dead.

I shall expect you to write.

My love to you,

P.

c/o DR J. L. RANKIN, NEW YORK, 30.iii.40
TO SPUD JOHNSON
My dear Spud,
No doubt this is a surprise. It's almost as big a surprise to myself, as I didn't know until three days before I left that I could get the necessary permits. Now I've just been three days in New York.

One reason why I have come over is that *Happy Valley* is coming out here, with the Viking Press, in June, and I wanted to make some personal contact with the publisher. I also mean to try to do something with the play, which is probably going to have a trial in London before long. I expect I shall be back in time to see that before I go into the Army, for I suppose I shall be called up about June!

This is a letter that I hate, and have put off writing, Spud. Now there seems nothing to do but go at it baldly in the way of explanation – which should have come earlier, anyhow. You've noticed a change in me, and there <u>has</u> been a change. I haven't explained before, because I was waiting to see if time would do something to either of us, and it hasn't worked that way. Not long before I left New York last year, I met someone I became very fond of. And that's gone on building up during the last six months. It's another reason why I wanted to come over here. I'm now staying with Joe. He's a doctor, a Southerner, from Georgia.

Is this too unpleasant a letter? I hope not. Because I <u>am still</u> very fond of you, and I hate hurting you. I know I'm to blame for this. But there it is – I suppose I'm made that way.

I remember you once said what a pity it was, after having an intimate relationship with someone, that person faded out completely when the relationship was over. I hope this can be an exception, my dear, and that we can still make something out of friendship. That's the way I would like it to be if you can get past my rather scurvy treatment of you.

So I'll hope to hear from you. As I said before, I'm still very fond of you, and you're much too valuable a person for me to want to feel I have been cut completely out of your life. Though I suppose I deserve to be.

Love,

Patrick.

BEN HUEBSCH OF THE Viking Press was the rock on which White's career was built. Huebsch had published in America the early novels of White's heroes Joyce and Lawrence; he had fostered two generations of American talent; at the Viking Press Tom Guinzberg was the business genius but Ben Huebsch did the 'literary crystal-gazing'.[6] Ben Huebsch deeply influenced the writing of White's next five novels, not by heavy editorial intervention which he deplored, but by being what he was: a civilised New Yorker and the one reader White wanted to impress.

From Huebsch came strong unspoken pressure for White to return to England to fight. He vacillated. Wouldn't his asthma keep him out of the services, he asked Betty Withycombe? He was free to stay in America, she replied, but he must not fudge his motives: he must be absolutely honest with himself. In Rankin's flat he worked at the final draft of *The Living and the Dead* while he waited for *Happy Valley* to appear.

48 EAST 53RD STREET, 22.iv.40

TO SPUD JOHNSON

My dear Spud,

Thank you so much for your letter, which was much more generous than the situation deserved. But I <u>am</u> glad that my behaviour hasn't finished Everything, as I was afraid it might. I wish we could meet again soon, though I don't see how that is going to be possible, unless you suddenly appear in New York, or the war ends, and I am able to feel at last that I can spend as much time as I want in the United States.

Unfortunately all these things seem very far distant. The war stays perpetually at the back of my mind and just manages to spoil every bit of happiness I am enjoying at the moment. Even so, that is considerable, and I wouldn't miss any of it, though it is, as I say, just spoiled.

When I shall be called up, I don't know. Or what my attitude will be when I am. I'm inclined in the evening to decide that nothing is going to be allowed to spoil my own personal life, and in the morning I read the news and have a fresh fit of wretched patriotics. It is all very difficult.

[6]PW to Stern, 29.x.1961.

I am now busy typing my new novel, the one I was working on when I was over last year. I don't know how it will strike anyone else as a book, but to me it seems the drabbest, dreariest thing ever written. I'm afraid my six months war depression must have got into it. On the other hand I can see interesting points in it, which make me hope it may be more interesting to a reader than I, as its author, am ready to believe.

Incidentally, would you please send me that parcel of journals I left with you? I'd like to look through them again soon and start thinking about doing them up in some form or other. Now that I'm more or less an adopted American I expect I shall find myself blushing for some of my first impressions and criticisms!

I still can't work up a thorough-going enthusiasm for New York. It strikes me as being lacking in a dimension, and the people are without roots. But it has a queer, irritating fascination about it. I repeatedly get the kind of sick feeling in my stomach I used to have as a child going to the theatre in a taxi. That's what I feel is wrong with New York. One's reactions are feverish and intestinal.

48 EAST 53RD STREET, 14.v.40
TO JEAN SCOTT ROGERS
Why, why, why anything? To-day is the day of the fall of Sedan and I feel particularly gloomy. Almost more than our own predicament, I find that of the German people depressing. Because they are being pushed about in the dark. At least we can see what awfulness is happening. When I read of all those bodies washed up in Oslo Fiord, and whole armoured trains blown up on the Dutch frontier, full of dumb, driven, German cattle——

Well, to get to my own unimportant, insignificant doings – the book is due on the 20th. It looks very handsome in heavy black canvas, with pink labels, beautiful type, and a jacket with a picture of the snake episode. I have hopes of a certain amount of success. Last Sunday in the *Times* and the *Tribune* it headed advance lists of forthcoming books. To my great satisfaction, I was put above two such best sellers as Angela Thirkell and Phyllis Bottome.[7]

I'm about halfway through the typing and revision of *The Living and The Dead*. Hope I can finish it. My agent has also suggested I make a book out of my American Journal of last year.[8] The other evening at dinner at

---

[7] Thirkell's tenth Barsetshire novel, *Cheerfulness Breaks*, and Bottome's *Masks and Faces*.
[8] This was never published and later burnt by PW.

the Stewarts,[9] I read bits of it and it was a great success . . .

I can't help feeling this is all so much stupid prattle at this moment. But I suppose there's also room for a little of that. Spring is in New York – rather an over-green, synthetic spring, like everything else here. But this time, I have felt more at home. Some of my friends are the best value. It is very gratifying when somebody one hasn't seen for months, says spontaneously in the first few moments: Now what about money? If you find you're short, you must come to me at once.

I hear from Ronald regularly. Did he tell you Bronson Albery[10] was thinking of producing my play? But every time that happens, war seems to flare up again.

I'll try to write again soon and let you know about things. I apologise for this effort, but much is implied.

Love,
Patrick.

HE COULD NOT HAVE hoped for a better reception for *Happy Valley*. The critics praised the strength of his characters and the beauty of his prose; they predicted the brightest future for Patrick White. Though his style might be greeted with scepticism elsewhere (in Australia with deep hostility), it was very much to taste in America.

48 EAST 53RD STREET, 26.vii.40
TO SPUD JOHNSON
This is a letter of good-bye, as I am off to Montreal on <u>Wednesday</u> to catch a boat for England. I am doing this from no personal desire – my life here has been too happy and in every way satisfactory – , but just because I don't feel I can ignore the war altogether. I've got to go through some of that before I can enjoy something else – I hope – as a permanent state.

My plans are no more definite than to go to London and offer to do something. Then when it is over I shall come back here, and probably take out my papers. Anyway, I know from my last six months in England that I can't breathe in Europe any more.

---

[9]Peggy Stewart, née Purdell, had retired from the stage to marry and read scripts for RKO. The Stewarts were always having rows: she would rush off to Grand Central Station with her suitcase and he would coax her home. PW remembered this when writing his 1982 play *Signal Driver*.
[10](1881–1971), an impressario who controlled several London theatres including the New (now the Albery) and the Criterion.

It's a pity we haven't been able to manage a meeting during the last four months. At least, I think so. And I would like you to meet Joe, and for you to like each other. This isn't prompted, either, by a general desire to patch up.

I have just got the Viking Press to say they will publish my new book, *The Living and the Dead*, though I have not yet signed a contract. Still, I know that Huebsch personally is enthusiastic . . .

That little G-string you presented me with last year is a great help in a New York heat wave! I wear nothing else about the house, and find myself wishing I could turn on some of that dry, desert heat.

66 EBURY STREET, 12.ix.40
TO SPUD JOHNSON

I still can't believe that what happens every night is happening to us, in London. The bad raids began about a week ago, and we now live almost exclusively in the cellars and basements at night. Last Saturday I was out when the first big raid began, was walking through the street where I used to live, about 11 P.M., when a screaming bomb made itself known, and I found myself getting down on the pavement with a couple of soldiers coming from the opposite direction. There we lay with shrapnel spattering round us and the building rocking against our ribs.

But it is not always as exciting as this. There are hours of boredom at night in the basement, where all my fellow lodgers sleep on the floor. And there is no means of getting about – no buses or taxis – , if one ventures out. I have been out most nights, as the alternative seemed to be extinction by staying in, and the deserted streets have been very beautiful, in a white moonlight and a yellow flashing of guns.

In the daytime we go more or less about our usual business. That makes it all the more extraordinary – to think that civilians are transacting normal business in what now corresponds to the Front Line. Suddenly you are reminded of this by the remains of a house that has been mashed to the ground, or a crater gaping in the middle of the street . . .

While I'm waiting I am doing a job with the Red Cross, in the Foreign Relations Department, which traces the missing in the various dead countries of Europe. I send the cables to Geneva and record the answers, which is much more interesting than it may sound as a cold statement. I am continually coming across interesting, and often tragic stories, letters asking us to trace families and lovers, and often letters which the senders hope will go direct, with very intimate messages, and sometimes even pressed flowers. But unfortunately we can only send a formal message to the occupied countries through our organisation in Geneva, and all the flowers and *chauds baisers*[11] are wasted on our office files.

Life is very full, with all this. I can now understand the people who, after the last war, having no resources of their own to fall back on, were left stranded, living on a kind of wartime hangover. During a war there is so much to do. Either you can bolt into it head first, get caught up in it, and avoid having to think for yourself; or else you can make it a very intense emotional orgy. I think a great many people are inclined to take one of these lines. And each type will suffer afterwards, in the post-war backwash . . .

I had a long letter from J.[12] a couple of weeks ago. You've been so good about all that, my dear, and I do appreciate it. I imagine myself in the same situation and the ungraceful line I probably couldn't stop myself from taking. Even when you tell yourself: If I love So-and-So enough––

66 EBURY STREET, 23.ix.40

TO BEN HUEBSCH

I think I have only twice been up against war since I got back – the occasion when I lay on my face, and one afternoon in and around Oxford Street, where there are now a number of impressive ruins. When you see a house that has collapsed, with mirrors and pictures still hanging hopefully on an inside wall, objects on the mantelpiece, and a solemn collection of furniture in a half-torn upper dining room, you begin to get the reality and unreality of war.

As for doing things myself, I have been before one medical board in a remote suburb, where they kept me standing for an hour and a half naked in their smelly drill hall, without being able to make up their minds whether to pass or fail me. This on account of my asthma. I am supposed to go again at the end of the month. Then I am also expecting to hear from the Air Ministry about a job I am hoping to get with the R.A.F Intelligence. But this takes time, much time, I think even longer than it does to place a novel by Patrick White. At the moment, I am rather hoping I shall be able to leave this wintry island altogether by getting myself drafted off to Egypt or somewhere else in the Middle East. But again, I suppose this will take time – perhaps the whole winter in question.

I have felt rather guilty about my inability to write something introductory for *The Living and the Dead*, as you had asked. If you were here, you would understand how difficult it is to make the brain function

[11]Warm kisses.
[12]Rankin.

creatively. I have been wondering if it mightn't be better to have an introduction written, anyway, by a third person. What do you think?[13]

STANMORE, MIDDLESEX, 3.xii.40
TO SPUD JOHNSON
I joined the R.A.F. about three weeks ago, after giving up hope of ever hearing from them. When I did, it was asking me to appear in full uniform as a Pilot Officer at very short notice. And since then I have been stationed just outside London, [censored].[14]

I have an Intelligence job which involves much more concentration than anything I have ever had to lend my head to. Consequently, when I come off duty I am not good for much more than a hot bath and bed. I am on duty for pretty long stretches, the worst of these a night shift lasting from 8.30 to 8.30. On a night of bad Blitz this is a particular strain, as one has to keep pace with everything that is happening all over the country, so as to write an informative account at the end of the period. The first night I was put on alone at this, will go down as one of my special and historic nightmares.

However, I seem to be getting into the way of things at last. Actually, I shall not be in this part of the world much longer. I volunteered for the Middle East soon after joining, and to-day I was told to expect to leave before the end of the month. Where I am being sent, I don't know. It might be [censored] or [censored], or anywhere. But wherever it is, I shall be glad to go, as it is bound to be more colourful than these dreary static months in England . . .

The war has loosened people up a lot and at the same time consolidated them, which I suppose is some advance – if there isn't a corresponding reaction afterwards.

Personally I seem to get a great deal more out of small things – like seeing my friends, chance encounters, a few minutes in which to do nothing, even bacon rations. And above all I have come to the conclusion that there is no material tie worth hanging on to, that nothing matters, nothing is harmful or annihilating, except something that touches what I think one has to call one's personal integrity. (I think I would have lost this altogether if I had stayed in America this year as I was tempted to).

How trite all this sounds! But having only just experienced this for myself, really for the first time, it is a great temptation to set it out, even

[13]Huebsch had asked for an introduction, rejected PW's compromise and issued *The Living and the Dead* without.
[14]Headquarters Fighter Command, Bentley Priory.

though I am speaking to someone who has no need of it.

Again I am annoyed because this is such a woolly, abstract letter.
You would probably much rather have concrete accounts of air raids and
things that are happening. But you see, there are so few people on which
one can work off abstractions, that one has to take the rare opportunity.

HIS CONVOY SAILED FROM England a few days before Christmas and
zigzagged up and down the Atlantic. 'You know nothing about bombs until
you have been bombed at sea,' he told Jean Scott Rogers. 'That is
something.'[15] Eventually he was put ashore on the West Coast of Africa
and waited for a plane to take him to Egypt. Idle in Takoradi he began a
diary which he kept for the next four months.[16]

TAKORADI, GOLD COAST, 22.i.41
We sit and drink a glass of fizzy lemonade. The whites have paid for
coming to the Gold Coast. They are either pitiful or apathetic. The lingerie
strings of the women hang down their arms in pale festoons. An exasperated
face under the conventional topee.

The negro woman sitting by her brazier at the crossroads in T. In
light from burning oil. Potato chips in the pan of fat. The woman giggles
with embarrassment and turns away her face. We talk to the African
minister, a patient lost creature standing in no particular world . . .

I am beginning to recover the habit of living inside myself. There is
no other way. Otherwise I become as pitiful as W.[17] Live inside yourself
and it is possible, paradoxically, to come closer, to be more intensely aware
of the real outside. By this, I mean the landscape and those figures that
are innate in the landscape, the Africans, rather than the superficialities
like W.'s baths and talcum powder . . .

During the last month, that is, since leaving England, or perhaps
more correct to say since joining the R.A.F., I have lost what I know as
myself. I suppose something will emerge in time, not the known aspects,
I feel, but something new. I can't decide if this is good. Surely there ought
to be a continuity. I want to say to the people who know me during this
period. This is not I, I am somebody quite different.

So much for the ego. We fly off to-day – high time – there is mildew
over everything.

[15] 7.ii.41.
[16] A small exercise book discovered among PW's papers after his death, the diary also includes
unpublished verse and preparatory sketches for The Aunt's Story.
[17] Richard (Dick) Whittal, late of the League of Nations Commission on Bulgaria, who gave
PW a crucial letter of introduction to Charles de Menasce in Alexandria.

LAGOS, NIGERIA, 22.i.41

To L. by air. More swamps, more bananas, more of the brown mud houses, the little toy houses of Africa. From the air, surf is motionless, frozen. The Royal Hotel, L. brothel-cum-*bal musette*:[18] the vases of dirty paper flowers, the bead curtains. We are given a bare dormitory for six. Outside the window negroes scuffle and fight. All the usual African smells, the smell of burning wood and black bodies ... The negresses of L. dance on the hotel roof. The beginnings of European coquetry. The husky dusky laughter of the dancing negresses, twined and twirling to a gramophone. *De jeunes negresses en fleur* ...

LAGOS TO KANO, NIGERIA, 23.i.41

A day's flying in the cold air, so cold that one shivered, teeth clattered, and one was glad of an overcoat, till now superfluous.

Landed at K. Heat again, but of the dry, piercing kind. I am alive again. A nostalgic sensation of country streets in Australia, the same listless trees and thick dust, but this only in the European quarter. The walled native city of K. is exotic, Muslim, with dark unexplorable doorways. Labyrinths of mud. As we walk through the streets it is the prayer hour. Like most organised devotion, this is a mechanical rite, a formula. The pelican tree: a large rare tree, pure white from the droppings of roosting pelicans. Followed by eighty children, this is more dream than waking experience – the little yellow and orange fronds, the piles of indigo, the inevitable minerals and roots, old black beggar women, naked to the waist, with disgusting dugs and leprous feet, the tall dignified Hausa men in their white tunics, the horrid Tuaregs veiled, boys with arrow pencilled eyes, the young girls, apple-breasted and beautifully balanced. The stars – I have forgotten these until now. They are a mystical climax in the desert, at once self and detachment ...

TO EL GENEINA, SUDAN, 24.i.41

Landed at Iri L.,[19] where we spent an hour or so in repairing brakes. Here a desolation, this sad French colony, with the Croix de Lorraine floating, and small unshaven French airmen listless in the shade. A very noble type of native, vastly tall, good features and slender hands. For the first time I noticed women with mud ringlets. Two of these walking naked across the plain with their beautifully balanced head-burdens. Drank, of all things,

---

[18]A café on the banks of the Marne where the Parisian working classes drank and danced on Sunday afternoons, as immortalised in the paintings of Renoir.
[19]Almost certainly Fort Lamy in French Equatorial Africa.

Pernod at the little blue and white mess overlooking the river. This water cool and green, a jade green. That is the true, the most refreshing tone of water. White parachutes suspended like mosquito nets in the mess. Outside white sand along the shore, and the intersecting sand bars. Cactus and thorns growing in the dust and heat. But by this time I am myself a cool river of Pernod, green flowing between the dried up cassia trees . . . Landed for the night at El G. Farther and farther in the desert. The stars take complete possession on the edge of the world, I am no longer <u>under</u> the stars, but part of them, living, palpitating, in the same cool detachment. The breathing of a star where once was heat.

I spent the night in a round hut made of mud and thatch. For furniture a wooden bedstead, a hurricane lamp, and an enamel wash basin standing on the brick floor. Outside the smell of hay and donkeys and dust. An elegant monkey, very narrow-hipped, chained to a bare tree. The mess at El G. is warm and hospitable. This is part of the great charm of the desert. There is nothing to offer but hospitality and genuine welcome . . .

To-night I lay down in my clothes between two hair blankets. And still the stars, this experience of stars, so long unnoticed. The dark young Pole, Dominique, his smoky laugh. Potter, our charming, fat, civilised Flight Lieut. We sit in the desert and discuss the two Lawrences, Katherine Mansfield, Rilke, Aldous Huxley, and Auden! What could be more perfect than stars, sand and a few chosen fragments of civilisation. but they must be <u>chosen</u>, very carefully.

I have seldom felt so happy, so aware, and at the same time so unconscious of the <u>business</u> of living. How long can this continue, *je me demande*. There must soon be some dark question begging an answer.

EL FASHER TO KHARTOUM

Started at dawn and came down at F. for breakfast. Here there were polo ponies and a comfortable brick bungalow, and serious Arab servants who brought scrambled eggs.

Later at K. This is a flat, new town lacking in atmosphere. I began very soon to dislike it . . . Like most rivers, the Nile is disappointing at first. Why this fact is so, I can't discover. Mountains are not disappointing in the same way, but always rivers . . .

I shall be glad to leave for Egypt proper, which I feel now may be a myth, or at least a cross between the Ritz Bar and a museum of archaeology – and I detest both pink lights and labelled dust.

LUXOR, WADI HAIFA TO CAIRO, 25.i.41

Between L. and W. the sea has ebbed leaving the many estuaries and tidal flats that make the Egyptian desert. From these rise the moon-craters and haggard mountains of black lava.

The temple on the river. Forms carved in the grey rock, seated on the river's edge. I find Egyptian sculpture quite incomprehensible. Either it is bad, or else it has some redeeming mystical quality with which I fail to make contact. Definitely I don't understand it. And I dislike the smooth grossness of so much. North of W. the Nile flows between green banks. The effect of this after days of desert is like slipping, hot, into a cool bath. The body and soul are immediately at rest. And then the groups of pyramids in a greenish-golden afternoon haze. There is a kind of light in which you become immersed – this to-day. I forgot I had been up since five. I forgot I was hungry. Just this moment of dissolution in light. At the aerodrome the usual transport muddle. At H.Q. worse. Interviewed in a half-dead condition at 7 o'clock. I was about as intelligent as a post.

Driving through C. at dusk, my first impression is a French suburb with a Moorish flavour.

WHITE WAS APPOINTED INTELLIGENCE officer to a squadron of the South African Air Force stationed in the Sudan. He had first to report for training in Khartoum. So he set out to retrace his steps, this time travelling south by river and then rail.

ON THE NILE, 9.ii.41

The journey away from Cairo has been a long reassembling of ideas. No more of that French bastard. The Nile is Egypt. Waking early in the train, those green flats, smoky with blue mist. The women walking with urns on their heads, or seated against the mud houses. The strings of pink camels. The movement of a camel picking leaves from the under part of a tree is highly delicate ... Across the Sudan the plains turn grey and stoney. Pink walls of the buildings at the little numbered stations. The oleander bushes growing in waist high mud shelters. Acacias stampeding like ostriches in the wind. All day it has been sand and desert, and peat mounds of black, volcanic stone. A fierce landscape, but one that I enjoy rather than resent, after Cairo anyway. Khartoum will, I think, be a trial ...

KHARTOUM, 13.ii.41

The zoo at K. is both informal and stylised. Details from many friezes wander freely through the park. Small, skipping gazelles nibble at the roots of grass, standing ankle deep in water. Blue, tufted cranes, the most distinguished monkeys. Here everything is fresh and clean. Seen for the first time. The animals feed from your hand. I became Adam walking through the Garden.

Apropos of the wounded officer in the dining room: Suffering is the one surprise left in this existence of ours. Joy is rational, expected. Not so with pain, which we should have left behind at least a century ago. Perhaps this is impossible. It is too necessary, a test of the spirit . . .

20.ii.41

All day there has been great activity along the banks of the Nile, natives squatting naked, washing themselves, every few yards. One little naked boy playing on Pan-pipes beside a herd of goats. Sometimes it is good to get away into this native landscape. I am weary of the Services – the officers on the terrace, the same groups. A contingent of nurses has produced a feeling of uneasiness. For the most part, well-scrubbed, solid, unattractive girls, but the effect is inevitable. Here sex is such an obvious problem. Men shift and sidle in their chairs. So that it is good to get away into the more abstract landscape of the Nile. So much subtler than the game of bulls-and-cows . . .

KASSALA, 1.iii.41

To K. in the tail of a Wellesley. Sand and wind blowing among the huts at the airport give a feeling of temporariness. Then caught up in the wind ourselves, whirled above Khartoum and a rather sickly strip of Nile. From Khartoum to K. there is no more than desert – blinding wind, sand, sun. And yet it was cold too in my exposed position without adequate clothing.

Landed at K. beside a most unnatural jebel, great bulges of rock in the shape of sugar loaves. At the foot of these fantastic shapes, grows a mud town.

I was met, actually met – somebody knew I was coming – by le Mesurier,[20] acting O.C. of No.1 S.A.A.F., and the Adjutant – a middle-aged R.A.F., quiet and contained with a sardonic, resigned smile.

The mess is an abandoned Italian colonial villa, the floors thick with dust and the scattered possessions of its present inhabitants. Impossible to make this place really habitable. There is hardly a stick of furniture, hardly a bench. I pitch my tent on the verandah, the bed that is already broken in two places, the chair that breaks in the course of the evening. But at least this spot is something personal, peculiar to myself. Under the white washed brick arches it is not unpleasant. I lie on my bed in the afternoon,

---

[20]PW later used the name but not the character in *Voss*.

listening to a bird mourning continually in a tree . . . The concrete basin with the water flowing from the well. I sit in it up to my chest, in the flow of water, it is just dark, a sickle moon and stars, our soft feathery tree darker than the darkness. The tree moves. The water flows. In the distance, voices . . .

4.iii.41

I sit all day in this small, white, brick cell waiting for, or passing on information of operations. In the distance the aerodrome. Aircraft fly very low over the house, scattering the birds out of the trees. Outside my window the dusty oleanders quiver.

At night there are bottles of beer on the trestle tables in the mess, and under the trees, surrounded by mosquito nets. I listen to the talk, the stories. It is all in the distance. And at night the telephone again. I lie in two blankets on a camp bed. It is cold enough for blankets, very cold when the bell rings and I tread through dust and darkness . . .

B. arrived yesterday. He has the same assurance, more so to a certain extent than the others, and at the same time a kind of diffidence, which is charming. An air of greater experience, of what I don't know, and yet perhaps not. It is a temptation to read subtleties into people you want to like. B. has a good head, tawny, very fine ears. He sits well. It is possibly a faint air of the world that I find attractive in this wilderness.

11.iii.41

I know what it is now to be obsessed by a job. That is, something imposed, outside oneself, for I have always been obsessed by my own work, too thoroughly. Now I am a slave of a series of complex operations, that I want to keep going, the wheels rotating, feverishly. It is imperative.[21] All depends on me. (Surely we could never keep going, even objectively, without the ego.)

Now I enjoy liking someone unlike the people I usually like. B. for instance. He is a source of continual pleasure – his good humour underneath the toughness, a streak of great delicacy. Everyone is growing a moustache. There is nothing like a moustache for helping to pass the time . . .

[21]The squadron was covering the Allied ground advance on Keren as the Italians retreated towards the Red Sea.

13.iii.41

This afternoon one of our machines ground-strafing the road at – killed two men on a motorbike. Van's voice on the telephone describing this, overawed, not quite knowing what he had done.[22] But by this time – it is probably the effect of this wretched desk and telephone – I think of lives not so much as lives as notches in a stick. When we get to the top of the stick, we stop. But Van was shaken. He had seen the blood streaming on the road.

17.iii.41

First light: the *muezzin* that I heard this morning, and at the same time the cocks started up, and donkeys, and camels, and dogs, against a white sky. Nearly always I am very content now, except when I think of J.[23] and wonder if it is finished. I tell myself it is the mail.

On the aerodrome the aircraft stand like big, waiting grasshoppers in the midday sun. Dust blows in the eyes. There are moments when it is not possible to see. Then the landscape returns, rock and dust, tufts of dried grass, and a string of humped native cattle. An airman in a singlet hangs his washed shirt to dry on a stick. Even in its passive state, an aeroplane is very much alive and expectant. It basks in the hot sun. Two armourers, sweaty and almost naked, loading the guns with ammunition. An engine fitter stands astride a wing. A smell of warm grease, burning metal, and hot leather . . .

Badge for the Sudan: a dead cow and three empty petrol tins lying in the dust.

20.iii.41

The monkey sits on my shoulder with his face in my neck. He sleeps, hot and close. Put him on your lap when he is asleep, and he moans like a miserable child. He must sleep against bare skin. He can't get close enough to this. His little whiskers give him a solemn look, but he is very skittish when he is awake. His hands are never still, touching, opening, closing. He sits on the telephone in the office and plays with the bell. The touch of the small, delicate, skinny hands of the monkey.

23.iii.41

This morning the Superintendent of Gardens, who is one of those glossy, rippling, rather girlish young Sudanese officials, came and announced with

[22]Flight-Lieutenant J. Van der Merwe.
[23]Rankin.

a giggle that he would like to quarter a flock of sheep in our front garden, to do the work of lawn mowers. Just before breakfast the lawn mowers arrived, rushing like a swarm of hungry grasshoppers through the garden gate. There is something obscene, almost unnatural about Sudanese sheep, as if a sheep and a goat had gone astray, and these were the result. Two boys accompanied this lot, thin and biblical, in fluttering white rags.

During breakfast a ewe gave birth. She lay on her side, gave one or two grunts, and a boy, seizing a leg, whirled a lamb out of her. He swung it in a wide semi circle, new and glistening, and laid it beside the mother on the grass. The mother immediately began a series of little maternal sounds – sheep arpeggios – licking the lamb's wet skin and biting at the umbilical cord. Later the lamb began to suck. I held his mouth to the teat and he began hardly consciously, doing something he was now beginning to remember from a previous existence.

The native ewes here have their teats tied up with bits of old rag to prevent the half-grown lambs from sucking. The rams have their testicles tied to the penis with bits of string. Presumably some local attempt at birth control.

24.iii.41
The Living and the Dead to be published by Routledge early in the summer.[24]

27.iii.41
Keren fell this morning. The news came through over the telephone, very dry and factual after all the elaborate emotional preparation. It seems that this may be the beginning of a rout down the road to Asmara.[25] This road I have been over so many times on the map, no more than this, is very vivid in the mind's eye. The boulders, the bridges, the dusty bushes, and now a retreating of Italians . . .

30.iii.41
These days I often feel listless and unenthusiastic, in spite of stirring events. We are every moment closer to Asmara. But I personally am stagnant, flabby, I feel a pale, yellow-tongued creature dried up and half rotted by the heat . . .

---

[24] The critic Herbert Read (1893–1968) persuaded George Routledge & Sons to take PW's novel after it had been rejected by his previous publisher Harrap and a number of other London firms.
[25] The Eritrean capital.

31.iii.41

V. d. Merwe crashed on an early patrol north of Asmara. After an attack on 3 Savoias, in which he was hit, he crumpled up against a mountainside and lay among the trees. K.[26] who was with him, reports no sign of life.

In this milieu death has lost most of its conventional meaning. One approaches it from a different angle. By evening, much time had flowed over the head of V.d.M. I suppose this is the only way, the alternative to a perpetual emotional strain.

1.iv.41

Asmara fell this morning . . .

4.iv.41

News came of the finding of Van. An Italian guide discovered his body in a native Coptic church in the hills above Asmara. 'He was lying on a native stretcher,' the guide says, 'I helped to straighten him out, I buried him in his parachute and read the R.A.F. burial service.' This for Van, who was in his way, one of the most corporeal members of the squadron. I still cannot believe that a pilot has walked down to the aerodrome for the last time. It is too sudden, too unconvincing.

WITH THE ITALIANS ROUTED, all available Allied forces in the Eritrean theatre were being sent to defend Egypt, for the Axis forces were advancing on Alexandria and had already encircled the Mediterranean port of Tobruk. The South African planes flew north and the staff of No.1 Squadron followed by rail to Alexandria.

6.iv.41

Any moment of complete happiness is impersonal, detached. It is something beyond the happiness of loving and being loved. It is something so distilled and colourless that its intensity is absorbing. I experience this sometimes, but rarely. To-night for instance, alone at the aerodrome. There are no longer any boundaries between the senses, the dimensions. The warmth passes through, whether it is stone, or flesh. May this not be similar to the state of death? Just an infinity of complete understanding and content.

The drive to the station at night through the mud streets, past the skeletons of houses, with white shrouds stretched upon beds. The road is terrible. It is consistently corrugated. A sleepy, fretful and finally damp monkey bounces on my lap. Alongside the road are pale green bushes with

[26]Captain Ken Driver.

large juicy looking leaves. Empty petrol tins glisten in the moonlight.

At the station the airmen are already sitting among the little piles of kit, singing or complaining. It is all a bit removed and odd this landscape, the white teeth of a sleeping native stretched upon a bench, the white robes of the railway officials at their telegraphic machines. The white vibrant light of an acetylene lamp. The train will never go. S. and I sit in our compartments. We drink whisky and talk. S. tells me about his sex life, which is much like anyone's sex life, both precarious and stale. The Flight Sergeant contributes from his wallet the photograph of a blonde and naked prostitute . . .

9.iv.41

That bend of the Nile, or rather between the two Niles, where the big iron bridge swung back to allow the dhows to pass, as we drove to Omdurman. The golden elbow of the land, golden with the stubble of a native crop that had not been mown quite clean close to the water. Goats among the stubble were black. And the pale water of the White Nile touching the deeper water of the Blue Nile in a wavering line . . .

10.iv.41

Germany has re-taken Tobruk[26a] . . . Tonight has been uneasy with the news, the long train stationary at A. on our journey northward, lorries becalmed on metal platforms with odd pieces of equipment protruding in the moonlight – waiting for somebody to wind us up again. This horrible possibility is often a symptom of moonlight. Supposing this were true – if somebody forgot or refused to turn the handle.

SIDI HANEISH,[27] 23.v.41

To-night is perhaps inauspicious for self-analysis. I am drunk, and therefore prone to self-pity. I am likely to be pompous even when wanting to be honest. But for that matter, isn't the motive behind self-analysis, honest self-analysis, nothing but self-pity? It is a device favoured by someone on the squirm. All my life trying to persuade myself that honesty is desirable, it probably only amounts to this. And I have not achieved it, not even the illusion of honesty, or what one likes to think is unbiased self-analysis.

The wind has been blowing all day, dust, sand in streams from the sea, while we are fighting this absurd war. Absurd only in its necessity. I am not denying it has to be fought once that necessity has been established. But here I sit in the midst of it, in the desert, in the ruck of self-pity. I

[26a]Nearly, but the port did not fall until June, 1942.
[27]On the Mediterranean coast near the Libyan border.

go down into the mess. There is a welter of words, a devouring of food. I pray to be unseen. It is K.Q. of all people who insists, rather puzzled, on trying to draw me in. When I resist, he tries by small ruses. I am a child to be humoured. He shows me how he has had his wings moved higher up to make room for his new ribbon. This is all the more touching, finding it in K.Q. The puzzled father of a difficult child. It is this kind of thing that also makes me feel such an imposter. I am fond of these people. It is a fondness I have found in few relationships. But am I entitled to it? It is like reaching over into a world to which you don't belong, from oil to water, or even more opposed substances. I feel I am always likely to be this foreign body, always.

THE DIARY ENDS HERE. A few days later, after a wild birthday party in the desert, White was transferred to an RAF unit on the outskirts of Alexandria.

ALEXANDRIA, 15.vii.41
TO JEAN SCOTT ROGERS
Dear Jean,
I feel guilty about not writing more often. But the desert is relaxing. Very occasionally I am stimulated by it and feel I am rising to the heights, but more often than not I exist in a torpid and mediocre squalor, not improved by my immediate material surroundings – the flea ridden blankets, the indispensable petrol tins, the chipped enamel basin that can never be properly cleaned, the dust floor on to which everything falls ...

I moved from the Sudan to Egypt nine or ten weeks ago and, after being separated from my South African Squadron, which I regretted enormously, I am back again with the R.A.F. It is all very tepid and humdrum after life with the Squadron. Those three months are three of the most important I have ever lived. I was doing a necessary job. They liked me, and wanted me there. Whereas, here I am just another dreary supernumerary. However, sometimes I think it's for the best. My best friends in the Squadron have either been killed or gone back to the Union, and it would no longer be the same.

I have been trying without success for the last few weeks to transfer to flying. The war has become much more personal since losing these people. I now have a grudge and want to work it off in bombs. I am beginning to understand all the hatreds of the last war, those strange emotions that used to puzzle me as a child. One incident in particular sticks in my mind. Our nurse used to take us for a walk past the house of a German in Sydney, and we would all three solemnly spit on the gatepost.

I was amused by it. Then, in retrospect, I was disgusted by its absurdity, when I grew older. Now I can quite share the emotions behind the symbolism.[28]

Lately I've had a week's leave in Alexandria, which I spent with Charles de Menasce, a very kind little Jew, whom I met through someone else in the R.A.F., and who lives in a Proustian atmosphere, surrounded by Gobelin tapestries, virtù, and 57 portraits of his mother. They are a large and cosmopolitan family, and I was asked to many large and cosmopolitan parties, where I indulged in three languages, and rubbed shoulders with Greeks, French, Egyptians, Armenians, and Syrians. That is Alexandria – a Babel of the Middle East. Unfortunately I tended to be asthmatic, probably due to over-eating and the renewed contact with civilisation, but no doubt also as a concession to the Proustian atmosphere . . .

Lately I have begun to feel the war may be over by the end of the year. Pray God it may, even at the risk of hypocrisy in our attitude to Russia when we have won. I am sure the English government will never be persuaded to look at her as more than a kind of political 'Boule-de-Suif'.[29]

By the way, I recommended neither *Tristram Shandy* (which I find unreadable) nor *Humphry Clinker* (still unread). To me the title for Great English Novel is shared by *Tom Jones* and *Middlemarch*. Write again, and keep out of the way of bombs.

Love,
Patrick.

AT A PARTY IN the Menasce apartment that summer, White met Manoly Lascaris, a young man about to join the Royal Greek Army. The alliance that began that afternoon in Alexandria lasted until White's death nearly fifty years later. 'Patrick made me happy at once,' Lascaris recalled. 'And I think I made Patrick happy.' They were the same age. Lascaris was a Greek, born in Cairo to an American mother then raised by aunts in Athens after both parents abandoned the Lascaris children at the end of the First World War. The family was distinguished in the Byzantine world and rich until they lost their estates in the sack of Smyrna in 1922.

The repercussions of that afternoon in the Menasce apartment were profound in both their lives. By temperament and upbringing Lascaris was

---

[28]The castellated house belonged to the brewer Edmund Resch, returned 1917; Lizzie Clark's brother Robert was killed fighting in France.

[29]Maupassant's whore who saves a party of virtuous travellers. See PW to Shepherd, 1.iv.81, page 543.

one who served; in Egypt in 1941 he decided to serve this difficult man whose ambition was to write. He countered White's temper with his own Levantine calm; the world that drove the Australian to black pessimism and rage was observed by Lascaris with understanding and wry forbearance. White called him, 'My sweet reason.'[30] The two men were apart more often than not over the next seven years, but none of White's letters to Lascaris survive. 'They were very beautiful and I regret it. But I had promised Patrick I would destroy them, so I did.' White revealed very little to his old correspondents. In those wartime letters that survive there is no mention of Lascaris for almost a year after their first meeting.

Western Desert, 13.xi.41
TO JEAN SCOTT ROGERS
My dear Jean,

I sent off an airgraph to-day as hors d'oeuvres. Airgraphs are horrible, impersonal pieces of paper, with no room for saying anything, but they do appear to arrive, which is more than can be said of many letters. However, I hope this one has better luck.

I have had two letters from you, so I suppose the others have either been sunk, or else they are lying round somewhere, and nobody will take the trouble to readdress them.

I am still in the Western Desert, and it looks as if I shall be for the rest of the War. Sometimes I feel bitter about this, thinking of all the places I might be, places like Syria and Iran. Nothing could be of less

[30]*Three Uneasy Pieces*, p.15.

interest geographically than this part of the world. It is all stones, sky, and endlessness. Perhaps so much negation will ultimately have a good effect on the character, iron out one's own tendencies to negativism. Two minuses, I mean, may make a plus.

There is very little I can tell about my life, just because there is so little to tell. I am writing this in a covered lorry, that creaks and groans in a high wind, and every few minutes I have to break off and telephone to some almost inaudible voice miles across the desert. Rosita Forbes[31] once said: Each journey I make, I leave little bits of myself behind. Well, that is exactly how I feel after one of these long distance, desert telephone calls.

The greatest problem is keeping clean. In fact, I have given up attempting this, when the water ration is about a pint a day. It is much easier in the circumstances to let the dust lie, and certainly warmer. For the nights are now very cold. Sleeping dirty has its practical side.

It is almost impossible to achieve any privacy living like this. I have to confine myself to thinking about what I am going to do afterwards, though there have been lulls when I have taken to verse (one of these poems has just been published in Australia),[32] and the other day I wrote a story, which may or may not be lucid – it is too soon to tell.

Whenever I get leave, I hitchhike to Alexandria, a long and uncomfortable process, and stay with Charles de Menasce, where I can come and go as I like. Alexandria is one of the better minor cities of this world. I'd put it in the same category as New Orleans and San Francisco – the same mixture of cultures, and the same easy tempo. People spend a lot of time chatting at street corners. By this time I have a number of friends there – Egyptians, Jews, Greeks, Syrians, and Armenians, but mercifully, no English. I get enough of the English in this Service existence. It is nice to escape occasionally to the πολλοί[33] . . .

I hope this will do, Jean, for the time being. I shall blow right out of this lorry in a minute. As it is, I am reduced to a couple of frozen kidneys. And I still have to put through the worst kind of shouting telephone call.

Write again, and tell me about *tout le monde*. Your letters read like Gibbon, lodged as I am in this later civilisation.

Ever,
Patrick.

---

[31](1890–1967), aviatrix and travel writer: *Forbidden Road*, 1937, etc.
[32]'Lines from Egypt' in the September 1941 issue of *Australia*.
[33]*polloi* = lesser breeds, rabble.

ALEXANDRIA, 7.iii.42

TO JEAN SCOTT ROGERS

Since I have been back in civilisation, and while not at lectures, I have been overeating, going to cinemas and watching the strategies of uniforms (amorous and otherwise) in hotel lounges. Sometimes this is amusing in an ironic way. Sometimes it is so sickening that I go off to the Arab quarter and sit in a deserted mosque. There is one particularly beautiful mosque, so bare and nobly proportioned and soberly decorated, that hardly anyone ever goes there. And this is my favourite place.

ALEXANDRIA, 17.iv.42

TO BEN HUEBSCH

Dear Mr Huebsch,

Your letter and the copy of The Living and the Dead arrived at last. I was delighted with the way you have done the book, binding, type, and jacket all very good. I enjoy looking into it sometimes, for it is all so old now that it begins to be new.

I can't start to tell you all my history of the last few months. It is stale enough, and will be staler still by the time it reaches you. But I was in the Second Battle of Cyrenaica, and got to Benghazi and beyond, with what seemed like adventures at the time, though they were probably insignificant enough. All I have seen of that country, is all I want to see. All I have seen of War, for that matter. But it seems to drag on with no respect for individual tastes.

I often wondered about you at the time when America was taking the plunge, knowing how you felt about active participation. I was both glad and sorry to see it come. But whatever may be, I am sure it will do America good, as a country, in the long run, to take part actively.

At the moment I am leading a comparatively quiet existence, after months of movement and discomfort. However, it is still not quiet enough, or I should say, private enough for me to do the things I want to do. I want to get started on my next book, and that must wait, perhaps too long for it to be anything but a period piece. I envy people who are able to get a book off their chests with the moment itself. I am always either forced, or inclined to keep mine back till they risk appearing to be dated.

I have resigned myself to another year in Egypt – which I like well enough in spasms, though it is second rate, even in its great periods never great. In the year 1942 I suppose it is as good as anywhere.

I have given up talk of meeting at specific dates, but I hope it will be some time soon, and with easier prospects than when we last met in New York.

With best wishes,
Yours,
Patrick White.

AT MEX ON THE western edge of Alexandria, where the rich once came to
eat fish in cafés along the water's edge, an aerodrome had been built to
defend the city. White worked here in an underground operations room as
the Axis and Allied forces prepared and fought the Battle of El Alamein.

MEX, 26.vi.42
TO JEAN SCOTT ROGERS
These are gloomy days out here, with the Germans advancing, and nobody
knowing much about the real state of affairs. My faith in armies deteriorates
as the machines encroach. We still seem to go out to war as if to a picnic,
however many times we are upset. Or else there may be a final subtlety
in this which we have not yet appreciated. I hope so.

After three months of this Wing, I am pretty tired of it – the
unchangingness of most of the people here. When not on duty, I make a
point of getting away from it if only to my cell, which fortunately I share
with a very tolerable human being called Sid Croix, a lawyer with humour
and an outlook.

I also manage to get into Alex. sometimes, and breathe something
approaching to an air of peace. My Greek friend, Manoly Lascaris, has a
new flat with the kind of atmosphere I like. The best part is a marble-
floored verandah overlooking a semi-tropical garden in a court of houses.
I can sit there any length of time doing nothing, playing with the future
perhaps in my imagination, or not even that, just dissolving in the general
green and rustle of banana and mulberry leaves . . .

My reading lately has been mainly 18th Century and Victorian, which
puts me even further out of touch with the people I have to see – people
who say: So you're reading Trollope, well, then you must also like Jane
Austen. This makes me realise again with a shock how flat, dim, dumb,
dull, and blind the world can be.

Do you know 'Mr Gil-fil's Love-Story' in George Eliot's *Scenes of
Clerical Life*? If you don't, read it, and see if you can get someone to make
a film of it for Irene Eisinger.[34] This book has made me a confirmed George
Eliot fan.

The weather is hot, but not tediously so, or perhaps after eighteen
months I have got used to sweating it out and my own lack of energy. My

[34](1906–), Austrian soprano appearing on the English stage from the mid–1930s.

taste for Egypt now is something that I could not have believed in a year ago. If only it weren't for the War, I could easily settle down here, and summon enough energy to write my next book.

MEX, 20.vii.42
TO SPUD JOHNSON

I'm sorry you didn't like *The Living and the Dead*. Most people prefer it to *Happy Valley*. As for myself, I have forgotten both these, and think only of the seven others I am saving up for the first opportunities of peace.

You mentioned a thought that passed through your head of writing to Joe Rankin for my address. Well, it's perhaps a good thing you didn't, because he wouldn't know. The last time I heard from him was November '40. Since then, not even an explanation of the silence. I know he was still around in New York, because a great friend, Peggy Stewart, spoke to him on the telephone a few months ago. What hurts me, is that there is no reason given. I can take reasons, however unpleasant, but there is something so flabby about a dead silence. (I suppose I am the last person on earth to talk to you about this, but there it is!).

Apart from the war, I could be very happy. I have made good friends in Alexandria, one in particular, a Greek called Manoly Lascaris, with whom I spend my spare time. I hope we may both turn up in the States after the War, for Manoly has an American mother living on Long Island.

I like to think of you still living in that peaceful house of yours, or have you been dragged into some kind of war work by this? Somehow, though, I don't feel the war can reach out as far as Taos. Are all those people still playing about in their beaten Mexican silver being transcendentalists?

I feel I am split up in little pieces all over the world. My sister, who has made me an uncle, is still living in England, my mother is in Sydney, and I'm glad to say I still have several important footings in the States. I sometimes hear from the Stewarts in New York and the Meltzers[35] in Charleston, and again, you in Taos. But my own New York life appears to be dead and buried. Perhaps it is all for the best. It was something too hectic to last.

Write again, as you promise, now that you have tracked me down, and give me a picture of Taos. I want to see that pink earth and those blue mountains again.

How is Brett? Please give her my love if she hasn't forgotten who I am.

Patrick.

[35]Ginny and Harold Meltzer, whom PW met on his first American travels.

ALEXANDRIA, 1.i.43
TO JEAN SCOTT ROGERS

I have managed to coincide on leave with Manoly Lascaris, and have been staying in his flat in Alexandria. To-morrow it is up for both of us, so that this evening I am not in the best of spirits, and have made much headway with a bottle of whisky on my own, Manoly having gone to say good-bye to some of his Greek relations – I thought it better to stay away and leave the flow of Greek unimpeded by attempts to speak English.

My liking for the Greeks is as strong as ever. They are a realistic people, warm without being soft and sentimental, and very loyal if they believe in you. My great lack is that I have never been to Greece. I feel that in relationship with my Greek friends I can't be all I should.

To-morrow I go back to the English and all that thinness, heartiness blathering through cardboard. Ugh!

You ask if I am writing, but I have no time for anything continuous of my own, and I am no good at anything that is not cumulative and continuous. I just go on storing up in about a dozen different compartments, and hope that some day I shall have time to get it all out. Any spare moments I have I spend reading, various things, most recently *The Last Enemy*,[36] which I think will be one of the books of the War, and Lamb's *Letters*, which are very good company when the only present company is R.A.F. officers, whose inanity just about drives one crazy. I have read much better letters than Lamb's. His whimsicality can be over-elaborate, and he hasn't the spontaneous gaiety of Gray, and he isn't visual like Cowper, or brilliant like that old bitch Walpole, but his letters are kind, and he <u>is</u> good company.

WHITE LEFT MEX FOR a job at Allied Headquarters in Alexandria compiling reports, dealing with the press and writing for the HQ news rag. He began to learn Greek. 'A terribly difficult language,' he told Scott Rogers in April. 'But I struggle along, and can now read children's books, and find writing a letter not too much of an ordeal.'[37]

ALEXANDRIA, 2.vii.43
TO JEAN SCOTT ROGERS
Dear Jean,

I am just recovering from a bout of sandfly fever.[38] To-day I am sitting up,

[36]Richard Hillary, 1942.
[37]26.iv.43.
[38]A high fever for three days with headaches and sore eyes.

and to-morrow I get up properly, and have been given 48 hours off. The whole thing is very annoying as, apart from asthma, I am not susceptible to disease.

Of course it should go and happen too just when the Bea Lillie concert party was within reach, and now they have been and gone, and I have missed them. Bea had a great success with the troops, it appears. But Vivien Leigh fell rather flat reciting some of *Gone with the Wind,* and an embarrassing piece called 'Plymouth Can Take It!' Doug was also in it, Leslie Henson, Richard Haydn, Nicholas Phipps, and Kay Young. As far as I can gather, everyone did things I have seen twenty times before, including that little sketch 'Snaps', which Mr Waters has worn to such a tatter, 'Rachmaninoff', 'Whitehall Warrior', the 'Double Damask Dinner Napkins', and other nauseous pieces, but I'm sorry I didn't see Bea again.[39]

I still have not typed the play.[40] What do you think of the novel from which it's taken. I thought it very subtle, and not *too* subtle or Henry Jamesy. The question is: would it be too subtle for that child's playground the theatre?

I have had two letters recently from Ronald, who is still rushing all the stars to Cambridge. The war grows remoter and remoter, though occasionally he makes some vague reference to an audience of troops.

I have been reading some more Trollope while ill – *The Way We Live Now,* which is a terrific panorama of vice, the sort of thing Thackeray would have liked to do but made a bore. (I can never forgive Thackeray since struggling through *The Newcomes.*) This book has an amount of violence unusual for Trollope, swindlers, forgers, really bitchy society women, the most hopeless black-sheep son I have ever met, and an American widow who fought a pistol duel with her husband, and shot a man through the head in Oregon! It's a long way from Barchester, but also excellent.

Well, we continue to wait for the invasion, but this time with much impatience, for my part. But then I was always hit or miss rather than patient. I am a bit afraid of Churchill's statement that the Germans must throw themselves on our justice. Injustice on a super-German scale is the only thing to fix the Germans.

Love,
Patrick.

---

[39]*Spring Party* was nearing the end of a three-month swing across North Africa performing as often as three times a day from Gibraltar to Cairo. Doug was Douglas Byng. The skits and songs from London revues went back to the 1920s. 'Snaps' once performed by Waters was by Herbert Farjeon.

[40]Juliana, an adaptation of *The Aspern Papers*; never performed and now lost.

HE WAS POSTED TO Palestine and spent the winter of 1943–44 interrogating refugees to find targets to bomb in the German towns these men and women had fled. Though White's support for the Jewish state was unwavering for the next thirty years, he loathed his time in Palestine. Terrorists of the Irgun began to throw bombs that winter and Haifa was under curfew. In early June White was back once more in Alexandria.

ALEXANDRIA, 17.xi.44
TO SPUD JOHNSON
My Dear Spud,
I am starting this straight after reading yours, partly because I enjoyed getting it, and partly from a sense of guilt. Is it really so long since I wrote? I don't believe it. I feel sure I did write again, and it must have been while you were away from Taos. Or is this one of the things I intended to do and then, from thinking about it, imagined that I had?

I am just finishing my fourth year in the Middle East and am due for the boat – which I am trying to avoid. I have hopes of a political or liaison job in Greece – if only people will make up their bloody minds before I am packed off. After 18 months trying, I can now read and write Greek, and speak it in pidgin fashion, so this should be useful.

Manoly is now somewhere in Greece. I was lucky enough to see him in Palestine just before he left, and brought back with me his very delightful 8 months old Schnauzer, which he couldn't take with him, and which now lives with me.[41] Again I have been lucky in that I have been able to live in Manoly's flat for the last 5 months.

Before that, 9 months in Palestine, the most awful country on earth. It makes one wonder where the few noble Jews one knows really come from.

I have written very little in the last couple of years. There has been time enough on and off, but one's mental state is not right in uniform. I have one short story supposed to be coming out, vaguely, in London, another one looking for a market (which it probably won't find as it satirises Palestinians),[42] and I am working on a third at the moment. Also I adapted Henry James's *Aspern Papers* for the stage. Nobody will touch it.

---

[41]Franz, later given the pedigree name 'Ironsides of Erehwon'; he remains a dog of legends in Sydney schnauzer circles.
[42]A Pair of Shoes which, PW explained to Jean Scott Rogers, 22.vi.44, 'are the currency of love in Zion'. Not published; now lost.

So on the whole I suppose I am a frustrated failure and would be very bitter indeed if it were not for one or two personal relationships, which are my anchor.

I am very grateful for the way you have persisted, Spud, in spite of my behaviour. Some day I hope we shall all three meet in the States.

You never heard anything more of Joe R., I suppose? That remains an unexplained mystery, and to satisfy my curiosity, I would like it cleared up. Apart from yourself, my sole surviving connexion with the States is Peggy Stewart in New York.

In England I now have two nieces, Gillian (aged 3) and Alexandra (4 months), of whom I find myself very fond although I have never seen them. My mother is still in Sydney so, for a family, we are pretty thoroughly scattered.

Please write to me again and let me know that these letter-cards do actually reach the States.

Love and best wishes
Patrick.

ALEXANDRIA, 18.xii.44

TO PEGGY GARLAND[43]

I shall certainly like to come and see the children and eat the pancakes, as you suggest, when I return, but when that will be, I can't say. My four years are up in four days. However, I have been trying for months to get to Greece, and if this is still possible and I am not put on a boat, I shall go that way. But it looks now as though the British will stink for many years to come, as far as Greek noses are concerned. Still I think this is all the more reason for me to try to go there. I feel that individuals may do much to repair the damage that has been done – if our policy will allow sympathisers to go there. How I wish I could get out of this uniform and go my own way.

I read the Layard book with interest and some surprise.[44] I had not realised that all these developments have been taking place while I have

[43]His cousin was now living outside London. After her years in Cape Town, where she took over the sculpture department of the new Michaelis School and was selected as an associate member of the Ecole de Beaux-arts in Paris, Peggy returned to England, lived for a time sculpting on Majorca, and in 1934 married a beautiful and radical doctor Tom Garland. At this time they had five children: Tomson, Nicholas, Sally, David and Tanya.

[44]*The Lady of the Hare: being a study in the healing power of dreams* by John Layard, 1944, argued the duty of analysis to illuminate as well as cure; he examined the appearance in various cultures of the hare as a symbol – particularly of sacrifice. Layard was a friend of Garland.

been sitting in my blissful Freudian backwater of the last few years. I suppose Christian symbolism for Christians is quite logical, and if this side of it was not emphasised before, most of the pioneer work was done by the Jews.

Personally I don't see why you should be afraid of a religious revival. (I speak as one who is nothing in particular.) It is almost as bad as being afraid of Communism. Perhaps the two going hand in hand may be the final answer, and certainly it would be more substantial, even taking into account the mysticism that you can't accept, than that vague ghost Democracy. Perhaps after all I am heading for Christianity myself! I don't know. But I do know that as far as my political views are concerned, the last few years have made me want to hear less theory and see more practice. With so much dead wood cleared out of the European countries by the War, I hope we may see this afterwards, in spite of the current diplomatic efforts of our government.

Suzanne announces that she is taking the children back to London to-day, which I think is very foolish, especially as there is no need. Or have the rockets stopped coming over? I hear nothing these days of what attention the Germans are paying to London, neither from letters nor from newspapers . . .

Well here is the end of the page. When I come back I shall remind you of your invitations.

Yours,
Patrick.

ALEXANDRIA, 3.i.45
TO MOLLIE McKIE[45]
You will not be able to believe that I am still where you left me, with even less justification than before. (I now spend most of my time compiling a lexicon of Modern Greek.) My hopes of getting to Greece were pretty high at one time. Then they were dashed by the Civil War, for nobody over there had any time to think of putting me in. Last week I thought I might at last be going, to replace Deakin, who was believed to be a prisoner, but I was foiled by him turning up again . . .

I am trying to get something as a stopgap in case the job in Greece should suddenly materialise, but this is very difficult. S.[46] managed to get

---

[45](1904–90), WAF intelligence officer in PW's unit, she became a teacher in Australia and Britain after the war. McKie was a birdlike woman of strong but cloistered enthusiasms for people and literature; a cheerful Christian and prolific letter writer; PW corresponded with her until they split over Australian politics in the mid–1970s.
[46]PW's commanding officer Basil Reay, known as Sunshine.

me a reprieve of a couple of months from the boat. If I do get sent back, I propose to try to get back to Greece from that end. I <u>know</u> that I can do something to further relations, much more than the people to whom Greece means nothing – but perhaps that is part of the policy.

I had a bad attack of asthma with bronchitis before Christmas, and they sent me to hospital for a week, after which they gave me a week's sick leave. It panned out very nicely as my friend Manoly Lascaris turned up on leave at the same time. When he went back he took his dog along with him, a support that I miss very much, though perhaps it is just as well as he has taken to tearing pieces out of Warrant Officers' pants.

Steve has started giving dancing lessons here. I went along to the tango, but did not find the Admin. block and standing in a line listening to one-two-slow turn conducive to learning, so I departed while everyone was in the midst of a slow turn.

THREE

A Patch of Soil

February 1945 – December 1951

WHITE REACHED GREECE IN February and was posted to an aerodrome on
the outskirts of Athens to train Greek pilots in operational intelligence. In
June he was transferred to Allied HQ in the city to draft speeches, in
Greek and English, for the RAF commanders. His off-duty hours he spent
in a room on the upper slopes of the Lykabettos. Here he began writing
again and produced about half a dozen short stories.

ATHENS, 17.ii.45

TO MOLLIE McKIE

As you will see by the address, I got here at last, but in most disappointing
circumstances, for I went into hospital shortly after my arrival with another
attack of bronchitis, and here I still am after nine days. It must soon come
to an end. But in the meantime it is very exasperating, not having had
time to get into the job nor to see anything.

I left Egypt after two days in a P.T.C.[1] (a phenomenon that I imagine
is very close to a Fascist state), interspersed with visits to Sunshine, who
was laid up with tonsillitis. Nobody could have worked harder over my
posting, and I hope I shall be able to repay him some day. When finally
I left it was to go and report to M.A.A.F. and B.A.F. on my way here.[2]
Nothing could have been more unnecessary than this circular tour, for at
each place I did no more than talk about nothing for half an hour with
someone who was not particularly interested. All it did really was to give
me this attack of bronchitis. The country was cold, miserable, desolate,
the inhabitants more squalid than the Arabs and not as amusing. I was
very pleased to get out of it and on to the plane for Greece. The last lap
of the journey was like a beautiful, feverish dream with old maps coming
to life underneath . . .

From what I see of the landscape through the window in the hospital,
the country is all that I desire. I feel that if it weren't for the War I would
be here for ever. But everyone else grumbles and grumbles, and the nostalgia

[1]Personnel Transit Centre.
[2]Mediterranean Army Air Force and British Air Force at Caserta outside Naples.

59

for Surbiton is very high. I think time and motion have rubbed all the nationality out of me, and I could live anywhere, provided it isn't Palestine and (probably) Italy . . .

Now I have to bow to war routine and go to bed. Two sessions in hospital this winter and I have about had enough. I get no better at accepting it either. I have reached the stage where my way is definitely the right way, which is a sign that the War ought to stop.

Yours,
Patrick.

ATHENS, 9.iii.45

TO JEAN SCOTT ROGERS

Of course conditions are still chaotic – fantastic prices, poverty, everyone very shaken by the Civil War on top of everything else. But the charm comes out on top of it all.

I had a number of friends here right from the start, the families of friends in Egypt, and they could not have been more spontaneous in their kindness and hospitality. I only wish I could do more for them in return.

I found my Greek blossom on my arrival, as if it had only been waiting for the right atmosphere. It is still far from fluent, but I can spend an evening holding a Greek conversation, and altogether it is a great asset. I am having lessons with a Miss Pesmazoglou from Smyrna, a very worthy spinster who wears mittens and a grey page-boy bob!

I shall not try to describe the Acropolis, which is an experience beyond words. I was sceptical on first seeing it through snow and a lavatory window. Then I climbed up to it on a blue and gold afternoon – Write again soon.

Love,
Patrick.

ATHENS, 27.iv.45

TO JEAN SCOTT ROGERS

This evening a shepherd has been playing his pipes underneath my window, and sometimes I walk through the oatfields at dusk, and smell the stocks in cottage gardens, and respond suitably to the black and melancholy cypresses lining the path. It is a beautiful, beautiful country – and I can't see Katie Pfister[3] belonging to it!

War news is increasingly good. Germany has almost ceased to be on

---

[3] A London friend of Rogers with a Greek mother.

the situation map we keep up in the office. I get great satisfaction out of visualising the destruction of Berlin, a city I always hated.

ATHENS, 2.v.45
TO THE PRIME MINISTER OF AUSTRALIA[4]
Sir,
I take the liberty to make a suggestion which, if the Australian Government saw its way to carrying it out, would be both a noble gesture on the part of Australia and a measure of assistance to a country which has suffered great hardship under the German occupation.

I am at present stationed in Greece, for which country I think all Australians who fought in the 1941 Campaign will still retain affection and admiration, and where I am continually discovering proof of friendship and appreciation of Australia. I am myself an Australian. My father, Victor White, was part owner of the property Belltrees at Scone in New South Wales, of which my cousin Alfred White is now owner. I have had a little experience of sheep raising myself, and believe that parts of Greece resemble parts of Australia, the southern mountainous area of New South Wales, for instance, where the winters are cold and the summers hot. It is my belief that Merino sheep might be bred profitably in Greece, and that the experiment would be worth the making.

I understand that there is a law against exporting sheep from Australia. However, I put forward the suggestion that in the circumstances it would be a generous act if the Australian Government were to present the Government of Greece with a small experimental flock of Merino sheep. Greece was badly depleted of stock by the Germans. It will take her some time to build up her resources, and particularly to revive her agricultural and pastoral life, which for Greece as for Australia is of the utmost importance. Greece's output of wool before the War was comparatively small. An increase and improvement of this output, if the introduction of Merino sheep were to prove a success, would be a considerable economic asset to a small and poor country. It is unnecessary to point out that an increase in wool production in a country of the size of Greece could not affect the interest of Australian wool producers.

Appreciating the pastoral difficulties which Australia now has to face as the result of recent drought, I would still beg the Australian Government to consider my proposal. It would, of course, be necessary to send with such an experimental flock an experienced Australian manager as adviser. In this case I would be willing myself to approach the Minister of Agriculture

[4]Ben Chifley (1885–1951), prime minister from 1945 until his defeat by Menzies in 1949.

for Greece and suggest that the Greek Government provide a salary for an Australian adviser, and consider sites for an experimental farm in a climatically suitable area.

In conclusion, I venture to suggest that such tenders of international assistance may well help to strengthen the peace in the difficult years which follow this long War, and that a country of Australia's size and growing importance will gain in the eyes of the world by showing herself able to make her own spontaneous, international gestures.

I am, Sir,

Yours respectfully,

Patrick White.

ATHENS, 9.vii.45

TO JEAN SCOTT ROGERS

On my free Sundays I have been making a point of hitchhiking round Attica. It is by far the best way to see the country, as going with one's friends only means chatter about the things one chatters about every day. As it is I have been meeting the peasants and talking to them. On one occasion a Greek even asked me if I was Greek. On these occasions I have taken myself to the Gulf of Corinth, Marathon and best of all, the temple of Neptune at Cape Sounion. Another high spot was the walk over the mountains from Marathon to the dam accompanied by the greengrocer's boy and a donkey laden with apricots, and attacked by fierce sheepdogs which we had to drive off with stones.

I have just finished my first story with a Greek setting. I hope and think it is good. But it is so difficult to suggest Greek conversation in English – there are too many words and phrases for which we have no equivalent.[5] I have got the money for the story that is to be published in *Bugle Blast*, but there is no sign of its appearing.[6]

I hope this will atone for some of my silences.

Love,

Patrick.

[5]'On the Balcony', the tale of a failed courtship in a city of women anxious to find husbands, is the only one of the stories he wrote in Athens to survive; *Harper's Bazaar*, August 1957, p.112.

[6]'After Alep', about the collapse of service marriages which he had followed week by week censoring the letters of the men in his unit, appeared in the third *Bugle Blast* collection of wartime writing published by Allen & Unwin, 1945, p.147.

ATHENS, 22.x.45

TO MOLLIE McKIE

My negotiations for the sheep are still in progress. I have at least had a letter from the Prime Minister's Secretary to say the matter is being considered, but I am afraid that if they are ever sent here they will be stolen and eaten long before they can produce any wool.[7]

ATHENS, 24.x.45

TO SPUD JOHNSON

My dear Spud,

It was a great pleasure to see your beautiful writing again after such a long time, but in this letter you told me very little about yourself. However, writing to me recently has been rather like dropping letters into space.

I have been in Greece for almost nine months now. I got what I wanted by dint of pestering people and have never regretted it. Except that it has been a disappointment for Manoly not to be here too. His regiment was kept in the islands, then withdrawn to Egypt, and apart from a month in summer when he came to Athens on leave, I have not seen anything of him this year. But the day after to-morrow I am supposed to be leaving for Alexandria on leave. M. has been demobilised in the meantime, and will be at home when I arrive.

In spite of all the obvious drawbacks – revolutions, invasions, and economic insecurity – , I am planning to live in Greece after I get out of the Air Force. What I want to do is buy the agency for certain commodities to import into this country,[8] have M. manage the business for me, and settle down to write all the things I have been prevented from writing during the war. No doubt it will be some time before all one's plans can materialise. I shall probably have to fight to get out of England again once I am inside it, and there will probably be difficulty attached to taking money out of the country. But again, one can achieve anything if one pesters long enough.

I expect to return to England at the end of the year, and get my freedom about January. I can think of nothing more exhilarating and really unbelievable than escape from the Service and the automaton existence among uncongenial people one has led for so long. In civilian warwork however mechanised and regimented it may have been, I imagine the

[7]The Australian government maintained its absolute ban on the export of rams.

[8]Pharmaceuticals: the plan was to buy them in Egypt and sell them in Greece where everything from aspirin to penicillin was in short supply; but the Greek government soon stepped in to end the drought.

individual did not experience the esoteric nightmare of tradition, behaviour, procedure, or whatever you like to call it. This is something that has always horrified me. I suppose it is some kind of a colonial's complex or related to the anarchist hidden inside me.

I feel I ought to tell you something about Greece, but I don't know where to begin. It is an absorbing country. Difficult to know why. But it is an increasing obsession, in spite of the fact that the people are frequently maddening and that one can see no real hope for them or ultimate solution to their problem. They have this terrible innate desire to destroy themselves, just as they have destroyed or attempted to destroy so many of their great men from Socrates down. But one continues to want to do all one can for them. I can't say more than I have already said – I want to stay here the rest of my life.

I wonder when we shall meet. Sooner or later no doubt. Taos will have to become a half-way house to Australia.

I hope you will write again and tell me more about your life.
Ever,
Patrick.[9]

ATHENS, 9.xii.45
TO JEAN SCOTT ROGERS
Writing has become very difficult. I have to struggle to express myself accurately, except when I am bitter, and then I express myself all too freely, but it is distorted. One of the major problems is how to cure oneself of bitterness after the last few years. Without the benefit of religion, and with too low an opinion of mankind to become a convinced Communist – how? But perhaps all this is a last burst of resentment at Service life, and I shall acquire a fresh frame of mind with my civilian clothes.

HE WAS SHIPPED BACK to London, demobbed in early January 1946 and found a room in his old digs in Ebury Street. There he raised a schnauzer pup, Lottie, and while trying to find a boat to take them both to Alexandria, began to write *The Aunt's Story*. Even while he was with the South Africans in the Sudan he was sketching the unhappy odyssey of Theodora Goodman, a wandering spinster going mad in a world on the brink of violence. The politics of the 1930s played a role in the novel, but at heart it was a portrait of a kind of woman familiar in the White world: an ageless but distinguished figure whose life has been wasted honourably at the beck and call of others. As White drafted the novel's opening

[9]This is PW's last letter to Johnson whose existence was never mentioned to Lascaris.

section set in the New South Wales of his childhood, memories of the country he had not seen for fourteen years poured onto the page. 'An alarming departure,' he told Mamblas, 'after writing R.A.F. prose for so long and not being free to think as I chose. But the despair and difficulties of writing one's own book are so much preferable to other despair and difficulties.'[10]

The only way to get the dog to Alexandria was to charter a light plane. They arrived in April. White continued to work on the novel – drafting the virtuoso central section of fantasies and dreams called 'The Jardin Exotique' – while the city was in turmoil around them. Lascaris had convinced White that Greece was an impossible destination and clearly they could not stay long in Egypt. Their home might have to be Australia. Ruth tried to discourage him. 'She can't say too much against it,' White told Scott Rogers. 'So I want to see first for myself whether it is as bad as she says. She, of course, has not experienced England as it is now.'[11]

White found a berth in a dormitory on the *Strathmore* and leaving Lascaris behind in Alexandria set out for home. Sitting on deck as the ship crossed the Indian Ocean, he drafted the third part of *The Aunt's Story* in which Theodora Goodman, too, is heading back to Australia. Theodora baulks and disappears into the dust and pink mountains of New Mexico seeking 'humility . . . pureness of being'. White stepped ashore in shabby Fremantle and discovered at once that he was home. A week later the ship reached Sydney and he moved into his mother's house on Darling Point.

SYDNEY, LATE 1946
TO JEAN SCOTT ROGERS[12]
I had not realised how Australian I am underneath until I came back and saw it and smelled it again. An ugly corner pub with iron-lace balconies was quite an emotional experience when I caught sight of it on landing at Fremantle.

There are plenty of drawbacks, but the sun and the plenty atone for most of them. There are almost worse Governmental restrictions and bureaucratic opposition than in England. No houses to be had. No houses to be built, because of the restrictions on materials. All sorts of hindrances to business, as I know from trying tentatively to start an export business.

[10]5.ii.46; Mamblas was now the Duke of Baena and Spain's ambassador to the Hague.
[11]27.vii.46.
[12]The opening page or pages of this letter are lost.

If you can get the goods, you find after going to four Govt. departments, that the last one will not give you a licence. If you get the licence, the manufacturer may not let you have the goods. And then of course there are shipping complications.[13]

But in spite of this, I would advise anyone who is not ineradicably English, or who wanted to lead a certain kind of scholarly life, or to make a name for himself in the theatre, to leave England and come to Australia.[14]

I have not yet been to the theatre for there is not much theatre to go to . . .

I am staying with my mother at present, but towards the end of January she will be giving up the house, preparatory to leaving for England. Then I don't know where I shall find a roof. Probably in Egypt, where I must return anyway, to take the dogs to England, to bring them out here! So you will see me sooner or later, for a little.

I have got nearly halfway through the book in re-writing and typing it. My phases of hope and despair have been many. At one stage I nearly threw the whole thing away. At present I am sobering down a little after an exhilarating rebirth of enthusiasm. When all is said, I have not the slightest idea what the book is like.

Are you still living with your family? I am definitely not made for living with mine. I have done it so little that I have lost what little art I had. I am no good now for anything but coming out when I have something to say, then going back and closing the door. And women perpetually in the house, what a jangle, what a curse!

I am sending you a box of food, which will arrive too late for Christmas, of course, but no doubt it will still be eatable. Write and tell me what you are doing. I have really been working quite a lot, which is some small excuse for not writing letters. Only when I read in my Sunday horoscope that I would do something I had been putting off, did I feel the time had come.

Love,
Patrick.

---

[13]The new plan was to bankroll an Alexandrian Cypriot wanting to import pins, paper clips and rubber bands into Egypt where they were in short supply. The first consignment was the death of the scheme: Australian pins were too blunt for Egyptian paper.
[14]PW tried to persuade Suzanne to bring her family out to Sydney. 'I still fail to see how the Pecks could not live happier lives out here, bringing up their children in sunlight and plenty, and saving 25% of their income,' he told Jean Scott Rogers, 17.ii.47. 'I think probably my mother is at the bottom of it, with her hatred of Australia, and rosy visions of a pre-War Bond Street.'

PUBLISHED 30.x.46
TO THE EDITOR
SYDNEY MORNING HERALD
Sir,

One point which appears to have been overlooked in the correspondence that has arisen out of the childish and unjust accusations made against the *Strathmore* immigrants,[15] is the vital necessity for easing the European situation immediately by the admission of immigrants to under-populated countries. After five years in the Eastern Mediterranean, I feel that I can speak with some knowledge of the problem . . .

Full bellies, a roof, and a plot of land breed content. As these requisites are generally more accessible to the British and Americans, they are sometimes unable to understand the nostalgic desire of the have-nots to achieve the same state. Although I am myself a British national[16] and an ex-Serviceman who shared a dormitory with nearly 100 foreign immigrants in the *Strathmore*, and although I argued for nine months to get a passage to Australia, I must still maintain the necessity for allotting a good percentage of passages to foreign immigrants whether it is to the British Dominions, the United States or South America, and that at once.

If a few Britons suffer temporarily by not travelling where and as they wish they have at least the mental comfort and moral support that a 'safe' nationality brings in a world in which problems are still distressingly national. But the immigration issue is not a national one. We must learn to think in international terms if we are to avoid an accentuation in world suffering.

Patrick White.

SYDNEY, 11.i.47
TO BEN HUEBSCH
Dear Mr Huebsch,

Yesterday I sent off to you the MS. of my new book, *The Aunt's Story*, which has taken me just a year to finish. Needless to say, I hope you like it! It has meant a lot to me in the writing, and has cost sweat and blood, as my first book after five years of inactivity. But I am still unable to judge it from the angle of a publisher or a public. So we shall see.

If there is any business to be discussed would you please do this with Curtis Brown, whose address I have lost, or if you don't like the book,

---

[15]Passengers complained to the paper about Eastern Europeans spitting, throwing fruit peelings on the decks, taking berths from British immigrants, etc.
[16]Australians at this time were still British nationals.

would you return the MS. to them? I believe Naomi Burton still deals with novels.[17]

I forget when I wrote last but believe it was while I was still in Greece. I left that country at the end of 1945 and went back to be demobilised in England. I dislike England intensely. I don't mind physical discomfort, but there was a kind of mental apathy and deadness that got me down. I left after three months and went to Egypt, then on to Australia.

Re-discovering my home country was an interesting experience, and full of nostalgia. I have been impressed by a great many things. The people are beginning to develop, and take an interest in books, and painting, and music, to an extent that surprises me, knowing them fourteen years ago. One gets the impression that a great deal is about to happen.

I have made up my mind to settle here, but am going away again first, probably in a few weeks time, to collect up various possessions. I have, among other things, two schnauzers stranded in Egypt. They are not allowed to come to Australia from a foreign country, but will be eligible if they spend six months in England. So all this has to happen first . . .

It is difficult to write anything but a bald and uncommunicative letter, with such gaps of years in our correspondence, but I hope one day we shall meet again. If one does settle in a place like Australia one has at least to pass through other countries to get anywhere. I look at it like that. So no doubt I shall see you.

Hoping you and your family are well,
Yours sincerely,
Patrick White.

HMT ASTURIAS, INDIAN OCEAN 3.iv.47
TO JEAN SCOTT ROGERS
I left Sydney in the *Asturias* on the 22nd March. So far the only positive thing about the voyage is that I am on my way. Conditions are steerage, except that, when not eating or sleeping, one can wander about in the more select parts of the ship. The dormitory is far worse than the one in the *Strathmore* as it is built round the shaft of a hold, and has a fierce smell of rank old men (this is a mixture of stale woollen underclothes, old newspapers, and shag). We serve ourselves with food (and such food), and take it in turns to do our own washing up in a greasy bucket, beside the

[17]Naomi Burton at Curtis Brown was PW's New York agent 1939–59; no successor pleased him so much and alone in the world she addressed letters to him, 'Dear Pat'.

table. Now that we are in the tropics I should think dysentery will spring up at any moment.

ALEXANDRIA, 9.v.47

TO PEPE MAMBLAS

I wonder if you remember a play I wrote about nine years ago about a Spaniard at St Jean-de-Luz? It surprised me by getting produced in London a couple of months ago.[18] Just a try-out of three weeks. And it flopped, as I feared it might. It is too slight, and has too little action for these times. However, I am told some people liked it very much, and that Queen Mary went to it. Why she should have chosen that particular play, and what she must have thought on seeing it, I wonder.[19]

The novel on which I was working all last year is to be published by Routledge, my pre-War publisher.[20] They are described as being <u>extremely enthusiastic</u>, but have not yet given the date for its appearance. As there is still a severe paper shortage in England, I gather it may be many months. This book is called *The Aunt's Story*. It is the one I think will only appeal to a few, though I cannot explain why, anymore than I know why a Picasso will sometimes appeal to a charwoman and not to a University don.

At the moment I am idling, or would be if I had not begun to wean seven schnauzer pups, which Lottie produced on my bed a couple of nights after my arrival. They are very pretty at this stage, getting about on wobbly legs, with their whiskers just starting to sprout. I am sorry that I cannot keep all seven, and am a little bit afraid of the day when I shall be in a position to indulge in whole litters of my own pups . . .

Quite honestly I wish I could skip the rest of this year, and find myself settled on a few acres of land in Australia. I am still determined on that completing of the circle. I like patterns, and Europe seems to me a prospect of unending shapelessness.

With love,
Patrick.

WAITING IN LONDON FOR the dogs to clear quarantine, White wrote *The Ham Funeral*. The play grew out of a painting of a fat corpse he had seen in Sydney. The painter, William Dobell, explained he was living in Pimlico before the war when his landlord died; the widow let down her hair announcing there would be a 'ham funeral' and sent the young

[18]*Return to Abyssinia* was directed by John Wyse at the Boltons Theatre from 11–30 March.
[19]According to Wyse, she liked it very much.
[20]No. He first went to Routledge with *The Living and the Dead*, 1941.

Dobell to fetch the relatives. White made the young man a poet, and the play the drama of his escape from the Mother, the family, the country and the life that would stop him being an artist. As White wrote the play he brawled with Viking over *The Aunt's Story*, first about the title – 'It fastened itself to the book when I first conceived it eight years ago,' he told Huebsch. 'Somehow I can't think of one without the other'[21] – and then about corrections.

68 EBURY STREET, 1.xi.47
TO MARSHALL BEST[22]
Dear Mr Best,
I am distressed to learn from your letter of the 17th Oct, that *The Aunt's Story* may appear before my corrections can be made. The only consolation is that a sharp proof-reader has been over it for you and spotted the worst mistakes. Although there are not many, I suppose, there are enough serious ones? What Australian will not laugh, for instance, on reading of a 'fiord' in Australia. And there are enough printer's errors in the French to make the author look ignorant and pretentious. I hope you will do everything possible to add some kind of a correction. I feel this is a far more important matter than any invasion of privacy.[23]

    Yours sincerely,
    Patrick White.

'ENGLAND I FOUND A nightmare,' White told Mollie McKie.[24] He sold or gave away all his furniture, left *The Ham Funeral* with Curtis Brown – his agents could do nothing with the play in London or New York – and despatched the dogs and paintings to Sydney. *The Aunt's Story* appeared in New York soon after he sailed, and the reviews were good. At Port Said Lascaris came to the ship for a few hours. The Alexandria flat had been sold and Lascaris was waiting for a seat on the flying boat. Their

[21] 30.vi.47.
[22] (1901–82), apprentice and successor to Huebsch, he saw through the Viking Press all PW's novels from *The Aunt's Story* to *The Vivisector*.
[23] PW had alerted Viking to 31 mistakes, some his own, but some the typesetters' including a cart crossing the paddocks and splashing through 'the brown water of the fiord'; Best agreed to tip into the first printing an errata slip with fourteen corrections. He told PW, 4.xi.1947: 'We have learned our lesson . . . You have an eagle eye.' On the matter of privacy: PW had to clear with John Holstius of San Francisco the use of his name in the novel.
[24] 19.i.48.

cook, Athena Borghese, was to follow some time later by sea. White arrived in Sydney in February 1948 and took a room at Petty's Hotel.

SYDNEY, 4.ii.48
TO BEN HUEBSCH
Dear Mr Huebsch,
Thank you very much for your letter and the batch of cuttings, which were waiting here for me when I arrived yesterday. The major reviews are certainly very gratifying, but it looks to me, from the attitude of the lesser critics, as though the book will hardly be a seller. I suppose my own mother would be representative of the reading public, i.e. those women who go to the library and get out another novel, and her reaction was: 'What a pity you didn't write a story about a cheery aunt'.

Who is Orville Prescott of the *N. Y. Times?*[25] I should be inclined to point out to him that the Viking published both my other novels (which he announces were not published in the States), and that they were well reviewed in the *Times* by Ralph Thompson and Jane Spence Southron. In fact, Ralph Thompson included *Happy Valley* in his books of the season in July 1940.[26]

Now I am thinking of houses rather than novels. I have already started the search. To-day I went out to look at a 20-acre farm on the outskirts of Sydney, but somehow I think it is not for me. I know the smell of ducks need not prevail for ever, but it starts one with a prejudice. And then there is the bath on the end of the verandah, and the lavatory down the yard. However, my ambitions may grow humbler as the search is prolonged. Also I am anxious to get somewhere to house the dogs, who should arrive next week, and who will only have to do two months quarantine.

I forgot to say that I think the book looks very striking. It's a pity, though, we had all those mistakes. I can't quite let that stay dead.

LASCARIS ARRIVED IN SYDNEY in the last week of February. Within days they had found a few acres at Castle Hill where they could run a small farm and breed their dogs. To Huebsch White wrote, 'I suppose all this has been lying dormant in me all these years. Coming to think of it, I am

---

[25]Prescott (1906–) had been the paper's daily literary critic since 1942.
[26]Thompson reviewed *Happy Valley*, 22 May 1940, p.21, and also in his 'Books of the Times' selection, 1 July, p.17: 'Tart and unusual'. Southron reviewed *Happy Valley* in *New York Times Book Review*, 26 May, p.7, and *The Living and the Dead*, same section, 9 Feb. 1941, p.6.

almost the only renegade from the land my family has produced.'[27] Lascaris had a job waiting for him in a French bank in the city, but White insisted he stay on the farm. Both men looked after the garden and the dogs. Lascaris drove the van – White never had a driving licence – and ploughed and planted the big paddock; White took care of the chickens and milked the cow. The only steady income the farm ever earned came from cream sold illicitly for two shillings a jar.

THE GLEN, 6.viii.48
TO BEN HUEBSCH
Our acres are just beginning to come alive after a severe winter. I suppose that will mean <u>less</u> time for writing. And on top of it all, my favourite schnauzer bitch has just had eleven pups, which I shall soon be hand-feeding, each one separately, five times a day. And I am also about to take on a hundred day-old chickens. So you see.

I may, however, start another novel in time, if my hand has not lost its shape, and if I can find the energy to root the junk out of an old outhouse to make a workroom.

I don't know whether you heard that *Happy Valley* and *The Aunt's Story* are being published in French by Gallimard. I have not heard who will translate. Still no sign of an English edition of the latter. I should be filled with disgust if I had not lost interest, after being well satisfied by the results of your edition.

This has brought me much strange and interesting correspondence. One lady wrote pages telling me how she resembled Theodora and her mother Mrs Goodman. Then she went on to curse the British, in rather a mixed letter. Funnily enough her name was Mrs Louisa Fluck.

I am sure I have been right in returning to the land. Now I look with horror at the rootless, pointless years, for they <u>were</u> pointless even at their most <u>significant</u>. What surprises me is that so many people continue to miss the point. Do you own a small piece of land as well as your perch on Manhattan rock? If you don't, I beg you to acquire a few acres at once and see what I mean.

Yours ever,
Patrick White.

[27]9.iii.48.

THE GLEN, 26.ix.48
TO JEAN SCOTT ROGERS
I have not yet seen any English reviews of *The Aunt's Story*. In America
the ones that mattered were as good as any I have seen of anybody's book.
Even so, very few people seem to have read it. And I imagine, though
there have been fan letters, that there were a great many, like you, who
did not like it. There are certain states of mind that one does or does not
apprehend, just as one does or does not respond to pure music or abstraction
in paint. Rational explanations don't help. So even if I went, step by step,
explaining this piece and that, I still don't feel you would accept my
contention that lunacy is richer than reason in a world in which reason
has become lunatic.

THE GLEN, 27.x.48
TO MOLLIE McKIE
At last we have our Athena Borghese. She arrived the day before yesterday
in the *Napoli* carrying a pillowslip of dried herbs. Already her cooking has
restored our morale and we seem to have hours extra to spend on outside
work. We did have a New Zealander for two months, but she made us
suffer a great deal, always telling us what a 'lady' she was, and about her
daughter-in-law, whose father is 'Manager of the Chemical Works, England.'
   At the moment we are surrounded by bush fires. Fortunately we are
pretty clear round this place, but it adds to the tension under which we
have been living. We have had a series of disasters lately – a kerosene

brooder in flames (from which the chickens were miraculously saved), pups with distemper (one dead), myself bitten through the wrist in a dog fight, and as a final touch, one of the cows has just had a miscarriage!

The Aunt's Story finally came out in England. I have had rather a silly review in the Times Lit. Suppl.,[28] and I believe there was an excellent one by John Betjeman (Continual Dew) in the Daily Herald.[29] The reviews take such a long time to appear nowadays, and then trickle on over months. However, I couldn't care less.

THE LONDON REVIEWERS' RESPONSE was mixed but at least they paid attention. All The Aunt's Story had in Sydney was a brief and obscure review in the Sydney Morning Herald condemning the 'lingering feeling of staginess and unreality' that pervaded the book 'as though the artifice has plastered itself too thick'.[30] Australia's critics were never really forgiven this tepid welcome home. White told his friends he had no wish to write, that all he wrote these days were cheques. 'It seems to be the chief evening pastime,' he told Mollie McKie. 'Sometimes I feel I shall be glad when there is nothing left and one can sit down in peace and live off one's milk and vegetables in a romantically neglected wilderness.'[31]

He now grew close to Peggy Garland who came to celebrate their first Christmas at the farm. She was very like her cousin Patrick: quick, possessive, curious, game, generous if she trusted but cold when her Withycombe suspicion was roused. Yet the two cousins looked at the world through contrary eyes: she presumed good where he suspected evil; she saw a welcome where White assumed hostility.

Tom Garland had been told he might lose his sight unless he lived in a mild climate, so the Garlands moved to New Zealand. The marriage was already in trouble. Soon after reaching Wellington, the Garlands' sixth child, Philip, was born brain-damaged. Peggy no longer sculpted, but soon became a figure in New Zealand as a radio broadcaster, reviewing books and paintings, giving talks and sitting on 'brains trusts'. The Garlands' house was a meeting place for writers, local grandees, left-wing unionists, university people and hordes of children.

---

[28]Suggesting, 2 Oct., p.553, that PW discipline his 'often stimulating' but 'sometimes ridiculous' prose.

[29]21 Sept., p.2: 'Patrick White must be one of the best living writers of English prose. But this does not mean he will necessarily be popular. He demands effort and he has his mannerisms. He is a dead loss to the libraries; a great asset to English literature.' Betjeman's collection Continual Dew appeared in 1937.

[30]7 Aug. 1948, p.6.

[31]16.ii.49.

Dogwoods, 2.v.49

TO PEGGY GARLAND

Dear Peggy,

As usual now it has taken me weeks to answer a letter. The days when I sat down and wrote one spontaneously seem to be over. But it did take me some time to get my energy back after this attack of asthma, and now with pups and things to feed, the days draw out longer and longer ...

While I was in hospital they gave me some skin tests to find out what gives me asthma, and decided it is feathers, kapok, rye grass, and pork! The last is easy enough to avoid, but the others are practically inescapable. Since I came home I have been having a series of injections, and may have to continue for 18 months, the local doctor tells me. The first few weeks I felt terrible – congested, and wheezing day and night – now, I hardly dare say it, I feel a change is taking place – my nose and chest drying up. It almost sounds like a newspaper testimonial. But perhaps it will work.

The place was strangled by weeds when I got back, as Manoly could only concentrate on the animals. The milking was done by a little girl called Joan Whorff, one of a family of 14, who live in a tin shed behind us, and whose father owns the bull we patronise. Joan W. did not do her job very well. Both the cows went off very badly. I expect there was too much giggling and chatter, as she used to bring her brother and sisters, Ken, Heather, Hazel, and Marlo as bodyguard. (Marlo is presumably short for Marlene.)

Both the cows are now in calf, I hope. But I have had a lot of trouble with Mabel, and am getting rid of her as soon as I can. She has developed a passion for breaking through fences. Several times I have found her on the road, and on the last occasion I discovered Athena trying to coax her in through the front gate. The climax came yesterday when M. broke through into the orchard, trampled all over some stocks Manoly has put in for market, and ended up outside the garage.

The pullets began to lay at 5½ months, and by this time are almost all producing. I don't think the one with the crooked neck has achieved an egg yet, nor the one we treated for diarrhoea. The latter has developed into a kind of flamingo shape, presumably from avoiding the others, who persecute her continually. The old hens all went to market a couple of weeks ago, and we have broken up their yard and sown it with grass and clover in readiness for this winter's chickens.

Solomon and Maggy distinguished themselves at the Castle Hill and Sydney Shows by each winning a Challenge at each. At Sydney the English judge, who did know the breed, pleased us by saying Maggy has the makings of a great schnauzer bitch. Monkey had eight pups seven weeks ago. We have only just started to try to sell them in earnest, and have sold one to a German Jewess who wanted to buy Maggy.

Many shrubs have gone in since you were here. We are making a hedge of them from the garage to the corner of the fowl yard, that is, along the edge of the citrus orchard, trying to incorporate all the seasons. We also have a Judas tree at last, though a poor, sickly, doubtful thing in place of the out-of-place deodar, and a golden elm at the end of the back lawn, in place of the barren plum. We have to wait till the winter for the arbutus, a crab apple, an English mulberry, and three Lombardy poplars on the boundary across the creek where the carobs have failed. Finally we have put in four dogwoods, and have just changed the name of the place to *Dogwoods*, as *The Glen* had always stuck in our throats, and this is more appropriate in more ways than one.

Our Irish neighbour Mrs Risbon is still having trouble with the grub in her cabbage. She told Manoly recently, however, that a man she met in the bus had said the pests we shall get soon will reduce us to bread and water. And did he know? Manoly asked. Well, said Mrs R., he looked as though he did. I called on her a few days ago, and found her looking magnificent, her hair hanging down, a greenish, grizzled brown, under a brown velvet cap in the Rembrandt manner. The poor thing has had out her teeth, by correspondence, I should think, and is now replete with some uneasy uppers in the shape of a shoebuckle, which fly out as she speaks, and which she hiccups back behind her hand with a: Pardon me.[32]

Last week I had a letter from a Mme. d'Estournelles de Constant, who has almost finished translating *Happy Valley* and *The Aunt's Story* for Gallimard.[33] How curious I am to see Australian disguised as French. Have you written any more? And what becomes of what you write? I feel I shall never put pen to paper again, and can't much care.

Anyway, this letter has run on, and you are probably much too busy coping with children to read it. Tomson[34] certainly looks handsome – a Withycombe, crossed with a Slav.

I can see no chance of my ever coming to New Zealand, but perhaps in fifteen years time you will take another holiday here. By then we should have a garden worth looking at. Incidentally, our New Zealand lidy, Lumsden, drove past recently in a *cear* and looked at us. (I have discovered

[32]These details attached themselves to Mrs O'Dowd in *The Tree of Man*.
[33]See PW to Stern, 24.ix.58, page 149.
[34]Her eldest son.

how one pronounces that New Zealand-Australian a̱. One tucks it against
the roof of the mouth somewhere under the right nostril, and then one
lets go.)

To-night is a butter night, unfortunately, so I must stop.

Please remember me to anyone who remembers me

Yours,

Patrick.

DOGWOODS, 18.vii.49

TO PEGGY GARLAND

Dear Peggy,

I have put off writing this letter hoping that I might have the burst of
oracular wisdom you seem to expect. But as time goes on I feel less and
less oracular. And anyway, I don't think it possible to give advice. People
make their own way through the fog. I expect even now you see more
shape in the muddle than you did at the time of writing, and wonder just
how much you wrote.

I imagine your situation (for want of a better word) is fairly general
to marriages that have lasted, just as irritation and counter-irritation develop
out of most human relationships. You, at least, hold the trump card of six
children. I should have thought it possible to disregard unsatisfactory
husbands in those circumstances, and concentrate on the children's lives.
Of course I barely know Tom, so all this is pure generalising, and probably
as correct as your impression of me is me!

What else can you do, anyway? Any manner of life is led in the cage,
to pursue another is, as far as I can see, merely to exchange the cage. Not
that one can't vary the monotony of the cage existence, until one accepts
the illusion that one is doing something. I think it will be an excellent
idea if you can develop the radio racket – even something positive if you
can din into the heads of New Zealand lahidies that there is such a thing
as civilisation. You will become The Oracle, through knowing as one does,
alas! that I am I.

I am sorry that I know Tom so little. He remains only an outline,
like a man in a novel by a woman, or a reference that one finds in a
correspondence. But again, I suppose, if I did know him, I should be unable
still to settle your behaviour, and one tough might even become two.

I am trying to think what I do when I find myself in the worst kind
of impasse. I think probably I fall back on objects, not possessions, but the
ordinary objects of daily acceptance. They are extraordinarily solid, or
matter-of-fact, and consoling. However, if this is the sort of thing you don't
see, it will sound most ridiculous.

A great deal has happened on this <u>Olympus</u> since I wrote last, but nothing that could be of interest to anyone else. The chief development is that we are now growing roses for market, that is, we have put in 165 bushes of Talisman and are awaiting growth. They are the best rose we grow here, and also seem to be in demand. At the same time we are developing another speciality – shasta daisies, chiefly because they do grow so big here, and lahidies say 'it's nice to have something white in the house at Christmas time.'

I hope your letter was an over-dramatisation. If not, I am very sorry, and sorrier to be so unhelpful, unless it was some help to blow off steam at somebody.

Remember me to anyone who remembers.

Love,

Patrick

P.S. All three of my books are now being translated into French.

DOGWOODS, 25.i.50

TO PEGGY GARLAND

We had a long period of domestic upheaval towards the end of the year. We finally had to get another job for Athena,[35] who was going quite batty on her own here. Not that she is any better in Sydney, I gather. Everything in Australia is wrong, and she only dreams of returning to a Greece that existed perhaps in the 'twenties, or more likely, in her imagination.

After her departure we immediately and unwisely took on an English family, and went through hell for three weeks. The Browns consisted of Mr and Mrs; aged about 70 and 60, Lancashire bred, and a grandson, 16, and grand-daughter, 24. They had come out to live with the old man's brother at Dural, a village a few miles on from here. On arriving they found a tin shed, instead of a 'five-room home', in which they were expected to sleep on the floor. Old Brown of Dural was also, according to our Mrs Brown, a 'most repoolsive man,' an asthmatic, who kept a spitting bucket in the middle of the kitchen, and his bucket was always full.

Personally I am inclined to think the bucket a device to get rid of his relations, on finding how 'repoolsive' <u>they</u> were. Mrs B. who was the dominating spirit, was one of those flat-faced, pasty Lancs. women, with ends of greasy hair straying about, and a set of teeth from which several had come adrift from the purple gums. She was intensely active from five in the morning till nine at night, during which time she got absolutely nowhere, but between nagging and nattering at her family and conducting

---

[35] At Romano's restaurant.

long monologues on the theme of Old Brown, would contrive to smear everything she touched with grease, scatter tea and sugar everywhere, and let the blowflies in. I have never seen squalor take possession so quickly and completely. In a couple of days all one's standards were broken, and one couldn't quite see where it all might end.

The old husband had either lost his memory, or pretended to. He could not even feed the fowls. So he proceeded to sit in the kitchen amongst the sugar and the tea, while the useless little boy almost sent the cows dry, pulled the heads off the weeds, and got ready for the pictures. Of Our Joyce, the granddaughter, we saw less, as she was learning to be 'secretarial' at a 'Business Ladies' College' in Parramatta. We saw her arrive and depart, or sometimes seated at the dressing table trying on peasant handkerchiefs in ways she had learnt from Lana Turner and Linda Darnell.

At least the Brown nightmare ended quickly, in weeks, if not in experience, and we settled down to an age at the sink, until we got the Kubiks. They have been with us since the beginning of December, a pair of Poles, whom I can't praise enough. The floors shine, the cupboards glitter with glass and china, the beds are weeded and the fields ploughed. Really too much goodness to last. And the K's themselves, young, pleasant to look at, and agreeable to live with. The only thing is, we are not teaching them The Australian Way of Life, whatever that is.

It is odd to think you were here just a year ago. Then I look at the shrubs and realise it must be as long as that. There is now quite a hedge of half-grown shrubs from the coral tree, where you sometimes used to sit, down to the big fowlyard. Here there are oranges and lemons instead of peaches and plums, and schnauzers instead of fowls.

I decided to cut down on the latter as not worthwhile, except for a few to keep us in eggs. Then there was a terrific storm last November which brought a giant gum tree crashing across the dog yard and smaller of the two fowl yards. Only casualty – one pullet. So, hastily, we had to patch up, put all the fowls in the small yard, and the dogs in the big fowl yard, the only remaining enclosure that would keep them in. And that way it has stayed.

We have made a bit out of stocks, snapdragons and roses this spring and summer, but not yet enough. And Lottie's last litter sold to the last pup. I have tended to withdraw from farming activities since Jan started to help Manoly. For better or worse, I have begun another book. It is slow and painful, and not a bit what I want to say, but that is always the way, I'm afraid. Also the prospect of having it with me for months, if not years, disgusts me – until I begin to realise that when I am not in that state I really feel rather lost. It is a case of one misery or another.

DOGWOODS, 2.ii.50

TO JEAN SCOTT ROGERS

Dear Jean,

I was very sorry to hear of your father's death. I am prepared to think he had qualities that justified your love for him, though he did his best to hide them. But the whole question of the love of most women for their parents has always been a mystery to me. I can almost always understand the love for a husband, even when it is at its most unbelievable. But the love of daughters for parents who make them suffer most of their lives is something quite irrational. There is only one form of love more exasperating and ignoble, and that is Mother Love.

I liked the latest touch to the Portrait of Margot.[36]

The financial side to your family life is something else that mystifies. How on earth could a man with your father's practice have <u>nothing to leave</u>! I can only feel he must have been most discreet in his vices[37] ...

I have just got up from a week in bed with what now seems to be my Annual Big Attack of Asthma. The last three summers have been the same. When they are over I cannot believe they were as bad as they were – but they are. Very good as a spiritual clean-out, but they leave one feeling physically like three or four sticks ...

We are sweltering in a steam of summer, turning yellow with the leaves. And there is so much to be done – three shows before Easter, six dogs to be groomed, snipped at, paraded and coaxed every day. A calf too, in three weeks time, and a litter of pups in a couple of months. We have at last sold a schnauzer before its birth!

Hope you are still happy in your flat.

Love,

Patrick.

DOGWOODS, 29.iii.50

TO BEN HUEBSCH

I started a novel with the advent of the Poles. It lapsed with the man's departure for the factory. Now there is a crop of 4,000 stock plants to be rescued from the weeds. So I don't know what becomes of the novel. Somewhere I read of a journalist who said to Fannie Hurst:[38] 'How nice

---

[36]Rogers' sister, twice unsuccessfully married. PW described her as 'a river girl in organdie hats who looked exciting but turned out to be frigid'. Scott Rogers wrote a play, *One Fair Daughter*, 1953, based on her sister.

[37]No: unwise in his investments.

[38](1890–1968), American writer whose love stories were read, according to the *New York Times*, 24 Feb. 1968, p.1, 'under every hair-dryer in America'.

for you to go down to your farm, and relax, and write.' To which Fannie Hurst replied: 'When I want to write, I take a room in a New York hotel.' I appreciate that – on my farm.

DOGWOODS, 1.vii.50
TO PEGGY GARLAND
I forget where we left off. Perhaps with the departure of Athena and the arrival of the Kubiks, our Poles. Athena is still moaning in Sydney, as far as we know, and the Kubiks are still with us, though we have weathered storms. The big crisis came when they realised factory workers here earned three times as much as anyone on a farm or in service. Of course they wanted to leave. But we reached a compromise. I got Jan a job in a factory conveniently up the road, where he works 4½ days, and at the week-end he works for us. Gertrud continues to look after the house. There are occasional wild fits of calculation, but I doubt they could do better, as they are making between them about £14 a week, with their food and somewhere to live.

The worst enemy is boredom, as they are loath to spend even a bus fare to go anywhere. All the Poles, apparently, are like that. Fortunately they were persuaded yesterday by Emmy Paukip, a German friend of Gertrud's married to a Ukrainian, to go to a ball in Sydney. This has pepped them up a lot, although they did not enjoy the actual ball, which was full of Ukrainians with Asiatic faces and red-haired Australians with skirts slit up the thigh. However, they thought Sydney very *schön*, like Hamburg, and ate steak in the vicinity of Central Station . . .

Betty tells me you are modelling again. I wish I could say I am writing. Too many things got in the way, and I gave up. I suppose if it had been anything worth writing I shouldn't have. So it is nothing to worry about . . .

It is far too late to be drooling on like this. I must de-tick dogs, and go to bed. Manoly sends his love. He is about to become an Australian, after answering a number of very silly questions.

Yours,
Patrick.

DOGWOODS, 12.x.50
TO MOLLIE McKIE
Australia has become very expensive, even living as we do here. So we grow all the vegetables we can, and yesterday we discovered a dish of garden snails is every bit as good as *escargots de Bourgogne*. While there are snails and dandelions, obviously one need not starve.

DOGWOODS, 3.vi.51

TO PEGGY GARLAND

I prefer the abstract in sculpture. There is something a little too uncannily possessive, perhaps also dispossessed about good portrait sculpture – sitting there, looking at you. I never feel this about a portrait in paint. Not that a sculptor will want to hear this . . .

The house is beginning to look shabby, but more like something we have lived in, and so I like it better. We are thinking of painting it in the spring, though are rather put off by the thought of damage to all those shrubs that have grown up against it. I wonder if one could ignore the bits of wall that are covered.

Betty and I do not correspond so regularly now. It is difficult at this distance. And I too no longer know what she is like. Probably she feels the same of us! Anyway, I am sure she has a full life, what with the forestry,[39] and all those names of acquaintances that spring up in her letters, and whom one can rarely identify. It is a great pity she can't make the trip she once spoke of, then we could all see for ourselves what we have all become.

You say your wishes have always come true. Mine used to, I think, then stopped, or else I have nothing left to wish, apart from trivialities. Sometimes I feel: If only I could wish to write another book. But I don't. And of course that is why I don't begin. Have you ever been in this colourless state of wishing for nothing more? Not that it isn't very agreeable. 'Colourless' is perhaps a wrong word– –

I have spent two evenings idle in front of a wood fire since beginning this, a third in trying to listen to The Cocktail Party[40] on the wireless. What do you make of it? I was driven to bed about three-quarters of the way through, so missed the dénouement, and cannot honestly say I know what it is about yet. I was impressed by Murder in the Cathedral[41] and thrilled by Family Reunion,[42] but there seems something dreadfully pretentious about The Cocktail Party and guaranteed to persuade the middlebrow he is being highbrow, almost as if it were by Charles Morgan out of Shangri-La.[43] And there is something so stale and old-worldly about a group of people revelling in their emotional and intellectual states in a vacuum. The sink would

[39]She was working for the Commonwealth Forestry Bureau in Oxford.
[40]T. S. Eliot, 1950.
[41]1935.
[42]1939.
[43]Morgan (1894–1958) was the London Times' drama critic 'Menander' before the war and wrote self-consciously serious but rather sentimental novels.

claim them, in fact, before they got too far. Perhaps mine is the wrong frame of mind, but I doubt I shall ever regain the right one.

We listen to the wireless a lot now after being rigidly anti-wireless for so long, and I am drinking up music like a piece of blotting paper drinks ink. It is really the spoken and written word to which I remain averse, possibly because it has become so false. But I can't have enough of music. And I often feel I should like to buy another picture and look at it. If there were not so many humdrum things to buy, and bills to pay off.

DOGWOODS, 15.viii.51
TO PEGGY GARLAND
My 'acedia' continues. Funnily enough this was diagnosed by an Anglican priest who stayed with us a couple of years ago. There are moments when I do take interest in a book I have in my head, and of which I wrote a certain amount while the Poles were with us, then I succumb to the feeling of: What is the use? Since the war I cannot find any point, see any future, love my fellow men; I have gone quite sour – and it is not possible, in that condition, to be a novelist, for he does deal in human beings.

While I was in bed lately I succeeded in reading what is an awful lot, for me, now, and discovered Scott Fitzgerald, of whom I had heard vaguely, but never met. You must acquaint yourself, if you haven't done so already. *The Great Gatsby* is in the Penguins, a work of art out of unexpected material – rich Long Islanders and phoney New Yorkers – but read it and see. Then I read his *Tender is the Night*, not in the same class as a whole, rather too much virtuosity, but vastly entertaining, and having flashes of wisdom. I am still glowing from my discovery. It is so good, when you think you have left no stone unturned, to find that there is one.

In this same spasm of reading, I read an excellent book on the ancient Greeks by H. D. F. Kitto, a crazy, but true book on Modern Greece by Henry Miller called *The Colossus of Maroussi*, and re-read Davidson's excellent biography of Edward Lear, and Symons' brilliant excavation of the nauseating Corvo.[44] Finally, I re-read the two books that have meant more to me than anything in the last ten years, George Moore's *Evelyn Innes* and *Sister Teresa*. Do you know these two? They are out of print. I am tempted to send them to you, as I think you would like them as much as I do, but on second thought, I don't feel I could part with them.[45]

[44]*The Quest for Corvo*, 1934.
[45]Before starting to write *The Tree of Man* and *The Twyborn Affair*, PW reread Moore's double-decker novel (1898 and 1901) about the great diva who becomes a nun. Common to Moore's and PW's work – apart from a fascination with nuns, artists and adulterers – is the twin search for vocation and purity.

It is months since I heard from Betty, although I wrote to her, and have sent her a birthday present. I think I am no longer one of her Good Works. I am tempted to throw that stone and see what the reaction would be . . .

The garden, in parts, is looking much the worse for a very frosty winter, in others there are clouds of prunus and cherry, and thickets of cerise and pink japonica. And I am particularly pleased with a bush of gorse, the yellowest of yellow in flowers, as if someone had taken a saucepan of scrambled egg and flung it at a bush of thorns. Some day, God willing, the garden will be a sight to see, and I look forward to that very definitely, even though we be in tatters ourselves and the house collapsed.

I have *Parsifal* in the background on the wireless, and it is a struggle to write. I don't really like Wagner, do you? There are seductive bits riding here and there, but I have to force myself to most of it. I feel that unless one is German, one has to be of that period when to like Wagner was to revolt against the conventions, really to enjoy it. (Floundering, Wagnerian sentence, but perhaps you can unravel it.)

We are half-expecting Manoly's youngest brother. He is a brilliant pianist, but is unable to conduct his life successfully, so we have suggested he come out here where we can at least see he gets some broadcasting, gives some concerts when we have made the right contacts, and fills in with pupils. The alternative seems to be starving in Paris, which he has been doing since the War. I hope this comes off, as we have the room, he is a congenial person, and I should like to have music in the house. The snag is going to be the piano, which we shall be paying off for ever after.[46]

No more can I write. *Parsifal* has become a nest of snakes.

I hope I have not kept the photographs too long. Some day I must try to take Dogwoods and avoid turning out a suburban box surrounded by puny shrubs quite unlike the magnificent ones of fact – or imagination.

Yours,

Patrick.

---

[46]Mario Lascaris (1918–70), a talented but quarrelsome player whose Paris and London debuts were financed by PW; instead of Sydney, he moved back to Athens to teach piano at the Conservatorium.

DOGWOODS, 29.xii.51
TO MOLLIE McKIE
Do you ever think of coming out? I have a great longing to see Greece
and France again, but never England. I should also like to wander off
round Australia and really see that. The trouble is: one cannot have roots
and not have roots at the same time.

FOUR

Ordinary Lives

April 1952 – February 1957

A FEW NIGHTS BEFORE Christmas 1951, at a time of bushfires and storms, White fell in the mud carrying slops to a litter of pups. As he clambered to his feet cursing, he sensed a Presence about him in the storm. This ecstatic moment was a turning point in his life. He became a believer – at first an orthodox Christian – and he returned to his desk. The MS. begun and abandoned in 1950 was reworked over the next two and a half years as *The Tree of Man*. All that had happened to them on the farm went into the novel. He put aside the dazzling prose of *The Aunt's Story* to write the lives of Stan Parker, a farmer of Durilgai, and his wife Amy. 'My aim was to keep things as primitive as possible in writing about these people.'[1] This new beginning was the toughest creative struggle of White's life.

DOGWOODS, 3.iv.52

TO BEN HUEBSCH

A short time ago I began painfully to write another book, squeezing out an hour a day in which to do it, and then not every day. Still, it is going ahead. I suppose I have written roughly a quarter. But I shouldn't care to say when it may be finished. And of course, with me there is always the chance of an abortion.

However, it gives me great pleasure to find I want to do it again. For a long time I felt this is only a world for builders, to build houses, farmers, to grow food, and priests, to heal the spirit. Of course there is also the artist with a message, but that is usually the artist without art.

But lately I began to think about it less, and actually started to write. It may be trash. I don't talk about it in case it is . . .

I dare not tell a publisher how little I read nowadays. I have E. V. Rieu's translation of *The Odyssey* beside my bed and sometimes read a page before falling asleep. However, reading is perhaps not good for writing. We shall see.

---

[1] PW's answer to a query from his Swedish translator Magnus Lindberg, c.1971.

DOGWOODS, 25.vi.52

TO PEGGY GARLAND

A visit to our house will one day be an experience of terror for the innocent Australian, what with you in the garden[2] and Roy de Maistre in the house. We have a map of Alexandria in the sitting room and one of Crete in the dining room, to which the timid cling desperately on making their first entrance. But now the maps will have to come down, as two more paintings of Roy's are going to arrive. One is a recent abstracted religious painting, and the other he calls *Variations on a Theme by Courbet* – the starting point is that one of a woman lying in a hammock in a leafy glade.

Roy is in a desperate state of impoverishment, diabetic, and threatened with losing the use of his feet in the next few years. One doesn't know what to do about it, (he is old and cannot be transplanted) except buy a picture. Then he insists on sending two, and one cannot help feeling that one is getting too much out of what should have been his deal. I am looking forward very much to the arrival of the pictures, as I have not seen any of his latest work. There is a crucifixion at the Sydney Art Gallery, but that is kept permanently in the basement to make way for the Streetons and Lamberts[3] . . .

The book I am writing continues to develop. It has no plot, except the only one of living and dying. But perhaps that is because I am no good at plots. I can't see anyone being interested in it, which is a depressing thought. On the other hand, I am lifted up at times to considerable heights, and that may be a sign. If it is another failure, I suppose the wrestling alone will have done something to one.

You may be surprised to hear I started going to Church about six months ago. I wonder whether you have also. If not, it is something that will happen to you sooner or later, it is bound to, in spite of all the things that put one off for half a life time. I am quite convinced. Your coral island may only be part of a necessary detour.[4]

I have probably been dozing in the middle of all this, and have certainly been listening to Brahms. The real cause of my bronchitis is the Greek contralto, Elena Nikolaïdi,[5] whom you must hear if she goes to New

[2]Garland never finished the figure PW commissioned for the garden.
[3]The Old Masters of Australian landscape painting.
[4]She had been asked to join an American anthropologist on an expedition to Mangaia in the Cook Islands to make portrait heads of the inhabitants; instead she joined a NZ cultural delegation to Mao's new China.
[5](1914–   ) from Smyrna, a protégée of Bruno Walter, she toured Australia several times in the 1950s for the ABC.

Zealand. Such a slashing, dashing, dazzling, golden-skinned creature I have never seen, and a voice that must be the greatest in the world at present. We got seats to the three recitals she has just given, and I had to hear all, whatever the results. I just managed to stagger to the last yesterday evening – and to-day to bed. You must hear her in Mahler's *Songs of a Wayfarer*, Schumann's *Frauenliebe und Leben*, Wolf's *Mignon*, Schubert and Brahms. I always thought I hated the *Erlkönig*, but Nikolaïdi gave me shivers of excitement.

We were surrounded by milkbar Greeks, mothers and grandmothers from islands, very bewildered, and daughters and granddaughters with accents and furs, determined to applaud culture, and prod the mothers and grandmothers when they demanded why she had to sing what she was singing then.

I suppose I must get into the frame of mind of 'going to bed', although I have been here all day. What a luxurious state of affairs if only one were not ill.

Love,
Patrick.

DOGWOODS, 8.xii.52
TO BEN HUEBSCH
My next move will be bees, I think. One can't sit eating one's own olives and goat's cheese without adding one's own honey.

I often wonder how I lived in cities, yet at one time I was quite unhappy in the country, and could only think of trains back. People come here now, and I can see the same restlessness. You, I suppose, are quite an incurable New Yorker, so I shall not wish for anything so unnatural as a visit from you. Still, I should like to see you again, and wonder if anything will ever bring you this way. I am rooted so deeply I doubt I shall ever be able to pull free.

DOGWOODS, 1.v.53
TO PEGGY GARLAND
Dear Peggy,
I have owed you this letter for many months, I fear. One grows increasingly Australian and neglectful every summer, I feel, just dragging through it towards the end, in what looks like laziness, but is really exhaustion. In the beginning we laughed at them for wearing bags in the rain and watching their houses collapse into the paspalum. Now I begin to see how it happens.

I also had a heavy bout of influenza-cum-bronchial cold towards

Easter, which, with the Sydney Show, is the climax of our year anyway. I managed to get through on my feet, but in a trance.

Then during Show Week we had Madame Henri here to help,[6] and mind the house while we were away, but this is always a doubtful blessing on account of the battering one gets from an unfailing monologue. You did not sample this on the occasions when you met her as she is forced to draw breath in English. In French she neither looks back nor listens, but seizes a word here and there from one's hopeless interjections, to pursue fresh but never fully-explored avenues of her own. If one pushes a paper at her she will read out the headlines, or solve a crossword puzzle aloud. If one gives her a book, she drops it after six lines to remember other books that she has held in her hands. If one turns the wireless on, she will begin to hum *une petite chanson de Tino Rossi* that she heard many years ago. Of course on the occasions when one leaves her for the day, she is pale with desperation at the end of it. She cannot sit. She must roam, in case there is an opportunity to pounce on someone at the fence and tell them of some incident in her life which, mercifully, they will not have heard before.

However, she is a good creature, and one is sorry one wants to hit her several times a day.

Betty has been slightly more communicative lately, though not as communicative as she could be. There are casual references for instance to a visit to Rome with some 'tertiaries.' I was forced to write back saying: Tell me all about these tertiaries; are you really only visiting Rome, or have you also 'gone over' to it? The fleeting nature of some of her remarks does make me feel that this is so – that she is embarrassed to tell, and is dropping clues for anyone who cares enough to pick up.[7] I hope she has not. That is one plunge I could not take. I suppose in my heart I am a bigoted Protestant.

I thought you would be interested in Simone Weil,[8] but did not expect you to subscribe to all of it. After all she is discussing the Roman Catholic attitude to religious faith, and your faith (which you have got although you may not yet have admitted it) is a personal one. That is where the dogma of any religious sect seems to me ridiculous and

[6]Marie-Thérèse Henri, who came to Lulworth for *conversation* when PW was a little boy, was tutor in French at the NSW Conservatorium 1922–44 and raised chickens in her retirement.

[7]Betty Withycombe had become a lay member – a tertiary – of the Anglican Franciscans in 1950; she remained an Anglican.

[8](1909–43), French mystic and philosopher deeply suspicious of organised religion; starved herself to death as an act of protest during the war.

presumptuous. Faith is something between the person and God, and must vary in its forms accordingly.

I am sorry I can't find your letter to try to answer points that you bring up. As far as I remember, you revolt at the universal injustices. I try to explain these by bringing them down to a personal level. I have not myself suffered any of the great injustices, such as hunger, or torture, or the devastations of war, to name a few, but I do feel by this time that all the minor injustices to which I have been submitted, and which at the time have seemed terribly unjust and unnecessary, even agonising have in fact been necessary to my development. I do feel that every minute of my life has been necessary – though this conviction has only very recently come to me – , and that the sum total can only be good, though how good one cannot presume to say.

None of this is new. It is quite simple. You may even find it ludicrous. But it is better to say it, in case it may help simply by its simplicity and obviousness. I think it is impossible to explain faith. It is like trying to explain air, which one cannot do by dividing it into its component parts and labelling them scientifically. It must be breathed to be understood.

But breathing is something that has been going on all the time, and is almost imperceptible. I don't know when I began to have faith, but it is only a short time since I admitted it.

I should really begin another letter to say other things, but if I stop now I may not start again for many months. We had the inside of the house painted a few months ago, and the result is very refreshing. The living and bedrooms are all white, which is really the only background for pictures (though some insist that this is red damask.) The only startling piece of interior decoration is in the back veranda, which has bright yellow walls, a deep blue ceiling, and red curtains. Put this crudely, it is rather crude. In fact, it is good and bright, just the thing for a back veranda, through which one tramps, and where one hangs about, reading papers and letters, and having tea in the last of the winter light. The kitchen is white again, with the veranda yellow repeated in doors and windows.

I wished you here for the exhibition of French contemporary paintings that we have had at the Sydney Gallery.[9] Lots of it unimportant, but still exciting. Some of the important people like Picasso and Matisse badly represented. But the great importance of the exhibition as a whole was that it gave many people the shock of their lives, and liberated many more after shocking them. One forgets really that the average Australian has

[9]'French Painting Today' arranged by the French and Australian governments at the Art Gallery of NSW.

seen so little. He can have heard quite a lot, and read quite a lot, but on the visual side he is a complacent Victorian.

DOGWOODS, 15.xi.53

TO PEGGY GARLAND

I don't know what to say about you and Tom, the more so because I don't know Tom, so am unable to calculate how monstrous or alternately, reasonable, his conduct may have been. But without knowing, my impulse is to say: Endure everything, because any other solution will be far worse, for either of you. At this point in your lives, you cannot drift off from one another without each leaving such chunks of personality in the possession of the other, that you could not hope ever to be whole again.

I am sorry you cannot work at your sculpture, because I feel that if you got hold of the largest and hardest piece of marble you could find and bashed at it till something came out, you would probably resolve this drama of difficulty – from your side, anyway. I feel the book on China[10] was too much the indulgence of your own wishes to be of much use in this respect.

As for Tom's complaining that he is overpowered by your personality then you must just humble yourself till he is not. You will still remain yourself to yourself. Humility, moreover, is a most catching virtue, and may work wonders.

The mention of your book came as a surprise. I had no idea you were so close to one coming out. I shall look forward to reading it, but rather wish it was instead the millionth Buddha that you don't want to do.

I did hope to finish the first version of my book by Christmas, but don't think I shall manage it so soon. It sprawls out. It is so long by this time, that I find myself suddenly remembering incidents I had forgotten, just as one remembers forgotten incidents in life, and derives a very fresh kind of pleasure from doing so.

I don't think this is an unhappy book, as you suspect, because at present I am happy, and I think one's personal happiness must get into a book whatever the theme.

There is still an awful lot of hard work to do, though, awful, boring, desperate work. I am sure there is nothing similar to the drudgery of writing in any of the other arts. I hate writing intensely, and if I had the glimmering of anything else in me, would be off into that to-morrow.

I am re-reading the letters of Van Gogh to Émile Bernhard[11] and the

---

[10]*Journey to New China*, 1954.

[11]Bernhard (1868–1941) published his complete correspondence with Van Gogh in 1911, trans. 1938 by Douglas Lord.

Autobiography of Grandma Moses (sent by Betty), and am filled with a yearning for paint. Nothing doing there, of course.

And at the same time music makes me feel frustrated. Do you know Bruckner's *Ninth Symphony* and Hindemith's *Harmonies of the World?* You must hear both more – both very noble and exciting.

We are about to trade in our wireless and start a radiogram. When that is done, I intend to buy just one or two difficult works like those and play them over and over till I am saturated.

The big event in our lives recently has been the refurnishing of the two living rooms, as we felt the time had come to throw out all that meaningless stuff we had lived with for so long. So we sent the whole of the dining room to an auction, and were a bit depressed to receive £23. I got a good price from an antique dealer for the mahogany desk, the Queen-Anne-Style spare bedroom suite was bought by a rather timid suburban couple for £95 (they proposed to push the beds together), and the sitting room went in bits, including the carpet to a taxi driver, who came in the middle of the night with a wife called Pet.

The new rooms are very pleasing, and so open that one can take great walks through them and feel the wind whistle past. We had the floors repolished, leaving them a natural colour, and I succeeded in finding two very attractive Indian jute rugs hidden away amongst the floral Wiltons. The one in the sitting room is filled with purples and reds in a grid pattern and leads up to a couple of big curved sofas, upholstered in greens, which can be used together or apart, under the Bokhara. In this room we also have a red armchair, a green chair shaped like a violet leaf, and another very elegant little chair made of black iron and yellow cord.

In the dining room we have some simple maple furniture, the chairs livened up with coloured webbing, two red, two blue, and two green. And I have designed an immense desk, which will take up most of one end of the room, and which I am going to have painted a stone colour, outlined in white, with red linoleum inset in the top.[12]

We have nine goats at present, and should have more, only one unfortunate doe was delivered of premature triplets and nearly died herself. I was nursing her on blackberry leaves and milk for a week.

Lottie, the old bitch who came to stay with you as a puppy, is expecting a litter at any moment. And Camellia has had one very ugly tabby kitten with a red face – Osmanthus, whose sex we have not yet agreed upon. Presumably it is the offspring of Agapanthus, a most useless

[12]This was a rough copy of the desk, now sold, that Francis Bacon designed for PW's Eccleston Street flat.

cat – the only thing he has ever done is get this kitten.

I can't think of anything more to write at such a late hour, being a bit stupefied by the weather. All day we lived in a furnace, with a westerly blowing, and the grass turning yellow under our eyes. In the evening a southerly came with a roaring like the sea. One watched the two winds meet like Kattegat and Skagerrak, the trees blown inside out. The night is still, but icy.

Are you going to the Sound this year? I almost said to the Lighthouse. What Christmas card will you make, I wonder, after that masterpiece last year.

I must go to bed. There are dogs asleep everywhere.

Love,

Patrick.

THE TWO MEN WERE not now so isolated in Castle Hill. They had met Fritz and Ile Krieger, neighbours a few paddocks away. He was a businessman. Both were survivors of the lost world of Austria-Hungary. The crowd at their table, mostly Central Europeans, talked music and writing but also sex, religion, politics and money. At the Kriegers White met the tiny, dogmatic, energetic and kind-hearted Hungarian Klári Daniel who devoted the next ten years to their friendship. The letters that survive from this time occasionally mention unnamed 'intelligent Hungarians' – White was always very slow to mention new friends to old.

DOGWOODS, 15.vi.54

TO PEGGY GARLAND

Dear Peggy,

My chief and quite good excuse this time for not writing, is that I am hard at typing the book, have been for months, and cannot bring myself to give up a working hour for anything else. However, the typewriter ribbon has now given out on me, and I am seizing this opportunity, before I can buy another. Not very flattering to one's correspondents – but you know what it is like to be finishing a book . . .

Thank you for inviting me to convalesce in New Zealand, but I'm afraid convalescence is a pleasure we can't enjoy the way we live here and now. Anyway, it now seems a long time since I was ill, and I feel very well – even Manoly has recovered from all the work he had to do during those two gloomy months of last summer. As far as I am concerned, I can't help feeling it was necessary – I see a lot of things a lot more clearly than I did before.

But I can't explain away the Fig Tree and the Gadarene Swine, as you ask me to.[13] I suppose if Christ was also Man he would have been less convincing without the inconsistencies, particularly to Jews reared on the Old Testament. Both the incidents you mention are in the Old Testament tradition of fire and thunderbolts. It could be that they would impress themselves more deeply on the minds of simple Jews if touched with a little of that same fire. And the swine to which the unclean spirits transferred themselves were, after all, the unclean animals of the East, and the association of the two uncleans would have impressed more vividly and emotionally, and seemed more apt. I am sorry I cannot do better than this, but I am confessedly, very ignorant on the subject. I have to take on trust some of the obscurer details (which I don't doubt I shall clear up eventually) and which are not sufficiently important to interfere with the goodness and rightness and immensity of the whole. Here, of course, one arrives at the super-rational which can only irritate those it does not convince . . .

The garden of Dogwoods is quite dead at the moment, but at least when dead, it is comparatively calm, and one can walk about in the winter landscape feeling almost free. We have had an autumn of colours, which is unusual in these parts, and one is tempted to put in all sorts of cold climate things on the strength of one year.

Have you ever heard Solomon?[14] We have just had him here, and I think his playing of the 1st Brahms Concerto the greatest musical experience I have known. He is really possessed by music to a most extraordinary degree. Rather an unpromising-looking man, carved out of a pumpkin, then the spirit starts to burn inside– –

I am becoming disjointed and should go to bed. The winds are whistling through the spaces of our newly-decorated house this winter, but I feel the better for it – and the desk with its endless red linoleum top.

Hope you are all well.

Love,

Patrick.

Dogwoods, 21.viii.54
TO NAOMI BURTON
Dear Naomi,
I was glad to get your letter and hear something about you at last. Your

---

[13]The tree: Christ, hungry one day, found a fig bare of fruit and killed it with a curse. *Matthew* 21: 18–22. The swine: Christ was persuaded by a devout madman to consign his madness into 2,000 passing swine who rushed to their deaths in the sea of Galilee. *Mark* 5: 1–16.

[14]The English pianist Solomon Cutner (1902–88).

life sounds quite cosy for New York! The house must be a help, for in an apartment, I feel, one just would not live, but roam the streets and end up in the gutters in the small hours. Or perhaps New York does not have the bad effect on other people that it has on me.

I sent off the MS of *The Tree of Man* a couple of days ago, so that in a few weeks we shall know the worst.

Mr Huebsch wrote just after you did, and sounds genuinely interested. May he continue so. I gather American publishers are not so frightened of length as English ones and this is rather a long book, 715 quarto pages in typescript.

We have a lovely spring at present, all blossom and pregnant goats, but I no longer look forward to the blast of summer, and the plodding up and down in it.

Do you ever see Peggy?[15] I have not heard from her for years. Very few of my friends have survived my rustication. It is something they just can't understand.

I hope the book does not burst open on the way; and of course, that it will sweep all America.

Yours,

Patrick White.

DOGWOODS, 24.xi.54
TO BEN HUEBSCH
Dear Mr Huebsch,
Your cable was a great excitement and relief, and since then I have had a letter from Naomi with details of the terms.[16]

I don't know whether other authors experience what I do: a feeling that they may be writing a secret language that nobody else will be able to interpret. Consequently the strain is very great until one discovers it is intelligible to someone else. And this time the strain has been increasing over four years.

I wonder whether sufficient people will know the source of the title, or whether some may even think I have pinched the poem and kept quiet. I could not very well write in the text: 'Thelma Forsdyke then sat down and read the following poem by A. E. Housman.' So perhaps we should acknowl-

---

[15]Stewart.
[16]Huebsch cabled, 11.xi.54: 'VIKING CONGRATULATES YOU ON BEAUTIFUL PROFOUNDLY IMPRESSIVE FULFILMENT OF EXPECTATIONS.'

edge it somewhere on the jacket when the book comes out.[17] However, there will be many small points to discuss, I expect, between now and then.

Will there be someone very accurate and painstaking to correct proofs? You may remember things that got into *The Aunt's Story*, like a cart crossing a 'fiord', because I did not correct the proof myself.[18] And of course it will be even less satisfactory to send proofs all the way to Australia than it was to send them to England.

I was knocked over like a ninepin about a week ago by an attack of asthma, and have been in bed ever since. My only consolation is that these attacks are a great help creatively. Yesterday I was seeing quite clearly whole stretches of a novel I am planning to start after Christmas, and which had remained misty until now. In the same way, *The Tree of Man* got finished during the two months I was in bed last summer.

Still, I am on the verge of selling out here, and trying to find somewhere where I am free.

I hope you have been keeping well, that I shall hear from you soon, and that there may even be some opportunity of meeting again.

Yours,

Patrick White

Have just received your letter. Thank you very much. Shall write again – about farming!

[17]This was done on jacket and verso. The verse from A. E. Housman's 'Shropshire Lad', 1896, was:

There, like the wind through woods in riot,
    Through him the gale of life blew high;
The tree of man was never quiet:
    Then 'twas the Roman, now 'tis I.

[18]See PW to Best, 1.xi.47, p.70.

DOGWOODS, 1.i.55

TO PEGGY GARLAND

You are wrong in supposing we shall set sail for Greece and never return. Oddly enough, I feel I am intended to stay in Australia and write about it. I am vain enough to think I can write about it in a way that the others can't – and anyway, I can't write about anything else. Of course, expatriate artists are common enough, but they do tend to thin out.

This is what we intend to do if we get what we want for Dogwoods – Put aside enough for a small, very simple, contemporary house in about an acre of native garden, all of which can be abandoned for a couple of months if necessary, in the event of sickness or travels. Start the Grand Tour in a Greek ship which sails between here and Piraeus. See Manoly's family in Athens, and wander a bit amongst the islands . . . To England, to my family and half a dozen surviving friends. New York, for obvious reasons of policy . . .

I wonder how much of this will come to pass. It is good to dream about, anyway.

DOGWOODS, 15.ii.55

TO BEN HUEBSCH

Dear Mr Huebsch,

I am sorry I forgot to answer your question on the origins of characters in *The Tree of Man*. I did, I think, take it for granted that you would take it for granted 'there is no character, or incident related to any living person.' I can't draw a character from life and make it look convincing. On the other hand there <u>are</u> the fragments that drift up out of the depths; I don't know how one can answer for those!

I have been in bed almost a whole month with asthma and the last two weeks in hospital. Actually, the asthma has gone, but a very slight temperature persists. This is not as sinister as it might sound, but it does seem to have been a feature of the asthma I have had in recent years, and nobody can explain it.

In the meantime, Dogwoods is a wilderness – goats and fowls gone, all but three dogs given away or destroyed. I don't look forward to returning to it. When I do, I plan to shut up the house and go with my partner Lascaris to Adelaide till the humid weather is over in these parts. Adelaide has a dry, blazing heat which should clean out my breathing apparatus. Then when the autumn comes, we shall get to work to make Dogwoods as attractive as possible for sale. I feel I can no longer cope with much more than a house, and the three old and manageable dogs, who will die off quietly by degrees. Because I still have books to write, and am now working on the skeleton of the new one.

London publishers are giving trouble over *The Tree of Man*. It is all a matter of length, breadth and thickness with them. What they want is *Novellen*[19] that they can get away with publishing disguised as novels. Gollancz became quite excited at one point over my book, and got as far as offering terms, but the printer demanded the text should be cut by 25%, so of course I declined.

As I feel I no longer have much to say to the English, and there is the Viking edition to look forward to, I don't much mind. Also I think the British edition should come from Australia, and shall probably try to work something along those lines soon.

I hope you are in good health, and that I have now answered all questions.

Yours sincerely,
Patrick White.

VOSS CAME TO LIFE as White lay in the public wards of Sydney hospitals in the summer of 1954–55 battered by the most violent asthma attacks for nearly twenty,years. He had been planning an explorer novel since the early days of the war but put it aside in bitter apathy after the failure of *The Aunt's Story*. Once he began to write in early 1955 the work went swiftly: the novel was finished by the end of 1956. *Voss* is, more than any of White's other novels, an account of the virtues of suffering. The German would find only deserts and swamps as he tried and failed to cross Australia, but in the suffering endured on the journey he hoped – as White hoped also for himself – to discover his genius, possess this new country and conquer his pride.

DOGWOODS, 16.vi.55
TO BEN HUEBSCH
Dear Mr Huebsch,
I had been waiting for the books to arrive before writing. I had always heard that surface mail between the States and here was erratic, but the word is mild. They took two months to the day, arriving just before your letter of June 10th.

It was very exciting to see *The Tree of Man*, and for the moment my life has no more to give. I seem to be re-living the exhaustion of those

---

[19]PW usually used the German Novellas.

years of writing. The cover looks very interesting, and should help. Only an Australian critic, if he saw it, would be bound to pounce on the 'essential' tree and say 'that is not a <u>gum</u> tree, therefore, this is not an Australian novel,' and condemn it on that account. Just as I am condemned and accused of being un-Australian because I have spent half my life outside the country. That is the way their minds work.

I had not been prepared for such a Bible of a volume. Could not the paper be a bit thinner? Or perhaps it will be in the commercial copies?

A STORM OF APPLAUSE for *The Tree of Man* broke in New York in mid-August. Leading the critics was James Stern of the *New York Times*: 'To reveal in a novel this life . . . of the soul in such a way that by the time the last page is reached all questions have been answered, while all the glory and mystery of the world remains, is not only the prime function of the novelist but the artist's greatest ambition – and surely his rarest achievement.'[20] America's enthusiasm for the book made White at once a name in the literary world, but he never had *Time* on his side.

DOGWOODS, 12.x.55
TO PEGGY GARLAND
Dear Peggy,
Of course you would see the review in *Time*.[21] The whole world has, and I continue to get letters which say: 'We saw the review in *Time*– –' So, I enclose a selection of others, including for value the one from the female whose periods are giving her trouble in Baltimore, and the one from the College Funny Man in Dallas, Texas. (<u>Please return these reviews.</u>)

You should have received a copy of the book, but the distribution seems to have gone wrong. Let me know if you still have not got one, and I shall send you a spare copy if you have not. Perhaps you are just lying low! I don't think Betty liked it. On receiving hers she wrote that she <u>thought</u> she was going to enjoy it, but now, many weeks have gone by, and as there has been no letter to say she did, I can only presume she did not. To dash off a letter at the beginning is a certain technique you may have encountered.

As you see, we are still at Dogwoods. Since April, when we offered

---

[20]*New York Times Book Review*, 14 Aug. 1955, p.1.
[21]'Australian with a Hoe' by Theodore (Ted) Kalem, 15 Aug., p.54: 'Stan's mute wisdom is knowing that endurance is all. Author White's literary unwisdom is in worrying this theme for so long that his novel itself becomes a kind of endurance test.'

the place for sale, only one person has been to inspect it. I do not mind much, as I would not really like to sell unless forced to. All the winter I have been feeling very ill. I had a course of treatment from a Viennese doctor, with what results I am anxiously awaiting the summer to see. If I can manage to get through the summers here, and make enough money out of the book to go for a trip, that would be ideal. (Incidentally, they sold over 10,000 copies in the first fortnight – probably it is bad.)

On the other hand, I am tempted to use the money on a few things we need, like a new car, new clothes (I have not bought a suit since before the War), furniture for the bedrooms, pictures, and gramophone records. It would be lovely to run amuck in those directions.

DOGWOODS, 25.x.55
TO BEN HUEBSCH

I have almost finished the first version of a new book. Am pleased with it only by fits. But of course, I am never pleased with anything really. I think it will be a long time before this one can be called finished. I shall have to re-write it at least once, probably twice.

I have had all sorts of reactions to *The Tree of Man*, wild enthusiasm, complete silence, anger, and insults. I rather feel that the English are not going to have anything to do with it, but hope I am wrong for F. Morley's sake.[22] Two who have been with me wholeheartedly over the other books have gone quite cold and silent on this. I had hoped that Morley's own enthusiasm was English, but you tell me he is more or less American!

DOGWOODS, 28.xii.55
TO PEGGY GARLAND

Amy Parker had to turn out like that. It is quite possible to be consumed by love for an individual and to be led to a fatal wallowing in something else at some point in one's life. A kind of desecration of the noble ideal one can't attain to. Amy Parker is led progressively and fatally to this, I feel, through her fleeting relationships with Madeline, the Young Digger, Con the Greek, O'Dowd and finally the commercial traveller.

It is strange you should be impressed by Stan Parker as a character 'of unfailing strength'. To me, he is at many points weak and wavering. Certainly I wanted him to appear admirable as far as his human limitations allow, but perhaps I have tried too hard.

[22]Frank Morley (1899–1980) was an American living much of his life in England; a director of Eyre & Spottiswoode, the London publisher which Huebsch finally persuaded to take the novel. As Australia was then – and to some extent remains – a suburb of London publishing, it was always the London edition of PW's work that sold in Australia.

From the way your letter proceeds to develop, I feel you are interpreting the book too much in terms of your own problem.[23] Of course, from all author's point of view this is most gratifying. Last night we were with a most intelligent Hungarian woman who has read the book, and she was interpreting it in terms of her quite different problem.

We have had some lovely Christmas presents this year, including Mahler's *Song of the Earth* with Kathleen Ferrier, and Bartok's *First Quartet*.

I feel that Tomson's career is right. I have never met him, nor have I met a cameraman, but I feel a good cameraman is of that character. Perhaps he will come here to film *The Tree of Man*. I have a wild dream in which I see it done as I can see it, without regard for expense or public.

DOGWOODS, 29.xii.55
TO BEN HUEBSCH
The best thing about this New Year is that I have been miraculously free from asthma so far – all through the summer in fact. It must be due to my strange Viennese, whose name is Morgenstern, incidentally. (While in his waiting room I have been looking through *Marjorie Morningstar*[24] in one of the women's magazines. Am I going mad, or is this the utter, utter trash I feel it to be?!)

Next week I start the re-writing of my new book, and my stomach turns over at the thought of it. You know I would really like to spend my life just sitting, and looking and listening to music.

DOGWOODS, 15.vi.56
TO CLEM CHRISTESEN[25]
In the last few weeks, more seems to have happened than in the same number of years, and in addition, I have been finishing another novel.

It was very thrilling to read the announcement of Marjorie Barnard's essay on 'The Four Novels of Patrick White'; until recently, it was quite a rare thing to meet an Australian who knew he had written one novel, let alone four. Yesterday evening the essay itself arrived, and I find it very surprising and pleasing. There are one or two minor points of criticism,

[23]She and her husband were on the point of separating.
[24]By Herman Wouk, 1955.
[25](1911–   ), poet and asthmatic, founder and for 35 years editor of *Meanjin*, the literary magazine that mattered most in Australia at this time. PW cultivated a careful, professional friendship with the prudish Christesen and forgave many irritations out of gratitude for publishing this first survey in the June 1956 issue of *Meanjin*. They did not meet for another six years. PW then wrote to Dutton, 26.x.62: 'He is an absurd old thing in some ways, but I'm rather fond of him. I also liked his wife very much. She reminded me of a good apple.'

but I shall write them to Miss Barnard as she lives in Sydney, and I can send the corrected MS. to her at the same time . . .

I must confess I have never written an article in my life. If you would give me more clues to the sort of thing you want, I might have a try one day.

I am so sorry to be of so little use to *Meanjin*. Poetry I have not written for twenty years, and I cannot convey what I want to convey within the bounds of a short story. My mind is not much more than a rag bag, and all the bits and pieces eventually go into a novel.

However, I had been thinking of offering you a fragment of my new book when everything is settled. It has to be put aside for a couple of months, then typed, then accepted by a publisher. I am not very keen on cutting bits out of novels, but there is a passage in this one which would convey something of its own, I think. So, if the publishers agree, and you would like, you may have it, in time.

I enclose rather a belated subscription. If you ever come to Sydney, please let me know.

Yours sincerely,
Patrick White.

DOGWOODS, 15.vi.56
TO MARJORIE BARNARD[26]
Dear Miss Barnard,
I enclose the copy of your essay with a few corrections. In addition, I have one or two queries of a minor nature.

I am not altogether happy about the juvenile poems you have dug up. They should not have been published, but as they were, I suppose I am responsible for having written them. I do not want to upset your excellent plan. So, if you <u>must</u> quote from the poems, you must.[27]

On page 4 of your MS., referring to the affairs between the doctor and Alys Browne, and Vic Moriarty and Clem Hagan,[28] you talk about those affairs beginning and ending on the same day, which is not so. They certainly ended, but they had been in progress for some time. You will see I have introduced some brackets suggesting you delete 'begin and'.

---

[26](1897–1987), novelist and historian who wrote five novels with Flora Eldershaw (1897–1956) under the joint name 'M. Barnard Eldershaw'; PW at this time was drawing on their *A House is Built*, 1929, for details of early Sydney for *Voss*. PW unsuccessfully urged Viking to take up their novel *Tomorrow and Tomorrow*, 1947.
[27]She did.
[28]In *Happy Valley*.

P.13 'station' is too impressive a word to use in connexion with Meroë, which was really only a run-down bit of a dairy farm at Moss Vale (the Sorrel Vale of the story).[29] I suggest 'property', a word which would cover the situation with discretion.

P.15 I don't like Theodora's 'Kafka nightmare'. Do you really feel there is any likeness to Kafka? I have only read one short thing of his (about a man who changed into a beetle) but after reading a lot <u>about</u> him, I found him most antipathetic. Also, he is a kind of fetish of the English intellectual. He was always dragged in, willy nilly, everywhere.

P.16 Theodora destroys her travel tickets on the road up the mountain but it is not until a little later, when Mrs Johnson introduces her to her husband, that she repudiates her own name.

P.18 'architected'. Would not 'constructed' look neater?

P.20 The instances given in the last para. do not seem to link up with the illustrations on the following page. Could you clarify? Or perhaps there is a link between the two that got left out in typing.[30]

P.23 'He has not forced his talent– –he has written enough to declare himself– –' You may want to alter this when you read of all the abortive novels and unpublished plays in the enclosed biographical note.[31]

Again I must say how impressed and gratified I am by your work. A great many people have become excited over *The Tree of Man*, but it is the first time anyone has shown that I have been working towards it over the last twenty years. Your phrase 'the vanity of writing has passed away' is a magnificent and telling one. Nor has any other critic, however sympathetic, put his finger so firmly on the point of *The Tree of Man* as you have in your: 'Each man's life is a mystery between himself and God.' I had begun to feel that perhaps I had not succeeded in making this clear, or perhaps it just is that people recoil from it.

One theme you missed, one that means a lot to me, is that of the 'mysticism of objects'. It crops up on p.398 *Tree of Man* in the scene between Amy Parker and her grandson. In fact, the consolation of the essence of objects recurs a lot in that book, with Stan in his workshop and about the farm, with Amy in her house. In *The Aunt's Story*, Theodora Goodman is also obsessed by 'objects'. Two instances that I can remember offhand, are where she goes to work in the ruined house at the end, and where she lays out her own possessions in the bedrooms of hotels. However, that is only by the way.

---

[29]In *The Aunt's Story*.
[30]She adopted all the changes suggested by PW.
[31]A short memoir reworked by Christesen for the June *Meanjin*, p.223.

I shall look forward to meeting you, and would like to read your essay on Seaforth Mackenzie.[32] I have not read any of his books, but I once met Roy Howarth[33] who told me he was particularly interested in Mackenzie's books and mine. It struck me as a strange co-incidence that you should have chosen to investigate the same two.

Yours sincerely,
Patrick White.

DOGWOODS, 27.vi.56
TO MOLLIE McKIE
Dear Mollie,
You certainly seem to be running into the Whites, but appear to like it more than I would. Hope is one of the George Whites. When I was a child at Tudor House, they used to live at Exeter, and sometimes I had to go over and spend a week-end with them. Coming from a family of two, it was very alarming to go to one of thirteen – or rising that way. Although they were very well off, the children were made to do all the work, which added to the strangeness. Most of Sunday was spent learning and reciting collects, but I hardly knew what a collect was. Their mother was particularly terrifying – a <u>good</u> woman with a passionate temper. Imagine a Brünnhilde who had left the Ring and joined the Salvation Army, taking with her, however, plenty of Wagnerian sex and hysterics – that was Ivy.[34]

While I was at Cambridge, it was once arranged that George, the father, Hope and another of the girls should come to tea with me at King's. All was ready, but nobody came. Finally I looked out the window and saw the George Whites disappearing through the gateway of the court. No explanation was ever given, because, like almost all Whites, they are barbarians.

Faith was the best. She had red hair, and used to swear, and get her mouth washed out with soap and water by Ivy – Brünnhilde. Later in life she developed a mezzo voice (possibly from all the soaping) and was studying at that College of Music near the Albert Hall. Just before the War she got some kind of contract with Covent Garden, but was sucked back into her family when war broke out. She has been through a preliminary fiancé (engagement broken), one husband killed, one husband

---

[32](1913–55) poet, novelist and alcoholic, author of *The Young Desire It*, 1937, exploring *inter alia* homosexual infatuation in an Australian school. Barnard's essay: *Meanjin* 59, p.503.
[33]Actually Guy (1906–74), Sydney University academic and first editor of *Southerly* who appears to have given in the early 1950s the first lectures anywhere on PW's work.
[34]PW was making use of her maiden name: Voss.

divorced, and the last time I saw her, I felt she was looking out for a third. Quite vile, but not forced, barbarous like the others, and she has that disconcertingly broody habit of humming during silences.

I always like to think of myself as a Withycombe, certainly not a White. Anything I may have certainly comes from the Withycombe side.

Well, *The Tree of Man* came out in Sydney with a review to end all reviews, by a 'Professor' A. D. Hope, who called it 'pretentious and illiterate verbal sludge.'

NO SHAFT OF CRITICISM ever wounded White so deeply. Hope praised the novel's memorable characters, mocked the fires and floods and Irishfolk so familiar in Australian novels, and flayed White's style with memorable ferocity: 'When so few Australian novelists can write prose at all, it is a great pity to see Mr. White, who shows on every page some touch of the born writer, deliberately choose as his medium this pretentious and illiterate verbal sludge.'[35]

DOGWOODS, 30.vi.56
TO BEN HUEBSCH
Dear Mr Huebsch,
As most of the Australian reception of *The Tree of Man* is now over, I can write and tell you what happened. Eyre & Spottiswoode drew it out and drew it out, until everyone was thoroughly exasperated, booksellers thought they were being imposed upon, reviews came out too soon, and the public was bewildered. Finally, the book was released last week.

But let us return to the reviews. Melbourne was the first, with a very grudging one in the *Age* by somebody who must once have written a novel, I think. His line was: 'This is quite unlike anything by any other Australian novelist, therefore it cannot be good.'[36] The fact that it was not a naturalistic novel seemed to get him down more than anything, and he finished up accusing me of copying Faulkner, Carson McCullers and Capote. This review was bad enough, but there was worse to come.

After a very sympathetic one by a man called John K. Ewers in the *West Australian*, the *Sydney Morning Herald* sprang upon us. I am enclosing it to show. Admittedly the *Herald* has jumped upon everything I have written, but they excelled themselves this time. A. D. Hope is an embittered schoolmaster and poet of a <u>certain</u> distinction. During the War he was

---

[35]*SMH*, 16 June 1956, p.15.
[36]Geoffrey Hutton wrote, 12 May, p.17: 'This huge three-generation novel is completely unlike any other Australian novel I can recall . . . almost eccentric.'

Professor of English at the Teachers' College Sydney, I am told, and now he is at some College (not the University) at Canberra.[37]

Somebody I know on the staff of the *Herald* says they have been flooded with letters of protest since the review appeared. Only two of these letters were published,[38] while the Editor was away. The latter, an importation from England, called Pringle,[39] replied in this vein to one man who had written: 'A. D. Hope is the best critic in Australia, one of the four best poets, and a Professor of English Literature– –'

In Melbourne the situation was saved by a novelist-columnist called John Hetherington[40] who put something in his column to the effect that other novelists were to me as street-corner fiddlers are to Yehudi Menuhin!! This burst on Melbourne like a bomb. Everybody rushed, and I believe their stock is practically sold out.

Here I think some of the damage done by the *Herald* may have been repaired, again by a column, and ironically, in the *Herald*. A few days ago I received a letter from the National Library for the Blind, London, asking for permission to transcribe *The Tree of Man* into Braille, and for standing permission to do any of my past or future books. They enclosed last year's list of authors, including names like Joyce, Kafka, Sartre, E. M. Forster, and Walter de la Mare. This in itself is about the most gratifying thing that has happened to me personally, but I had also to make use of it, and I managed to get it onto the front page of the *Herald* yesterday. I have not heard what the Editor's comments were, for that particular column is an independent affair.[41]

Here is a curious coincidence: the work by Joyce transcribed into Braille last year was *Dubliners*. The day I received the letter from the Library I read in an article on Joyce that '*Dubliners* was first published by an American publisher called Ben Huebsch.' That is something I never knew and was very pleased to discover.

I expect you will have gone to Europe as usual. Next European

[37]Hope (1907–) was a lecturer in Sydney but a professor at the Canberra College which soon became the Australian National University; his first collection *Wandering Islands* had just appeared to great praise.

[38]One for PW on 21 June, and another defending Hope on 25 June.

[39]A Scot of the sweater clan, John Pringle (1912–), formerly of the *Manchester Guardian*, was twice editor of the *SMH* from 1952–57 and 1965–70; his influential impressions of Australia, *Australian Accent*, appeared in 1958; in retirement he became a distinguished book reviewer.

[40](1907–75), war correspondent, biographer and novelist; his column appeared on the front page of the *Age*, 19 June.

[41]'Column 8', known in Sydney as 'Granny's column'.

summer I must make the effort to get to England, as my mother is now very old, and my sister has had a lot of bad luck recently.[42] So perhaps we shall meet there.

A few weeks ago I finished the second version of the new novel, *Voss*. I have put it aside, and shall start typing it in August. As usual I have no idea what it is like, but perhaps it will turn into something. I could have cut my throat after finishing *The Tree of Man*, and that turned out all right.

WHITE WAS NOW A man whose letters were kept and it seems fame also changed the scale of his correspondence: several hundred letters survive from the years before *The Tree of Man* – roughly the midpoint of White's life – but several thousand survive from the years after.

DOGWOODS, 11.ix.56
TO BEN HUEBSCH
As you know I hate talking about books before they are ready. For one thing, if one tells, anybody can see at once on reading the MS. how far one has fallen short of one's intentions. But perhaps I shall give you some idea. Some years ago I got the idea for a book about a megalomaniac explorer. As Australia is the only country I really know in my bones, it had to be set in Australia, and as there is practically nothing left to explore, I had to go back to the middle of last century. When I returned here after the War and began to look up old records, my idea seemed to fit the character of Leichhardt. But as I did not want to limit myself to a historical reconstruction (too difficult and too boring), I only <u>based</u> my explorer on Leichhardt. The latter was, besides, merely unusually unpleasant, whereas Voss is mad as well

I also wanted to write the story of a <u>grand passion</u> – don't jump. So this is at the same time the story of a girl called Laura Trevelyan, the niece of a Sydney merchant, one of the patrons of Voss's expedition. It is different from other grand passions in that it grows in the minds of the two people concerned more through the stimulus of their surroundings and through almost irrelevant incidents. Voss and Laura only meet three or four times before the expedition sets out. They even find each other partly antipathetic. Yet, Voss writes proposing to the girl on one of the early stages of the journey, partly out of vanity, and partly because he realises

---

[42]Geoffrey Peck died suddenly of a cerebral haemorrhage at 47, after which Suzanne discovered she was pregnant and her third daughter Frances was born in 1956. She was also responsible now for both her aged mother-in-law and mother in London.

he is already lost; She accepts, partly out of a desire to save him from his delusions of divinity, partly out of a longing for religious faith, to which she feels she can only return through love.

At this point, I see I could easily become involved in an ocean of detail and analysis. Better not. As the two characters are separated by events and distances, their stories have to be developed alternately, but they do also fuse, in dreams, in memories, and in delirium – most closely, for instance, where Voss is lying half dead of thirst and starvation, and Laura is suffering from delusions as the result of a psychic disturbance, diagnosed as the inevitable 'brain fever.' Voss is finally dragged from his golden throne, humbled in the dust, and accepts the principles Laura would have liked him to accept, before he is murdered by the blacks. Laura recovers. She becomes a headmistress, and figure of some respect in the community, if also one that nobody really understands, because of some mysterious past.

You will see that there is a lot that has to be <u>made</u> convincing. I want to include the crimson plush and organ peals, while making them acceptable to the age of reason by a certain dryness of style. To a certain extent the style is based on that of records of the day (it may even make the Australian critics feel I am saved from illiteracy), but I have also left some loopholes through which to get my own effects.

Two of the greatest difficulties have been to try to make an unpleasant, mad, basically unattractive hero, sufficiently attractive, and to show how a heroine with a strong strain of priggishness can at the same time appeal.

As for the look – the sound of the thing, I have tried to marry Delacroix to Blake, and Liszt to Mahler. Now I really am committed to my own shortcomings! And on reading over what I have written, I see I have failed to convey that there are <u>lots</u> of subsidiary characters, minor alarms and excursions, deaths by thirst, a suicide, an illegitimate child, picnics, balls, and weddings.

I have been reading a book on Judaism by Abraham Heschel, in which I have found references to Louis Ginsberg's *Legends of the Jews*. Is that anything to do with Ginsberg of the Viking?[43] I have been giving a lot of time lately to Judaism, in connexion with the book I want to write next. So I suppose I shall come a cropper over the Jews, if I have not done so already in *Voss*.

I am still planning vaguely to be in England for about a month next summer, but I must admit the prospect of missing what happens on these few acres, if only for a few weeks, is a most unpleasant one. Living in an

---

[43]No, the co-founder of the Viking Press was Harold Guinzberg.

apartment, you will be free of all such handicaps. I actually have to decide whether to miss the autumn colours, or to get back in time for the azaleas. No doubt I should find better of everything in other places, but that is not the same.

Yours sincerely,
Patrick White.

DOGWOODS, 17.xii.56
TO NAOMI BURTON
Dear Naomi,
To-day I sent you by registered air mail the MS. of the new book, Voss.

I hope Ben Huebsch is all right. It is some time since I heard from him, and I have a feeling he may be ill. Or perhaps it is just the international situation.

I shan't write any more now. Finishing the book, has put me behind with all my Christmas correspondence. And besides, we are having a heat wave, and a drought. I seem to spend most of the daylight hours carrying cans of water to remote trees and shrubs.

A Merry Christmas and a Happy New Year!
Yours,
Patrick White.

DOGWOODS, 5.i.57
TO KEITH MICHELL[44]
It was really the War that made me lose interest in the theatre. I felt, I think, that the kind of High Drama necessary in it, had been played out by us all during these years, and that anything we might put on a stage could only appear colourless and feeble. So I kept on at novels. (I had published three before The Tree of Man), and in those I think I can convey things more subtly than I ever would in the theatre.

Of course, I suppose also I have not got the technical flair for a play. And that does rankle. Particularly as I know when someone else has done something wrong. I still feel sometimes I would like to pull it off, just once, to show myself, and perhaps your letter has pandered to that ambition! If I do finish something in play form, I shall send it to you for your judgment.[45]

I have never seen you act, but have read about you, and heard of you

[44](1928–   ), actor and director who left South Australia to become a leading classical actor in Britain, star of musicals, director of the Chichester Festival Theatre, etc.
[45]As a result of Michell's enquiry, PW decided to look once more at The Ham Funeral.

from English friends connected with the theatre, with the result that I hope you are not quite lost to us before we have a theatre for you to act in. I almost succumbed to the glitter of London, Europe and all that, but of course, it is different for an actor, who is fed on glitter to a great extent. Since the War, I have hardly stirred from these six acres outside Sydney, and as a writer, I feel I am the better for it.

DOGWOODS, 8.ii.57
TO BEN HUEBSCH
Dear Mr Huebsch,
It was a great relief to get your cable, and even more so, your letter – to hear that several of you have found something in *Voss*. As you have realised by now, I am always on tenterhooks until I know that my books are not just private illusions.

You talk about the 'symphonic structure' of *Voss* – well, in the last ten years I think music has taught me a lot about writing. That may sound pretentious, and I would not know how to go into it <u>rationally</u>, but I feel that listening constantly to music helps one to develop a book more logically.

I expect your conscientious editor will find many more mistakes to add to those you have already spotted. '*Wie lang sind wir schon hier?*' is certainly better on p.381; and by all means <u>restore</u> the *Umlaut* <u>throughout</u>. I suppose I did away with it living in a country where such a thing, or any form of printed accentuation, simply does not exist.

You ask: 'What will the Australians say now?' Quite a lot of them are beginning to look for works of art, and will accept *Voss*, and even exalt it, but there will be the usual outcry from those who expect a novel to be a string of pedestrian facts, and from the critics, themselves mostly writers, or worse still, 'professors'.

Some time ago I cut out the enclosed, as it seemed to me to convey something of the climax of *Voss*, although the latter is certainly not a 'Triumph of Death'. Perhaps Brueghel and the artist who does the jacket for V. may get together in some way.[46]

Then, I have a couple of publicity photographs to send later. They are better than that horror taken after the War, and which might be described as 'The Triumph of Fat and Civilian Life' – also more suitable than the one I sent recently.

Thank you very much for the Rebecca West[47] which arrived a couple

---

[46]Huebsch suggested they save this scene of slaughter for a fresh edition of *Mein Kampf*.
[47]*The Fountain Overflows*, just published by Viking.

of days ago, and which looks most enticing wherever I open it. I hope soon to get down to it.

Manoly Lascaris, who helps me to exist here, is off next week on a few months holiday with his family in Greece. I don't like to think of the chaos which will probably result when I am left on my own, and can't see myself writing anything for a long time to come. Actually, I am toying with the idea for a play – jotting bits here and there. My Jewish novel will take a lot more thought and reading, and even then I may not have the courage to embark on anything so esoteric. Time and other powers will decide.

Yours sincerely,
Patrick White.

DOGWOODS, 25.ii.57
TO BEN HUEBSCH
I must also thank you for *The Fountain Overflows*, which will become one of those books I particularly cherish – like *The Swiss Family Robinson*, and *The Secret Garden*[48], and *Le Grand Meaulnes*,[49] and even *War and Peace*. I wonder what it is they all have in common. One seems to pass over and go on living in them for ever after. I think possibly it is because they give one glimpses of a heartbreaking perfection one will never achieve, whether it is the rather comic, homespun achievements of the Swiss Family, the perfect refuge of *The Secret Garden*, the interiors and scenes of family life in Tolstoy, and Rebecca West's lovely portraits of people as one hopes to find them.

[48]By Frances Hodgson Burnett, 1911.
[49]By Alain-Fournier, 1913.

Lost and Found

March 1957 – September 1958

TEN YEARS OF LIFE at Dogwoods had taken their toll on Lascaris. He left, exhausted, for Greece and both men feared his departure might mark a permanent breach. But these months apart, which White passed off in his letters as a bout of homesickness, confirmed Lascaris' authority in the relationship: White found he could not do without him. For White, this miserable time was made worse by the suspicion that the old trouble with his lungs was TB. At this low point, alone at Dogwoods, he began three important correspondences: with his friends the Moores, fellow-Christian Freddie Glover and the painter Sidney Nolan.

White had admired Nolan's work for years and wrote hoping to persuade the painter to design the jacket for *Voss*. But it was Cynthia Nolan who replied from London, setting a curious pattern that continued for nearly twenty years. Though White came to love them both, Cynthia was the link: this singular, fierce woman who guarded her husband, built a garden on the Thames, wrote books and the letters Sid always *promised* to write. White said of Cynthia: 'She reminds me of myself.' The painter was to break all White's rules – an artist living abroad, accepting honours, courting publicity – but the friendship with the Nolans was so strong that White accepted all of this. Until things went very wrong, nothing was wrong.

DOGWOODS, 7.iii.57
TO SIDNEY NOLAN
Dear Sidney Nolan,
You do not know, and probably have not even heard of me, but I have written several novels, of which the last, *The Tree of Man*, had a certain amount of success here and there. Another novel, *Voss*, is to be published in London within the next eighteen months by Eyre & Spottiswoode, who brought out *The Tree of Man* in such a filthy jacket,[1] I have suggested they

---

[1] Don Finley, an amateur artist working at Australia House in the Strand, painted a crude stand of gums for the English jacket.

approach you and ask whether you would be prepared to do a jacket for the new book.

Of course, I don't know whether a noted painter would contemplate such a thing, but I personally would very much like it. It may amuse and interest you to know that Vance Palmer in his review of *The Tree of Man* for the A.B.C. found affinities between your painting and my writing.[2] Although I cannot see the connexion in *The Tree of Man*, I often felt in writing *Voss* that certain scenes were, visually, in the Sidney Nolan Manner.

Briefly, *Voss* is about a megalomaniac German explorer who comes to Australia in the Nineteenth Century. The character is based, but only based upon that of Leichhardt. The book is really the development of a relationship between Voss and a woman he meets briefly while passing through Sydney. It is the story of a grand passion consummated only in the minds of the two people concerned as the expedition advances into the interior. Stylistically, I try to satirise the chronicles and correspondence of the period.

No doubt Eyre & Spottiswoode will suggest you read the MS. If you quail before such an undertaking, Chapter 12 contains an incident which I think might be very effective as a subject. In it Palfreyman, a naturalist (in no other way connected with Leichhardt's Gilbert) is murdered by blacks. As Palfreyman is by innocence and instinct the essential Christian, I can see his death depicted after Greco's 'Burial of the Conde de Orgaz', though in the Sidney Nolan manner, with the members of the expedition lifting up his body, and instead of Greco's heavenly choirs, the detached blacks standing in judgment on a cloud of mist in the background. However, that is just a suggestion. If your imagination responds to the idea of doing a jacket, as I hope it will, you will probably choose to do something quite different.[3]

Incidentally, one thing we do share is an enthusiasm for Greece. I spent a year there after the Liberation, and so far it has been the most important year of my life.

Yours sincerely,
Patrick White.

DAVID MOORE WAS A civilised Englishman who had known White's work

[2]Palmer (1885–1959), eminent literary nationalist whose proletarian novels, verse and criticism PW found profoundly unsympathetic. He broadcast his verdict on the novel, 29 July 1956, in *Current Books Worth Reading*.

[3]He did: a thin Voss sent to PW on a postcard, then a disappointing fat Voss for the finished design. But PW told the painter, 28.x.63, 'the jacket in its finished state is, indeed, so much better than I would have got if E. & S. had been left to their own devices . . .'

in England. Moore came to Australia to write film scripts and on the set of Ealing's *Bitter Springs* he met Gwen Moore, a woman of swift sympathies, a teacher from Western Australia. Ealing folded; they married. While Moore worked on the *Australian Encyclopaedia* for Angus & Robertson, he mobilised the publisher's Sydney shop to promote *The Tree of Man*. White invited them to Dogwoods and the friendship that then began between the two couples lasted the rest of White's life. In early 1957 the Moores left for England where David was to take a diploma in anthropology.

DOGWOODS, 7.iii.57
TO THE MOORES
Dear Gwen and David,
I hope this will get to England in time to meet you. Since Manoly left a fortnight ago, I seem to spend all my time writing to meet ships on their arrival at ports . . .

My mother writes that she is looking forward to seeing you. Of course, by this time she is pretty old, and may be rather boring. My sister is the kind of mother who talks about her children. The only thing she ever reads is a best seller with a tinge of pornography. It is really the children I would like you to inspect and report on.

I hope you had a good voyage unembarrassed by too many quoits. Manoly is surrounded by Roman Catholic pilgrims, young men hung with holy medals, and elderly ladies bound for an audience with the Pope, who rub up against him, he says, 'like cats in season.' Still, he seems to be amused by it, and there is free vino at table.

FREDERICK GLOVER OF THE Rural Bank, Parramatta, a frail and formal man, headed reluctantly into the bush at this time to manage his first branch. Glover took in tow a mother-in-law ('Mother') and his wife Mollie slightly crippled by polio. He had worshipped with White at St Paul's Castle Hill and was devoted to the theatre. Glover advised White on his investments; they shared a subscription to the *New Statesman*. White felt protective pity for this gentle 'crypto' – 'He thought everyone was in love with him' – and encouraged the hopes Glover had of being a playwright.

DOGWOODS, 24.iii.57
TO FREDERICK GLOVER
I wonder you let yourself get carried away about your family – you see very little of them. If you did not like your father, nor did he like you, so there need be no feeling of guilt. The details may be sordid, as you say, but

objectively they are very interesting, so perhaps they may be of future use to you. What I mean to say is that it is better to use them than to brood over them.

I had bad news a few days ago: my sister wrote to say my mother had been knocked over by a man bumping into her in the street, and in the fall had broken her hip. They operated on her immediately, but the doctor seemed to think there is a possibility she may not walk again, on account of her age (she will be 80 next month). However, my sister feels, from what we know of her, she will manage to get about somehow. I suppose the pressure will now be put on me to go over, but I shall resist that. I am sure it will be better for everyone if I do not.

I have signed the English agreement for *Voss* at last, the terms now quite satisfactory. Also had a row with the German translator of *The Tree of Man*, who sounds as though he is trying to change what he is incapable of translating[4] . . .

Thank you for the review of gramophone records. According to that and a book by Max Graf that I have just been reading,[5] Stravinsky is the composer of the age. I must really try to listen to some more of his later stuff. Most of what I have heard has sounded so terribly sterile. Lately I have bought records of the Brahms *Second Concerto* (Serkin), the Mahler *Ninth*, and a lovely recording of some Bach cantatas sung by a counter tenor called Alfred Deller.[6] Have you got this last one? If not, I would like to give it to you when I can buy another record of it. I find I play it at least once a day. So let me know. It is something you can play back at Vockler[7] so as not to let him have all his way with Palestrina.

I must say V. sounds awful. Perhaps the worthy, boring Evangelicals are preferable after all to the worldly, pretentious Anglo Catholics.

Manoly wrote from Cape Town. His brother[8] had failed to get over from Durban, which was a disappointment – couldn't get anyone to take charge for him at the Bank, which must be a tin-pot affair. However, M. had also had a letter from their cousin the Princess,[9] who is going to descend from Rome and carry him off at Naples for the duration of his stay . . .

[4]The novelist Heinrich Böll (1917–85).
[5]*Modern Music: composers and music for our time*, 1946.
[6]English singer (1912–79) who restored that voice to the concert platform.
[7]The Rev. John Vockler (1924–   ), curate of All Saints', Singleton.
[8]Aristo.
[9]Eleana Guistiniani was married to the Italian diplomat Prince Goffredo Biondi Morra.

I lunched yesterday with the Kriegers, where I also found the Josephs.[10] Ile is off at the end of the week. I have arranged for her to meet Huebsch while she is in New York.

Too tired to type anymore. The grass is more or less under control, and I don't think I shall have to call anyone in to help. Anyway, in another fortnight the worst will be over as far as the grass is concerned. I find the time is going terribly terribly slowly, but perhaps it will speed up as I grow used to the situation.

Yours
Patrick.

DOGWOODS, 9.iv.57
TO DAVID MOORE
Manoly should now be in Athens. I had several letters from him in Rome, where he was staying with his cousin the Principessa, and having an orgy of galleries and churches. Last week-end he was to have left for Greece. It is intolerably dreary here on my own. It is not the work, just the slow passage of time. At night I wash up, and drink, and play Mahler and Bruckner, till my head thunders – I shall probably be ready for Alcoholics Anonymous at the end of it all.

No chance of starting anything fresh in the circumstances. I think perhaps it is a good thing. I should pause for some time before the next, and do a lot more reading . . .

I see *The Doll* is about to open.[11] The other night I went to a cocktail party in Castle Hill, at which I was the youngest by about 20 years. One dear old lady with white hair and a fringe, who had started off being very shy, said to me just before I left: 'Mr White, I am the wife of a canecutter. If you ever come to Queensland, I shall show you cane with the knickers down.'

If this typing looks unduly peculiar, it is because Tom Jones[12] is rolling about on top of the desk, and I am baking a batch of bread at the same time. Lovely smell. I always bake my own bread nowadays.

Let me hear from you again soon. I have taken a ticket in the Jackpot Lottery, so if things go better than they usually do, I shall be able to pay your passages back.

Love to you both,
Patrick.

[10]Maurice Joseph (1912–   ), physician who was soon to solve the riddle of PW's lungs and handle his major bronchial crises for the next thirty years; he and his wife Isabelle lived at Castle Hill.
[11]Ray Lawler's *The Summer of the Seventeenth Doll*, in London.
[12]Cat.

DOGWOODS, 1.v.57
TO FREDERICK GLOVER
Had a very depressing ten days, a combination of no news from Manoly
and disasters happening to people I know. Of course, I began to connect
disaster with M. Then, two letters arrived yesterday, and another one, the
first written, to-day. When there are three or four air mails a week from
Greece, I don't know why the letters should arrive in lumps and after such
delays.

M. has had a hectic, if interesting Easter. First, a visit of some days
to the island of Poros, on the coast of the Peloponnese, which is almost
one large lemon grove, and where he collected all sorts of seeds and bulbs
for the garden. During Easter he seems to have gone the rounds of the
churches in Athens, and to a famous monastery some way out. At one
church the father and cousin of Elena Nikolaïdi are the cantors. The father
taught her before she went to the Athens Conservatoire, and he says one
can see the origins of her style. The big Easter procession from the
Cathedral this year was rather messed up. Instead of singing traditional
music, they played the Chopin funeral march for Cyprus and Makarios[13] . . .

The other night I listened to the Shostakovitch Violin Concerto with
Fritz.[14] It is a very shoddy work, almost a violin solo, for Oistrakh of course,
but even so. Fritz was in ecstasies. I have come to the conclusion that
what he likes in music is only virtuosity and sensuousness. He came out
with some extraordinary remarks about chamber music, such as: it cannot
be great because it has nearly all been commissioned by dilettantes. In
such moods he becomes a schoolboy, and it is quite impossible to argue.

The house painting starts to-morrow, and it is now very late, so I
must go to bed.
Yours,
Patrick.

DOGWOODS, 30.v.57
TO PEGGY GARLAND
Dear Peggy,
I am glad there was not a date on your letter as it would make me feel

---

[13]A year earlier the *SMH* had published a magisterial letter from PW condemning the
British for provoking conflict between Greeks and Turks on the island, 2.vi.56: '. . . history
has proved that no oppression can destroy the spirit of Greece, but it is to be feared
that in the present instance her traditional friendship with Britain may have suffered a
damage too severe to be repaired.'
[14]Krieger.

guiltier, although I really have a perfectly good excuse for not writing before; I have been here on my own since February, and feel myself getting slower and slower at doing what has to be done. Now I am ticking off the days till July 2nd, when Manoly will return. His trip was very necessary, and had to take place just when it did: there seemed less chance of a war breaking out in the immediate future, several of his relations might die at any moment, and for once there was some spare money in the bank.[15] Now I can tell he wants honestly to come back. Before, I could always sense he felt something of an exile from Greece. He says he finds he really does not have much in common with his family any longer, or indeed, with anyone over there. The country was as beautiful as ever, but the poverty of the majority of the inhabitants so miserable that he could only feel ashamed . . .

Voss is being published in New York in August, in London not till the New Year. A few weeks ago I had a cable from New York to say the American Book of the Month Club had chosen it as their book for August. From the point of view of sales, this is most satisfactory, as the Book Club guarantees quite a considerable sum, which I shall halve with the publisher.[16] Harper's Bazaar is publishing something about me in August or September, with a photograph, and a ten year old short story[17] for which they are giving $300! Extraordinary to think this stir is taking place over the same person who could not create even a mild one a few years ago.

Do you know the work of the Australian painter, Sidney Nolan? We have persuaded him to do a jacket for the English edition of Voss. I was determined not to leave the jacket to the publisher after what happened to The Tree of Man . . .

I don't feel strong enough to-night to discuss Brutality in Art and Literature at all intelligently. I certainly find the existentialist attitude most repulsive. Perhaps I am not a realist. When we came to live here, I felt the life was, on the surface, so dreary, ugly, monotonous, there must be a poetry hidden in it to give it a purpose, and so I set out to discover that secret core, and The Tree of Man emerged. I suppose the school of brutality to which we object is just another attempt to rise above monotony and boredom by substituting a more exciting ugliness for the existing one. No doubt the disciples persuade themselves they are being more 'honest.'

This letter should really go on for pages in order to fill the gap since

---

[15]Lascaris had exhausted his capital at Dogwoods; only after a grim confrontation did PW give him sufficient money for the journey.
[16]PW's share was US$20,000.
[17]'On the Balcony' in August, p.112.

I last wrote, but that is quite impossible. Nowadays I feel my letters are no more than a kind of shorthand of information. I must write to Betty, too, for her birthday. She wrote me a good, objective letter about Suzanne and her girls. Did you know my mother had broken her hip just before her 80th birthday? She is home again, however, walking on crutches, and hoping soon to be using a stick.

Have you read *The Fountain Overflows* (Rebecca West)? Or *Dead Yesterdays* (Natalia Ginsburg)?

Hope I see you before long.

Love,

Patrick.

DOGWOODS, 7.vi.57

TO THE MOORES

So Gwen has been going through the bluebell phase. I suppose she had to – together with the thatch, and the hedges, and all the other adorable trimmings. They make me shiver when I think of the walks in cold, rainy afternoons, and the dismal tea-room at the end. Of course I know there are many things far worse in Australia. But I cannot get sentimental about bluebells. Nor have I ever really been able to take to daffodils: they remind me of those long, cold Englishwomen with pale, unshapely arms . . .

My life has been hell for the last several weeks, with a painter, a week-end carpenter, and now a bathroom-tiler all taking a hand. At present the bathroom looks like an Egyptian prison cell, the walls stripped to the brick, smelling of age and damp, and the basin removed and lavatory cut off. Very miserable, particularly as there is a gastric epidemic raging along Showground Road. I can only hope I shall be spared until All Conveniences are restored.

DOGWOODS, 13.vi.57

TO FREDERICK GLOVER

With things as they are, I can no longer read, write, think, and can scarcely listen to the gramophone. I drink a lot of brandy early in the evening, which puts me into a stupor for the middle; then I wake up, wash up, and scribble lines furiously in the small hours . . . There is no news, as I am unable to go anywhere now, am unable to receive, and am too unwashed for most people to receive me even if they remembered my existence.

LASCARIS RESOLVED IN GREECE to continue life with White but their reunion in early July was not easy. Nothing of their difficulties surfaced in letters that survive from this time – or any time. White remarked to

Glover, 'Things are at last returning to normal . . . Manoly home, sharing the work, which makes it so restful, it is quite like having a holiday.'[18] For years White had dreamt of a Grand Tour of Europe; now he decided both of them would return there in 1958. At this point, a bundle of copies of *Voss* arrived from New York.

DOGWOODS, 19.viii.57

TO BEN HUEBSCH

I don't think I have written since I received the copies of *Voss*, so I have not said how pleased I was with its appearance. (Incidentally, I read last night that the colours blue and yellow are the colours of introverted and extrovert spiritual perception. I wonder whether the designer was conscious that he had hit the nail so subtly on the head!)[19]

I must also thank you for your article in the *Book of the Month Magazine*, which gets away with quoting from letters without making the writer of them writhe.[20] That is, indeed, a triumph of discretion. It is dreadful to think, however, that one's letters still exist. I am always burning and burning, and must go out to-morrow to the incinerator with a wartime diary I discovered at the back of a wardrobe the other day.

To return to *Voss*: I feel the reviews will probably be all right, but am very doubtful of the public. Half the friends who have received advance copies preserve a cold, dead silence, or make desperately nostalgic references to *The Tree of Man*. That was what they expected – again – with a dash of water. I don't know what they will think of my next, which seems to be forming – still only in my mind – as a kind of cantata for four voices. I think it may be some time before I start, as one of the themes is the Jewish esoteric one, which I believe I mentioned.

The German *Tree of Man* is supposed to come out this month under the incredibly German title of *Zur Ruhe kam der Baum des Menschen nie!*[21] I suggested it might wrap itself round the jacket like a piece of string, but they claimed that everybody was *begeistert*.[22] Since then we have had a row. They sent me the proof so late it was impossible to get the corrections back to them in time to please the printer, so that probably it has been

[18]7.vii.57.

[19]George Salter's design had shreds of Voss's letter to Laura floating in a golden haze over blue distance.

[20]The article in *Book of the Month Club News*, July 1957, p.4, drew heavily on PW's letters to Huebsch since the war.

[21]This is the line by Housman from which PW took the book's title: 'The tree of man was never quiet', see fn. 17, page 96.

[22]Enthusiastic.

printed mistakes and all, and there were a number of ludicrous ones, since the translator, an arrogant individual and novelist called Heinrich Böll, would not consult me until the end. Do you know Kiepenheuer & Witsch? Dr Witsch seems quite a correct <u>German</u> but always takes *Urlaub*[23] in a crisis, and leaves somebody with the glamorous but unconvincing name of Alexandra von Miquel to pour oil and womanly tact on the troubled waters. Unfortunately it is all too obvious.

DOGWOODS, 31.viii.57
TO DAVID MOORE

It was heartening to know *Voss* made such an impression on you, because with many people it has fallen quite flat. Some who have had copies will not refer to having read it. Kylie Tennant says it is 'most horrifying.'[24] One of my cousins (the one in Oxford) whose judgment I have always valued writes rather bitchily: 'I have quite stuck in *Voss*. Your style which has always bordered on the precious has toppled right over. It reminds me of

[23]Holiday.
[24](1912–88), novelist, whose friendship with PW began when she sprang to defend *The Tree of Man* in an eccentric interview, *SMH*, 22 Sept. 1956, p.10. 'I dreamt about you last night,' she said the moment they met. 'You had blue hair and it was quite terrifying.' PW always thought Tennant a bit crazy but admired her courage.

a custard that has cooked too long, and curdled.'[25] On the other hand, Robert Liddell, who could not read *The Tree of Man*, is full of enthusiasm for *Voss*,[26] and Keith Michell is trying to persuade Pinewood to let him film it.

American reviews – some good, some downright bad, the latter usually as a result of the critic's not understanding what he is reviewing.

I am feeling exhausted at the moment, what with the strain of all this book business, and having my cousin Peggy Garland here for a fortnight to recuperate from her troubles (her husband has left her after 25 years . . .) I always enjoy having Peggy here, although some of her behaviour is a little vague, and she makes the house look as though a Poltergeist has been through it.

DOGWOODS, 2.ix.57
TO BEN HUEBSCH
Dear Mr Huebsch,
This afternoon I had your letter about the accident.[27] It is a terrible thing to have happened, but, if it is any consolation, my mother, aged 80, broke her hip at the beginning of the year as the result of being pushed over in Kensington High Street, was very soon out of hospital, walking on crutches, almost immediately exchanged these for a stick, rushed to a performance of the *Italian in Algiers* at Glyndebourne, and is now doing practically all of what she wants to do, almost as if the accident had not happened. Still, I am sorry you have had to experience so much unpleasantness so far from home. I can imagine such an accident, in the dark, at an <u>Italian</u> railway station, with everybody expressing himself . . .

My new book is stirring unmistakably, but I think it will be some time before I try to put it on paper. I want to read and think a lot more yet. At present it is called *Riders in the Chariot*.

For the last seven months I have been involved with an Anti-T.B. clinic, spending a lot of time travelling back and forth between Sydney and Castle Hill. In the beginning apparently, as the result of X-rays showing shadows on my lungs, they suspected either T.B. or a malignancy, but

[25]This is the only surviving fragment of Betty Withycombe's criticism of PW's work.
[26]Robert Liddell (1908–92), novelist, travel writer and former Professor at Farouk I University, Alexandria, advised Lascaris in 1941 that PW was a fine writer which judgment encouraged Lascaris to commit himself to the Australian. Liddell was now in Athens. His *Aegean Greece*, 1954, was the first of three distinguished travel books, the others being *The Morea*, 1958, and *Mainland Greece*, 1965.
[27]He had broken his knee.

finally they have decided it is only an allergic condition, something called Löffler's Syndrome.[28] My old Dr Morgenstern is now trying to clear this up, and I don't doubt he will succeed as he did with the asthma, and the rheumatism in my feet. I only regret the time spent in waiting rooms.

DOGWOODS, 4.ix.57
TO FREDERICK GLOVER
Dear Frederick,
Peggy's visit has made it impossible for me to answer your letters singly, and even now, I shall not be able to deal with them in detail. I seem to spend all my time washing up and preparing for the next meal. We have been entertaining a great deal, but have also been entertained.

The Tildesley[29] lunch was quite a success. Miss Evelyn appeared on our doorstep in a flowerpot-coloured flowerpot hat, clutching a giant billbergia plant,[30] and looking very paintable. Mrs Salier was suitably silly, and had an argument with Peggy about Our Lovely Queen, which unfortunately I missed as Miss Beatrice was earnestly sounding me out on Arrau in the public lavatory.[31]

The T.s very quickly returned our hospitality as they are friends of a Professor Davis who was in China with Peggy, and whom she wanted to meet again.[32] This lunch took place at the Macquarie Club with all due pomp and ceremony, but I would have preferred to re-visit their house. At one point where the conversation flagged, Miss Beatrice leaned towards the Professor and asked, with a gleam in her eye: 'Tell me— — what do they <u>drink</u> in China?' I shall only be able to do justice to the bird in Miss B.'s hat when we meet ...

To-day Rodd brought Father Hope, an exceedingly civilised old fellow

---

[28]Simple pulmonary eosinophilia, transient shadows in the lungs which look very like TB or sometimes cancer. This was a step towards identifying the condition that had dogged PW most of his adult life, but the precise cause was not pinpointed for another two years.

[29]Sisters Evelyn and Beatrice, the twin pillars of amateur theatre in Sydney.

[30]A vulgar epiphyte.

[31]The papers that morning carried reports of Claudio Arrau's appeal against a conviction for offensive behaviour in Sydney the year before. He was on a concert tour of Australia when he was arrested and fined £5 after winking at a police provocateur in a lavatory at Lang Park. He abandoned the tour. Evidence was heard at the appeal of an eye affliction; the Crown conceded Arrau's former good character and the judge declined to enter a conviction.

[32]Albert Davis (1924–   ), professor of oriental studies at Sydney University, translator and biographer of the poet Su Shih. Garland recalled PW's irritation this day because 'he couldn't talk about China and we wanted to – so he cut it short.'

for an Australian church man[33] – drank a glass of wine, obviously enjoyed his food, and seems aware of the world in a way the evangelicals are not. In spite of his worldliness, however, I feel he is genuinely honest and good. (Do you know that the hideous evangelical Churches of Sydney are referred to as 'Mowll's God boxes'?)[34]

DOGWOODS, 9.x.57
TO KEITH MICHELL
The reviews of Voss in the States have been mostly very good, but it is not selling wildly. I think a lot of people, after being trapped into expecting a popular novel in The Tree of Man, are fighting shy this time. The legion of middle-aged, eiderdowny females is probably laying off, and it is they, after all, who make a book into a financial success. A strange development is an order of 1000 copies of Voss for the U.S. Army Libraries. (And, in passing, a Sydney bookseller told me the other day that The Tree of Man is very popular with truck drivers.)

The English edition of Voss was not to have appeared till April, but the Book Society has decided to make it their choice for December. I have had a most disgruntled letter from the publisher complaining of the indecent haste in which they will now be forced to publish (they have had the MS. since last Christmas, and the Americans were able to bring out their edition in August.) I managed to persuade Eyre & Spottiswoode to get Sidney Nolan to do the jacket for Voss, and I feel that will be more suitable than the one provided for The Tree of Man.

What are you doing now that the Vic. season is finished? I still have not got anywhere near writing a play. I can no longer think in terms of theatre. But a number of people here seem to be writing plays, how interestingly remains to be seen. I have an idea Australians lag behind in that field, not because we haven't a theatre, but because we are un-dramatic, too boring. The average Australian can't tell one anything

[33]John Hope (c.1891–1971) was the priest at the Anglo-Catholic city parish of Christ Church St Laurence where Kylie Tennant and her husband Rodd worshipped; they took PW and Lascaris there about this time for he had despaired of his local Evangelical C. of E. He found Christ Church too Roman for his taste, and so abandoned formal worship altogether.
[34]Howard Mowll (1890–1958), Bishop of Western China, came to Sydney in 1933 and kept the archdiocese on a path of Biblical purity for 25 bleak years. PW had a particular grudge against Mowll: before the war Ruth gave the family's Mount Wilson cottage to the church as a holiday home for clergymen, but somehow Mowll took possession of the place, and later sold it, as his own.

without making it sound pointless. Such a chronic shapelessness can breed novels, but the drama will hardly flourish in it.

I have just read *The Doll*, which I thought much better than when I saw it acted. As acted, it seemed to me an occasion of lost opportunities, both for humour, and poetry. (I am right off <u>realism</u> anyway. I read the other day that somebody had referred to it as 'reality in degeneracy', and that is perhaps what I feel about it.) But, from hearing everyone else's reactions to *The Doll*, and now from reading the script, perhaps I was wrong about it. Certainly I saw the play on a night of intense heat, everyone sweating to death on both sides!

DOGWOODS, 1.xi.57
TO MOLLIE McKIE
I am afraid we are no closer to finding the right people to look after 'Dogwoods' while we are away, but I expect somebody will materialise. Everything now looks very nice, and I shan't particularly want to leave it. Still, it will be a change not to do the washing up for a few months. I did go away for a few days recently, but found myself washing up in self-defence as my hosts were so bad at the sink.

Yours,
Patrick.

DOGWOODS, 13.xi.57
TO PEGGY GARLAND
A most exciting broadcast from Salzburg last week. I wonder whether you had it? A von Einem piano concerto played by somebody called Gerti Herzog, unknown to me, and Honegger's *Liturgical Symphony*.[35] The first was extremely brilliant and gay, the second quite stupendous. Honegger seemed to be saying a lot of what I want to try to say in my next book (I am still a long way from starting, but enjoy brooding over it, and think I shall be forced to eke out that luxury for some time, in any case, if we do go for the trip – on which I paid a deposit last week.)

No more from Betty, but I received from her a copy of Lawrence Durrell's *Bitter Lemons* – about Cyprus. A very moving, beautiful, and on the whole impartial book. My criticism is that he only made one perfunctory reference to the devil of the piece (Eden), who stirred up the Turks against the Greeks, making a deadlock inevitable and possibly permanent. Of

[35]Herzog was enjoying a brief moment of celebrity; Honegger's 1946 work, a passionate response to the war, was considered for a time one of the great symphonies of the century; Karajan conducted the Berlin Philharmonic.

course I am a sucker for anything about Greece, so I should sympathise with Prof. Davis's tears over China. I can produce them almost any time for Greece, and nearly cried my head off reading *Bitter Lemons*. It is the Mediterranean really. Everything on earth that matters is concentrated [there as][36] far as I am concerned – and when I say earth, I mean space too.

DOGWOODS, 12.i.58
TO THE MOORES
The Chalk Garden is here now, and we have been twice.[37] The first time in ten years I have felt happy at a straight play. Here at last is imagination, wit and mystery, and that is what theatre means for me. I don't want realism anymore than I want the photographic rigours in painting. We went the other night to see the current Australian opus at the Elizabethan *The Shifting Heart*.[38] As a sermon it is excellent, and should be heard by all those Australians who, unfortunately, will not hear it. As a play I found it ineffably boring, and amateurishly acted by everybody except the author. We are building up a tradition of shouting to disguise the lack of tension, and that together with the dollops of backyard sentimentality, and the realistic framework, makes me very depressed. Perhaps Ray Mathew will save the situation.[39] Do you know he has two plays coming along?

Voss is about to arrive here, and I can feel the critics poised for ritual murder. All the Sydney papers have been very careful to keep the British opinions dark, so this time a good time should be had by the jackals ...

Otherwise, I have another book boiling up, and in the circumstances, don't know whether to let it or suppress it. I think probably I should not begin yet, and should read and think for a bit longer. But I could do that so much better at Dogwoods than trotting round a world which has given me as much as I am going to get, and besides, I feel more and more, as far as creative writing is concerned, everything important happens to one before one is born. Only journalists need to feed on events and facts.

---

[36]The letter is torn.
[37]By Enid Bagnold (1889–1981), performed by Sybil Thorndike and Lewis Casson.
[38]By Richard Beynon (1925–81): the hopes and hard times of an Italian family in Australia.
[39](1929–   ), playwright and poet for whom PW had high hopes; after some success in Australia, Mathew moved to London in 1960.

Dogwoods, 17.i.58

TO PEGGY GARLAND

God knows what has become of the book I ordered for you for Christmas. I am always told it has not yet arrived. I am sorry I did not know about a lovely book on Goya by Malraux[40] which I bought yesterday, especially as you probably will not like this one I have ordered. All those Goyas – I feel I want to eat them, and bury my face in them, and sniff them up, they are so good. And now I am filled with a rage to write just like he painted.

Dogwoods, 27.i.58

TO FREDERICK GLOVER

Dear Frederick,

I am sending Enid Starkie's *Rimbaud*, but as there are great chunks of untranslated poems strewn all through it, I don't feel you will get an awful lot out of it. His life is fascinating, of course, particularly as the latter part of it cannot be satisfactorily explained, even by reading the poems that go before. And you will get the bare life from the book.

Today we have had a visit from a German, a Dr Joachim Schulz, who is writing a book in German on Australian literature.[41] He has been here seven years, doing odd jobs of teaching – at a German school outside Brisbane, and at Armidale University. Rather a pathetic old man of 60, very exposed to life, I feel, and trying to build the subject with which he is occupied into something much bigger than it is. Some of his judgments are very queer. For instance he accepts Colin Roderick's *The Lady and the Lawyer* as a work of art,[42] and I should never have thought of Helen Simpson as contributing anything to the literature of anywhere.[43] He has also dug up people one has never heard of, and who, he claims, are fascinating. Of course, they may be! One thing of which I am glad: he is taking up the cudgels over William Hay. My instinct has always told me that there is something, although I have only read <u>about</u> his novels. If I did not have several more to write, I would go into the matter myself.[44]

---

[40]*Saturn: an essay on Goya*, trans. C. W. Chilton, 1957.

[41]*Australien*, Welt im Buch, 1963.

[42]Historical novel, 1955, set in colonial Sydney; Roderick (1911–   ) was an editor at Angus & Robertson, later an academic teaching Australian literature.

[43]Simpson (1897–1940), prolific novelist born in Australia but living mostly in England; *Under Capricorn*, 1937, set in colonial NSW, was filmed poorly by Alfred Hitchcock in 1949.

[44]Later he discovered Hay's *The Escape of the Notorious Sir William Heans* was 'one of the best Australian novels'. To Maie Casey, 31.x.66.

Shall read your play when it comes. However, I do feel you should be getting on to something quite fresh. Perhaps that is because I am always hit or miss myself.

Kriegers and Loebels[45] set off to spend the long week-end at some place at Kangaroo Valley, although I warned them to expect something pretty terrible. They were back the following day, and spent the Sunday together, in a huddle, playing the *Rosenkavalier*. (One day I think I shall write a comedy about the Viennese in Australia.) Apparently the guesthouse was a white weatherboard with rooms like ovens, a dining room under plastic covers, and of course, the most excruciating food. After one night Ile did one of her transparent bits of diplomacy, told the woman her husband had broken his glasses and could not see without them, then they paid up for the whole weekend and got out.

We went to a terrible party the other evening at Warrawee at the House Beautiful of my stockbroker cousin.[46] Why we were asked, I don't know, as we always feel that his wife, who is the soul of suburbia, hates us. Anyway, one looked at all the people and wondered to whom, out of about 50, one might possibly talk. They were all middle-aged, or elderly, North Shore business and the men all similar – they could have been wearing *papier mâché* masks for an expressionist play – , the women all in false teeth, and little hats made of flowers, either pink or blue. We stood under a crepe myrtle and drank about a gallon, but nothing happened. I was introduced to a Mr Horn who announced with pride that he had been made to read *Dombey and Son* at school, and as a result had not opened another book since. Finally, in desperation, we took to urging the daughter of the house, who was dressed in what looked like a Bebarfald curtain, and who will probably become a permanent spinster, to run away to Italy or France and live by her wits.[47]

You don't mention how Mother settled down on her return.[48]

Have signed agreements for German and Portuguese translations of *Voss*. I don't think it will ever arrive here, which I begin to find humiliating and exasperating. Nor have we found anybody yet to look after the house.

---

[45]The Loebels were Poles who survived the war teaching in Tashkent before making their way to Australia.
[46]Ned White of the White family firm C. B. Quinan & Cox.
[47]Morna White survived as Mrs Morna Lambert, but Bebarfalds, the home furnishers for careful shoppers, is now defunct.
[48]PW spoke very firmly to Glover about his difficult mother-in-law Mrs Almond, e.g. 26.xi.57: 'You must deal with Mother exactly as I advised. You are now the Bank Manager.'

But that does not worry me so much. The thought of a winter at Dogwoods is at present most desirable.

Don't leave *The Chalk Garden* till too late. And what about *The Doll*! The *N. Y. Times* said just what I felt and the 'language barrier' was just a gesture of kindness.[49] However, I am sorry for the poor wretch, knowing how one feels after that kind of a jolt.

Yours,

P.

There is said to be a big scandal brewing – Warwick Fairfax and the wife of a Jewish barrister.[50]

DOGWOODS, 8.ii.58

TO THE MOORES

Thank you for sending the Third Programme review of *Voss*, which I found very interesting, and he seemed to me to mix praise and criticism in right proportion.[51] I am only sorry, though, that I have not read half the people of whom I remind them – Malraux, only *La Condition humaine* about twenty years ago, when I did not care enough to follow him in his career; Conrad, several books in my teens, when I could not understand what all his conflicts were about, and consequently did not like him. (The one Conrad I do like, and which I read just at the end of the War on the advice of Robert Liddell, is *Under Western Eyes*.) Of Nietzsche I read *Also Sprach Zarathustra* when I was an undergraduate without being drawn to it. Funny that Whiteman alone should pick on Rimbaud. I <u>am</u>, indeed, soaked in Rimbaud, and it could well be that that comes out.

The book has arrived out here at last, and the reviews have begun. In the Melbourne *Age* a person called Alan Nicholls has produced a piece of monumental stupidity. He accuses me of being <u>child of a faithless generation</u> – like Sartre. Fancy pulling that one out of the bag. He seems to think Oedipus a philosopher, and refers to Gilbert, the naturalist of

---

[49]Brooks Atkinson's 23 Jan. notice in the *Times* killed the show on Broadway: 'If *Summer of the 17th Doll* were in an incomprehensible foreign language, it might conjure up mysterious images of life in far-off places among elusive people. It is the English language that is confusing. We think we know the full meaning of what the Australians are telling us. We don't.'

[50]Warwick Fairfax (1901–87) was the twice-married patriarch of the *SMH* who amazed Sydney by courting Mary Symonds (c.1920–), wife of a Sydney divorce solicitor, Cedric; Fairfax married her in 1959. PW's letters are peppered with references to this affair and his fascination with kittenish Mary Fairfax influenced his portrait of Lady Miriam Surplus of Comebychance Hall in *The Memoirs of Many in One*.

[51]H. G. Whiteman, published in *Comment*, 26 Dec. 1957.

Leichhardt's expedition, as Griffiths. As for the <u>writing</u> of *Voss*, it is the most terrible thing that ever happened, although, he allows, it does convey my ideas to anyone who has the patience to wade through my turgid prose. Finally, he thinks it a pity I did not cultivate the style of R. L. Stevenson.[52] (Actually the prose of *Voss* at its most turgid is supposed to suggest the mid-19th Century Australian chronicle from which, it struck me while going through one after another, is descended the Australian official prose of to-day.)

The *Herald* review appeared to-day, done by Kylie Tennant, and seems to me to be as good as one would get here.[53] At least it was a great change not to be farted at by the *Herald*, and anything of a less open, more intellectual nature would only frighten off the Great Australian Public of the Lousy Lending Library.

Did you, by any chance, come across a review by Eric Lambert, the Australian novelist,[54] in the English *Tribune* (24th Jan)? If not, it is worth getting hold of as a study in malevolence and frustration – nothing I have written is the least bit Australian, *The Tree of Man* is like a burlesque of D. H. Lawrence by Perelman, the Great Australian Novel has often been written, acclaimed with affection by humble people, and absorbed into the Australian Dream etc. etc.

How sick I am of the bloody word AUSTRALIA. What a pity, I am part of it; if I were not, I would get out to-morrow. As it is, they will have me with them till my bitter end, and there are about six more of my un-Australian Australian novels to fling in their faces ...

The Tildesleys asked us to a lunch the other day to meet Sybil Thorndike and Lewis Casson. I sat next to Sybil and was burnt up by that wonderful personality. Even at that age, she is ablaze with everything that is vital, and so beautiful, one had not realised. Lewis, who is several years older, would like to settle down to being an old man, I rather get the impression, though I am sure he would never admit to that. Anyway, I would like to think of him sitting in a garden instead of trailing on to the

---

[52]*Age*, 1 Feb., p.17.
[53]A mad piece: she reported *Voss*'s arrival in Australia *SMH*, 8 Feb., p.12: 'the praises of the literary world dripping off its long serpentine form'.
[54](1918–66) prolific Left realist writer, best known for his first novel, *The Twenty Thousand Thieves*, 1951.

next engagement.[55] (Have you read, incidentally, a little book called *Tea with Walter de la Mare* by Russell Brain? There was a graceful and enviable old age. Perhaps a little bit too graceful. But pleasing to read about.)

DOGWOODS, 11.ii.58
TO BEN HUEBSCH

If I were not going away, I think I might start *Riders in the Chariot* at this point. Always when I meet with lack of understanding in Australian critics, I feel like sitting down and starting another of the novels they deplore, to give them further cause for complaint. But perhaps it is a good thing in this case that I am being restrained by circumstances. I would like first to go to Jerusalem and speak to one or two people. It will not seem to contribute much to the book, only I am never altogether happy if I do not know about past stages in the lives of my characters. And my 'hidden zaddik'[56] – because that is how he appears to be developing – did pass through Jerusalem.

Oh dear, it is going to be a very trying book to write, but I am living with it all the time now. It is shaping and altering, and the four voices of what I still like to think of as a kind of cantata are beginning to sing in the way that, finally, they must.

Hope to hear good news of you soon.
Yours sincerely,
Patrick White.

WHEN KEITH MICHELL TEMPTED him with talk of writing a play, White retrieved his only copy of *The Ham Funeral* from Doris Fitton's Independent Theatre in North Sydney where it was still waiting after nine years for Fitton to make up her mind. She was the last survivor of the women who once dominated 'little theatre' in the city and though White often

---

[55]PW had met Thorndike (1882–1976) and Casson (1875–1969) in London twenty years before. To Mamblas, 19.xi.37, he reported Thorndike's 'queer mixture of sincerity and technique. The conversation was mostly political. They are very ardently Left. Sybil works herself into a frenzy which one suspects may develop into an epileptic fit. She sits on the edge of her chair, trying to bring out words which refuse to come, and clutching at the air as a substitute. The uncomfortable part was that I found myself also straining to sit on the edge of my chair and could almost feel my face growing into the shape of hers. Lewis Casson sat there like a block of granite against which, occasionally, she cannoned, to quiver off again. By the end of the evening I was in a state of complete awe and exhaustion.'

[56]Mordecai Himmelfarb was to be the novel's hidden zaddik: one of the 36 Jews of exemplary righteousness, secret saints, believed to be on earth at any one time.

mocked her and her semi-amateur productions, he admired the old girl's dedication to the stage. Having rescued *The Ham Funeral*, White now sent it to Glover who was immediately enthusiastic.

DOGWOODS, 16.iii.58
TO FREDERICK GLOVER

If *The Ham Funeral* is all you say it is, then I must certainly try to do something about it. Have you sent it back? If so, I have not received it yet. I may be able to re-write in Athens while Manoly is occupied with relations, then present Keith Michell with it when I arrive in London.

It is useless for me to try to discuss the play with you here, as it is ten years since I read it, and I can hardly remember what it is about. I am sure it is too short – my plays always were. I imagine that whatever directions one gave for a set, the producer would probably jettison everything and decide on what he wanted. Actually I don't remember this one as being so naturalistic, but I rather liked the idea of the fourth wall torn out, leaving a frame in jagged wallpaper. I know you are prejudiced against whores – and I just love them. But I think I already have a substitute for that scene, a kind of brutally comic vaudeville act with a blood-curdling denouement, involving the Young Man. Saw a picture of Keith Michell the other day, and he is the Young Man. So perhaps all the pieces of this rather strange and delayed jigsaw are going to fit together in the end.

DOGWOODS, 19.iii.58
TO BEN HUEBSCH

I am told that *Voss* is selling well in England, though how well, I could not say. Here it has been at the top of the best seller list in spite of the worst reviews anyone has had since Hepburn was here in Shakespeare.[57] They took a sledgehammer to H.; on me they have only used the small, claw variety. I am enclosing a selection so that you can see . . .

On and off, I am thinking about the partial re-writing of a play called *The Ham Funeral* . . . It really only needs writing up a bit here and there, and perhaps one complete new scene substituted for one of those already in existence. It is the sort of thing I can scribble at on bits of paper in aeroplanes, type out in Athens, and thrust at a certain young Australian star in London, as he is very keen to have a play of mine. If nothing happens, I don't mind; plays don't really mean anything to me. However, I would like to have a theatrical success in New York just to make the Australian press die finally of apoplexy.

[57]Katharine, in 1955 in *The Merchant of Venice*.

DOGWOODS, 5.iv.58
TO THE MOORES
I expect you have heard something of the things that started happening to me all of a sudden – I mean, how *Voss* was given the Miles Franklin Prize for best Australian novel of the year. As it was the first time awarded, the bull that went with it was most alarming, and I only got through with the assistance of half a bottle of whisky and a pill. I was summoned on Wednesday last to a conference room on the tenth floor of the Rural Bank, and there, in limelight, after speeches by Menzies,[58] Evatt,[59] and Colin Roderick, was presented with a cheque for £500. Most awful was a speech of half a dozen feeble lines by myself. As you know I have spent my life avoiding them, but I could not get out of it this time, as it was obvious the whole incident was going to be such a crashing rejoinder to the journalist-critics of Australia. Well, I did get through, and was actually on television without my knowing it. I had seen something out of the corner of my eye, and thought it was a newsreel. Then, the following day, two people rang up and said they had seen me on the telly and that I looked real nice . . .

Personally I felt as though a slow tin of treacle was being poured over me. But on the whole, it was all very pleasant, and gratifying, and strange, and tiring.

WHITE AND LASCARIS LEFT for Jerusalem on 11 April 1958. The plan was to spend a few days in Israel and then two months in Greece before making their way to England for the rest of the summer. They were to return home through the United States.

ATHENS, 20.iv.58
TO THE KRIEGERS
Dear Fritz and Ile,
I hate receiving typewritten personal letters, but I suppose if I send you one written by hand you will not be able to read it, and after all, I did decide to bring the Olivetti. (Incidentally, we had a big blow from excess baggage right in the beginning; they made us pay £51 overweight as far as London, and that was without the typewriter. Our big cases and the overnight bags were in order, but we had not reckoned that the little Orbit

---

[58]Robert Menzies (1894–1978), conservative prime minister since 1949; he had PW's vote until the elections of 1959: as PW told Glover, 22.xi.59, 'I feel I cannot contribute any longer to the career of that Slyguts Menzies.'
[59]Bert Evatt (1894–1965), leader of the opposition.

bags would be weighed, and into those we had stuffed a lot of medicine bottles, dictionaries, papers and things. Now we have learnt from a travel-seasoned Jewess to carry an Orbit bag under the coat one is wearing, although this does make one look as though one is possessed of a third buttock.)

The journey as far as Bangkok was quite uneventful, but pleasant and comfortable. From our experience so far, Qantas is easily the best air company. As soon as we parted with them we started running into irritations. At Bangkok we were told that we should have to wait 24 hrs to catch the Air France plane, as this had 'broke' on the way from Tokyo. In the heat of the moment this was very distressing, and a great wailing broke out amongst the Jewish pilgrims to Israel. I suppose I must have done my share of wailing, for in the middle of it all they asked me if I wasn't 'Mr Winkel'. At the height of the crisis, too, the skirt fell off the elderly *Blaustrumpf*,[60] Mrs Cohen, who was trying to lead her flock, and she was left standing on Bangkok airport in a flesh-coloured slip. Finally, we were all disposed of in hotels, and Manoly and I at least were glad of the delay as we were able to look at some wonderful Buddhist temples the following morning – all glass, and porcelain, and marble, with bells tinkling, incense rising, crowds praying – it happened that that day of all days was their New Year. For twenty-four hours I became, I think, a Buddhist.

Air France arrived fairly late that night, complete with glamorous hostesses – we had Michele Morgan[61] as far as Teheran, and Ingrid Bergman from there on – , but they were not nearly as efficient as the Australians, and I was surprised to find that after all the latter have a much more agreeable kind of natural charm. The food, however, was far superior.

At Teheran next morning we found we had emerged from the steam baths of Thailand, and were now surrounded by snowy peaks on a vast, bare, wind-swept plain. For our stay at the airport, we were herded into a small, square, sinister room, like something at a lesser Arab railway station, by a kind of female Commissar, with a very bad temper, and food-spots down her front. Doors were slammed. We were commanded. We were given cups of cold tea with egg-stained tea-spoons, all in the Arab tradition, while Persians stood around looking, drinking little coffees, and, one of the Jewesses insisted, talking a kind of bastard Russian. There was a general air of anxiousness about the pilgrims, and I think we were all glad to return to the plane, having picked up a Swedish honeymoon couple, who were punching each other in their exuberance, and a kind of seedy maestro

[60]Bluestocking.
[61]French film star (1920–   ).

with a hysterical wife, who kept screaming in French that he was not going to have another sou of her money, as he only drank it. Later that afternoon, after flying over the snows of Southern Turkey, and turning at Cyprus, we began to approach the Promised Land. The Pilgrims, who had been putting on their best in the lavatories for the last hour in preparation for the reunion with *Verwandten*,[62] now began to jump from side to side of the plane, and finally weigh it down, one feared, on the side of Tel Aviv.

It was a relief to get down, and soon be on our own again, although there were first many formalities at the airport, incredible efficiency, very agreeable and helpful hostesses, and civilised customs officials. Israel is really most impressive. We were sorry we could not spend longer there, and intend to return sooner or later. Everywhere something positive and constructive seems to be happening, the young Israelis are most stirring, and everyone looks happy – which was an impression I never had when I was there fifteen years ago.

Unfortunately the dusk became darkness as we drove towards Jerusalem and we were not able to approach it by daylight as I had hoped. In spite of being told we should never find accommodation during the Celebrations,[63] we were accepted by the first hotel at which we asked, very clean, and reasonable – a co-operative – with good food and excellent service. Soon we were swallowed up in a comic mixture of Diaspora – American Orthodox eating in caps, but accompanied by elegant social wives, discreetly disguised English Jews, correct Germans, and a terrible Johannesburg couple, she like a Black Orpington, and he like a dinkum Austrilian mite, taking his teeth out for comfort after dinner.

We took a couple of motor trips while in Jerusalem, which did give us a general impression of the Jewish side of the city, only a very general one, however, and it was most disappointing not to be able to visit the Holy Places, which are all in Arab hands. Although we went to the British Consul, the most he could offer was to get us a permit to pass into Jordan; from there the Arabs would not have allowed us to return and use the tickets we had for the journey on from Lydda to Athens. The most impressive thing we saw on the Israel side was the new, half-built university, of which there is not one detail that is not in perfect taste. I must say the sight of so much Israeli enterprise, imagination, and industry made Australia seem like something out of the Middle Ages, except that the Middle Ages

[62]Relations.
[63]Passover.

did produce also things of beauty, and here they were being produced in Israel to-day.

We spent a very interesting evening with a friend of Klári's,[64] a Dr Spitzer, who had worked for Schocken, the publisher, in Germany, and who is now employed by the publishing house of the Jewish Agency. At one time also he worked with Martin Buber,[65] who is at present in New York. We sat up with Dr S. till about 2 a.m., drinking brandy, looking at prints, and talking about everything under the sun. The following day we lunched with him at an oriental restaurant, after which he took us to see one of the old quarters, and into a Yemenite synagogue, where I found an air of peace and perfection such as one seldom finds in a church.

Another interesting friend of Klári's we visited was Recha Freyer, a woman who succeeded in bringing thousands of children out of Europe during some of the most difficult years. She now works for some kind of organisation for destitute children, and has started a fund to support Israeli composers while they are composing their works. (They were expecting Kubelik[66] in Tel Aviv a couple of days after we had to leave; he was to conduct the Beethoven *Ninth*, with Elsie Morrison[67] and another Australian singer, Lauris Elms,[68] in the women's solo parts.

Approaching Greece a couple of days ago, we were every bit as bad as the Jewish Pilgrims arriving at the Promised Land, jumping from side to side in the same way, as we identified islands in the incredible Aegean. Athens is much changed – it has lost a lot of the village atmosphere which I so much liked, but it has still got the ability to squeeze my stomach into a ball, and to make me sing as I walk through the streets. I know of no other place in the world which does this sort of thing for me.

So far we have been much taken up with relations. Manoly is staying at the above address,[69] which is that of his youngest sister, Elly, and I have a very pleasant room and bathroom in an empty flat belonging to a friend, in a house directly opposite. In a few days time we shall start moving about.

---

[64]Klári Daniel.

[65]Jewish theologian, writer and philosopher (1878–1965) who had fled to Palestine in 1938, professor of social philosophy at the University of Jerusalem.

[66]Raphael Kubelik (1914–   ), Czech conductor.

[67](1924–   ), soprano.

[68](1931–   ), contralto.

[69]In full: c/o Dr Polymeropoulos, Ploutarchou 3, Kolonaki, Athens.

ATHENS, 23.iv.58
TO THE MOORES

Apart from the fish, I think we can eat better at home ... But the fish – – ! That is really something, and we have more or less decided to eat nothing else while we are in Greece. To think that Australians believe they know about fish; it is pathetic. Last night we went to a place near the water in Piraeus and feasted with many cousins on clams on the shell, fried baby kalamaria, prawns about six inches long, little red rock cod, of tender, melting flesh (these are perhaps the best of all), and an enormous fish, I don't know what, grilled in the piece, with crisp, salty black and golden skin. All this with plenty of retsina, of course, and raw salads.

MYKONOS, 15.v.58
TO THE MOORES

For me the landscape means much more than the antiquities, as I did not have more than a very rough classical education, and besides, I am a romantic at heart. For that reason Delphi leaves the greatest impression. It is such a stupendous panorama, and the same goes for all the country between Delphi and the Ionian Sea, where we took a ferry to get to Patras. I don't think I shall ever see anything to equal what we saw in those two days, and quite untouched by tourists, officials, politicians, and all the decadent, parasitic life of Athens.

In the Peloponnese we went to Olympia, (which is merely lyrical, pretty, and Italianate after Delphi) Tiryns, Mycenae, Epidauros and Corinth. Sparta again was a wonderful landscape that one had to bow down to, though the town itself shows no apparent traces of antiquity. Just near it we clambered up a mountain in the dusk and drizzle to the Byzantine city of Mistrá, with a church perched every few hundred yards. The topmost church was of particular interest as an ancestor of Manoly's, another Emanuel Lascaris, founded it. His tomb is there, and a fresco portrait from which the Turks scratched the eyes during the Occupation. Now there is a gaggle of nuns in possession. The Abbess entertained us with ouzo in a very stovey little room, and sold us embroidery when the heat and drink had broken down our resistance. (Very beautiful embroidery, too.)

I have become very enthusiastic about the Myceneans since seeing what the Athens Museum has to show, and the remains of Mycenae are also wonderful, above an Argive plain looking like a quilt of red, purple, green and yellow patches. One also gets a thrill out of seeing the floor of the bathroom in which Clytemnestra murdered Agamemnon, though one wonders why she didn't do things more cleanly, simply by pushing him over the cliff on the edge of which the bathroom stands. Not far away is the immense and expensive tomb in which she put him afterwards.

Since I began this, we have come back to the rigours of a social life in Athens, though I am not sure that the rigours of a Simple life on Mykonos, drinking gallons of retsina every night with boatmen and fishermen, was not more destructive. The island itself is almost quite barren, few trees on account of the fierce wind that blows half the year, and oriental-looking white cubes of homes, jammed together so close in the port that one feels the whole town is just one block of flats. It did not suit me personally, everybody running in and out all day and all night, knowing everybody else's business. I began to long for life on a mountain peak . . .

I . . . must now say something about Delos, which we visited from Mykonos, and which was a perfect idyll. A long rocky barren island covered with yellow grass and thistles, but at the same time masses of pink convolvulus, purple statice, yellow sea-poppies and the common field red, as well as a little flower resembling the gentian. The air full of a sound of what could have been deafening larks. Cisterns full of green water and enormous, green, coupling frogs. Crimson dragonflies above the water, intent on the same game. And all through it, the remains of what must have been a great city, columns, temples, mosaics (fabulously beautiful ones that one wants at once for a house of one's own), with down by the sea, propped up against stones, the marble torso of a giant Apollo, worn down by the weather to a texture of cuttlefish. We came back to Mykonos, suitably pricked by thistles and burnt by the sun, over a classic sea.

ATHENS, 7.vi.58
TO SIDNEY NOLAN
Dear Sidney Nolan,
Thank you very much for writing. I am always glad to hear when people get something from my books. And I am often haunted by your painting, particularly the first I saw – one called 'Robbed'[70] – and some of those escaping convicts.

When you had the exhibition at the Whitechapel Gallery, I read something about the woman, whose name I forget, who survived shipwreck on the coast of Australia in company with a convict. It sounds like material I could use, and one day you must tell me more about her – although I

[70]One of the Kelly paintings from 1947, first seen in Sydney at the Macquarie Galleries, Easter 1948.

have made a vow never again to go farther back in time than the last World War.[71]

It is exciting to think you may do some paintings from *Voss*. I always see most of what I write, and am, in fact, a painter *manqué*. Visually, *The Aunt's Story* is a kind of Klee. Long before it was written I was seeing it in terms of Klee, and after the War, when I began to write it in London, there was a tremendous exhibition of Klee's paintings which poured oil on my flames.[72] At the same time I was also much influenced by a painting by Roy de Maistre which I bought then, still own, and of which Roy painted a second version on reading *The Aunt's Story*.[73]

I am afraid I shall not reach London till August, when you will be gone, but perhaps we shall meet in the States. I shall be in New York for a fortnight in September, then a fortnight in Florida, and a couple of days in San Francisco on my way home to Castle Hill in October – though all these plans may come to nothing if the dollars run out. You might leave your address with Eyre & Spottiswoode. My New York publisher is The Viking Press, 625 Madison.

Have not met the Johnstons.[74] I thought I might do so when I was on Kálymnos recently, but was told then that they had moved to Hydra. Now I don't think there will be time. We go to Rome on the 18th, and my travelling companion, a Greek from Australia, has family in Athens who must be placated by a series of farewell celebrations before we leave.

Your sincerely,
Patrick White.

ATHENS, 17.vi.58
TO FREDERICK GLOVER
Dear Frederick,
This will be the last letter from Athens, and I may even have to finish and post it in Rome. We have stayed on here really a little too long,

---

[71]The seed of A *Fringe of Leaves*: at Nolan's Whitechapel exhibition in mid–1957 was exhibited a number of paintings inspired by the fate of Eliza Fraser, lone survivor of the crew of the *Stirling Castle* marooned in 1836 on the great sand island off the Queensland coast that now bears her name. Nolan discussed the wreck and the paintings at their first meeting in Florida in 1958.

[72]Organised by the Tate and hung at the National Gallery, December 1945–March 1946.

[73]'The Figure in the Garden (the Aunt)' 1945, Art Gallery of NSW.

[74]The novelists George Johnston (1912–70) and Charmian Clift (1923–69) who had invited the Nolans to Hydra for the winter of 1955–56. PW, without meeting the pair, conceived an abiding dislike for the Johnstons.

chiefly to go to Epidauros – and that, alas, was a washout. Set off from
Athens the day before yesterday at lunchtime, with clouds already looming;
by the time we arrived in the late afternoon they had begun to spit; then
began a wait of an hour and a half in the amphitheatre to keep our seats,
in a slow sad drizzle; and half an hour after the play had begun the
downpour came. The leading critic got up and stalked out of the arena,
which seemed to release everyone – actors melted away, and the audience,
which had been huddling under hoods of newspaper all the way up the
mountainside, poured down through the amphitheatre in a ribald rout,
stormed cordons of police, and threatened to invade the temple of Tauris
itself in search of shelter.

It was really most frustrating, for the whole expedition from Athens
and back takes 14 hours, and the little we saw of the play gave one an
idea of how wonderful it would have been in its entirety. The first thing
it showed us was that Anglo-Saxons must never never attempt Greek
tragedy, because the English language cannot convey such emotions, and
Anglo-Saxon bodies are all wrong. Iphigenia was played by Synodnou,
who they all say is now the leading actress in Greece.[75] Physically she is
very pleasing, and she has a voice of considerable power, rather darker
than one would expect from that type, and never forced to shout. The
Orestes and the Herdsman were also just right, from the little we saw of
them, but most impressive of all was the Chorus. In movement it reminded
me a lot of the corps de ballet in the slow movement of *Choreartium*,[76]
which I expect you have seen. Their timing was wonderful, for they were
almost continually in motion, and all their movements in perfect accord
with their words. They were dressed in a kind of gunmetal grey, with
stylised wigs of some lacquered material showing from under their hoods.
Iphigenia wore a pale gold. I am sending you the programme for the whole
season, so that you will be able to get some idea of how things look. It
will only be coming by surface mail, however.

I don't know that we have been doing much of interest since we got
back from the Dodecanese, chiefly giving Manoly's family the opportunity
to see him. How right I am about families, if I am wrong about everything
else. I am glad I have never allowed myself to submit to my particular
octopus. To-night is the last, and there is going to be a tremendous
gathering, with aunts in floods of tears, Manoly warns me. Elly, the youngest
sister, and Elias, her doctor husband, have been wonderful all along, and

[75](1927–   ), later a politician and the alternate minister for welfare in the late 1970s.
[76]Massine's ballet to Brahms' 4th Symphony, first produced in London by the Ballet
Russe in 1933.

I wish we did not live so far apart. They are quite selfless, very intelligent, and it is so easy to be with them doing nothing, which is the real test. But all the aunts would love to possess to the death. Mario, the pianist, who has destroyed himself by his own fecklessness, has to go through the long list of those who have been his ruin, even including family servants, and, I feel, ourselves when not present; while Katina, the eldest, is a crazy rattle, who gives Manoly a headache after the first half hour. Still, I am very fond of them all, and to-morrow will be a harrowing day.

FLORENCE, 3.vii.58
TO PATRICIA WHITE[77]
Dear Pat,
My mother forwarded your letter, which reached us when we got to Florence. We were very sorry to hear you had to have another operation. You say you have every confidence in your doctors, but I wonder if you got to the right ones. I am sure you only choose a doctor because you have played golf with him or know his relations. Personally I would never go to an Australian doctor unless he were also a Jew. However, doctors are a person's own business.

I don't know whether you have heard my mother has half-lost her sight. Apparently she had a kind of haemorrhage near the seat of vision, and now she cannot see to read print, although she can manage a typed letter with a magnifying glass, and she can write a letter by bright daylight. Still she refuses to have anybody to live with her, so I don't know what will happen to her. Suzanne says she thinks she would be dead if it weren't for her will. She still insists on going to Glyndebourne with wheel-chairs posted along the route, and the person who accompanies her suffering agonies . . .

Rome was a pleasant place to be in, but most disappointing in many ways. I expected to be swept off my feet, and was only knocked over backwards by the vulgarity of its churches, and the ugliness of its ancient remains, which all look as if they are made out of stale gingerbread. If ever one sees a statue of any grace and aesthetic appeal, one goes up to it and discovers it is of Greek origin, and if ever there is any detail that pleases in a Roman church, it is because that detail is Byzantine. In one or two churches there are some really wonderful Byzantine mosaics practically

[77]PW's second cousin (1907–   ), descended from Archdeacon White of Muswellbrook: no acres, no fortune. As a young woman she was part of Ruth White's circle at Lulworth and worked most of her life at Royal Sydney Golf Club. She was the only White with whom PW remained in close contact.

obscured by Baroque excrescence. The most sympathetic church of all was commissioned early on by two Greek brothers. Of course, the Etruscan remains are a different matter, and we went to a lovely museum of Etruscan art at the Villa Giulia, one of those many minor palaces of some Pope or other,[78] and which I should like to own, as it is completely walled, with a garden inside, and a good safe place for dogs.

VENICE, 11.vii.58
TO THE KRIEGERS
I refuse to go in a gondola, as they are now almost the exclusive property of elderly American ladies, they look so funereal (much more than Liszt suggested), and in the smaller canals they keep one so close to the water and move so slowly one would be asphyxiated by the smells. Everything must go into those canals – kittens, corpses, abortions, to say nothing of the more obvious forms of refuse. When we arrived here and found our room looked onto a narrow street (the Calle Goldoni, incidentally), we were very disappointed, but after the first twenty-four hours we realised how kind the management had been to spare us a canal.

You must not think from this that Italy is smelly. Until we came to Venice, we had encountered hardly any smells. In fact, it is one of the cleanest countries I have ever been in. The hotels, although we are only staying in second-class ones, are all excellent. The railways and trains are most efficient. The food is splendid. Nor are the Italians a bit like the Anglo-Saxon conception of that race – black, noisy, and dirty. Those must come from Naples and the South, for the farther one travels north, the better-looking the people become, it is quite a rare occurrence to set eyes on a 'black' Italian, and even more to encounter one that is conventionally voluble. Their politeness is extreme, though one can't quite believe in it; one feels that underneath they don't care a button for the foreigner, and that the latter is only there to be bled as dry as possible. In this they differ very much from the Greeks. If the Greek shows he likes one, he means it. He is fundamentally sincere and honest.

However, to return to Venice, the smells, and some rather unreliable food are the most one can complain about here. The food has been wonderful to eat, but we spent one night recently vomiting severely, and Manoly has had some more prolonged stomach troubles.

Perhaps another drawback is the number of German tourists. These Goths pour down into Northern Italy in thousands. We came across them first in any numbers in Ravenna, now in Venice they even swamp the

[78]Julius III.

Americans. Except at the Lido, where the fabulously expensive Excelsior seems to be inhabited exclusively by Germans, they appear to be doing it on the cheap – the kind that wander round with shapeless bags full of *Wurst* which they gnaw in their rooms at the pensione at night. There are the clear-golden ones, the men a kind of aging *Heldentenor* with *Bauch*[79] and wedding-ring, the women of quite agreeable texture, but with those hypocritical fish's eyes. Then there is the grey-skinned variety, made out of lumps joined together, both sexes inclined to B.O., the men in *Lederhosen* with all the stains of the *Italienische Reise*,[80] the women in what are supposed to be 'gay' dresses, but which by any other standards are a screaming jangle of bad taste. The women are all so sweet and innocent. When occasionally I cannot resist giving them a look to suggest that I know exactly what evil their wombs have conceived, there is no sign that anything has ever happened; if anything, they grow sweeter and even more innocent.

We are leaving here to-morrow and going straight to Milan, cutting out Verona which we had intended seeing, because Huebsch has turned up at Milan, and I gather is hanging on there only in order to see me. Otherwise we probably shan't meet on this trip, as he gets to London after our departure, and to New York again after we shall have left. Personally I am quite glad of the excuse to do a little less sight-seeing. We have exhausted ourselves pretty thoroughly. Still, if one is foolish enough to set out on such a trip (they should really only be made by the young and by Americans), one has to go through with it to the bitter conclusion. I have seen many wonderful things, but I don't feel it was really necessary. One reaches a stage when external experience is no longer necessary.

In the end you forgot to give us your cousin's address. We went to Fiesole, which I think is where she lives, and saw some traces of how restful and beautiful Florence must have been up to fifty years ago. Now it is a hell-hole, the noise worse than anything I have ever encountered, and petrol fumes to make one suffocate. The pictures are wonderful, of course – the Ufizzi one of the sights of the world, and the Fra Angelicos in the Cloister of San Marco miracles of art and faith. On the whole the small places have pleased me better in Italy – Perugia, Ravenna, Sienna, Pisa all have a great charm. Rome is a monster of bad taste and dishonesty (more of the spiritual than the material kind). Yet, life there, if one can ignore the Holy Roman Church, can be civilised and peaceful, I think, in some backwater.

Ile will be pleased to know there are three orchestras on the Piazza

---

[79]Heroic tenor (traditionally blond) with stomach.
[80]Italian journey.

of San Marco of which at least one is playing *My Fair Lady* during the day or night. They seem to have come to an arrangement whereby one takes over when the other stops. I must say I hope never to hear another note of 'I Could Have Danced All Night' since the half-dozen of which it is composed have been dinned into me so mercilessly.

MILAN, 13.vii.58
TO FREDERICK GLOVER
We arrived in Milan only yesterday afternoon, and had dinner last night with Huebsch, who has come here really only because it will probably be our only chance of meeting on this trip. Last time we met was eleven years ago outside the ruins of St Ann's, Soho; this time it is outside the Duomo, Milan. He has aged a lot in between, but still seems to have great energy and charm, and keeps abreast of everything . . .

A nice anecdote from Huebsch last night: he told us how he once brought Joyce and Werfel[81] together in Paris. It was a very painful evening, as they were very cold, and would hardly address each other, until quite late on when they discovered they had music in common. Both Joyce and Werfel had good voices, and they proceeded to sing at each other over wine in the deserted restaurant until quite a late hour.

MILAN, 17.vii.58
TO FRITZ KRIEGER
You will not accept my political opinions, but I must express some of them. No diplomatic expediency will make me accept the Germans. I forgive Eden nothing. It is immoral to invade other people's countries (as Russians and Germans do) even if the object is to preserve a balance of power. It is immoral to hang onto other people's possessions (such as Cyprus) with an eye to keeping that same balance of power in the future. It is immoral to stir up one country against another, as Eden did Turkey and Greece, particularly after those two countries had succeeded in submerging a tradition of bitter hatred. It is better to die. (For a long time I have had a pretty strong suspicion that nothing is better than death, anyway.)

If I hate the Germans, I also hate the Russians, perhaps a little bit less, because they are less hypocritical, less 'innocent'. However, although I hate the Russians, and see that their doctrine represents evil the way it is expressed, when I am in Europe my sympathies are Communist. They

---

[81]Austrian poet, novelist and playwright (1890–1945), best known for his novel *Das Lied von Bernatte*, 1940.

were before, and they are now that I am back here again and can see things for myself. There is no necessity to feel the same way in Australia, because everyone has enough, and a reasonable expectation of justice. I can see no solution but Communism for the European problem. In fact, the only way to destroy Communism is to live through a period of universal Communism; then it will kill itself, and something more acceptable will evolve – and last until those human beings who survive the change have had the time to embroider on it their normal patterns of bestiality and hatefulness.

We leave for Vienna this afternoon, for which I shall be very glad. Milan is a dreary place, though the worst part of it is its climate. The heat and humidity are far more vicious than in Sydney, with the result that I have had asthma all the time we have been here, and have only been able to get some sleep with the help of pills. Yesterday Anuska[82] lent us her car, and we and Huebsch drove to Maggiore. The change in atmosphere was wonderful; it was as if a vice that had been holding my chest was gradually unscrewed.

LONDON, 12.viii.58
TO DAVID MOORE
Manoly and I arrived here about ten days ago, and are by now in the thick of London life. It has been wonderfully pleasant to meet old friends again, and find we can slip back into friendship without any effort. That has been the best part of it. London itself not so good. I wonder how I succeeded in living in it for so long, overlooking so much, for it is so terribly dirty, ugly, the people so drab – also ugly and dirty – the women like uncooked dough, the men so often suggestive of raw veal. Manoly thinks it becomes beautiful at night, and that it is only saved in the daytime by its trees, and I think he is right. Certainly an awful daytime skyline of black or red brick can wear a lovely purple bloom at night; even the telly aerials grow mysterious and right; and the trees make perfect oases in squares and parks, particularly after this drizzly summer.

I have been seeing a lot of my family, and so far have had no rows with my mother. She is now very pathetic, half-blind, going deaf, and walking very slowly with her two sticks. Suzanne is quite remarkable in the midst of the very dreary life she has to lead. It always amazes me to think I am related to her – she is so cheerful, and nice – whereas I am every bit of my mother, which is one of the reasons why we have never

---

[82]Mrs Anna Deakin, sister of Klári Daniel and mother of the Sydney businessman Peter Abeles.

been able to get on together. Any way, this time we are keeping clear of politics. (I am wondering how she took some of your remarks on her beloved and stainless British in the letter she gave me yesterday to read.)

She also gave me the Ross Campbell article, which is remarkably polite, for him. The thing that interested me most was the glimpse of a band of supporters that I did not think I possessed – apparently young, aggressive, patrons of the espresso bars – in fact, just the age group with which I always felt I failed to communicate! This has been a most heartening discovery.[83]

We have been to several theatres – (*The Chairs* and *The Lesson* by Ionesco, which are both built round brilliant ideas modishly expressed, but somehow there is something bad and fungoid about Monsieur I.[84] – *Duel of Angels*, I think a posthumous Giraudoux, which I found theatre at its most elegant and satisfying, though morally rather perverse – and *Irma la Douce*, a first-rate, witty, original musical, of which one of my fans, Keith Michell, is co-star.) Keith gave us tickets for the latter, and afterwards he and his very beautiful actress wife took us out to supper. I forget whether I told you I had exhumed a play and sent it over to K.M. Well, although he is a great fan through my novels, I rather gather he feels the play stinks.[85] So I suppose that is that.

Since I began this, I have lunched with Eyre & Spottiswoode. Douglas Jerrold, the Chairman, is a kind of Grey Eminence, with beaky nose, withered arm, and habit of chewing his words in the best English manner – as if they were a difficult and unpleasant meat. One hears hair-raising stories about him – how he literally drives others to drink, crushes all personality out of those around him, and how he once reduced Laski[86] to gibberish in an unscripted radio discussion. He is a rabid Roman Catholic, and clashed badly with Graham Greene when the latter was a member of the firm. After he had dislodged Greene, he once said: 'I was a Catholic before it was <u>fashionable</u> to be one. Greene pops in and out of the Church just as he pops in and out of bed.' However, to-day at lunch, he spoke very kindly of his Great Hate, saying: 'Greene is perhaps the only real novelist writing in England to-day.'

Also at lunch was Temple Smith, the junior partner of the firm, with

[83]Campbell (1910–82), critic and humourist who had panned *Voss* and now reported, *Daily Telegraph*, 26 July 1958, p.14, 'From the coffee shops and wine bars frequented by Patrick White's devotees came at first angry mutterings, then the thunders of anathema and excommunication . . .'

[84]Eugène Ionesco (1912–94) Roumanian French playwright of the Absurd.

[85]'Just not for me,' Michell reported years later; his wife is Jeannette Sterke.

[86]Harold Laski (1893–1950), English political scientist, author and formidable lecturer.

whom I have been corresponding for some time now. From his letters I always took him to be a dry, dusty individual, probably at least ten years older than myself, but I found a glamorous young man still in his twenties, with rather sunken blue eyes, and a full under lip, who spoke very intelligently, and bridged some of the gulfs between the Grey Eminence and myself. On the whole we all got on fairly well, except that I have had to scotch a horrible plan of theirs to give a party so that people can satisfy their curiosity.

IN NEW YORK, TOO, White was fêted by publishers when he and Lascaris arrived in early September. To be back after nearly twenty years away was exhilarating, yet White was reassured in these hectic days that he had done the right thing as an artist not to settle on Manhattan. He waited until he reached Florida before catching up on his correspondence.

FLORIDA, 13.ix.58
TO FRITZ KRIEGER
Dear Fritz,
As I mentioned in my post-card, we went to visit your family, and spent a very agreeable evening there. The journey was not very heartening, first, through those horrifying up-town slums of New York, with even a real corpse on the line at one of the stations, and cops cutting his pockets open, then all those Tudor mansions at Bronxville . . . We found your mother very sympathetic – young, and gay. In some ways I should think she is a lot like you . . . after dinner we were shown the paintings . . . during the exhibition . . . your mother went off to her room, and was sitting there playing patience, with a cigarette hanging out of her mouth, and a terrific smoker's cough. I think probably, like you, she is more for music than for the visual arts.

FLORIDA, 15.ix.58
TO DAVID MOORE
Some interesting things happened in New York. The most interesting was a meeting with Zachary Scott, the actor, who I had already heard was interested in my books.[87] He is, in fact, interested in making *The Tree of Man* and *Voss* into pictures . . .

We came down here last week, and shall remain till the 26th, when we leave for San Francisco. I have been very pleased to meet the Sidney

[87](1914–65), one of film's distinguished heels, best remembered for his role in Renoir's *The Southerner*, 1945. Scott had recently returned to the stage and was considering film production in order to remake a typecast reputation.

Nolans at last. They were travelling from Louisiana to New York, and came over this way so that we could see each other. We spent most of yesterday together, driving through Florida, and also lunched the day before. I think you would like them as much as I do . . . or would Gwen perhaps dislike Cynthia? I was a little bit prejudiced against the latter before meeting, as the result of all the bitchy things I had heard about her as we travelled round the world. However, after knowing her, and thinking back I realised that all the bitchery came from other women. I found her forthright and intelligent, perhaps a little ambitious (a fortunate quality in an artist's wife), perhaps also a bit jealous, but she is the wife who is slightly older than a very attractive husband, and she says that other women are always offering to mend his shirts, and trying to put their hands up under his coat to massage his shoulders. Sidney N. seems to be completely honest and without nonsense. He is of simple Australian–Irish stock and makes no bones about it. In fact, I can't think when I have met a man so much Himself, which of course is why his work is so much his own. Physically he is medium, fresh in colouring, or rather brick-coloured, and with eyes of a blue that I can imagine might suck the unwary right under.

Here we are staying with Manoly's middle sister, Anna, and her husband Bill Reagan, who is very ill – may pop off without any warning – so the atmosphere is rather a tragic one. Anna has been utterly absorbed into America; I didn't think such a thing could ever happen to a Lascaris. To-morrow Mom is due to arrive from St Petersburg, and we are prepared for drama, as she has not seen Manoly for forty years. I feel anything may happen, from the awful to the disappointing.[88]

Florida itself I can't say I like one little bit. The climate makes one feel like a beachcomber, a tropical wreck, with green whiskers on one's lungs, and a grey-purple bloom upon one's cheeks. Most of the state seems to be swamp, but swamp would certainly be preferable to this re-claimed coastal strip, which is a shambles of motels, hamburger joints, gas stations, super-markets, and girlie girlie shows. One good bit yesterday when we discovered a botanic garden full of peacocks and exotic fruits. But I can really only say: Roll on the plane to San Francisco.

Hope all is well –
Patrick.

[88]Now Mrs Randolph Bronson of Florida. PW reported to Glover, 20.ix.58, 'Quite a satisfactory meeting. I was surprised to find that an American Mom does fit in with Manoly and the other Athenians; the jigsaw is almost complete.'

FORT LAUDERDALE, 24.ix.58
TO JAMES STERN

Dear Jimmy,

It seems an age since we were in New York, about which you asked me to write. I don't know whether you have ever been in Florida. If you have, you will know how one feels after ten days of it. One seems to go to pieces in the steam, or else to turn into a kind of fungus, observing in a vegetable way the semi-human awfulness with which one is surrounded.

But the visit to New York was most stimulating, if unfortunately brief. The people at the Viking Press were very hospitable, and we had a couple of sessions with Zachary Scott. The first time we went to a drink at their apartment, and also met Ruth Ford.[89] It was all very New York, slightly brittle, but pleasant to experience again as a social game. I can't say I appreciated most of the pictures; the tea-tray school of painters has never appealed to me, especially those with surrealist overtones. The second occasion we met Z. was at a lunch, at which we discussed his movie project in more detail. I think his enthusiasm seems real, but it is very difficult to make sure with Americans, or rather, their enthusiasm can often be real enough, but that does not mean it will last ... The thing that pleased me most was his announcement that the director he wants to interest in my work is Jean Renoir – the only man I have always felt might translate it into film.[90] Z. suggested that I should write the script, which I refused, as that is something I would not know how to go about. Then he asked me whether I would be willing to come to the States for six months to work with a professional scriptwriter, but I had to refuse that too. I always feel that America has the worst effect on any artist who comes here after a certain age. In fact, one has to be born in it to produce anything worth while; otherwise the life, the surroundings, and the language kill. Besides that, I want to start on a new book when I get home, and I cannot let anything else interfere with it. After all, I am 46, and still have five or six books left to write[91] ...

The other thing you wanted to know about – the dedication of Voss. Marie d'Estournelles de Constant was a Frenchwoman who became very enthusiastic about my work in the days before The Tree of Man. She was

[89]Stern had given PW an introduction to the Scotts; Ford (1915–) was Scott's wife; he had plans to cast her as Laura Trevelyan in his film of Voss.

[90]Renoir (1894–1975) was busy at this time on the great Le Déjeuner sur l'herbe.

[91]By the time PW left the US his hopes for films and plays were very high. Scott also took an option for a Broadway production of The Ham Funeral. The fading and occasional revival of these hopes over the next few years was always in the background as PW wrote Riders in the Chariot.

a reader for Gallimard, and persuaded him to buy my first three books for publication in French. At the time[92] I felt I was getting nowhere, and that there was not much point in my continuing to write. Nobody read what I had to say. I was also up to my ears in the place at Castle Hill. However, d'Estournelles continued to pester me by correspondence, and I suppose it was her efforts as much as anything else that decided me to embark on *The Tree of Man*. In the meantime, she translated *Happy Valley* and *The Aunt's Story*. Gallimard published *Happy Valley*[93] which was such a flop I was shown none of the reviews, and Gallimard decided not to do any of my other books, in spite of the option money, and what he had paid for the finished translation of *The Aunt*. d'Estournelles had gone into hospital with some kind of tubercular complication, I had a few more notes, rather incoherent, under the influence of dope, and that was the last I heard. Finally, I got Douglas Cooper to make some enquiries, and he found out from Raymond Queneau that d'Estournelles had died.[94] Then *The Tree of Man* came out, and when I wrote *Voss* I felt that, although we had never met, I owed her a book, and dedicated the latter to her. From the many letters that she wrote me she was an amazing person. As well as translating from the English, she seems to have been a designer of stage costumes, and used to get up at crack of dawn to make an abstract of world news for the French Foreign Office.

If you ever feel inclined to write, our address is:

'Dogwoods,'

Castle Hill,

New South Wales.

We get out of here the day after to-morrow, God willing, and fly to San Francisco via Fort Worth – leave San Francisco on the 29th, and arrive home October 1st. Florida has been a nightmare.

---

[92] 1948.

[93] As *Eden-ville*, 1951.

[94] In 1954. PW had known Cooper (1911–84) in London when the collector and critic was putting his Australian fortune into a pioneering collection of Cubist paintings; the writer Raymond Queneau (1903–76) was a leading editor at Librairie Gallimard which did not resume publishing PW's novels until Suzanne Nétillard's *Le Char des elus* in 1965; most of the novels have since been translated into French; shortly before his death PW was wrestling unhappily with translator's questions about *The Living and the Dead* which appeared in 1990.

Chariots

December 1958 – February 1961

ONCE BACK AT DOGWOODS, White began to draft *Riders in the Chariot*. In the novel's great contest between good and evil, the underlying evil is the persecution of the weak by the strong, epitomised here by the Holocaust. Though White was writing fifteen years after the revelations of Auschwitz, he was one of the first novelists to come to grips with this century's innovation in horror. His four riders – a scholar, a painter, a washer-woman, an eccentric spinster – are outcasts and believers, each saved at some point in their lives by ecstatic illumination: the chariot across the sky. They shared White's own frustration that this vision was only ever half-glimpsed, even by the most devout believers.

DOGWOODS, 17.xii.58
TO BEN HUEBSCH
Dear Mr Huebsch,
It is time I wrote to wish you a Happy New Year. I should, of course, have written to you sooner, but arrived back here on October 1st with cracked ribs, after falling down in a concrete shower in Fiji on the last morning of our trip; then went off on a short spell of my usual bronchitis. After that there was all the business of getting settled again, breaking our way through the jungle of a garden, finding out what had happened in the house, looking for lost cats. Then – a few improvements to the house, with all the exasperation that workmen provide: we have had air conditioning installed in three of the rooms, fly screens on the other windows, and finally a new stove, which is a great pleasure to use.

In addition I have started on my new book – I don't like using the titles of unfinished books, but I think I did mention this one once – , and have written how much it is difficult to say, perhaps a third, perhaps not so much, but I can see it will take some time, and perhaps need as many as three writings. I shall want somebody here to check the Jewish parts after a second writing. I feel I may have given myself away a good deal, although passages I have been able to check for myself, seem to have come through either by instinct or good luck, so perhaps I shall survive. After all, I did survive the deserts of *Voss*.

DOGWOODS, 18.ii.59

TO FREDERICK GLOVER

We have just had a shattering day. We had to put our poor Solomon to sleep at last. The last two or three days he had been suffering, never seemed to be able to settle down at night, would go round and round in circles on my bed looking for a comfortable place, and often I would put on the light and he would be sitting there looking at me with what sight he had left, wondering why I was not able to do anything. A few days ago, he developed pains in one of his hind legs, and although we were giving him drugs and an infra-red lamp, it did not have any effect. Then I noticed that there was a raw place on the inside of his mouth, on the jawbone really, near where the lump was on the cheek. This morning we set out for the vet. In Victoria Road, we had to pull up rather sharply, he fell off the seat, and by the time we reached Spira's a bad haemorrhage had set in.[1] They gave him an anaesthetic, and said there was a hole in his jaw as big as a pea through which the blood was pouring. Apparently the cancer had eaten into a blood vessel. They said they might patch him up, but we decided not to let him come out of the anaesthetic. I shall never have another dog to compare with him. He was not a spectacular temperament, just a perfect character. I realise now the whole place has become permeated with him – but of course I have no intention of rushing to the estate agents to-morrow![2]

DOGWOODS, 11.v.59

TO BEN HUEBSCH

By now I have written about 90,000 words of *Riders in the Chariot*, and think it will work out at about 120,000. When I say 'written', though, a lot of it is very rough and will probably have to be re-written and re-written. The Jewish parts in particular will have to be gone over very carefully. The more I read on the subject the more mistakes I seem to find in my own work, and sometimes I wonder whether I didn't make a colossal mistake in attempting to portray a Jew at any depth. In the beginning he had me petrified, with the result that the writing suffered, but as the book developed my blood began to circulate again, and the other characters

---

[1] PW's vet and friend Harold Spira (1923–91) pioneered the long-haired miniature dachshund in Australia.

[2] PW had mocked the Kriegers who considered abandoning Castle Hill in 1958 after the death of their dog. PW had written then to Glover, 15.viii.58: 'One would expect some half-crazed spinster to rush from her house, hair streaming, but not a hard-boiled business man who has been advising us on all subjects all these years, and his sophisticated wife.'

seem in a curious way to have helped me understand Himmelfarb.

I am going to get help in the corrections from a sister of Anuska, whom you met in Milan. Although Klári is something of a blue stocking and militantly Jewish, I am sorry not to have been able to unearth a male Jew with sufficient knowledge, as she really has not been introduced to the core of the matter being a woman. However, she says she has somebody who will help out. Male Jews in Sydney seem to be either completely materialistic, or assimilated, or else the devout ones are suspicious of the motives of anybody who is taking an interest. But I do grow more and more interested. At the moment I am up to my ears in an abridgment of the Talmud, which I find most rewarding, and that is leading to other reading.

So, you see, you must not expect anything from me for a long time yet. Nor does the book have an exclusively Jewish theme as this letter might suggest. What I want to emphasise through my four 'Riders' – an orthodox refugee intellectual Jew, a mad *Erdgeist*[3] of an Australian spinster, an evangelical laundress, and a half-caste aboriginal painter – is that all faiths, whether religious, humanistic, instinctive, or the creative artist's act of praise, are in fact one. The half-caste aboriginal, who is diseased and degraded as a human being, will be perhaps the real test – whether I can make his creative genius strong and convincing enough. That is something – and nothing of the book! Even so, it is more than I like to tell, so I would rather you keep it to yourself.

PEGGY GARLAND WROTE IN June asking White to explain an insulting remark about her daughter Sally. A chain of gossips from Athens to England had passed the quip to Betty Withycombe who then wrote angrily to Peggy calling their cousin Patrick: 'this unnatural person'. Peggy sent her sister's letter to Australia along with her own. These letters shattered White's by now fragile relationship with 'the demi-Nun of Oxford'.

DOGWOODS, 17.vi.59
TO PEGGY GARLAND
Dear Peggy,
Thank you for your calm letter. As far as I can remember I wrote some time ago to Katina,[4] who is a nice, but crazy, babbling creature, a remark such as this: 'It is a long time since we heard from Peggy. I hope nothing has gone wrong with one of the girls this time' – suggesting: since the

---

[3]Earth spirit.
[4]'Lascaris' sister Katina Photiades.

boys' efforts lead one to expect complications in the Garland family. Katina, Manoly says, half-reads everything, and then pours forth. That, I am sorry to say is how it must have happened, probably heightened by Freda Cooke.[5] Of course I was wrong to make the remark in the first place. But who doesn't let such things fall? I'm sure Sally herself will do it before she dies. I am only sorry she has acquired this unmerited international fame. The Hampstead part of it is certainly a problem.

As for the demi-Nun of Oxford I am writing to let her have a piece of my mind, as perhaps you intended me to. She has been bitchy enough about you in her day, and even since the Christian metamorphosis. She is really lousy with her miserable religiosity and self-sacrifice. If anybody wanted their knots untied by a 'free Jungian analysis', it is Betty (poor Joyce, we know, has been luxuriating in masochism for years)[6] but Betty, this super half-veiled thing-- Do you know, when we were there she announced to Manoly, as if she were firing a gun: 'My sister is married to a homosexual; I doubt whether she has ever been consummated.'[7]

I am keeping your letter to write a second answer, about Greece and so forth, when I have cooled down.

Please thank David[8] for his admirable letter which I shall also answer in time. We shall look forward to having him here, provided you dare let him plunge into such a cesspool, and provided also I am not laid low.

I have been having colds for months, which have ended in some rather peculiar lung complication. A specialist[9] looked rather glum at first, then when he had heard the rest of my history, decided that a lobe of one of my lungs had been collapsed by a bronchial cast. He is now trying to dissolve the latter with antibiotics, but if that fails, he will have to stick a pipe down, and suck the piece of spaghetti out.

Again I am sorry for all the trouble that has been caused, especially to Sally. But I am not sorry for anything that I am going to say to Betty. It is nice to know how she has been feeling about me all this time, and now at least we can untie our unnatural relationship.

---

[5]New Zealander, mutual friend of Peggy Garland and Katina Photiades.
[6]The third Withycombe sister had devoted much of her life to her husband, the pacifist and religious playwright Richard Ward (1910–69).
[7]This was provoked by a polite enquiry about Joyce from Lascaris as they walked round Kew Gardens. At the time, PW made excuses for Withycombe's response to Lascaris – she had not shaken his hand at first meeting – and PW reported then to Garland, 26.ix.58: 'I think Manoly was downright frightened, and I got the impression B. did not care for him much; anyway, they were most wary of each other.'
[8]Her son.
[9]Maurice Joseph.

Writing to you again.

Love,

Patrick.

P.S. Apart from everything else our septic tank blocked up the day your letters arrived.

DOGWOODS, 27.vi.59

TO FREDERICK GLOVER

There is really no question of our selling Dogwoods. We should both be too unhappy anywhere else – in fact, I think the place means even more to Manoly, as it is to him what my writing is to me. This is something you will not be able to understand, as you have never wanted to plant lasting things. Otherwise you would have been forced to do it over the years you were at High Tor.[10] A person who feels such a compulsion never tells himself: 'There is no point in doing it; we shall be leaving here in a couple of years.' He just goes ahead and does it.

I can see that the visual side of life means very little to you (either inside a house, or outside), whereas it means a tremendous lot to both of us. We must have a shell, and a shell takes years of drudgery to make. If we gave this up I do not feel I could face making another satisfactory shell. Just to wander about Australia in discomfort, from one empty town to another, watching a landscape slowly destroyed by a race whose most pronounced gift is that of creating ugliness would be out of the question. And the thought of the food – If we were forced to leave Dogwoods, I feel the only thing we could do would be to leave the country, and live in Greece or Italy or Spain, or wandering between the three. There it would not matter being without a shell because one would be surrounded by natural beauty, and if man intrudes, a Mediterranean peasant, even, cannot help creating something aesthetically pleasing when he puts one stone on top of another. Then there is the food – the kind we like to eat. And civilisation easily accessible.

Actually the outside work is not the tiring part of life at Dogwoods. The work in the garden revives us after the drudgery of work indoors. (What that is, you don't realise either because Mollie has always done that.) But, as Manoly says, if we go into a box in a block of flats, or some dreary little suburban house with a backyard in which one could only roam up and down without escaping, we should still have housework to do, and none of our trees and shrubs to revive us.

So that is that! Of course if one were completely incapacitated, that

[10]The Glovers' house at Castle Hill.

might be a different matter. But I would rather die early, I feel, where I am happy, than drag out a lifetime as a lost soul.

DOGWOODS, 9.vii.59
TO PEGGY GARLAND

We had not heard of the Greek painter. I hope he is a good one. On the whole they are not. It always surprises me as there is so much to paint in Greece to which only a Greek could do justice. The trouble is, I think, that no Greek seems able to detach himself enough from politics to be able to practise an art. Apart from poets, of whom there have been some very good modern ones, there are no writers worth speaking of for the same reason. When I am in Greece I get dozens of ideas that I could work up if I were a Greek, but would not attempt otherwise, as I only like to work from inside. If I try to give any of these themes to a Greek, he will shrug and say: 'We can't write about modern Greece, because we should get into trouble politically.' I still feel I could write volumes about modern Greece without becoming politically involved, but perhaps I should feel differently if I were a Greek. Anyway, there is no reason why a Greek should not see the marvellous Greek forms and light as I see them, and be able to translate them into paint on a level that is above the merely quaint and parochial.

If you feel you want to live in Greece, you should rent a house there first before you buy one. There are lots of things to be overcome, and one can sometimes come down with a bump out of one's philhellenic cloud. 1946, for instance, which sowed the seeds of philhellenism in me, was a very different kettle of fish from 1958. There was a great deal that I found intolerable then. But Robert Liddell tells me that things have improved again. I always imagine though, that if one lived there one would experience alternately waves of love and waves of hate. Those of hate were dashing themselves over one's head last year. Then I found too, that Athens had degenerated enormously with its development. Probably the Greeks are a people who only shine in adversity. When they are prosperous they grow fat behinds and an oriental indifference. They make the most terrible bourgeoisie. The best of them are peasants, or else aristocrats, who have almost died out. Still, I would like to live in Greece, if I came from, say, England, and not an undeveloped place like this.

When I last wrote I think I was already in the thick of medical complications. As the bronchitis had lingered on for weeks I decided to go to a specialist, who had x-rays taken, and as a result became a bit concerned about a patch that he thought might be a tumour. As the patch did not clear with treatment, he decided to do a bronchoscopy last week.

It was a most unpleasant business, but did at least prove that the patch on the x-rays was caused not by a tumour but by an accumulation of mucus, some of which the doctor drew off. Now I am trying to clear up the rest taking antibiotics and doing breathing exercises. I must say it was a great relief to know there was nothing worse.[11]

Poor Katina is in a great state about the International Chain of Gossip. She is writing to you. As far as I can gather Freda Cooke is the chief embroiderer. As for the Prioress of Upper Oxford, she and I have exchanged some very cold letters. I had decided to write no more, but her last one was so Jesuitical in tone and full of misunderstanding, that I think I shall be tempted to have one last fling. If I were the heartless monster she professes to find me, I doubt whether I should have a friend, and I do have quite a number, nor are they by any means sycophantic, superficial ones. It is also dreadful to think that she has endured with Christian fortitude all these years what she describes as the 'deformity' of my nature. The trouble is, I feel, I have never been impressed by her exhibitions of hysterical intensity, nor wanted to be swallowed up in her possessive cloud. Hence, I lack feeling. Admittedly there is a great deal in life that I find grotesque, but that does not mean that I do not also find it tragic, sometimes, or at least, pathetic. I suppose even Betty is that.

It is rather late, and again there seems to be a lot I have forgotten to say. You mentioned music: it has almost died out here, except when the Musica Viva[12] brings somebody from overseas. But we listen a lot to the gramophone. I am playing mostly Bach and Bartok at present, and Beethoven quartets. All the Bs one likes – Bloch and Berg too. But I can no longer listen to Brahms. Next week the Czech Wind Quintet is in Sydney.

Must stop now. Hope you are all well –

Patrick.

FOR GEOFFREY DUTTON'S NEW *Australian Letters* White had written the polemic 'Prodigal Son' in 1958. This attack on the Great Australian Emptiness, 'in which the mind is the least of possessions', has been quoted more often than anything White ever wrote. Dutton was a young university lecturer in Adelaide, a poet and editor who had written a number of books. The Duttons had been graziers at Anlaby outside

[11]Joseph had at last identified precisely the shadows on PW's lungs as the work of a rare allergy to mould spores in the bronchi: allergic bronchopulmonary aspergillosis. In July Joseph gave PW the first shots of 'some stuff just arrived from America': cortisone.
[12]Entrepreneurs of chamber music in Australia.

Adelaide as long as the Whites of Belltrees in New South Wales. White
had appealed to Dutton to help two Lascaris family retainers, Greeks from
Alexandria, stranded in Adelaide without English and without work.
Dutton arranged for the old couple to garden and cook for his mother at
Anlaby.

DOGWOODS, 12.viii.59
TO GEOFFREY DUTTON
Dear Geoffrey,
We were very glad to get your letter. The fate of the Joachimidis seems to
have been decided quite miraculously. It sounds just the right kind of job.
Manoly received a letter this evening from Panayota, who feels they will
be able to give satisfaction in their work, but only hopes the language
difficulty will not be too great. I don't feel it need be, as the two Greeks
will have each other to talk to and can work things out together. It is
when there is one foreigner and no means of communicating with anybody
that the trouble begins ...

I don't feel, however, that all my early books are altogether worthless.
Although I could no longer read *Happy Valley* or *The Living and the Dead*
if I were shut up in a cell with them, I have a weakness for *The Aunt's
Story*, Australians do not like it, of course because they have not experienced
all those European cross-currents of the 'Thirties which go to make up
'Jardin Exotique'. Perhaps in twenty years time they will begin to see the
point. I find that a lot more have come to accept it since it originally
appeared.

Strange the way the Roman Catholics have taken me up. I was
brought up vaguely an Anglican – my mother lowers her voice when
mentioning that So-and-So is a Roman Catholic – , but the Anglicans, at
least the evangelicals, tell me sweetly that my books are not Christian. I
really know nothing about Roman Catholicism except what I have gathered
from painting and literature. So perhaps I am an R.C. manqué!

DOGWOODS, 23.ix.59
TO FREDERICK GLOVER
Did you hear about the murder in Castle Hill? A farmer called Grunsell
in James Lane tried to strangle his erring wife (née Shirt), finished up
shooting her, then drove to Manly to drown himself, but gave himself up
when he failed.[13] Both of them strict Methodists we are told.

---

[13]Grunsell was sentenced to only seven years for manslaughter after the court accepted that
the poultry farmer's mind was unhinged by 'malicious and unfounded gossip' about his wife.

DOGWOODS, 5.x.59
TO PEGGY GARLAND
By the end of the month it will be just a year since I started the book I
am now working on, and with luck I shall finish the first version this
month. It has given a lot of trouble on and off, possibly because I have
been feeling rotten physically, but I think probably the difficulties would
have been as great in any circumstances. An awful lot will still have to be
done, and it may take a couple more years to do it, but the main thing is
to have got the shape of it onto paper. It is so long I find I have almost
forgotten the beginning now that I am at the end . . .

I get quite drunk with music, and play it a lot to lead me up to my
work. Funnily enough I have always felt closest to Berg, and on the sleeve
of the last record I bought I found out that he was also a bronchial
asthmatic. I had played his *Violin Concerto* all through the 'illness' of Laura
Trevelyan in *Voss*, and have been using it and the *Concerto for Wind
Instruments* a lot in this book too.

Yesterday was the Jewish New Year, and I spent part of the day at
the Great Synagogue. I was taken there by a Bessarabian taxi-driver, who
is also a scholar of Hebrew; he taught it for many years to members of the
Synagogue. As one of my characters is an Orthodox Jew I wanted to go
to some of the High Feast-day services, and I was handed over to the
Bessarabian, with whom I have another date for the Day of Atonement.
The Synagogue is a lovely building inside, in much better taste than the
Sydney churches. It was strange to sit in one's hat, and I felt rather naked
as I was the only man in hundreds who was not wearing a shawl. Apart
from these formalities, everything was very informal. The members of the
congregation made endless conversation during the service, and children
ran up and down between the body of the Synagogue and the gallery
where the women sat, carrying messages between parents and relations. At
one point the buzz rose to such a pitch, the Chief Rabbi had to make a
speech about the difficulties of carrying on a service at the same time.
When it was all over, everybody scuttled about shaking hands with
everybody else, wishing each other a happy New Year, and looking much
happier than Christians usually do after a Church service.

Our garden is shooting into unaccustomed glory this spring. The last
couple of weeks have made a lot of difference, the trees in the forest really
look like trees now, and we have not yet had any of the steamy weather
which usually is the best for growing. Magnolias have been particularly
good, and a weeping cherry. To-night I am afraid a lot of damage is
probably being done; it is raining in torrents, with a gale blowing at the

same time, and we have had six black-outs between three and nine, during which I have been trying to cook the dinner.

DOGWOODS, 9.xii.59

TO FREDERICK GLOVER

You are certainly wrong about my attitude to people being coloured by the fact of their being Jewish. I was merely trying to find a reason for A.D.'s[14] always trying to avoid me in London before the War, and wondered whether it was because he knew I knew he was Jewish, and thought I might tell. However, it is more likely the reason was the other one: that I might report back here on his behaviour in London. If I dislike Joan Hallenstein, it is certainly not because she is a Jew, but because she is mean, suburban, gushing with social cliché, and repulsively ugly.[15] One of my greatest supports over the years has been Huebsch of the Viking Press, a noble Jew if ever there was one. Klàri Daniel, an orthodox Jew, is more Christian than most Christians. And I have many other Jewish friends whom I love and respect. What I do not like is when Jews pretend not to be Jews. That has always been a source of great embarrassment both to Manoly and myself in our relationship with the Kriegers. Fritz even makes derogatory remarks about the Jews, apparently under the impression that we don't realise he is one.

DOGWOODS, 13.xii.59

TO GEOFFREY DUTTON

I am glad you like The Aunt's Story better.[16] It is the one I have most affection for, and I always find it irritating that only six Australians seem to have liked it. I can't think how you should be puzzled by the ending, but without knowing more, can't very well explain. S. Nolan's jacket I like in itself (I have the original hanging in the sitting room), but it is not my character. Theodora was a distinguished creature in spite of her dowdiness and ugliness; this one it seems to me, is pure Shanty Irish. The jacket for Voss I do not like. S. sent me a preliminary drawing on a post-card which got the character to perfection – thin and prickly. Then the final version turned into that fat, amiable botanist.

[14]Unidentified.
[15]A neighbour and friend of the Kriegers.
[16]Republished by Eyre & Spottiswoode, 1958.

DOGWOODS, 7.i.60
TO PEGGY GARLAND

Dear Peggy,

I don't think I have had such smart notepaper as this since my palmy days in Eccleston St. Manoly gave me this for Christmas, and I do find it quite an incentive to correspondence.

Thank you very much for your long letter and *The Catcher in the Rye*.[17] I had read the latter, but shall be glad to own a copy. It is something I often find myself wanting to lend. In your letter you make yourself sound like a character out of a Rodney Ackland play – all that bed and books, and going out alone to the cinema.[18] Certainly you are lucky to be able to spend so much time in bed. I never seem to get more than four or five hours there in the twenty four, unless, every now and then, I just fall on the bed and have to sleep for a very long time.

It already seems ages since all the excitement over the W. H. Smith Award. As it was given for the 'most outstanding contribution to Eng. Lit. in 1957/58' and the judges were Harold Nicolson, C. V. Wedgwood, and William Plomer,[19] it was one in the eye for the Australian Professors of English who continue to accuse me of illiteracy. Smiths wanted to pay my passage to England for the presentation, and ten days expenses in London, but I did not think it wise to land in November fogs after a winter of bronchitis here. It was a heaven-sent excuse, for they had told me I should have to appear on television, give radio interviews, and then, of course, there would have been the nightmare of the dinner itself.

One good thing that has happened since is that Lanes have decided to do *The Aunt's Story* as a Penguin. (*Voss* comes out in Penguin in April.)

I liked the account of the various members of your family. Tanya sounds most intriguing but I hope she doesn't turn into another Betty with 'black-looks-not-'arf.'[20] I'm sorry David failed to get into the University if that is what he and you wanted. I should think it would be just as well for him to start in advertising, if he is intended for something else, it will show in time, but I think it is important not to sit about hoping for guidance. Tom's return would certainly be a disaster for everybody, and I

---

[17]J. D. Salinger, 1951.
[18]A reference perhaps to the early plays of Rodney Ackland (1908–   ) when he was known as 'the English Chekov'.
[19]Awarded for the first time. The judges were Harold Nicolson (1886–1968), biographer, diplomat and gardener; C. V. Wedgwood (1910–   ), historian; William Plomer (1903–73), poet and novelist.
[20]Said of Betty Withycombe by one of the servants in the 1920s.

should act very cold and firm if it shows any signs of happening. Or turn Tanya onto him.

I had an odd and foolish note from the Nun of Oxenford, written on Christmas Day 'with the rain lashing at the window.' She wants me to visit a friend of hers called Sandy Someone, a professor of bio-chemistry, who slipped and broke his leg, and is in the Western Suburbs Hospital Sydney. Virtue is to be its own reward, but I think it is really hoped that the recumbent professor will be a gimmick for reconciliation. Imagine the situation. The unfortunate Sandy: 'And how is your Cousin Betty?' I: 'I don't know. She is such a bitch I no longer bother to enquire. However, it is her charity which brings me here.' It is so grotesque I don't feel I can reply to her miserable letter any more than I can visit Sandy Someone. In any case, I don't imagine a professor of bio-chemistry would be the least bit entertained by my presence. The Nun, incidentally, was rounding off her rain-lashed Christmas by dinner with the Hunts . . .

I bought Bach's *Christmas Oratorio* with the present my mother didn't send me this year. However, it is a wonderful and consoling work in any circumstances. What a pity you can't enjoy Bach. Whenever there is somebody like that, I feel I want to cut some nerve, the absence of which will allow B. to become absorbed at last. I think now there is nothing in life that I love more than the music of Bach. But it can be grim, of course, in the hands of the worthy mediocrity.

Must stop now, wishing you all a Happy New Year.

Love,

Patrick.

DOGWOODS, 20.i.60

TO BEN HUEBSCH

In November I finished the first version of *Riders in the Chariot*. I was almost frightened to re-read it, and not altogether delighted when I did at the end of another month – still too close to be really detached. There are some terrible patches of writing here and there, which will need a lot of working on – and which I have already improved to a certain extent – , but I was pleased with the general shape of the book. This is what I had been trying to get, and what the superficial newspaper reviewer will refer to as shapelessness. If you can imagine a section of castle wall with four merlons (that is the correct word for the raised parts; I have just looked it up in the dictionary!), that is the kind of shape it is: the four merlons being the 'lives' of the four Riders set at regular intervals. The reviewer already mentioned, on coming to the second merlon, will certainly think: What is all this? He has gone off his head, throwing everything away in such a digression. But we hope the right kind of reader will carry on, and realise in the end that all is balance and intention.

Now I suppose I must break the sad news to you that it has run into about 200,000 words! Otherwise you will wonder why I am taking such an unnaturally long time. It may even take very long, if I have to re-write again after Klári Daniel has read it for the mistakes in the Jewish parts. But I do not want my castle to fall to the enemy even at the worst battering. So you must have patience.

I continue to study Judaism on and off. I have had a 1 vol. edition of the Epstein *Judaism* for some time. It is an excellent little book. I wonder what the 3 vol. Pelican edition is that you mention? Mine is a Pelican. Perhaps you misunderstood your friend, and the Pelican 1 vol. is abridged from some 3 vol. work of the authors.

I forget if I told you I was at the Great Synagogue for Rosh Hashana, Yom Kippur, and Succoth. Also, Manoly and I were asked recently to a Bar Mitzvah, the son of some friends to whom we once sold a Schnauzer – they still don't know how useful their invitation was. I find the Synagogue services much more 'live' and moving than our Christian ones. At least the Jewish faith seems to be part of life, and ours is just tacked on, if it is at all. But perhaps if I saw more of the Jews at their worship, I might come to the same conclusion. It is easier to be impressed by what one does not know.

Last night I went to Sydney to a big meeting of protest against the outbreak of anti-Semitism in parts of Australia.[21] I found it depressing on the whole, for there seemed to be only a handful of Gentiles to the thousands of Jews, and if there is to be an end to anti-Semitism, at least it must come from us. However, I am told that a lot of Gentiles arrived late and were put in the basement to hear the speeches relayed. (As I watched the Jews pouring in before the meeting, and a sprinkling of Gentiles beginning to arrive as time was up, I began to have a suspicion that the Foolish Virgins[22] were probably Gentile.) The speeches, by politicians and the representatives of religious bodies, were mostly abysmal – ignorant and innocent, which only added to my depression. It made me wonder who is going to save this country from the wolves,

---

[21]Swastikas had been daubed on synagogue walls in Germany in late 1959, the first appearance of anti-semitic graffiti since the war; the 'swastika plague' spread to Australia in January 1960.

[22]Five unprepared women whose lamps ran dry as they waited for the bridegroom; they were off buying oil when he finally arrived so they missed the wedding. *Matthew* 25: 1–13.

especially when the proceedings were rounded off by a woman exhorting us six times over to remain just ordinary Australians. That hateful religion of ordinariness, which I believe is also practised in the States, if no longer to the same extent. Last night I wanted to jump up and draw attention to the extra-ordinary Russians, except that it would have given too much satisfaction to some of the Gentiles present. Anyway, I hope the mere holding of such a large meeting may have some effect in the country, and there are always small, practical ways of educating. Do you know Lord Russell of Liverpool's book, *The Scourge of the Swastika?* It seems to me the last word on Nazism, and I am sending copies to the 35 Municipal Libraries of Sydney. Whether anybody reads them, is, of course another matter.

I suppose you would not deign to read Alma Mahler Werfel. Somebody gave me *And the Bridge is Love* for Christmas, and I have to admit I wallowed in it as if it had been a prolonged Sunday newspaper, full of scurrilities.[23] She certainly has a streak of supreme vulgarity, and usually succeeds in bringing others down to her own level. Mahler comes out of it unscathed, but she turns Werfel into a most repulsive object while apparently doting on him. Perhaps he was repulsive. You will know better than I . . .

This letter should smell good and garlic-y, as I have been cooking a dish of Imam-Baïldi in between typing.[24] In my middle age I have developed the inconvenient and a-social habit of going to bed after dinner. Then I get up and use the middle and small hours. These are the best for writing letters and cooking, also for revising, though not creating novels; first thing in the morning is best, I find, for that.

I hope this finds you well. You sounded well in your last letter. Please thank Marshall Best. I shall write to him separately, but later, by which time I should also have read some of the Whitman.

DOGWOODS, 25.ii.60
TO MARSHALL BEST
Dear Marshall Best,

If I did not write sooner to thank you for the *Leaves of Grass*, it was because I wrote at the time to thank Mr Huebsch for his share in the present. There are some wonderful lines in it – lightning flashes – , but also, I'm afraid, a great deal that makes me laugh. Can anyone take seriously, for instance, a man who concocted a title like 'I Sing the Body

---

[23]Alma Mahler Werfel (1879–1964) was wife or mistress to Mahler, Walter Gropius, Franz Werfel and the painter Oskar Kokoschka.
[24]Aubergine stuffed with tomatoes and parsley.

Electric'? I think perhaps one has to be American really to appreciate Whitman, because he is as much a part of your literary and social development as he is a poet. Any way, I am glad to have the handsome book, and enjoyed reading Malcolm Cowley's[25] interesting introduction.

Are you by any chance publishing George Painter's *Proust*? I found it almost as good as the novel itself.[26] Funnily enough books on these great literary 'liberators' came into my hands almost at once – your Whitman, Painter's book on Proust, and Ellmann's *Joyce*, which looks as though it is going to be something. Like Whitman, Joyce is a writer I now find fascinating to read about, but not to read – although in my youth I considered him practically God.

DOGWOODS, 13.v.60
TO FREDERICK GLOVER

The Kriegers and Andrew and Elly Fisher[27] were here to dinner a couple of nights ago. Andrew brought us a brilliant record of Barry Humphries doing his characters Mrs Norm Everidge and Sandy Stone. He has crammed all the horrors of Australian suburbia into a very short space – really quite uncanny.

DOGWOODS, 23.vi.60
TO MOLLIE McKIE
Dear Mollie,

What a pity all the members of your family go away.[28] Distinguished Australians should be trying to make something of their country, hopeless as that task may seem. But I suppose I must not say all I could, in case I am forced to drag up my own roots. There are times when I feel I shall not be able to stand it to the bitter end.

Here we seem to live continually under threat. One may wake up any day and find the land has been taken out of the Green Belt. Then, of course, it would be impossible to stay on and pay the rates.[29] This

---

[25](1898–1989), critic and translator, Best's colleague at Viking Press.

[26]This was the first volume taking Proust's life to the turn of the century; the second volume was not published until 1965.

[27]Fisher, a farmer in Victoria, was Ile Krieger's brother; it was he who preserved PW's letters both to the Kriegers and his own family.

[28]One brother, William, was Organist and Master of Choristers at Westminster Abbey; another, John, was leaving Melbourne to become assistant Bishop of Coventry.

[29]Dogwoods lay in a cordon of bush and farms which planners hoped would contain Sydney's sprawl; to be released from the Green Belt made fortunes but attracted high rates; Dogwoods was never released while PW owned it.

morning, even, we went out and found shrubs smashed, and surveyor's pegs knocked in for road-widening without our being told anything about it . . .

We had a visit recently from John Hetherington who announced that he wanted to write a profile for the *Age*. I gave him lunch, and thought we were getting on like a house on fire, but when I received a draft of the profile, I found him accusing me of 'chill reserve.'[30] So really one will never have any idea what impression one makes on others. I am still accused by the Sydney press of being a 'hermit' although a constant stream of people roll through this house. I even met a man the other day at a party who told me he had heard I had left for Greece to enter a monastery.

Dogwoods, 3.viii.60
TO BEN HUEBSCH
Dear Mr Huebsch,
I expect by this time you are taking it easy in Sweden. How I envy you. To do nothing, and to be waited on, would be very agreeable at this point. At least I have finished the Second Version, but there is no question of doing nothing, for the weeds have begun to grow again, and there are always the aeons one has to spend at the sink and at the stove. Also I feel I have to catch up on my reading, and sometimes find myself still with a book in my hand at three in the morning.

---

[30] 16 July, p.17: 'It seems possible behind the mask of his rather chill reserve, PW worries about the manifest failure of many people to understand his novels.'

About *Riders in the Chariot*: it does, I'm afraid, work out at about 230,000. I have tried it on Manoly and a Jewish friend. The latter flew into ecstasies, and announced that I am the 'first *goy* to have understood the Jewish mind.' Allowing for exaggeration, I am now comforted by the thought that my attempt should be acceptable to Jews. I am more sceptical of the reader's literary judgment. I have known her go very wrong at times. Manoly, always a sober judge, does like the book, I <u>think</u>. But he is worried because he foresees that it will offend a great many Australians. I can't help that. There is so much that has been offending <u>me</u> over the years, and now I must give expression to my feelings.

I don't think the Third Version will take very long, for I don't have to make any radical alterations in the Jewish parts, as I had expected. It will be largely a matter of clarifying language throughout and correcting small details.

I have read *Dr Zhivago* at last. I hope you were as spellbound as I. There was hardly a page which did not leave me wanting to shout and sing. I also finished the Durrell quartet, of which the brilliance has begun to appear slightly meretricious after Pasternak's more mature wisdom. Still, I am thankful for Durrell too. Now I am reading a riotous thing called *Absolute Beginners* by Colin MacInnes, author of *City of Spades*.[31] If you haven't already come across them, I recommend both those.

I really have very little of interest to write to somebody who is moving around, seeing and doing. Last night at dinner we were made very restless by the Professor of Greek from Sydney University who is about to start for Greece.[32] Next time I want, if possible, to do Sinai and Petra, Christian Jerusalem (which we missed in 1958 by going first to the Jewish sector), Israel again (and in particular Safed), Constantinople, of course a good slice of Greece, Spain, and Russia, since Pasternak's landscapes are haunting me.

In the meantime I can only lose myself in a sea of violets – they are flowering here in sheets at the moment – , and the cherries are beginning.

Yrs,

Patrick.

---

[31](1914–76), novelist, son of novelist Angela Thirkell, educated in Melbourne.
[32]George Shipp (1900–80), at Sydney from 1955–65.

DOGWOODS, 19.viii.60

TO FREDERICK GLOVER

I don't think I have written to you since Rostropovitch and Markevitch.[33] That was stupendous, and I have bought R. playing the *Sinfonia Concertante* of Prokofiev. However, I think I preferred the performance we heard in Sydney. David Moore, who listened to the Shostakovitch Cello Concerto broadcast from Melbourne, says that that was even more terrific. The only recording is an American one for Columbia, which I think I shall try to get now that I have Sam Goody's catalogue,[34] and have found out what to do. But one should really see Rostropovitch. He plays like an enraged bear, then comes out at the end to acknowledge the applause like a gay, and gentle human being.

To-day we got back the Roy de Maistre paintings.[35] On opening the crate we were upset to find five of ours, and another one substituted for 'The Aunt'. However, I remembered hearing a de Maistre was coming out to the Art Gallery after the exhibition in London, I rang them, and found that the import agents had made a mistake; the Gallery has 'The Aunt', and we were sent theirs. For the time being we have the latter hanging in the sitting room, and it makes me feel I want to keep it. It is one he painted not long before I got to know him, and I can remember it hanging in the old studio in Ebury Street, when I was still terrified of modern painting. Now it looks like an Old Master, such wonderful colour and textures, although the subject is abstract with a strong flavour of the surrealism which had blown up at that period, and which one does not find normally in Roy's paintings. As I made some money recently by selling some Beale shares,[36] I have written making him an offer for a couple of others, or at least asking what he wants for them. Probably I shall not be able to afford, even if he wants to sell, as one of them is a very important one . . .

Have finished reading a borrowed copy of *Lolita*. I started sceptically, but found a major work of art. All the Viennese ladies who managed to lay hands on it before anybody else, and who bolted into it in search of a smell, say that it is a bore and they couldn't finish it, but of course they were quite unable to recognise its scholarliness, and the brilliance of its satire.

[33]The cellist and later conductor Mstislav Rostropovitch (1927–) on his first tour of Australia; and the conductor Igor Markevitch (1912–83).
[34]New York record dealer.
[35]Lent for a retrospective of de Maistre's work earlier that year at the Whitechapel Gallery, London.
[36]Beale & Co. Ltd, financiers.

GEOFFREY DUTTON WAS COMMISSIONED to write a short book on White's work[37] and came to Dogwoods in August. White was ill in bed much of the time, but this first meeting was a success: 'We liked G. Dutton very much indeed.'[38] Soon they met his wife Ninette who also wrote, gardened and was an enamellist of note. White's and Lascaris' lives became happily entangled for the next twenty years with this beautiful couple. Geoffrey and Nin were intelligent, rich and dashing. They came from White's world – the bush, Oxbridge, writing – and were masters of the arts of friendship: good letters, a few books, a box of wine, holidays on Kangaroo Island, easy meetings with interesting people, with painters and writers who in turn became friends of White and Lascaris. Within two years White was calling the Duttons, 'Some of my best friends'.[39] His letters to them – nearly three hundred – are a vivid record of almost everything he encountered in his life: books, places, plants, dogs, paintings, films, infirmities – moral and physical – food and people. And he spoke to the Duttons with some candour about his life and writing.

DOGWOODS, 19.ix.60
TO GEOFFREY DUTTON
Dear Geoffrey,
First, some points which cropped up in reading the biographical sketch. Probably you won't want too much detail because of the problem of length. But there is no harm in your knowing, and you can pick the bits you need . . .

p.5 'He admires D. H. Lawrence's letters etc– –' Although I admire T. S. Eliot, I have not read an awful lot, because I have never really warmed to him. I suppose the poet who has meant most to me in recent years is Rimbaud.

p.5 'He likes Beethoven etc– –' Beethoven certainly, and particularly the quartets. Mahler, yes; I found him very helpful when I was writing *Voss*. But I cannot say that I like Liszt, only that his bravura and a certain formal side helped me in conveying some of the more worldly, superficial passages of *Voss*. The same with Delacroix. The latter is a painter I admire, but for whom I have no affection. Blake I never think of as a painter, rather as a literary genius who also expressed himself visually. I suppose the painters who mean most to me are people like Goya, and Greco, Picasso, and Klee. I always feel I began to write from the inside out when

[37]*Patrick White*, 1961, in the Lansdowne Press series 'Australian Writers and their Work'.
[38]To Glover, 12.ix.60.
[39]To Huebsch, 31.viii.62.

Roy de Maistre introduced me to abstract painting about 1936. Before that I had only approached writing as an exercise in naturalism. Anything else was poetry. (This is probably still the attitude of many Australians and most Australian critics.) Then came the terrors of abstract painting. As far as I was concerned, it was like jumping into space, and finding nothing there at first (the same thing when one first plunges into Zen.) Then gradually one saw that it was possible to weave about freely on different levels at one and the same time.

To return to the composers, I suppose those who mean most to me to-day are Bach and Bartok. I have leant heavily on both of them while writing *Riders in the Chariot* (also on Bloch to help me understand a certain character.)

I don't know that you could refer to *Riders* as a 'bitter comedy'. There is certainly bitter comedy or satire running all through it, for it is about contemporary Australia. But it is too big and rambling to support the term 'comedy'; that suggests to me something compact and complete in itself. Nor can one say it takes place in a suburban town. Rather, it converges on Sydney and the suburban outskirts from England, the North of Germany, and somewhere in the north of this state. More than anything it is a profession of faith, and so it will probably turn out to be my bitterest flop. I can already hear the rationalist knives being sharpened for me from Perth to Brisbane.

The only play of which I still have a copy is *The Ham Funeral*. It is the last I wrote, from an idea given me by Dobell, of the same period as *The Aunt's Story*, so it looks as though I have got the theatre out of my system. This is the play on which Zachary Scott took an option. If I can find my copy, I shall send it. But sometimes I look for things on or in my desk and do not find them for years.

Dogwoods, 3.x.60
TO GEOFFREY DUTTON
Dear Geoffrey,

We were glad to hear your good news. I feel if people start to breed, they should, if possible, go ahead and have a batch,[40] although personally I should not like to think I had brought somebody into the world. But of course that is wrong! And you will make a good father, whereas I should be an abominable one. When will the baby be born? Perhaps it will be a girl this time, and you will have the pleasure of avoiding Joyleen. (Since

[40]Their son Francis was born 1958; Ninette was now pregnant with Teresa (Tisi) 1961; Sam was born 1963.

you were here I have found Hilma, Iffla, and Lima in the *SMH* Deaths Column, my great source of names.)

I finally unearthed the copy of *The Ham Funeral*. I send it with diffidence, as it seems to me more of a private matter than the novels, almost an act of indecent exposure . . .

I have just been reading about Joyce's play *Exiles*, which hung fire for years, then was a flop in Munich, and, one suspects, in London too. I think perhaps *The Ham Funeral* is the same kind of piece, and should be discreetly forgotten. Apparently, at one point, Joyce said to a young French translator who had read the script: 'Don't you think *Exiles* is as good as Hauptmann?'[41] To which the young man replied: 'Some scenes are even worse.'

You must really make another attempt at Ellmann's *Joyce*. I, too, was bored at first – he could perhaps have been more selective in the passages dealing with childhood and youth – but after the first couple of hundred pages, I sailed along. It is truly a magnificent piece of portraiture, though the subject may be a bit repulsive. And towards the end I was even very touched by the relationship between that, *au fond*, rather mad genius and his hopelessly mad daughter. (It was surprising that one so superstitious and at the same time steeped in opera should have ventured to call his child 'Lucia'.)

DOGWOODS, 6.x.60
TO FREDERICK GLOVER
Dear Frederick,

I seem to get very little time for writing letters nowadays. Any time I spend at a desk, I want to give to my book. Then I lie down on my bed, and spend the rest of the time asleep. However, I have also got through the Ellman life of Joyce, which is quite an exhausting physical undertaking, holding those 800 pages, especially when lying in bed. What a book it is . . .

The other night we were summoned to dinner by Beatrice Davis of all people.[42] We had met at parties once or twice, and never had much to say to each other. She had always been most artificial – refaned – , although Manoly and she appeared to have some normal conversation at the Penguin party. The invitation to dinner came about because Hal Porter had been in Sydney, and wanted to meet me. Hearing about him, I had never taken to him, but along we went to Folly Point, which is part of Cammeray,

---

[41]Gerhart Hauptmann (1862–1946), German playwright who won the Nobel Prize in 1912.
[42](1909–92), distinguished editor, midwife to Australian literature of the 1940s and 1950s.

sticking out into Middle Harbour, and spent a most agreeable, if alcoholic evening. Hal Porter certainly <u>looks</u> very strange – older and mellower than I had expected, but with a most curious hair-do – or is it wig? – brought forward, and round, and about, of a dead lemon-spaniel colour. Very sympathetic as a man, however, and I'd like to see more of him[43] . . .

The irises – the good ones – are just beginning. I have some of the big white you gave us in the black-and-white Dutch pottery bowl on my desk. This spring has been a wonderful one in the garden – masses of every kind of blossom, bluebells in the grass, and even lilac in six-inch sprays outside my window. I am hoping that when all the leaves come we shall really be lost in the forest this year.

It is very late, and I must go to bed, or I shall miss the little time I get for reading. Hope things are going all right for you, and that Mollie is not too exhausted. Also that we shall see you one day.

Yours
Patrick.

DOGWOODS, 26.x.60
TO FREDERICK GLOVER
I expect you read about Kylie's husband getting an arm, half a foot, and several fingers and toes taken off by a train.[44] I went yesterday to Sydney Hospital to see him. It is a grim situation. It is difficult to tell how he is really taking it, although he is still obviously in pretty considerable pain. Kylie is wonderful, as one would have expected from knowing her. She has got a hard time coming, with those two children to bring up, and perhaps also the husband to keep. However, we don't yet know how he will come out of it. He may be able to pull himself together, and they can work wonders to-day in the rehabilitation line. A schoolmaster with a hook might even be at an advantage with the children.

I have finally broken with the Kriegers.[45] The stages are too long and

---

[43]PW never met the novelist and playwright (1911–84) again. That night PW had remarked to Porter that the poet John Thompson and his wife Patricia were probably marrying off their young son 'to make a man of him'. With signature malice Porter then told the Thompsons that PW thought their son was queer and perhaps also that PW lusted after the boy – who was not, as it happens, homosexual. This ruined PW's friendship with the Thompsons. Before posting a letter reproaching Porter, PW showed it to the novelist Thea Astley who felt she would have been 'completely crushed' to receive something so fierce. Porter later boasted selling it to the Mitchell Library to pay for another boozy weekend in Sydney. The letter is not among his papers there. Porter did what he could to keep this feud alive.
[44]L. C. Rodd had thrown himself onto the tracks in another attempt to end his life.
[45]No, but their intimate friendship was finished.

involved, perhaps even too silly to go through. All this mystery, 'withdrawal' and so forth was beginning to irritate me. I lent Fritz that little book on *Zen in Archery*[46] which I thought might help give him a new approach to lots of things. I received back quite a nice letter, but in which he said he felt we had been getting on one another's nerves lately. It sounded so terribly Viennese. Such dreadful things have been happening lately to people we know, all these Central European nerves have become doubly laughable. So when Ile rang up on her return from Melbourne, full of that female diplomacy which sticks out a mile, asking us to a meal at which we should obviously be expected to sit round with Elizabeth and Fisher Flora[47] and pretend nothing had happened, I declined. Ile now accuses me of being without understanding. The trouble is, I think I have too much understanding of the Kriegers. For a long time now we have been asking one another to meals and exchanging presents at the appropriate times without its meaning anything at all. It is just a routine. They no longer give anything of themselves as they did in the beginning. Ile has become quite unreal in her jungle of wrought-iron and lacquered pot-plants. I cannot feel they have anything left but their material selves. Fritz, who would make a good, warm-hearted Jew, has got lost trying to play at Christianity, which is an abstraction even to Christians, unless they are very simple, or the most worldly Jesuits.

DOGWOODS, 19.xi.60
TO CLEM CHRISTESEN,
Dear Christesen,
I am sorry if you have been upset by any criticism of *Meanjin* I may have made to Marcel Aurousseau.[48] With this on top of various pieces of recent reportage, by other friends, on other matters, I can see the day approaching when I turn Trappist. As far as I remember, I said to Aurousseau that a paper kept alive by grants led a somewhat artificial existence, but it is too long ago to recall the details of my remarks.

    Does the opening paragraph of your letter mean I shall be asked to appear on TV? If so, I am afraid that is something I can never do. Of course I wish *Meanjin* well, and contributed to your fund[49] out of a windfall

---

[46]*Zen in der Kunst des Bogenschiessens*, Eugene Herringel, trans. R. F. C. Hull, 1953.
[47]Ile Krieger's sister Elizabeth, widow of Jenör Léner (1894–1948) of the Léner Quartet, and their mother.
[48](1891–1983), geologist, writer and Leichhardt scholar; they met at Sydney Symphony Orchestra concerts.
[49]10 guineas.

at a time when you said responses were poor. I realise you did a lot to help my books in the beginning, and for that reason I offered you an extract from *Voss* before it was published, although I never feel happy about that practice. (When I wrote offering to keep my promise, while you were away, I received a letter from a stand-in professor[50] saying they would print it only if they approved of the work, and that I must not expect payment, for which I had no intention of asking.) If I have not given you a passage from *Riders in the Chariot* – still unfinished – I have also refused *Australian Letters* and Australian *Vogue*. My reason is that I might give passages to all three, and create the impression that I had written three entirely different books. It is only by reading the whole work that the parts will be seen to connect. In the case of *Voss*, the extract you published seemed to me to convey the spirit of the whole,[51] and so, the lifting was aesthetically permissible.

If I have not sent you articles, if I haven't reviewed books, it is because I am not a professional intellectual. I am an artist trying to get down on paper a number of novels I have in my head, and wondering, when I get held up by illness more and more each winter, whether I shall have the time.

It seems to me one of the chief difficulties in running a magazine like *Meanjin* is the absence in Australia of a race of professional intellectuals such as you find in older countries, and that you have to fall back on university professors trailing an academic aura, and creative writers hot from their own involvements. Certainly some of the contributors to intellectual publications in the old world and America are themselves creative writers, but they seem to be able to maintain a detachment few Australians are able to achieve.

I hope I have not put you off by all this, and that I shall have the opportunity of meeting you here one day. If I refuse to appear on TV, or speak in public, it is because I know my own limitations.

Yours sincerely,
Patrick White.

DOGWOODS, 24.xi.60
TO SIDNEY NOLAN
Dear Sidney,
Thank you for your card, and please thank Cynthia for her letter. The

---

[50]Geoffrey Serle (1922–   ), history lecturer at Melbourne University, an editor of the *Australian Dictionary of Biography*, vols 3–11.
[51]'The Death of Palfreyman', *Meanjin* 16, 3 Sept. 1957.

Leda and the *Soldiers* are now sitting on one of the bookcases in the sitting-room. Leda grew visibly the first evening about sunset as the light poured in through some rattan curtains of a bordeaux colour not unlike what I take to be the 'wine-dark sea' in the background of the painting. I had put her between rather a severe small tree, of a succulent variety, and an old celery glass full of roses, already on the blowsy side, and some of them spilling. Don't you think celery and full-blown roses is the right combination for Leda? I still like the *Soldiers*, in spite of the fact that you now say it does not really come off. All the same, I shall wait with interest to see what you may do from the clue I have given.

About the jacket for my *Riders in the Chariot* – I shall not have finished the final version until end of December, perhaps even beginning of January. I don't want to hurry it anymore. In fact, I couldn't if I wanted to. However, as they don't propose to bring it out before the end of 1961, you and the book ought to be able to coincide somewhere in the world during the year. I shall tell Temple Smith to let you have a proof copy or something as soon as he has one. Or, if you decide to come here from Africa, and I can separate you from friends and public appearances for a few days, and intern you here, you might read my copy of the MS. I am only doing three – one for Eyre & Spottiswoode, one for the Viking, New York, and one to keep myself.

I have heard no more from the Zachary Scotts, so take it that nothing will come of *The Ham Funeral* in New York. I think the option has just about run out. Recently I sent the play to Adelaide to Geoffrey Dutton, who has been writing a book on my books for the Jacaranda Press,[52] and who wanted to see the play, out of curiosity, and to round out the picture. He, Max Harris[53], and a producer called Ballantyne[54] immediately got excited about it, and said they thought it ought to be done at the next Adelaide Festival. Strangely enough, as soon as an opportunity offered itself, I began to feel appalled at the thought of being sucked into the theatre – rehearsals: 'I can't possibly say that, darling' etc. etc. So here was I holding back, when another letter arrived to say that the play had been read by all those responsible for the staging of the Festival, and all were agreed that it should be done. I decided to try letting that one die down,

[52]No, Lansdowne.
[53]Poet & commentator (1921–95), principal victim of the Ern Malley hoax, fellow-editor with Dutton of *Australian Letters* and proprietor of the Mary Martin chain of bookshops. PW counted Harris as an ally for years, then became exasperated with the attitudes he struck in his column in the *Australian*.
[54]Colin Ballantyne (1908–88), Adelaide theatre director whose hopes of directing *Ham Funeral* were dashed by PW's insistence on using John Tasker.

when a third letter arrived, the following day, to say that they wanted to take an option on it for March 1962. So it looks as though there is no escaping fate.

The Tucker exhibition has burst upon us in Sydney.[55] The two critics who matter were most enthusiastic, but I'm afraid I was terribly disappointed. Except for one or two, I found the paintings self-conscious, laboured, exhibitionistic. Of course I am allergic in the first place to paint laid on like mud, and more so to collage. Some of these had textures reminiscent of fun-fair side shows. Some of the minor things looked as though they had just been knocked off to catch an extra buyer. However, I am told that three of the big works have been bought by galleries, and so far five others have gone to private collectors.

We went yesterday to a small exhibition of a much quieter and more painterly nature: a retrospective show of de Maistre, Wakelin and Grace Cossington Smith, who all started out about the same time. For de Maistre they had to draw on works already in Sydney, and five that I own provided the core. The piddling Herald accuses Roy of being influenced by Chirico and Sutherland, two painters that I happen to know would not influence him either consciously or unconsciously.[56] I am buying a little Cossington Smith. It is on a small scale, but it is one of those paintings which could not have been otherwise in any detail.[57] I am quite excited about it. Have you ever seen her? She herself has something of Theodora Goodman, only a Theodora who has not gone in on herself. At the opening, she was carrying a string bag, and wearing a hat of white, papery poppies, with long, dead-green, trembling stalks.

We have been wondering where exactly you will be going in Africa. It is so vast! But I suppose if a painter goes to exhibit and sell paintings, Johannesburg would be the place, and I don't think I could stand that, even if the whole family of Oppenheimers came and ate out of my hand.

---

[55]At David Jones Gallery. PW was predisposed to be hostile to Albert Tucker (1914–   ), for the painter worked at Heide on the outskirts of Melbourne in the 1940s and PW had absorbed Cynthia Nolan's suspicions about her husband's Heide companions. PW recanted a little after seeing a big retrospective of Tucker's work in later life. He admitted 'you could sort out a few good ones'.

[56]Reviewing 'Pioneer Contemporaries' at the Macquarie Galleries – works by Roland Wakelin (1887–1971), Grace Cossington-Smith (1892–1984) and de Maistre – Wallace Thornton wrote in the SMH, 24 Nov., p.2: 'The representation of works by Roy de Maistre is rather uneven in changing styles – the austere abstraction of "Seated Figure" contrasts with the de Chirico mood of "Conflict" until in the "Crucifixion" of 1957 there is a Sutherland-like figure surrounded by a tritely harlequin-patterned background.'

[57]'Bonfire in the Bush', 1937.

During the War, I was stranded briefly on the Gold Coast, from where I flew across to Egypt, through Nigeria, Chad and The Sudan. Kano was wonderful, particularly a ghostly tree made white by the droppings of the pelicans that had roosted in it. And Chad was rather like a dream. I remember parachutes hung to dry against a blue lake, and getting rather drunk on Pernod, which is perhaps what has turned it into a dream.

Well, I do hope the jacket business will come off in spite of all your moves and the few difficulties. Fortunately time is on our side and I don't imagine a jacket has to be ready as far in advance as the text.

Hope you find your travels interesting and profitable, and that we may even see you at Castle Hill.

Yours,
Patrick.

DOGWOODS, 3.i.61
TO BEN HUEBSCH
Dear Mr Huebsch,
This is really only a line to say that I am about to send the MS. of *Riders in the Chariot* by airmail (first or second class depending on the sum involved!)

Thank you very much in advance for *Finnegans Wake*, which you mentioned sending when you wrote last. It seems a long time, but things take an age to reach Australia from the States. I don't quite know what happens; it's as though we had gone back to the old sailing days. Last year I ordered some records from the States, and it was months before they arrived.

Must go to bed, as I have to get up early to go to Sydney for the despatch. They are so stupid at this local post-office they just look blank if one wants to send anything unorthodox.

Yrs,
Patrick.

DOGWOODS, 5.i.61
TO GEOFFREY DUTTON
I posted the *Chariot* yesterday, both to London and New York. The parcels crashed down into the bowels of the G.P.O., making me feel they had probably burst open at the start, and even if they hadn't, they were probably setting out on an ominous career. I am still too close to the thing to see it as a whole. On my last reading it appeared a mess with some bright patches.

Dogwoods, 7.i.61
TO EDNA O'BRIEN[58]
Dear Edna,
A lot of things happened in a rush: I finished my book, your letter came,
I posted the book, I read *The Country Girls* at last. It is really miraculous
what you have done; I don't think there is a dead line in it, and I am still
rubbing my eyes for all those bright pictures. I wonder what it is that
makes writing come alive. I like to think it will happen if one lives the
story intensely enough in the process, because if that is so, the book I have
just finished should swallow people up. But I am not at all sure. The light
in *The Country Girls* is something I am afraid you will never recapture. It
is something that happens in the beginning. Just as one never sees things
so clearly as one did in childhood. If only one had the technique and the
experience to put down during childhood what one was seeing then. I
suppose that links up with Baudelaire's remark: 'Genius is recaptured
childhood.' In which case you seem to have done it and got it. I only
tremble for your next!

Funny the way nuns and convents are always sure fire in a novel. I
have never been a Roman Catholic, was brought up vaguely an Anglican,
but nuns always fascinate me. Do you know George Moore's *Evelyn Innes*
and *Sister Teresa*? They are really Parts I and II of the same book,
unfortunately out of print, but you must get hold of them somehow if you
haven't already read them. In spite of the queer wooden novelettishness
of much of the writing, and corniness of theme – the great singer who
becomes a nun – , I think he succeeded in writing a great novel there. I
try to persuade Eyre & Spottiswoode and Lanes to re-publish, but so far I
have not succeeded.

I should think Eyre & Spottiswoode would eat you up. I did not like
them in the beginning because I fell into their hands more or less against
their will, but since then we have grown to respect one another, and their
list is improving all the time. The man to approach is Maurice Temple
Smith. From his letters I expected him to be old and rheumaticky, but
when I was in London two years ago, he turned out to be young and
handsome, and in spite of that, has, I feel, quite a lot of understanding for
books. I shall be writing to him probably tonight, and shall give him your
address, but if nothing happens you might try from your end. The Viking
Press has been marvellous all through the twenty odd years they have been
publishing me. It will be a good thing if you can get with them. Unfortunately

---

[58](1932–   ), Irish novelist, who had written to PW declaring herself a fan and enclosed a
copy of her first novel.

Ben Huebsch, the partner who has always had my interests at heart, is now retired, although he still considers I am one of <u>his</u> authors, and I hope he will till he dies. I feel I am bound up with him <u>in</u> some way . . .

Where does your husband's name come from?[59] Is he Jewish? Half my friends seem to have been Jewish, and I have attempted to put a number of Jews into my new book – a thing I suspect only Jews themselves should do. All this has led me to immerse myself in Judaica over the last few years. It is a fascinating religion, particularly the mystical side of it.

Well, it is 4 a.m., and I must dash off the letter to Temple Smith, if it is to be written to-night.

Yours

Patrick White

P.S. I can't get your 'mountainy people' out of my head. When I was a boy I worked for a time on a sheep station in the south of this state – very cold and primitive it was. I used to have to take horses into the village some miles away to have them shod, and would stand about outside the forge while they were being done, and look at the village people. I know exactly about those 'mountainy people' from being a bit 'mountainy' myself at that time.

DOGWOODS, 10.i.61

TO CLEM CHRISTESEN

Thank you for telling me how you have overcome your asthma. As it happens, the asthma part of my trouble is not nearly as bad as it used to be. What I get now is a kind of bronchitis, with an infection of the chest which sets in, and is liable to lay me low for three weeks at a time. However, even this is much improved, or seems to be; I am looking forward to the winter to see whether this is really so. Last February, after getting nowhere with orthodox doctors over the years – the most they could do was stick a needle into me every time I fell by the wayside – , I decided to try a naturopath of whom I had heard wonderful reports, and in my case too, he certainly seems to have had results – through manipulation, ray treatment, herbal medicines, and diet. I agree with you that diet probably plays the greatest part. I am allowed to take milk, however, though I never use more than a dash of it, in coffee. No sugar, no starch, and absolutely no citrus. I used to drink a great glass of orange juice every morning, as we have our own citrus orchard. Now I am supposed to concentrate on red meat and green leaf vegetables (with the exception of

[59]Ernest Gebler, Dublin novelist and playwright, son of an Irish mother and Czech father; he and O'Brien divorced in 1967.

spinach). At breakfast, even, I eat a green salad – with plenty of garlic! Half an hour before breakfast, I drink two glasses of warm water, with a little salt, then eat eight prunes, then drink a third glass of water. How disgustingly faddy it all sounds! But it has had results, and I had grown desperate.

DOGWOODS, 5.ii.61
TO BEN HUEBSCH
Dear Ben,
(To burst into first names so late in the day! I am always chary of doing so, and always jump slightly when I hear somebody call me by my own.)

Your letter and cable[60] were a great relief. Of course I realise it has to be read and accepted by other people too, but you have been the true judge over so many decades, and true judgment is what interests me most. Himmelfarb was a worry, because he had to be just right. Of course I had studied Judaism over the last few years, and talked endlessly with Jewish friends, but in the end what helped me most was the fact that throughout my life I have been an outcast myself in one way and another: first a child with what kind of a strange gift nobody quite knew; then a despised colonial boy in an English public school; finally an artist in horrified Australia – to give you just a few instances. There have also been occasions when anti-Semitism has touched me personally in a mild way: when Manoly and I settled here in Castle Hill the postman of that day would not speak to us, because, we discovered, he thought we were foreign Jews speculating in land (I, if you please, was pretending to be an Australian); again when I once protested against paying over again the fare of somebody who had travelled in the same taxi, the driver stood on the kerb screaming at me: 'Go back to Germany!' (In those days practically any foreigner here was of Jewish extraction, and added to that there was my strange diction which many seemed to find practically incomprehensible.) These little instances do have an influence on one's outlook.

I am glad you like my two devils, Mrs Jolley and Mrs Flack. I must tell you how they originated. When I was in the States in 1939, you may remember it was suddenly found out that a number of respectable Philadelphian widows had been quietly poisoning their husbands to get the insurance. At the time I tried to work up a short story, of which I thought under the title *Duet for Harpies*, but gave up in the end because I felt it required a very definite American idiom. But the idea clung on, and

---

[60] 22.i.61: *RIDERS* IS A GREAT BOOK YOUR BEST CONGRATULATIONS LETTER FOLLOWS HUEBSCH.

came out finally as Mrs Jolley and Mrs Flack, each of whom had been the death of her husband, if not by poison.

I have not broken my connexion with Curtis Brown, London. I don't feel that Juliet O'Hea is interested in books except as an investment (between ourselves), nor does she particularly care for or understand mine, but she has tagged along over the years.[61] So did Naomi Burton, and I should be with her still if she were with Curtis Brown, New York. The new man rather irritated me, as I thought the least he could do was get in touch with his authors.[62] Juliet has had *Riders in the Chariot*, which she had to read quickly to pass on to Eyre & Spottiswoode, who had to catch Sidney Nolan for the jacket before he goes to Egypt. I don't think anybody at E & S has read it yet, but to-day I had a letter from Nolan's wife, his right-hand man, telling me how excited they are, and that he has almost decided what the jacket is to be. Their enthusiasm is most gratifying, as they are the first Australians to read it.

One point I did not mention before is the dedication. I have always felt I would like to dedicate the book to Klári Daniel, the sister of the Hungarian Anuska whom you met, and to yourself. Klári has been my mentor, as it were, in Jewish matters, and you have been – you. I wanted to see how you reacted to the book first, otherwise it would have been too much like holding a gun at your head! Even now, perhaps you would not like to be associated with it to that extent. I leave it to you. If you agree, let the dedication be simply:

FOR

KLARI DANIEL

AND

BEN HUEBSCH.

If you prefer to be left out of it, simply say so, and pass on her name alone.[63] Please don't forget this, because I have promised it to her, and she would be most disappointed if the dedication were left out.

Finnegans Wake finally arrived, and I am now drifting along with it

---

[61]O'Hea (c.1911–) was agent to Lawrence Durrell, Doris Lessing, Mary Renault, etc., and represented PW from 1941 until her retirement in 1975. At this point, PW was still smarting from her lack of enthusiasm for *The Tree of Man*. Her literary opinions were tough – she thought PW's plays and stories all but unsaleable outside Australia – but in business matters she was a source of unfailing commonsense.

[62]Perry Knowlton of Curtis Brown represented PW in New York until 1965 when John Cushman took over the 'London' writers of the agency; that arrangement lasted until 1978 when Knowlton took the list back again; PW remained with Knowlton and Curtis Brown until he broke furiously with the agency everywhere in late 1986.

[63]Huebsch accepted the dedication.

by slow stages. What a work. In spite of its flashes of wit and poetry, I can't help feeling he could have given us something more if he hadn't plunged into the Liffey. In the end I suppose I shall have to get even further involved. Whose would you say is the best commentary on *Finnegan*?

I was hoping to send you some Australiana for Christmas, but when it comes to the point, there is very little that would interest you. Now I think I am on the track of something – only it is New Zealand.

Well, I am anxiously waiting to hear what your colleagues think, and expect I shall any day now. By the way, I received the book by Margaret Kennedy[64] sent by the Press. Quite a surprise that she should launch out in that way. She says some shrewd things here and there, but some of it is a bit sprightly and womany. The only other thing I have read of hers is *The Constant Nymph*, which I devoured as a schoolboy. Incidentally it occurred to me recently that the girl in that was perhaps the first of the nymphets.

My bronchitis is very much improved, but I suppose winter will be the test. I wonder, too, how much of it was due to the book I was writing. I want to give the naturopath his due, but I certainly feel a hundred times better since I wrote that book out of my system.

Yours,
Patrick.

---

[64]*The Outlaws of Parnassus*, 1960, a defence of the novelist as entertainer.

SEVEN

Stage Machinery

March 1961 – March 1963

WHITE NOW TURNED HIS mind to the tale of Eliza Fraser and her wreck on the island off the Queensland coast that now bears her name. He had heard the story from Sidney Nolan the day they drove round Florida together: how the *Stirling Castle* ran aground in 1836 and the blacks slaughtered all the survivors but Mrs Fraser who survived as a slave stripped of everything but a 'fringe of leaves' tied around her waist until a runaway convict took her back to civilisation. Nolan had painted his first Mrs Fraser paintings on the island some years before; now the writer planned to follow in the painter's footsteps. But first White made a long-promised visit to Peggy Garland in New Zealand.

WELLINGTON, 15.iii.61
TO BEN HUEBSCH
Dear Ben,
I came over here yesterday on a short visit to a cousin. It is so beautiful it makes Australia seem like a rubbish dump, and yet with all this unspoiled natural beauty there are the most astonishing outbreaks of human violence and youthful degeneracy, as you probably read about from time to time in the papers. I am in the thick of the Katherine Mansfield country. To-day I was taken to the Bays, of her stories . . .

I am staying here till the end of the month. My cousin has been having a hard time – abandoned by her husband after six children, the older children now leaving for Europe, while she is left behind with the youngest, a retarded boy of 14 who recently became mentally ill. He has very lucid moments, however. The other day in the dentist's waiting room he took a bishop to task for saying that it was 'fun' to go to church, the boy maintaining that as one went to church to get help in combating one's sins, it was a matter that could only be taken seriously.

WELLINGTON, 25.iii.61
TO FRITZ KRIEGER
The great drawback to the place is the wind. There are grey, tearing days which perhaps explain the high suicide rate and undercurrent of neurosis.

Dogwoods, 3.iv.61

TO PEGGY GARLAND

Otherwise the journey was uneventful. We ate Canterbury chops with decontaminated peas. The Customs were actually polite, and I shared a taxi into the city with two ladies called Maureen and Thelma (the latter had a cleft palate), who had apparently married from Sydney into New Zealand many years ago, and were trying to remember which street we were in. They did not seem to think much of New Zealand, while I was privately thinking very little of Sydney.

Dogwoods, 5.iv.61

TO FREDERICK GLOVER

Peggy is going ahead dividing the big rambling house into flats, after which I am advising her to think of going to England herself, as she may find proper treatment, and a school of some kind, for Philip. At times he is a great trial, cannot be left without flying into a passion, or worse, a state of nervous anxiety which leads to a breakdown. Certainly his brain was damaged at birth, but a lot of the trouble seems to be psychological. He is very childish in many ways, but has moments of great lucidity and insight. He will listen to music by the hour, and likes to talk about God, and to feed animals. The guinea pigs he keeps would get fed at all times of the day and night, sometimes in the most undesirable places, such as his bed, or on the kitchen table. The day Peggy went up to Auckland to see Tanya off,[1] I had promised to take him to the zoo, and we set off, but he was really only interested while he was stuffing the animals. Then he must always be stuffing himself, preferably with sweet things, with the result that he already has the figure of a Buddha. If they try to stop him, he goes into people's houses, or shops, and steals the sweet stuff. So that really you have a comparatively peaceful time, with Mother Almond safely in bed ...

Very hard up at the moment, in fact, as the result of the trip to N.Z. and the paintings I have bought recently, I have only enough in the bank to see me through the next fortnight, so I hope to God some dividends will start coming in, or the advances on the book. Otherwise I shall have to break into a sum I have put aside towards the big trip.

[1]Peggy's daughter Tanya was leaving for England.

DOGWOODS, 7.iv.61
TO MARSHALL BEST
Dear Marshall,

Thanks for your letter of March 16th. I forget exactly what I said about painting and music in connexion with writing. Still, if I disapprove of myself in what you concoct, I suppose I can say so. I tend to believe that what an author has to say to the public, he puts in his books. Letters are the devil, and I always hope that any I have written have been destroyed, excepting those which for business reasons have to go on file. Somerset Maugham had the right idea when he appealed to anybody possessing letters he had written to destroy them when he dies.

Katherine Mansfield is a good example of the letter-writer traduced. Did I write to you when I was in New Zealand recently? While I was there I handled a lot of her original letters and notebooks, which have lingered on to accuse her as a monster of sensibility and egotism. I would prefer to remember her by her stories, although I confess to being tremendously intrigued by the private, sometimes almost automatic outpourings. The cousin with whom I was staying in Wellington has a lodger in Anthony Alpers, who wrote an excellent life of K.M. which Knopf published a couple of years ago.[2] When I left the other day to come home, I was very pleased and touched by his giving me a little greenstone and silver paper-knife which had belonged to K.M.

You say in your letter that you are awaiting a photostat of the Sidney Nolan jacket from London. I am afraid you may continue to 'await' it, as Nolan has gone off to Egypt, and still no sign of a drawing of any sort. It is most disappointing. He is the one to do a jacket if he would only get down to it. I know he would understand the book. I know from his wife that it appealed to them. But he has been committed to so many things at once, including sets for a play, and now I feel too many Egyptian images will get in the way. However, there is just a faint hope. Things have a habit of rising up out of a painter's unconscious suddenly and without warning.[3]

NEWS BROKE ON 14 APRIL that the Governors of the Adelaide Festival had rejected *The Ham Funeral*. This was not the first time these Adelaide

---

[2] *Katherine Mansfield: A Biography*, 1953. Viking published Alpers' (1919–) second biography of K.M. in 1980, *The Life of Katherine Mansfield*.
[3] Temple Smith finally went to the studio and over Cynthia Nolan's vociferous objections chose a picture for the jacket of the E & S edition – perhaps the best-designed of any of PW's novels.

figures – brewers, businessmen, stockbrokers – had vetoed a Festival production: Alan Seymour's *The One Day of the Year* was earlier banned for casting a slur on the men and women of Australia's fighting forces. Now after a protracted brawl within the Festival organisation, the Governors decided to reject *The Ham Funeral* fearing, 'Its complexity will limit its appeal to a few high intellectuals and even they would find it difficult to interpret the so called psychological aspects of the play.'[4]

Crucial support for the Governors came from Neil Hutchison, the English chief executive of the Australian Elizabethan Trust (known as the Trust) established in 1954 with the high purpose of promoting theatre, opera and ballet in Australia. Short of cash and staffed by English imports, the Trust had had only limited success. By their action, the Governors and the Trust turned *The Ham Funeral* – whatever its qualities as a play – into a rallying point for those Australians exasperated by the nation's official culture.

News of the ban was carried across Australia and into the wider world of literature. Critics, commentators and cartoonists came to White's defence. For a few weeks he affected indifference and claimed he had expected nothing less from the Festival.

DOGWOODS, 2.v.61
TO GEOFFREY DUTTON
I find, after all, I got rather a battering over *The Ham Funeral*. My final reaction has been to sit down on May Day and start a new play, the first for fourteen years. The last two days it has been pouring out in almost an alarming way, and will probably shock more than the *Funeral*, as this one is purely Australian, and at the same time has burst right out of the prescribed four walls of Australian social realism. If I don't get this one on, and twist the tails of all the Adelaide aldermen, Elizabethan hack producers, and old maids dabbling in the Sydney theatre, I shall just about bust. The new one, by the way, is called *The Season at Sarsaparilla*, as it becomes rather tedious always to refer to 'the play', the 'book' etc.

DOGWOODS, 19.v.61
TO PHILIP GARLAND
Dear Philip,
I wonder how you have been getting on since I left Wellington. I hope the guinea pigs are flourishing, and continue to give you as much pleasure.

---

[4]Point (1) in 'Reasons Against *The Ham Funeral* as a Festival Production', the minority (2 to 10) report of the Drama Committee adopted by the Governors.

Recently we got another cat to replace the one that died while I was in New Zealand. We picked up the new one quite by accident, though, which is perhaps the best way of taking on a cat. One night we were taken to eat at a Chinese restaurant in one of the slummier parts of Sydney, and as we were leaving we heard a kitten's voice calling from down a very dark, smelly alley. We went down to investigate and found what should have been a white kitten, padding up and down, very friendly but apparently abandoned. We did not want to take him, as we have three others, but it was difficult not to, once we became friends with him. So we put him in the back of the car, and he has been with us ever since. At first he was a filthy grey colour, as if he were full of coal dust, and certainly swarming with fleas. He also had a sore on his lip, and rather persistent diarrhoea. But all that is past now. Manoly gave him two baths, and he is as white as Pearl, the other white cat we have. The new one is called Dixson, after the street where he was found.

Most of our pullets are laying at last, in fact, we now have too many eggs, and have to give a lot of them away. Still, it is good to be wallowing in eggs for a change – lots of omelettes and scrambled eggs – instead of counting every one and wondering whether you can manage it. Most of the fowls are white, with a few blacks, one enormous red, and a very pretty speckled grey hen, which is really the nicest, though the others dislike her, and persecute her because she is different. Fowls are very colour-conscious. The different colours all roost together, and won't allow one of the wrong colour to get anywhere near them.

Are you still listening so much to music? Lately I have been off it a bit, chiefly because there is something wrong with the gramophone. I think it must need new valves. The sound does not carry so well now, but perhaps it is just because I am getting deaf. I don't know that I am, but it could be that, I suppose. Mostly I listen when I am doing things in the kitchen, and you have to have it on fairly loud for that.

Next month I am going for about ten days to Queensland, the state to the north of New South Wales if you look at the map. I am going by sea, as I want to look at the coast from a ship, and it will take two days from Sydney to Brisbane. I have an idea it will be pretty awful, there is only one ship, and one sailing a month, but it can't be helped; that is the way I want to go. I shan't spend much time in Brisbane, except that I want to try to see a painter called Ian Fairweather who lives on an island off the coast. He is an old man of about 75, and hardly anyone has seen him. He has spent his life living on islands, and in swamps, and about ten years ago, tried to cross the sea from Darwin to Timor on a couple of petrol drums. I don't know whether he will want to see me, but I shall have a try. He is one of the best Australian painters. I have a big picture of his called 'Gethsemane' taking up the whole of one wall in my bedroom. So at least we shall have that link. After that I am going to take the train, and go to a place about a hundred miles north of Brisbane, and which I have an idea I may write about later on. It isn't all that necessary to have to see a place to write about it, but this time I feel I want to.

I hope you are still going to your lessons with Mrs Wood, and that you have learnt a lot by now. I am typing this because I think you will find it easier to read that way; a lot of people can't understand my writing. Now you will have to write back, as you promised, and tell me about everything. I shall always be interested to hear what you have to say.

I hope your mother and Sally are both well, and that you are a help to them. Remember that good sauce you made one night? I expect there are a lot of things like that you can do. You ought to make your own garden, and grow a few carrots for the guinea pigs.

Love –

Patrick.

MARYBOROUGH, 22.vi.61

TO PEGGY GARLAND

I am writing this from Maryborough, a deadly small town on the North Coast of Queensland, from which I hope to escape by to-night's train. I came here to go to Fraser Island, about 25 miles from M., without realising just how difficult that would be. The island is uninhabited except for some forestry workers, and a few people go there fishing, and camp in shacks on the ocean side. Boatmen wanted £25 to take me over to the island, which made me very depressed, as I didn't have enough money with me, and didn't want to pay so much in any case. Finally I arranged for £10 with a young man who pilots a small plane about the size of a taxi to fly me over most of the island (it is about 80 × 20 miles), and to land there on a rough air strip. We then walked several miles inland through the scrub, and by extreme good luck met a forestry truck – a kind of Emmett bomb,[5] held together by wire and string, with a fuel tank tied to the roof – which rushed us into the interior, a magnificent jungle of tallowwood, box, satinay, and blackbutt, with gullies full of palms, and vines strung from trunk to trunk. It was a rewarding day after all, as I now know what I want to know.

---

[5]Rowland Emett (1906–90), the *Punch* cartoonist who drew fanciful locomotives made of teapots, etc.

Brisbane on the way up here was much more sympathetic than I had expected. I imagine it would be terribly dull intellectually, but it is full of interesting ramshackle latticed houses built on stilts, and the people, just to meet them in the streets, are an amiable, extrovert race. I am afraid Sydney is really the blot on the Australian landscape. In some ways alive, it is full of hatefulness – and ugliness and bile.

The story of *The Ham Funeral* seems to have been broadcast far and wide. The latest is that an Adelaide group called the Adelaide University Theatre Guild is going to put it on in November to spite the Festival Board. The Guild has the use of what is supposed to be the most up-to-date theatre in Australia, and they are bringing the producer[6] and leading lady of my choice. (The only snag there is that the leading lady may be whisked off before November to appear in a play which is going from here to London.)[7] I am looking forward to none of it, as you can imagine and having to go all the way to Adelaide, sit in at rehearsals, and alter lines . . .

On the way back I have to break my journey at Grafton for a couple of days to placate the Glovers, but I am itching to get back – to peace, and one's own oasis. Except for the day I was on Fraser Island the radio hasn't stopped drooling in my ears – in hotels, in buses, in the streets, even in trains there has been the transistor in the next compartment.

Now I must go down and take a good stiff brandy before my last meal with the commercial travellers.

DOGWOODS, 28.vi.61
TO MARGERY WILLIAMS[8]
I am glad you met Roy,[9] and hope you will see more of him. I expect he does make women feel maternal. Many have doted on him, and I can see there must have been a strong element of the maternal in their doting. The way they would try to out do one another with the most delicious jar from Fortnum's. He has been very ill in recent years, and I always hope

---

[6]John Tasker (1933–88).
[7]Nita Pannell (1904–94), whose performance in *One Day of the Year* impressed PW; she was taken to London with the show; though unable to be the first Mrs Lusty, she was the first Miss Docker in *A Cheery Soul* and the first Miss Quoddling in *A Night on Bald Mountain*.
[8](1906–88), Sydney literary hostess who was to succeed Klári Daniel as the most devoted of PW's lady disciples. She was the lively wife of Norman Williams, British Council representative in Australia until his death in 1969. Her gossip was the seed of many short stories. PW told Peggy Garland, 20.xii.60, 'In the Middle East the British Council was always something of a joke, but we like these people, and it is exhilarating suddenly to stumble across somebody who speaks the same language.'
[9]de Maistre.

we shall see each other again. I am putting away as much as I possibly can from my new book, and perhaps we shall be able to make a proper trip in a couple of years time. (We want to go back to the Middle East, Greece of course, and see Southern Italy, Sicily, Spain, and Russia.)

DOGWOODS, 1.viii.61
TO BEN HUEBSCH

To return to *The Season at Sarsaparilla*, that is a kind of charade of suburbia, the season being a bitch's heat, and running parallel to that is the incident of a suburban nymphomaniac. It is a kind of folk piece with overtones, except that the Australians will probably miss the latter. There has not been time to get many reactions. The young producer who is being kept out, and whom I am trying to launch at the same time as my plays, is enthusiastic about it, I don't think altogether from policy, and so is Manoly, whose attitude to life and the arts is very sound. On the other hand a theatrically-minded friend who insisted on reading it found he was rather shocked.[10] The theatre is maddening to deal with, and I regret my desire to break into it. Too many (astrological) stars have to be in the right place. I can see I shall be driven mad by *The Ham Funeral* before it comes off in November. The theatre and the body of the cast are in Adelaide, the leading lady (if she is not whisked off to appear in a play in London) is in Perth, the producer and the author are in Sydney. So you can see there are some difficulties. This week I have to face the ordeal of a reading of the play by students of the Drama School at the University of New South Wales.[11] John Tasker, the producer, who is also a lecturer at that institution, has arranged it so that we can at least hear how the play sounds before it goes into production.

I gave the proof copy of *Riders* to Geoffrey Dutton who wrote the booklet I sent you, and he has gone off his head about it, but of course he is a very superior Australian. He feels there is going to be a lot of resentment in certain quarters. My greatest hope is that history will allow them the luxury of resentment.

JOHN TASKER WAS THE pale, flirtatious, caustic, beautiful, obstinate young man who brought the excitement of theatre back to the centre of White's

[10]This was Frederick Glover. PW replied, 22.vii.61, 'You have been so wound up in that high-falutin' Cocteau fustian, in which not one of the characters shows signs of having a natural orifice, that you were not prepared to consider the vulgarity of everyday life.'
[11]NIDA, the National Institute of Dramatic Art.

life. Lascaris called him 'the virus'. The son of a coalminer, he was rescued from the Hunter Valley at the age of eighteen by a lover who took him to study at the Central School of Speech and Drama in London. Tasker returned to Australia in 1959 full of energy and European ideas. 'One notices it,' said White, 'after the corny local productions.'[12] When the Adelaide University Guild took over *The Ham Funeral* from the Festival, White insisted they have John Tasker.

DOGWOODS, 13.viii.61
TO FREDERICK GLOVER

The reading of *The Ham Funeral* was quite interesting, if also an ordeal. I shall be relieved when the whole business is over and done with. At least quite a lot of it is effective, as the reading, or near acting on a rudimentary set, helped to show. The bits that came off best are the music-hall acts, such as the scene with the two scavengers (whom I substituted for the prostitutes), and the parts where the relatives do their stuff . . . The Young Man made a good attempt, but did not enunciate well enough or vary his facial expression, with the result that he became stodgy at times. However, it is an impossible, irritating, congealed part. If there is ever any self-pity in a character it shows up at once on the stage, and becomes a bore. I must try to loosen some of the Young Man's too literary speeches, and there are words and phrases throughout which do not go. The whole effect is that here is an opera looking for its music – but I don't suppose it will ever find that unless some young composer happens to become fired when the play is produced in Adelaide.

Another thing about the reading, it has convinced me *The Season at Sarsaparilla* will be ten times better as theatre. John Tasker thinks the latter is 'much more actable'. I asked him pointblank what he thinks of the young people. He said he thinks those of between age are too articulate and not sufficiently involved in the lives of their families, with the result that they will not get sympathy. But I feel that young people of that age very often are not involved. I never was. I just came and went. I remember once my mother burst into tears at breakfast, and said: 'Aren't you ever going to say anything to us?' One couldn't though, because they used to talk by the hour about vegetables and the weather. I have not yet had any other reactions, only a letter from Curtis Brown, London, to say the play had been received. Probably I have laid an enormous egg, but I have far

[12]This to Glover, 14.iii.60, after seeing Tasker's production of Sartre's *Lucifer and the Lord* at Sydney University.

more faith in it than I have in *The Ham Funeral,* which is at most a curiosity . . .

I have never read any of Genet's plays, but to read about them, he sounds as though he is doing the kind of thing I am aiming at in the theatre. But although I have three more plays in my head, I wonder whether I will continue. I find everything to do with it infuriating. Too much depends on what is beyond the author's control . . .

I forgot to mention that the students who read *The Ham Funeral* came back to John's flat afterwards, to discuss, and I found we actually spoke the same language. It was a most stimulating discovery, because the conventional, uncommunicative young always make me feel a hundred.

DOGWOODS, 15.viii.61
TO HARRY MEDLIN[13]

I am sorry not to have answered before, but the word 'lecture' always does something to me. I wonder why people always expect novelists to lecture. If I were able to lecture, I feel I should not be able to write novels. Anyway, I have never lectured in my life, and am afraid I must now disappoint those who expect me to in Adelaide. Nor can I speak on radio, or appear on television. In fact, I am in no way a public figure. I hope these deficiencies will not make things difficult for you. I do want to be present at rehearsals in case things have to be altered, but if more is expected of me than I am able to give, perhaps I could at least pay my own fare.

DOGWOODS, 13.ix.61
TO JOHN TASKER
Dear John,

I am enclosing a list of amendments to *The Ham Funeral.* I have taken out the few lines which you don't like in the prologue, and given a version somewhere between the two others. But I am not at all satisfied with the solution, and I would like Max Harris to arbitrate when you go over there for rehearsals. I thought this production was by way of being an Anti-Festival, and so my hit at the Governors was permissible. I have never been one to sit and smile sweetly when there was an offending eye to spit in, and there is, besides, a tradition of satiric rejoinder in English literature and drama. The attitude I always adopted with my novels was take-them-or-leave-them, and I did get there in time, although it was a long time. Now I would like to adopt the same attitude with my plays.[14]

---

[13](1920–   ), scientist, chairman of the Adelaide University Theatre Guild.
[14]The lines stayed out.

DOGWOODS, 28.ix.61
TO GEOFFREY DUTTON
Dear Geoffrey,
Your letter arrived yesterday, and today I received my copy of Meanjin with your 'Leisured Ladies', which I like immensely.[15] I feel the poem might develop into something larger. There is so little satire in Australian poetry. The pity at the moment is that none of our leisured ladies will read Meanjin – although I can make sure to dangle it in front of the one or two I know.

There must be many chariots of which I don't know. The reason I chose it as a symbol in the beginning was because it crops up so often even within my knowledge. Ezekiel's is the most obvious one to anybody like myself of a sketchy classical education,[16] but I have been haunted ever since I was a young man by the painting of an Apollonian chariot by Odilon Redon, which I saw in a Bond Street window.[17] It finally became the chariot by the unnamed French painter Dubbo sees in the art book. Redon was a minor painter, but his work has a peculiar magic, and apparently the idea of the chariot appealed to him too, as I saw another one in a gallery in Paris when we were over there in 1958. I had not started Riders, and it helped to spur me on. I wish I had known about Ovid's Phaeton. I must get hold of Sandys' translation:[18] the bit you quote is magnificent. Symbols must certainly work on an 'imaginative rather than an intellectual level', as you say. Surely one must deal with any detail of a work of art firstly on the 'imaginative level', and that is what is wrong with most Australian critics. Their lack of intuition makes them rush to dissect intellectually. Or am I saying this because I am stronger in intuition than in intellect? It is something that shamed me in my youth, but which age has made me accept as a blessing as well as a weakness. It is also one reason why I will never let myself be drawn into writing critical articles; when I am right about a work of art I am usually right, but cannot present my reasons in an intellectually satisfying manner. The feminine in me, I suppose! . . .

I must tell you about a remarkable thesis on The Tree of Man I read the other day.[19] It is by a housewife in Hawaii called Mrs Vivian Olsen,

---

[15]An account in verse of an empty day spent in monied Australia; Meanjin 3, 1960, p.310.
[16]Ezekiel 1, also 26:10.
[17]Redon (1840–1916), French precursor of Surrealism.
[18]Of Ovid's Metamorphosis from which Dutton had quoted a few lines describing Phaeton's calamitous drive across heaven; later he found a copy of the 1692 edition to give PW.
[19]Patrick White's The Tree of Man: A Study of Style, University of Hawaii, 1961.

who did it for the University of Hawaii, encouraged by a professor who came here as a Fulbright Scholar. She complains of working under great difficulties – two small children, and a neighbour on one side who conducts group ukulele lessons, and one on the other who listens to a radio programme which specialises in Hawaiian songs on the organ. Later on, when the children grow up, she thinks she may expand the thesis into something larger. She certainly gets on to things with a very sure nose, although she has confined herself here to a comparatively small area . . .

To-day I did a dreadful thing. I started another novel,[20] and am in that state of hope, fear, and frustration which goes with only the beginnings of fulfilment. You know all those admirable small touches which flood through one's mind, and which will only be forgotten before one can get them down on paper– – I can never decide whether to rush at it, or go cautiously. Well, there it is, the same awful muddle as usual, which somehow, one prays, will turn into a novel.

Yours
Patrick.

RIDERS IN THE CHARIOT appeared in early October in Australia, North America and Britain. The critics were enthusiastic: on the whole, this was the best batch of reviews White had ever had. 'Has there ever been, one wonders, a like work of literature,' asked his champion James Stern in the New York Times.[21] But in private Stern expressed misgivings.

[20]A Fringe of Leaves.
[21]New York Times Book Review, 8 Oct., p.4.

Dogwoods, 16.x.61

TO JAMES STERN

Dear Jimmy,

Thanks very much for your letter, as well as for the review in the *N. Y. Times*. As reviewing I did not find it as good as the one on *The Tree of Man*, but you yourself have said that. However, it was most generous and enthusiastic, and did me a lot of good after the stinking little piece they gave me in *Time* magazine. I don't know whether you saw that. It starts off with a thumping lie: that no American critic had ever been very impressed by any of my books: the most these had done was elicit a few expressions of polite surprise from the English. It then goes on not to review, but to dismiss the book in a couple of paragraphs, on the grounds that it is unintelligible and that I am more interested in words than people. The whole thing smelled a bit fishy – as if there were literary or publishing politics behind it, somebody had a German grandmother, or perhaps even an Australian writer had infiltrated.[22] So far there has been nothing else from anywhere. Whether there has been a delay or I have simply laid a large Egg, I don't know. I am inclined to think there are some other shocking reviews, as my agent has sent your review – twice – and failed to mention *Time* magazine at all, quite forgetting that everyone in the world sees that wretched rag.

I am going to try to answer the criticism in your letter (including the things to which Mrs B. objects). Himmelfarb tries to make Rosetree admit to his Jewishness when overcome by a longing to associate with somebody of his own, particularly in what has remained for him rather a forbidding country. That longing grows even stronger on the *Seder* night,[23] when he is shattered by his surroundings and the attempt to celebrate on his own what should have been a family feast. So he sets out for Rosetrees', as they are the people who would come most obviously to mind. I refer to Himmelfarb constantly as 'the Jew' on account of what was being prepared for him. I wanted to establish in the reader's unconscious a connexion between him and the other 'Jew'.

'Housekeeper' in Australian usually means a 'working general'. In Miss Hare's engaging a housekeeper at the end of the War, I wanted to imply

---

[22]Complaining to Huebsch, 3.xi.61, about this unsigned 'monstrosity in *Time*', PW wrote: 'It sounded to me very like an Australian writer. At one time a woman novelist called Christina Stead was cornering and demolishing other Australian novels in *Time*. She had started off being quite brilliant as a novelist in her own right, then married – and dried up creatively.' But the reviewer, 6 Oct. p.66, was American Brad Darrach.

[23]The first night of Passover.

another attempt on her part to make human contact. Mrs Jolley's duties, which you say remain vague, were to clean and cook, and God knows I have shown her sweeping and baking, wrestling with cobwebs, and so forth. There was, besides, a tradition of servants in the Hare family and this was a little attempt on the part of Miss H. to restore it. Mrs Jolley's remaining with her appears a little mysterious at first, but it finally becomes clear that she is afraid of something that has happened, in fact, a feeling that she may have 'murdered' her husband. Then, of course, her daughters are unwilling to have her and she thinks more than once about getting into the clutches of Mrs Flack, in spite of her infatuation. Mrs B. complains that I do not show anything, or enough of the domestic side of Miss Hare's life, but she is there primarily because she is the *Erdgeist*, and I am more interested in her inner life. If I had become involved in a lot of little domestic details à la *Tree of Man*, there would have been no end to *Riders*. I had to interweave four pretty important lives, and so I concentrated on what would reveal their essence.

Dubbo does some very squalid things. One reason is that the Australian aboriginal in contact with civilisation is a very squalid creature. (I have even read an account of aboriginals in their normal state in the last century eating maggots, and the lice on one another's heads.) I also wanted a contrast between D.'s physical squalor and depravity, and his devotion to his gift. I feel his gift would have been the less if he had not experienced the depths. (I am convinced of that in my own case.)

I wonder if Mrs B. is a renegade Jew uneasy about her own apostasy. Some of her remarks about Himmelfarb make me think so. Surely it is possible for anybody who has been a rebel to discover or re-discover faith? It is more than possible: it is happening all the time. I was brought up as an orthodox Anglican, went through youth believing in nothing but my own ego, because I had to rebel against my family and imagine I was an intellectual. In the beginning, I suppose, I had 'believed' only in the conventional, infantile sense. Then, towards the end of my thirties, when everything was going wrong, I can remember a day when I stood in the rain, the water up to my ankles, and pouring off me, as I proceeded to curse God. Not long after that faith began to come to me. So it is surely possible for Himmelfarb to return to a faith as possessive as the Jewish one. Certainly in my own case I did not return to orthodox Anglicanism, but the Anglican church is a feeble organisation compared with the Jewish faith. I made the attempt, found that Churches destroy the mystery of God, and had to evolve symbols of my own through which to worship.

There is obscenity in *Riders*, for reasons I have partly explained in the bit on Dubbo. It is permissible to use discords in music, why can't one use obscene words where necessary to convey a certain effect? I don't think I have used them recklessly, certainly not in the few instances I can remember offhand. Himmelfarb returning from the hopeless visit to the Rosetrees on the *Seder* night: 'The train farted extra good– –' etc. The whole return journey is expressive of hopelessness and despair, both for what has happened to him, and for the ugliness and awfulness with which he is surrounded. The 'fart' is followed by the psalmist's version of the popular song heard on the radio. The whole thing is an indictment. He admits later, on touching the *mezuzah*,[24] that hate has got the better of him. (As it does get the better of me from time to time in this in many ways hateful, philistine, ugly and complacent country. I have to confess I wrote the description of Himmelfarb's journey home on the *Seder* evening before I began to write the book, although it had been forming in my head for some years. I was in bed with bronchitis at the time, and there had been a particularly vicious attack on *Voss* by one of my chief Australian detractors. Then suddenly I found myself reacting in a notebook in the disguise of Himmelfarb) All that is by the way. To return to the point, I have deliberately used the word 'shit' in a couple of places to produce a shock discord: the smell of it to emphasise the 'slime of despair' as the Jewish mother wipes her sick child when they are waiting in the shed for the train which will cart them off; again where Miss Hare is chasing Mrs Jolley through the house and the 'brown word' shoots out of her memory as she tries to defend her dear, her good Jew, and for the first time she begins to accept the Christian image which Peg had always offered without success.

To return to the question of hate: there is also love in the book, Mrs Godbold – as Mrs Chalmers-Robinson realises in her old age: 'the rock of love on which we have all foundered.' (I think it is Mrs Colquhoun who helps her complete the image.)

It would have been quite impossible for me to write *Riders* in the same vein as *The Tree of Man*. Stan and Amy are like characters out of my childhood or from recollections of my parents. I was always fascinated hearing them talk about the last century. It had a glow of morning. But only the saints, the Mrs Godbolds, are innocent to-day . . .

Manoly's back is a lot improved since he started to wear a corset on the advice of a specialist. The drawback is that the corset, while easing the strain on the displaced vertebra, causes discomfort of other kinds –

[24]A little case of scriptures on the doorpost.

wind, and so forth. It has to be worn very tight, and there is a great steel plate up the back.

Best wishes for your wedding anniversary and the trip to the Loire.

Yrs

Patrick

My enthusiasm seems to have got the better of my ability to type!

DOGWOODS, 30.x.61

TO JOHN TASKER

Riders in the Chariot keeps on exploding at every letter delivery. I have now had all the important American reviews, most of them very good. I have even had, for the first time ever, a remarkably good review in the *Sydney Morning Herald*, from Charles Higham of all people, when I imagined he would neither like nor understand the book, but his review is very well constructed and worded. He is a bit extravagant in his praise, but as we know, that is nice once in a while. Now the English have begun. A very good one in the *Manchester Guardian* by somebody called Jeremy Brooks. A very familiar name, but I can't place it. Very enthusiastic, but inaccurate in the *Express*, good but dreary in the *Telegraph* from Daniel George, and one of those grudging, <u>pallid</u> pieces in the daily *Times* – the kind I always get from them – as if they are afraid to go along with somebody who has been so indiscreet as to commit himself. I am told there is a very good one by Pringle in the *London Magazine*. Not yet arrived[25] . . .

It was unwise of me to have started the new novel at this point, but having started I cannot leave off, although the only time when I can protect myself enough from outside events is from midnight till 4 a.m., when I rise from my bed and really get to work. I have not yet seen or met Vivien Leigh, but funnily enough she is mixed up with all this; I can't stop seeing her as the woman in the novel. It would make a good film if it weren't for the fact that she and her leading man – Burt Lancaster for preference – would have to go through most of the action practically stark naked.

Had a very nice letter from Sid Nolan, and the original of the *Riders* jacket so my collection of Nolans is growing without my ever having bought one! This painting is so much subtler and to the point when you actually see it; one would say it had actually been designed for the book,

[25]Higham, *SMH*, 28 Oct., p.12; Brooks, *Guardian*, 27 Oct., p.7; Peter Forster, *Express*, 26 Oct., p.6; George, London *Telegraph*, 27 Oct., p.21; *Times*, 26 Oct., p.16; Pringle (who as editor of *SMH* had commissioned Hope's 'verbal sludge' review), *London Magazine*, Nov. 1961, p.68.

which in fact was not the case. I do hope the Nolans will come back here.
His painting gives me such a lot in my work, and he claims I do the same
for him . . .

Must stop. There's a whole kitchenful of washing up. Looking forward
to seeing you all next week, not only to escape these depressing duties,
but because I feel you are really making something happen. (Have taken
a ticket in the Opera House Lottery to float my New Venture Players in
Chekhov, Ibsen, Dürrenmatt, Ghelderode,[26] Genet, Brecht – and even –
you must allow the impresario one touch of vanity – Patrick White.
Direction, of course: John Tasker. And a talent of players, including the
lustiest of <u>true</u> Elizabethan-style actresses – Joan Bruce.[27]

Yours

Patrick.

DOGWOODS, 30.x.61

TO GEOFFREY DUTTON

I am reading your *Whitman*[28] with great interest . . . I had only seen
photographs of W. as an old man, so the photograph on the cover of your
book is particularly interesting. There he is – trying to seduce even the
anonymous reader with that repellent mouth and his bedroomy, woman's
eyes. Even his brand of mixed-up homosexuality is irritating; one longs to
hear of him having an honest-to-God root with one of his bus-drivers
instead of sitting there fumbling with the tickets.

DOGWOODS, 3.xi.61

TO BEN HUEBSCH

Next week I fly to Adelaide for last rehearsals and first performances of
The Ham Funeral. I hear exciting reports of it. The young man who is
producing it seems to have felt his way through to its significance at last,
and the play has hatched, as it were. I am now looking forward to what I
had been dreading. Since all this began the same people in Adelaide have
asked for an option on my second play *The Season at Sarsaparilla* . . .

We are vaguely planning to start on a trip about April 1963, if it will

[26]Michel de Ghelderode (1898–1962), macabre Belgian satirist of human folly. PW told
Stern, 9.v.62, 'I think more of him than of Brecht. For all his wonderful bits, the latter has
some terrible longueurs.'

[27](c.1926–), an English actress working in Australia since 1954 was now to play the
Landlady in place of Nita Pannell; her performance in *The Ham Funeral* established her
considerable reputation in Australian theatre.

[28]Oliver & Boyd, Edinburgh, 1961.

still be possible to travel. I am even thinking of sticking my head in the lion's jaws this time, but only if I am allowed to go to the places I want. I want to see Kiev, the Caucasus, the Caspian, and the Crimea. Also I don't want to go to Russia as a writer. Actually I am described as a farmer on my passport. I suppose they might find out that I am not, or else they wouldn't find out, and I should be sent to look at endless collective farms, either of which fates would be awful. This time we shall return to the Middle East, as I want to see a number of places I have missed, like the monastery on Mount Sinai, Petra, Trebizond, Constantinople, and Athos. I also want to go to Spain which I don't know at all. So let us hope we shall meet again in Europe. Rome? That I think would be pleasanter than Milan, though I wouldn't mind a few days on one of the lakes.

Hoping you are well, and not too troubled by all the international horrors.[29]

Yours,
Patrick.

Dogwoods, 20.xi.61
TO FREDERICK GLOVER
Dear Frederick,
We have been wondering how all this rain has affected the Clarence,[30] and whether you are preparing to send Mother off in a duck. I hope you are escaping some of the deluge. I returned on Friday – two hours late, after flying all the way through cloud, and such headwinds that we were forced to land at Wagga, and refuel. This morning Manoly flew off; I hope he has landed safely, and presume he has, as I have not heard.

Well, Adelaide was a whirl of excitement. I shall probably never be able to remember it distinctly. It was wonderful the way everything went right after fourteen years of waiting, and so many attempts to prevent the play coming to life. The whole thing looked beautiful, although John and Stan Ostoja[31] were daggers drawn by the end of it, the acting very good indeed, the audience enthusiastic, the critics behind us ... The best performances came from Joan Bruce ... terrific in the scene where Mrs Lusty has hysterics at the funeral feast. But there are many bits that I shall re-live.

[29]The Russians that week exploded two nuclear bombs: 50 megatons one day and about 30 the next.
[30]The river that flows through, and often across, Grafton.
[31]The designer Stan Ostoja-Kotkowski (1922–94).

I think the repercussions are going to be most interesting. Last night we went to a party given by the British Council for John Betjeman (whom we liked immensely), and there we found all the heads of the Establishment. We arrived about an hour late, so that they were already conveniently drunk. Poor old Evelyn[32] was quite alarming – like a tottery ferret: I'm afraid she'll end up having a stroke at one of these parties, although I expect shock at the success of The Ham Funeral was largely responsible for her behaviour at this one. I had to say: 'You see, John Tasker did have it after all.' She replied: 'At least you must admit I saved you from Kevon Kemp.'[33] (At one time the latter tried to coax me into putting up money for a theatre, but as I hadn't the money I was really in no danger.) After that Manoly heard her muttering: 'I must make Patrick like Neil.' Because the Fat Boy[34] himself was there. He came up rather whimsically and said: 'Are you going to let the Trust do something about it?' I did not act all that keen, so he started scribbling telephone numbers and arranging lunches. Moses[35] was also there, kept squeezing my arm and trying to make me promise to spend a day at the wood-chopping at Sydney Royal. You can imagine how I reacted to that, and he stood there saying: 'See, he won't promise, he won't promise.' Finally I said: 'If I promise to come to the wood-chopping, you must promise to give us a conductor.'[36] So then I was told the tale of woe. At one stage he said: 'Neil, you know, was a wonderful radio man.' I could not resist: 'Why not take him back into radio?' In fact, it was a game of Aunt Sally such as I have never experienced . . .

Another great event: on Tuesday I am dining with Stravinsky! Hannah Lloyd-Jones has asked me.[37] She said he was most anxious to meet me, but I expect that was just a way of laying the social bait. Anyway, I am going, however difficult it may be as Manoly will still be in Adelaide, and I shall have to trail to Edgecliff in a series of cars, trains, and buses. Still, I would walk to Katoomba for Stravinsky.

More than ever I felt I want to live in Adelaide. One feels happy just walking about the streets, as we discovered when we were there five or six years ago, and now of course I have many friends. Max[38] is really a

[32]Tildesley.
[33](1922–78), critic and wine buff.
[34]The Fat Boy =Neil Hutchison, ex-BBC, ex-ABC.
[35]Charles Moses (1900–88), general manager of the ABC, director of the Elizabethan Theatre Trust and a keen amateur axeman.
[36]For the ABC's Sydney Symphony Orchestra.
[37]Hannah Lloyd-Jones (pre-1900–1982), widow of the proprietor of PW's favourite Sydney store, David Jones.
[38]Harris.

marvel at organising any kind of campaign, and the Duttons are a home from home. We went out to Anlaby one day – very manorial, and old Mrs Dutton is straight out of *The Chalk Garden*. There is such a similarity you would have laughed. I also had a long talk with Panayota, the ex-coolie of Manoly's Aunt Anastasia – rather a tragic little woman, who can barely speak English, and so is unable to communicate adequately with her mistress. However, the mistress's family say it is better that way.

DOGWOODS, 20.xi.61

TO PEGGY GARLAND

Since I began, the famous dinner with Stravinsky has taken place. He was quite different from what I expected – which was something tall, cold, and cerebral. In reality he is a dear old thing, but very old, tiny, and arthritic. His wife is a kind of St Bernard; one imagines her carrying him about the house in her teeth. Robert Craft, the young American conductor, who is the Boswell to Stravinsky's Johnson, and chief interpreter of his music, seemed somewhat peevish last night. Perhaps not enough attention. Stravinsky and I sat together at dinner. He told me: 'I am a professional drunkard. All the time I drink whisky, whisky, whisky!' I must say he held it very well. During dessert he passed me shelled walnuts on the palm of his very soft hand. Lots of rings.

DOGWOODS, 18.i.62

TO THE DUTTONS

I tried to get back to the novel, but the theatre upheavals have left me too unsettled. I am better able at the moment to work off my feelings in the short stories, in short bursts of rage and disgust. I hadn't written one for about twenty years when I suddenly put 'Willy Wagtails' on paper. I never felt I was suited to the short story, and those I had written were too weak to worry about. I think probably I have come to it now, apart from the emotional reasons, through the artificiality of the theatre. There is something a bit dishonest about the short story, just as there is about a play. Last night I finished another story called 'Being Kind to Titina', which I am sending to Christesen in case the moans start coming from Melbourne. I'll send you a copy some time to have a look at. It is based on Manoly's childhood and youth in Alexandria and Athens. There is a novel I want to write one day, about a boy growing up in those places, in a large family, and ending with the German invasion of Greece. I think of it under the title of 'My Athenian Family', and see it as a kind of Greek version of a Turner sunset with a lot of brown Byzantine figures in the foreground – at least the closing scenes, with the Germans approaching

Athens, and refugees leaving.[39] Don't know when I shall get round to all this, and I would like to spend a couple more years in Greece first. Anyway, the 'Titina' story is a sketch for the novel. Next week I imagine I shall have to start altering lines in *The Season at Sarsaparilla*, but I have at least three more stories I want to get off with this batch.

I hadn't realised you were going to Tasmania. Is that in connexion with the University? I must say I envy you. I have always wanted to go back there after spending an idyllic, Rocky-Point[40] kind of summer at a place called Brown's River near Hobart when I was five years old. In those days there was hardly anything there beyond a few wooden houses, beach, jetty, and fields of raspberry canes, to which I would be sent early in the morning by my mother to bring back punnets of fruit. There was also a wonderful deserted place called Blackmans Bay, to which we used to go for walks with a lot of other children and nurses. I expect you will see McAuley down there.[41] He struck me as being much happier and more human when I met him recently – the result of getting Sydney out of his system, I expect.

Sooner or later the Council is going to grab some of our land, I feel, and then I think the move must be made to Mount Lofty.[42] Or will that, too, be overrun in a couple of years? Perhaps Tasmania is the answer.

I have a pile of unanswered letters, some of which I must attempt to answer. Some most embarrassing poems by an erotic North Sydney teenager: all about virgins holding their thighs. I shouldn't, but can't resist telling you that her name is—Willing. (Please don't pass that on; I find I can say nothing nowadays.)

DOGWOODS, 2.ii.62
TO BEN HUEBSCH
A friend of mine,[43] a Viennese Jew who has lived here for the last twenty-five years, has just returned from a trip to the States and Mexico. He says it has confirmed his belief that Australia is probably the most boring

---

[39]One of PW's favourite paintings was Turner's 'Interior at Petworth'. He told Mary Benson, 30.vi.71: 'I used to go and look at it almost every Sunday when I was living in London in my youth: besides being a subtle painting I feel it taught me a lot about writing.' Late Turners, he told Penny Coleing, 23.vi.71, made him, 'grow breathless with delight every time I see them'.

[40]The cliff on Kangaroo Island where the Duttons had a holiday house.

[41]The poet James McAuley (1917–76), one of the perpetrators of the Ern Malley hoax, recently appointed reader in poetry at the University of Tasmania.

[42]In the Adelaide Hills near the Duttons.

[43]Fritz Krieger, but their friendship was almost at an end.

country in the world, but for all that, he would rather have it the way it is to live in. I cannot agree with him on both points. But we <u>are</u> a boring race, and the constant realisation of it makes me desperate. I do feel, however, that the change is taking place, only very, very slowly; there is so much dead wood keeping the live growth back. The heads of Establishments are still telling us what is good for Australians. English throw-outs still flock here to teach us, and there is a dreadful atmosphere of Adult Education in which no art can flourish. One had hopes of the Jews who came here after the Troubles, but on the whole they have been a disappointment. They have given us doctors, handbags, and *Torten*. But in the arts, they lurk in a thicket of Brahms and Richard Strauss; visually, wild horses wouldn't drag them farther than Kokoschka . . .

Had a letter yesterday from Mrs Untermeyer.[44] She finds the ending of *Riders* 'contrived'. This seems to be a very fashionable word. But isn't a work of art contrived, unless it is a naturalistic novel, or an academic painting? What about all the great set-pieces of Crucifixions in painting down the ages? What I tried to bring off was a literary, contemporary version of one of those set-pieces which we know so well. 'Contrived', certainly.

DOGWOODS, 19.iii.62

TO FREDERICK GLOVER

When I said I have given up drink, I really have. One night while John was rehearsing *The Break*[45] we went with him to a meeting of Alcoholics Anonymous. I was so impressed by what I heard, and convinced that I had crossed the borderline that I have not drunk a drop since that evening, just a month ago. Life at times is very dreary without, but I realise it had begun to get hold of me; I was depending on it too much, and starting to drink earlier in the evening every month or so. I think the boredom of life in Australia is really what made me take to it – the endless household drudgery, and that sort of thing. It is always getting between one and the work that really matters, and of course there is no way out. The houses in which one lives to-day are not made for servants, even if one could afford to pay for one[46] . . .

John was here to-day discussing *The Season at Sarsaparilla* which he

---

[44]Jean Starr Untermeyer (1886–1970), American poet and translator who had given PW his introduction to Huebsch in 1939; PW told Spud Johnson, 24.xii.39, her verse has 'too much watery abstraction and not enough feeling for objects.'

[45]Drama by Philip Albright set in Potts Point, directed by John Tasker.

[46]This was the first of several occasions PW gave up alcohol for a few months.

will produce in Adelaide probably about June. I shall have to try to alter various things, which I always hate doing, so boring tucking into cold pudding. We also had the Prerauers here during the week with their German translation of *The Ham Funeral*. It reads wonderfully well in Berlin dialect. In fact, I think it sounds better in German than in English.[47]

    Yrs

    Patrick.

DOGWOODS, 29.iv.62

TO BEN HUEBSCH

I have begun to feel the five or six novels I still have inside me might just be novels, and that I must do quite a lot of stocktaking before I start anything else of that nature. I think perhaps when I do write a novel it will be something I have never contemplated writing before. I don't yet quite understand what has happened, but something has, both inside and out. I have just celebrated these suspicions by having the worst asthmatic blow-out I have experienced in ten years, and still feel rather groggy, while at the same time, stimulated! I suppose it all amounts to this: if I went on as I have been doing I should soon find myself a comfortable mediocrity, whereas I am looking for an unopened door, through which I can step and find myself rejuvenated.

DOGWOODS, 14.v.62

TO PEGGY GARLAND[48]

Dear Peggy,

There was no date on your last long letter, so I don't know how guilty I am in not answering it before, but I think it came quite a long time ago. In it you say Philip had been two months at the Bethlehem Hospital. I wonder where that is exactly.[49] Anyway, it sounds a good thing to have got him in there, if he likes the doctor so much, and I hope the plan for the Rudolf Steiner school will also work out all right. Strange and terrible that he should have tried twice to kill himself. He cannot be so very

---

[47]Translated by the critic Curt (1901–67) and his wife, the singer and critic Maria. They also translated *Season at Sarsaparilla* but neither was performed. The agents Kiepenheuer of Berlin spoke of difficulties presented by the 'language of emigrants who had not had the opportunity to observe and to feel the development of German language after the war'. But the Prerauers' colloquial translation of *Summer of the Seventeenth Doll* enjoyed great success in Germany and Austria. In 1969 Kiepenheuer & Witsch published their translation of *Riders in the Chariot*.

[48]Now in London.

[49]At De Crespigny Park, SE5.

backward to have had the urge. I suppose it was during some of those flashes of intuition he has.

I am glad you have got something out of the Maritain.[50] I am certainly not intellectual enough to be able to follow it all, but it did not seem to matter – the way one takes it for granted, or at least I do, that one cannot understand every inch of paint or note of music. Everything I have done has been done through intuition rather than through reason, so perhaps that is why I was particularly enthusiastic about the Maritain. It is also why I cannot get most Australian intellectuals to accept him, and why so many of them hate my books. Still, there are more and more coming round, and I get fantastic letters from all kinds of people, some sophisticated, some who look as though they can barely write, and yet from what they say, one can see they have understood what I have tried to convey. It is, I suppose, that the mind which works by reason alone the average Australian mind I should say, is incapable of understanding . . .

After writing about one third of a 19th Century novel last year, I began to feel it was too remote, and that one should do more about one's own period. There is too much dabbling in the past in Australia I think, almost a National Trust in literature. So while I take stock I have been writing short stories, and becoming quite fascinated by the form. Of course they remain superficial by comparison with the novel, but one can very often convey some interesting overtones. I have just sold one called 'A Cheery Soul' to the London Magazine, which I think will be in their September issue. I think it is one of my better stories, and they have asked for more. I am now roughing out a play version of the same story, and find things fall into place as though the original idea had already been in my mind as a play. Perhaps this short story phase is the result of having Katherine Mansfield's paperknife on my mantelpiece . . .

The last couple of days we have been having about the worst downpour we have experienced at Dogwoods. Very depressing and exhausting. One feels in the end as though the sound is boring into one's head, and all the animal business at once becomes so complicated. As well as the ancient surviving schnauzer, Maggy, we now have two small dogs, a miniature pinscher, Lucy, and a pug called Fanny. I had always wanted a pug. This one has something of our great-aunt Annie at Cheltenham except that she is far more lively and intelligent.

---

[50]Creative Intuition in Art and Poetry, 1953, by Jacques Maritain (1882–1973), philosopher, Catholic theologian and teacher in France and North America.

Dogwoods, 24.vi.62

TO GEOFFREY DUTTON

I am up to my eyes in plays at present. I am halfway through the second version of my new one *A Cheery Soul* . . . it seemed to be all ready in my head, tucked away behind the story version which I sent to the *London Magazine*. The other day I was a bit disturbed, however, to read that there is a play about a home for old people by Arden called *The Happy Haven*, and mine takes place partly in a home for old people. Still, from what I read we make two very different approaches. Mine is a portrait of one woman – a wrecker, who first of all almost destroys two private lives, then a home for old people, and finally the Church, by her obsession that what she is doing for other people is for their own good. Only at the end for a moment she gets a glimpse of the truth when a dog lifts his leg on her in the street.

The rehearsals of *The Ham Funeral* are going well, I am told.[51] I am keeping well away from them as I don't want to be interrupted in my present work. One thing disgusts me, and that is the publicity that is being put out about the play. It looks as though they are trying to sell it as a 'spicy evening', and in doing so I feel they are going to put off a lot of the genuine supporters without bringing in more than a few of the morons at whom the publicity is aimed. I suppose one would have to expect an attitude like this in a place like Sydney. It is really one of the lowest places on earth. (Incidentally I have written to Hutchison to say we had better get together. It is far too complicated standing off from each other when involved in a thing like this.)

The reading of *The Season at Sarsaparilla* was very effective indeed. John had been having the jitters about it, and now I feel he has more faith in the play. Thank you for your invitation to stay when Manoly and I go over to Adelaide. I expect we shall work it as before, in relays, as it would be too complicated to make arrangements for the animals and both go over at the same time.

We had heard from Panayota about the arrangement with your sister.[52] We are only trying to puzzle out how Panayota comes to refer to her always as Mrs 'Planwit'. Presumably that is a version of 'Blackburn', or is it a corruption of a Christian name we don't know?

I had an interesting session last week with a young nun from Canberra who came up to the Dominican Convent at Strathfield to cross-question

---

[51] The play opened in Sydney at the Palace on 6 July.

[52] Old Mrs Dutton had died at last and the elderly Greeks were now to work for Dutton's sister Helen Blackburn.

me on my novels, on which she is writing her M.A. thesis. I had always imagined the Dominicans were a very austere, enclosed order, but not a bit of it. To begin with she announced by letter that she would be prepared to come to my home if I preferred that, but I preferred to get my foot inside the convent to see what that was like. The interview took place in a large cold, incredibly clean room, which we had entirely to ourselves – another surprise. She was an extremely intelligent young woman, far more intellectual than I, and I'm sure many of my answers must have been most disappointing to her. She was trying desperately hard to keep things on the rational plane, whereas I was bringing it back all the time to the intuitive one. I also had to admit that I am not a Christian, but that I believed in Christ as a means by which God reveals Himself. After the interrogation I was given a sumptuous lunch in a private dining room, waited on by three elderly, superior nuns. One of them, I gathered, was the Mother Superior who brought Sister Mary Catherine Norton up from Canberra. We made a great deal of polite conversation, which rather interfered with my tucking into the lunch. However, it was all very delightful, and I suppose I should now be drawn into the Church. I am certainly sorry I shall have no excuse for going back there to see my nuns.

Hope all is well with you all –

Patrick

Thank you in advance for the wine. It is a bit alarming to have reached 50, especially as my eyes and ears seem to be celebrating it by going off. I must see about new glasses very soon.

ZOE CALDWELL, ONE OF the 'loves' of White's life, had joined the Sydney cast of *The Ham Funeral*. She was the daughter of a Melbourne dancing teacher, made her debut at eleven, joined John Sumner's Union Theatre Company, then spent five hectic and successful years in Britain and Canada before returning in 1962 to play St Joan in Australia. White was entranced by Zoe. She wanted to play the slattern Nola Boyle in *The Season at Sarsaparilla* and White agreed, though she wasn't built for the part: 'Zoe is minute, with a sharp, rather fine face, whereas Nola Boyle is a big blowsy overflowing blonde about ten years older.'[53] But first she played the Girl in *The Ham Funeral* in Sydney in July.

The designer Desmond Digby was a second friend made at this time. 'The campest number I have ever met,' was White's first impression.[54] And he loved the banter, the hectic conversations: theirs was one of the great

[53]PW to Medlin, 15.v.62.
[54]PW told Glover, 7.ix.61.

telephone friendships. Digby grew up in New Zealand – he knew some of Peggy Garland's children – studied set design at the Slade and worked at Glyndebourne before coming to Sydney in 1959. His paintings sold well, but to White's chagrin Digby's real ambition was to design for the opera. Now, despite furious protests from Tasker, White asked Digby to design the first *Sarsaparilla*. His 'brilliant effort'[55] set the seal on this enduring friendship.

DOGWOODS, 18.vii.62
TO THE DUTTONS
Dear Nin and Geoffrey,
I hope you will have understood why I haven't written before to thank you for the magnificent present of wine. There has been a terrible lot of running to and fro, arguments, and even rows in connexion with play productions, and finally *The Ham Funeral* was launched. I complicated matters by starting to write another play *A Cheery Soul* in the middle of it. Between ourselves I think it was a protective measure, so that I could shout at people: 'Don't come near me; I'm writing a play!' I must say it was a godsend, being able to burrow into something positive and forget the chaos . . .

I expect you heard something of the launching of *The Ham Funeral* from Beryl Pearce.[56] It was a wonderful night from my point of view. I was well bricked up in a pillar of alcohol, and watched from the back row of the circle. I don't think I have ever been in such a full theatre in Sydney, and the audience was with the play. (We had a most depressing dress rehearsal audience, which laughed in all the wrong places, and sent us home to bed in a state of despair.) Since then houses have been very good on the whole, and I am wondering whether they will extend their miserably short season. The *Herald*, *Sun* and *Mirror* all gave excellent reviews.[57] The *Telegraph* panned it, but that was to be expected,[58] and the semi-literate, exhibitionist gossip females like Mrs Dekyvere and Andrea are doing their

[55]PW to Glover, 5.ix.62.
[56]Secretary of the Adelaide University Theatre Guild.
[57]All 12 July: *SMH*, p.7; *Sun*, p.34; *Mirror*, p.9.
[58]12 July, p.43. David McNicoll (1914–), poet and editor-in-chief of Frank Packer's sclerotic but popular *Telegraph* and *Sunday Telegraph*, had known the Whites at Lulworth – where he courted Suzanne briefly – and promoted in Packer's papers the verdict of Sydney society that it was ludicrous for a grazier's offspring to live and write in PW's way. McNicoll occasionally needled PW in his 'Bennelong' column and gave rein to those journalists PW called 'the Packer pack' – Ross Campbell, Cyril Pearl, etc. – who disliked the novels and mocked the plays.

best to keep people away. Certainly I snubbed Mrs D. on the first night by refusing to be photographed with her[59] ...

Beryl told me you had resigned from the University. I wonder whether that means you have decided to settle at Anlaby. We also heard from Panayota that you and the 'Planwits' had all been out there, and that some men had been there to 'count the furniture'[60] ...

I am sending A Cheery Soul to Perth to Nita Pannell, as she is the one I have always heard in the part of Miss Docker, the cheery soul. I think it is the part she has been waiting for.

Manoly has been coughing and sneezing for weeks with a flu cold which won't go away. Miraculously I have escaped it. I think I have been so busy I haven't found time for a cold. Sunday was a sad day; we put the last of the schnauzers to sleep – she[61] would have been fourteen to-day. Twenty years of the one strain is quite a long time, and I feel depressed and guilty on being without at least one of them. However, one can't go on into old age with large hairy dogs to be stripped and de-ticked. The house is empty of dogs at the moment, as the pug and the pinscher are in the catharsis cage having a season.

Hope you are sorting out your affairs satisfactorily, and that we shall meet in a few weeks time. Incidentally I was sent a copy of Hemisphere, and thought you had written a well-condensed article.[62]

Yours

Patrick

Saw Max[63] for a few seconds on the first night, emerging with walking stick from the lavatory.

---

[59]Nola Dekyvere (1904–91), tireless charity queen and columnist, one of the younger circle that gathered round Ruth White during the war, attacked The Ham Funeral for 'sordidness and bad language' in one of the first columns she wrote for Packer's Sunday Telegraph, 15 July, p.51. A few days later they came face to face at an exhibition of Desmond Digby's paintings and had a civil disagreement reported on the front page of the Sunday Mirror, 29 July, under banner headlines: SOCIETY FEUD. NOVELIST ATTACKS HOSTESS.
[60]Anlaby was owned jointly by Dutton siblings and their children; the Geoffrey Duttons had decided to move into the big house – an eccentric homestead in large gardens – while John Dutton continued to manage the property's diminishing acres.
[61]Maggy.
[62]'A Distinguished Australian Novelist' in this journal of Asian and Australasian writing, July 1962, p.12: '. . . one of the few novelists of genius in the present age', etc.
[63]Harris.

DOGWOODS, 17.viii.62

TO GEOFFREY DUTTON

I think this is the best season for sarsaparilla we have ever had at Sarsaparilla. It is trying to smother all the shrubs near enough to the street fences, and I am superstitious enough to dislike hindering it. The day I had the last conference on the play with John and Desmond Digby before J. left for Adelaide, a dog was trying to rape a bitch outside the gate as I set out for Sydney. So all the right omens are there! Desmond has produced the ideal set, by the way, both simple and attractive, and one wonders why one had to go through such hell before Desmond stepped in.

    Yours
    Patrick.

DOGWOODS, 30.viii.62

TO BERYL PEARCE

John tells me there is a big drive for dinner jackets and long white gloves. I have a 30-year old dinner jacket which has been shut up in a suitcase since the outbreak of War, and which has probably turned to lace by now; I daren't look at it. I have my 5-year old black suit which I intend to wear – it is very presentable – and if that is not formal enough I can lurk at the back of the theatre – I would anyway. I don't want to wear a dinner jacket again in my life-time. Sorry if this sounds bloody-minded, but you know how I appreciate you all without my telling you.

    Yours
    Patrick.

DOGWOODS, 18.ix.62

TO WENDY DICKSON[64]

Dear Wendy,

Thank you very much for the telegram. The first night was another of those strange dreams. Everybody was there, including the Governor,[65] who was heard to whisper when the dogs began to bark and the little girl ran on at the beginning of the play: 'Ah, THE WIND IN THE WILLOWS!' The Governor's Lady was in 'donkey brown', we read, and somebody of the

---

[64]Resident designer with the Trust; she designed three of PW's plays: *The Ham Funeral* in Sydney 1962 – 'rather like an early Sickert, with the clearer colours of Vuillard', PW told Dutton, 18.vii.62; *Night on Bald Mountain* in Adelaide in 1964; and Sharman's revival of *The Season at Sarsaparilla* in Sydney in 1976.

[65]Edric Bastyan (1903–80) whose reward for serving Mountbatten in South-East Asia and the Queen in Hobart was this second Australian vice-regal tour of duty in Adelaide.

entourage in 'beaded raspberry velvet'. In Adelaide the papers really go to town over the dresses.

Far more important than the first night was the second, when people actually paid to stand! I think this is a play which will have something for everybody – if only the stupid Elizabethan would see. Old James Mills[66] made me a very flowery speech at a party afterwards, and I am told he was going round murmuring: 'Most interesting play– –' a remark somebody suggested he had had by ticker tape from Europe.

Desmond's set was perfect. It conveyed exactly what I wanted. In fact I now see Castle Hill as a reflexion of THE SEASON AT SARSAPARILLA and not the play as a reflexion of Castle Hill. Some of the actors were so good I feel more than ever I must have my own theatre, and bring everybody together to do the things we ought to be doing. We shall never get anything out of the Establishment. Even at the Opera House there will be some deadhead standing in the way.

I hope you are getting on with the ballet.[67] Do you know who could have sent me a telegram from William St signed 'Livin Doll'? Wondered whether it might be Beryl Meekin.[68]

Yours
Patrick.

DOGWOODS, 23.ix.62
TO GEOFFREY DUTTON
On my second visit I spent more time watching the audience, and there was no mistaking the warmth of laughter, and you couldn't ignore the handkerchiefs coming out here and there, particularly in the big showdown between Zoe and Cliff Neate.[69] That was exactly where I had my cry at the first rehearsal I saw, and where I have my cry I know I have got my audience! You see I am really very Common Man inside, perhaps even Common Housemaid.

DOGWOODS, 8.x.62
TO BEN HUEBSCH
Dear Ben,
I hope you are by now safely returned from your travels. I seem for ever

---

[66]General manager of drama for the Elizabethan Theatre Trust.
[67]Assisting Ray Powell in the design of *Just for Fun* for the inaugural season of the Australian Ballet.
[68]Former Tivoli comedienne who played one of the dustbin girls in the Sydney *Ham Funeral*.
[69]Neate (1925–) played Nola's husband Ernie Boyle.

setting out on mine. Last month I went over to Adelaide for the opening of *The Season at Sarsaparilla*. This week I leave for Melbourne, and the production of the same play down there. At Christmas we are going over to spend a week with the Geoffrey Duttons at a place they have on Kangaroo Island, just off the South Australian coast.

The Season was a tremendous, not to say a vulgar success in Adelaide. It was seen by 4,266 people in eight performances and a hastily organised matinée. The second night, usually the doldrums of a theatrical run, people were paying to stand. I am enclosing some of the reviews, so that you can get an idea of what the play is about. There were a couple of bad ones too, one in a paper that does not matter, and the other, not exactly a review, but the reaction of one member of a panel of four who discussed it on TV. The outraged minority described it as 'the most deplorable evening I have spent in the Australian theatre.'

Now the Elizabethan Trust is buying the play – they are always the last to come round – and it will be given the full works in Sydney, followed by a tour of the lesser cities like Newcastle and Brisbane.

So the plays are getting around at last, and people are being affected by them. I heard last night about a woman who had made a date to meet a friend after they had both seen *The Ham Funeral* (separately), but the friend did not turn up, and telephoned later to say she had been so overwhelmed by *The Ham Funeral* the night before, she had not felt like going out! I must confess all this excites me very much, and that I have four more plays waiting to be written. I do intend to get back to novels, but for the moment I must respond to so much heady stimulus.

I am not going to write any more at the moment, because there is a lot to clear up before I leave for Melbourne. While I was in Adelaide Manoly turned a double somersault in the car. Mercifully he only lost a few pieces of skin from his shins.

Yours
Patrick.

DOGWOODS, 26.x.62
TO FREDERICK GLOVER
The Melbourne production was not nearly so stylish or brilliant as John Tasker's, but it has some very pleasing touches. Sumner[70] is a sincere

[70]John Sumner (1936–   ) left the British Merchant Marine for the theatre and established in 1953 the first professional repertory theatre in Australia which became the Melbourne Theatre Company. Sumner had directed the first productions of Ray Lawler's *Summer of the Seventeenth Doll* in Melbourne, London and New York.

producer, with greater depth and mellowness than the Tasker. His lighting is good – he plots it all himself – and he can bring out the most in any passages where there is a lot of action. I enjoyed working with him – none of the hysterics of the Tasker; he is not protecting his own uncertainty from any encroachment on the part of the author, which is what I think is wrong with the Tasker . . .

I was very happy staying with the Caldwells. Mum certainly talks a lot, but I found most of it to my taste. She comes out with some superb lines. On one occasion I met a woman whose daughter had committed suicide by jumping off, I think, the *Age* Building. I made some banal remark to Mum about the tragedy of it, and she replied with a touch of pride for her friend's daughter: 'She was the first Melbourne girl to throw herself off a building. Several have done it since.' Dad is a very sweet character. In fact, I liked them both enormously. Zoe drove me about madly all over the place, hands frequently off the wheel, and we would suddenly have a swig out of a whisky bottle while standing at the red lights after a rehearsal where everything had gone wrong.

I met Barry Humphries and his wife a couple of times, and got to like them very much. He is a genuine fantastick. I have just finished the first draft of the story which I shall eventually turn into a film for him, with Zoe playing his mum, his wife, and the character out of a subjective novel he spends most of his life writing.[71] This thing has turned out very peculiar indeed, but I feel it is going to be right. It will have to be photographed in some of the rundown bits of Mosman, with glimpses of that awful Military Road.

Dogwoods, 11.xi.62

TO PEGGY GARLAND

At Christmas we both hope to fly to Adelaide and stay with the Duttons on Kangaroo Island. Klári Daniel we see quite often, and she always asks about you. We have not seen the Kriegers for many months. Fritz can no longer bear to be in the company of anybody who doesn't hold the same ideas as he. He trembles with rage if one disagrees, and the strain became too great, especially when he referred to Yehudi Menuhin as a sixth-rate violinist, and when he tells me I am tone deaf for liking Bach. He is one of the most neurotic men I know, and simply wants to exist like a turnip with nothing to disturb his mind. Ile has gone pretty dead too as a result of all this.

[71]This was Clay; PW later saw it as one of three sections of a film, Triple Sec, to be directed by the young Bruce Beresford; nothing came of the project.

Dogwoods, 1.i.63

TO EDITH HAGGARD[72]

Dear Mrs Haggard,

I arrived back from a Christmas visit to find *Harper's* proof of 'Being Kind to Titina' waiting for me. I started to correct, and was shocked to find the guts had been cut out of it. Quite apart from the bowdlerisation, every attempt had been made to destroy the atmosphere of the story, and to iron out my style into a kind of, well, 'magazinese' to coin a sufficiently awful word. I cannot believe their readers are as stupid or puritanical as they would like to think – or do American magazines to-day cater for cohorts of Helen Hokinson clubwomen?[73] It is a sad, even a terrifying thought. Would you please make sure the story is not printed by them? I have written direct to a woman called Lucy Moss to say this is what I have decided.

All this is very depressing, because I now see there is no market for my stories in America. Would you please let me have back 'Miss Slattery and Her Demon Lover'? I have a magazine waiting for it here, and the *London Magazine* wants it and another of my stories afterwards. This is a breakdown of their usual policy, which is only to print unpublished stories. I don't like to blow my horn as a rule, but Cyril Connolly told the editor of the *London Magazine* that my story 'A Cheery Soul', which they published in their September number is the best short story he has read.

I do hope you didn't <u>know about</u> *Harper's* behaviour! In any case, I wish you a Happy and Successful Year.

Yours sincerely,
Patrick White.

Dogwoods, 4.i.63

TO CYNTHIA NOLAN

We spent Christmas on Kangaroo Island with the Geoffrey Duttons. It is a fascinating place, not quite like anywhere else, though one discovers bits of Attica, the Aegean Islands, and Cornwall amongst its individual qualities. It was looking quite dry and burnt-up after this eastern coast, but I prefer the dead colours to the lush. The Duttons have an old rambly stone house, on a rocky point, amongst wind-swept tea-trees. There is nothing else visible in miles of bay, and from the sea it looks a little like a Greek

---

[72]Of Curtis Brown, New York; she had been trying for some time to place his short stories; her only 'success' had been this with *Harper's*.

[73]Hokinson (c.1899–1949), cartoonist of the *New Yorker* specialising in the mild tribulations of innocent, plain American matrons.

monastery. We were eight adults and six children for Christmas. Fortunately everybody agreed, but in any case it was possible to live one's own life if one wanted. I spent most of the time sleeping and fishing. The last afternoon, rather a dull one for light, all silver water and leaden sky, we took a net down to the bay, and hauled in quite a miraculous number of fish.

JOHN TASKER HAD DECLARED *A Cheery Soul* unplayable and the Adelaide University Theatre Guild rejected it too: 'The university scientists who usually take the first plunge with my plays seem to have been shocked by the fact that God plays a certain part in this one; a randy slut and a bitch in season were different matters.'[74] But John Sumner accepted the play for a Melbourne production in late 1963. His anger hardly mollified, White began to write *Night on Bald Mountain*. 'If it comes off,' he told Peggy Garland, 'it will be the first Australian tragedy.'[75] The scene is something like the Mount Wilson of his childhood where an alcoholic and her husband drive an innocent young woman to her death. A wise woman keeps goats in the bush.

DOGWOODS, 5.i.63
TO MANFRED MACKENZIE[76]
Dear Manfred Mackenzie,
Thank you for your letter and the Christmas card with its seductive chariot of doves.

I think you are playing a dangerous game – fascinating to the player, no doubt – in all this symbol-chasing. Most of the time, I'm afraid, it leads up the wrong tree! I can't see any connexion between Alf Dubbo and Rimbaud, although I have Enid Starkie's splendid book, have read it several times, and grew drunk on Rimbaud when I first discovered him. Rimbaud would have had more influence on Le Mesurier,[77] I think, although the latter is a comparatively undeveloped character in the novel in which he appears. He just had to be there. But I can well see one might develop him and give him a novel to himself.

[74] To Peggy Garland, 11.xi.62.
[75] 11.xi.62.
[76] Sydney academic (1934–   ). 'Today I had a visit from that symbol hunter Manfred Mackenzie, who turned out to be a pleasant young man neither American, nor English, nor yet Australian,' PW reported to Dutton, 18.i.65. 'He apparently has a wife and child whom I did not meet, but who spent an hour and a half in the car while he was in chasing symbols.'
[77] Poet on Voss' expedition to the inland.

I believe I did refer to Dubbo somewhere as 'that dark fellow', but only in a literal sense – that is, in the sense of 'coloured.'

I read *The Wasteland* when I was an undergraduate. I have never read *Four Quartets*, although a learned Australian has found that I have lifted all the symbols from that work and put them straight into *Voss*. I have not read Laforgue,[78] although your remarks tempt me to. Nor have I read *The Golden Bough*, and only a very, very little Dante in the translation by Dorothy Sayers.

Happy Valley received its name only because it recurs so often in Australia, and indeed in other parts of the world. There was a specific Happy Valley where we used to go for picnics in my childhood, at Mount Wilson in the Blue Mountains. At the time when I wrote the book I don't think I had read *Rasselas*.[79] At the end of *Happy Valley*, as far as I remember, the characters simply drive away in a car – of no symbolic significance whatsoever. I should hate to have to read *Happy Valley* to-day; it is too full of obvious stylistic enthusiasms for certain writers, though shorn of those, the bald story might make a good film.

I am sorry not to be able to confess to most of the influences you suggest. I may have arrived at certain conclusions via other writers who had read those you mention. Otherwise I suppose symbols can pop out of the collective unconscious.

I am less taken up with novels at present than with plays and short stories. They offer greater difficulties, at least to me. It is particularly tempting to try to be literate and subtle in the theatre, while remaining contemporary and workable. That is where Eliot fails, I feel, and what I am trying for. I had two plays produced in 1962, hope to have another one done towards the end of this year,[80] and have just finished a fourth. I am also aiming at a triple bill of films, adapted from some of my short stories. The film offers tremendous opportunities for visual symbolism, and for conveying the inexpressible by that means.

I wish you a Happy New Year.

Yours sincerely,

Patrick White.

[78]Jules LaForgue (1860–87), innovative French poet highly valued by Eliot.
[79]Samuel Johnson's 1759 fable of the Abyssinian prince from the Happy Valley who explores the world and finds home's best.
[80]Sumner had agreed to stage *A Cheery Soul* in Melbourne.

DOGWOODS, 10.ii.63

TO PEGGY GARLAND

I had a shock last week on receiving an invitation to lunch with Our Lovely Queen on the yacht while she is in Sydney. My first impulse was to take the train somewhere, but now I think I shall go, to see who else is there (I believe they only have twenty guests), and to watch how the colonial notorieties react. One might use bits of it later on. There seem to have been wild scenes in N.Z. with police dogs brought in to restrain the crowds. They have also had some particularly New Zealand murders there lately.

DOGWOODS, 17.ii.63

TO BEN HUEBSCH

Dear Ben,

The time of our departure is coming close. We have decided in the end to go by air, as five weeks at sea would be too big a bite out of the six months, and fly from here to Athens on March 28th. We aren't yet able to say anything very definite about dates. We want to see some of the Festival of Epidaurus, and that I think will be end of June-beginning of July. We should probably reach Rome about the first or second week in July. I hope you still think of meeting us there – though if you would rather choose somewhere else, we shall be moving on London via Vienna, Geneva and Paris. Again our plans are a bit fluid. Manoly has some Italian cousins in Geneva – he is the Italian Consul-General[81] – but if they have left Geneva for their summer holiday we shall then have to go to their country estate, somewhere near Naples, instead of Geneva. I have been wondering whether it mightn't be more peaceful and cooler to stay somewhere in the hills outside Rome at that time of year. Do you know the Campagna at all? I can find out, but it will take time and a certain amount of correspondence . . .

I am thinking of sending you a novel by a New Zealand novelist called Janet Frame which bowled me right over the other day. She publishes in England with W. H. Allen, and the other day they brought out one called *The Edge of the Alphabet* which I have not yet read. The book that impressed me so much is, I think, her first – called *Owls Do Cry*. It makes me feel I have always been a couple of steps out from where I wanted to get in my own writing, but it is the kind of book that could only have been written by somebody who is a bit crazy, and I have heard from Antony Alpers that she has been in and out of mental hospitals. I find

---

[81]Goffredo Biondi Morra.

this book particularly interesting because of my own New Zealand cousins. Although they are intellectuals and of a different social level from the family in the book there is the same despair and confusion under the simple, uncomplicated New Zealand surface. I shouldn't be surprised if any New Zealander took a gun to his neighbour. Guns are to New Zealanders what axes are to Poles.[82] I laughed when Our Lovely Queen made her speech the other day about 'this happy country' when she was in Auckland . . .

P.S. The Elizabethan Theatre Trust has asked me to consider writing the libretto for an opera to open the Sydney Opera House. I have an idea,[83] but it will depend on whether I can accept the composer. There are some truly dreadful ones at large.

DOGWOODS, 1.iii.63
TO CLEM CHRISTESEN
You mention the purity of your secretary, but the whole point of the story[84] is that here are purity and incorruptibility germinating on the rubbish dump . . . I wish you would make a test case of this! It would do *Meanjin* ultimately so much good, infuse such new life into it. Just fling it in the faces of the puritan-materialists. They'd probably pipe down altogether if they knew I am lunching with the Queen on the yacht this coming Sunday. I'm sorry I shan't have a copy of *Meanjin* to present to her on the occasion, with 'Down at the Dump', words and all, as my English publisher says she is probably the first of the Windsors to invite a serious writer to lunch. I'm inclined to think Geoffrey Dutton is nearer the mark when he points out there is probably a jockey of the same name, and some confusion has arisen. It is going to be a strained occasion in any case. I shall have to stop and take something at the Newcastle Hotel, but the question is what, and how much? There is a theory that Vodka doesn't leave a smell − −

To return to the 'words': if you must make changes I suggest 'flickin' on pp 2 and 3 − it looks less muddy, and sounds less turgid than 'mucken'. But in the other cases I can't see a way round. On p 15 where Ossie lies

---

[82]Bogdan Mazurski ran through the Regent Theatre in Sydney on 9 Sept. 1959 axing patrons at an afternoon session of Bing Crosby's *Say One for Me*. One man was killed when he threw himself between his wife and the Pole. Fourteen others were injured. The Pole with the axe, an image of innate, mindless evil, crops up often in PW's writing, e.g. in the *Six Urban Songs* where 'He chopped the gent in the mac,/Whose teeth flew out in surprise . . . ' etc.

[83]To adapt the abandoned 'Fringe of Leaves'.

[84]'Down at the Dump'.

in the horse-stall amongst the 'shit' he is supposed to have sunk as low as he can get, lice and all in his disgusting hair, when Daise takes pity on him. Daise has come for 'manure' for her garden, so that can't be used. 'Dung' would sound too Biblical, too poetical. I suppose it could be used at a pinch, but the scene is recalled by Ossie himself and must sound contemporary and brutal. On p.18 where Ossie says to Daise: 'I couldn't get a stand – ' I can't see any alternative but to use just that. The people who might object probably wouldn't understand what it means anyway – and on p.22, Mrs Whalley's: 'Poison? My arse!' is far too epigrammatic to destroy. If the story is hacked about to any extent we shall look silly when it comes out with its original trimmings in the volume of my stories Eyre & Spottiswoode are waiting to publish when I have collected enough. The English expect Australians to be Australian, and we have got our layers of obscenity. If I used all these words in a story of no moral intention, then I agree it would only be a piece of exhibitionism. But Meg Hogben and Mum Whalley are the pure, the truthful, those of whom we may have hopes in the future.

Funnily enough I had an anonymous letter from some idle woman in Melbourne who plagues me about three times a week. She . . . accuses me of adopting the attitudes of a Zen monk. I have shown over and over again that the point I am trying to make is the distinction between rich, ripe, fertile vulgarity and sour trash which silts up, chokes and kills.[85]

Dogwoods, 8.iii.63
TO DESMOND DIGBY
Dear Desmond,
How are things at the El?[86] Pretty wet, I'm afraid, after reading about the Royal Progress yesterday at Coolangatta. Here it rains, but only in a mild drizzly way, and I am able to run about between showers and start another fire in the incinerator; my desk is being turned out for the first time in five years.

I managed to get to the Luncheon on Monday after a dreadful Sunday night, when I started a kind of bronchial complication and vomitted up everything besides. However, I took everything. Manoly took me to Parramatta and I went in by train, looking like a waiter going on duty, as my only presentable and cool suit was a new black one I had bought to wear to the theatre and concerts in the summer. There was quite an amiable atmosphere in the Sydney streets for once, and I hung about the

[85]*Meanjin*, June 1963, p.153, bowdlerised the text which E & S restored.
[86]The El Dorado Motel, Surfers Paradise, where Digby was staying.

Circular Quay for a bit waiting for Them to approach. Finally they did, standing up in a very leisurely car. She was all in blew, he in a kind of tweedy number the colour of dry cowshit. After a bit I approached the yacht in fear and trembling, and ran into the Utzons,[87] who had received a summons in the air on their way from Tahiti, and had been rushed straight from the plane. In our nervous condition we ganged up quite a lot, and he promised to show me over the Opera House. His wife is of that plain, dank-haired mermaid kind one sees from Denmark, very pleasant. As her English is a bit vague, she smiles. Then we went on board, up a red carpet, with sailors slapping their rifle butts, and were received by I don't know how many members of the household: a tall, toothy, elderly man in a lounge suit, and glamorous young Navy and Army equerries among them. The Army equerry, who was Australian, appeared to have read some of my books, and told me that other members of the household were 'very interested'. In fact, he said, the copy of *Voss* had disappeared mysteriously. (I should think the Juke had probably thrown it out the porthole after reading half of Chapter I.) The guests were very oddly chosen indeed, and I couldn't think for the life of me why I had been asked. I had imagined there would be other artists of various kinds, but Doris Fitton and Murray Rose[88] were as close as we got to that – with of course the Utzons as a last minute inspiration. Otherwise they were all business tycoons (that Kirby, looking like a purple fig about to burst,[89] Warwick Fairfax, Hallstrom)[90] civil servants, and an admiral and general or two. We were lined up on either side of the saloon for the introductions to Ma'am and the Juke. There were drinks before and after, good stiff ones too, and one needed it. Mary Fairfax was tottering and using her smelling bottle before the drink was produced, and the headmistress of Cheltenham High,[91] a nice hearty old thing with whom I had conversation, confessed that she was petrified. Doris, of course, was in her element, doing all that *grande dame* stuff she'd learnt in rep, tremendous curtsey while Lady This and Lady That were tottering and nearly falling under their chiffon hats. Lunch was really very good – rolls of smoked salmon with scrambled egg at the side (it's worth remembering), tournedos on foie gras with a salad, and *profiteroles* with chocolate sauce. I have never sat at such a long

[87]Architect of the Sydney Opera House Joern Utzon (1918–   ) and his wife Lis Fenger.
[88]Olympic swimmer and actor (1939–   ).
[89]James Kirby (1899–1971), machinery manufacturer.
[90]Edward Hallstrom (1886–1970), maker of Silent Knight refrigerators and benefactor of Sydney's Taronga Park Zoo.
[91]Bessie Mitchell.

mahogany table. There were some rather ugly gold urns down the centre, and vases of yellow and white flowers. They sat on either side, and I was at the lower end, so could look right down and observe. I was between Murray Rose, who is a most civilised young man, able to talk about things, and a Mrs Parbury, a youngish woman with heavily loaded eyelashes, who is a niece of the Duchess of Gloucester. She came out here originally to be with her auntie, and fell for Parbury, a tall dark handsome Australian of family. I used to know his great-aunt (now dead) and aunt (now crazy, but at large – she was always a thin spinster drifting from park to park, for no wrong reasons, just to pass the time, and now poor thing she is so mad she no longer knows which park she is in.) My mother used to know the Parburys in her youth on the Hunter and I can remember her telling me in shocked tones that whenever the Parburys wanted to go for another trip they sold off a paddock. I used that in connexion with the Goodmans in *The Aunt's Story*. However, I couldn't tell the Hon. Mrs Parbury any of that at the luncheon. I couldn't find out any of her interests, only that she has two children whose education is worrying her. I told her to send them to the ordinary schools, but she is afraid they would develop split personalities. I replied that I had developed one at the best of schools. That didn't get us very far either, nor the fact that one of her relations is one of my oldest and closer friends. After lunch we stood about in the saloon again for coffee, and I spoke to Admiral McNicoll and his wife.[92] He is the brother of the bastard on the *Telegraph* who is one of the leaders of the opposition to my books. I think the admirals would show themselves to be of the opposition also if the politenesses were down, but we were soon led up to Ma'am, who began to discuss with McNicoll the oiling of stabilisers. She is fed up because the stabilisers in *Britannia* are apparently of an old-fashioned variety, which have to be taken out for oiling, while the latest can be oiled in position. After they had been through all this another lady who had been led up, all coffee lice and chiffon hat, spoke about the Barrier Reef, so I thought I had better put in a word as obviously a word wasn't going to be put to me. I told Ma'am she must make a point of seeing Fraser Island one day, and about the interesting wreck which had taken place there, and of the Nolan paintings which no doubt she had seen. At which she gave a shriek, or as close to a shriek as she could come, and said: 'Ohhh, yurse! The Naked Lehdy! We saw one in Adelaide.' Poor girl, she might loosen up if one took her in hand, but as it is she struck me as being quite without charm, except of a perfectly stereotyped

[92]Alan McNicoll (1908–87), soon to be Australia's Ambassador to Turkey; and Frances, née Chadwick, a former correspondent for the *Economist*.

English county kind, and hard as nails under the Little-Thing-in-Blew appearance. I suppose it's just as well that she's tough. One wasn't led up to the Jokey Juke – he approached, and I think he made up his mind early on that he was going to keep well away from anything that might be an intellectual or an artist.

When all this was over I went up to the Cross and had a long gin session with Jack Lee, the English film director,[93] whom I liked, and with whom I have a feeling I may get together over something eventually.

DOGWOODS, 15.iii.63
TO DESMOND DIGBY

To-day Utzon showed us over the Opera House. Of course I really only went because you would have been so shocked to hear I hadn't found time for it, but how infinitely glad I am that I did. It has made me feel glad I am alive in Australia to-day. At last we are going to have something worth having. If only they had got going on the whole thing a few years earlier, so that we could be certain of having a part in it! I was particularly glad to have been shown over by Utzon, a kind of Danish Gary Cooper, although his English is a bit woolly at times, and difficult to follow. How shocking to think of those miserable little aldermannish devils attacking such a magnificent conception from their suburban underworld. Funnily enough as we were walking up and down all those steps in such a very contemporary setting I kept thinking of Phaestos, Mycenae and Tyrins. It occurred to Manoly too, without our having discussed it. I suppose the contemporary and the ancient do have a lot in common; it is the in between periods which went astray under the mass of detail.

Another exciting thing recently: I went to the Olsen exhibition, and got quite drunk on those pictures. I now think he is the Australian painter.[94] All those Spanish entanglements have gone, and the colour and light has come pouring in. Unlike Hodgkinson he is teeming with ideas.[95] I wish I could have bought half a dozen. One would not have been enough, but in any case, if we had not been going for the trip, there was scarcely one left to buy. I was intrigued by a reference by Bob Hughes in Nation to the

[93]Lee (1913–), brother of the writer Laurie Lee, came out to direct Robbery Under Arms, 1957, married an Australian fortune and settled in Sydney.
[94]John Olsen (1928–), exhibiting at the Clune Galleries; this was a conversion for PW who described Olsen's work to Peggy Garland, 30.x.60, as 'a kind of brown knitting. I cannot share the raptures of the disciples, because I just cannot get excited about brown, even, I have to confess, when Rembrandt used it.'
[95]Frank Hodgkinson (1919–) who had just exhibited at the Hungry Horse in Paddington. PW changed his mind later: see PW to the Nolans, 6.xi.64, page 268.

'savage portrait of Sue Du Val.' Of course I went rushing round the walls looking for that number, but couldn't find it. So I asked Thelma, and was told somebody had bought it, and that it had already been removed – on a solicitor's advice! Apparently the Du Val raised hell, although Thelma said the portrait was no less 'abstract' than another one I saw in the exhibition called 'Portrait of Bob Hughes Approaching Vadim's.' Anyway, Olsen must have found his way intuitively right on to the Du Val nerve, although he only met her once and very briefly.[96]

DOGWOODS, 17.iii.63
TO THE DUTTONS
Dear Nin and Geoffrey,
Thank you very much for your letters and postcards. Yes, I dote on the Douanier Rousseau, and I think his 'Joyeux Farceurs' (incidentally not particularly 'joyeux') looks besides like a forestful of black schnauzers.[97]

I have corrected the additional piece to the Lansdowne Press booklet, and sent it on to Lloyd O'Neil.[98] There were only a couple of minor points on p.2. The actual landlady did in fact send Dobell to fetch the relatives, she didn't go herself. To this day I haven't seen Bill, although I receive queer little messages from time to time through other people, one of them to say he had not been to the first night of *The Ham Funeral* because he did not like the people who invited him to go, though there is no indication that he went to any performance during the run. Nor have I received the promised drawing for the painting which hangs in the Haywards' cloakroom.[99] However, I'm told that Bill decided at one stage to install a W.C. in the

[96]Du Val (c.1920–   ), society gastronome, says she objected not to the painting – 'pricks and tits and balls' she called it – but to Olsen's failure to ask her permission before hanging it in Thelma Clune's gallery. 'I loved the portrait. It was just bad manners. John was naughty.' Bob Hughes called the painting 'ferocious' in Sydney's *Nation*, 9 March 1963, p.20. When PW later met 'Sue the Gastro' he was at first horrified, then told Eleanor Arrighi, 9.vii.67, 'we met again, have met several times, and she is real, and real bawdy, which I like. She is also one of the uncrowned cooks, not of Australia, but of the world, and I've eaten round it several times. I can't help admiring a great artist.'
[97]Perhaps, but actually monkeys in the jungle; the painting is in the Philadelphia Museum.
[98](1928–92), founder of the press now preparing a second edition of Dutton's *Patrick White*.
[99]Bill (1903–83) and Ursula Hayward (1907–70) had a house filled with treasures at the foot of the Adelaide Hills; he was the proprietor of the city's leading store and she was a collector, wit and patron of painters and writers. Above the cloakroom lavatory hung a small Dobell oil, about 10cm square, called 'Boy Weeing'.

house at Wangi, and all the pieces lay about for months, if not years, while he and the aged sister continued to stagger out to the dunny in the wind and the rain, just because they couldn't think where to put the new W.C. . . .

Our departure is hurtling towards us alarmingly. The date is March 28th. As usual I am going through a kind of 'cherry orchard' nostalgia which will get worse until we actually arrive. Almost every night we go out, and I am living in a perpetual hangover. Odd nights we have hordes of people here, and I shall be relieved when it is all over – particularly the murder of our hens – we are now down to three.

The last I heard from the Adelaide Guild was that *Bald Mountain* is more or less safe for the Festival. However, it may not be, so don't talk about it yet as a *fait accompli*.

That's about all the news, I think. As soon as I get away I am going to start work on the screenplays, then write another stage play, and I have a novella which will probably work out long enough for me to offer a volume of short things to Eyre & Spottiswoode. Some of the action of the novella, called 'Dead Roses', is going to take place at Rocky Point. I also have an idea for a short story called 'The Terrible Algebra' which I got the other day from a letter of Henry James, in which he advises a warm, outgiving woman friend not to become too involved in the lives of other people but to do something about the 'terrible algebra' of her own. I find after reading Vol 2 of Leon Edel's life I am out of sympathy with Henry. One can't call him a phoney – he was far too innocent – but there are some astonishingly awful traits to his character. Whenever in future I start to suspect I may be one of the fringe-dwellers of life, I shall take heart in remembering Henry James.

DOGWOODS, 24.iii.63
TO JOHN TASKER
We have almost got to the end of our farewells, and will surely be overweight from all the flasks of brandy and St Christopher medals we have received. I must say I never like to set out on a long journey without the Saint in my pocket.

EIGHT

Loose Ends

March 1963 – September 1964

WHITE HAD DELETED RUSSIA from the itinerary but the plan was still to explore the Byzantine world with pilgrimages to Mount Athos, Istanbul and the city of Smyrna on the Anatolian coast from which the Greeks were expelled in the Catastrophe of 1922. Back in Australia, John Tasker was rehearsing the first Sydney production of *The Season at Sarsaparilla*.

ATHENS, 31.iii.63
CARD TO THE MOORES
A very smooth, but exhausting journey. Manoly developed dysentery from a Singapore sandwich, and now 'flu. I have had a streaming cold. Arrived to find the aunt[1] had died the week before. So all we could do was take flowers to the cemetery. Everyone fortunately very calm. Athens much altered. Only the lights the same, and the Acropolis.
P.

ATHENS, 27.iv.63
TO THE MOORES
Dear Gwen and David,
It was good to find the letter here when we returned yesterday from the islands. We were away a fortnight in the end, instead of the intended ten days, but travel in Greece is like that. Nobody knows what happens a hundred miles away. The traveller arrives at the next point of departure to find there isn't a boat for another two or three days. I used to find it madly irritating, but have now found it possible to seal myself off and settle down to work after exhausting the sights on a small island. (These islands of Greece are really only for a couple of days or a couple of years; anything in between is futile.) We have just been to Mykonos, Delos, Samos and Pátmos. Mykonos is not an island that appeals to me – it is packed with tourists and rather decadent Athenians, but we always have to go there as

---

[1]Despo, sister of the late Elly Lascaris, the maiden aunts who between them had raised Manoly and his siblings.

Manoly's sister Elly[2] is devoted to it. She has a most attractive and peaceful house in which I could spend a lot of time, but as she is the godmother of practically every child in Mykonos we are carried off all the time to eat and drink and listen to a particularly unintelligible dialect shrieked at top voice to compete with the wind. We both really became rather depressed and ill in Mykonos. Our getaway to Samos was particularly Greek. The boat was supposed to be coming at ten, then we heard on the wireless that it was expected at twelve (midnight), then at three. We got up for three, and descended to the port, where we sat in a café drinking Nescafe. Finally the boat arrived at five. But we did get a miraculous dawn thrown in . . .

Samos is a very different kind of island, quite large, very beautiful scenically, with lots of trees and high mountains which always seem to be trailing tatters of cloud. Unfortunately it is a dead island. Houses crumble, the bombed palaces along the waterfront at Vathy have never been rebuilt, and the town itself has an intolerable provincial air, only coming to life on Saturday night when everybody parades up and down the waterfront for several hours. It was a rigid ritual, one felt, and that one was probably dressed all wrong for it, and walking on the wrong side. The most noticeable thing about Samos was the exceptional number of handsome people, which was a change from the ugly, embittered Athenians, and the amiable but uninteresting bears of Mykonos. However, the Samians make up for their beauty by being unusually stupid. Another disappointment was the wine, 'Samian wine' is a myth. Everyone brings their brew into a co-operative, where it is all tipped in together – a nauseating sweet red, which almost all goes to Germany, a mediocre white, and a pleasant enough rosé. We went to two very interesting but almost deserted monasteries, and drove right round the island in a hired car, during which our driver took us to his village, and we had a most wonderful, thick egg-and-lemon soup made from a fish brought straight from the sea. Unfortunately on such occasions one is never alone. The inhabitants gather round one like flies on the sore on a mule's back, and one is forced to make a lot of very rudimentary conversation.

From Samos we went to Pátmos as we discovered a little boat, unknown to Athens, plies between the two islands once a week. It was very small, the sea very rough, and our fellow passengers, mostly theological students bound for Pátmos, spouting over the side like whales. In addition one was distressed by the sight of country cheeses standing exposed on top of the hold round which all these seasick youths were

[2]Polymeropoulos.

milling, and a pathetic lamb tied to a stanchion by a string, being taken from one rock to be slaughtered on another.

Everybody has his island, and I think Pátmos will remain ours. There is a small and comparatively modern port, where we stayed, right on the quay, with people expecting boats and screaming at each other all through the night. But the main village is on the top of a mountain which rises behind, a warren of narrow white streets winding round an enormous grey monastery with crenellations like a fortress. Halfway up there is the cave in which St John had his Revelations and dictated the *Apocalypse.* Two very charming novices led us to the cave, and afterwards presented us with wallflowers picked from outside, which I feel we shall have to keep pressed between the appropriate pages and bring out to show to bored and sceptical visitors.

Pátmos was full of curious coincidences. I have often said I shall have to live in Greece for a couple of years to write a novel I have in my head about a family of Anatolian Greeks (much like Manoly's). Just after we came out of St John's cave another very good idea for a novel came into my head, but one for which I shall have to do a lot of research into the theology of the Greek Orthodox faith and the present-day monastic system. Well, we went several times to the village, visited the monastery, and were received at two convents. The last day we discovered a most wonderful 18th Century house, which will be comparatively cheap to buy, although one will have to spend a fair amount on doing it up. But I felt it was our house the moment we went inside. There are twelve rooms, including a long glassed-in veranda-place at the back, paved with brick, a courtyard paved with flint in a formal pattern, three wells, one of them inside the house, and a walled garden full of almond trees, pomegranates, and quinces. The last owner spent some years in Odessa before the Revolution, and the house does have a great deal of the Chekhov atmosphere. It would make just the right set for *The Cherry Orchard,* for instance. We are going to try to buy the house, although we can't really afford it after this trip and paying my latest income tax, and then there will be the expense of trying to live on two sides of the world, the problem of where to keep the animals, and so forth. But it is just one of those crazy things one has to do every now and again. If it comes off, you will both love the house.

I found letters from both Nolans on arriving back here. Sid is doing the cover for the Penguin edition of *The Aunt's Story.* I had seen an early painting of his which seemed to convey much more of Theodora Goodman than the jacket he did for the E.&S. hard-cover edition, and now he is going to try to do something along the lines of that early painting of a woman caught in her net veil . . .

Cats and dogs seem to have settled down, though Fanny was very shy at first. We miss them a lot at times.

Hope all is well –

P.

You might let Thea see this as I have to write several more letters to people unknown to one another. Glad she at least shared the Prize, even though it was with the author of whom she disapproves.[3]

The night we reached Mykonos two little girls, both Elly's godchildren appeared at the house. The younger was called Elly. Manoly asked the older and shyer her name, but the younger of the two answered very promptly: 'Her name is Sophia, and she pisses in her pants.'

PÉLION, 8.v.63
TO GEOFFREY DUTTON

I think we have more or less choked the influence the house has over me. The woman who owns it, and who prefers to live with her children in Athens, said she couldn't take less when we said we couldn't give so much. However, she is going to discuss the matter with her children, and if they have climbed down by the time we return we shall have the agony of decision all over again. I hope not. It would be crazy to be landed with that house, and we might have to end up living exclusively at Pátmos.

We only spent a week in Athens before setting out again, for the north this time. Every fresh direction in Greece makes me feel that this is Greece at last, and that I haven't seen anything beautiful until now. We are on Pélion at present, making very exhausting expeditions up and down the mountain, through forests of chestnut, and straggling slate-roofed villages, down paths cobbled with chunks of marble which seem to have dislocated every bone in my feet and sent shooting pains up my shins. Yesterday we decided to engage a couple of mules to bring us up to the top again, and I must say that mule's back was the greatest luxury I have ever experienced . . .

[3] Thea Astley lived not far from Dogwoods. 'We both liked her very much,' PW told Glover, 14.iii.60, after her first visit. 'She has wit, and flashes of intelligence for a Brisbane girl turned schoolteacher.' She and PW enjoyed a close gossips' friendship, more intense on the telephone than face to face. *Descant for Gossips*, published the year of their meeting, was Astley's first success; her next, *The Well-Dressed Explorer*, shared the 1962 Miles Franklin prize with George Turner's *The Cupboard under the Stairs*. PW's friendship with Astley came apart in late 1964 when she made disparaging remarks about Dutton's poetry: see PW to Laurie Collinson, 27.xi.64, *page 272*.

Oh – something that will interest you – while we were in Samos we discovered that Katsimbilis[4] was staying in our hotel! We didn't meet him, but often used to look at him. He is not a bit Colossal – rather like one of those large, grey, shiny ticks filled with borrowed blood. He has a wife with a peacock's voice and an ugly face who was much more interesting. She had a clever technique of dropping the peacock-voice and tearing strips off the maids in sweet, affectionate tones. But Robert Liddell says everybody likes her, and that he has known two people dying of cancer who couldn't bear to have anybody else at their bedside.

I must stop now as we are setting out for a remote village to see the surviving mural of Theophilos, one of the few good Greek painters. He is a primitive, came from the Pélion, lived during last century, and almost everything he painted was done on Pélion walls, which have been allowed to crumble or moulder. We have a little book on him, published while there were still enough of the paintings to reproduce. This is typical Greek behaviour. They are only good for sitting on their bums in Athens, chattering about absolutely nothing, and complaining how poor and neglected they are.

SALONIKA, 14.v.63
TO FREDERICK GLOVER
Dear Frederick,
We are still feeling rather battered after returning yesterday from our visit to Mount Athos. Certainly a visit to the Holy Mountain is advisable if only to get it out of one's system and to explode a myth. The Myth of the Monastic Life is of the same order as that of the Noble Bedouin. As far as I am concerned I disposed of the latter during the War. Now the other has gone the same way, as we discovered the monks of the Holy Mountain are little more than a bunch of dirty old, half-crazed vipers without a trace of the Christian spirit in their behaviour either to outsiders or one another.

The journey to the Mountain is very long and involved, made more so by the fact that nobody is able to give one any accurate information on how to get there. One just has to find out painfully for oneself, and improve on the approach next time, if there ever is a next time, and for us I doubt there will be. We started off from Salonika in a bus which takes about four hours hectic driving along dreadful roads to reach the port of Ierissós at the neck of the peninsula. (One has to remind oneself all the time that Mount Athos <u>is</u> on a peninsula, because both physically and

[4]Editor, translator and endless talker, portrayed in Henry Miller's *The Colossus of Maroussi*.

spiritually it is more of an island than most islands.) At Ierissós one is seized upon by the owner of a caïque, and then starts the voyage of about five hours to the place where one lands to reach Kariés the civil capital of the theocracy. We made the mistake of taking more than we could comfortably carry, so that all the time we were either lugging too much luggage up and down the sides of a mountain or bargaining with rapacious mule drivers. After landing on the peninsula from the caïque we had our first experience of Mount Athos walks, about two hours up a mountainside along a path cobbled with chunks of marble, to reach Kariés, where one presents the permit one has been granted by a Ministry in Athens, and which has to be replaced by another paper signed by every member of an ecclesiastical synod, which is then presented at every monastery one visits. We arrived at Kariés at dusk and quite exhausted, put up at a very primitive inn, and started the business of sitting to wait for our permit next morning. Monks either have no idea of time, or else they enjoy torturing the lay pilgrim – I am inclined to think it is mostly the latter. The only Christianity we came across while on the Mountain was in the slaves who work for the monks and one or two of the pilgrims. Of the latter about the nicest was a Greek who plays the vibraphone and trumpet at an Athens nightclub called the *Flamingo* and who was visiting the Mountain to beg for some miraculous raisins which are supposed to ensure a safe delivery for his pregnant wife.

Our first experience of monasteries was in a Russian one outside Kariés, an enormous labyrinth of neglected buildings, of a late period and not particularly good architecturally.[5] It is now lived in by five aged monks, and its speciality, when anybody can get in to see it, is an icon which cures incurable diseases. However, the abbot who seemed particularly crazy even for a Mount Athos monk, shrieked at us that we were wasting his time – he was bottling wine from the cask – and that he wasn't going to show us anything. Nor did he, in spite of the shrieks and curses of our ally, a funny thin old Mongolian-looking Russian from China, who could at least speak Greek, and who confided in us that the abbot was really a Communist and that he, the Mongol, was always trying to make up his mind to go to the police and tell all. The church at Kariés, which we were allowed to visit after Manoly had had a strip torn off him by a monk for wearing a short-sleeved shirt, has some very fine Byzantine frescoes, as well as a miracle-working icon which had just returned from a visit to Athens.

After this we set out on the journey to another monastery called Vatopédhi, up hill and down dale, over the usual marble chunks, with a

[5]Agios Panteleimon, once home to 1,500 monks.

mule carrying our baggage, Manoly and I taking turns to ride a one-eyed horse, and accompanied by a brigand of a lay muleteer. It took about three hours, pretty rough going, but is one of our pleasanter memories of Athos, as we returned to nature, away from the dreadful atmosphere of the monasteries.

Vatopédhi was certainly the best of those we saw, the vastest, but also the cleanest and most peaceful. It would have made a good hotel if run by laymen, and it also contained one of the few clean, pleasant, and civilised monks we came across. But this man had only been about 25 years on the Mountain, he had been three times a refugee, that is, he really knew about and had suffered from life, and he came from Smyrna, the place from which all good Greeks, including the Lascaris, have sprung. We spent a pleasant day at Vatopédhi, but experienced the usual monkish unwillingness to show the outsider their treasures. (Unfortunately our friend from Smyrna was only the doorkeeper.) In the end we did succeed in getting inside the church just before leaving, and that is a fabulous building in the best Byzantine taste we have seen so far. We were also given our best lunch in a monastery, a dish of fried potatoes, some excellent sardines treated like anchovies, and a good rank peasanty cheese, which you would not have liked at all – no wine, however, at Vatopédhi.

In the afternoon we caught a caïque to the Grand Lavra. (We found it best to travel by sea, though it is often difficult to catch the boat, and often a storm will spring up to prevent it arriving.) The Grand Lavra is supposed to be the showplace, although we personally hated it, and did not think it a patch on Vatopédhi. We arrived at dusk, and had a nightmarish struggle up a steep incline to get into the monastery before the gates closed, for the rule is that they close at sunset. Lavra is older than Vatopédhi, has more valuable relics and manuscripts, but it is also dirtier, crazier, and altogether most unpleasant.

On the positive side there was an appealing little monk in charge of the outsiders and a really Christian lay cook (a shocking cook in spite of his kindness). We shared a room with a policeman from Sparta, who started off by being as unpleasant as Spartans can be, suspicious of our intentions, and wanting to know all about us. The fourth in our room was a peasant from another part of Macedonia, come to the Mountain to supervise the cutting of wood from which the monks make a tidy penny. In the course of our acquaintanceship this man tried to persuade Manoly to stop off at his village on our way back and choose one of his five sisters as a wife.

It was almost impossible to sleep while we were there. At about 1 a.m. the monks started intoning in a chapel outside our room, and continued until about 7.30. When it was not the monks it was a party of fat Livádhian merchants, tourist-pilgrims like ourselves, who kept up a babble on the balcony outside, when they were not spitting over the edge without any regard for the passers-by below. On the Sunday morning we got up about 5 a.m. and spent from 6 till 7.30 in the chapel with the monks. Again very little evidence of spirit, only elaborate procedure. The chapel itself did not excite us after the breath-taking interior at Vatopédhi. The larger church is closed for cleaning, though we actually succeeded in getting into it during our stay. Again it was not up to Vatopédhi, though there was a beautiful collection of old icons put away in a cabinet, as opposed to mostly ornate horrors on display. There are also the remains of their saint, from who flames issued when they tried to transfer him to a reliquary some years ago, and a piece of the True Cross, which for some reason or other we were not allowed to see.

There are many other monasteries, but after a day and a couple of nights at the Grand Lavra watching crazy monks, sensing something of the feuds between them, and listening to the explosion of one or two temperaments which I'm sure only Callas could surpass, we did not feel we wanted to trail round the other side of Athos.

We had also become involved with the fat merchants from Livádhia, who wanted to add us to their party, and from who we had every reason for wanting to escape. The last evening was really a nightmare, in the pilgrims' refectory, pinned in between the merchants, supping at an awful mess of corn soup, and a Jehovah's Witness delivering an interminable sermon on the Last Judgment. In the end Jehovah was routed by the more orthodox merchants, who accused him of his heresies.

During the afternoon a gale had sprung up, as always happens when one wants very badly to escape across the Aegean, and we spent several hours anxiously awaiting the appearance of the regular boat which should arrive at sunset and take us away in the morning. Just about sunset the wretched thing did arrive and we retreated into the monastery as the filthy old doorkeeper tried to slam the door on us. The rest of the night we spent trying to be awake in time for the caïque's departure at 5 a.m. However, the gale was howling by then, and when we struggled down the mountainside with our baggage in the dawn, we were told by some sailors that the caïque had fled in the night rather than risk the dangers of an increasing storm in the rocky little harbour. We were most dejected at this, and toiled back up the mountainside to wait for the following day. But our luck changed, and a couple of hours later we were able to slip away in a very small caïque which turned up out of nowhere, and which agreed to take us back to Hierissos. I think we would both rather have gone to the bottom than spend another day and night at the Grand Lavra. Anyway, the caïque turned out to be most buoyant, and the seas not as bad as they looked, and after many hours we reached dry land, and better still, normal secular life.

I am really too close to all this to be able to write about it, and I feel this is a horribly flat and rambling letter. Our next important port of call is Constantinople, although we are stopping off at Kavalla and Thásos on the way. Salónica is as squalid as ever, but at least there is possibly the best restaurant in Greece, at which we have been making up for all the corn mush and cold haricot beans we ate on Mount Athos. Nor is it bad to be back in a room with bath, even though our lavatory had in it an unsinkable French letter, and shit on the seat – still that is better than a black hole over a cliff and heaps of shit all round, monastery-style.

It is strange to think that *The Season at Sarsaparilla* will be opening in a week's time,[6] or that I ever had anything to do with it. Perhaps I didn't. In a letter I had the other day from John he announced that he and Carmel Millhouse[7] were working on the character of Girlie Pogson to see how they could make her 'more human and tender' when she was always meant to be a suburban bitch with the soul of a vacuum cleaner.

ATHENS, 2.vi.63
TO ALICE AND DENIS HALMAGYI[8]
Constantinople is one of the most squalid places I know – it makes Cairo seem hygienic – but then there is the Bosphorus, just to drive along it washes one clean, and Ayia Sophia, which I think must be the most noble building on earth. You can keep all the mosques, and even the Seraglio, wonderful though it is, but I shall take the several excellent restaurants in which we ate, particularly fish, and always cooked by Greeks. We had a tremendous drive from Constantinople to Smyrna, fifteen hours of it in a bus, with Turkish music blaring all the way, and a hostess to squirt cheap eau de cologne into our hands and offer us chewing gum. Again one felt very squalid, but the landscape is on the grand scale, if too nostalgic – one is reminded continually of the rightful owners.

Almost the whole of Smyrna was destroyed when the Turks set fire to it and drove out the Greeks, but along the waterfront there are a number

[6]At the Theatre Royal.
[7](c.1924–   ), radio and stage actress who played Girlie in Adelaide and Sydney.
[8]His GP Alice (c.1922–   ), married to a physician Denis (1921–   ), both refugees from Hungary after 1956. She was the source of much of the medical information in PW's fiction.

of old houses, mostly foreign consulates and mansions of rich Levantines at the time of the Catastrophe, façades of white, and rose, and creamy marble, with iron doors and shutters, which show one what Smyrna must have been at the turn of the century when it was still in Greek hands. We looked for Manoly's grandparents' house, but there is no longer any trace of it.

ATHENS, 8.vi.63

TO GEOFFREY DUTTON

We finished our travels in a blaze of excitement on Lesbos, the most beautiful and varied island so far. (By now I realise the only way to live in Greece would be on a large and comfortably adapted caïque, cruising round to all one's favourite places, living on board, and cooking all the wonderful things one finds in the markets ashore.) But Lesbos is really exciting, in places very savage grey, distorted rock formation and combed-out trees, in one place a monastery sitting on top of an extinct volcano, here and there gently bucolic, very fertile valleys with trees and streams, reminiscent of Ionia. The most beautiful place of all is Mólivos, one of those villages rising up to a fortress beside the sea. I am only afraid it will become swamped by foreign intellectuals and would-be artists. There are already a number of them there, and at lunch we met Peter Green[9] – I could remember him reviewing *Voss* for one of the London dailies – with his wife and three small children. They were hoping to find a house in Mólivos in which to spend the next seven months. Just along the coast is another village called Petra where we were told there was a collection of the paintings of Theophilos, the 19th Century painter, who came from Lesbos and migrated to Pélion. He dealt mainly with subjects from the War of Independence, and is a most engaging and fertile primitive. The collection belongs to a painter called Elevtheriadis who received us in the rather frightened way of most Greek intellectuals – wondering which political side we were on. The only disappointing thing about Lesbos is Mitilíni, where we were staying. It has the squalor and bourgeois pretensions of most of the island capitals. But it was some compensation to stay at the Lesbian Hotel, with the Sappho in opposition next door, and to find a statue of Sappho looking terribly like Marjorie Barnard. It has given me an idea for a play. Can't you see the opening? Lesbos at night, a starlit court, one of the followers reading from those deathless, palpitating, passionate poems to celebrate the arrival of the poetess in their midst, then – enter Margaret Rutherford. I remember reading Forster's guidebook

[9]Since 1953 fiction critic for the *Daily Telegraph*; his review of *Voss*, 4 May 1956, p.8.

to Alexandria in which he says, roughly: 'At the time of her death Hypatia was not the glamorous slavegirl of fiction, but an elderly lady with a gift for mathematics.' In the same way I expect Sappho was a blowzy bluestocking with a gift for exciting that semi-intellectual semi-sexual frenzy in which Lesbians thrive . . .

You need have no real fear about my living permanently in Greece.[10] It is a wonderful temptation, but I realise it wouldn't work – too many irritations, complications, and then, I am far too deeply rooted in Australia. I think the real reason I have always kept dogs is that the dogs will always force me back, being of a sentimental nature where animals are concerned. And a couple of weeks ago I ordered a dozen advanced pullets for our return in October, as I don't feel life is quite right without a fowlyard. If we sell Dogwoods and move to Sydney, the place we have our eye on should allow us to keep a disguised pen for a few fowls.

The Season opened in Sydney with a great bang – shouts of joy and screams of rage intermingled.[11] But I gather some of the cast are far from good enough, and the whole thing was thrown onto the stage after only a fortnight's rehearsals. The Tasker is now trying madly to cover up by letter, praising in particular those actors everybody else has picked on as bad, and in general doing a Tasker. He left Sydney for Europe a few days after the play opened, which alarmed me exceedingly, both that he shouldn't be there to watch over the production, and because we shall probably have him dogging our footsteps. He will catch up with us in Rome I should think. But I shall be very firm if he bobs up in London. Anyway, I expect we shall have had a bumper row in Rome. He has made a proper fool of himself again in the Sydney press, and was photographed in the foyer on the first night with a kiss-curl plastered on his forehead. Sumner seems enthusiastic about the prospects for *A Cheery Soul,* and has engaged Nita Pannell for Miss Docker. I shall probably go down to Melbourne soon after arrival in Sydney, as Sumner actually wants me to be in on the rehearsals from the beginning!

ATHENS, 28.vi.63

TO MARGERY WILLIAMS

I expect a lot that will be trying in London. My mother has called for her black hat with feathers, because she has heard the King is dead and there is going to be a Black Ascot. So you can imagine some of it.

---

[10]By now he had decided against the Pátmos house.
[11]The Sydney *Mirror*, 23 May, devoted page three to attacks by columnist Ron Saw and critic Frank Harris under the banner headline, 'A PLAY THAT STINKS'.

THE TRAVELLERS LEFT ATHENS on 1 July 1963. Lascaris' father was ill, but White had business in London he would not delay: theatres must be found for his plays; stars persuaded to take the lead in *Night on Bald Mountain*; and Benjamin Britten coaxed into collaborating on the *Fringe of Leaves* opera for the opening of the Opera House. White poured his energy into these projects but they all, in the end, came to nothing. Much of what spare time he had he spent with his mother.

LONDON, 26–30.vii.63
TO BEN HUEBSCH

Since I began this I have been rushing around, mostly wasting time, but always quite pleasantly. I have to go to my mother every other day. She is now 86, more or less blind, and only gets up for a little in a wheelchair. She is a great problem as, at the moment, she has six slaves waiting on her and one another, and my sister and I would like to persuade her into a good nursing home, to save some of the fortune which is being poured out in maintaining the slaves. However, she is very stubborn, and I don't feel I can broach the matter until I have a satisfactory nursing home to offer. I have just persuaded her to start dividing her jewels, furs and furniture between her daughter and grand-daughters, so that the things won't disappear in death duties. All this should have started happening some time ago, but she clings to the possessions she no longer uses and can barely see.

LONDON, 3.viii.63
TO PEGGY GARLAND

Dear Peggy,

Thanks for your letter. I am the one who should have written, but I think you realise how artificial our visit has become from trying to see too many people in a short time. Somebody said the other day that it's like making a series of long distance calls and forgetting to say the important things.

About meeting Betty – I can't say I care for her any more or want to see her, but if you want to ask her to the family reunion I shall be polite. However, I can't act warm when I feel cold, and often, I think, what one doesn't say is worse than what one says. That is the situation, and if you want to make anything of it, it is up to you to decide. I am not good – I only know what good is. That is probably what is wrong with Betty. She knows what it is, and would like to be good, but remains an exercise in goodness.

Have sent you the Jung biography (?) auto-biography (?) memoirs

(?) – difficult to know what to call it.[12] It should be coming from Heywood Hill,[13] and I hope it arrives – H.H. seems terribly vague.

Do you know the taro cards? Yesterday at lunch with the Duttons we met the Australian painter Lawrence Daws[14] (there is a big green abstract of his over the radio at home) and he showed us reproductions of some paintings he has sent out to an exhibition in Brisbane. There was a fascinating series of gouaches which he did after looking at the taro cards, and one of these I am buying on the strength of the reproduction and my nose. He says one can get the cards at Foyles' for 2 gns. – think I am going to have a try!

I expect David told you they are going to do *The Season at Sarsaparilla* at the Mermaid next year.[15]

Hope to see you when we get back from Scotland.

Yrs

Patrick

Went yesterday to the de Staël exhibition, which I like as much as I disliked the Francis Bacon.[16] I could have eaten some of those paintings – the paint looked so thick and good.

LONDON, 14.viii.63

TO ZOE CALDWELL

London is pretty awful – the people so unattractive and lifeless, dirty too. But the theatre is exciting, if high decadent. Australia would have a fit at all the incest, abortion, adultery and language which gets let loose over here on the stage. The 'bloodys' have given way to the 'fucks'.

LONDON, 4.ix.63

TO MARGERY WILLIAMS

My mother has been giving a lot of worry the last few days. She collapsed just before the week-end, and I thought on Sunday she was probably going

---

[12]*Erinnerungen, Träume, Gedanken*, 1961, had been translated in 1962 as *Memories, Dreams, Reflections*.

[13]The London bookshop where PW kept an account; scraps of his correspondence with the shop are now in the library of the Australian Defence Forces' Academy in Canberra.

[14](1927–) whose great importance in PW's life was to reintroduce him to Jung. PW bought Daws' paintings; they argued aesthetics and the need for Australian artists to work in Australia. Their friendship came to grief at the time of Daws' divorce.

[15]PW had given this news to her son but this prospect, like all the others, came to nothing.

[16]De Staël at Gimpel Fils, South Molton Street, and Bacon's bloodied bodies at the Marlborough.

to die, but she rallied, and is taking a bit of notice again, and living on egg and brandy. Her heart is weakening, though, and I think it won't be very long, also she may get pneumonia or uraemia. I wish it would happen as soon as possible, as there is no point in lingering like this, and at least if she dies while I am here, I can help my sister clear things up. The latter is away in Italy at present with an aunt, and I am not saying anything as she has had too many deaths in her life. Nor do I think she is emotionally involved with our mother any more than I am.

LONDON, 28.ix.63
TO GEOFFREY DUTTON
Last night the Nolans took us to see Stravinsky's *Rite*. Sid's sets and costumes are terrific, and altogether I felt I was back in the days when ballet was ballet, not a bunch of English getting into polite positions. There is probably a lot to tell you, but I can't sort it out at the moment. There is hardly a minute to spare away from one's schedule. My mother lingers on, quite brightly at times. We had a good session the other day when I thought of going through all the cooks and maids who had ever worked for us. She enjoyed that, and when I had exhausted them kept asking: 'Haven't you any more reminiscences?' I don't know whether to let her know we are going back to Australia, or just to disappear. In that case she will probably think I haven't called to-day.

APPROACHING ATHENS, 1.x.63
CARD TO CHARLES OSBORNE[17]
We have just eaten the Qantas dinner – life is a little melancholy. A dramatic moment at the airport when we were asked to pay £27 overweight. Fortunately Sid threw his weight about and they let us off. It is dreadful to think we shall have to sit here for another 32 hrs. Must get out the pills after Athens.

    P.

DOGWOODS, 6.x.63
TO THE NOLANS
Dear Cyn and Sid,
Here is the letter to Stravinsky. I hope it does not begin disrespectfully, but I can never bring myself to use that arse-licking word *maestro*. The idea looks somewhat naive when committed to paper, but I hope there is something in it to set him off. It might just become an old man's last profession of faith, although I know it is the wrong faith – he went over to Rome.[18]

    We had a painless journey back. The first night I took the pills, slept heavily, woke groggily. The second night I slept perfectly, without assistance. There were no photographers on arrival, which was surprising, as Hoad and Rosewall were amongst our fellow passengers.[19] The last I saw of Hoad he was stalking through the customs at Mascot in rather elegant manure-coloured tweeds looking resentfully neglected.

    Returning to our house has been quite easy, though I must say it is still pretty cold and mildewy. The garden is a wonderful wilderness of overgrown trees and lank grass, through which our recovered cats stalk, sniffing suspiciously at the leaves of the agapanthus. At night my pug gets beneath the sheets and plasters herself to my side like a strip of hot rubber. So far I haven't had to cook as our friends have been turning up with food, in some cases even complete, cooked meals. Soon I must start about going to show myself, as that arch-liar the *Telegraph* put it about that I had bought a 'palace on a mountain' and was not coming back. (This is all part of the fictitious image they have concocted for me, of rich, scornful dilettante spurning the equally fictitious Little Man and Decent Australian.)

---

[17](1927–), Australian Londoner, broadcaster, arts bureaucrat, biographer, editor of the *London Magazine* where PW's stories appeared in the 1960s. Osborne reviewed many of PW's novels in London. The two men cultivated one another but were not close friends.
[18]This was an idea for a ballet; the composer did not reply.
[19]Tennis stars Lew Hoad (1934–94) and Ken Rosewall (1934–).

The sad part is that many believe it. Our butcher's father died three weeks ago apparently remarking: 'What a pity Patrick White has said good-bye to Australia in that way.' I wonder whether we shall live to see the toads of Packer, the industrialist Philistines, and the landed louts drop off this otherwise acceptable body.

There isn't any more news for the moment, except that I had a cable from my agent which runs: 'Miles insists decision funeral envisaging autumn production advise consent stop Codron signing.' I wonder what it all means. I have agreed to give in to Miles if Codron agrees to take on John Tasker, as I can't dish the latter twice over.[20]

Love from us both,
Patrick.

WHITE HAD RETURNED TO Sydney expecting to hear of his mother's death at any moment. He knew he was about to come into his father's estate and was now, after years of shilly-shallying, determined to sell Dogwoods and make the move into town, put the theatre behind him and return to writing novels of which three or four were already queuing in his mind. Much had to be done before the plan could go into effect: there were stories to collect and polish for his first volume of short stories, *The Burnt Ones*. And he had to face *A Cheery Soul* in Melbourne and *Night on Bald Mountain* in Adelaide. Once again the City Fathers had rejected a Patrick White play, but this time the Guild was mounting it anyway in their own theatre during the Festival. White was brawling with Tasker.

DOGWOODS, 20.x.63
TO GEOFFREY DUTTON
The last few evenings we have been much taken up with trying to do the right thing by Fanny – rushing to Strathfield to mate her with a pug-dog of the noble name of Teng Wah Lo-Sze. Unfortunately Fanny has so far been terrified and Lo-Sze not all that interested. I wish you could see the house in which all this takes place. It is a real Home Beautiful in the right kind of brick, with pixies, storks, and toadstools on the lawn, dog ornaments

---

[20]This tangle led to nothing. Bernard Miles of the Mermaid theatre had taken an option on *Sarsaparilla*, declined rather rudely to meet Tasker and let the option lapse. Now he took an option on *Ham Funeral* which was in turn to lapse unexercised in late 1964. Michael Codron agreed to produce *Bald Mountain* with Tasker directing but, after seeing a reading of the play staged by Tasker in London, Codron's enthusiasm disappeared. So PW's only real chance of London productions was botched by trying to juggle a role for Tasker.

inside – literally hundreds of them, from small china ones to enormous cloth Dismal Desmonds, the size of a man, standing in corners. Quite eerie. The matings take place in what the pug-lady refers to as the 'dogs' TV lounge'. Certainly there is a TV working madly all the time, which is perhaps what puts the dogs off. On the last occasion there was some dreadful musical, with a number, the chorus of which went: 'Sit down! Sit down! Sit down!' Teng Wah Lo-Sze obediently did, and that was the end of the mating for that evening. We are also learning 'terms', such as 'showing colour' for bloody discharge, 'tied', and 'a slip mating' – all too Dekyvere.

MELBOURNE, 21.xi.63
TO PEGGY GARLAND
Dear Peggy,

I am in Melbourne at present, returning home to-night after an exhausting couple of weeks with the play – Manoly sent your letter on. It was fortunate my mother died when she did, and apparently quite peacefully, she simply went off one morning as the nurse was talking to her.[21] As you said, it is certainly the end of something when one's mother dies, even when it has been a mother one has disagreed with all through life. However, I think we both enjoyed the conversations we had during the weeks I was in London.

I am sorry Betty has been giving such trouble. I suppose the old bitch is taking out on you what she feels about me for not going to see her. Unfortunately I have packed your letter God knows where and am leaving for the train in about half an hour. I can't remember all the financial details, but know you would like the loan of a couple of thousand.[22] At the moment I'm afraid I couldn't do anything about it. I do have about £3000 put away, but want to keep it for a particular purpose. We are going to start trying to sell Dogwoods when I get back. It may take a couple of years to get what we want for it, so, I want this money to pay a deposit on a house in Sydney if the right one should turn up in Sydney while we are negotiating over Dogwoods. If the probate on my mother's estate is settled in reasonable time that would be a different matter, and I might

[21]Sitting on her commode, just as Mrs Elizabeth Hunter died in *The Eye of the Storm*. To Ben Huebsch he wrote, 16.xii.63: 'We understood each other in the end after being quite unable to get on all my life.'

[22]To buy a house in the village of Eynsham outside Oxford. Peggy Garland had come here from London in 1962 after placing Philip in a Rudolf Steiner school near Aberdeen. She had been living in a cottage belonging to Betty; she bought her own despite PW's refusal to help.

be able to help you. But I have no idea how long it will take. (It may be very complicated as the money I shall inherit will be from my father's estate, half of which was divided between Suzanne and myself, the rest going to my mother for her lifetime. That kind of will, so safe once upon a time, seems to cause endless complications in Australia to-day.)[23] In any case I hope you won't sell 'Hopwood'[24] in trying to buy a house in England. If you can hang on to 'Hopwood', I'm sure it will be worth a lot more in a few years time.

A *Cheery Soul* opened the night before last. It has been a wonderful experience working with John Sumner after the other director. He seemed to know almost always what I was trying to say, and on occasions when he didn't was willing to accept my explanations. We have a splendid cast, quite passionately devoted to the play. Desmond Digby's sets are about the best he has ever done, starting fairly naturalistically in the first act, and becoming more and more abstract and open as Miss Docker reduces and is finally reduced. Lighting was most difficult, but they succeeded in bringing off what was wanted. Then the first night– – Halfway through I began to smell a greater hostility than I ever encountered at any of my other plays. I am told there were people stamping up and down in the intervals saying the theatre should be locked to keep such stuff out of it. We got through without any too noisy demonstrations during the performance. Almost all the Melbourne critics condemned it (one of them in one line)[25] saying that I am without wit, humour, love, or even liking for human beings, in fact what so many Australian critics said of my novels in the past. Only the *Sydney Morning Herald* gave what one could call a serious review, and one which I can accept on most points.[26] I had some extraordinary individual reactions afterwards, many of them from people who matter in the theatre. The director of the Elizabethan Theatre Trust wouldn't let my hand go, and kept telling me it was a great play.[27] Desmond immediately jumped in and asked when he was going to bring it to Sydney. Haag said:

---

[23]This is not as Dick's will reads but PW's interpretation may reflect some more generous arrangement Ruth made in her lifetime. According to the will she had *all* the income until her death when the estate was divided equally between son and daughter; her own considerable estate she left entirely to Suzanne.

[24]The Garlands' house in Wellington.

[25]'A *Cheery Soul* is a sad play,' said the Melbourne *Sun*, 20 Nov., p.18.

[26]'Faults notwithstanding, the play is illuminated by PW's characteristic humour and finely focused observation . . .', 20 Nov., p.14.

[27]Stefan Haag (1925–86), opera producer, had become executive director of the Elizabethan Theatre Trust earlier in the year; it was Haag who had commissioned PW to write the libretto for an opera to open the Opera House.

'I have wider plans for it.' So we shall see. Last night I went to the second performance, we had a normal audience, with the play all the time, and the actors were much more relaxed. It is going to run a month, and I think we should get quite good houses after this fuss in the beginning, caused mainly by the pretenders of society and provincial would-be intellectuals.[28]

I shall be glad to get home. After that Manoly comes down to see the play, and about the middle of February I shall have to think of leaving for Adelaide and the next trial by theatre. In the meantime I have managed to get down on paper two *Novellen* to provide the backbone of the volume of short things which I am going to call *The Burnt Ones*.

Love
Patrick

The more I think of the answers I got from I Ching that afternoon, the clearer they seem to be.

DOGWOODS, 25.xi.63

TO FREDERICK GLOVER

My mother's death was more a conclusion than anything else. After spending so much time with her in London I realised exactly where we were. There were moments when I felt she had gone already, and others when it seemed as though she had hung on just waiting for our visit. For the first time in my life we reached understanding – at least I think so. Manoly says I am exactly like her, so perhaps that is what was always wrong. One of the most pleasing things about her last days was to see the great affection she had for Manoly. She would really come to life every time he appeared.

WHITE CAST ABOUT FOR a collaborator to work on the Mrs Fraser opera. Peter Sculthorpe was the first Australian composer White found 'in any way exciting'.[29] His music was native, brooding and elegant, but Sculthorpe's voice was essentially contemplative not operatic. He was the wrong man for the project, but at thirty-five Sculthorpe was flattered by the invitation to collaborate and in awe of White. Disaster followed.

---

[28]The play was a financial disaster for the company: it lost £4,228.
[29]PW to Ian Donaldson, 20.i.64.

Dogwoods, 5.xii.63

TO GEOFFREY DUTTON

By now there have been quite a lot of good reactions to A *Cheery Soul*. The *Jewish Herald*, Melbourne, is giving rousing support.[30] But I think it will be many years before most kinds of Australians will realise what the play is about. Even the Jewish paper talks about 'anti-religion', when I thought my own faith would come out through the characters of the clergyman and his wife, and in Miss Docker's final moment of illumination.

I have been pegging away at the rewriting of 'Dead Roses', but was held up last week-end by suddenly wanting to write a song cycle. All Sunday as we drove to Mount Wilson and back it wouldn't leave me alone, and I wrote it down on Sunday night after we got back; it is called *Six Urban Songs*. I suppose really they arise from my disappointment at the inability of most people to understand A *Cheery Soul*, and there is more than a little spleen in them.

A very curious coincidence: the day after, Covell[31] brought Peter Sculthorpe to lunch to discuss the possibility of an opera. In the course of the conversation Sculthorpe said he had been commissioned by a Melbourne group to compose a song cycle, but that he didn't know where he was going to find the words! I was able to say I had them. However, he still has to see them, as I wanted to have another look before typing ... We also talked about the possibility of the Mrs Fraser theme as an opera. He is not very happy at the thought of what he calls a 'historical' opera. I explained that my approach is not historical at all, that I deal with states of mind, and that the content is very contemporary although in a Victorian setting. Now he has taken the synopsis away to Tasmania, stopping in Melbourne on the way to investigate A *Cheery Soul*, which I feel could also become an opera ...

You will probably despise the *Six Urban Songs* as poetry.

Can you please tell me the name of some small S.A. railway siding? The father of a character who is making his way in life, is stationmaster there. The parents are solid gold, and the character goes back occasionally to visit them. He says: 'Dad's the stationmaster at— —.[32] Mother used to clean out the toilets at the Black Bull before she married. They're a bloody boring pair, but they're good. I go down there from time to time, when

---

[30]22 Nov., p.15: 'a play of shattering impact; savage and merciless – but dramatically exciting'.

[31]Roger Covell (1931–), distinguished theatre and music critic in Sydney, later professor of music at the University of NSW.

[32]Buckleboo.

my sense of duty needs refreshing, and learn about the truth at its source. And eat baked parsnip, which I don't particularly like.'

IN THE COURSE OF rehearsals for *A Cheery Soul* White became infatuated with one of the actors, Brian James, who was playing the tongue-tied vicar, Mr Wakeman. James was alarmed by these declarations of White's affection. White's passion for the actor caused fierce arguments at Dogwoods until Lascaris quenched the blaze.

DOGWOODS, 16.xii.63
CARD TO BRIAN JAMES
I am sending this because it seems to express what I had on Saturday afternoon! And this evening I came across this line in Rimbaud: 'A little kiss like a crazy spider will run round your neck— —'[33] All the things I would like to have said are coming out to-night, and it isn't possible to say them. We had lunch yesterday at the Windsor Hotel amongst the hats and the cutlery. It was sad after our two delicious meals the evening before. At the next table there was a party of landed gentry including a lady who complained that the *Himalaya*[34] had been too 'chilly' for her on account of the 'hair conditioning.' Adelaide-Hamlet-Sydney-TV – I shan't think – it must work itself out for us.

DOGWOODS, 21.xii.63
TO PETER SCULTHORPE
Dear Peter,
I was delighted to get your letter – or letters. This won't be exactly a frilly reply, as my pug Fanny gave birth to a litter of seven three days ago, refuses to do anything for them, and we live now by the alarm clock, feeding, and wiping the bottoms of pups. A pug is something to get ready-made. In the circumstances, I shall answer your letter point by point:
   Six Urban Songs: I don't think it necessary to have a chorus if you feel it will jeopardise the work's chances of being performed. But I do think a fairly large orchestra is necessary to bring out what is there, especially in 'Night and Dreams', 'To Watch the River', and the explosive,

[33]*Un petit baiser, comme une folle araignée,*
      Te courra par le cou— —
Et tu me diras: 'Cherche!' en inclinant la tête,
—Et nous prendrons du temps à trouver cette bête
   —Qui voyage beaucoup— —
            from Rimbaud's *Rêvé pour l'hiver*, 1870.
[34]One of the last P&O liners on the London run.

and indeed the supplicating bits of 'God'. I also feel two voices, preferably soprano and baritone, would have to be used. I think one soprano could do 'Song of the Housewives' if the music helps her with the right chattery-nattery, twittery-jittery tones. Perhaps here and there a rumble from the baritone would help – to introduce *Angst*. (However, please disregard any of this if you don't like it, or find it corny. The composer is the one who matters.) 'Night and Dreams' and 'To Watch the River' are obviously for the baritone, but perhaps the soprano could help with odd phrases in 'Night and Dreams', to increase the perfume, and to introduce a cry of ecstasy and fulfilment into the last couple of lines. 'Rhinestones' is light, bright, brittle, glittery, and ought to be the soprano's song. In 'Sick Song' the soprano could help with lines like O Lwow, O Cracow, The pines are bending under snow! though fundamentally the song should belong to the baritone or desperate Pole. The soprano again might help to convey the prayer phrases in 'God' – 'the flowers of the field etc.'

A Cheery Soul: I agree it could not become grand, popular opera, just as the play can only appeal to a certain public. In any case, I am the only public I ever write for. When it comes to opera, you, as the composer, must decide what you want to do, what inspires you to do it. (I can't see *The Aunt's Story* as an opera. It is too introspective – too subtle, I like to think! If I had had technical experience in films, I should like to make it into a film, but I should have to do it myself.)

A Fringe of Leaves: what you say about money, technicians etc – aren't we setting out to have the best goddam opera house in the world? Well, they can't run it on a shoestring with a couple of amateurs operating the switches. So let us set out to give them something for the best opera house in the world . . .

I, too, am busy, until after *Night on Bald Mountain* is launched in Adelaide. Then I should be able to start on the libretto.

DOGWOODS, 9.i.64
TO BRIAN JAMES
My dear Brian,
It seems like ages since I wrote or heard from you. We seem to have been through several crises here – not the least of them being Christmas and continual heat waves . . .

My volume of short pieces is now ready for typing. In fact, all the stories are typed, but as I didn't feel I could type my way through again to make a presentable MS. for a publisher, I have sent them to a typist. As I was finishing the main *Novelle*, which is called 'Dead Roses', it occurred to me it is made for a film needless to say an uncommercial one . . . There is even an unworthy part for you! (One day I must do something I can feel is really yours.)

I am booked in at a motel in Adelaide from 24th Feb till 11th March. Perhaps if your engagements prevent you coming, I can creep in somehow to Melbourne on the way there or back. But I do hope for Adelaide. Alec Archdale[35] has suggested I drive there with him, but he would have to start earlier than I. I can't leave Manoly with so much on his hands for so long. (Incidentally, you are known to exist. I mean M. and I talk about you. He claims to have known when you were introduced in the dressing room.)

Don't bother to send back 'Miss Slattery'. I'm going to send 'Dead Roses' to John Sumner to see what he thinks of it as a film, and whether he has any ideas on how to get it done.

Yesterday I had a receipt from the South Yarra Gallery which brought you terribly close!

Love—

P.

DOGWOODS, 5.ii.64
TO GEOFFREY DUTTON

The Tasker has arrived in Sydney, in a leather hat, a rosebud in his lapel, and an Alister Kershaw accent.[36] He seems to have interviewed the press and spoken on the telly from coast to coast, so that there must already be a considerable body of opposition. We met for a discussion to-day, and it ended up in a shouting match in the restaurant of the Rex Hotel at the Cross. We go over and over the same old points, which I thought we had exhausted by correspondence, and which have caused enough bitterness already. The chief matter for contention is that I refuse to set my play between the Wars instead of in the present. I think the implication is that I am too old-hat to bear the clear white light of to-day. I keep asking him why he condescended to direct the fucking thing. But he harps on telling me 'my cast is most unhappy about it' – other people are always enlisted, now even Max,[37] whom he hates, sees his point of view. It is all part of the Tasker technique – to bash everybody to pulp in the preliminaries,

[35](1905–86), veteran actor playing Sword in *A Night on Bald Mountain*; PW admired Archdale and later supported the theatre company he established on Sydney's North Shore.
[36](1921–) Australian poet whose 1958 essay on the charms of living in Paris provoked PW's polemic, 'Prodigal Son'.
[37]Harris.

and then when he has reduced them to doubt and despondency keep them where he wants them. By now I know enough about it to be anything but a stone wall to his treatment. He started shouting at me; 'You don't trust me! You have no faith in me like you did during *The Ham Funeral*.' I could only reply: 'In those days I didn't know so much about you.' There was much repetition. 'How can I give my actors confidence if you don't have faith in me?' A possibility, of course, and a sad one. 'If what I see at rehearsals gives me faith, I shall have it.' 'Ah, no, but I must have it <u>now</u>!' Already I can see efforts ahead to discourage me from coming to all those rehearsals at which <u>meaning</u> is discussed, and to have me at the run-throughs, by which time the thing will have set, and any call for alteration can be brushed aside. It is too boring to bother you with any more.

DOGWOODS, 14.ii.64
TO BRIAN JAMES
There is a reason for my delay in writing. I told you I had mentioned you to M. as he and I had decided to discuss such things. However, as it turned out, that didn't work at all. He could accept it intellectually, but not emotionally. There have been scenes and accusations. I don't blame him, I should have made far worse ones. As things have turned out, I would like to try to put your and my relationship on a different basis, so that we can all three meet in friendship when you come to Sydney. At least I don't <u>feel</u> that you are particularly involved with <u>me</u>. Perhaps I am wrong, in which case I hate to think I may have caused you any unhappiness, because I am and always shall be <u>very</u> involved with M. I do hope things will sort themselves out, and that you will feel you can come here when you are working in Sydney. I think you and M. will like each other.

Are you still thinking of coming to Adelaide?! If you can make it, I should like you to sit with me on the first night (March 9th) – that is, if you can bear to be near anyone so jittery at the opening of one of his own plays. There is a party afterwards given by the Guild – the card says 'black tie', but I personally don't possess such a thing . . .

Looking back at the earlier part of this letter I think there is probably a lot of vanity in it. At least I hope we can continue to meet without any effort on your part. Please let me know about Adelaide, because if you won't be there I shall ask Desmond to use the ticket. (M. can't go till I get home to look after the animals.)

Write soon and let me know what is happening to you.
P.

I leave here on 24th. My address in Adelaide is: Scotty's Motel, North Adelaide.[38]

DOGWOODS, 13.iii.64
TO FREDERICK GLOVER
Dear Frederick,
It is all safely over. I got home the night before last feeling more exhausted than I have ever been. I spent practically the whole fortnight in the theatre as we were rehearsing day and night, sometimes into the small hours of the morning. As the stage director went off to Melbourne to teach law over a fortnight before we opened and the prop girl was almost useless, there were times when I was driving all over Adelaide looking for suitable furniture. This added quite a lot to one's exhaustion. Then, although it was impossible to go to any of the other productions, one made a dash during intervals to see the various exhibitions of paintings. I carefully avoided Writers' Week, which began a couple of days before I left, but had some pleasant meetings with the Duttons, the Wightons,[39] the Bryn Davies,[40] the Haywards, and Sid Nolan. But being in the theatre during rehearsals is really like belonging to a religious order.

I was very pleased with the way they did the play. Wendy's sets were most effective in the end, though fiendishly difficult to construct and manage without experienced mechanists, and the actors complained a lot during rehearsals at the difficulty of acting in some of the areas.[41] There was one young man in a less important part rather stodgy and amateurish, but everyone else did very well. The Tasker had his moments of odiousness as far as I was concerned, but I think he realised from our meeting in Sydney that I was not going to stand for too much, and that kept him in check. However, he got under the actors' skins on several occasions. Alec was muttering that he would kick him in the teeth before we had finished, and Nita[42] at one stage burst into tears and threatened to catch the plane to Perth. The trouble is the lout just hasn't the vaguest idea how to handle

[38]This letter, which PW showed Lascaris before posting, marked the end of the episode. James did not go to Adelaide.
[39]Dugald and Rosemary Wighton. She (1925–94), one of the editors of *Australian Letters* and *Australian Book Review*, was closely involved with Writers' Week for the next few decades and became a Governor of the Adelaide Festival.
[40]Belle and Bryn Davies. He (1904–92), an eccentric academic late of Cairo University, was also an editor of *Australian Letters* 1957–64.
[41]Dickson had to place on the stage a mountain hut, the interior of a large house and a stretch of bush.
[42]Nita Pannell who played the goat woman Mrs Quodling.

people. I think his production was very good, though, and the critics have picked on him unfairly. Still, bad, good, or Zeferelli, I should never have him again. I don't know which notices you have seen. I think Covell was just in his,[43] and for the first time in history I have been reviewed seriously in the *Telegraph*. I was given Martin Long[44] instead of the usual illiterate hack. But the two Melbourne papers to have reviewed us so far (*Herald* and *Sun*) have behaved in their usual way, though perhaps the notices didn't stink as high as those for *Cheery Soul*.[45] Audiences seem to be with us . . .

The day before I left for Adelaide Stefan[46] came out and talked about the opera and said the Trust was prepared to support us. I also had a meeting with him in Adelaide with Sculthorpe and Nolan to discuss some of the technical details. He appears to want to direct it himself, and remembering *The Consul* I should like him to.[47] As soon as I have looked through my four plays so that their final versions can go to the publishers I must get on with the libretto. I have already written a couple of scenes to get the feel of sung lines, and I believe Peter has set them to music, but there was too much of a hurlyburly in Adelaide to be able to discuss things seriously . . .

The first Sunday I went up to Anlaby for the christening, which was a large affair of about a hundred and forty guests. How the Duttons do all these things I don't know, because they had prepared all the food and only had a bit of hired help on the day. The christening took place in the pre-Raphaelite church the grandfather built in the burnt-up Australian paddocks. I spent the night at Anlaby, and it was very restful after the guests had gone.

DOGWOODS, 18.iii.64
TO BEN HUEBSCH
Dear Ben,
It is a relief to find you see the stories in the light I hoped you would. I

---

[43]Roger Covell, *SMH*, 11 Mar., p.12: 'this flawed, in places clumsily constructed, but in many ways admirable piece of theatre, seems likely to outstay in the memory most of the more superficially appealing events of this festival.'

[44]Long (1920–   ) called the play, 11 March, p.2, 'a passionate and skilful contribution to the small but growing stock of Australian drama'.

[45]H. A. Standish in the *Herald*, 10 March, p.14: 'The play as a whole has a somewhat noxious air.' Howard Palmer in the *Sun*, 11 March, p.28: 'A few good lines and a good plot do not make a play. A pile of bricks is not a house.'

[46]Haag.

[47]Haag directed Menotti's opera in 1953 for the Australian National Theatre Movement.

am a bit surprised, however, that you should want to have some of them printed first in magazines. That is, I can see the point, but for years I tried through Edith Haggard of Curtis Brown to get my stories into American magazines, and was told repeatedly that American magazine readers would not understand them. Finally I took it that the reader of American magazines was a particular kind of moron. Magazine after magazine turned the stories down. All my friends who read 'Miss Slattery and Her Demon Lover' thought it was a certainty for the *New Yorker*. But I think 'Miss Slattery' must have been turned down by almost every magazine in America. On the other hand when it was published in the *London Magazine*, I began to receive messages of congratulation from all over the world. 'Dazzling' was the word most frequently used. The only story which got anywhere in the States was 'Being Kind to Titina', which was accepted by *Harpers*. But when I received the proof and found that every foreign word and every reference to sex had been cut out, I preferred to withdraw and send back the money, although I had already spent it . . .

I am just back from Adelaide where my play *Night on Bald Mountain* is filling the theatre. Although the original intention was to run it only for the duration of the Festival, they have now decided to keep it on for another week . . . The day I caught the plane home I was taken to lunch at the Adelaide Club (the stronghold of the opposition) with two of the more liberal Festival Governors in the party and a number of the dying elephants looking on.

WHITE COOKED A MEAL for Sculthorpe soon after they returned from the Festival. Over dinner all their differences were revealed. White now began to see that Sculthorpe was not the composer he wanted and accused him of failing to understand his characters. Sculthorpe found White unwilling to accept any changes to the first scenes he had written, scenes Sculthorpe considered impossible to set.

DOGWOODS, 3.iv.64
TO PETER SCULTHORPE
Dear Peter,
I am sorry about last night. Of course it was fatal to try to discuss such things after I had been cooking a meal, by which time I am always at my worst. But I should have felt shattered in any circumstances to find you had gathered <u>nothing</u> about Mrs Roxburgh from the synopsis.[48] You say you see the other characters, but all the others are there only for her sake.

---

[48]The Mrs Fraser of PW's version.

She is the only one who really interests me. Even the convict is no more than a necessity of Mrs Roxburgh's. You must have a mind the complete antithesis of mine – analytical, whereas I approach everything intuitively. Perhaps in the long run this may be a good thing – if it is not a complete disaster!

In the meantime I must try to tell you something about Mrs Roxburgh. It's a pity the novel I wrote is in my very bad longhand; otherwise I could have given you that to read and saved a lot of trouble. When, in answer to your question, I said Mrs R. was a bitch, it is not strictly true, only that in the end she does give way to her latent sensuality. She was a farmer's daughter, a wild and rather passionate little girl on a farm in North Cornwall. When she was a child her father once drove her in their gig to Tintagel, and told her the legend of the place. Always at the back of her mind there has been the vision of a boat beaching, and some kind of radiant male figure landing to play a part in her life ... After the shattering experience of her husband's death, Mrs Roxburgh becomes an automaton for a little – while she is the aboriginal slave. She is probably sustained by her origins – the farmer's daughter on a windswept, struggling, North Cornish farm. Then she meets Masters. There is the natural relief of the situation, and by degrees he becomes the Tristan figure of the Tintagel legend which has always been at the back of her mind. Soon it is easy enough to transform the legend into fact. But at the same time she experiences guilt. She feels she is betraying her dead husband, whom she did genuinely love ... When the fever leaves her,[49] and the kind conventional people come to take her away. She persuades herself for a moment, that as she stands transformed in her crinoline, that she will be able to return to that former life, in which she channelled her sensuality into contact with things 'my necklace of topaze, my necklace of emerald' etc etc., but realises at once that when she descends the marble spiral the trees she has climbed with the incredible Masters will be rooted in the hall. As the voices of kind friends are prescribing remedies, and Miss Sibilant is sounding her conscience-notes, Mrs Doke can't resist sounding Mrs Roxburgh on her second husband of whom she has spoken in delirium. But Mrs Roxburgh replies: 'It is too sad to tell.' This is the last line she utters as she goes out, and should and could be made most poignant. It must contain the whole of Mrs Roxburgh's future in it. I think the opera should end on that note.

I hope you see something more in the character of Mrs Roxburgh after this. I could write about her endlessly, because I understand her

---

[49]After returning to civilisation.

so well. I think the only thing will be for me to write the libretto in some form or other; then you can see.

If I referred to the treadmill idea last night as corn, that again was an unfortunate word. What I feel is that to introduce that motif right at the start would be to fire off too heavy a gun too soon.

Yrs
Patrick.

DOGWOODS, 7.iv.64
TO PEGGY GARLAND
We have just started something which may turn out a bit tricky. There is no sign of anybody coming to buy Dogwoods, but rather than spend years of the few left to us waiting for a buyer, we started looking at houses in Sydney. The other day we found one which I think can be made very comfortable and attractive, so I decided not to wait, and am raising the money on my mother's estate. God knows when we shall be entitled to lay hands on that officially – and I don't know what will happen when the time comes to move into the new house and nobody has come for Dogwoods. The estate agents all say nobody will give us our price for it as a house with garden, the place's only value is as land to be cut up when the 'developer' can get it out of the Green Belt. Of course I realise all that. The people with money all want to show off in bogus Tudor mansions in another part of Castle Hill. Lots of people who covet Dogwoods don't have the money. So it looks as though it will have to go to the spoilers. But when? We shall have to try an auction just after we move out, rather than leave it for hooligans to smash up.

The new house is on the edge of Centennial Park, which is the largest park in Sydney, and there is another park behind us. The address is unfashionable and the house of the wrong period – it must have been built some time during the first decade of the century – but it has the makings of what we want, and it will be like living in the country while only ten minutes' drive from the G.P.O. There is a forty foot living room with wonderful wall space for paintings, and another large room which I shall use as a workroom. Both the kitchen and laundry are large compared with what one usually finds, an excellent, if very pastel bathroom, two spare rooms on the ground floor, and the bedrooms which we shall use are large interesting atticky, with glassed-in balconies looking out over the park. There are two garages, when you rarely find one in Sydney – one of these we shall be able to use for tools and luggage and things – , the garden is enough to keep us happy, and already wired to receive dogs. Perhaps the greatest advantage is that very little will have to be done beyond altering some ceilings, architraves of doorways, and painting, before the place will be habitable. I hope there will be some way of your coming eventually to stay at the house on Centennial Park . . .

I had started the libretto for an opera which I had been contemplating for some time, but the composer came to dinner last week and informed me that <u>he</u> didn't begin to understand my central character. I would have withdrawn there and then if it had concerned only myself, but Sid Nolan, from whose Mrs Fraser paintings I got the idea originally, is very keen on doing the opera, and the Elizabethan Trust has just announced they will support us. Anyway, I am doing nothing for the moment, except send the composer a biography of the character he doesn't understand.

There is this curious business of 'understanding' with Australians. What they really crave for is factual journalism.

The volume of short stories and *Novellen* called *The Burnt Ones* seems to have registered with my London and New York publishers, and it will be coming out towards the end of the year. Then there will also be the volume of four plays later on. However, I wish I could see where to go next, although I have several novels and a couple of plays in my head. This wretched libretto hanging fire has bemused me for the moment.

DOGWOODS, 30.iv.64
TO MARSHALL BEST

I am determined to move and start building the shell for my last years while I am still young enough to do it. This may sound over-pessimistic, but I only consider it realistic. From experience I know that it takes years to make the shell, and I suppose I can reasonably expect another twenty years before senility sets in – or the chopper descends.

DOGWOODS, 14.v.64
TO SIDNEY NOLAN
Dear Sid,

I was very glad to get your letter to-day as this whole opera contretemps has been very upsetting. After reading the Strauss-Hofmannsthal correspondence,[50] and another illuminating book, on Berg, by a man called Redlich,[51] I feel that to bounce into writing a complete libretto on the off

[50]*The Correspondence between Richard Strauss and Hugo von Hofmannsthal*, trans. Hanns Hammelann and Ewald Osers, 1961.
[51]*Alban Berg: The Man and his Music*, Hans Redlich, 1957.

chance of pleasing would be madness unless one were completely in tune with the composer. I am sure that you and I could do it if you were the composer, but I am just not sure of Sculthorpe as the composer for this particular opera. We have met again, and it was all very agreeable, but I would like to hear some more of his music. I think probably he may do something about the Urban Songs after he has composed the quartet which Musica Viva has commissioned,[52] and then one may have more of an idea – though the Urban Songs are a far cry from Mrs Fraser. If I bring up Pelléas and Mélisande I am told by the experts that that is something which happened at a certain point in music, and we have gone on irrevocably from there. They could well be right.[53] I feel that opera to-day, and in Australia, should develop more out of the idiom and mentality of a Berg, and of course the Mrs Fraser story does not connect up with that. I think perhaps in the end we must hope for somebody who will connect up with us and it and the present; it might be done as one isolated work.

In any case shall we wait just a little to see how Sculthorpe develops? By that time too, I may have got to know him better, find him less superficial, and he will have shown which way he means to go. The Trust, as far as I can see, are quite prepared to destroy him as a real composer for the sake of quick and easy returns from a popular work. Before Haag left for Europe he thrust on him a copy of Nino Culotta's Gone Fishin' as an inspiration![54] The most horrible piece of 'European-Australian' vulgarity on Haag's part that I have yet come across. (I shall come back to H. in a minute.)

I told you about the story which is circulating about my having thrown a dish of rice at a Donald Friend painting the night Peter came to discuss the opera. Apparently this was concocted by a woman called Lillian Peart, wife of the Professor of Music at the University. She is a great

---

[52]String Quartet No.6, financed by the Alfred Hill Memorial Award administered by Musica Viva.

[53]Debussy, in setting Maurice Maeterlinck's symbolist play Pelléas et Mélisande, had faced the same challenge now facing PW's collaborator: to set a literary text of many thousand words. 'Patrick loved Pelléas, and understandably loved the quasi-recitative of the word-setting,' Sculthorpe told me, 18.i.94. He commended PW for looking to then-unfashionable Debussy: 'extraordinarily perceptive . . . all the more extraordinary being contrary to the zeitgeist.' Sculthorpe noted that Maeterlinck's falling out with Debussy almost led to a duel.

[54]A comic novel, 1962, by John O'Grady writing in the guise of an Italian migrant. Haag was making the point that even in this novel the characters, unlike those in PW's libretto, had an operatic quality: they could be made to sing.

interferer and source of gossip.[55] Peter says he did mention something about 'arguments' but nothing more. He was mystified when I brought up the rice, but then said it tied up with a remark he had heard the same day and which he had not been able to understand at the time. A girl pupil who had been with him for tuition asked how the opera was coming along. He said it hadn't started, and then she replied: 'Oh . . . I did hear something about a dish of spaghetti', and immediately stopped as though she had overstepped the mark. So these stories circulate and change their shape en route.

The really upsetting one is the one I heard the other night at a concert. It may be just another dish of rice-spaghetti, but I must ask you to keep it well under your hat for the time being. The story is that Haag himself started to write *A Fringe of Leaves* a few weeks ago. I can't feel he would be so underhand, without even a word to me. If it is true, and you agree to it, I am willing to abide by that, especially as I don't feel that this is the moment for me to embark. However, if Haag is writing the libretto, and you don't like the smell of it, I shall be prepared to sue, hoping to catch the Trust acquiescing at the same time. But as I have said, and as I hope, because I like Haag, it is probably one of those malicious stories.[56]

I must also confess I shall probably write another novel if I don't start the opera now. It is not that I am staving off the opera in favour of the novel. I think I am really taking refuge in a novel after the bashing up I have had over my last two plays, and feeling that the world of opera would be ten times worse than the world of theatre proper. The latest attack has come from Bob Hughes in a piece he has written for the *London Magazine* on *Night on Bald Mountain*.[57] It is all written in the brashest, most vulgar, facetious undergraduate style. Some of his assertions are quite fantastic. He claims that the girl was 'not a virgin', and so her behaviour was incomprehensible. Short of having her stand on a rock and shout: 'I am a virgin!' for the benefit of the Bob Hugheses, I don't see how I could have made it clearer. A lot of people complained because she was a virgin but I suppose Bob couldn't believe such a phenomenon exists. In another classic passage he comes out with:

[55]The story came to PW via Doris Fitton and Lillian Peart (1912–93); though denied by PW in his lifetime and Sculthorpe since, the story remains alive today. PW never owned and disliked the work of his Tudor House contemporary Donald Friend (1915–89).

[56]It was.

[57]Robert Hughes (1938–   ), painter and critic whose review of the play appeared in May 1964, p.60.

'Sword's knowledge is no use to him; it cannot save his marriage; only sensuality could have done that.' Whose marriage was saved by sensuality I would like to know. The piece is full of this kind of thing, and there is no point in going on about it. At least, after this, I shall look with renewed interest at those little white-maggoty bitten-to-the-quick fingers and his dishonest kleptomaniac paintings.[58]

We are moving very slowly towards the new house. All the investigations take so long. I feel I am dealing with a pre-Revolution Russian bureaucracy half the time, and my solicitors sit like owls in some cluttered Dickensian nest. To-day I have been with the architect, and at least he has some good practical ideas for alterations. If we can get the last and most important document out of the City Council I hope we may be at Centennial Park by the end of July. That is when my sister arrives with her three daughters. I would like to be able to house her, if they want, though actually I don't think they will want. The two elder nieces are terribly conventional Kensington young ladies. It is the little one, rising eight, I want to lay hands on. She is all the time drawing and reading, and I think there is something there. She has never lived amongst books and paintings, and this would be the chance.

Your 'Chain Gang in Galaxy' has impressed all the people I wanted to impress – impress is the wrong word, because it has made them visibly enthusiastic – whereas all the dead-heads have recoiled, and that too, is how it should be.[59] I think the canvas needs stretching, to reconcile the details with the edges, but I shall wait now until we move, then hope to rope in the expert from the Gallery. At the same time my big Fairweather wants treating to preserve it from disintegration.

Did you know that Godfrey Miller died last week? He was old and

---

[58]Hughes had enthusiastically defended PW in the *Ham Funeral* crisis but soon after, in Sydney's *Nation*, 21 April 1962, p.19, he attacked the work of Tom Gleghorn (1925–) as 'the painting of an illiterate with good handwriting', etc. PW at this time admired and collected Gleghorn's abstracts and retaliated by accusing Hughes in a number of letters of borrowing too much in his own paintings. To the Duttons, 4.v.62, PW described Hughes as 'not a painter at all. He is an intellectual who would like to be one, whereas Tom is 100% artist. It is time Bob decided to be an intellectual and simmer in his own bile and frustration.' Hughes abandoned painting; PW changed his mind about Gleghorn; he never revised his opinion of Hughes.

[59]Originally called 'Soldiers Shelled while Bathing', it was renamed 'Galaxy' after PW saw it in the catalogue of an exhibition and wrote to the Nolans, 18.ix.59, it 'looks like a celestial chain-gang knee-deep in the Milky Way'. He mentioned the painting often; Nolan took the hint and gave it to PW.

mad and I suppose it was the best thing. I once tried to buy his 'Nude with the Moon', and shall always regret not having done so – but before he worked it up into the dried-out composition which now hangs in the Gallery.[60]

I have just finished a book you gave me in London – *Sacred and Profane Beauty* by Gerardus van der Leeuw. A lot of it I found ponderously American-Germanic, and the final theological arguments were frankly above me, but all along the way I found remarkable flashes of wisdom. It has been a great standby, together with my recordings of Bach, in the last nightmarish weeks. Are you a Bach enthusiast? Whenever I am feeling mentally ill, I play him endlessly. His sanity and simplicity make me sane again.

I have also been playing the Strauss operas on and off, lent me by Desmond Digby – *Ariadne auf Naxos* (fascinatingly elegant, when it doesn't slip over into vulgarity), *Arabella* (rather light-operettish), and *Die Frau Ohne Schatten*. The last I find wonderful musically, except for the denouement, and fascinating as a libretto – but as an opera it has been a great failure, and so, perhaps, here is evidence again that I am on the wrong tracks.

So glad you have begun on the Ladies.[61] I shall look out the 'Six Songs' and send them in the next few days, also the synopsis for the much criticised libretto. It is wonderful to think you will both be coming out here, I hope you will feel you can come to us in the beginning until you have put your own house in order.

We have a very good friend who will probably be getting in touch with Cynthia while she is in London. She is Margery Williams, the wife of the British Council representative in Australia. She is both intelligent and perceptive, and I think you will like her.

Yours

Patrick

European experts warn me that *Frau Ohne Schatten* could easily be our downfall!

---

[60]Miller (1893–1964), a rich man who lived in squalor painting difficult paintings, was a principal source for the portrait of PW's Hurtle Duffield who lived and worked in much the same territory, was courted by the same clients, clung to his own paintings, etc. PW brought fresh eggs and oranges from Castle Hill hoping to persuade Miller to sell 'Nude with Moon'.

[61]Portraits of women in hats inspired by figures in PW's novels.

Dogwoods, 24.v.64

TO GEOFFREY DUTTON

Now a word of criticism from me. All this commerce – flying about – Melbourne twice – Kangaroo Island almost immediately after, and the Festival before that – how is it all going to affect your work, the work which really matters? I wrote some time ago that I had seen signs of deepening and maturing in your criticism and when you settled at Anlaby I hoped you were going to give more time to this. Now I am beginning to have my doubts. It is very difficult to write this kind of thing without sounding pompous and awful, but I feel that you and I can quite easily get sucked back into something from which we thought we had escaped. I know I have to sit down to a serious stocktaking. I feel just about clapped out creatively – partly through the recent critical battering, partly through the temptation to become a kind of social flibbertygibbert. I've got to humble myself, and more or less start painfully all over again.

Now that I've got that off my chest, perhaps we can talk of other things! . . .

Further: Expect you heard from Ursula[62] about our funny evening at Hannah Lloyd Jones'. Apart from a conversation with Sid on the veranda, with the moon coming up behind some tall gums, and a good gossipy gin-up with Ursula herself at the end, it was a bloody awful evening, full of Baillieus[63] looking like their bulls. Dinner was all little tables, and I seemed to get stuck at the wrong one. The other man opened with: 'Well, Mr White, I hope you will consider returning to live among us.' I answered feebly that I had been doing just that for the last 17 years. I had beside me Hannah's very bedroomy niece Mari (Livingston) Gibb, an ageing blonde, who looked as though she would oblige quickly under the stairs.[64] On my other side was rather a rigid young woman in blue, from Adelaide, a Gosse[65] or a Hay – Dull, but to be trusted. People who read the Sunday papers tell me that this party was the social highlight of Show week. Wadda-ya know! Still, I like old Hannah when she stops having the social jitters, and one can get down to talking about a few new lines for the shop. Ursula, I have discovered, is a Geminian, which explains that certain empathy.

How this letter has drawn itself out. I think I am staving off the evil moment when I start answering some dirty ones.

[62]Ursula Hayward.
[63]Melbourne dynasty that survived disreputable beginnings as land dealers to become stockbrokers, bankers, miners and graziers.
[64]Not her reputation.
[65]Christel, wife of the industrialist Edmund Barr Gosse.

Our pug strain has enjoyed a triumph at the Royal. Ethel's grandfather won the Dog Challenge, her father the Reserve, her grandmother the Bitches' Challenge, and practically every other prize was carried off by a relation. I expect, unconsciously, I am buying that house at Centennial Park so that I can walk across next year with Ethel and a basket of lunch, and carry off the Bitches' Challenge. She is preparing for it every day.

Love to all –

Patrick.

DOGWOODS, 12.vi.64

TO BEN HUEBSCH

I hear quite often from the Nolans, who are returning next year as the result of an idea I gave him for a new series of paintings. The painting in the background of my photograph, by the way, is one of his, which he gave us recently.[66] Expect the N.s will hate Australia, and the Australians are waiting to bash them good and hard as compatriots who went away and became a success. It is really a hateful country, and I think if I were 15 years younger I would go away and stay away for good. As it is I hope to take root in this new house, which will be closer to the source of something I want to write during my remaining years. But before that, when I can find the peace and time, I shall probably have to write the last of the Sarsaparilla novels.

THIS WAS *THE SOLID MANDALA*, a search for wholeness and serenity in the story of Arthur and Waldo Brown, twins whose lives remain entwined to the end, two halves of an odd whole. The figure of simple Arthur owes a great deal to White's memory of Philip Garland; to create the monster Waldo – an unsuccessful, unprolific, jealous Australian writer – White drew on his own worst fears of himself. Hate poured into the pages of *The Solid Mandala*. White was gloomier than ever about the human race, and the frustrations of the theatre years just passed had left him with a darker, more pessimistic view of his fellow-countrymen. But the theatre had also sharpened his prose.

DOGWOODS, 3.vii.64

TO MARSHALL BEST

Dear Marshall,

I have corrected the proof of *The Burnt Ones* and have posted it back to-

---

[66]This was 'Galaxy'; the photograph by Axel Poignant (1906–86) appeared on the jacket of *The Burnt Ones*.

day. Both you and the proof reader seem worried about explanations to
Greek words. Well, I have explained a few more, but as many of them are
food dishes, and don't have a compact enough name, I prefer to leave out
the explanation rather than embark on something like: Meat rissoles, with
lots of garlic and cumin, stewed in tomato sauce – which would turn the
thing into a tedious and humourless cookery book. There are clues in the
context to most of the other unexplained words – that is, for the intelligent
reader, of some worldliness; the other kind would not be interested in the
book anyway.

The proof reader is also worried about some of the Australianisms.
But I refuse to pander to the American reader to that extent. There is a
lot in the American language I have had to puzzle out for myself, and am
none the worse for doing so. Why can't the American do the same when
it comes to ours? When there are things I don't understand in any language,
it doesn't detract from the context as a whole. I had to quote two lines
from *Miss Slattery and her Demon Lover* for the proof-reader: 'Oh dear,' she
said, 'you're a whale for knowing. Aren't there the things you just accept?'
That's my way, though perhaps I would be less ignorant if I had been less
acceptant.

Yours

Patrick.

DOGWOODS, 9.viii.64

TO THE DUTTONS

Dear Nin and Geoffrey,

I am afraid I have fallen badly behind the birthdays – those fifteen Leos
with whom we are acquainted – but I hope you have had and will have
happy ones. I am wondering whether you have read Manning Clark's Vol
I.[67] Last year he sent me a copy, and I groaned loud to myself, stuck it on
a shelf, and there it stayed until suddenly the other day I realised he is
expected back in August. Felt I must at least look at the book, and found
myself plunged into a fascinating, perhaps even a great work. I could have
sat and read it from cover to cover if it hadn't been for the interruptions.
If you have not read it Manoly and I would like to give it to you as a Leo
birthday present, but I expect you have already had it, and may even

---

[67]*A History of Australia. Vol 1. From the Earliest Times to the Age of Macquarie*, 1962.
About 1960, the historian (1915–91) was introduced to PW by James McAuley in
George Street. Clark told me he was struck by the hunger on PW's face, 'a hunger for
forgiveness in a man who places himself, through his pride and pessimism, beyond the
reach of forgiveness'.

dislike the book. Anyway, please let me know so that we can think of something else.

I am now feeling more or less normal again.[68] Those cortisone hangovers, however, are so long and so depressing one feels for a long time as one plods round zombie-like that one will never do anything worthwhile. In addition to that I had to have the sharp remains of my broken tooth pulled out. The dentist left the root behind, with the result that I had to pay a visit the same day to a surgeon who carved it out and sewed me up. No sooner over that than I had a violent attack of the fashionable diarrhoea. But the last few days I have felt so far restored that I have got back to my old routine of working through the small hours of the morning. Novels are really very peaceful and gentlemanly after plays, though one forgets how difficult and what a prolonged labour they can be. What had seemed fairly straightforward in the beginning is developing into something infinitely complex as details accumulate and side-roads open up. Still, it is satisfying to become involved again. I only wish I could close the door in Martin Road and sit down to it in comparative peace of mind.

But I suppose it will be weeks yet before the house is finished, let alone furnished adequately. We have been there the last two Wednesdays and things are going slowly. Fortunately we like the builder and feel he is honest, but all those bodies like plasterers and plumbers fail to turn up when they are expected. I suspect the house has a somewhat fishy past. They have come across lots of strange little hiding places, and all the ground-floor windows had been screwed up with screws which, the builder says, must have been there a very long time. I am almost prepared for somebody else's shady past to turn up one night and show us the point of a gun. Since we first went there the neighbours seem to have pressed very close. On one side we find there is a barbeque, and a kiddy, at which the dogs would stand and bark, so we have had to order a paling fence. That same side there is also a Shetland pony in a garage. The other, the Greek side, there is going to be an Alsatian and although there will be a fairly high dog-proof fence I fear it may not stop an Alsatian, and that our girls may get raped when they are in season.

My sister and nieces are staying with the Taits somewhere down in the direction of Canberra.[69] They have been so rushed I must say I have only seen Suzanne twice. I think she is getting rather sick of some of the people to who she is being subjected, and of being taken to lunch at the

---

[68]An asthma attack had landed him in hospital for a fortnight.
[69]Daisie Tait was the Pecks' cousin and an old friend of Suzanne; their properties were not near Canberra but further west at Cootamundra.

Macquarie or the Rose Bay Golf Club alternately. Sydney people no longer seem to entertain in their houses; I expect they have lost faith in their tin-openers . . .

Treania Smith[70] has produced a possible buyer for Dogwoods – the P & O agent from Aden who wants to retire to Castle Hill with a medium house and large garden. But I still have hopes that the Dutch woman with the riding school will be able to buy it, as I think she would be the right one.

Happy Everything at Anlaby– – What has become of the Eyre book? It is some time since I heard it mentioned, and I hope it has not become submerged in commerce.[71] On the other hand I may have been too submerged in my own affairs to take in those of other people!

Yrs
Patrick.

ON THE MORNING OF 7 August 1964 a valet at the Athenæum Court Hotel in London found Ben Huebsch sitting at his desk, a cigar in one hand and a pen in the other. He had died in the night while writing a letter to his son. The body was cremated in London but the publishers of New York held a memorial meeting of their Grolier Club later in the year to honour Huebsch.

20 MARTIN ROAD, SEPT. 1964
TO THE GROLIER CLUB
I first met Ben Huebsch in 1939 when I landed in New York, rather scared, to try to publish my first novel.[72] I had been turned down by practically every publisher in New York when Jean Starr Untermeyer, to whom I had an introduction, decided to bring me together with Huebsch. I was very frightened. But the strange thing happened: he took me seriously, he saw something in my book, and then began a relationship which lasted until he left us. Ben stuck to me through the unacceptable years. He

---

[70]Treania Smith (1910–90), partner with the intimidating collector Lucy Swanton (1901–81) in Sydney's Macquarie Galleries. Though PW often complained the 'Macquarie girls' were out of touch and their exhibitions dull, he wished the place well. PW thanked Maie Casey for agreeing to visit the gallery, 8.viii.66: 'the mink locusts will decide they ought to descend.' PW portrayed the proprietors in The Vivisector as the 'steel eagle' Ailsa Harkness and the 'red ferret' Biddy Prickett.
[71]The Hero as Murderer: The Life of Edward John Eyre appeared in 1967: 'a noble work', PW told Dutton, 12.viii.68, 'I hope you will write others in that vein.'
[72]PW probably met Huebsch on his return to New York in 1940 after Happy Valley was accepted.

became as much a part of my writing as those other necessaries, paper and ink. It was so important in my uncertain youth, to say nothing of my vacillating middle-age, I realise now, to feel that here was one of the certainties.

Living at opposite ends of the earth we met rarely, but each meeting when it happened had something rare and memorable about it. After the war, after I had been demobilised in London, I was living in Ebury Street, in a bed-sittingroom which had not yet recovered from its bomb damage. I had begun painfully to learn to write again, and it seemed so right that Ben should turn up in my rather bare, carpetless room next to the bomb site. We strolled about London, and I began to suspect one might return to the things that matter most.

Years later – Ben much older, walking with a stick, but no less tough in spirit or agile of mind. I had travelled across Italy to meet him in Milan – perhaps the least rewarding Italian city. But there was the perfect day, eating trout in the sunshine on the edge of Maggiore. Afterwards we took the little steamer to the Borromean Isles. It will remain one of my great pleasures, to have seen the white peacocks and the rock crystals of Isole Bella in Ben Huebsch's company on that gently perfect day.

We met again in London in the summer of 1963. Again happy, memorable occasions. When Ben was preparing to leave on some incredible but typically Huebschian journey across Spain. We were planning our next meeting – but only superficially, humanly planning. I felt, as he closed the door, we had been telling each other that this would be the last time. Such qualities as were united in Ben Huebsch, of warm heart and worldly wit, of subtle perception and simple directness, of immense steadfastness and intellectual renewal, are never more than partially withdrawn into the core of truth.[73]

DOGWOODS, 13.ix.64
TO MOLLIE McKIE
In what the builder calls ten days to a fortnight and the architect a fortnight to three weeks we are supposed to be leaving Castle Hill and moving to Centennial Park ... I shall be glad to go. I realise I have never liked Castle Hill, only this place, which has been good to my work and necessary for it. What I have left to write has more connexion with the city, and I want to be there to knit up all the threads.

---

[73]The original is lost; this text comes from a privately published booklet, B. W. Huebsch, 1876–1964, A record of a meeting of his friends at the Grolier Club, New York City, on December 9, 1964.

NINE

Martin Road

October 1964 – January 1967

A BONFIRE OF LETTERS and manuscripts burned for two days in a pit
behind the house before the two men left Dogwoods in early October.
Details of this 'nightmare' move appeared in White's letters for months.
He told James Stern, 'I hope never to move again until I go to the nuns
in my senility.'[1] At 20 Martin Road, the novelist was stimulated by having
neighbours over the fence for the first time since his childhood and he
wove a fantasy of suburban life about them, a soap opera broadcast
episode by episode in his letters. The park where he exercised the dogs
became a personal landscape of romance and mystery. As the two men
were settling in to Martin Road, *The Burnt Ones* appeared in London to
very mixed reviews.

20 MARTIN ROAD, 25.x.64

TO PEGGY GARLAND

Dear Peggy,

Your letter arrived a couple of days ago. For weeks I had been saying to
myself every Sunday: This Sunday I must write to Peggy – but so much
has been happening lately, I always failed in the end. First of all I had to
go to hospital at the end of the winter with a virus on top of the bronchitis
which had been hanging about ever since the cold weather began. Then
the day I came out Suzanne arrived with the girls, and they were in Sydney
for a couple of months. The new house involved a lot of running about
in connexion with the alterations. Then I have been working on a novel,
of which I have almost finished the first version. And finally just a fortnight
ago we moved down from Castle Hill, an experience I hope never to have
again. Eighteen years in one place means an awful accumulation of stuff,
to say nothing of the mental accumulations, and I think we both feel quite
a bit older as the result of the upheaval.

I am sure we have done the right thing, though. This is a house of
an unfashionable period, probably about 1912, it is not large, but the rooms
are very spacious, and it is sandwiched between two parks, one of then

[1] 14.xii.64.

the largest in Sydney, with wild bits which make you feel you are out on a moor, and lakes full of water-fowl which we can hear honking in the distance at night. From our upper windows the park is a wonderful sea of mist and trees in the early morning, and at night the views give an impression of somewhere on the outskirts of Paris rather than Sydney N.S.W. . . .

For the first time in about twelve years we are trying out a cleaning woman. She is a Jewess from Harbin, whose grandfather went there from Minsk. They are a family of printers, and Mrs Fraenkel's daughter is a pianist. They are only really working to get themselves established, and then I suppose we shall lose her. But perhaps by that time we shall be ready. I can never really get used to having somebody working about my own house. However, she will do the ironing, and that will be something, now that we no longer have our good old laundress of many years.

I am amazed to hear that 'Dead Roses' is the story of your novel. I don't think you ever told me the story, and certainly I didn't read it. (What, by the way, happened with Anthony Blond?)[2] If anything the characters of Anthea Scudamore and her husband were based on those of a couple I used to know. I have had good reviews from England – except for a stinker in the *Sunday Times* and a very destructive one from Naipaul in the *Spectator*.[3] But I have never known the latter let anybody go free. I don't know whether it is professional animosity or whether it is a case of the coloured intellectual taking it out on the white man.

My new novel has been obsessing me for months, with the result that it has poured out rather chaotic, and the process of oxywelding will probably take longer and be more painful than usual.[4] All the distractions nowadays mean that I have to get up and work at night, I am sometimes pretty exhausted.

I am sorry to hear of your trouble with Philip.[5] It does look as though you should try to see him less, as I have always felt. But I shan't try again to offer advice on your family. I am not clear whether David has married

---

[2]After moving to Eynsham, Garland had written a novel which PW suggested she should send to Anthony Blond (1928–   ) who read the MS. but declined to publish.

[3]Jeremy Rundall, *Sunday Times*, 4 Oct., p.49, under the heading 'Characters sapped by the sun'; V. S. Naipaul, *Spectator*, 16 Oct., p.513, concluded: 'it is in the contrast between the simplicity of what he has to say and his involved way of saying it that the particular embarrassment of this collection lies.'

[4]oxywelding=second draft.

[5]Now diagnosed as schizophrenic; this was the start of a period of intense suffering for the boy who remained in institutions until his death in 1986.

Sarah yet, or whether they are still only intending to marry.[6] I often wonder how his painting is developing. The photographs were very interesting. You look thinner, younger, and better in every way than when we saw you in England last . . .

All our paintings have taken on a miraculous new lease of life since we came into this house. There is so much space and light after the other rather dark little tree-choked house, and of course the freshly painted white walls make a great difference. You will have to come back here one day to see what we have got. Unfortunately this is a house which asks for people and parties, and at the same time I have so much work left, there is going to be a tremendous conflict between the two.

MARTIN ROAD, 6.xi.64
TO THE NOLANS
Dear Cynthia and Sid,
I can't believe it is almost a month since we came to this house. There has been so much to do I suppose the time has passed more quickly than usual. I am going to like it very much if only we can settle one or two things – such as the feud with a neighbour over a fence. We put up a paling fence to prevent us seeing . . . his backyard, he flew at it and started hacking it down with a tomahawk, and there the matter has rested – with gaps of great unsightliness, and our dogs barking at his small children as they smash bottles or push things through the wire netting we have stretched across. Yesterday we met at the gap in the company of my solicitor, who was full of tact, and I think the situation may have improved. We may even have persuaded him to accept the paling fence painted white, though he continued to murmur that it wouldn't be 'eyesthetically pleasing' and that it would remind him of Redfern.[7] I felt like pointing out that his own backyard was essentially Redfern, and that if he cared to glance around, every second house in this New-rich Row has a paling fence, most of them unpainted. There is suburbia for you, but if only we can solve the fence problem I feel we can ignore it.[8]

The house is lovely. In it the paintings have taken on a life they never had before, and we still have plenty of space for those we shall collect in time. I must get hold of a colour film and try to coax a photographer I know, so that you shall see.

[6] He married Sarah Hough (1944–   ) this year; she wrote and illustrated children's books as Sarah Garland.
[7] A shabby Sydney suburb.
[8] The neighbours made an uneasy peace.

One of the reasons I am writing now is about the enclosed cutting on Young Man who Fell Down Volcano.[9] I was going along in the bus after reading it, when I began to see a whole series of Nolan paintings unfolding out of the incident. Don't you think there are great possibilities? – Young Man on the Edge – Falling – Falling – Fallen – hair streaming, teeth bared, much play of eyelids or eyeballs, gulfs of lava, caverns of fire, all the people sitting inside them – all the metaphysical overtones which can be implied. I hope I can send you on this idea eventually.

Since I came here I finished the last section of The Solid Mandala – very crudely, and in need of expansion, but I wanted to get the whole thing down on paper and forget about it for a couple of months before starting the rewriting. There will be some very difficult things to get right. In the meantime I want to read solidly. I don't seem to have had an opportunity for years. I am afraid to read fiction while I am writing it, and I am never able to concentrate on other things with more than half my mind while I am working.

A man we know who got back the other day was raving about the Shakespeare Sonnet paintings. I wonder whether we shall ever have a chance of seeing some of them.[10] There has been a good exhibition of gouaches by Frank Hodgkinson, sent over from Spain. He is a painter I have not cared for in the past, but suddenly colour has flooded in, and these are ravishing and subtle at the same time. I was forced to buy one when I should be saving money to pay for the necessities.

Poor Ray Mathew! By now I have had a number of reports and read several reviews of his Spring Song. I always felt it was pretty anaemic on paper but hoped it was one of those things which to spring to life on stage. Apparently not. However, for that bastard Bernard Miles' sake, I can't help also feeling a little bit glad.[11] ...

[9]Into the crater of Mt Matupi near Rabaul fell John Hamilton, 24, a tourist from Sydney. The SMH reported, 2 Nov., p.1, that he was about to take a photograph, 'Overbalanced on the sharp crumbling edge and plunged 200 feet down the inside walls . . . it was believed he died of loss of blood, exposure to the scorching sun, and sulphur fumes.'

[10]They reached the Macquarie Galleries in Sydney in late 1967. PW told Glover in early October that year, 'I decided to try for one. At the Macquarie they won't sell in advance, so I got there at 7 a.m. with my goat-milking stool. There was one man ahead of me, but we settled down on friendly terms after discovering we were interested in different paintings. Mine celebrated Sonnet 146, so you see it wouldn't suit everyone . . .' The sonnet argues against the pursuit of material happiness: 'Why so large cost, having so short a lease, Dost thou upon thy fading mansion spend?'

[11]Miles had produced Mathew's play in place of PW's Night on Bald Mountain.

We went to hear Malcolm Williamson's symphony 'Elevameni', but I wasn't with it at all. It seemed to me a dreary bit of pastiche after a composer like Richard Meale, who is truly contemporary.[12] My great recent musical excitement was hearing the Hungarian Quartet play through all the Bartok Quartets as I have never heard them played before. If I had to choose records for a desert island I think those quartets are what I would take – and I have been feeling deprived of them as my pick-up hasn't been working. Peter Sculthorpe has finished his quartet commissioned by Musica Viva, and which we shall hear next season. He came here the other night amiable as ever, but I can't come any closer to feeling he would be right for our particular work.

Manoly is busy with our garden, which can be made to look quite interesting, particularly at the back, where we are going to have a kind of Greek terrace on the roof of the garages, with vine-covered pergola and lots of pots. In front I think we shall have to concentrate mainly on native shrubs to avoid getting that tight suburban look. It is a help being perched on a rise with a path winding up by grass terraces and already three very nice little gumtrees well-established ... In the afternoons I walk in the Park, with pugs, down avenues of paperbarks and date-palms, along a lake full of enamelled-looking moorhens and baby ducks. At one end one might be lost on a moor or *Heide*.[13]

If I haven't spoken about the actual move, it is because it now seems too much of a nightmare.

Love from us both
Patrick.

20 MARTIN ROAD, 18.xi.64
TO THE DUTTONS
Dear Nin and Geoffrey,
Thank you for the letters. You must be the first to receive *The Burnt Ones*, which is in a way fitting.[14] Yes, I think the jacket is marvellous as itself, but I can't feel it has a great connexion with the contents of the book.[15] Still, it is so arresting I am sure it will sell a great many copies. I am

---

[12]Williamson (1931–   ) was later Master of the Queen's Musick. PW began championing Richard Meale (1932–   ) after hearing his 1964 *Homage to Garcia Lorca*. Meale, he told Garland, 25.x.64, 'is the real thing'. Meale was to compose the opera *Voss*.
[13]Pun? Both the Melbourne artists' colony and the heath country PW had known round Hannover.
[14]The collection was dedicated to them.
[15]Four distraught heads by Nolan; another of his jackets to disappoint PW.

anxious to see the cover of the Penguin *Riders* which I am told is excellent in every way.

Your letters must have provoked a very idyllic dream about Adelaide which I dreamed last night. I can't remember what happened in it, only that I was walking along an empty sports ground with somebody anonymous somewhere near a university. There was dew on the grass, and an early morning light.

It was dreadfully frustrating only to talk to Geoffrey on the phone and not have him see the house, and more so to hear of you both making all those trips to Melbourne instead of Sydney. Thank you for the offer of prints, but I never think they really go with originals, even if the prints are of masterpieces and the originals are comparative mediocrities. Somehow the real paint makes the prints go flat.

We still have lots of jobs to do, and I very rarely leave the house during the working hours of the day in case some tradesman who has promised to come actually turns up. Usually he doesn't, and when he does I find myself wishing he hadn't. Two days ago we got the painters back, and half the house had to be dismantled. You've never seen anything like the mess the furniture movers made of the stairway on the day of the move, and a clot of a plumber, who did almost everything wrong, excelled himself by turning on the main before connecting up the upstairs lavatory, and flooding the diningroom ceiling just after it had been painted. Now all this has been made good at last. I must say painters are the most amiable, the most house-trained of all the tradesmen. They insisted on putting back all the curtains and paintings we had to take down for them, and some of the paintings give one a rupture just to think about moving them. (That is why some of our paintings stay in the wrong position for ever after. The new Frank Hodgkinson is all wrong for light, but I'm afraid it will probably stay where it is just because it was such a bugger to hang.)

The Finnish light fittings and curtains are the greatest success. It is strange that that little country, with such stodgy and rather unpleasant inhabitants (at least the few I have met) can produce things in such infallibly good taste. Their things are shockingly expensive in the shops, but we were fortunate in that our architect introduced us to the man who imports most of the stuff . . .

I am resting between versions and enjoying a read such as I haven't had for years. I have just finished *The Brothers Karamazov* for the third time in my life. Each reading has given me a little more. I hope I have the opportunity of reading it again in twenty years time. By then I should be able to get into every corner of it. The sad part of the book is that one realises one hasn't, and never will arrive anywhere very much in one's own writings.

Now I am re-reading *Varieties of Religious Experience*[16] and mopped up a funny, sour, bankrupt little novel of Edna O'Brien's *Girls in Their Married Bliss*. I finally got hold of *Notre Dames Des Fleurs* – in English though, as the English for some perverse reason are not allowed to import the French version. I thought in the first place I might succeed in getting the French into Australia, though never the English. However, it sailed in without a hitch.[17] I don't know what you think of Genet. I have never been able to get much out of the plays from reading them. I once tried some *nouvelles* lent me by a man I very much disliked, and took a great dislike to Genet. But I must say there are some glittering jewels in *Notre Dame* lurking amongst the shit . . .

We have some entertaining children belonging to the neighbour with whom we haven't quarrelled. The boy, aged about twelve, asked Manoly the other day if he was my butler. He then became awfully formal, and said: 'Well, I hope you are enjoying the comforts of your new home.' After that he went on to tell how his mother was reading *Riders in the Chariot* – 'but she finds it so heavy she has to take a rest after every couple of lines.' The father, an Australian-born Greek, is a very nice man and tremendously profitable gossip. I foresee some happy talks ahead.[18]

20 MARTIN ROAD, 27.xi.64
TO LAURIE COLLINSON[19]
Dear Laurie,
You sound in a bad way, and I suppose you must make up your mind to come back if you can't reason your way out of the situation you are in. I don't see why you shouldn't if the doctors say there is nothing wrong with you physically, and surely your mother has had such a good innings in possession of you, it is time you took some time off. But I'm afraid I have never been sympathetic towards mothers. As for the English, they certainly don't fall all over the stranger, but suddenly you find they have accepted you, and their friendship lasts better than that of most people. You ask how I felt when I first went to England. The circumstances were entirely

---

[16]William James, 1902.

[17]Australia banned Genet's novel – in English not French – two days before PW wrote this letter and it remained a prohibited import until 1972.

[18]But they moved away soon afterwards.

[19](1925–), poet, playwright and Marxist, who had recently gone to England to live; he and PW met during the season of *A Cheery Soul* in Melbourne.

different in my case. My parents took me there – we arrived on my thirteenth birthday – and dumped me in a school. After a year they went back to Australia, and I stayed on for the four years at school hating every minute. Schoolboys of course are far worse than adults, and there was never a day when I was not called 'a bloody colonial' or a 'bloody cockney'.[20] As I was a rather proud child, I ended by hardly ever opening my mouth. I made only one lasting friend – the Ronald Waters whose address I gave you. It was only after I pestered my parents to let me leave school and return to Australia that I could accept the good points of the English. Then, of course, I began breaking my neck to get back . . . You talk about getting a safe job and becoming reconciled to your failure to be a professional writer. Surely very few of the writers we respect could live off what they earn from their writings, unless of course they take to journalism and other things on the side. I know I should lead a very meagre existence on what I earn as a writer.[21] It just happened I was fortunate in inheriting something on which to live.

Manoly and I moved to this new address on October 12th, a dreadful day which I shall never forget. It seemed to last for about a week . . .

I have not seen anything of Thea for quite some time. We had one of those telephone rows in which a few home truths were spoken, and I think she may have wiped me. I did ring up again to make the effort, but we parted with her very sour remark: 'So it's up to me next time is it?' It all began over the wretched *Well-Dressed Explorer* and the Penguins. She has it in for Geoffrey Dutton because he has never asked to do the book as a Penguin.[22] Such a wave of envy and spite came out that I let fly, as Geoffrey is one of the fairest men in Australia, and quite devoid of the usual literary spite and malice. In defence of Geoffrey I had to say that if I had been managing Penguins I shouldn't have wanted to do *The Well-Dressed Explorer*. (I have always thought it a wretched book, and couldn't have finished it if friendship hadn't forced me to.) Thea poured forth more than ever on Geoffrey, declaring a kind of war.[23] I have always found she

[20]Perhaps; but PW's contemporaries recall finding nothing very foreign about Australians – their mockery was reserved for Jews.

[21]PW told Glover, 27.ii.63: 'Since I began to work for the theatre I average £400 a play, whereas with novels I averaged £4000 every second year . . . Manoly has no more than I am able to allow him.' But after Ruth White's death, PW assured Lascaris' financial independence by settling on him a sum roughly equal to the entire proceeds of selling Dogwoods.

[22]Dutton was now editor for Penguin Books in Australia.

[23]She recalls it began with a disparaging remark about Dutton's poetry of which she had read very little.

resented anybody's having a vacuum cleaner until she had one herself, when she had, she forgot about the vacuum cleaner and went on to something else. I found resentment building up over our move to Sydney, as though we might be doing better for ourselves. There had been remarks like; 'You poor things, I do pity you going to live in Sydney,' whereas in the past she had been lamenting the fact that she lived in a remote suburb and was forced to miss so much ... I don't think she will ever write anything worth while because she is so obsessed with herself.

20 MARTIN ROAD, 10.xii.64
TO FREDERICK GLOVER
The copies of *The Burnt Ones* have been terribly late in arriving. I received my own only the day before yesterday, and there is no sign of them yet in the Sydney shops although I am told the Melbourne ones are displaying them. The mails have been most erratic. I have just received some parcels from my London book-dealer posted in September – some gorgeous volumes of Jung in which I am now wallowing. I want to get in as much reading as possible between now and Christmas, because after that I shall start work again. The longer I live the more difficult I find it to read fiction, unless it is something I know from experience to be of value; I have unread novels on my shelves which were given to me years ago. One's own fiction is, I suppose, a kind of fantasy-habit like masturbation. It would be impossible to live in this abominable country (or country of abominable inhabitants) without developing some such vice. If I were fifteen years younger and hadn't burnt so many bridges I'd go away for ever. You who live amongst the vegetables are not so conscious of how the vipers squirm. At least one has one's friends, and now we have this house, which I shall hope to make a meeting place for those who need encouragement. Unfortunately one can't encourage everyone, and those who are not encouraged turn into Lovejoys[24] and start spreading the recluse stuff.

20 MARTIN ROAD, 14.xii.64
TO JAMES STERN
Dear Jimmy,
We were glad to hear from you again. Had often wondered how you were getting on since your illness, but I didn't write as we had a few upheavals ourselves during the year ...

[24]Robin Lovejoy (1923–85), Sydney theatre director, had given an interview in the United States in which he called PW a recluse.

I was interested in your comments on *The Burnt Ones*.[25] I had always sensed you did not like my stories, but I had to write them for one reason or another. At one time I had ideas of writing 'Dead Roses' as a novel, and think it may have been a pity I didn't. It also occurred to me to deal with the central part of it, the marriage, as a play. However, at least you seem to approve of it as a novella! You speak in your note about 'creating the good'. Unfortunately we live in black times, with less and less that may be called good, and I suppose I must reflect the blackness of those times. I tried to write a book about saints, but saints are few and far between. If I were a saint myself I could project my saintliness, perhaps, endlessly in what I write. But I am a sensual and irritable human being. Certainly the longer I live the less I see to like in the human beings of whom I am one. You say I have dislike even for the Greeks. Why should the Greeks be ideal, untouchable? Many of them are most hateful, as Manoly too will tell you. I should have thought the Greek stories 'A Glass of Tea' and 'Being Kind to Titina' were full of compassion, and if I had put more into 'Dead Roses' and 'Down at the Dump' they would have run over with American sentimentality.

Well, I probably shan't write any more stories. Time is running short and I have other things to do. I have finished a first version of a novel, which I am calling *The Solid Mandala*, and which is probably blacker than any of those stories you have been complaining about! I shall probably be working on this till the end of 1965. During the year E & S propose to publish my four plays in one volume. Again there is talk of doing one or more of them in England, but I shall only believe when the curtain goes up, and anyway I am no longer all that interested in the theatre. I must concentrate on the several novels I still have to write.

Are you translating anything now? As translators of Freud do you approve of Jung? I have been reading a lot of Jung lately and he seems to me to have a lot of the answers.

I do wish we could meet and have another meal somewhere. (I thought of Tania[26] the other day when I was making a Russian soup which needed sorrel and I had to use endive because I didn't have the other.) I am trying to save up, as soon as we have everything for the house, to go to Europe in 1966. When I say Europe – I expect it will be our beaten track, through Greece, to Rome, Paris and London. Or perhaps we shall leave out Paris this time, and eat in Marseilles and Lyons instead.

---

[25]Private comments – Stern did not review the volume.
[26]Stern's wife Tania Kurella, gymnastics teacher and translator.

This time there won't be any Ben Huebsch. I feel the blood has drained out of the Viking, but hope I am wrong.

The room is full of snoring pugs. It is too late to write any more. We have a wonderful dawn here – Centennial Park is a kind of Corot, though on the other side, what has been the Champs Elysées by night, is turned back into Anzac Parade.

Love to you both, and best wishes for 1965 –
Patrick.

20 MARTIN ROAD, 7.ii.65
TO FREDERICK GLOVER
If you have an enlarged cock I feel you ought to take it to a doctor, as you might have an enlarged prostate. We are of an age for that. On the other hand, from what I have seen in baths and public lavatories, many old men must have enlarged cocks and it is probably a normal occurrence. Even ageing women grow body hair in unexpected places. But I advise you to see a doctor in case it is prostate.

I'm afraid there are no frills of sensibility on this letter, but I am not in a frilly mood!
Yrs
Patrick

20 MARTIN ROAD, 14.ii.65
TO GEOFFREY DUTTON
I have got into a very rough patch in the novel, and have been feeling very low about it. I had to stop and read right through again. I think half the trouble was I had become too obsessed with words and textures and had forgotten what I was trying to build up into a whole. Also I have been having asthma for the last couple of weeks. Perhaps it was brought on by the struggles with the novel – or perhaps the asthma has been making the novel seem more desperately bad than it is. I do know that two doctors have told me all their asthma patients have started up.

20 MARTIN ROAD, 22.ii.65
TO FREDERICK GLOVER
You can't expect me to rush off taking holidays and abandoning everything. I can't bear living in other people's houses, for one thing, and I can't bear Australian hotels, so it is really less exhausting not to go away. Of course I drink, and you must not expect me not to. It is one of the great creative looseners, along with music, and sex. I love and need them all.

I spoke to a doctor about your enlargement, and he said there could be some endocrinological reason for it. So I still think you would be wise to consult a doctor instead of talking sentimentally about 'compensations'. There is so much of the whole business I just don't understand. I thought everybody had an erection every night, just as they have a shit in the morning. It doesn't mean a thing. But I should begin to get very worried if I didn't have them.

20 MARTIN ROAD, 21.iii.65
TO GEOFFREY DUTTON
Yesterday morning I finished Version 2 of *The Solid Mandala* in a state of acute constipation as a result of so many days' tension. Now I have taken a Brooklax and hope to function normally for the next month. After that, the final round. I think this one is going to be either very good or very bad. There are matters in it which I am trying to clarify, but which might perhaps best be left cloudy . . .

We went the other night to find out about the great Japanese ballet, and found a kind of Folies Bergères Unrevealed – showgirls milling about rather clumsily, half-naked muscular glamour-boys, and *la grande vedette*[27] raised above everybody's heads on a platform at the end scattering silver glitter in the direction of the audience. Of course the audience went mad – any Australian audience will if you show them a bit of tinsel. But

[27]The star.

to drag in Zen and dress it up in silver glitter – only the soul of an Australian lahidy could come at that. If this goes to London I am sure the intellectual papers will give it that popular label High Camp.[28]

At last I have got hold of some of Peter Porter's poems – the earlier ones, in a Penguin with some by Kingsley Amis and Dom Moraes.[29] Some of Porter's are <u>very</u> good, others a bit young and over angry. What on earth does Australia think of somebody so savage? But you are the only Australian, as far as I know, aware of his existence . . .

There have been more fires in the park, including one so close I had to order a fire engine. So relaxing after Castle Hill, where you felt you had to do it yourself rather than send for the horse-and-buggy volunteer brigade.

20 Martin Road, 8.iv.65
TO FREDERICK GLOVER

I agree Sid says too much to the press and TV nowadays, but as they seem to be brought here and there free by Qantas I suppose he feels he has to be a public figure. So far I have succeeded in avoiding the Johnstons.[30] The Nolans say she is better than he, and has suffered a lot having to live with George. They visited them once when they were living on Hydra, and there was a kind of Belsen atmosphere, with the whole family more or less starving, and George in a state of TB. Now that they are back here and living on the fat of the land, Charmian has set in the solid flesh of an Australian lahidy, quite unlike the rather off-beat photograph they publish. Every time one opens a paper they're in it, but I suppose that is so that they can continue to have it good. One wonders what one might do in similar circumstances. I don't <u>feel</u> I could turn into a Johnston, but I have always been able to sit back and get on with that I wanted to do, without any of the material worries.

---

[28]*Yügen* by Robert Helpmann to music by Yuzo Toyama performed by the new Australian Ballet and designed by Desmond Healey; the Moon Goddess scattering glitter as she escaped the earth was danced by Kathleen Gorham; reviews in Europe later that year were mixed – Clive Barnes wrote, 'Noh play equals no ballet.'
[29]*Penguin Poets 2*, 1962.
[30]George Johnston and Charmian Clift had returned to Sydney after living for ten years on Hydra; his novel *My Brother Jack* won the Miles Franklin in 1964 and Clift became a successful columnist on the *SMH*.

20 MARTIN ROAD, 18.iv.65
TO PEGGY GARLAND

We have almost been through the ten days of hell which the Sydney Royal Agricultural Show brings to people who live in these parts. It is only a stone's throw from the showground, and we have floats, trailers, trucks and caravans parked all down this street for the duration. During the day the cars of the showgoers are added to these, often literally on the pavements, and in front of our garages in the back lane so that we can get neither in nor out. One is a prisoner for ten days, except for the breathers of Sunday and the night of Good Friday. Of course it brings a lot of life to the neighbourhood, and some of the inhabitants obviously flourish in it: ladies who normally stroll listlessly down the street and back start spanking twice round the block, and our next-door neighbour sits on her terrace at an iron table in her pastel bubble-nylon nightie, I suspect when her husband (to whom she isn't speaking) is out. One starts speaking to neighbours one had never addressed before, and I wonder whether one will speak to them again before the next show. It's all probably like the war in London.

We continue to like our house and to feel it had been waiting for us. To-day I found out it was even built the year both Manoly and I were born (by a prosperous jeweller for the sum of £900). So there does seem to have been some sort of design about it. The only worry at the moment is how to heat it most satisfactorily and cheaply during the winter. A few days ago we had a preliminary cold snap, which immediately started me off with bronchitis, and I went off and bought a couple of oil-filled heaters which one plugs into the electricity. They sound very good in theory, but I have a suspicion they may turn out ruinously expensive. The cold came with a downpour of several days, which broke the drought, and was in every other way a relief. The lake in the park which had dried up was again full of water and duck. I went down with a bagful of stale bread the evening the rain cleared and had ducks flying and swimming at me from all corners, a wonderful pattern of converging wakes on silver water, but quite a solid wall of cold. I also found a Queensland wheel-tree in flower. Do you know it? Very Jungian. I have had to bring one into my novel.

20 MARTIN ROAD, 6.vi.65
TO MARSHALL BEST

I ought to be able to send you the typescript of *The Solid Mandala* end of the month or the beginning of next. The end is now in sight, but after that I shall have to correct and do one or two things. It has turned out shorter than I had anticipated (about 300 quarto pages of type) because my handwriting seems to have developed a spread with age. I am still too close to the book to be able to get much idea how good or bad it is. I like to think my own involvement means the involvement of my future readers, and the writing of this one has certainly torn me to shreds.

ON 21 JUNE 1965 HE sent *The Solid Mandala* to New York. The novel was dedicated to the Moores. David Moore was now curator of the Australian and South-East Asian collections of the Australian Museum. White, after having new teeth fitted, left to stay for a few days at Anlaby before returning to Sydney to await New York's verdict on the novel. This came in mid-July.

20 MARTIN ROAD, 1.viii.65
TO GEOFFREY DUTTON
Dear Geoffrey,
To-day is the perfect day. After weeks of bashing wind and tearing rain there isn't a leaf stirring, and a still blue-gold haze lies over the Park. We have even lost our neighbours ...

After their great enthusiasm for *The Solid Mandala* the Americans are playing a bit safe over their percentages. However, I realise I am not much of a proposition to an American publisher. I am also having agent trouble. Curtis Brown London has had a final showdown with Curtis Brown New York, so I have to correspond with them both about the *Mandala* till the situation is tidied up. C. B. London has taken up with somebody called William Morris in New York. Ever heard of him?[31]

We went the other night to dinner at the Drysdales.[32] The only other guests were Ralph Smith,[33] an ageing dilettante-rentier with whom we met Tass in the first place (in the days of Bon),[34] and a woman called Moffat,[35] originally from Scotland. By some miracle Slimy Sculthorpe didn't appear, even uninvited. Tass is really much better on his own ground, talked a lot, and became quite human. Maisie chattered, showed us some of the Purves-Smiths, and made rather a mess of a pie. She said: 'Every time I look in the oven at this pie I feel I have to have another sherry.' I think

[31]In fact, John Cushman left the William Morris Agency to handle the Curtis Brown list in New York and represented PW from 1965–78.
[32]Russell (Tass) Drysdale (1912–81) and his second wife Maisie, widow of the painter Peter Purves-Smith.
[33](1900–93), bachelor collector of books and paintings.
[34]Drysdale's first wife Elizabeth (Bon) who had died two years before.
[35]Anne Moffat, nurse to the Drysdale children during the war.

she and I have quite a lot in common. Talking things over afterwards Manoly and I found we had come to the same conclusion independently in three instances. We both got the impression that Maisie is more interested in the painting of Purves-Smith than in that of Drysdale. We are both a bit worried about what will happen to the Drysdale exhibition in London. It looks as though he will be in for the tooth-and-claw treatment. The paintings really are a long way off what is fashionable now, and for that matter a long way off the best Drysdale. Manoly said afterwards: 'They all looked to me like reproductions.'[36] Finally, each of us had a eerie feeling that Bon was present all the time. I keep stressing our shared reaction, otherwise I know you would think I am making prejudiced remarks or indulging in fantasies! ...

Nin's dishes are a great success above the icons. The marbled one I have on a bookcase in my workroom. The Moores and Klári Daniel[37] are all very pleased with the ones they bought.

To-night we go to Desmond's to have a pre-preview of the paintings which are going to the Macquarie Gallery for his exhibition.[38]

I have started work on a novella which I call 'A Woman's Hand'. At least I hope it is going to be a novella and not a novel; that would be too soon and too exhausting.

Yours
Patrick.

20 MARTIN ROAD, 15.viii.65
TO GEOFFREY DUTTON
Max sent me Hal Porter's outpouring, wanting himself, me, everyone to fly into action.[39] Of course the Porter is just a sac of green pus throbbing

---

[36]Critics treated his London show at the Leicester Galleries in Oct. 1965 with respect but regarded Drysdale as a talented old exotic.

[37]These were the last days of PW's friendship with Daniel. Her possessiveness now exasperated him; he accused her of being mired in nostalgia for Hapsburg Europe. A trivial scrap over lunch sent her into exile: she refused to taste a new cauliflower salad – another version of the story cites raw fish – and PW took this as final proof of her conservative prejudices. Daniel was crushed but told Maria Prerauer, 'I don't hold it against him. I did it gladly. He squeezes you out like a lemon and when it is dry he turns to someone else.' When Daniel was dying, PW refused to allow Lascaris to visit her in hospital.

[38]'The Australian Lady'.

[39]Harris had sent a copy of the London Magazine, Sept. 1965, where Porter at p.43 gave an account of the fateful night at Folly Point – see PW to Glover, 6.x.60, page 171 – omitting nothing but Porter's own malign role in the affair. Porter was in London for the season of his play The Professor.

with jealousy. It would be in one way a good thing to go for him, but in another it would be to descend to his own very low level. Anybody reading the article in England would get a pretty good idea of the kind of person he is. His moment of limelight must have sent him madder and drunker than ever, or perhaps it is London going to his head, making the baroque middle-aged queen pose as the blustering Colonial Boy, as in the days of the Edinburgh Festival. He will probably go off in a fit of drink during rehearsals of the play, or afterwards on reading the notices.

20 MARTIN ROAD, 24.viii.65
TO BARRY HUMPHRIES
Can't think of any sketches – only that I should like you to do something about the odious Nock & Kirby, which you would have to see in its present state of bazaar awfulness. They have a slogan: IT'S FUN TO SHOP AT NOCK & KIRBY'S, whereas it's pure fuckun hell, and I mean to write shortly and tell them so. Since last October I have been trying once a month to buy two quart tins of something called Spartan 'Floorclean'[40] (does this bring back the Australian flavour?) and they still can't keep it for me. You can see how conservative I am, and willing to try. Recently they have turned jokey. Above the cagebird and goldfish department there is a large sign FISH AND CHEEPS. Unfortunately they have quite a lot of interesting goods, all the best in plastics, if you can push your way through the pastel plastic ladies who wander round, looking. Yes, I must take you there.

　　Funny you should pick on Emily.[41] The Duttons have a Tessa, and Geoffrey's mother was an Emily, a great and capricious beauty who had everybody terrified. On one occasion she sent somebody to Kapunda, about ten miles away, to buy her some stamps. The hireling returned with some of those which celebrated the Olympic Games. Emily Dutton looked at them and said: 'What are these ridiculous circles? Take them back at once and bring me stamps with the head of Her Majesty the Queen.'

WHITE'S COUSIN NELLIE COX of Mudgee danced in Sydney musicals and modelled for Schiaparelli in Paris. Marriage to an Italian diplomat made her Eleanor Arrighi but he died soon after the war leaving her, a great beauty in her prime, to survive as a real estate agent in Sydney. White had not met his cousin until introduced by Desmond Digby in 1961. He

[40]Concentrated cleaner of very low alkalinity and excellent detergent power applied by long string mop; now no longer available.
[41]For the name of his second daughter.

was captivated by her and her daughters: the designer Luciana and the painter Niké. The dramatic beauty Boo Hollingrake in *The Vivisector* is in most respects a portrait of 'Nellie' Arrighi whose friendship White enjoyed for twenty years until her death. Soon after finding White his new house in Martin Road, she retired from business to live for a time in London and then from 1967 in Rome.

20 MARTIN ROAD, 30.viii.65
TO ELEANOR ARRIGHI
Dear Eleanor,
Nearly two months since I got your letter, but August was turned completely topsy turvy when Manoly was struck down by a serious illness. He was three weeks in hospital with pericarditis, or inflammation of the membrane round the heart. It was intensely painful in the beginning, and so sudden the symptoms looked very like a coronary. In fact for the first couple of days we thought that was what it was, so you can imagine things were pretty gloomy. He came back from shopping and complained of a neuralgic pain in his neck. Then it began to intensify in the afternoon and gather round his heart. I spent an hour telephoning doctors, but they were all out on their rounds or away skiing. In the end I had to get an ambulance and take him to the casualty department at St Vincent's (remember that if you ever want to gatecrash a hospital without a doctor). They had him in a kind of death ward for the first couple of days, with most of the other patients in a coma, and all the emergency gadgets. After that it went much better, in a room with one other patient, only the food was uneatable, and I used to have to take a hot meal every night when I went. He has been back a week now, and in a few days is going to South Australia to recuperate with the Duttons for a fortnight. The cheerful part of pericarditis is that when they get their strength back there are no after effects as from a coronary.

I had started work again, but naturally it has not been going awfully well. I was thankful I had got the novel off my hands before all this happened. Now it is mostly a matter of daily routine, except for a couple of hours I manage to keep for work in the middle of the night.

Our ... neighbour has returned ... We are not on speaking terms with either of them since the woman began keeping a mongrel puppy in a cage hardly bigger than itself. ... We sent for the RSPCA, which incensed her considerably. She told Manoly she came from a grazing property and he couldn't tell her anything about the care of animals. She then retaliated by sending the Health Inspectors to us, presumably to catch us out for keeping four dogs ...

Desmond has had a very interesting and fairly successful exhibition.[42] It should have been more successful only it wasn't solemn enough. Because you could laugh, people were inclined to overlook the fact that the pictures were very brilliantly painted. I bought four. I also have three new Daws, a Henri Bastin,[43] two by Max Watters,[44] a coalminer from Muswellbrook, and one by an unknown and very young painter called Stephen Earle.[45] So the house is beginning to look a bit like a gallery . . .

I met your sister one day at a dreadful exhibition of Justin O'Brien's.[46] That seemed to be just what the society ladies wanted: a kind of sentimental Catholic oleograph of Greek Orthodox subjects, with a dash of Burlington House 1925 and Sydney Camp 1940. I think everything was sold.

I wonder whether you saw the Hal Porter play. It sounds quite a flop from bits we have read about it. He has been making the most fantastic statements to the press about all the money he has made from it in Australia, when it was only done briefly by the Adelaide University Theatre Guild, and I know what they pay. He has also had a book on Australian theatre published out here, in which he says an English-cum-Australian novelist Patrick White got hold of the Trust and persuaded them to do his plays, causing them to lose I don't know how many thousands. He then goes into a tirade against 'the fifth-rate English homosexuals who run the theatre in Australia.'[47] Everybody is trying to work out who they are. In years I can only think of one, and he is probably only gossip. Jealousy and drink must have sent Hal off his head, or perhaps he is hoping to coax somebody into court. He must have made more money out of that case against the Tasmanian journalist than he ever did out of his writing.[48]

20 MARTIN ROAD, 3.ix.65
TO MARSHALL BEST
Dear Marshall,
This is just a line to say I have corrected the proof, but want to keep it a

[42] A rogues' gallery of Australian matrons, at the Macquarie Galleries.
[43] (1896–1979), pioneer of naive art in Australia.
[44] (1936–   ), naive painter who worked in the Whites' territory of the Hunter Valley.
[45] (1942–   ), he became one of the stable of painters exhibiting at Sydney's Watters Gallery.
[46] (1917–   ), the art master at Cranbrook School, about to leave for Rome.
[47] *Stars of Australian Stage and Screen*, 1965.
[48] Porter sued Ron Broinowski, deputy editor of the *Hobart Mercury* over a cheap review of his memoir *Watcher on the Cast Iron Balcony* and won £1,000.

couple of days as I am not happy about one important word, and hope the right one will slip into my head. In any case, you should have the proof by Sept 14 ... I believe the proof-corrector of *The Solid Mandala* is the same one I have always had. One day you must tell me about him or her.

Yrs
Patrick.

20 MARTIN ROAD, 7.x.65
TO GEOFFREY DUTTON
I have had a letter from John Gielgud asking me to call on Osbert Sitwell when he is here. I don't know whether it will be possible to get him off the ship and up this mountain to a meal in his state of Parkinson's disease. Strange how the Sitwells all wait till they are almost corpses before coming to Australia, when there was never a country which so demanded all one's life-blood.

DICK CASEY WAS APPOINTED Governor-General in September and Maie Casey sailed into White's life a few weeks later. The Caseys had always divided the duties of a post between them: as British minister in Cairo during the war, governor of Bengal and Australia's minister for external affairs, Dick Casey dealt with the politicians while Maie collected the great. A stylish woman but no beauty, she wooed White with her drawings, poetry and tepid prose. White was intrigued by this remnant of his own Anglo-Australian world, and came to trust and like her. Maie Casey demanded a worldly, thoughtful response; he never whinged to her.

20 MARTIN ROAD, 17.x.65
TO GEOFFREY DUTTON
The biggest of the latest events was the State dinner for the Caseys. I had almost had enough of such things after the other function, but went to this one because I have always felt there was something civilised and sympathetic about the C.'s. My table companions were not particularly interesting. For some reason I was put between two ladies of the War Widows' Guild – the President, an old girl called Mrs Watkins dressed in exactly the same colour as her plastic gums, which gave her a certain fascination,[49] and quite an attractive younger one called Una Boyce, who

[49] A perfect description of Aileen Watkins – president of the guild 1949, 1952–73 – but there's some doubt she was there that night.

prattled brightly about all the White cousins she had been at school with.[50] On the other side of Una there was Bill Dobell, with whom I couldn't talk till afterwards – opposite him MacMahon the surgeon who saved his life, with wife, both pleasant[51] and opposite me some people called Walker. She is an attractive woman, a sister of Mrs Rapotec. Walker I found a monster.[52] He is President of the Graziers' Association, would have liked to become sentimental over some of the worst of my relations, almost foams at the mouth in enthusiastic support of the Bush Schools of Aust Painting, and subsided for good and all when I said that I thought the arts had moved into the cities. I found out afterwards that during the War, when he was a dashing young sergeant, W. was known as the Goodooga Bull.

Towards the end of the dinner a man suddenly came and hissed in my ear: 'Lady Casey specially wants to have a word with you afterwards. Somebody will come and take you to where the meeting will take place.' Quite the Dumas touch, in fact, and I must admit it gave me a thrill. When everybody got up, a minion did appear and Bill Dobell, who had been hissed at also, and I, were whisked away into a private room. There we had a long and fairly uninterrupted conversation with the Caseys. He is rather like a British statesman of another era, but a great relief after the Australian politician. (I expect really I am a True-Blue Peg at heart.)[53] Maie Casey I felt at once was a person I could see a lot of, and it is a pity to think I have discovered this too late, although she did say, as though she meant it: 'I hope we shall be able to see something of each other later on.' She may like to come out here and spend a few peaceful hours. At one stage she made the remark: 'Before we became involved in this silly business– – ' then stopped herself. Towards the end of the session McKell[54] erupted on us, and the Packers.[55] Lady McKell, whose name is Min, is very thin, and drops a very professional and professionally humble curtsy. McKell became amiable, and told me how much he had enjoyed the realistic approach of my articles on Vietnam in the *Australian*, at which point Lady Packer sprang in and said: 'Oh, that's the other one – a journalist.' Lady

[50]State secretary of the guild, 1961–89.
[51]Edward and Elizabeth MacMahon.
[52]Bruce and Pip Walker; her sister Andrée and her husband the abstract expressionist painter Stanislaus Rapotec (1913–   ) were friends of PW.
[53]Dutton called his very conservative sister-in-law True Blue Peg.
[54]William McKell (1891–1985), ex-boxer and ex-Labor premier of NSW who succeeded the Duke of Gloucester as Governor-General, 1947–53.
[55]Proprietor of the Sydney *Daily Telegraph*, Frank Packer (1906–74), and his second wife Florence.

P. was all smiles and diamonds . . . Have you ever seen Packer Himself? There is a putrid carcase for you. If I were Lady P. I'd hold out for a whole lot more diamonds.

We went the other night to the first of the shop-window performances by the Community Theatre intended to bring in more members. They did the plays with style, but the programme was badly chosen *Krapp's Last Tape* and *A Phoenix too Frequent*.[56] If I am not to have more of a say choosing programmes I shall have to resign. Have you ever seen *Krapp*? Never was a thin piece of elastic stretched so far. I must say it doesn't break, and found the mood of it very close to some of my blacker ones, with a bottle, at the kitchen table, at 3 a.m. Fry can be quite funny when he comes down to earth, but the gush in between is intolerable.

The new notepaper looks very good. I must get on to the agent again to see what is happening about Penguin and the plays[57] . . .

I am having great trouble getting all the medical information I want in connexion with the next one, 'Dolly Formosa and the Happy Few.'[58] Next week I go to Callan Park to talk to a psychiatrist called Bell who sounds helpful and who may possibly be profitable. But hardly any of them in Australia seem to have had any experience of cocaine addiction, and the literature on it from overseas is very sketchy.[59] I expect in the end I shall have to go gingerly hand in hand with my intuition and my own schizoid nature. Since I sketched out the three in my mind, I have got an idea for a fourth *novella*, which I may include, depending on the length of the originals.

It has been raining here for a day and a half. I wonder whether you are getting it. We are having appliance troubles – a leaking hot-water system, a very rusty leak, and I fear the worst – then, two air-conditioners which we had put recently in our upstairs bedrooms reduced the temperature during the heat-wave last week to 82!

Love to everybody at Anlaby. The Anlaby pinks are flowering, and the sarsaparilla has put out several feelers –

Patrick.

---

[56]PW was a director of Alexander Archdale's theatre at Killara on Sydney's North Shore; *Krapp's Last Tape* by Samuel Beckett was performed by Archdale alone; of Christopher Fry's *Phoenix Too Frequent* PW remarked to Glover, 13.x.65, 'so lush at times it makes one wince'.

[57]Dutton and Brian Stonier had set up the paperback imprint Sun Books, for which PW was trying to secure Australian rights to his *Four Plays*.

[58]This was one of the short novels PW planned to write for Sun Books.

[59]PW saw David Bell (1931–   ), psychiatrist in charge of psychiatric research, and discussed drug addicton; Bell's field was actually addiction to amphetamines not cocaine.

20 Martin Road, 18.xi.65
TO GEOFFREY DUTTON

I am doing all I can, in my own way, to let you have the *Plays* eventually, but I am going to make sure, naturally, that we get the most out of the hardback edition. I also want you to know that anything I may do I am doing for <u>you</u>, and not for Australian books, as I am out of love with practically everything Australian by this. Perhaps if I lived in Europe or London like the financially successful Australian writers and painters, and made an occasional graceful progress through these parts, I might feel more sentimental-patriotic. But one would have to earn quite a lot to manage it. As opposed to Moorehead's £3000 advance,[60] presumably on a paperback, the best advance I have ever had on a <u>hardback</u> is £1500 recently for *The Solid Mandala.* I got £350 for the plays. The book bazaars of Sydney, I mean the big places like A&R and Dymocks, hardly bother to put my books out, I take it that is because they don't sell enough copies. So you see I should be hardly a gold mine. I think a lot of people imagine I am a Successful Author because I was fortunate enough to inherit some money, and am able to live and write on that, using it with care, and doing most of the work ourselves. And I am still determined to scrape together every possible shilling to be able to escape from this damned country every few years, otherwise I should go mad. I toy with the idea of going to live somewhere like Rome, to enjoy the pleasures of the world while there is time left, but feel the expense might be too great once I found myself there. Also, when it came to the point, I shouldn't want to leave my friends who alone make all the jimcrackery and hot air of Australia bearable.

20 Martin Road, 28.xi.65
TO THE DUTTONS

I am delighted with the Maie Casey book, of which I have read over half.[61] It is something I shouldn't have thought of reading if you hadn't published it, but she is full of wisdom, and those houses and her portraits are fascinating. I am more than ever sorry I didn't get to know her before she was removed to higher spheres. The book has also solved something of my own puzzle, I feel. It is not that I am not Australian, I am an anachronism, something left over from that period when people were no longer English and not yet indigenous.

---

[60]Alan Moorehead (1910–83), war correspondent and historian whom PW met during the war in Egypt. This advance was probably for *The Fatal Impact*, 1966.
[61]Her family history, *An Australian Story*, republished by Sun Books, 1965.

I don't know that anything of interest or importance has happened since my last letter, except that we have had heavy showers two nights running and a day of intermittent drizzle in between. Everything is sitting up in the garden, and there are long caravans of snails across the paths.

We had the old Tildersleys and the Evanses of the Museum[62] here to-day to a brawn I made from a pig's head. Very successful in the end, but such a shambles in the making I doubt I shall ever undertake such a thing again.

Oh, I had forgotten – Rudy Komon[63] asked us to lunch one day at his house, a decrepit looking semi-detached brick villa on the waterfront at Watson's Bay. Inside there are paintings to make a thief's eyes fall out. Dobell miniatures and drawings by the dozen, things one didn't know existed. A Conder in a frame made by Conder himself out of what looks like the woodwork from a stable. Little masterpieces by several painters I had always tended to dismiss. One of the best of Williams's[64] abstract landscapes. A most unusual Blackman[65] of a schoolgirl looking like Thea Astley surrounded by phallic drums on a very yellow beach. Where Rudy goes wrong, I think, is over Molvig[66] – whom he considers 'possibly the greatest, certainly the most misunderstood Australian painter.' We ate a mass of delicatessen and drank several bottles of wine, but it was the paintings which made me drunk.

[62]John, about to retire after ten years as director of the Australian Museum in Sydney, and his wife Faith.

[63]The Sydney art dealer (1908–82) was courting a suspicious PW who often complained about 'that old bastard Komon' because he didn't put prices in his catalogues. To Dutton, 28.ii.65: 'I don't buy paintings when the price is not on the catalogue. I know this isn't fashionable – but there are still a few dealers old-fashioned enough to be honest . . . R. was a sports reporter who never thought about a painting until he came to Australia and got onto a good thing.' But Komon knew the value of paintings before he left Europe: during the war he traded them for fresh vegetables. PW's tribute to Komon is Benny Loebel in *The Vivisector*.

[64]Fred Williams (1927–82).

[65]Charles Blackman (1928–) was one of the painters PW admired less the more successful they became. For the time being PW was still able to praise; after seeing the catalogue for Blackman's 1966 exhibition at the Johnstone Gallery in Brisbane, he told Maie Casey, 8.viii.66: 'For years I have wanted to give Blackman a shove in a direction I could never exactly define. Now he has got there; the vision is whole. He has also been living in a very small house in Brisbane, which has prevented him painting the enormous canvasses he likes to paint.' PW was beaten to one of these small paintings, 'Girl Frightened by Windmill'. 'I have always been fascinated by the windmills of my childhood.'

[66]Of Jon Molvig (1923–70) PW remarked to me, 'He had so many different styles I could never really take to him.'

20 MARTIN ROAD, 9.i.66
TO JULIET O'HEA
Geoffrey Dutton is one of my loyalest friends and supporters, and I must
let him have something. I had started the *Novellen* with the idea of letting
him have the paperback rights eventually, but after finishing the first, I
have been overcome with some kind of inhibition in the second, and feel
I can't go on. The truth is I must never go down any sidetracks, and the
next thing on my list was another full-length novel. That is what I must
begin now.

BUT NOT AT ONCE. In the middle of January White and Lascaris spent a
week on Kangaroo Island with the Duttons. Then, with the publication of
The Solid Mandala only days away, White plunged into the new novel
The Binoculars and Helen Nell which was to follow the many lives of a
Sydney woman who was at various times an actress, a cook and later a
thief with an accomplice who worked as a lawyer by day and burglar by
night. Through the binoculars of the title she looked at life – as White
himself so often felt he looked at life about him – through the wrong
end. Other titles White had in mind for the book were The Far and the
Near or The Varieties of Sexual Experience.

20 MARTIN ROAD, 28.i.66
TO FREDERICK GLOVER
Kangaroo Island was very beautiful, though exhausting. I know of nobody
like the Duttons for vitality. Apart from two, and sometimes three fishing
sessions a day, Geoffrey is up to light fires, empty garbage, read to children,
and Nin thinks nothing of cooking several times a day to feed a houseparty
of fourteen, half of them children, which really means cooking two sets of
meals. We went fishing most days, though neither of us is any good at it.
We also went for long walks without clothes along deserted beaches looking
for shells. As a result of all the sunburn we both look like pieces of dried
cod.

20 MARTIN ROAD, 20.iii.66
TO JAMES STERN
Dear Jimmy,
I should have answered your February letter – and now there is this other
wonderfully heartening letter of the other day. In January we went and
spent a week with the Geoffrey Duttons on Kangaroo Island – still idyllic
and unspoilt – it's the island and house in 'Dead Roses' – but I arrived
back here with a slight pneumonia which our two faithful Hungarians

Denis and Alice Halmagyi routed pretty smartly. Unfortunately asthma set in, and stayed, through the foulest changeable weather till the other day. There were times when I thought I should never breathe normally again. Now I am feeling as though none of all this had ever happened!

There are so many things to answer in your two letters I don't know where to begin. *The Solid Mandala* – I think it may turn out to be my best book. Certainly it was hell to write, or perhaps I am still too close to it. Probably every book is hell to write. (Yet I am constantly meeting ladies who say 'how lovely it must be to write' – as though one sat down at the *escritoire* after breakfast, and it poured out like a succession of bread-and-butter letters, instead of being dragged out, by tongs, a bloody mess, in the small hours.)

I have had some wonderful reactions from people like yourself, after a bad start in the States, with the most vindictive outpouring yet in *Time Magazine*. It was so evil, so personal, I can only think it was written by an Australian novelist who got hold of the book from Alwyn Lee while passing through. It was worse than Alwyn Lee could have perpetrated.[67] Do try to find out who it was. (Don't reveal that anybody thinks it was an Australian novelist, because they may clamp down tighter than ever on their 'secret'. My brilliant intuition could be a bad guess, but I think I can connect the kind of drunken gibberish with a certain person who has been trying to kill me for some time.) The novel came out in New York on Feb 3rd, and *Time* reviewed – or didn't review it – almost simultaneously.

I have very little contact with New York since my wonderful old Huebsch died. Marshall Best, who now looks after my interests at the Viking, has been on a trip round the world since before *The Solid Mandala* came out – he arrives here the day after to-morrow for twelve days – and nobody else in the office thought to write me a word about what is happening. An old girl I know in Philadelphia sent me a Viking advertisement the other day which quotes very enthusiastic reviews from somebody called William Ready in the *Library Journal*, Bernard McCabe *Saturday Review*, and Roderick Cook *Harper's*.[68] That looks as though the New York Sunday papers have either poured their scorn on it, or ignored

[67]No. Alwyn Lee was again PW's tormenter, dismissing him 11 Feb., p.58, as 'The Shaman of Sarsaparilla' and a 'receiver of stolen religious goods'. Lee, who had also written very hostile notices in *Time* for *Voss* and *The Burnt Ones*, was an Australian freelance journalist in New York, well-read, a big figure on *Time*, a drinker, womaniser and guru, a communist who died in the arms of the Catholic church. Lee was linked by friendships formed at Melbourne University before the war with two other unsympathetic critics: Ross Campbell and Cyril Pearl of Sydney's *Daily Telegraph*.
[68]*Library Journal*, 15 Jan., p.282; *Saturday Review*, 12 Feb., p.36; *Harper's*, March, p.151.

it. Anyway, I have never expected the Americans to get with *The Solid Mandala* – or anything else I have to write. I think the English will understand, though.

I wonder how you will find *Maurice Guest*; on re-reading it.[69] After sending it as a Christmas card to a number of people I respect, I began to read, and found it the most appalling and unreadable novelette. Somebody told me a film had been made of it with Van Johnson and Elizabeth Taylor.[70] Well, that is just about it – the story of the film – 'he knelt and kissed the gravel where she had stood.' Particularly that gravel!

Manoly and I are coming to Europe next year whatever the obstacles may be. I have been saying vaguely: 'Oh yes, we shall go in 1967, if we can scrape the money together, and find somebody to look after the house-cum-art-gallery.' Now I suddenly feel: 'What the hell? We may be dead in a few years. Break into capital, instead of leaving it for some square nieces to inherit, and leave the house to be broken into.' So we shall be coming in 1967.

You ask about the house and garden. There is not much garden, and the soil is sandy, but we are getting somewhere at last. The house stands on a rise, a hill even, with a ramp winding up to it – very bad for Central European hearts – but dramatic, especially at night with one or two lights. We have three beautiful mature gum trees, the only things growing here when we came, and we have planted roses, several special hibiscus, and a number of native things. Azaleas are our great standby. They are so wiry, and stand up to the gales which sweep us. At the back, which is full of statuesque cats and pregnant pugs, we have a 'Greek' Terrace on top of the two garages – that is, vines growing over a pergola, and lots of pots with geraniums, herbs etc. There is also an ugly but necessary clothes line, a patch of grass for dogs to do their business on, more hibiscus, frangipanni (which I don't much care for – too much like Hanualulu and Flahrida) and a flourishing lemon tree. The general effect and the vibrations are right. (I think the Feinsteins' Sarsaparilla house was something like our house in Martin Road. Their town house was one of the monstrosities in another street not far from here known as Millionaires' Road.)

Thank you for the offer of Svevo's biography.[71] I have always found him fascinating as a character, though I can't read his books. Incidentally, in my old age, I can't read Joyce, but love to read about him. (Do you

---

[69]Henry Handel Richardson, 1908; the novel was recently republished by Sun Books.
[70]*Rhapsody*, 1954.
[71]P. N. Furbank's *Italo Svevo: the Man and the Writer*, 1966: a biography of the Trieste novelist and protégé of James Joyce, Italo Svevo (1861–1928).

have the Ellmann *James Joyce?* Physically Waldo Brown at all stages is, for me, Joyce at all stages.)

To-day we had a delightful visit from Yevtushenko,[72] and I can't resist repeating his inscriptions on my copy of the Penguin edition of his poems – ('Zhima Junction' is probably my favourite poem, as it links up with all the great Russian short stories, novels, <u>and</u> music)[73] – anyway, here is the inscription: 'Too great writer Patrick Wait from all may russian Learto Ev Yevtushenko.' That will help me endure Australia a little longer.

After we got back from Kangaroo Island I started writing another novel. It will be rather different – I hope. I abandoned the idea of a volume of three *Novellen*, after finishing one, which I think is good. I'll send it to you in time. It is called 'A Woman's Hand', and the full-length novel The Binoculars and Helen Nell.

We look forward to seeing you both next year.

Oh, the teeth sucking – Australian ladies with badly fitting sets always do suck them to express approval or disapproval. Sometimes you see old men in the street with their teeth sitting out at the end of their tongues. But I haven't done that one yet.

Love to both–

Patrick

What a labour the Kafka letters must be but then you are used to labours.[74] I am tempted to send you poor Jean Untermeyer's book of reminiscences. But I shouldn't. She has her virtues along with the MacDowell Colony side.[75]

---

[72]Yevgeny (Zhenya) (1933–).

[73]But when he found 'Bratsk Hydroelectric', he told Dutton, 2.i.66: 'Little could be done about such rhetoric, sentimentality, and copybook patriotism. It may provoke orgasms in the youth of every Bratsk in Siberia, but to me it is the kind of stuff which is not for export.'

[74]James and Tania Stern translated Kafka's *Letters to Milena*, 1953, and he was now working on Kafka's *Letters to Felice*, 1973.

[75]*Private Collection*, 1965; Untermeyer was devoted to the MacDowell Colony, the writers' and musicians' retreat in New Hampshire; see PW to Charles Osborne, 10.x.68 p.337.

20 MARTIN ROAD, 3.iv.66

TO GEOFFREY DUTTON

Yevtushenko turned up here the Sunday before last with Frank Hardy[76] and no Krugerskaya.[77] I was glad it happened that way on the first occasion, because he can understand English quite well on his own, and I feel Oxana does falsify things a lot. Last Sunday I got together a fairly representative gathering of younger artists to offset what must have been a pretty unattractive diet of Australian Writer in Adelaide. I asked the Emanuel Rafts and the John Stockdales (painters), Richard Meale and Nigel Butterley (composers), Don Gazzard (architect) and his wife Marea (potter), Helge and Darani Larsen (silversmiths), David Moore (anthropologist) and Gwen who is a teacher. I had several big dishes of cold food, and only red and white wine and beer for drinks. All went very smoothly, except that at one point in their operatic duet-cum-ballet the guests of honour turned on an embarrassing tirade of hate against America, knowing we had an American in the house.[78] I was particularly disgusted after reading an interview in which somebody asked Y. about the trial of Sinyavsky,[79] and he replied that when he accepted hospitality he didn't expect someone to throw a piece of watermelon rind under his feet. However, we parted with tremendous love arias (all the more comic knowing what Krugerskaya really thinks about my work – doesn't she remind you of a big black velvet spider?), and invitations to Russia. A nice little touch at the end, when Oxana was laying it on extra thick: 'Frank Hardy was the first to get to love you' – whereupon Frank looked very grave, and murmured: 'Your books'.

[76]Frank Hardy (1917–94), communist, raconteur and author of the celebrated 1950 novel about the corruption of church and state in Australia, *Power Without Glory*. PW disliked Hardy in his role of Fair Dinkum Aussie.

[77]Oxana Krugerskaya was an overbearing interpreter supplied by the USSR Writers' Union.

[78]His publisher, Marshall Best: 'He couldn't have been a more discreet guest,' PW told Glover at Easter. 'In fact, too discreet, because one couldn't discover what he really thought or liked.'

[79]Andrey Donatovich (1935–   ), novelist and critic exiled for seven years to the labour camps for slandering the Soviet system abroad; his 1956 trial provoked international outrage.

20 MARTIN ROAD, 27.v.66

TO JAMES STERN

Dear Jimmy,

Thank you for sending me the article on Joyce.[80] I remembered reading it when we stayed with you, but enjoyed going over it again.

With the exception of the review by the peevish Irving Wardle,[81] the English have done me proud over *The Solid Mandala*. The Americans were most disappointing. Certainly there were exceptions, but most of the critics over there understand less and less of what I am trying to say. I am sure there has not been a review in the *New Yorker* or I should have been sent it. (The book came out, as far as I remember, on Feb 3 or 12.) That piece in *Time* was by Alwyn Lee, I found out.

Your remarks on your mother and her entourage bring back my own mother's last days. She was not too far gone in senility, but the entourage – there was always another one to look after the latest member. I have an idea for a novel I am going to write one day, about a similar mummy, half senile, but with moments of blinding, brutal perception, and the attendant priestess keeping the flame alive. It does become a kind of religion.

Manoly and I have both been ill – first of all he with flu and a severe strep throat, then I developed flu with bronchitis. Fortunately I was able to stay on my feet till he got up and took over. Now I am up again, and I'd like to feel we were finished, only next week M. has to have an x-ray for probable gallstones.

During all this *Helen Nell* has fallen by the wayside. However, I have written over 85,000 of the first draft, probably about one-third. My bronchial fever brought me a splendidly obscene rabble to populate some of the more shadowy areas.

I've got a Polish translation of *The Living and The Dead* which I must send Tania when I find the energy to do it up. Or perhaps she can no longer read Polish?

We are in the chaos of house-painting – only the outside, which wasn't done when we moved in. By now we are almost nervous wrecks, as we watch our rosebushes smashed by ladders, fuchsias shrivelled by blow-lamps, wet window-sills marked by prowling cats, and the laundry door scratched by dogs asking to be let in. By the way, it looks terribly like the

---

[80]*The Listener*, 28 Sept. 1961, p.461: Stern's spare and beautiful account of a meeting with Joyce.

[81]In the *Observer*, 15 May, p.26: 'the book seems just the kind of coldly exhibitionistic thing that Waldo might have written.'

Feinstein villa at Sarsaparilla. When we settle down again I must coax somebody to take a snap.

Love to both
Patrick.

20 MARTIN ROAD, 2.vi.66
TO FREDERICK GLOVER

We went last night to hear Brendel play the same programme you heard. To give Sydney her due, the Town Hall was practically full. It was a wonderful evening, although I developed a cough which made the last movement of the *Hammerklavier* hell to sit through, at least for me personally. I still think I prefer my Backhaus recording, although it may not be such a perfectly achieved interpretation. A certain craggy mystery remains. I also found Brendel inclined to draw out the *andante* into something too sentimental, just as he made the Berg too lushly beautiful; it is much bonier music. I find Brendel's platform presence disconcerting. I tried not to watch him, but found my eyes returning in fascination. I feel he has the soul of an ageing virgin, a kind of bridesmaid manquée. There was one point at which I almost saw the white net and satin shoes.

20 MARTIN ROAD, 14.vi.66
TO RALPH SMITH

Nothing much has happened since my last letter, and this is really to ask whether you can remember something from your youth. When I returned to Sydney in 1929 after leaving school, I remember seeing at Clifton Gardens or Balmoral an old abandoned weatherboard structure with Palais de Danse painted on it. Can you remember if this was in existence as early as 1919? About that time I can remember the nurse of some children we used to play with getting into evening dresses and going to dance at a 'Pally' somewhere. I think it was the one at Clifton Gardens. On the other hand, I was only seven at the time, the name of the nurse's employer was "Clifton", and that may be why I have come to think Lally used to dash off and dance at the Clifton Pally. Any information from you gratefully received. I want my fictitious characters to go across by ferry and dance in that old ramshackle weatherboard.

20 MARTIN ROAD, 10.vii.66
TO FREDERICK GLOVER

Geoffrey has fantastic tales of Yevtushenko in Adelaide. Y. seems to have gone to bed with most of the ABC girls, one of whom was so exhausted she had to stay in bed for 24 hours. His main-string, however, was a waitress, who had to be carted round by Nin Dutton to all the official functions. Judith Anderson[82] and Zhenya detested each other. He always insisted on calling her 'Judy'. When they first met at the Haywards during a party she commanded him: 'Go on stand over there in the corner and recite some of the poems.' He refused, whereon she started clutching herself and saying: 'But I'm an actress, I have to feel what I'm reading.' At one stage in the evening, Zhenya disappeared into the kitchen with Judy's niece. When he returned without her, Geoffrey went out and found her on all fours. He asked what on earth she was doing. She replied: 'I'm trying to find a button.' The climax of Judy's fury came when the waitress was shoved into the limousine to be taken from the recital hall to the Festival Club while Zhenya came on with Geoffrey. Apparently Judy turned on the girl, and said: 'Who are you?– –And what connexion do you have with the occasion?' Nin reports that the girl carried it all off in a very dignified way, and that conversationally she was superior to a lot of the Establishment.

Do read Christina Stead's *The Man Who Loved Children* if you haven't. It is one of the great novels of the world.[83]

Yrs
Patrick.

20 MARTIN ROAD, 12.vii.66
TO MAIE CASEY
Dear Maie!
I have now read the little book and am returning it separately.[84] In her relationship with Proust I find Marthe Bibesco the more interesting of the

---

[82]The great actress (1898–1992) born in Adelaide, best remembered as Mrs Danvers in Hitchcock's *Rebecca*, 1940, had volunteered to give four 'classical drama recitals' at the Festival: a disaster.

[83]Stead (1902–83) was hereafter championed by PW but he found none of the other novels matched the high achievement of *The Man Who Loved Children*, 1940, reissued 1965. Of *For Love Alone*, 1944, PW told Dutton, 5.ii.67: 'when she gets to England it teeters on the edge of becoming novelettish. Even so, it is a remarkable book. I feel elated to think it is there.' After reading *Seven Poor Men of Sydney*, PW told the Moores, 22.v.68: 'It's very good, but a lot of the romantic fantasies are wearisome, and the intellectual discussions of Communism. A lot of it comes too close to the world of Christopher Brennan, Hugh McCrae and even Norman Lindsay. I also find the characters far too much alike, too much projections of what is probably her own forceful and egotistical character.' *Letty Fox, Her Luck*, 1946, surprised PW who told Dutton, 13.i.75: 'It's extraordinary to think of that quiet, sedate woman writing anything so hilarious.'

[84]*Au Bal avec Marcel Proust*, revised edition, 1956, by Princess Marthe Bibesco, whom Maie Casey passionately admired.

two and wish she had shown us more of herself. We have read so much already about P. I did not feel she added much (I realise of course that her few touches must have contributed to a grand portrait such as Painter's) and the letters from which she quotes make him sound sentimental, even trivial and childish at times. I suppose he was all of that along with the rest!

I have broken off the novel to catch a story which keeps on rising to the surface. This was the right moment. Now that I have a version on paper I can go back to *Helen Nell*, who is not looking as dreary as I felt when I wrote last. The story I mention is of Athens during the Occupation, and is called 'The Full Belly'. I must send you a new novella of mine, 'A Woman's Hand', when it comes out; part of it takes place in Egypt.

Geoffrey Dutton spent three days with us last week – the usual whirlwind of events and people. One night he took us out with David Campbell whom I hadn't met before. Do you know him. He is a great charmer, and very witty. I was glad to find I like him so much as he is one of the few Australian poets I can read with pleasure.[85]

Geoffrey has discovered a girl called Anne Gordon[86] (one of those Gordons from Bungendore way) who, we think, is going to be really good. G. is publishing some of her poems. She is still a student, very beautiful and shy. Has had a tragic life: her father died not so long ago of leukaemia, then her mother a year later of some obscure disease. She was engaged to be married, but withdrew from that. The poems I have read are technically rather raw, but there is nothing 'routine Australian' about the imagery; here and there she makes you see things for the first time.

We look forward to your coming here in August. Please give us as much warning as possible so that I can think up something good for lunch.

Canberra must be hellishly cold. Do you ever come across hares? I mean, to eat. There is a Greek way of stewing them very slowly with a lot of lemons which I want to try, but I can never find a hare in Sydney.

Have had a letter from Cynthia Nolan which I haven't yet completely deciphered; there are so many corners, pockets, and borders, some of the latter completely gummed over by the flaps of the aerogramme. I gather she is happy to be back under the 'deodar' beside the Putney mud.[87]

Yours
Patrick.

[85](1915–79), poet and grazier, amateur boxer and former RAAF pilot who lived on a windswept stretch of country out from Bungendore. To Glover, 10.vii.66, PW wrote, 'if I were a woman I should be breaking my neck to commit adultery.'
[86](1945–), now a painter in England.
[87]The garden of the Nolans' house in Deodar Road, Putney, ran down to the Thames.

20 Martin Road, 30.vii.66
TO GEOFFREY DUTTON

The reason I am writing so soon is that Maie Casey was here yesterday . . . The lunch turned out very well. The hares arrived two days in advance. After I had cut them up our kitchen was a horrific sight; Duncan's chamber can't have looked bloodier. And the twelve lemons and twenty-four cloves of garlic gave spectacular results. We had chlorophyll for Maie, but she refused to take it. I'm sure those she met later in the day must have suspected the lunch of being a republican plot.

White's sister Suzanne returned to Sydney to live in August 1966 with two of her daughters, Frances and Gillian. White volunteered to take Gillian while Suzanne found a house. 'It will change our lives a bit,' he told Marshall Best. 'Less alcohol and farts, more shaves and edifying conversation. Or perhaps it will end by her teaching us a thing or two about life and squalor, the way the young seem able to now.'[88] Gillian was twenty-four and had made the move to Sydney reluctantly, leaving behind a job at the BBC and the man she was to marry. White overwhelmed her with plans just as his mother had once swamped him. Gillian withdrew. Ruth used to accuse her son of being stubborn and silent; now he raged in letters about his 'inert' niece. These were unhappy weeks for both of them, made unhappier by White's automatic disapproval of the man Gillian wanted to marry.

20 Martin Road, 18.ix.66
TO FREDERICK GLOVER
Dear Frederick,

I wanted to write last Sunday to catch you before you left for your holiday, but became entangled with my family. They had a meal here in the evening, then went over to the Moores', who hadn't yet seen all of them. I forget whether I told you Gwen Moore broke her kneecap a few weeks ago, and is still only hobbling about very painfully.

Some time ago I thought you said in a letter that you were coming on to Sydney from Canberra, but there was no mention of that in your last. Is that off now?

Suzanne has a six-months' lease of a hideous and cramped furnished flat in a new building near the Edgecliff post-office. I can't think what it must have looked like before all the plastic flowers and one-button satin

[88] 17.vii.66.

cushions were put away. There is a wall-to-wall which makes one dizzy, and which even extends through the kitchen! However, it is very close to Ascham, where Frances will start the day after tomorrow, and in the six months of the lease one hopes they will find a house to live in permanently. But they are so hopeless at organising themselves, Manoly and I feel we shall have to find the house and push them into it. They came out here not even knowing how many pieces of luggage they had, or what was in them. It was only last week they discovered one of the suitcases was missing. (Fortunately it turned up in the baggage room at the Belvedere, where Suzanne spent the first few days.) Suzanne is terribly lazy, I'm afraid, and mentally indolent. Consequently she has got very fat and wheezy, and will probably get steadily wheezier, going from lunch to lunch with other ex-Frensham girls.[89]

It would be quite out of the question to expect them to cope with this house. The most I can hope for is that Gillian will have got into the way of things by Christmas, when we go to Kangaroo Island for a week, and that she can be persuaded to look after the house and water the pots, perhaps with a friend for company. As for holidays in Australia, I don't think it is possible to have such a thing. I always come back feeling exhausted. What I am planning to do if I ever really feel I need one is to move into one of the spare rooms, sleep and read, and go out to all meals. We do enjoy going to Kangaroo Island, but that is the most exhausting marathon of all.

Gillian is still with us, but with fits of conscience: she feels she should be huddling with the others in the nasty little flat, especially when Frances starts school and will have to be received at 3 o'clock. I hope she doesn't decide to go there, because I don't know how they would move at all with her mountain of luggage added to what is already there, and they seem incapable of separating the things they don't need from what they do. G. is a very nice, well brought up Kensington girl, but it is difficult to see where she will fit in here, unless into the most negative kind of Eastern Suburbs or country society, to which all her mother's friends belong. It gives me the horrors to see the build-up of all I spent my youth throwing off. Because Gillian deserves better than this, though it is difficult to explain what. She has a kind of distinction . . . a kind of vague yearning after music, probably because the man she was in love with was a [musician].[90] We both feel she hasn't got him out of her system, and might suddenly rush back if something else doesn't happen and here all the men

[89]Boarding school, wisteria covered, in bracing country near Tudor House.
[90]No. She had studied music before they met.

of the right age are already attached, if they are not bad eggs or queens.

I expect you will have got hold of *Australian Letters* by now. The print is dreadful, to cut expense by saving paper I imagine.

We went the other night to the Community Theatre's *Romeo and Juliet*, and for the first time they have done something I have enjoyed and can honestly recommend. There are a lot of rough patches, but I can see from this they have got something to give ...

Frances bore up very well, though she did look at her watch rather a lot. Tomorrow we are going to *Boris Godunov*, so she will have been thoroughly initiated into the rigours of theatre à la Beatrice Tildesley.

In spite of all the upheavals I have been working a lot lately, though not liking what has come out. But I am going to ignore everybody, take my time, and spend years on the book if necessary.

I hope you enjoy Canberra. I hated it when I was there, but that was about eighteen years ago.

Yours
Patrick.

20 MARTIN ROAD, 23.ix.66
TO JULIET O'HEA

I am working at the novel quite consistently again in spite of many distractions. The chief one is my family ... they have to look for a house, but they are so passive I'm sure they will do nothing about it unless Manoly and I find one and push them into it. Nor does Gillian do anything about approaching the ABC for the job. The ground is dug, but she spends her time washing her hair, and, I imagine, hoping somebody will spring up and marry her. I realise I have been spared a lot in life, not having to push children of my own in directions they didn't want to go.

20 MARTIN ROAD, 17.x.66
TO MAIE CASEY
Dear Maie,

Thank you for the *Art in Australia*. Not the least interesting thing about your article[91] is that it shows how much of Drysdale comes from Purves-Smith. That Paris Street is a thrilling painting.[92] If I had discovered it as a child I should have stared at it by the hour.

There is something in which you could perhaps help me as you have

---

[91]'George Bell in Bourke Street', Sept. 1966, p.120: about Bell's school in Melbourne in the 1930s at which she, Drysdale and Purves-Smith were pupils.
[92]'Paris', 1940, by Purves-Smith, in the Caseys' collection.

been interested in cars. In the book I am writing there is a flashy and rather hysterical new-rich woman called Ethel Taylour who owns several cars for different occasions. There are those she shares with her husband, and which are driven by the chauffeur. But she has something fast and exotic which she jumps into and drives herself when she wants to blow off steam. The period is 1928. Would an Isotto Fraschini (spelling?) have been owned by somebody rich and capricious in Australia at that time? How large, how open would it have been? I want her to go on rather a damp, windswept drive down the coast taking with her Ellen her cook (Helen Nell at this phase of the story). If the car could not have been an Isotto – what? Do you know of any book where I could find photographs of cars used in Australia at that period? Can one refer to a 'glove box' in a car of then? The drive in question takes place in the early hours of the morning after a disastrous formal dinner party. There is a point where Ethel Taylour stops the car and takes off her jewels for greater freedom. She has to put them somewhere. I am sure you will be able to give me some advice on all this car business.

Nin Dutton broke her journey here on her way home from Russia. She has fantastic Travellers' Tales: roasted oxen devoured in the Caucasus, lighting candles to Pasternak with Yevtushenko in a Moscow Church as a first rite on arrival. Apparently one can't admire anything or they give it to you. Nin has an icon which Yevtushenko's wife yanked down from the wall over the bed.

No more room. Hope to see you when you come here next.

Yours

Patrick

20 MARTIN ROAD, 24.x.66

TO FREDERICK GLOVER

Last night we had some people in, and I played the whole of *Tristan* through. It was an evening of assault and battery, but I think they enjoyed it, although one lady got a bit hysterical between the music and change of life, and Emily Lane-Brown,[93] aged a few months, tried to outdo Flagstad in the beginning. I gave them a meal during the intervals, and it worked out very well that way. For the main dish I made a big Sauerkraut with pork and Frankfurters. Next month I am going to play through the recording of *Boris Godunov* Desmond Digby and James Allison[94] have given me for Christmas.

[93]Child of Penny Lane-Brown, later Coleing.
[94]Digby's partner, librarian at Woollahra Library.

MARTIN ROAD, 5.xi.66
TO CYNTHIA NOLAN
Dear Cynthia,
I suppose if you <u>want</u> to put that piece in your book there is no reason why you shouldn't.[95] However, there are one or two things which ought to be changed or corrected. I should leave out the word 'great' and put 'Patrick White, the writer'. Nobody knows who will appear great until many years later, and yours may appear a reckless choice a few years hence (this is on l.5 p.169). Manoly says he and Anna didn't go on that drive, and now I seem to remember they didn't (l.16 p.169). I saw the picnic at Point Piper as a Boudin not a Delacroix (l.16 p.170). There was a moment when it seemed that the death of Voss would never come right. I was in bed with bronchitis at the time, I got out and put on a record of Bartok's violin concerto, and immediately I began to convey what I wanted. (Same para).

Geoffrey has just left for Adelaide. He spent twenty-four hours with us to break his journey and tell about his trip, Nin had done the same a couple of weeks earlier. G. gave us news of you. I hope you have scotched the cold by now.

If you hear of Edna O'Brien receiving a copy of my last *Novelle* by air mail, it is because she sent me her latest novel by air, and I felt I had to reciprocate in some small way. I sent you the same thing by sea a few weeks ago, when it came out.

There have been some very upsetting developments recently, and I am feeling thoroughly exhausted by them. The other day Clement Semmler and the representative of the Encyclopaedia Britannica came out here to offer me the award, but I refused it as it is money that smells.[96] Just after that poor Semmler walked through the same screen door you bumped into. He went literally through, however. I am sorry we met for the first time on such an occasion, as I liked him, and would like to know him. This morning I see to my horror that they have divided the prize between

---

[95] Her account of travels in North America and incarceration with TB in a New York hospital was published in 1967 as *Open Negative, An American Memoir*, but Cynthia Nolan had cut this passage about her first meeting with PW in Florida.
[96] The Britannica–Australia Awards for achievements in the arts and sciences were made each year by the US publishers of the encyclopaedia. Semmler (1914–   ), critic, biographer of Banjo Paterson, deputy general manager of the ABC 1965–77, admired PW above all living novelists. Later they enjoyed a friendship of some warmth.

Randolph Stow (fair enough)[97] and that monster Hal Porter. To think that I am responsible for putting $5000 in the hands of Charlie's Aunt! I imagined they would give it to somebody like Martin Boyd[98] or Christina Stead, both of whom have been ignored in the past. Then the art award has been given to Ursula Hoff of the Melbourne Art Gallery.[99] That too astonished me. One would think that, if they are determined to ignore Sid, they would give it to somebody like Fred Williams who has just had a most wonderful and very creative exhibition.

My other embarrassing incident, coming on top of the first, was a letter from the National University offering me an honorary Doctor of Letters. I always feel completely foreign to the academic world in Australia, or anywhere else, and couldn't imagine going down to Canberra, making an oration, and hobnobbing with A. D. Hope, their Professor of English, who has put on record forever in his History of Australian Lit., his earlier opinion of my 'pretentious and illiterate poetic sludge.' I was sent for by Nugget Coombs right on top of the letter, and urged to accept the honorary thing.[100] It was well meant on his part, but I just felt I didn't want any of it.

Sydney has broken out in a rash of op and pop – boring geometry, and paintings of girls exhibiting their bushes over the tops of their stockings. Apart from the Fred Williams, there has been a very good exhibition of pottery by Marea Gazzard,[101] from which I bought a piece. There is also a spate of ill-digested Whiteley-Bacon.

We always see Maie Casey when she comes to Sydney, and I like her immensely. He too is growing on me. Last time we went to Admiralty House and he and I talked quite a lot. But she likes best to come here alone to lunch with us. At Admiralty House on the last occasion we met the daughter, whom we found most unexpected.[102]

---

[97]Randolph (Mick) Stow (1935–), novelist. PW told Glover, 13.xi.59, that To the Islands, 1958: 'If one forgets about some novelettish minor characters, is magnificently done.' But then in Tourmaline, 1963, Stow had, 'Come to grief in a lush labyrinth of poetic prose', PW told Dutton, 9.v.65.

[98](1893–1972), novelist offspring of the distinguished Victorian family of painters, potters and writers. PW admired Boyd more as literary figure than as writer: the books seemed 'rather watercolour' to PW.

[99](1909–), assistant director of the gallery, authority on Rembrandt and Charles Conder.

[100]Herbert (Nugget) Coombs (1906–), chancellor of the Australian National University, governor of the Reserve Bank and founding chairman of the Elizabethan Theatre Trust. PW came to admire him particularly for projects he initiated in Aboriginal Australia.

[101](1928–), potter, sculptor and teacher exhibiting at Gallery A.

[102]Jane Macgowan (1928–).

I still have Gillian my eldest niece staying here. My sister has found a house in Woollahra which is now being investigated by the solicitors. I hope there won't be any snags, and that they will be able to move in soon. Suzanne and Frances are living in a horrible tower, with doorhandles which come off, and wall-to-wall in the kitchenette. Gillian is the most passive and helpless creature I have ever come across. She has to be pushed in every direction. I am hoping John Hopkins will soon be back at the ABC, and that she will then be able to go and present the letter of recommendation she has from her bosses at the BBC.[103] But I expect she will have to be dragged there by me. The other night she was going out to dinner – we were somewhere else – she found some cat shit on the bonnet of her car, was too helpless to go and get an old newspaper to rub it off, drove all the way to her dinner, then back afterwards with the cat mess still on the car.[104] What her real interests are beyond the man in London . . . I have been unable to find out. She . . . makes no attempt to go about and see things. There is music, but her taste runs to people like Elgar and Vaughan Williams . . .

This to me is another terribly depressing situation. Nor is my book going at all well. I think I may suddenly destroy it one day.

Sorry to be so gloomy, but there it is. Hope things are better with you.

Love
Patrick.

FOR FOUR YEARS AUSTRALIA had been sending men to fight in Vietnam. When the new prime minister Harold Holt introduced conscription to feed the war machine, he won overwhelming public support for backing the Americans in a war to contain the 'downward sweep' of communism. White had never seriously questioned this until Geoffrey Dutton sent him a copy of the *Ramparts Vietnam Primer*. 'That model sarge on the cover is just a bit too clean-cut to convince,' he told Dutton.[105] But the *Primer* began the transformation of this private conservative into a public radical.

20 MARTIN ROAD, 20.xi.66
TO GEOFFREY DUTTON
Dear Geoffrey,
I have now read the *Vietnam Primer*, and see I have been wrong, chiefly

[103]John Hopkins (1927–) was director of music at the ABC.
[104]She has no recollection of this.
[105]13.xi.66.

through ignorance. I am writing to *Ramparts* for more copies. However, I should like to know more about some of the contributors. Do you know anything more than the little biographical pieces inside the cover? The 'model sarge' is the one who impresses me most as being first hand and sincere.[106] My only criticism of his accusations is that the cynicism of the American army in Vietnam is the cynicism of any Western army in any country of the wrong colour. I experienced it with the British all through the Middle East, in Italy, and in Greece.

20 MARTIN ROAD, 18.xii.66
TO GEOFFREY DUTTON

Last Sunday in the middle of a dinner party for the Milgates,[107] the Blackmans and the David Moores, we started a premature whelping. It was pretty hectic cooking the dinner and running out to open the packages and cut the cords. We had three live dogs, one live bitch and one dead. During the night Ethel sat on one of the dogs. The following day they seemed too slack and cold to be normal, and it looked as though they had been affected by the streptococcus infection Ethel has been suffering from. We immediately started feeding them with an eye dropper and they all seemed to be responding. However, Ethel sat on another dog the following night, and the third died yesterday morning. The surviving bitch, Grace, seems very tough, and I have hopes of rearing her. I now take her up to my room at night, and she sleeps on a hot-water bottle in a little box. Every two hours she wakes me, and I feed her with the eyedropper. It is all very disappointing for Tessa,[108] as you will not want the trouble of keeping a pug bitch with the dachshund dogs. I'll have to see whether I

---

[106]Sgt Don Duncan's passionate anti-communist beliefs led him to join the US Army but, after 18 months fighting this war, decided, 'The whole thing was a lie. We weren't preserving freedom in South Vietnam. There was no freedom to preserve . . . The world is not just good guys and bad guys. Anti-communism is a lousy substitute for democracy.' *Ramparts*, Feb. 1966, pp.13–24.

[107]The Milgates were the actress Dinah Shearing (c.1926–) and the artist Rod Milgate (1934–) whose friendship with PW lasted nearly 20 years. She was one of PW's great stage enthusiasms but he admired her husband's writing more than his paintings. To Dutton, 13.xi.66, PW declared that Milgate's 1966 play *A Refined Look At Existence* was, 'The first play I have seen which is both Australian, theatrically creative and intellectually satisfying.' Their friendship came to grief over Milgate's indifference to politics. Shearing, being berated again about this on the telephone, told PW to stop: 'You shout at Manoly, you shout at other people, but not me. If you don't stop I'm going to hang up.' She did. Tentative contact was restored ten years later with an exchange of flowers and photographs.

[108]The Duttons' daughter, Teresa.

can pick up a ready made dog pup. I know after two litters that pugs should only be got ready-made. Strange, when they are such straightforward, sturdy little dogs after their early puppyhood.

20 MARTIN ROAD, 15.i.67
TO FREDERICK GLOVER
She was so lively at first we had hopes of her, and did in fact keep her alive for a fortnight feeding her every two or three hours with an eye-dropper – very exhausting – and after a bit one saw there was no hope. We buried her on Christmas Eve . . .

Suzanne tells me Gillian has booked to go back by Sitmar on Feb 1st.[109] Gillian herself has not mentioned it, and I don't expect she will. She came here on Boxing Night and chirped her usual nothings. If any sort of farewell crops up I shall not be of it, as I couldn't sit there pretending everything is lovely in the garden. I shall now concentrate on Frances, who escaped from Kensington in time. She has already started to think for herself, and has very strong ideas on what is right and wrong. This might sound priggish in a child of ten, but there is no trace of the prig in her.

This New Year seems to be one of upheavals and decisions. Yesterday I finally decided I can't go on with the book I have been writing. It is something I have been trying to face for some time; it is only unfortunate that it took me almost a year and 160,000 words to realise I had a miscarriage on my hands. It happened to me once before some years ago when I wrote two-thirds of a novel about Mrs Fraser. The reason why I gave up has never been clear to me. I still have the fragment, and what there is pleases me in many ways, but I have never been able to make myself go on with it. I expect I shall never go back to this one either, but in the present case it is a monster of overblown detail and luxuriant fantasies.

All this is not as bad as it sounds, because I have had something else boil up in me with great insistence. I am going to do nothing for a month, then start on this other book.

Suzanne now has possession of her house, but they haven't yet moved in as the furniture she brought out has to be fumigated, and there are various jobs to be done in the house. Frances is very excited at the prospect of having a garden. She is always watering such as there is already. Manoly gave them a hose as a house-warming present, and neither of the flat-bred

[109]And was paying her own fare.

girls knew what to do with it at first. Suzanne managed to remember from her childhood. One wonders how they will get on.

As you have perhaps gathered I am not in the mood for writing a letter. Yours about the Kriegers and Fishers was most interesting. If the Kriegers are hard up I expect that is why we haven't seen them since Ile brought her family here, although I made it clear I should like to see Fritz here after he returned from his trip. He sent us an affectionate Christmas card, and we sent *Once Around the Sun*, that collection of Australian schoolchildren's poems – which you must get hold of if you haven't got it already. I don't doubt we shall get together with the Kriegers eventually, and the relationship will probably be an easier one.[110] They will be less suffocating for being less upholstered. I am coming to the conclusion that all European Jews suffocate one in the end by being over-possessive and over-furnished.

20 MARTIN ROAD, 25.i.67

TO LAWRENCE DAWS

Since you left, the drizzle has turned to a downpour, but I don't complain as I can watch our wind-stunted trees growing. Last night we went and ate fried fish on a rickety pier at Rose Bay: very paintable in the Impressionist past – perhaps even in the hard-edged present.

---

[110]The friendship was over; the Kriegers later moved to Melbourne; over the next decade the only contact came when PW sent Ile Krieger Hungarian translations of his novels.

Words and Paint

February 1967 – January 1970

IN THE MIDDLE OF a steamy Sydney February, White embarked on *The Vivisector*, a writer's account of a painter's life. For the painter Hurtle Duffield, the pursuit of truth is an act of worship. White believed an artist who celebrates the world in all its squalor and beauty draws close to God. In *The Vivisector* he was setting out once again to show unbelievers the faith he believed buried in them all.

At some point in the first draft of a novel White expected to suffer an asthmatic 'blow out'. This came after only a day at his desk. He was taken to hospital. Lascaris, as always, packed, along with White's pyjamas and his father's ivory hairbrushes, a bundle of Martin Road writing paper. Propped up in bed at Royal North Shore, Prince Alfred, Prince Henry or St Vincent's, White continued to write.

PRINCE ALFRED, CAMPERDOWN, 20.ii.67
TO MARGERY WILLIAMS
My hospital life is full of small events. This time I wasn't able to get a room to myself, which is perhaps all to the good. I have an amiable room-mate with a lot of Sandy Stone in him, although his grandfather was a Swede. His Beryl is from Tumbarumba, and still apple-cheeked.[1] There are two sons, three nursing daughters, one of them married to a school chaplain, and two grandchildren. This morning Sandy took communion and I found it very awkward at such close quarters as I did not feel I was in a position to take part. We have long nostalgic dialogues about N.S.W. earlier in the century. All in all, things might be worse.

PRINCE ALFRED, CAMPERDOWN 26.ii.67
TO GEOFFREY DUTTON
By now I have shared the room with three different men. The first two were easy enough, but at present I have an elderly maniac of about 14

[1]Sandy and Beryl Stone, a decent couple from suburbia, were created by Barry Humphries and entered Australian folklore.

mentally, a South Coast chemist who gobbles lollies and plays pop on the transistor all day. I hope I can restrain my explosion a little longer. In the meantime it is almost impossible to read, think, rest, or write a letter . . .

To return to Australian lit., somebody brought me Judith Wright's *The Other Half.* I found it all very impeccable, but depressing, particularly 'Turning Fifty' in which she toasts the rising sun in coffee.[2] The same day, in Maritain, I came across a quotation from Plato: 'Commonsense is the greatest obstacle to poetry.' It seemed to be aimed right at the heart of Australian creativity.

20 MARTIN ROAD, 6.iii.67
TO GEOFFREY DUTTON
Dear Geoffrey,
Thanks for letter and Akhmadulina.[3] I like *Fever* best, then *Longing for Lermontov.* Here and there in the poems I detect that kind of Russian rhetoric which I dislike when it occurs in Yevtushenko. I wonder how it is in the original, and whether it is stressed in translation. (Why have I never read Lermontov? He crops up so regularly, and the name alone is fascinating. Perhaps he is another of those one can't translate.)

I escaped on Wednesday from the hospital as planned, and ever since have been feeling guilty about my relief, as they really looked after me very well while I was in there. I am still pretty groggy, there are times when my legs feel as though they are filled with air, and my chest doesn't clear up altogether as the weather continues so foul. But at least I can breathe now.

Yesterday evening Iris Murdoch and John Bayley were here briefly for

---

[2]Wright (1915–   ), poet and conservationist wrote:
I raise my cup–
dark, bitter, neutral, clean,
sober as morning–
to all I've seen and known–
to this new sun.
She was a product of the same NSW pastoral world as PW (indeed, PW's grandfather once owned the patch of New England where she was born) but neither greatly admired the work of the other. PW told Margery Williams, 6.xi.64, that Wright, on accepting the Britannica–Australia award for her contribution to literature, 'announced that nothing novel had come out of Australian letters since the early 'Forties, which I must say I found a little hard to bear'. PW later supported her work for Aborigines and conservation.
[3]Bella Akhmadulina (1937–   ), poet and once wife of Yevtushenko; Dutton and Igor Mezhakoff-Koriakin were translating a book of her new poems published as *Fever* by Sun Books in 1968 and later in London and New York.

a drink.[4] I think you would like them. We did. She is rather plump, homely, and dowdy. He is a strange-looking little man, rather nervous in the beginning, and probably ill. I felt we were all on the same wavelength, and was sorry they are on this mad tear through Australia so that we can't see more of them. I told them they ought to see Geoffrey Dutton in Adelaide, but left it at that. You can go in search of them if you feel like it.

I still haven't received my copies of the *Ramparts Vietnam Primer*, and wonder whether they haven't been seized. On the other hand, after reading an article on *Ramparts* in the *N. Y. Times*, I may simply be a victim of *Ramparts* chaos. It is run by a bunch of 'colourful' young men who keep a pet monkey in the office.

Had a very engaging post-card from Sid Nolan from Marakeesh – a carob tree full of black goats in the middle of a completely bald landscape. The London winter had begun to get Cynthia down (you know she was struck down by TB a few years ago in New York) so they had gone to Marakeesh to breathe some better air . . .

I must go and baste the bloody beef. It is wonderful to be able to eat again, what one likes, and in quantities.

Yrs
Patrick.

20 MARTIN ROAD, 12.iii.67
TO JULIET O'HEA
A couple of days ago I cleaned the house from top to bottom, which can only be done when I am in full possession of myself.

20 MARTIN ROAD, 26.iii.67
TO GEOFFREY DUTTON
The Show has been worse than ever this year, perhaps because of the perfect weather. Yesterday – Saturday – was the most hideous Arab bedlam I have ever had to endure. People I know who were at it got no pleasure at all, and fell on their beds with exhaustion the moment they returned home. There were cars parked even on the pavement down Martin Road. The final frenzy of fireworks, loudspeakers, and screams, made me long for a downpour on Easter Monday to wash the whole thing away.

We had drinks recently at Admiralty House, the Drysdales also there, and Clem Semmler. Manoly discovered the latter has exactly the face and head of a grasshopper. I quite like him, though. When we were leaving

---

[4]Murdoch (1919–   ), the philosopher and novelist; Bayley (1925–   ), the critic.

Maie embraced Tass. She said: 'I don't know why I always kiss Tass and never Maisie.' Maisie replied: 'Let's keep it heterosexual, shall we?' Maie rang the day they were flying up to open the Show. She was unhappy at having to make a speech about the scones, because 'there's nothing you can say about a scone.' I told her everyone concerned would be satisfied to hear the scones were extra dainty this year. She could probably give herself quite an amusing time camping her way through official functions, and nobody to understand the language . . .

Have been working fairly intensively to take my mind off the Show, but writing becomes no less terrifying than it was, if anything, more. Still there are moments when things slip out of their own accord, and one wonders: how on earth did I think of that?

20 MARTIN ROAD, 24.iv.67
TO HAROLD HOLT
PRIME MINISTER OF AUSTRALIA
Dear Mr Holt,
I have felt all along that we Australians are ill-informed on the origins and conduct of the war in Vietnam. A few months ago the enclosed booklet came my way,[5] and I am sending it in case it isn't known to you. It is worth reading and thinking about.

I'd like to add that I have always voted Liberal but can't go along with the war-in-Vietnam policy, nor can I stomach the invasion of Australia by the United States, although I have nothing against Americans in their own milieu.

Yours sincerely,
Patrick White.

20 MARTIN ROAD, 7.v.67
TO JULIET O'HEA
Yes the Miles Franklin business was quite astonishing. I hadn't entered *The Solid Mandala* because some of the books which have won the prize in the last few years have taken any glory out of it. About ten days before the announcement was to be made I was rung up by a blithering Knight called Oliver Crosthwaite-Eyre.[6] He wanted me to meet him at very short notice, which I couldn't. He then congratulated me on the award I was about to win. I could only reply: 'Which award?' When I told him I hadn't entered my book, he said: 'Oh, but I think my colleagues have.' I told him

---

[5]Copies of the *Ramparts Vietnam Primer* had finally arrived from San Francisco.
[6](1913–78), Conservative MP, Verderer of the New Forest, chairman of Eyre & Spottiswoode.

his colleagues must withdraw it at once and he blathered off. After a couple of days I rang up the trustees who look after the prize, and one of the judges I know. I was told nothing could be done as the judges hadn't been able to agree on a runner-up. The manager of the trustees even went so far as to tell me I should accept the money at the function, then return it to the fund if I wanted to. I said they could easily divide the prize between Peter Mathers' *Trap*[7] and Elizabeth Harrower's *The Watch Tower*[8] which are both well above the average book which wins. These arguments went on for a couple of days by telephone. Then there was a silence, and when they came out of it they announced that *Trap* had won the prize. I was very glad. I had read it a short time before and felt it was one of the few creative novels about Australia. He was born in England and went away again since growing up. Perhaps that is why he can write.

I haven't had a word from E & S or their distributors to explain their strange behaviour. I already refer to them as my ex-publishers but until I have another book to offer I'm not going to bother thinking about someone else.

Yrs
Patrick.

20 MARTIN ROAD, 7.v.67
TO MAIE CASEY
Can you remember about telephones in Sydney in 1914? I think I can remember one in our house about 1915. It had the ear and mouthpiece joined by a bar, and there was a handle to wind when one wanted to make a call.

Do you know – or perhaps you could find out in London – whether Sargent's portraits could be seen in public galleries by 1913 and whether the paintings of Toulouse Lautrec were hanging in public galleries in Paris by then? In each case, I think they would have been, but I'd like to make sure.

---

[7]Mathers (1931–   ) grew up in Australia but had returned to England for a few years; PW tried unsuccessfully to persuade Viking to publish *Trap* in North America. He told Best, 1.ii.67: 'Apart from the reprints of Christina Stead, *Trap* is the only Australian novel I have read for years which I feel is really creative. It is very crude, but he has tremendous vitality and imagination.'

[8]Harrower (1928–   ) had met PW a few years before and joined his band of loyal women friends; she knew not to be possessive and their cool intimacy lasted until PW's death. His one regret was that *The Watch Tower* was her last book. Years later PW gave her a copy of *Memoirs of Many in One* inscribed: 'To Elizabeth, luncher and diner extraordinaire. Sad you don't WRITE.'

By the way, if Roy asks you about the portrait he painted of me years ago, pretend you have seen it, and I'll show it to you one day. I suppose it flattered my vanity in my youth,[9] but I got to hate it as I grew older, and for a long time it has been 'under the stairs.' I believe Roy started asking James Fairfax[10] about it once, and James had to get out of it somehow. It's difficult to know what to do with it. I have a vague plan for giving it to James, who will present it to the Gallery of N.S.W., because one can't very well present a portrait of oneself, yet for Roy's sake I feel perhaps it ought to go there. It will, in any case, with all the other paintings after I am dead.

We are naturally very depressed over Greece.[11] No word from any of Manoly's family since it happened, and some of them may well be under arrest. One of the cousins is quite a seasoned gaolbird. You may have met her in the M.E., as she was a friend of the Smarts. She is a poetess of sorts, and her name is Elly Papadimitriou.[12]

A strange little experience the other evening: a young girl arrived on my doorstep in the dark. She had come all the way from Marrickville to show me a poem she had written, and because, she said, she wanted to look at a living author she had admired. So there I sat, a not very impressive 'living author', suffering from an attack of diarrhoea, and the potatoes disintegrating in the kitchen. The girl's name was Elizabeth Power – a very good one, I think.

20 Martin Road, 16.vii.67
TO MARGERY WILLIAMS
Dear Margery,
You did make Scotland sound idyllic, although you then set out to correct the impression. I was very much taken with it – to my surprise – when we were there a few years ago. I felt I could have taken over and started living in one of the stone houses in the valley in which we were staying,

[9]'One of the looser Goyas in a more contemporary idiom,' he told Spud Johnson, 12.x.39.
[10](1933–), connoisseur and heir to Sir Warwick. PW told Dutton, 1.v.67. 'He grows on one. There is much more in him than he cares to admit, but I expect he gets so outrageously flattered because he is a millionaire and a Fairfax, he has withdrawn into himself in embarrassment.'
[11]On 21 April 1967 the government of Greece was overthrown in a military coup d'état.
[12](1906–) poet and communist, was part of Lady Smart's lesbian milieu in Cairo. Amy Smart was the Coptic second wife of the oriental scholar and spy Sir Walter; they entertained writers, artists, politicians, etc. Papadimitriou was then working with Greek refugees to Egypt, was imprisoned during the Greek Civil War and imprisoned again by the Colonels. PW disliked her.

but of course there would be dreadful drawbacks. Whenever I picked on a particularly attractive-looking house I was surprised to be told it was, or had been, a manse . . .

I have been working a lot and liking some of it. I find that I am using bits of my miscarried novel of last year, so perhaps I was trying myself out in that, and it won't be wasted. However, my chief incentive is gone. I used to want to contribute something to Australia. Now I no longer care. There is only something I have to work out for myself. But perhaps that is all to the good, because chauvinism is bad.

I have had an exchange of letters with the awful little Holt. I sent him a booklet, published in the U.S., showing why the war in Vietnam is an immoral one. He retaliated by sending me six issues of a publication called *Vietnam Studies* through which I am at present wading – very departmental – except where Michael Stewart[13] or Menzies suddenly start talking intelligibly. Of course each side is right and each side is wrong and only God will decide. But I who am not God can't help feeling that the Americans are more immoral than the Communists for resurrecting fascism (how could they help it – they're so Germanic) to combat Communism. Democracy is every day more firmly nailed in its coffin.

I also sent the Vietnam booklet to the leaders of the Churches and find most of them are in my camp. Only Cardinal Gilroy replied: 'Yes, Vietnam is very sad, I have been there,' perhaps because the liberal Catholics of the U.S. accuse Spellman[14] of engineering the war in support of a Catholic minority in South Vietnam.

Poor Rabbi Porush didn't reply to me, because he must have received my letter the same day as he had a war of his own on his hands.[15]

I have found the Israeli episode most inspiring. I know you are in sympathy with Egyptians, but I have always found them lying, bullying, blackmailing cowards, and this is what that brief campaign has proved them to be. I think it has also proved the Russians to be incredibly stupid, unless of course their stupidity was forced on them. I only hope the Israelis will be able to keep Sinai, Gaza, the whole of Jerusalem, and the West bank of the Jordan, for I have been there and know how painfully exposed and vulnerable they were. If the Arabs had won this little war they would have cut every Israeli throat. And now all this boo-hoo from the British

[13](1906–90), British Foreign Secretary.

[14]Francis Spellman (1889–1967), cardinal archbishop of New York, vicar to US Armed Forces, homosexual, defender of Joe McCarthy, advocate of US intervention in Vietnam.

[15]Israel had launched the Six-Day War on 5 June 1967; Israel Porush (1906–90) was chief minister of the Great Synagogue in Sydney.

press about Arab refugees. What about the Jewish refugees of the past. And the Palestinian refugees, all of whom could have been absorbed by the Arab countries if they hadn't wanted to keep them hanging around as a source of trouble.

Don't think I am anti-British. I feel I am more 'English', by my upbringing, the more collapsed, sleazy, swinging, and hepped-up England sounds . . .

The Tildesleys arrived back a few weeks ago, rejuvenated. We fetched them from the airport. I have never unloaded, and loaded, and unloaded so many bottles of liquor. They seem to have seen the two worst plays in London and are probably now proclaiming how superior the Sydney amateur theatre is.

See you in August, I hope. Love, Patrick.

20 Martin Road, 3.ix.67
TO PEGGY GARLAND

If Betty is as gloomy as you say, show her this letter and it will cheer her up to find I am as bad as she thought I was. But why does she have to go into the office after her retirement? Does she think she's indispensable? Hasn't she enough inner resources (I thought she specialised in these) to tide her over her remaining years? Blindness, of course, does reduce. I am sure I shall go blind too, but I like to think I shall be able to interest myself in my old age. Anyway, I am planning for it as my eyes grow worse and worse.

A couple of weeks ago we sold Dogwoods after trying for six years.

Hard to believe it has actually happened, or that it is no longer anything to do with us. It was bought by a speculator, so it is only a matter of time before everything but the ghosts will be bulldozed. The house itself was falling down anyway and I am relieved it didn't do so while still on our hands.[16] The new owner has taken over the tenant, who seems prepared to go on living in it and the jungle of garden.

Frances my youngest niece seems to have settled down in Australia. I think she is probably the best of the three. Dreary Gillian the eldest . . . went to Greece for the honeymoon, and I can't think of anything more incongruous. Alexandra the second one seems to have made a good marriage, though it's still early days. Her husband is recording manager for EMI.[17] Unfortunately she has just had a miscarriage in Rome where they went for him to make a recording of *Aïda*.[18] Much as I like Italy I shouldn't want things to go wrong for me there.

I hope we <u>shall</u> manage to get to England next year, for it seems a very long time since we were there.

Love,
Patrick.

20 MARTIN ROAD, 16.x.67
TO LUCIANA ARRIGHI[19]
Dear Luciana,
Thank you very much for several attractive cards over the months, perhaps even the years by now. As one grows older one seems to slow up, stand longer at the sink, know more people who have to be cooked for, one even sits longer at one's desk, though the act of writing becomes more than ever an act of oxywelding.

There was a journalist[20] running round this town trying to find out my silent number, and for once nobody gave it. However, he got my address and sent me a telegram in the middle of the night, a very startling

---

[16]PW got his price: $20,000; but not for another six years was the land chopped up into building blocks; the house was still standing in 1994.

[17]After Finishing school in Paris and a brief stint as a secretary, Alexandra Peck married Christopher Bishop, later managing director of the Philharmonia Orchestra. PW was to have rows with both her sisters but never with Alexandra, perhaps, she said, 'Because I was the one niece who never had to stay with him.' In 1987 she divorced and married an English company director, Guy Dawson.

[18]No, *Rigoletto*.

[19]Daughter of Eleanor, now embarked on her career as a designer in Europe.

[20]Sam White of Paris and the *Spectator*.

occurrence in Sydney. I didn't answer the telegram. I believe you sent the man originally. Please don't send me any more journalists, because whatever they try to tell always seems to turn out with the wrong complexion, and I particularly don't like the kind of international gilded gossip this particular one goes in for.

Last week we put the Nolans on a plane for South America. They had been here I don't know how long, perhaps a couple of months, but they gave an impression of permanence and it was very depressing to have them go after all. Of all the people I know I think Cynthia is the one who reacts to people and things most like I do. Sid has had wonderful triumphs right and left: a retrospective at the National Gallery, and smaller exhibitions at four other galleries.[21] It was staggering to see all the imaginative and painting genius that has poured out of one man. It has made the retrospectives of other Australian painters seem quite trivial and pathetic – and yet there are still people here who will not admit that he can paint. To me this has been the greatest event – not just in painting – in Australia in my lifetime. It has made up for a lot if not all my bitterness for having been dug out of this pit.

There has been a terrible opera season, to which I didn't go because I wasn't going to be blackmailed into subscribing for the whole season when you are lucky if there is one bearable production in the lot. Actually there is a good new young producer called Sharman but I suppose he will have to go away[22] . . .

The other night I had a nightmare in which we were in Rome, but did not know how to find Nellie Cox.[23] Then you appeared and were taking us to her, but I suddenly found I had lost you and Manoly in the streets. I went into a kind of trattoria, which also seemed to be a rendezvous for racing (push) cyclists. Everybody was very kind and said I could use the telephone, but this was high up on the wall, and I had to reach it by climbing on top of a substantial billiard table, then onto a collapsible card table. The card table almost always collapsed and hit me under the jaw, or if it didn't I would find on climbing to the top that I had left the piece of paper with the number somewhere down on the floor. This sort of thing went on till the end of the dream, or rather till I woke up, while the

---

[21]To mark Nolan's 50th birthday: a retrospective of 143 paintings, 1947–67, at the Art Gallery of NSW; drawings at the Hungry Horse; recent paintings at David Jones; 'Shakespearian Sonnets' at the Macquarie and theatre designs at Qantas House.

[22]Jim Sharman, (1945–) had directed *Don Giovanni* on a chess board; reviews were scathing; PW was intrigued.

[23]Nellie Cox=Eleanor Arrighi née Cox.

cyclists sat at other tables studying form in newspapers and not noticing a thing.[24]

I have been working all this year on a novel, which is very strange and unlike anything else I have written, and nobody is going to like it if it ever gets finished. However, what is there must be dredged up. At the same time I have been writing a novella when the novel becomes too depressing. The novella has almost reached its final version.

Desmond started something new for him in painting, then got into difficulties, and rushed back to the Trust, which I think is a great pity, but sticking pins into June Bronhill seems to have liberated him in some way.[25] If only he could get over his inhibitions he would be a very good painter. Sid Nolan walked up to one of the Digby paintings I have, and said it had the same quality as a Degas he has seen recently in New York.

I can't read your Paris address on one of the cards, so I shall send this to your mother to forward. I hope things do arrange themselves and that we shall see you in Europe next year.

Love –
Patrick.

20 MARTIN ROAD, 26.xi.67
TO MAIE CASEY

The end of *The Vivisector* is in sight. That is, I have come out of the jungle, but it doesn't mean there won't be a long and arduous march till one reaches the sea. At least one can see it, though I can no longer estimate how long the book may be. At least the first part must be condensed as I approached from the wrong angle, thinking I was going to project through the eyes of many people, whereas it all has to be conveyed through one man, though not told in the first person. It's an odd thing, but I can never do that. Immediately I become inhibited. So I could never think of writing an autobiography. I can't feel I should be the least bit interesting as the single identity I am supposed to be, only as the many characters of which I am composed. I expect that is why I became a novelist, and why I had difficulties at first in seeing things through the eyes of one man in *The Vivisector*, until I discovered ways of achieving the kind of fragmentation by which I convey reality.

I was about to send my new short piece 'Five-Twenty' to London

---

[24]A frequent detail of the dreams PW describes in his letters is the indifference of bystanders to his absurd behaviour.

[25]Digby was designing costumes for the Trust's *Don Pasquale* in which Bronhill (1928–) sang Norina.

when I was trapped the other night at dinner at the University. Professor Wilkes[26] who edits *Southerly*, a magazine one forgets exists, asked me to contribute something. I felt guilty, as *Southerly* has been very faithful over the years, so I am letting them have the story. If they like it – as I pointed out, it may have too much despair and too little grammar for the kids.[27]

The last few days at home and abroad have been so depressing they almost haven't been depressing – I mean, one almost couldn't believe they were happening. Manoly has now had letters from his American sister Anna, who went back to Greece for a couple of months to see the family. Apparently Athens is now run by police. They can bust in at any moment and search the house. One has to close all the windows and doors in order to talk, and if on any occasion more than four people are gathered together one has to inform the police. Anna had to report to them that she was going to a wedding to which she was invited. The telephones of the eldest sister and one of the aunts have been disconnected because of their political opinions, although they did at least restore the aunt's telephone as she is an old woman of over eighty. Anna went back to the States in a Greek ship, where there were even secret police planted amongst the emigrants. That voluntary loan, by the way, you may have read about it in the papers here, is far from a voluntary gesture on the part of patriotic Greeks. The police come to the house, and take it from you, giving you a suspicious piece of paper in return. And now the Turks![28]

I don't know how much backstairs Australian literary gossip you get, but there has been one recent event that has made me so disgusted I can no longer feel Australian. (In any case, my English upbringing makes me feel more and more English the lower England sinks.) I shall wait to hear some more, however, before I tell you about this disgusting piece of literary injustice.[29]

Looking forward to seeing you on the 10th, whatever human nature may be brewing on the side. –

Yrs

Patrick.

<hr />

[26]Gerry Wilkes (1927–   ), foundation professor of Australian Literature at Sydney University and editor of *Southerly* since 1963.

[27]Appeared *Southerly*, 28, 1, 1968, p.3.

[28]The Turks were poised to invade Cyprus, blaming communal violence there on the presence of Greek forces. In these matters PW always sided with the Greeks.

[29]Christina Stead, chosen by a panel of writers as winner of the $10,000 Britannica–Australia Award, was then disqualified for living too long outside Australia.

20 MARTIN ROAD, 13.xii.67
TO THE EDITOR
SYDNEY MORNING HERALD
Sir,
If the Higher Junta of Australian Intellect considers a novelist of genius like Christina Stead ineligible for its much-juggled American award, it helps explain to me why, for some time past, I have felt a foreigner in this pathetically chauvinistic parish.

And what about Sidney Nolan? Ineligible too, because he doesn't squat round the pump along with the other blokes?

Patrick White.

MARTIN ROAD, 16.xii.67
TO THE NOLANS
The mushroom cloud of Christmas is hanging over us more than ever this year, as I am at that stage in my First Version where everything outside it is exasperating. I might finish in three weeks, or it might be three months. The whole thing (two more versions) will probably take most of two more years. Then I should like you to read it to see how close or remote I am from the workings of a painter's mind. I should hate to find he is only a painter in a novel like most of the painters in fiction. I have also thought I'd like to dedicate the book to you, but you'd have to decide on reading it, as it will probably shock a lot of people, Australians in particular.

20 MARTIN ROAD, 29.i.68
TO PEGGY GARLAND
We had a very good week on Kangaroo Island – fishing, bathing, sleeping and reading. We hadn't been anywhere since Kangaroo Island two years before, so we were in need of it. Wonderful to read as much as one wants. I never get the chance, because I need all the time I can scrape together for writing. However, I was quite glad to get home and shut my own door after a week of extrovert living, with five children between eleven and four rushing in and out shouting and slamming, to say nothing of a fuel stove, oil lamps, and hot water from the kettle. The Duttons' vitality is unquenched at 45, while Manoly and I, at 55, creep rather sluggishly in and out of boats, nursing our incipient arthritis and too audible wheezes. (Manoly at least is free of the wheezes.)

20 MARTIN ROAD, 3.ii.68

TO THE DUTTONS

Dear Geoffrey and Nin,

We arrived back to find the house intact, the garden still alive, and none of the animals escaped from their prisons. Thank you for a memorable week. I found it difficult to get back to a normal diet after the fish. It is sad that it is almost impossible to buy a fish that is both interesting and fresh in Sydney. Somehow I must manage to get hold of some fresh whitebait, because the new deep-freeze machine is simply calling out for it . . .

Publishers are all courting madly:[30] I have received *Pasternak's Letters to his Georgian Friends* from Secker & Warburg, Ken Wilder has sent a book called *The Peregrine*[31] – 'I think this book will appeal to you for the outstanding quality of the writing', Desmond Briggs of Anthony Blond,[32] who is coming out for the Festival, is making advances in advance through David Moore, and Manoly and I have been invited by Harold Macmillan the week after next. However, I have switched the Macmillan invitation and he is coming here, because 4 o'clock tea amongst all that furniture at the Belvedere, in the middle of February, was too suffocating to face.[33]

We've hardly been out since we got home, except to what turned out to be an unexpected shivoo at Admiralty House. Not a bit what one expects of Maie, but the party was really for her friend the daughter of Otto Kahn, a distinguished and completely natural person whose name turned out to be Nin Ryan![34] Some of the guests curdled my blood: the Packers, for instance, the Helpmann, Cecil Beaton, now a strange blur indeed, Lord Maugham, who has a face like a wizened cow's twat,[35] Hannah Lloyd Jones spinning like a silly social top. On the other side of the fence,

[30]White's London agent Juliet O'Hea was spreading the news that he was unhappy with Eyre & Spottiswoode and would be seeking a new publisher once his novel was finished. Meeting his suitors was a principal reason for the next trip to Europe.

[31]Wilder (1927–) was head of Collins in Australia; *The Peregrine*, J. A. Baker's study of East Anglia, published by Collins, won the Duff Cooper Prize in 1968.

[32]Briggs (1931–), managing director of Blond, later the romantic novelist Rosamund Fitzroy.

[33]The Belvedere was an eccentric Sydney hotel with very good food but rooms crammed with furniture and bad paintings; here Sir Basil Hunter seduced Sister Manhood in *The Eye of the Storm*; when Macmillan came to Martin Road the three spent an hour or so talking about Mt Athos.

[34]Margaret Dorothy (Nin) Ryan (c.1900–), art collector, figure in international society, daughter of the New York financier (1867–1934).

[35]Robin Maugham, 2nd Viscount (1916–81), novelist and nephew of Somerset.

there were the Drysdales, rather jittery, Clem Semmler looking anxious, Hal Missingham also looking anxious,[36] the Coombs.[37]

That Helpmann is one of my least favourite human beings. He came up all sweetness and charm, and with equal sweetness and charm I congratulated him on his honours and 'achievements.' However, as soon as we got on to Honolulu, which needless to say is one of his spiritual homes, the electric light bulbs began to bulge and flash, and he almost did a panto ballet on the spot when I lumped it in with Florida. While you were on the Island you probably missed the Helpmann announcement that the Adelaide Festival has been too highbrow in the past, but that he will soon fix that.[38]

Another curious coincidence: the first letter I opened on arriving home was one from my agent to say the Czech radio wants to do 'Dead Roses' as a serial.

Got back to *The Vivisector*. Like everything always, it is coming good and bad. I think probably I am trying to say what can't be said, and in the circumstances all will depend on what I have been given to say. I wonder if everybody has such difficulty in forming an opinion of the work they are working on. The night before I got *The Vivisector* out of pawn, I started looking through The Binoculars and Helen Nell, and found it leaping at me, fresh and clear. So perhaps I may even go back to that later on, and finish off what seemed so desolatingly awful at the time.

20 MARTIN ROAD, 18.iii.68
TO JAMES STERN
Dear Jimmy,
I should have written sooner if I had realised you had sent the stories personally.[39] I received them some time ago, there was nothing to say they had come from you, and I took it that it was something Maurice Temple Smith had thought of doing. Your letter arrived the other day just as I was beginning the stories, and now I have finished them this evening, and can write more than thank you. What a remarkably modest person you are to

---

[36]Missingham (1906–94), painter, photographer, director of the Art Gallery of NSW.

[37]Nugget and Mary Alice (Lallie) Coombs.

[38]Robert Helpmann (1909–86), dancer, choreographer and actor, had been appointed artistic director of the 1970 Adelaide Festival. PW's letters contain many sallies at Helpmann. PW told Waters, 1.x.69: 'Dame Helpmann flies back and forth weighed down with medallions; has the CBE painted on the dressing room door, and is photographed making up for Coppelias with a towel round her tits.' But PW supplied Helpmann in 1973 with a synopsis for a ballet and something of PW's idea survived in Helpmann's *The Display*.

[39]*The Stories of James Stern*, 1968.

keep yourself so dark. Of course one knew you had written stories, but I didn't imagine they would be anything like these. Apart from the classic ones, so many short stories are so dead that one dreads having to read them. But I can think of no other writers in the Twentieth Century whose stories are so satisfying and at the same time so subtle as yours. Some of Pritchett's have made me enthusiastic, but I honestly can't think of any others in English, though no doubt there are some lurking around. In my teens I had a passion for Katherine Mansfield, but when I tried to re-read them a few years ago I found them too cold and chiselled, almost affected. The stories in your volume which give me most are 'The Man who was Loved', 'A Stranger among Miners', 'Under the Beech Tree', and 'Something Wrong'. Some of the English stories I find horrifying. I don't think anybody else has brought out that particular horror of English family life. I can re-experience the temperature of the bedrooms. Ugh! You made me cry three times – in 'The Man who was Loved', 'Next Door to Death', and 'Home' – whether that is a good thing or not, I don't know, but I like to think it is, and so I record it. If I didn't cry in 'A Stranger among Miners', perhaps it is because the people in it wouldn't have known how to cry. I think 'The Broken Leg' one of the most horrible things I have ever read. Broken legs apart, one has experienced the same nightmare and forgotten about it. Well, that is how I feel. It is a great relief to find that somebody one knows and likes is a master in his art. Now I am looking forward to lending the other copy, which I ordered as soon as I saw it mentioned in Secker's catalogue. There are quite a few who are worthy of you, but who haven't known about you because your remarkable modesty has prevented it.

Thank you for sending the pieces about Roy.[40] I do wish he could have hung on another year so that we could have seen him again. Always before we set out for Europe somebody we value dies, and we are left kicking ourselves for not getting there sooner. Roy played a great part in my life. He taught me to accept only the best, and I always feel it was he who taught me to write, although he himself found it the greatest effort to put pen to paper. I remember once in his studio a woman friend asked him to play a record of the Schumann piano concerto, which he did, and I went away seduced by the whole occasion. On another occasion when we were alone I asked him to play it again, and he turned on me and said: 'Nonsense! You must only listen to the greatest!' And I suppose ever since I have resented having to listen to the easily seductive. I fell hopelessly in love with Roy and spent a very unhappy few years. He himself was trying to recover from something unhappy, but said that, in any case, an intimate

[40]De Maistre had died on 1 March 1968 at the age of 73.

relationship of ours wouldn't have worked because he was twenty years older. It wouldn't have worked either. We were both too irritable and unyielding. Years afterwards it was a great satisfaction to me to find that Roy and Manoly liked and approved of each other. Roy is another who didn't blow his trumpet enough, but I think in time his best painting will be appreciated for what it is. After we were last in London, I was very touched by a letter in which he asked whether I would like him to leave me his house and his paintings. Although it was a tempting proposition I said I couldn't possibly keep up a house in London as well, nor could I house so many paintings . . .

Should like to write about *Larks and Heroes*, but I am prejudiced by all the publicity from this rather revolting little bog-Irish almost priest married to a renegade nun.[41] His book is powerful, but the scenes flicker on and off, and the novelette keeps on taking over, and I couldn't count the number of times somebody kicks somebody in the crutch – or spikes – and the girl even punches the hero in that place to show her affection. What Australia doesn't do to the Irish Catholics!

Love to you both –
Patrick.

20 MARTIN ROAD, 24.iii.68
TO MARY BENSON[42]
You mention Proust. If we were only living in the Nineteenth Century then there would be so much opportunity to cultivate sensibility and conduct a correspondence, but now I am always being dragged back to the routine of living, and it is a fight to keep enough time for work, let alone correspondence. However, I am now pausing between versions of the novel, answering letters, and trying to read a few of the books which have queued up.

I don't really know much about my own novels except the one I

[41]Thomas Keneally's (1935–) third novel, *Bring Larks and Heroes*, 1967 – deeply influenced by PW's writing – established Keneally's reputation in Australia. He had studied for the priesthood but was not ordained; his wife Judy was for seven years a Sister of Charity. PW was scathing about the critical enthusiasm for Keneally at this point; he told Dutton, 12.xi.67: 'I suspect a lot of this is because he is a decent little bloke who will appear at seminars, PEN functions, and gatherings of Australian writers, instead of a cold, peculiar monster who won't pander to them, and who tells them about their present-day brutalities. As that is what I feel I must continue doing, I suppose I shall continue sinking lower in their estimation.'
[42](1919–), writer born in South Africa, living in exile in London from 1966.

happen to be struggling with. I grow farther and farther away from those I have finished. It is as though they were put into me, and I brought them out, but apart from that there isn't much connexion. For that reason, I find it difficult to write about myself and work as so many writers seem to get satisfaction from doing. In any case I am not of great interest as a person; I like to think my books are better than I . . .

At one time I was attached to a SAAF squadron on the Sudanese-Eritrean frontier. Then we were posted to the Delta and finally the Western Desert, where I was reclaimed by the RAF. The South African pilots were dashing, innocent young men, even less sophisticated than the Australians of their kind. I felt they liked me, and I was grateful for it, in the way one values acceptance by those with whom one really has nothing in common. They got shot down one after the other, and it was all very depressing in the end. (One of them was a le Mesurier, whose name I used for a vastly different character in Voss. The South African was, I believe, the son of a bishop, very steady and dependable; he shouldn't have been shot down.)

In a way you are lucky to belong to South Africa, awful though it has become, because any South African who is worth anything is going through the fire, and out of that something valuable will be compounded.

Here we haven't yet got any real problems, though they're just round the corner. We are a smug, piddling country, blowing our own trumpet for all we are worth, while our achievements are few and mostly material. I stay here only because Australia is my blood, but at heart I realise after a long time I am Anglo-European.

Haven't yet read the book you sent, but I shall.[43]

Yours sincerely

Patrick White.

20 MARTIN ROAD, 7.iv.68

TO MARSHALL BEST

We start for Greece on May 1st. Until then I shall be warding it off with both hands, but I am always all right once the upheaval has taken place. What makes it all the more unpleasant this time is that my novel has boiled up very fiercely. I finished the First Version, and to my surprise, after all the agonies, it has roughly what I wanted to convey, only I still have a hell of a lot of writing and ordering to do. I have started on the Second Version, and the chaotic opening, which had been worrying me, is now coming good. But I can see a couple of years' work ahead. It is

[43]Her history of the African National Congress, South Africa: The Struggle for a Birthright, 1966.

long – don't blench – it is roughly 224,000. However, remember that the only one of my books the American Public (as opposed to Initiates) has really liked – *The Tree of Man* – they liked, I am sure, because of its length – about 206,000. (They also liked it, wrongly, because they thought it was a Frontier Novel, and they will like *The Vivisector* wrongly because they will think it Sex Life of Famous Painter.)

ATHENS, 3.v.68
CARD TO THE MOORES
Thank you again for bringing us to the airport. We got here safely after 24 hrs but it is such an unnatural way to travel. I have felt awful ever since. The steam-heat of Singapore, Kuala Lumpur, and Calcutta was unbearable. I expect my chest will dry out in Athens, but it will take several days. Great changes here. This time we look at the Acropolis from our roof through the bars of TV aerials, and on the other side Lycabettos has almost disappeared behind a rising building. Manoly's family are well, but the anonymous Athenians look grim and embittered. They have also become very rude but melt on seeing an Australian passport.
    P.

THE LIFE SEEMED TO have gone out of Greece. White and Lascaris settled into their old routine, making expeditions and returning to Athens to recuperate from the fevers and food poisoning that always afflicted them on their journeys. They saw the rock monasteries of Metéora, revisited the mountains around Métsovo and crossed to Corfu. After another break in Athens they set out for the islands of Skopelos, Skiros, and Skiathos.

ATHENS, 18.vi.68
TO MAIE CASEY
Dear Maie,
Thank you very much for your letter and the drawing which we found on arriving back from some island-hopping. I feel the drawing is rather too flattering, too young, the nose too fine – I have a lumpy potato of a nose. The eyes come out too dark. Funnily enough I find the eyes and nose together remind me of Manoly's! But of course it is impossible to judge a likeness of oneself. As a drawing I like it.

I arrived back from the Sporades with quite a high temperature, and have just spent a couple of days in bed. I think our normal life must be over-hygienic, so that when we come to a country like Greece we are easy victims to germs. It always happens, to both of us.

Skiros was by far the best of the three islands, and will remain one of my favourites. It is more primitive than many because of bad communications. Hardly any roads, so one has to get about on foot or by mule. The weather is also more variable. The first two days we had wind and rain and I thought I disliked the place, then it began to emerge. It is in any case rather a shy island. The village, like a wasp's nest of white cells clinging to a steep rock, was once a fortress. Some very interesting interiors, with inherited copper vessels, and old plates and pots made on the island. The present-day ceramics are pathetic by comparison, nothing more than souvenirs.

What we enjoyed most were some walks we did through cultivated fields in the evening – very peaceful and rural, with peasants walking their cows, ewes, and goats home to the milking. Lots of snakes about; we saw several dried skins, and on one occasion killed a live snake ourselves at a spring. For the first time I saw chick-peas growing, very graceful and feathery little plants. Now I want to see lentils.

We took one walk into the mountains to a church of Agios Demitrios. The approach was most varied, first through a narrow valley full of planes, oaks, walnuts, figs, and occasional plum trees. Then the valley widened out the sides covered with pines and chunks of marble.

We were walking along a dry riverbed through a forest of pink oleanders. On the way we passed one fascinating farm cultivated by a very old man and woman. The land was terraced above a running stream, and irrigated by water brought from higher up by stone conduits. On the terraces, beautifully kept olive, fig, and apple trees trained like lombardy poplars, aubergines, maize, tomatoes, everything one could want. On one side of the whitewashed house somebody had carved a Cycladic figure. In the evening as we came back the old man was feeding some of those real hens one sees in Greece, and the old woman milking her goats. It was one of those places in which I feel I want to sit down and never get up again.

We had several talks with an old man called Manoly Virgiliou who took parties of Australian and New Zealand soldiers from Skiros to Smyrna during the War. A very long way in a small caïque. They used to go by way of Psarra, the island off the northern tip of Chios.

Skopelos and Skiathos were banal after Skiros, except that in Skiathos we saw the house of Papadiamantis, who is about the best 19th century Greek novelist. He was born and died in this small house, which has something very monastic about it; it made me feel ashamed of my own. He was pretty austere in most of his attitudes, remained unmarried, and considered it sinful to be photographed (that, I think, will be my excuse in future when the wretched press and telly are a nuisance!) However, he wasn't all austerity, because the custodian, who insisted on telling us everything in almost unintelligible English, explained that he was 'a friend to the bottle.' Some day I must use that as a title.

Skiathos, I am afraid, is being over-run by what looks like ex-Army and Navy officers (English) with wives to match. Without knowing what they are up against, they have built villas in a kind of garden suburb, and are now desperately trying, without any Greek, to persuade somebody to repair their plumbing. A South African widow has been far more practical. She has taken an ex-Evzone[44] as lover, and also makes him work very hard about the place.

Poor Manoly is in the throes of family farewells. His aunt has a list of brides from which she wants him to choose. The old father had a mild coronary while we were away, and has now started a fresh phase. As he is stone deaf, no longer able to read, half senile, and pretty helpless, it's a pity the attack wasn't strong enough to carry him off.

I wonder whether we shall get to France. We don't plan to leave Italy till July 16th, so perhaps things will be more normal by then[45] . . .

Read about the composition of the Arts Council. As usual the emphasis seems to be on education![46] Apart from Geoffrey I shouldn't think any of them has any taste, or conception of creative imagination in the arts.

Yrs
P.

THEY LEFT ATHENS AT the end of June to spend a happy fortnight in Rome exploring churches and gossiping on Eleanor Arrighi's terrace in the ghetto. Then the two men set off to eat their way to Paris via Bologna, Parma, Lyons and Rouen. They reached London in early August.

PARIS, 1.viii.68
CARD TO THE MOORES
Paris has been an orgy of paintings and food – the latter at great expense. Everything is expensive, but particularly the food. A marvellous exhibition of Vuillard, also a Dubuffet. I'd like to have one or two Dubuffets to scare the Sydney squares with. We spent one day at Rouen, rather a depressing

---

[44]Former Royal Guard and, in this case, considerable beauty.
[45]PW was pleased by riots that spring in Paris. He wrote, 'My God, how glad I am that old monster de Gaulle has a mess of his own to cope with.' To Margery Williams, 26.v.68.
[46]But the founding purpose *was* educational – to take the arts to the people and the bush through tours, exhibitions and festivals – and most of the money came from State departments of education.

town, and the Flaubert museum was closed. Very good sole normande, however, and stuffed sheep's foot. Another day at Malmaison, my favourite palace.[47] Have had a couple of meetings with French friends, all very amiable and hospitable. London to-morrow.

    P.

LONDON, 8.viii.68
TO THE MOORES
Dear Gwen and David,
Thanks for the long letters. It seems ages since I could bring myself to sit down and write anything but a post-card. It isn't easy even now, as I keep remembering somebody else we have to see while we are in England, and so many people are offended if they think you have left them till the end . . .

    I think one would have to be young and untravelled to enjoy London as it has become: filth almost to equal that of Istanbul, most of the older affluent people looking down at heel and desperate, most of the young dressed to take part in some shoddy and unattractive carnival. Certainly it has rained almost since we arrived, and one gets terribly depressed waking up and looking out on yet another black morning. But at least the whole thing has made me feel I shan't complain anymore about living in Australia! (Manoly says: for another six months.)

    We have been to some always interesting, not always acceptable, theatre. Got into the last performance of Seneca's *Oedipus* through Irene Worth.[48] One wondered how much was Seneca, how much Ted Hughes[49] who adapted it, often in wonderful language, and how much Peter Brook.[50] The general effect was of souped-up *grand guignol* without the actual blood and raw liver. A number of very vital young actors, however, delivering the lines. John Gielgud rather out of his element in anything so stark. Irene Worth had some superb moments, although the producer seemed to have set out to degrade her by making her do some incredible things. At the end when the characters wheel on a giant phallus covered in gold kid, and a band plays 'Yes We Have No Bananas', the whole thing becomes a kind of stupid students' rag. In spite of his brilliance I now have great

---

[47]On the outskirts of Paris, residence of Napoleon and Josephine with opulent apartments in the Empire style.
[48](1916–91), American brought to London by Tyrone Guthrie; here she played Jocasta.
[49](1930–), poet, who adapted this version of *Oedipus*.
[50](1925–), director.

reservations about Peter Brook – also about Jim Sharman, who seems to have got everything from Brook.

The night after *Golden Cock* we went to *Golden Boy*,[51] the only bearable musical since *Oklahoma*. I thought I shouldn't be able to stand Sammy Davis, but he is terrific; I am now a fast fan. The whole production was exciting, particularly on the visual side . . .

Began this several days ago. Since then rain, rain, fur growing in one's bronchial tubes, until to-day, when the sun has actually come out and the pavements are dry. A very dull performance of *The Tempest*[52] wasn't worth the journey to Chichester. The production very fashionable on the surface: instead of a golden cock we got silver balls this time, one of which opened up in the end, like a kind of twee cocktail cabinet, disclosing Ferdinand and Miranda, rather cramped, playing chess with rock crystals. John Clements looked good as Prospero, but he's a stodgy actor with a monotonous voice. Ariel wore silver combinations and was made to behave like an imbecile. All that seems left of the English theatre is the tradition of diction and technical faultlessness.

Sid Nolan took us to the exhibitions of Matisse and Henry Moore.[53] The Moore is great, but I was disappointed in Matisse. Perhaps he is still too 'modern' for one to form a true opinion. Paintings one thought rich and seductive in the past have gone flat, and the later ones are too close to contemporary imitators. At the moment I should say he comes miles behind Picasso, and Braque, though attempting less, is a better painter.

Unfortunately the Nolans have had to go to Australia for a number of reasons just when we are here. However, we saw them almost every day in our first week, and put them on the plane yesterday in a heavy downpour. I think we may coincide again in San Francisco on our way back.

This is a comfortable place to stay[54] and said to be inexpensive. We have a bed-sitting-room, with cupboard-kitchen and bathroom, and plenty of wardrobe space. Its great advantage is that it is within walking distance of so many places. One needn't worry when the trains and buses give out, or depend on blackmailing taxi-drivers in the middle of the night. There is a leafy square in which a black pug takes his exercise in the middle of the day, and a view in which Westminster and Saint Paul's still hold their own amongst the skyscrapers. Eccleston Street looks cold and foreign now

[51]Charles Strouse (music) and Lee Adams (lyrics) based on the Clifford Odets play, designed by Tony Walton, at the Palladium.
[52]Directed by David Jones and designed by Ralph Koltai.
[53]Retrospectives: Matisse at the Hayward and Moore at the Tate.
[54]A serviced apartment at 20 Chesham Place, SW1.

that Roy is no longer there. Next week I have to meet his cousin Celia Broadbent at the studio in connexion with some things he has left me, one of them a painting. (Sid has also given us a painting.)

Well, in eleven weeks we shall be seeing you, and I shan't mind how quickly the time passes. I only want to get back into my own house and start work again. I have had enough of idleness.

Yrs
Patrick.

LONDON, 21.viii.68
TO GEOFFREY DUTTON

To-day we heard about the invasion of Czecho-Slovakia and have been plunged in gloom. Everything seems to be happening all over again. Surely there is nobody ridiculous enough still to think human beings can make any progress, though certainly at the moment the human beings pulling us back are Russians. At the same time I am approaching the end of Henri Troyat's *Tolstoy* in which the whole Tolstoy family is rampaging around Yasnaya Polyana like crazed animals. If exceptional Russians could behave so irrationally one can't expect much of lesser ones. Although I still admire Tolstoy as a writer, this book has torn to shreds the respect I had for him as a man.

We went the other day to lunch with the Daws in their new house, which has great possibilities when they get beyond the camping stage, though I suspect they may be the type who choose to camp indefinitely. Anyway, the rooms are large and pleasing, and there is also, less pleasing, a small wet London garden. I thought both the parents looked very thin and washed out, perhaps as a result of the move and the new baby, as well as the cheerless English-summer day. (How silly of them to huddle here, even though 'aesthetic standards are higher' – make his own in Adelaide!) William is already a large, jolly, interested child. The Jewish has come out in him much more than in Sam, who is an altogether different strain. They showed me a couple of paintings by the latter which are already better than much of what one sees in the galleries – if a doting father hasn't given them a dab here and there.

Went to my cousin's at Eynsham outside Oxford last Sunday. We also had to visit the parents of our next door neighbour's English gardener. He had told us his mother and father looked after a 'showplace' at a village called Eustone, but we weren't prepared for the palace we found. Do you know anything about Ditchley Hall? I have found out since that it is considered Gibbs' masterpiece. As it happened Duncan Burden's parents were away, and I found myself for some time all alone with this deserted magnificence, wandering through formal gardens with borders of clipped yew, and staring guiltily through the windows at rococo treasures. I was almost tempted to go right up and stick my nose on the panes, but thought I might find somebody doing the same on the other side. Croquet hoops on a mown lawn did suggest some kind of life. Finally I dug up somebody who sounded like an off-duty butler, and who told me the people I wanted had gone to Basingstoke.

Another thrilling occasion was an evening we spent at the Dickens House. One of my fans and his wife who keep the place clean gave us a meal there. The house is full of interesting objects and prints. I still haven't got it all in focus.

Hope Manning Clark gets the prize – for what it's worth.[55] I find in the Tolstoy book I'm now reading that the committee for the Nobel Prize overlooked Tolstoy for Sully Prudhomme when making their first award. That, surely, is the last word on all such awards.

I don't think I mentioned I have had a letter from a woman at a Canadian university who wants to write my biography, and proposes to come to Australia to get the facts! I told her my life has been a very uninteresting one, and even if I should be more interesting than my life, she will have to wait till I'm dead to put in the juicy bits. Hope that disposes of her.

Horrified the other day on meeting Roy de Maistre's cousin at his old studio to be given a MS. of an unpublished novel I wrote after *Happy Valley*.[56] I thought I'd destroyed the remaining copies before we left Castle Hill. Now I wonder what else may be lying around waiting for the wrong hands.

LONDON, 16.ix.68
TO JAMES STERN
We went to Edna's Place on Saturday,[57] and found about twenty people sitting down to dinner. Most of the ladies were in fancy dress, and several were lady-novelists-successful-with-films e.g. Penelope Pumpkin-Eater,[58]

[55]The 1968 Britannica–Australia Award for literature; Dutton was one of the judges; Clark didn't win.
[56]No copy of Nightside has since come to light. The novel was set mainly in the late 1930s in France where a dancer – Lil in Australia, Lys in Paris – is murdered by a German psychopath. Betty Withycombe read the MS. and remembers it as 'a horrid book, nasty'. She persuaded PW not to submit it to a publisher.
[57]Edna O'Brien.
[58]Penelope Mortimer: *The Pumpkin Eater* was filmed in 1964 by Jack Clayton with a script by Harold Pinter.

Nell Poor-Cow[59] and of course Edna Love-Object herself.[60] At dinner I was between Penelope and a wilting, youngish Jew called Francis Wyndham, a grandson of Ada Leverson.[61] Lashings of Irish Whisky, with the result that the conversation is a little vague by now. We only seem to meet Edna in a mob of people, so I have never been able to find out what she is like, how much is innocence, and how much calculation. The other night, in black velvet from the thirties and a pair of silver shoes, she had rather the manner of a kindly landlady. We have asked her to lunch alone before we go, to see whether we can solve the riddle.

LONDON, 21.ix.68
TO NINETTE DUTTON
Dear Nin,

It was nice to get your letter. I had been on the point of writing, but was held up debating whether to send the reviews of Andy[62] in the Observer and Sunday Times. I decided against in the end, because no doubt they will be sent from those less personal sources the press-cutting agency and publishers. Yes, I was badly disappointed in the book, but Geoffrey may be right in saying I missed the point because I didn't read all of it. One day I must try again in greater calm. But I do maintain that if there are to be revelations at the end the novelist must somehow convey a few hints of this in the beginning, through the general tone, not necessarily by clunking clues. And that was something I didn't get in Andy.

I can't remember my actual words to Geoffrey, but it was something like 'the book must have been written by some philistine buried deep in you.' I don't know why that should have hurt him. In myself there are many worse characters buried not so deep and always waiting to take over.[63] No doubt sooner or later one of them will escape my control, with disastrous results. I hope G.'s 'second novel' which you mention in your letter will turn out better than Andy, but I still feel that factual works will remain

---

[59]Nell Dunn: Poor Cow was filmed in 1967 by Ken Loach who also wrote the script with Dunn.

[60]On reading The Love Object PW remarked to Stern, 27.viii.68: 'One wonders where she can go from there in the race towards complete abandon. She can certainly write, but what will the boys at school say to her boys?'

[61]Wyndham (1924–), journalist, writer of short stories (unpublished at this time), editor of the correspondence of Jean Rhys, grandson of the novelist, wit and supporter of Wilde.

[62]Geoffrey Dutton's second novel, set in the RAAF.

[63]He admitted suspicion to Dutton, 12.viii.68, that 'some Elinor Glyn deep in myself may some day dash off a novelette to shatter the world'.

those in which he shines. I am always coming across people who speak in praise of *The Hero as Murderer*.

We are coming to the end of our stay here in a welter of eating and drinking: very livery work ... Also spent a couple of days with Steven Runciman[64] in the haunted tower in which he now lives, in Dumfriesshire. Somebody else was actually haunted while we were there, but ghosts never appear to me, receptive though I am.

HOLIDAYING ON THE ISLE of Pines in 1967, the promoter Harry Miller read *Voss* and determined to make the film. Miller was a salesman of genius – he began life selling nylon socks and lingerie in little wool towns in New Zealand – and made his name in Australia producing the musicals *Hair*, *Jesus Christ Superstar* and later *The Rocky Horror Show*. He had never made a film but now he struck a deal with Patrick White that locked the two men in an uneasy commercial embrace for the next ten years. One of the great themes of White's life was his loathing of 'the publicity machine' yet here he was embarking on the *Voss* project with a maestro of PR. As White's hopes faded over the years he raged wildly against Miller. He was on edge from the start.

LONDON, 26.ix.68
TO GEOFFREY DUTTON
My agent and Harry Miller's solicitor have now agreed on the wording for the contract to the filming of *Voss*. Whether we shall ever agree on a director is a different matter. They want me to produce a list, so I have named four. Probably Miller will think I am mad, as all my directors are so far from the kind of 'action man' they will want to turn *Voss* into a boys' adventure story. Actually Bruce Beresford has suggested a director, superficially startling and impossible, but who will be I think the perfect solution if we can get him.[65] This is my great obsession at the moment.

The other night we took the Daws and the Temple Smiths to dinner. They don't live far from one another and I think they may get together profitably later on. But I wasn't altogether happy about this occasion. Lawrence is always inclined to start waffling away with the cloudiest meta-physical ideas which he wants to relate to painting, writing, and to creativity in general, and this has the effect of making one reduce the creative act to a much lower level than I normally should to one of scrubbing floors, shitting,

---

[64]Historian (1903–   ), authority on Byzantine history and civilisation, hence of the rise and fall of the Lascaris princes of Nicea.
[65]Satyajit Ray (1921–92), 'To film the novel, not the exploration epic the script turned out to be.'

and vomiting. Even if this is a slight exaggeration, I still think creativity is 90% awful drudgery. I do think also that these metaphysical preoccupations have mucked up L.'s paintings. Any I have seen in recent years have been big half-empty canvases, sometimes coated with a milky film. I told him he ought to go back to Australia. He says he does regularly and spent a whole year there a few years ago. I felt like saying that the last of his paintings which showed any vitality and colour were those painted after that year in Australia but I managed, rightly or wrongly, to hold my tongue. But both the Daws are now strangely cloudy and I should say physically anaemic. At least their faces took on a little colour after the meal the other night. Or perhaps they were blushing for my triviality.

Have been to see the all-male *As You Like It* expecting something very fashionable and gimmicky. But it is one of the most satisfying and sincere productions of Shakespeare I have ever seen. And quite a dream to look at, using only the minimum of scenery and props.[66]

These last days in London are going to be hell. I can't sleep for making mental lists of all the things that have to be done. Have just had another letter from the agent to say Miller wants a list of six directors. How can one trot out six possible directors for what will be a very difficult film to make? I suppose they think they will sign up some unsuitable mediocrity I stick on the end of the list in desperation.

LONDON, 27.ix.68
TO JAMES STERN
Cecil Beaton's photographs make me look like a stuffed sea-lion. Perhaps that is how I look! I did not see Cecil when I went to look at the results. There are three which I quite like. But the secretary said: 'How Funny! I thought these would appeal to you,' and she brought forward two of the most sea-lionish. So that must be definitely how I look.

THEY SPENT OCTOBER IN the United States. Again White was trying to sell his plays to Broadway producers and again he met no success. But a hectic fortnight in New York was stimulating: 'I need no sleep and feel so well there,' he told Juliet O'Hea.[67] The two men then set out for Tennessee and Florida. After a round of Lascaris family reunions and another round of farewells, White and Lascaris flew to San Francisco to meet the Nolans. Only scraps of correspondence survive from these weeks in America.

[66]Directed by Clifford Williams, designed by Ralph Koltai with Ronald Pickup as Rosalind, Anthony Hopkins as Audrey and Derek Jacobi as Touchstone.
[67]29.x.68.

NEW YORK, 10.x.68

TO CHARLES OSBORNE

Hair is to me the greatest amateurish bore. The good bits would have squeezed into ½-an-hour. Last week-end my publisher drove us through Vermont and New Hampshire – wonderful autumn forests – also went to Tanglewood, Emily Dickinson's house at Amherst, and into MacDowell Writers' Colony (Ugh!) Zoe is the same as ever and we are relieved to find we like her husband[68] very much. Large, and impressive Dubuffet expo at Museum of Mod Art.

    P.

FORT LAUDERDALE, 21.x.68

CARD TO JOHN CUSHMAN

We had a peaceful interlude in Tennessee, with a drive to the Great Smoky Mts. (here in technicolour). And now fetid Florida. I haven't heard such fascist talk since Germany before the War. It feels as though Wallace is practically home.[69]

    P.W.

SAN FRANCISCO, 31.x.68

CARD TO RONALD WATERS

We leave to-night for Home. Have enjoyed S.F. The Nolans arrived from Sydney just as we got here from Miami. We have been mucking around together v. pleasantly. Wonderful drive to Lake Tahoe on the Nevada border. In spite of the hippies this city is about 30 years behind Sydney even ... Forget if I told you our house was burgled and now we are wondering what is happening to our dogs in the bushfires. Can't wait to get back.

    P.

20 MARTIN ROAD, 24.xi.68

TO ELEANOR ARRIGHI

Dear Eleanor,

Thank you for your letter which got here just after we did. Since then I have had one from Niké in which she says you have been down with the Mao flu. It seems to be all through the Northern Hemisphere, particularly New York, so I am glad we got out in time. My seeping bronchial tubes

---

[68]The Broadway producer Robert Whitehead (1916–).
[69]No. Nixon won in a landslide.

would have made a wonderful breeding ground for anything the Maoist thing might start . . .

We arrived home on the date planned, almost to the minute. The house had been left very clean and orderly. A few casualties in the garden, which we expected as nobody ever becomes enslaved to any garden but their own. Unfortunately there had been a burglary about three weeks before we got back. Four of our icons were stolen, also the record-player, and all Jenny Trew's[70] jewellery. They were obviously specialising in jewellery and money, because all the drawers had been pulled out, pockets turned inside out in suits hanging in the cupboards, and the paintings left hanging crooked after a search for wall-safes. I suppose it could have been worse; one hears of thieves turning up with removal vans and taking the lot. But now one will always feel it may happen again . . .

I got back my MS and read through it in the first week. Fortunately it is more or less what I intended, and now I am busy writing the second version. Work stretches ahead of me literally for years, because I find the book is about 246,000 words. The difficult part is to remember the thing as a whole when one gets one's nose down on the details.

This is Sunday, and my day for writing letters and paying bills, so must now get on with some of the others.

Love
Patrick.

20 MARTIN ROAD, 5.i.69
TO GEOFFREY DUTTON
Dear Geoffrey,
Your newsful letter arrived. I was afraid pigs might give a lot of trouble.[71] When we were at Castle Hill people used to rush into keeping pigs, but they usually started backing out mysteriously after a little. They seem to be prone to some alarming diseases, but I didn't know about the temperamental difficulties.

I shall be interested to read *Tamara* and can only say I am hoping I shall like it as much as I disliked *Andy*.[72]

---

[70]Nanny and general factotum to the Dutton children; she had minded Martin Road.
[71]Dutton had bought the rump of Anlaby from the other family shareholders and begun intensive pig breeding to try to make the place pay. He told me: 'Craziest thing I ever did.'
[72]Not really. *Tamara*, Dutton's third novel, was set in Russia. When the time came PW told its author, 6.xi.69, there was much he enjoyed, 'But I wasn't happy about the protagonists all the way: they seemed to me to come out of what the lending libraries used to call Light Romance. This was a pity, because they came good later on, and were real and moving. Still, I'd have been much better pleased if you'd written this as a travel book.'

I agree that one explorer is enough or it may be that one adventure into 19th Century Australia is enough. That is what I felt when I was halfway through that novel I began on Mrs Fraser: hardly exploration; I think it was the sheer weight of all the adversities people had to cope with in Australia in those days. Still, I sometimes take out the MS. of *A Fringe of Leaves* and look at it. It still attracts me, and I may come back to her one day when she has recovered from the mauling she got from various vulgar little careerists when I was foolish enough to suggest the theme might be one for an opera.

In spite of the festivities I've been working a lot lately. In fact New Year's Eve was the only day I wasn't able to put in some time at my desk, and I'm approaching the halfway mark of the second version. Fortunately it interests me more and more: I am finding all sorts of things I didn't realise were there, which link up along the way, and I must have put down unconsciously. I expect a lot of people will be furious and disgusted, but it has to come out the way it is coming. I feel more and more that creative activity in the arts is very closely connected with sexual activity, and that an awful lot of the insights I have had have come from that source. It isn't necessary to 'sleep around' but to investigate the variety of regularity.

On New Year's Eve about twenty-four people turned up, and as far as I can tell it was a success, though I was a zombie after two days' cooking. I wish I had lived in the days of slaves when I could have clapped my hands and invited 224 guests and seen what was going on.

This seems to have been a Christmas of separating husbands and wives. Our friend Penny Lane-Brown[73] has separated from her husband (I am godfather to their second child), and Ros Humphries has separated from Barry ... The little Humphries girls look two absolute Renoirs, and Emily Lane-Brown is also something of a Renoir. So Renoir is in in 1969 as fathers move out ...

Hope you have a good summer on the Island. I'd wish I was there too, if we hadn't got back so recently, and I didn't have this book on my mind.

Love to all –

Patrick.

P.S. Pushkin – more about next time – I think he is the most wonderful writer I have been left to discover in my old age.

---

[73]Later Penny Coleing.

20 MARTIN ROAD, 2.ii.69

TO GEOFFREY DUTTON

Harry Miller came up with option money the day after I told you he hadn't! After that he came here to lunch, and we had an amiable meeting; in fact, my agent's Aust. rep. Peter Grose said it was the first time he had seen H.M. behave naturally. So there! I'm always hearing about people I frighten the shit out of.

Now the big impasse in developing *Voss* as a film is the clause which gives me a veto on the director. However, I would never sell the rights if I didn't have that. Now, according to Harry, Universal Pictures are prepared to invest millions of dollars, and send a scriptwriter ('a very gentle young man') all the way to Australia to do re-search and consult my every wish, provided I give up that veto on the director. So we are stuck. Universal won't give a clue to the kind of director they would choose, except Harry M. said vaguely: 'Zinnemann[74] and Tony Richardson[75] were mentioned.' Zinnemann presumably because he directed a successful period film in *A Man for all Seasons*. I don't know if you got on to the crap Tony Richardson was talking while out here about 'extrovert Australia' and Ned Kelly as the 'symbol of opposition to materialism.' So you could imagine with either of those! When I brought up Ray*, Harry said: 'He hasn't even a track record! He makes art films! Aren't you interested in money?' So I had to say – yes, to give away, but that I have enough to be happy on, and all I am really interested in is art. Still, I like Harry Miller, and I think we shall get on together in spite of this.

Can't start another page. Let us know about meeting at the airport on the 17th.

Love to all,

P.

* I believe Ray is now making a film from Narayan's *The Guide* in Hollywood, and I'm v. anxious to see what happens. If it succeeds, they'll all be licking his ass.[76]

FASHIONABLY SLIM FOR THE first time in her life, Suzanne Peck had flown to London before Christmas to see her first grandchildren. With her on the journey was her daughter Frances. They plunged into a damp London

---

[74]Fred (1907–); he had directed *The Sundowners* in Australia in 1959 with Robert Mitchum, Deborah Kerr, etc.
[75](1928–91), his *Ned Kelly* with Mick Jagger as the popular crook had not yet been released.
[76]Puzzling: Ted Danielewski directed a joint US-India production in 1964 with a screenplay by Pearl S. Buck. If there were plans for a remake by Ray, nothing came of them.

winter and Suzanne was immediately ill with asthma. She appeared to recover, but late on 2 February White's niece Alexandra rang from London to say Suzanne was dead. White's grief came mixed with anger – he raged about her Sydney doctor – and fear that he might die at any time from such an attack. Suzanne was only 53. Particularly on White's mind was the future of his niece Frances and he did what he could to save her from the fate he had endured forty years before.

20 MARTIN ROAD, 16.ii.69
TO ALEXANDRA BISHOP
Dear Alexandra,
I was very pleased to get your letter explaining some more of the situation . . .

I hope it will be a long time before Frances goes to boarding school. My four years at boarding school in England were such hell, I shouldn't wish it for any child I know, though the schools may be less like prisons nowadays. The only thing I can say in favour of them is that, when anything particularly awful was happening during the War, like the Blitz in London, or when one was being shot up or bombed in the Western Desert, or escaping into Tobruk in the dark, I used to tell myself: at least none of this is quite so bad as the years at Cheltenham, because the enemy is only trying to destroy one's body, not the part that matters.

A gloomy letter, but one has to consider all these things!
Love to everybody. Shall write to Frances soon.
Patrick.

20 MARTIN ROAD, 23.ii.69
TO PEGGY GARLAND
Dear Peggy,
Thank you for your letter about Suzanne. I had misgivings when she went to London in the middle of winter, something I would never do, and she too was a chronic asthmatic; but she wanted to see her two grandchildren, both born recently. I tried to make her go to see the authority on asthma at Hammersmith, but I don't think she had been when she died. She went into hospital soon after arriving in those December fogs, and was bad enough to be given oxygen. She recovered, and was discharged, but was down to 6 st. in weight. Then, a couple of weeks before they were to come back, she caught 'flu, and died of complications from that. The charm doctor she went to here kept her on too big a dose of prednisone, and that was half the trouble, I feel. I have been on the same drug on and off for years, and know how tricky it can be. The reducing process is most

intricate, but fortunately I am in the hands of some very dedicated and brilliant doctors; I could never persuade her to see them.

I shall miss her very much. I never brought you together as you wouldn't have had anything in common, as I hadn't, beyond blood and a childhood; but she was the only close relation I have ever cared about. We never quarrelled after we grew up. She was very good humoured, and altogether without vice. I have been impressed by the number of people who have written saying she was the friend who mattered most, and in each case I felt they were being sincere.

Now Frances, the youngest child, who is only twelve, will have to stay with Alexandra the middle one. I like them both, and they will give her a good home, but I don't like to think of her growing up in London as it is now. However, there is nothing much I can do about it, beyond offering to bring her out here in two or three years time for the long holidays, and let her see what she thinks of it. Obviously it's better for her to be with her sisters for the time being, as they will be difficult years. Also, I don't want to be accused of meddling.

I envy you going to Spain, though only in a way. There must be so much to see, one might get swallowed up by it; one should have started earlier in life.

I am about three-quarters of the way through a second version of my book. Now that I've had this warning I feel I must press on as fast as possible, but it's very long, and I don't expect I shall finish before mid-1970.

Glad David has that job;[77] he is the one I felt had the greatest possibilities.

Love,
Patrick.

MARTIN ROAD, 30.iii.69
TO CYNTHIA NOLAN
Before it happened I shouldn't have thought Suzanne's death would be such a blow: we had no friends or interests in common, and yet our relationship was a very good and satisfying one. She had no vice in her; and she is almost the only person I never offended.

Since this warning I have been working as hard as possible, to finish at least the second version of *The Vivisector* in case I pop off too. Someone else could edit the Second Version if necessary; whereas my first versions are always so chaotic, only I could pull them into shape. Anyway, I am a

[77]Her son, teaching at the Bath Academy of Art at Corsham Court.

few sheets off the end of the Second version. This doesn't mean it will be finished in the next few days: the last part is full of 'unsayable' things, which will probably have to write me, instead of my writing them. In other words, I may have to sit and wait a long time for solutions to jump into my head, and it will all have to be done through implication and images rather than direct statements.

I think probably writers are charged with 'cruelty' more often than painters, though I'm sure painters like Dubuffet and Picasso must have come in for quite a bit of it. My painter-vivisector is horrified as well as fascinated by what he finds; at the same time because he is an artist he must go on finding.

I wonder whether Sid knows a painting called 'The Pretty Baa Lambs', which I think is in the Ashmolean, and I think by Madox Brown.[78] If he doesn't know it, I wonder whether he could find out who the painter was. It's a painting of some charm, though not of much account: I want to mention it in connexion with something in the book.

To me the only recent art excitement is a Rapotec exhibition: all of a sudden he has come a long way, and this is breathtaking.[79] I am particularly pleased because I like the R.s so much, and it isn't often that one can admire the work of the painters one likes . . .

Maie was here the other day looking better than I have ever seen her, though she says they are both exhausted and will be relieved to hand over.[80] We shall miss her visits. There is going to be a farewell thing (evening) at Admiralty House with 300 guests and a marquee: decorations to be worn, but I have nothing but the Desert Sore, which I didn't bother to collect, Manoly at least has the Order of the Phoenix, and he should I suppose wear his Imperial purple; that would shake them.[81] It is an awful prospect, but we are going because we like Maie so much.

MARTIN ROAD, 27.iv.69
TO CYNTHIA NOLAN
The shivoo at Admiralty House was, between ourselves, an agonising occasion; I have only had one worse experience, and that was Sid's retrospective: here at least there were no paintings involved. I suppose the

---

[78]By Brown but hanging in the Birmingham City Museum and Art Gallery: a pre-Raphaelite mother and child in a landscape with lambs.
[79]At the Bonython Gallery in Sydney.
[80]The Caseys were to retire on 25 April.
[81]The Desert Sore=The Africa Star; the Order of the Phoenix was awarded to Greek troops by the Patriarch of Alexandria; the Imperial purple (joke?) was claimed by the Lascaris princess of Nicea.

setting the other night was a brilliant one, with a scarlet band floodlit on the lawn under the angophoras, the Harbour and Opera House in the background and a pale blue marquee with a most sumptuous feast spread out. I'd like to be able to tuck into the food now, but on the evening I was only able to swallow a few mouthfuls, of what I couldn't say. There were so many people I dislike I took refuge in alcohol, and clenched my teeth so hard I sent the false ones wrong; the metal part began eating into my gum, with the result that I am toothless in my lower front till the dentist succeeds in putting things right.

At least the night is over, but it is depressing to think we shall probably see Maie much less often than before.

20 Martin Road, 7.v.69
TO MAIE CASEY

I finished *Madame Bovary* and it left me feeling cold as death. Shan't be able to read any fiction for a long time after this, except that I have to face my own. And what a lot of Emmas one knows. A few months ago I heard of a group of unappreciated wives bringing significance into their lives by studying *Madame Bovary*! I think I may work that up into something.

We shall miss you. The glamour has gone out of Australian public life since the Caseys stepped down.

Yrs
Patrick.

20 Martin Road, 14.vi.69
TO GEOFFREY DUTTON

I expect this will only be a mere note as I have dozens of letters to write, including two to the bereaved: that always makes me chew my pen, because more often than not one doesn't know what their attitude to their dead has been.

Tass[82] and his father, for instance? More difficult still to congratulate Tass on the knighthood, which I feel may be the end of him. The only kind of artist who can safely accept a title is the actor: actors can blow it out in a series of histrionic farts, but painters, writers, and composers seem to bottle it up and become museum objects.

I'm working hard now, but sometimes spend the whole day typing and re-typing the same couple of pages: very exhausting and depressing. Why did it look so good on previous readings, and finally so awful? I'd

[82]Drysdale.

like to know whether the lights go on and off in other people the way they do in myself.

Yrs

Patrick.

20 MARTIN ROAD, 1.vii.69
TO JULIET O'HEA
After careful thought Harry Miller has come to the conclusion that the Voss/Nobel Prize story is a rumour he started himself. I shall post a bomb through his letter box.

20 MARTIN ROAD, 13.vii.69
TO MAIE CASEY
I am always a bit uneasy when painters start painting flowers and poets write about birds; I feel they are avoiding the more important things they should be doing. When we met in San Francisco last year I felt Sid was a bit lost: he'd been hit by the present trend in painting, and didn't quite know where to go next. I had to try to tell him I was altogether lost, and just intended to go where I was led by whatever leads me (God, of course; though it hardly does to go round saying it directly.) Still, if Sid is painting all you say he is, I shouldn't be uneasy about his flowers; I shall accept them as a caprice; and I am slowly getting used to these particular ones!

The Vivisector is lugging me along. I am a bit frightened of it: it's a kind of Frankenstein's monster; and I'm sure a great many 'Australians' will be horrified. If all goes well, I should finish in October.

The Duttons have been here – nice to see them as always, but always bad for work; they play so hard it's a disruptive influence. This time, very tactfully, they said they'd stay at a hotel; as they seemed to spend half their time giving press and telly interviews I was glad. Geoffrey, as usual, is madly 'bookmaking'. I was driven to say I think far too many unnecessary books are being 'made', and that in ten years' time he will be embarrassed by The Clifton Pugh Book, for one.[83] The next in that line is going to be a book about the collection of somebody in Melbourne called Joe Brown[84] . . .

I had asked the Drysdales some time ago to let me know when they'd like to come to dinner. The other night he said they'd like to come this

[83]Bound in merino, issued by Sun Books in 1968 under the title *Involvement: the Portraits of Clifton Pugh and Mark Strizic*.
[84]Art dealer; *Outlines of Australian Art – The Joseph Brown Collection*, text by Daniel Thomas, appeared in 1973.

Wednesday, which is the night before they leave for Melbourne and the operation: very touching, I thought. I've always wanted to see more of the Drysdales, but they do collect some God awful people. I must tell Tass of a line I came across from Keats: 'My imagination is a monastery and I am its monk.' Hope you have both settled back.

Patrick.

20 Martin Road, 24.viii.69
TO JEAN SCOTT ROGERS
Dear Jean,
I'm sure if Lena Green[85] could sit up and offer to make you a cup of tea after a heart attack, she won't die yet, though for her sake I'd like her to, rather than go on existing in that sordid hotel bedroom.

Before this happened I had a letter from her, by the hand of the cousin, full of news of old Alexandrians, most of whom had died recently!

Sorry about the mumps. All those childhood ailments must be very unpleasant in later life; though mumps are supposed to be worse for men than for women.

Manoly was very miserable with boils for about a week recently. Nobody knows why they came, though a previous one was caused by a cat jumping on his lap and sticking her claws into his thigh.

I finished my book a few days ago, and should feel relieved, but am full of gloom: particularly at the thought of having to read through it again. However, everything has been making me gloomy lately, both the books I open, and world events. It seems as though we have to live with awfulness in the world, but books one thought good shouldn't suddenly appear bad. I suppose I am going through a bad phase.

We are having the house re-painted. The outside would be finished if it weren't for the weather; because of that, they have started on the inside, and tomorrow we have to face the worst – the kitchen, pantry, and laundry. At least the painters themselves are very amiable and conscientious; in fact, Ethel one of our pugs has a crush on the boss painter and is behaving like a woman when the Troops move in. Every evening when he leaves she sits looking terribly dejected, watching the crack beneath the back gate.

Yrs,
Patrick.

[85] An Alexandrian hostess of distinction whom PW and Lascaris found in 1968 living almost destitute in a hotel in Earl's Court. Since then PW had been supporting her with monthly cheques delivered by Scott Rogers.

WHITE CHECKED THE TYPESCRIPT making minor corrections in pen before handing it to Lascaris who never commented on a new book until he had read the last page. His verdict was favourable. White then bundled up two copies, one for New York and one for London, and took them into the city for the usual row at the post office counter: stamps for *The Vivisector* cost $30. He knew several London publishers wanted the novel and in Sydney, Angus & Robertson was offering him an open cheque. Waiting for the verdict White read, watched films, wrote letters and revised his story 'The Night the Prowler' drafted in Europe the year before.

20 MARTIN ROAD, 22.ix.69
TO GEOFFREY DUTTON
Dear Geoffrey,
Thanks for your letter. I wonder, indeed, what you will make of a play.[86] One has to have a try, but it is all so discouraging in this country, and will remain that way as far as I can see. A play with a lot of characters can only expect a troupe of amateur-students galumphing about; even if it were economically possible to put such a play on with professionals they wouldn't galumph much better than the amateurs. It would also require more daring than I have, to embark on a play set in XIXth Century Russia. I am ready to rely on my intuition to get me past any experience I haven't experienced (provided the experience isn't involved with mechanical technicalities or the sciences), but I go very warily where I don't have automatic command of the cultural background. That is why I seldom write about any country but Australia: I couldn't write about most others from the inside – I mean, I couldn't exist inside the characters I was writing about. Although I know the Greeks better than most foreigners who write about them, I am always walking on eggs when I become a Greek character. (I expect all my characters are really bits of myself, and it inhibits me when foreignness forces me into a certain amount of objectivity.)

Christina Stead's characters, on the other hand, are all people she has known. She wasn't prepared to believe that mine, the important ones anyway, are latent bits of myself. She came to lunch last week and we got on very well. I didn't ask anybody else because I imagined that she is sick to death of meeting people at the literary-social functions to which she is forced to go. Physically she is unlike most of the press photographs one has seen, although there is perhaps one early photograph which links up with the present Christina Stead. To talk to her is more like talking to a

---

[86] About 19th century Russian terrorists – particularly the women – and the murder of Alexander II; unfinished.

man than a woman, although there is nothing overtly masculine about her, and I shouldn't think anything lesbian. Her marriage seems to have been one of the best kind. Now that she is on her own I think she might come out here to live, to be near her family, though I suggested she give it plenty of thought before burning her bridges.

I have been reading the Frank Dalby Davidson sex compendium, but I am afraid I shall not be able to stay the course.[87] It is maddening to think how good it could have been, because he has some astonishing insights to show for all those years of ponderous work and bad writing. I have just come across a bit, about 'filmy underwear and dainty bra,' and that will be about as far as I can go.

I heard *The Vivisector* had arrived in London and New York. Still too early to hear any reactions. Two or three people always read it at the Viking before they commit themselves. Then, in London, my agent only returns from her holiday to-day, and she will have to read it before anything is decided there. In the meantime, I am feeling pretty bleak.

20 MARTIN ROAD, 27.ix.69
TO FREDERICK GLOVER
On this occasion we were seeing *If–* –[88] Well – I can't imagine why you didn't see the point: it's one of the best films I've seen, the smallest part perfectly cast and acted, the direction what I dream of. After the frightfulness of amateur professional theatre in Australia, it was miraculous to come across all this perfection. The buildings of my old school (Cheltenham) added to the horror of the story: the revolution part of it seems to have been simmering in me all these years, and I was on the roof with the other stengunners.

20 MARTIN ROAD, 5.x.69
TO JULIET O'HEA
I wanted to stress that we must get away from E & S by any means; I should have thought the behaviour of their director, the Hon. Thingummy Thingummy Eyre was excuse enough for my leaving.

I'd rather take less from a publisher I could respect, like Cape – though of course get all you can!

I suppose E & S are not altogether to blame for the fall in sales. I am neither new nor sensational, and I won't get with the publicity machine.

[87]*The White Thorn Tree* in its burly first edition published by the National Press Pty Ltd, Melbourne, 1968.
[88]Directed by Old Cheltonian Lindsay Anderson, 1968.

I notice that when their books come out the Macleans and Bellows of this world rush to London and jump on the telly, Edna O'Brien starts telling how she wants to become a nun and so forth. One of the most successful painters in Sydney[89] employs a personal PR; there are telly sessions in the home, beside the sea, with his blind wife; and they rush to buy his paintings. George Johnston one of the biggest sellers, cashes in on everything: his TB, his kids he has been left with, his wife's death just before his last book came out (actually it was a hushed up suicide). Again the public lap it up. But I find it all nauseating; and in any case my life is not the least bit spectacular: it is so humdrum, I suspect that is one of the reasons I write novels.

It is a relief you liked *The Vivisector*. Manoly thinks it's my best and Marshall Best says he was 'deeply shaken and terrified'! . . .

I should like to know how we stand before Graham C. Greene arrives in Sydney to do his stuff for Cape.[90]

20 MARTIN ROAD, 7.x.69
TO GEOFFREY DUTTON
Dear Geoffrey,
What a disaster! I once broke a couple of ribs (the time I fell in a slippery shower at Nadi airport) and know how painful that can be, but a wrist must be many times worse as well as more incapacitating . . .

Even so, I don't see why you need be plunged in such gloom and remorse for having it good in life and an amiable character thrown in. There are so many depressive, violent, irritable, sleasy, destructive people about, it's a relief to think of somebody attractive and enviable. So relax and enjoy your spiritual status.

I've never noticed your giving way to self-pity, or known about self-pity being the 'curse of the Duttons.' It used to be mine when I was a youth, and I think all my early writings were tinged with it. An old cousin of my father's, with whom I used to spend my school holidays in England, recognised it and took me to task very sternly. I was hurt at the time, but realised later that it makes the characters in novels awful bores. In time I tried consciously to avoid it, just as I have always tried to avoid 'blowing one's own trumpet' after a severe upbringing by a Scottish Presbyterian

---

[89]Charles Blackman.
[90]Graham C. Greene (1936–   ), former merchant banker, nephew of the novelist, managing director of Jonathan Cape, came to dinner at Martin Road later in the month – 'an austere occasion', he reported to head office, 19.x.69 – but one that clinched the matter for PW. Among other advantages, Cape promised not to involve PW in local promotion.

nurse. (To me, trumpet-blowing is one of the most painful traits of the Australian character, and one of the reasons why I don't like living here. How comfortable it might be if I'd had an Irish Catholic nurse instead.)

20 MARTIN ROAD, 10.xi.69
TO INGMAR BJÖRKSTÉN[91]
Dear Ingmar Björkstén,
Thank you for your letter. We heard some of the awful rumours in Australia and I had to make some quick plans for going into hiding if there were any truth in them. But of course there wasn't, so one felt rather embarrassed and humiliated. I saw a photograph of poor Beckett looking quite crazed after he had fled to Tunisia.[92]

I am feeling very empty at the moment after finishing a book I had been working on for almost three years. My New York publisher is enthusiastic, but I am trying to get away from the one in London to go to somebody else. This is causing delays as the old publisher wants to hang on and make an offer after reading the book, a very long one. It is called *The Vivisector*. My protagonist is a painter who lives most of his life in Sydney from the end of last century to the present day. It also deals with the Sydney plutocracy, which I don't think has been done before in any detail: Australian writers don't seem to have considered it aesthetically desirable to write about the rich. (There is an exception in Martin Boyd, but he came from Victoria and concentrated on Melbourne society.) At least with the rich, who are usually slightly more cosmopolitan, one can get away from what is referred to as 'the Australian image', which no longer interests me.

I still have your book, though I have never got as far as reading it![93]
Yours sincerely,
Patrick White.

20 MARTIN ROAD 26.xi.69
TO JEAN SCOTT ROGERS
Dear Jean,
I'm sorry you found Lena Green feeling so poorly last time. Have just heard of an old lady, blind for several years, who has died at the age of

---

[91](1936–), Swedish critic and journalist, discovered *Voss* on a visit to Australia in 1962, had tea at Dogwoods, and returned to become an advocate for PW's work in Sweden.
[92]PW *was* a contender for the Nobel in 1969 for the first time—just as Harry Miller had said— but Samuel Beckett took the prize.
[93]*Australisk Dagbok*, 1964. Not translated.

96. It will be dreadful if Lena lingers on like that; and what would happen to her at that hotel? I suppose there must be some kind of home which would take her. I can remember going to see a place run by some Blue Nuns at Holland Park, but I've no idea what they charged. Two old cousins of Roy de Maistre were there, and they would not have had much money. Actually Lena is Jewish, and I'm sure there must be homes run by Jews for Jews. Perhaps you might lead up tactfully to religion next time you go; I can't remember her ever mentioning her Jewishness, but it was well known in Alexandria that they were Jews.

If she comes out with it, you might ask if she had ever thought of trying to get into a home for aged Jews if she becomes unable to look after herself. (This doesn't mean I shouldn't still be willing to contribute what I am contributing.) If you bring up the nuns first, she may then confess to the Jewishness. But nuns will usually accept those of other faiths.

20 MARTIN ROAD, 11.xii.69
TO GEOFFREY DUTTON

Good news that you are resigning from all the committees and councils: they were draining you. I can understand your wanting to prevent a lot of the politico-intellectual wangling that goes on – who doesn't? – but you can't become involved with that sort of thing and remain creative.

Yes, I hated the public side of the anti-conscription campaign, but felt I had to do it.[94] I certainly shan't pay the fine, but don't think the Government will send us to gaol, though I am prepared to go: so many are involved, they would flood the gaols, and I feel in the circumstances they will continue to ignore what is happening. At most, we may bring Gorton down.[95]

We had a funny experience the night of the signing: we had taken Mary and Godfrey Turner to a farewell dinner before they leave for Europe,[96] then come home to bed rather pissed. About 1.30 the bell started ringing. We looked out and saw a van . . . I wondered whether I wasn't being arrested already – after all, a VAN – when it suddenly occurred to me it was the PMG, and I rushed down to grab the urgent cable.

[94]PW was one of a group of artists, businessmen, etc. who hoped to provoke fines and arrests by signing a statement on 9 December 1970 urging defiance of the National Service Act. The publicity was useful for the anti-Vietnam cause, but no arrests were made.
[95]When Harold Holt drowned before Christmas 1967, his place was taken by John Grey Gorton (1911–   ), an ex-fighter pilot and grapefruit grower. Popular at first, his government soon began to lose its grip.
[96]Mary Turner (1926–   ), one of the proprietors of the Macquarie Galleries from 1956 to 1978, and her husband the market researcher Godfrey (1914–88).

It was the first of three important publishers' cables. I can now tell you that Cape is going to publish *The Vivisector*. They are the ones I have wanted all along because I feel they have the best list, and I found Tom Maschler very sympathetic when we were over there last year.[97] E & S hung on to the bitter end; after a fairly miserable offer, they came up pretty well when the first one was turned down: they also tried to seduce me with the additional offer of a £2,000 publicity campaign (such as they gave Malamud for *The Fixer*.) We turned that down too. In the end, it happens, Cape is offering better terms than E & S when I hadn't expected it. All this is a great relief after weeks of tension and uncertainty. I'm only embarrassed by my own mysterious behaviour towards Macmillan and Collins, who were also on my list, but I expect they are used to writers behaving mysteriously.

20 MARTIN ROAD, 4.i.70
TO GEOFFREY DUTTON
Dear Geoffrey,
Christmas over, thank God! We had quite a mild time once the scrambling to do up and deliver presents was past. But we have both been suffering from stomach troubles as the result of over-eating and drinking, and rheumatic pains from the north-easterlies which have blown for days. My rheumatics only left after house-cleaning day: I suppose all the stooping and stretching drove them out; so you can tell Max that is another good reason why not to keep a 'char.' Wasn't that a stinking piece of his in *The Australian*? One of the most vulgar and embarrassing effusions I've ever come across.[98]

I've signed both the agreements for *The Vivisector* by now, but I don't know when it will be coming out. The Viking tempo has slackened off since the days when Ben Huebsch and Harold Guinzburg were living just round the corner from the office. Marshall Best, who is semi-retired, now spends half the week in Connecticut ... However, I am glad they are still publishing me: there is nothing flash or shyster about them.

Am now typing the final version of the much interrupted novella *The Night the Prowler*. I did think I might write a couple of short things to strengthen the volume, but rather than coax out stories before they are

---

[97]Tom Maschler (1933–   ), chairman of Jonathan Cape. PW told Maie Casey, 17.viii.69, that he was 'very much alive to contemporary fiction'.
[98]Harris in the *Australian*, 20 Dec. 1969, p.17, had mocked Swedish press efforts to come to grips with Australia and PW – whom some papers confused with the Catholic novelist Morris West – in reporting the candidates for the 1969 Nobel Prize.

ready to come naturally, I shall probably start a long novel which has been nagging at me in the most astonishing way the last couple of weeks. Whether it is a good or bad sign, I have never known so much about a book before starting to write it. It makes me wonder if I haven't read it somewhere and forgotten, or whether somebody else isn't writing it at the moment and I happen to have tuned in.

ELEVEN

Storms along the Horizon

January 1970 – December 1972

EVEN AS HIS MOTHER lay dying, White knew he must write the novel of
Ruth's death, attended by acolytes and besieged by heirs who wanted this
opulent convalescence to end in death or a bare room at the Blue Nuns.
The core of the novel would be the struggle between himself and that
almost-senile woman of immense will, a reckoning between mother and
son. *The Eye of the Storm* has the fundamental plot of all the books White
wrote after falling in the storm at Castle Hill: the erratic, often unconscious search for God. In the eye of the cyclone, Elizabeth Hunter
experiences 'a moment of sublimity which she had always been grasping
for in her rather self-obsessed materialistic life . . . it had to be a
tremendous upheaval to daunt such a dominant character.'[1]

20 MARTIN ROAD, JAN. 1970
TO RONALD WATERS
AND FREDDIE CARPENTER[2]
Dear Ronald and Fred,
Thank you very much for the Colibri – very elegant and useful[3] – and
with Ian Bevan thrown in, that was an extra surprise. My, how plain he
is: just as Manoly said when he met him in the street with his . . . Baby
Doll sister.[4] He's like a shih-tsu without any hair on. But I like him: he
talks sense and seems very businesslike; and in half an hour I heard
more about Harry Miller's plans for filming *Voss* than I have from Harry
Miller himself in nearly two years. Harry is too busy twisting about
playing at circuses and giving ladies hot pants to be able to get two
words put together straight. As a matter of fact it is over a year since I
had a word from him either written or spoken: not that I mind; I only

---

[1]PW to Rodney Wetherell, ABC Sunday Night Radio 2, 9 Dec. 1973.
[2]Freddie Carpenter (1908–89), dancer and heir to an Australian pub fortune, was Waters'
partner from the late 1930s until his death. Carpenter gave up dancing to become a
choreographer and director of London musicals; his work brought him often to Australia.
[3]MONOgas Cigarette lighter; PW did not smoke.
[4]The London agent, Ian Bevan, was Harry Miller's European representative.

hope the option won't be renewed. But first I should like to let him know I read how on the first night of *You Know You Can't Hear Me*[5] he had them play 'Waltzing Matilda' while he stood to attention; I want to be able to say: If I had been there, Harry, I should have been praying that a resounding fart would fly out of my arsehole at the right moment. So much for Sir (would-be) Harry Miller.

England sounds awful this winter. Hope you haven't had the 'flu either of you, or if you did, I hope it was at different times. There's nothing worse than everyone being ill together and wondering how one is going to stagger out with the dogs. Here we are having awful summer weather instead. Last Sunday there was such grey steam Manoly said: This is Florida without the trouble of getting there.

We are vaguely planning for a trip next year on Book advances; the great thing to plan is how not to have to go to Florida; but I suppose Mom and Sister Annie will create if we don't. M.'s father died just after Christmas we heard – eighty-eight and practically bedridden. For a long time his only remaining interests were his stools and the nurses, so there was no reason to lament his going; in addition he was just about the most selfish human being I have ever encountered. In April we are expecting M.'s youngest sister Elly for a couple of months. Elly is the one we particularly like. She is going via the States for the christening of her first grandchild. We had a lot of trouble getting her a visa for Australia. At the Embassy in Athens they seemed to think she wanted to migrate, and had to know her criminal record and the criminal records of her children. I think she would still be waiting for the visa in April if we hadn't written to the Ambassador in Athens and the Minister for External Affairs in Canberra complaining about the police-state treatment she was receiving. After that the Ambassador wrote personally and the visa went through very quickly ...

Somebody[6] wants to make a telly film about me and I have agreed to it provided I like their line of approach. It also depends on whether the BBC London will support financially, which they have suggested they will. Of course you couldn't expect anything of the ABC Sydney, they are shit where money is concerned and anything else. I am dreading the whole

---

[5]*You Know I Can't Hear You When the Water's Running*, ('An evening of convulsive mirth') by Robert Anderson at the Playbox in Sydney in 1969.
[6]Peter Thompson (1940–   ), an aspiring director but later a film critic. The following year, as shooting was about to begin, PW withdrew. 'They are very upset, naturally, and probably won't speak to me again,' he told Glover, 7.xi.71. 'But it would have been far worse if I had turned their film into a disaster by drifting through it like a mumbling zombie.'

thing what with my monotonous voice and always saying something else when it comes to the point, and no doubt I shall come out looking like Dracula's grandfather. Anyway, when you sit looking at your gorgeous technicolour box, as I come down the front steps I'll put in a special fart or two which only Elm Row[7] and Coral Browne[8] will understand. Who knows, we may appear together yet in a special revival of *Arsenic and Old Lace.*

Did the ties arrive, I wonder? A lot of things seem to have gone astray this Christmas what with the Sydney post-office and the London 'flu? I didn't receive one word from my three bloody nieces, but I don't think that was either 'flu or post-office, just a family disease that was kept at bay during my sister's lifetime. Haven't heard anything of Freddie Angles, but he has been rather peculiar when we have tried to approach in the past. Saw Thelma A. the other day; the young Angles are expecting another baby at any moment.[9] All the wives round here have had or are about to; I think everyone is so relieved when the Show is over in April, they throw the pills into Centennial Park and fuck solid. Anyway, this time of year they're all spilling out the babies.

Nothing in the theatre but *Hair* and *Not Now Darling,* the latter with a young man called Ron Frazer, who, I seem to remember, wagged his Gothic hip at you when you were here; the stills outside the theatre make it look about ten times overdone. I am still a skinhead; but all the doctor and barrister squares down Martin Road have grown mutton chops: such an aid to pomposity. Hope to hear from you before we see you.

P.

20 MARTIN ROAD, 26.i.70
TO JEAN SCOTT ROGERS
Dear Jean,
I can imagine Lena Green wouldn't take to a hospital ward, although that room in the sleazy hotel must have been terrible enough. Perhaps when she is well enough the cousin will get her into some kind of old people's

[7] The Hampstead street where Waters and Carpenter lived.
[8] (1913–91), born Melbourne, West End star and caustic wit. PW dreamt of her as Nola Boyle in a London production of *Season at Sarsaparilla;* to Waters he wrote, 26.ii.62, 'I know what is <u>inside</u> Coral, and how it would pop out if she got into that part.'
[9] Freddie Angles had danced in London with Freddie Carpenter, retired after the war to Sydney and appeared occasionally in pantomime. Home turf for his racing and theatre family was Centennial Park: his niece Thelma lived over the back fence from PW and her son, another Fred, had sold PW the Martin Road house before moving further along the street where he and his wife Annette were expecting a child.

home; what I had visualised was a cell of her own, from which she could emerge to talk to other old people if she felt like it. We used to suspect she had been in the chorus as a girl; perhaps she'll admit to that eventually as she has admitted to the Jewishness: then she might be eligible for an actor's home, where there's probably a lot of ginning up and fruity reminiscence . . .

Today is Stralia Day, a fitting one too, of steam and rain. This year I wasn't invited to the Premier's party,[10] I think because I have been opposing conscription for Vietnam or perhaps it was only because I have always sent my regrets in the past: the thought of standing round with a lot of politicians and big business successes congratulating themselves on being Australian was something I couldn't face.

Had a letter from Jonquil, who seems much revived.[11]

Yrs

Patrick.

20 MARTIN ROAD, 1.ii.70

TO MAIE CASEY

Have you had any experience of hurricanes, land, sea, or air? I am particularly interested in how far up they reach, and how they would affect flying; also the <u>eye</u> of the hurricane: whether a ship can sail along within the eye and miss most of the storm. I feel sure you know something about the air part, or that you will know somebody who has had first hand experience of hurricanes.

20 MARTIN ROAD, 4.ii.70

TO JULIET PAGE[12]

Dear Juliet Page,

Thank you for the draft blurb, which I have torn into considerably, as you will see. I think my version may whet the curiosity slightly more than yours; perhaps you will object to the introduction of characters' names, but to me they work up into a kind of incantation.

One specific point: there are no 'ranchers', there is no 'ranching' in Australia. References to ranchers only caused laughter and incredulity when one of Cape's press handouts appeared recently in *The Australian*.

I have dropped a reference to the 'English' novel because they might

[10]Robin (Bob) Askin (1909–81), Liberal premier of NSW 1965–74.
[11]Jonquil Antony (1916–80), scriptwriter and former wife of the director John Wyse who directed *Return to Abyssinia* at the Boltons in 1947.
[12]Blurb writer at Jonathan Cape.

object to it here (I shouldn't). I like 'plutocracy' better than the 'society of the cultured rich.' We do have a very small society of cultured rich, but a lot of people might laugh.

I forgot to tell Tom Maschler that the *Sydney Morning Herald* approached Curtis Brown, Sydney, for serial rights of *The Vivisector*. I refused because such a long book would only lose its character in the cutting it would undergo. Anyway, when there are so many people who say: 'We're waiting till your book appears in paperback', they wouldn't even do that if they read it as a newspaper serial.

Yours sincerely,
Patrick White.

20 MARTIN ROAD, 18.ii.70
TO TOM MASCHLER
Dear Tom,
I hope you will able to read this. We have friends sleeping in, and I don't want to wake them with my typewriter . . .

About *Portnoy*, I hardly know what to advise.[13] I think it is one of the wittiest books I have read, and you can repeat that if you want to when publishing in Australia. I'm doubtful about Adelaide as a launching place. One is inclined to think of the Adelaidians as being advanced because of a handful of progressive intellectuals one knows, but the majority are terribly starchy and reactionary. Sydney is the most emancipated city in Australia; I'm not saying that because I come from it; there is much that I detest about it. On the other hand, I'd like to see Portnoy come in the Adelaide Establishment's eye!

Yrs,
Patrick.

20 MARTIN ROAD, 22.ii.70
TO JAMES STERN
Even so, the inhabitants of the Northern Hemisphere pour out here nowadays every January February March – our worst months; it has reached such a pitch that I refuse a princess practically every week. Next week we have the musical queens Britten and Pears: I shall refuse them too if any advances are made, though I don't expect they will be: I think Britten is a nauseating county snob and Pears a nauseating voice. Of course there

[13]Cape was planning to export Philip Roth's *Portnoy's Complaint* to Australia. Later in the year, when Customs banned the book, Penguin printed a local edition and PW was a key witness at the obscenity trials that followed.

are also a lot we look forward to seeing and don't see enough e.g. the Nolans and Edna O'Brien who are coming to the Adelaide Festival.

Have you read Edna's new book, *A Pagan Place*? I've always been a fan of hers, though I haven't liked them all (*The Love Object* I thought bad, and *August is A Wicked Month* I couldn't bring myself to read) but this one carried me right away. It is the same country as *The Country Girls*, my favourite one till now. *A Pagan Place* is denser, subtler, really heartrending in places. How lucky the Irish are, and the American Jews, in having those rich tormented backgrounds to draw on; here are we, the bloody Australians, with nothing, having to conjure rabbits out of the air. As a writer I'd like to have been almost anything rather than an Australian – even a New Zealander or a South African (I must say being a Canadian wouldn't have much to offer).

Apart from the influx already mentioned, Manoly's youngest sister is coming to stay with us in April for a month or two; she is our favourite relation, who is always wonderful to us when we go to Greece. Blood relationship is mostly just a farce, but occasionally <u>one</u> comes good, and that makes up for all the rest. (What has happened to your sister since your mother died?)

As we are about to start one of our postal strikes, and you are probably floating round Bandol or God knows where, this may not reach you for months. I suppose it will eventually, and you will see that my typing hasn't improved, and – I hope – that we love you both as much as before.

Yrs
Patrick.

20 MARTIN ROAD, 1.iii.70
TO JEAN SCOTT ROGERS
Dear Jean,

I had your letter about Lena Green's death, which I had in fact been expecting any day. Strange that an old Jewess should have died on reaching Beulah Hill! I must investigate it when I am next in London, but expect it is just acres of that awful outer-suburb roughcast Tudor.[14] I also had a letter from the cousin; if she is rushing off on a world tour I feel she could have done more for Lena.

I am enclosing a last instalment of the money I have been sending, and would like you to buy something you want. It must have been an awful bore dealing with the monthly dole to somebody you had wished onto you . . .

In my new novel I have left the pleasures behind and reached the agonising difficulties. Every time I begin again I think: I am now so experienced, this one can only be easier; but it becomes increasingly difficult.

Yrs
Patrick

Have seen a photograph of a daughter of Rasputin living in Los Angeles: exactly like Lena Green!

MARTIN ROAD, 15.iii.70
TO CYNTHIA NOLAN

More and more threads have to be gathered in, which will make the book longer than I had thought: it's going to be in the shape of a spider's web. One of the great difficulties in writing novels, I find, is to prevent a superficial, but very important character from sabotaging the whole thing. That was my worry in dealing with the Sydney social scenes in *The Vivisector*, and in this one there are the characters of an actor and a rather flighty nurse who must be given a certain amount of density without the intellectual thought-processes which wouldn't be natural to them. I think at last I am finding the right tone, but getting there has meant an anxious time. To return to this question of superficiality and density: it is the great problem in writing about anything Australian; my (secret) solution is to ring in as many foreigners and eccentrics as possible and hope I can keep people interested through those. Perhaps the reason *Voss* has succeeded with more readers than the other books have, is that there are no Australians in it, except the aborigines, who are, paradoxically, exotics.

[14]Beulah Hill is Mitty Jacka's suburb in *The Eye of the Storm*.

20 Martin Road, 31.iii.70
TO MARSHALL BEST

Anthony Burgess seems to have ruffled the Australian Writers in a talk he gave,[15] in which he said: 'A country is only remembered for its art. Rome is remembered for Virgil, Greece for Homer, and Australia may be remembered for Patrick White.' The newspaper report continues: 'The entire gathering of writers, which did not include Patrick White, held its breath in shock for a moment before releasing it in a smothered gasp. No one clapped.' How I wish I had been watching and listening at a hole in the wall.

20 Martin Road, 5.iv.70
TO MARGARET SUMNER[16]

I expect I shall go nuts in the end like Barry Humphries. At least he is only split in two, whereas I shall break into fifteen.

20 Martin Road, 5.iv.70
TO GEOFFREY DUTTON

We met the Burgesses at dinner at the British Council, with only one other guest, an old girl called Polly Elwyn Jones, the wife of the British Attorney General, whom we had met already some years ago. I found Burgess very well informed, Liana most difficult to understand, though Manoly seemed to decode what she was saying until the vino got to work in her. Afterwards we gave them all a lift, first dropping Polly Jones at Darling Point. After that Liana began clutching her head and moaning: 'Sydney is all beetch-beetch. This old Mrs Pearl – She beetch.' The others immediately assured her the name was Polly Elwyn Jones, and she didn't seem anything of a bitch. However, I remembered Polly's professional name as an illustrator is Pearl Binder. Even so, I agreed there was nothing bitchy about her, if anything a bit too sweet. But Liana continued to moan: 'No, I sense all around me – all Sydney beetch.' I began to feel positively unmasked, and had to confess that I was one. Anthony said he was one too, whereupon Liana shrieked: 'Yes, you are beetch because you are novelists.' She was still regurgitating when we dropped them: 'This Mrs Pearl – she biggest beetch.' Then suddenly I realised what it was about – and only because I am a bitch. When I went to the lavatory after dinner at the British Council, I decided to flip back the page in the visitors' book to see who else the Burgesses had been given. There I found the inevitable

[15] At the Adelaide Festival.
[16] Wife of the Melbourne theatre director John Sumner.

Keneallys, Ken Slessor (glad somebody remembered)[17] <u>and</u> the Cyril Pearls[18] of all people! So now I said: 'Well, Cyril Pearl's certainly a bitch, from his column in the *Herald*.' And Liana followed up with: 'Mrs Pearl is beegest beetch . . . '

Did you hear about Margaret Dick[19] in a taxi with the earnest Lundkvists:[20] 'Explain to us this word "booger" which is always coming up.'

Yrs
Patrick.

WHITE WAS IN CONTACT through Clem Semmler with a young New Zealand academic at Cambridge 'intellectually obsessed' with the novels. The fruit of Peter Beatson's obsession was *The Eye in the Mandala*, a study of White's religious ideas that appeared in 1977. Here at the start of his research – and correspondence – Beatson asked Semmler to overcome his embarrassment at having lost White's first letter cataloguing the books and writers that had influenced his religious philosophy.

20 MARTIN ROAD, 10.v.70
TO CLEM SEMMLER
Dear Clem,
I remember receiving and answering a letter from Peter Beatson perhaps a couple of years ago. (At that time he was apparently still able to see, though not well enough to read, I gather.)[21] It's difficult to answer such a question as he wants me to; one reads books, perhaps absorbs something from them, then one forgets the source.

I can admit to Jung and Buber because I read a lot of each some years ago in connexion with books I was writing.

Last Christmas I was given a book called *Existentialism and Religious Belief* by David E. Roberts (OUP). It is full of interesting things, particularly a chapter on Gabriel Marcel. Elizabeth Harrower who gave me the book, thought he might be the one who would interest me most, and he does.

---

[17]Poet and journalist (1901–71); PW to Semmler, 10.iv.69: 'Far more of a poet than some of those who keep on uttering'.
[18]Cyril Pearl (1906–87), journalist, biographer and historian, one of the hostile Packer pack; and Patricia (Paddy) Pearl, his forceful second wife.
[19]Harrower's Scottish cousin and friend.
[20]Artur Lundkvist (1906–91), Swedish writer and critic who had joined the Swedish Academy in 1968 in order *inter alia* to secure the Nobel Prize for PW; travelling to Australia with him was his wife, the poet Maria Wine (1912–   ).
[21]Beatson was suffering from *retinitis pigmentosa*.

Since then I have got hold of another of Marcel's books *Being and Having* (Fontana) and am trying to track down two more, *Decline of Wisdom* and *The Philosophy of Existence*, which I think may have been published in translation in New York.[22]

I suppose what I am increasingly intent on trying to do in my books is to give professed unbelievers glimpses of their own unprofessed faith. I believe most people have a religious faith, but are afraid that by admitting it they will forfeit their right to be considered intellectuals. This is particularly common in Australia where the intellectual is a comparatively recent phenomenon. It is easier for me to make these admissions, because I am not an intellectual, only a doubtful Australian, and in many other ways beyond the pale. The churches defeat their own aims, I feel, through the banality of their approach, and by rejecting so much that is sordid and shocking which can still be related to religious experience. This is what I am trying to do, perhaps more than before in *The Vivisector* which is coming out this year.

Gabriel Marcel, whom I came across only recently, may help me more in the novel I am working on at present, though it is difficult to say at this stage (I haven't yet finished my usual chaotic first version.) Anyway, the book seems to have a more specifically religious content and pattern than the others.

The other day I picked up a very seductive little book called *The Cloud of Unknowing* (Penguin). It is written by a 14th Century English mystic, and deals with the contemplative life. I can't go all the way with it, because I feel that the moral flaws in myself are more than anything my creative source. In the same way, I don't imagine Beatson would want to renounce his intellect, though I think he should investigate the book, as a curiosity, and because it could be a source of illumination.[23]

20 MARTIN ROAD, 10.v.70

TO NINETTE DUTTON

I think a lot of women may not approve of the sexual incidents in *The Vivisector*; but Hurtle Duffield is essentially a puritan, and an artist

---

[22]Marcel (1889–1973), philosopher and playwright, described himself as a 'Christian existentialist' and was, like PW, sceptical of all *systems* of belief. After discovering Marcel, PW wrote to a priest, Paul Maloney, 11.ii.70: 'The nauseating Sartre had prevented me from investigating "existentialism" until now.' The works: *Être et avoir*, 1935, trans. 1949; *Le déclin de la Sagesse*, 1953, trans. 1954, and a collection of essays published in translation in London as *The Philosophy of Existence*, 1948.

[23]To the Nolans, 5.v.70, he added the remark: 'A fascinating book, but what it proposes would be the end of us.'

determined to protect the secret core out of which he creates. He has also been made suspicious of women by his treatment by his real and his foster mother. From what one sees today there is anyway very little that is sacramental in sex. Half the marriages one can observe are failing or failed. You of course are looking at things through the eyes of one who has had an exceptional marriage relationship. Perhaps living on the edge of a park and seeing the sordid goings-on we see has made me cynical!

20 MARTIN ROAD, 21.vi.70
TO MARGERY WILLIAMS
Dear Margery,
I should have answered your letter sooner, but we have had Elly staying with us for the last two months and there has been a lot of extra work on top of work. She left last week, and the house now seems very empty. We shall miss her; she was an admirable guest, and did some of the nastiest jobs of her own accord. The last night we gave a party for thirty-seven people who entertained her while she was in Sydney. Even though we got Penny[24] to do the food this time, it was a great strain, and I shan't give another party in a hurry.

I'm sorry if I offended you in trying to stir you up. The situation is one I find difficult to understand for the reasons I've already given.[25] Perhaps my being the greatest pessimist on earth has also made me resilient. When I was a child I had a mental list of things I would throw out of the window, and in what order, if fire broke out. (Perhaps this was the result of being in a fire at the age of nine months.) Anyway, I've always imagined the worst things that could happen to me and tried to work out how I should deal with them: if Manoly should die, if I should lose all my money, suffer a stroke, go blind, dry up as a writer, experience a foreign occupation, and so forth. Perhaps I should write a Book of Contingencies to prepare people like you for the worst.

Another thing I can't understand is you saying you will accept something if offered, but will never go out to look for anything. My experience has been that nothing has ever come my way without pushing, fighting, manoeuvring, exploding. Nor does it happen any easier now: not the things I really want, anyway.

I am writing away at my new novel, and may possibly have got two-thirds of it down on paper. Already I feel dreadful sensations in my stomach at the thought of *The Vivisector*'s coming out in New York on July 8th. I

---

[24]Lane-Brown, later Coleing.
[25]PW had lost patience with Williams' grief, she having been widowed for 18 months.

can imagine *Time Magazine* already sharpening its anonymous Australian knife. However, some very encouraging things have already been said by individuals.

Ken Russell's assistant flew out here a few weeks ago to discuss the filming of *Voss*. Russell is apparently very keen to do it, and would like to start shooting in October next year if the money can be raised. There is quite a good chance of this since his success with *Women in Love*[26] . . .

After a long dull period in the Sydney art game, there is quite a staggering Brett Whiteley exhibition.[27] I now think he's a great painter. In the past he was not much more than an imitation of Bacon, and to a lesser extent Nolan; though he put on the paint in his own way. Now he seems to have found himself fully, in Fiji, and on this present visit to Australia. He's the only other Australian painting on the same scale as Nolan, with equal diversity in his imagination. There's also a sleazy exhibition by Martin Sharp (the London virus double strength) which even a lot of the social squares have been getting groovy about, but it gave me the horrors: I felt we'd all be better dead, and that the Chinese should take over immediately.[28]

I hope to hear from you again soon, and that this letter has not been unkind; kindness, alas, can end by doing harm, and what I was attempting was to be realistic.

Love,
Patrick.

20 MARTIN ROAD, 28.vi.70
TO RONALD WATERS
Dear Ronald,
Thanks for answering the questions (legibly, too!) What should my ageing actor use to take his make-up off? I'm sure I can remember them using coconut butter in my youth, and I don't go back to Kean's day. This book is giving me a lot of trouble. It's not all about actors; in fact the action takes place away from the theatre. The trouble comes from having too many characters, and while I am involved with one in particular, I have

---

[26]After seeing Russell's television film *A Song for Summer*, 1968, and the *Observer*'s review of *Women in Love*, 1969, PW had persuaded Harry Miller that Russell was the man for *Voss*. The director's assistant was Harry Benn.

[27]'Paintings and Assemblages', at the Bonython Gallery.

[28]Sharp (1942–   ), painter and poster-maker, was exhibiting his London paintings at the old Clune Gallery in Kings Cross; PW dreamt about the end of the world after seeing the show; after Jim Sharman brought the painter into PW's orbit, his work appeared at Martin Road.

to leave the others for long stretches, then work myself back into the right frame of mind when I return to them. I imagine Esmé Berenger must have felt something the same when she played all the parts in *Hamlet*![29]

I must have expressed myself wrongly in my last letter: I didn't mean to suggest there was anything phoney about the really great actors when I used the expression 'conjuring trick;' with the really great it is a trick they can't explain. I think Zoe Caldwell is the only great actress I've known really well, and I know her background ('the plumber's daughter', and all that), and have seen her build up the part at rehearsals in three different productions. She would never be able to explain, and I wouldn't ask her to try, because I have recognised genius at work. How to convey it though, is the difficulty. I think I have brought it off with the painter in *The Vivisector*, and in the same book perhaps, also with the girl musician (who is a kind of Zoe of the piano.) But with actors one does come up against the 'conjuring trick' even though that may be unconscious. How they can change shape physically, for instance, without assistance; I've seen Zoe do that, and I can remember Margaret Rutherford changing shape in the wings at the Saville during a rehearsal for that peculiar revue[30] when she told me to go away and that she was so frightened: it was almost as though I'd caught her naked or having a shit . . .

Harry M. has become much more communicative lately as things seem to be going well in connexion with *Voss*. I think I can see through every move, and there are times when I could shit on him, but on the whole I like him, and even find him attractive. I suppose if things were different I'd be one of the Hieronymus Merkin stable.[31]

Poor Widow Pearman[32] with a young lover: She'll have it coming to her. Do you remember Lyn Harding[33] is supposed to have said he was only happy after he became impotent? But I don't think ladies do. And I'm sure I never shall. So here's to unhappiness.

(Of course that is only deep down amongst the fantasies, whereas in actual fact I am happier than most people have been.)

At last something has happened in the 'Australian Theatre.' You probably haven't heard of an experimental Theatre called Jane Street where M. and I have suffered some evenings of hell in the past. The other night

---

[29]The ancient British actress (1876–1972) played Gertrude in 1910, the prince in 1938.
[30]*It's in the Bag*, some of the dialogue PW wrote for Rutherford reached Manchester, but all was dropped along with her before the show opened in London in Nov. 1937.
[31]Hieronymus Merkin=Miller.
[32]Coral Browne was the widow of the agent Philip Pearman.
[33](1867–1952), English stage and film actor, a famous Moriarty in many Sherlock Holmes films.

we went to an 'entertainment' rather than a play *The Legend of King O'Malley* based on the life of an American who came here before the First War and went into politics.[34] It was a tremendous success full of vitality and humour, though I'm afraid of no interest in other parts of the world.

20 MARTIN ROAD, 24.viii.70
TO NINETTE DUTTON

The Menuhin concerts were chaos after the booking plans had been lost in the fire. Fortunately we were able to get seats for the first concert through Desmond, who knows the management. But it was a free for all: the tickets were for the Town Hall (which couldn't be used because of the strike) and the numbering of rows at the Capitol didn't match. As we knew all this was going to happen, we arrived early and got ourselves excellent seats. Some of the critics didn't: they have been sulking ever since and writing that the orchestra[35] is an inferior one and that Menuhin's bowing has gone to pieces. To us it was a night of pure musical bliss. I'm glad you liked him. I've never gone out of my way to meet him because on the whole musicians only come out of themselves with other musicians. But to me there is no other performer like him: he looks as if he had a light inside him. On the way home I said I wondered if he had any vices; M. said of course everybody has. Later on I was looking at the programme and must say I was very shocked to see all the vulgar PR work he had put into it: even a photo of him displaying his KBE in its satin box.

20 MARTIN ROAD, 4.x.70
TO GEOFFREY DUTTON

The other night we gritted our teeth and went to see *Woodstock*,[36] which is a must, even if you don't sit through the whole thing (we didn't.) It would be a much better film if they pruned each pop performance by half and concentrated on the crowd. Even so, it is a phenomenon amongst films. Depressing, too: I came home with visions of Western civilisation drowned under a flood of human sludge such as invaded the idyllic Woodstock landscape.

THE VIVISECTOR FAILED IN North America: after quiet but sympathetic

---

[34]By Bob Ellis and Michael Boddy; several in the cast came to play a part in PW's life including the actresses Kate Fitzpatrick and Robyn Nevin, and a former architecture student Willy Young who became PW's favourite photographer William Yang.

[35]The Menuhin Festival Orchestra of London.

[36]The 1970 documentary of the American rock festival, by Michael Wadleigh with Joan Baez, Jimi Hendrix, Joe Cocker, etc.

notices in June, it sold only 4,000 copies. These figures were White's worst since *The Living and the Dead* appeared in New York in the early years of the war. But he had not lost Britain. The publication of *The Vivisector* in London in mid-October was regarded as a literary event and the novel quickly sold 12,000 copies. Another 10,000 were sold a few weeks later in Australia. The move to Cape was vindicated.

20 MARTIN ROAD, 1.xi.70
TO TOM MASCHLER
Dear Tom,

Thanks for your letter and the cuttings. No, you needn't censor reviews. In any case, I should be receiving them from a press cutting agency, so don't go to the trouble of sending any more. They have certainly been a varying lot, from Tom Rosenthal's overwhelming praise[37] to mayhem in the *T.L.S.*[38] I'm pretty sure that piece was written by Bob Hughes. Please try to find out. I have had my opinion of him for years, and probably it got back to him. Shan't say more till I know for certain.

Now I must try not to think any more about reviews: both the good and the bad are the best encouragement never to write another word.

Also, I hope you won't quote that bit you've underlined about the Nobel Prize. To get what wasn't given to Tolstoy, Henry James, Proust and Joyce would only be humiliating, and I hope it is never mentioned in my connexion again.

I went down to Melbourne one day last week for the *Portnoy* trial. It was an ordeal till I actually got in the box, then the actor in me quite enjoyed the performance. The whole thing has to be conducted with great solemnity, I realise, but I couldn't resist saying what a funny book I think *Portnoy* is: I hope I didn't put my foot in it.[39]

Yrs
Patrick

I enjoy reading John Berger's 'point of view'. He always struck me as being

---

[37]*New Statesman*, 23 Oct., p.536: '*The Vivisector* like a great painting, must be looked at again and again, to be allowed to create its reverberations. White will find it difficult to do anything better than this haunting, obsessed and magnificent novel.'

[38]Under the headline 'Painter and Decorator', 23 Oct., p.1213: 'As a painter, Hurtle Duffield is a writer's fantasy – *this* writer's fantasy ... In the end he goes down in a flurry of language which may have been inspired by *Finnegans Wake* but which unfortunately recalls *A Spaniard in the Works*. It is an appropriate end for a hero whose whole existence was in language.'

[39]The book was convicted, confiscated and the publishers fined $100, but to suppress the book effectively there had also to be a conviction in NSW.

the most tortuously cerebral art critic, and I thought I might get him for *The Vivisector*. Didn't he too, write a novel about a painter?[40]

20 MARTIN ROAD, 29.xi.70
TO PETER BEATSON
Dear Peter,
Thanks for your letter with the most hair-raising and illuminating account of a trip I have read so far. Awful though it must be, I am tempted, yet I'm sure I know all about it from my dreams and most despairing moments. So I don't think the temptation will be a lasting one: I have too much to cope with without that.

Since you left[41] we've done nothing of very great interest. We've made one expedition to the country, very depressing, to see some old people I've known all my life, and who won't last much longer. On the way we passed through Castle Hill (Sarsaparilla), and stopped outside our old house long enough to steal some cuttings of winter buddleia.[42] The garden is now a jungle, quite awe-inspiring to see trees we planted as threads twenty-four years ago, but from the brief glimpse I got of the house I didn't want to look any more: it is tumbling down.

I suppose Mount Wilson, our goal that day, is beautiful; I used to think it the most wonderful place in the world, but by now it is so overgrown and dank the sun can hardly penetrate. We went first to see some old servants of cousins of mine, now dead. Flo and Matt are in their eighties. He is so crippled with arthritis he can only crawl about with sticks attached to his arms. She has something wrong with one of her legs: it is blown up into a balloon, but she hobbles about, manages to clean the house, and is still a Good Plain Cook. In their youth he was a footman she a housemaid at what was then Dorchester House. When I used to be sent to Mt Wilson to stay with my cousins as a child, they were the ones

---

[40]Berger admired *The Vivisector*'s energy and imaginative power, *Times*, 22 Oct., p.8, but quarrelled with PW's 'romantic decadent' view that the artist, 'challenging good and evil, must be a moral type unto himself. In extreme, it is the view of the artist as Lucifer.' Berger's Duffield, in his 1958 novel *A Painter of Our Time*, was Janos Lavin, a Hungarian who comes to London in 1938 and disappears on the brink of success in 1956.
[41]Beatson had stayed at Martin Road for a few days earlier in the month.
[42]Buddleia taken the previous year apparently failed. PW wrote to Cynthia Nolan, 27.iv.69: 'I felt sick going up to our front door to ask permission . . . a little slut in a pale blue dressing gown came out when I knocked. I can imagine what it would be like inside, or rather I *know*, because I had a dream recently in which the outside looked exactly as it is now; I'm sure the interior would have tallied with the dream.'

I used to spend my time with. They were full of stories of London High Life (how Lord Louis went out leaving the front door ajar and a candelabra burning on the doorstep) and regularly got the *News of the World* which taught me all about the sordid side of life at a very early age. These people are still very jolly in spite of everything, and in a way I always enjoy seeing them: we laugh at the same things (rather black English as opposed to sunny Australian).

After that we went on to my old nurse, and her husband, a sawmiller formerly, who was always a great source of bush lore. When I was a boy I explored all the mountain gullies with Sid, and was shown a lot of fantastic things and told a lot of fantastic stories. Nurse came from Carnoustie, Scotland, when she was sixteen, and was with us for ten years, only leaving when I was sent to school in England. I was really far fonder of her than I was of my mother. Now Sid and Lizzie are both in their eighties. He still has his wits about him to some extent, but she doesn't know what she is doing and saying half the time; she kept telling Manoly and me how we had grown since she saw us last (a year ago). She and her house used to be spotless, but now there are little heaps of dust she has forgotten to sweep away, and she is rather grimy, and done up with safety pins instead of the cairngorm brooch I remember. I expect she will go before long: she is as frail as a deformed sparrow. At least I hope she will die before her husband who can still look after her, and who has several younger brothers and sisters-in-law on the mountain who will be able to look after him. I am haunted by a wooden worm-eaten trunk, now in the dunny, which came with the scottish lassie to Australia in the beginning. I'd like to have it, but don't know how to ask.[43]

I've got as far as the last two chapters of the novel I'm writing. This seems to me the most difficult book I have attempted but I expect they have all been difficult at the time: I am closest to *The Vivisector* and I know that gave me hell. I think one expects ease as time goes on, and that is something that never happens: everything becomes more gnarled and inward-looking.

20 MARTIN ROAD, 27.xii.70

TO THE DUTTONS

A few days ago Barry Humphries suddenly came up on the telephone (it turned out he had got my silent number from that strumpet at the British Council!) He was in Sydney, and in a state, after blotting his copybook in several places. *The Age* had given him the sack after he had written a

---

[43]The chest was given to him after her death; it is now in the Mitchell Library.

column sending up the rich Melbourne Jews who celebrate Christmas. He had then rushed (perhaps even escaped) from his hospital in Melbourne[44] to come to Sydney and ask Harry Miller to take him on. Harry had given him an appointment at the office, but before this was due, Barry had burst into Harry's flat in Harry's absence and insulted the housekeeper by saying rude things about the paintings and furniture. According to Barry he was confused by his first day of freedom after a year of hospital. According to the house keeper, he was drunk. Next day he rang up the secretary and insulted her too, according to Harry; amongst other things he said: 'I'm trying to get in touch with a friend who's become an acquaintance: a Christian writer called Patrick White.' Barry's call to me was to see whether I would try to make the peace with Harry M. We had Barry out here to lunch. He arrived an hour late, after two more telephone calls announcing himself, and a taxi driver at our door to ask whether I still expected to see Barry Humphries. Barry, in a grazier's hat and monocle, was looking rather strange. He says he has been 'weaned off one or two toxic breasts' but I felt he must have got on to at least one of them again on his way to Martin Road. I'd be most interested to see his medical report. He still has flashes of great brilliance, but moments of despair, one feels. Very difficult to assess. He is such an actor one can't decide when the acting has stopped. I spoke to Harry Miller on the phone, and he agreed to talk to Barry. Whether he did, I don't know, and I didn't feel strong enough to ring Barry and ask. He was staying at the Gazebo, in spite of being on the rocks financially, and was planning a party for the following night, to which so far he had invited Sculthorpe, Peter Coleman,[45] and Peter Scriven.[46] He said: 'I suppose you wouldn't care to come?' I didn't feel I wanted to. Nor do I like to think what must have happened to Barry when faced with the toxic tits . . .

I haven't attempted to work the last couple of weeks: all those cards to write, and parcels to do up; but I have been reading back, to become re-acquainted with my chief character before killing her off. Parts are very good, others as raw as could be. The main thing is to get it all down before we go away in time, I hope, to pay a visit to Adelaide first.

Be very discreet if you mention any of the happenings in this letter, and I think it would be better if you destroy the letter itself. In fact, I'm starting to ask all my friends to destroy all my letters. On the whole I think it's a good thing most people don't write letters any more.

[44]Where he had been drying out for some months.
[45](1928–), co-editor of *Quadrant* and fledgling conservative politician.
[46](1931–), puppeteer who created *The Tintookies*.

The most indiscreet titbit of all (<u>and this you must mention to nobody</u>) is that I was asked to ring Canberra the day of Barry's visit, and had another alarm. I was told Our Lovely Queen would like to make me a Knight Bachelor. You can imagine my reply. I had only to remember the collection of Knights at the Caseys' farewell – or myself sweating and farting half my life over the stove and at the sink.

Yrs,

Patrick.

20 MARTIN ROAD, 3.i.71

TO THE NOLANS

Dear Cynthia and Sid,

The night you rang was rather a hectic one and no doubt you thought I sounded vague. We were having a dinner for Manning Clark, arranged weeks ahead, and which became a snowball over the weeks till we were finally ten at table. Both Manning and David Campbell became exceedingly amorous, David embarrassingly so at one stage with the wife of a senator (the husband sitting at the other end at dinner).[47] Manning kept asking Kylie[48] if she was promiscuous, and as he tried to pull her on to his lap in the middle of the meal I heard him tell her she reminded him of his father. The Canberrans certainly behaved like canecutters from the north, as Manoly said afterwards, but you would have to do something to make up for an existence in Canberra.

In spite of a certain amount of junketing we have had a very quiet Christmas and New Year. We didn't have the usual party for the New Year as I am fairly close to the end of the first version of my novel and I must make sure of finishing that before we leave in April (if we do). What I should really like is to finish it by Australia Day, because it was on last Australia Day that I began.

We went out to Margo Lewers' one night just after Christmas after staving off invitations to that dreadful drive for I don't know how long.[49] It was all right getting there on this occasion, but on the way back the

[47]Senator Jim McClelland (1915–   ) and his wife Freda through whom PW met the leadership of the Labor Party.

[48]Tennant.

[49]PW thought Margo Lewers (1908–78) a conceited but rather poor painter. Yet before the death of her husband the sculptor Gerald (1905–62), PW loved their house at the foot of the Blue Mountains, their company and their parties: 'Ideas hurtled, argument flared, voices shouted, sparks flew,' he wrote in Gerald's obituary, SMH, 18 Aug. 1962, p.12. 'As I see it, the house on the Nepean . . . provided one of the focus points of our still tentative civilisation.' The house is now the Lewers' Gallery.

rain came down in sheets, there were waves hitting the windscreen, and every so often crumpled cars, sometimes with ambulances in attendance. Nor was the party much fun somehow: too many of those Lewers acolytes (I don't know why Margo's friends nearly all turn into acolytes). One . . . particularly puts me off . . . The other night she was dyed a black black, and wearing black pyjamas and a bloody mouth, and looked as though somebody had hit her on the head with a hammer her neck has gone. I just couldn't make myself known. Tony Tuckson is now one of the sights, in hair and gear, looking less a swinger than a mad gaffer.[50] But for once he streamed conversation; it was all released apparently because he had read *The Vivisector*.

According to the press this has been the best-selling novel of the year, and some shops have been charging as much as two dollars above the published price and getting away with it. So I suppose I am in, but one wonders how desirable that is. At the same time people like Madame du Boisée are hissing about 'obscenity' in Double Bay.[51] I always thought that woman was a pretentious idiot. Last time we met her she had drawn green lines on her eyelids and was grooving with Ginsberg,[52] under the influence of Anne Wienholt who was here on a visit from California.[53] I am now waiting for old du Boisée with a trump card in the shape of a letter from a Mother Veronica Brady of St Mary's College Melbourne who has read and admires *The Vivisector*.[54]

I have some more information on Clive James[55] from Barry Humphries: '– –his hero is Scott Fitzgerald. He has copies of everything by Fitzgerald as originally published in *Esquire* (he got them at Tyrrell's Bookshop for a price he names proudly). He is vicariously interested in the careers of recently dead writers who lived romantic disappointed lives and I would have thought he was predisposed to envy. Despite his unctuousness I didn't care for him a scrap and felt that I was being introduced to him so that I could be summed up and dismissed from his crowded scholar's mind. He produces expressionist plays in Cambridge for bored adulatory students. He invited me to an evening rehearsal and I arrived a bit pissed and thought

[50](1921–73), abstract expressionist whose superb work was hardly known at this time.
[51]Mother of PW's friend Andrée Rapotec.
[52]Allen Ginsberg (1926–), beat poet.
[53]Wienholt (1920–) of Larkspur, California, Australian printer, painter and sculptor.
[54]Brady (1929–), radical critic and Loreto nun, had studied PW's writing in Toronto and returned to Australia a devoted interpreter of PW's work.
[55]PW had discovered that James, not Hughes, was the author of the attack in the *TLS*. PW told Maschler, 8.i.71: 'I'm glad I found out: I might have been rude to the wrong one.'

someone else was him, so I suppose it's my turn in the barrel next.' I don't think one need know any more. I must say it is a little galling to be dismissed by somebody whose hero is Scott Fitzgerald, but perhaps that is something one should expect from an Australian who is also the Perennial Undergraduate.

We have been told of a possible houseminder, and I must chase after her as soon as life has settled down again to being normal. In any case I am going to buy the tickets this week to leave for the States on April 17th, whether we go or not. I wish I were one of those people who are content to spend their life in one place; it isn't so much the places I want to see again, but the people, and at the same time I know that all the time we are away I shall want to get back to my book.

I'm afraid Noti Polymeropoulos, Manoly's nephew, will have left the States by the time we arrive.[56] He will be either in Germany or Sweden. In his last letter he then makes the mysterious remark: 'who knows, we may meet in Australia.' I must say I think it would be far better for him to cut loose from the U.S. before he is any older and come out here. You must give us Jinx's latest address so that we can get in touch when we are in New York.

Love to both,
Patrick.

20 MARTIN ROAD, 17.i.71
TO JOHN McGRATH[57]
Dear John,
Of course I should have answered your letter while it was still hot but various things got in the way. Now I don't know where to begin.

Harry Miller got back before Christmas full of plans for meeting, but I still haven't seen him, perhaps because one of my friends who wanted work from Harry insulted him. I tried to bring them together again; now I hear from neither. Harry did tell me on the telephone that you had finished the screenplay, but that it had to be shortened and he didn't want

[56] PW for a time nurtured a plan to make a match between Notis and Cynthia Nolan's daughter Jinx.
[57] (1935–), dramatist and director who wrote *Events While Guarding the Bofors Gun*, 1966, etc., and collaborated with Ken Russell on film and television projects including *Billion Dollar Brain*, 1967. McGrath believed *Voss* 'one of the greatest novels' and persuaded Russell to tackle the film. In mid–1970 he had arrived in Australia to explore desert and city locations. 'I like him immensely,' PW told Waters, 2.viii.70. 'He seems both professional and sensitive, and I'm sure from one or two things he has said that he will produce something good for the script.'

to show me the longer version in case I took a fancy to that. You made Ken Russell sound difficult in your letter.[58] Harry M. may have found him difficult too, and that may be Harry's reason for not wanting to see me. Certainly I feel Russell is undertaking more than he can manage if he is going to produce an opera at the end of 1972, with films of *The Boy Friend, Under the Volcano* and *Voss* in between. At least that is what I read in the paper, and of course half of it probably isn't true[59] . . .

I still think Russell is probably the only director who could attempt *Voss*, though we went to *The Virgin and the Gypsy*[60] a few days ago and thought that a better film than *Women in Love*. It must be easier to adapt a short story or novella than it is to make a novel into a film: you can pad the short story convincingly if it offers visual possibilities, whereas it is difficult to leave out bits of the novel. Anyway, *The Virgin and the Gypsy* appealed to me immensely. The gypsy himself wasn't much more than beefcake, but he glowered and made his body hair bristle, and I suppose that is what was required. Almost everyone else was excellent: that girl!

20 MARTIN ROAD, 1.ii.71

TO GEOFFREY DUTTON

You amaze me the way you rush from one holiday to the next with hardly a breathing space between. This would be none of my business if your every other letter didn't come up with the cry of poverty and what-will-become-of-Anlaby-and-the-children? I should have thought if you dug yourself in at Anlaby for two or three years you might improve the situation. When the pre-Revolution Russians were hard up they returned to their estates. Certainly they drove themselves mad with boredom in most cases, but you, like Pushkin have your 'embroidery.' Because Manoly and I are fond of you all, and wonder what will become of you, I felt I had to make these remarks.

Last week I finished my book (first version). It has taken almost exactly a year. I began last year to fill the awful void of the Australia Day holidays, and here we are in them again, with no novel to protect me. Now I'm going to make the MS. into a parcel which I shan't open till we get back from Europe.

---

[58]Relations between McGrath and Russell had soured after McGrath refused to write *The Devils*.

[59]Russell filmed only *The Boy Friend*; Peter Maxwell Davies' opera *Taverner* was directed by Michael Geliot, and John Huston made *Under the Volcano*, 1984.

[60]1970, from Lawrence's story, directed by Christopher Miles, with Franco Nero and Honor Blackman.

May I now pay the visit we've talked about? I want to go to the Proms, which take place in the earlier part of this month, so would it be all right if I come say February 25th till March 2nd when I shall leave for Melbourne, and do the same sort of thing with the Sumners? If that isn't convenient perhaps I could do it the other way round, though I haven't approached the Sumners yet.

This week I am supposed to be appearing again in support of *Portnoy* (the A & R case).[61] I find the whole business rather boring by now, but thought I'd better agree to do it as I've been so consistent in refusing A & R everything they want. I'm told Thea Astley has been trying to work everything to appear as a witness. She burst into the QC's office and told them about some schoolgirls which set fire to another girl's pubics. I was tempted to mention that an A & R director once set fire to his own pubics at a party.

20 MARTIN ROAD, 21.ii.71
TO ELIZABETH HARROWER
Dear Elizabeth,
I'm sending *The Glass Bead Game*.[62] I hope it's all right. Sometimes those things that Central Europeans go into a hush about are not for us e.g. *The Death of Virgil*.[63]

Halfway through *Nostromo* I became carried away by it. It's a stupendous narrative; I'm only disappointed in some of the characterisation, and for a long time I couldn't submit to the operatic tone. (One could hear the screams of anguish against the strings in that last part where the Viola girls fight over Nostromo and Papa Viola shoots him by mistake: I'm not surprised somebody tried to turn *Victory* – which I haven't yet read – into an opera.) Nostromo is not so much a man as a moral conflict; and the Goulds and Decoud are more ideas than characters; as for Antonia, who seemed at one stage to kindle, she needn't have been there. I think a number of novelists writing at that period got their characters into a fuzz of moral conflict and lost them there (not only Conrad, but Henry James and E. M. Forster); it's something the Russians and the French managed to avoid; their characters remain flesh and blood. Still, *Nostromo* is a wonderful novel of its kind: it got me panting and breathless at times with admiration and delight . . .

[61]After Melbourne there were two trials in Sydney both ending in a hung jury. *Portnoy* was then released for sale.
[62]Hermann Hesse, *Das Glasperlenspiel*, 1943, trans. 1949.
[63]Hermann Broch, *Der Tod des Vergil*, 1945, trans. by Jean Starr Untermeyer, 1946.

I hope your telephone will soon be on: life is no longer Edwardian enough for correspondence.

Yrs

Patrick.

20 MARTIN ROAD, 31.iii.71

TO JULIET O'HEA

Our departure is hurtling towards us and, as always, I begin to regret it: autumn is the best season in Sydney, and then I think of all those lovely winter dishes one can eat in the fug of one's own kitchen. But we leave for the States, willy-nilly on April 17.

SAN FRANCISCO, 18.iv.71

CARD TO THE MOORES

Thanks for taking us to the airport. We had a very comfortable flight: only about eleven passengers in economy most of the way so we could stretch out. S.F. 54° when we arrived which was a bit of a shock, but nice and sunny. We have slept, and gorged on fish, and today we are going to the redwood forests. Clothes shockingly expensive compared with Sydney. Beggars in the streets and whores at the corners.

Love,

P.

ST PETERSBURG, FLORIDA 25.iv.71

TO THE DUTTONS

Dear Geoffrey and Nin,

We are approaching the end of our Florida session, which should make me feel more cheerful than I do. This time the U.S., in spite of a day spent watching the Grand Canyon, and some pleasant moments and meals in San Francisco, feels incredibly dead. Nowhere does one see a soul who might share one's thoughts and opinions: just a lot of turnips. I can see why my books don't sell in the States: what is surprising is that any book should sell.

St Petersburg is less ugly than Fort Lauderdale, our usual fate, but it is also far more dead: one seldom sets eyes on anybody under sixty. However, yesterday, we discovered an oasis called Tarpon Springs, a Greek sponge-fishing community on the Gulf, and that was a pleasant interlude. We drove there with the children of Manoly's Italian cousins – the father is now Ambassador to Eire,[64] and we shall be staying with them when we go to Dublin. The son and daughter in-law, Fabrizio and Federicka, are here because the boy is taking some vague course in International Business at a Florida university. That makes them sound unpromising but you would like them if you met them, and perhaps you will: they have announced they are coming to visit us in Australia and to drive across the Nullarbor Plain. (They are rather given to desert drives, and once got as far as the Monastery of St Catherine on Sinai.)

Anna, M.'s sister has come over from Fort Lauderdale, and is drooling away in her particular brand of American which we find so difficult to understand. M. has a daily session with his Mom, who is still very lively (in her eighties) but as unreal as ever. The family by her second husband has removed itself for our visit, which is just as well.

So far the Grand Canyon has been the high-light. I forget whether you have been there. Tourists can't detract from it. It was fearfully cold while we were there (some of the people claimed to have seen snowflakes falling) and the light not at its best, but there were occasional breaks in the grey to ring the colour changes. There was also a fair variety of birds, including a fairly large, intensely blue one, and grey squirrels and chipmunks which would scuttle up the cliff-side and accept bread.

To get to Tampa, the airport for St Petersburg, we flew in four different planes, and had to spend a night at Phoenix, an unsympathetic city if ever there was one. In the course of all these manoeuvres we were stranded for four hours in Las Vegas, for which I am glad, in a way: You can't believe what you are seeing in the gambling saloons – all those zombies pulling automatically at the pokies, or heaped round the roulette wheels and baccarat tables in a fiendish artificial light at 11 a.m. and an even more fiendishly stale air.

This morning in the paper I read an article 'The Americanization of Australia.' We certainly have few of the similarities the article claims, but I feel now the danger is something we must fight against before anything else: the worst possible kind of pollution.

I forget whether I gave you our safe addresses: c/o Viking Press, 625 Madison Ave, N.Y. 10022 from now till May 20th, Bank of N.S.W. Sackville St W.1 May 20th till July 1st.

I'm preparing for the meetings with John McGrath and Ken Russell by re-reading *Voss* for the first time since I wrote it. It stands up well as a whole, though I should like to alter much of the punctuation and many a

---

[64]Goffredo Biondi Morra.

phrase. If K.R. will only convey it as it is I am sure it will be a success as a film: it is visual all the way.

Have also read another novel by the superb Kawabata,[65] called *The Sound of the Mountain*. Discovering the Japanese novelists in my old age is as exciting as discovering the Russians in my youth. I must see about cornering a lot more of the Tuttle Titles[66] when we get to New York – which will be the day after to-morrow, thank God. At least we know one or two people there who speak the same language, and I am looking forward to some mail.

Hope there have been no more dramas, and that the trip to Brisbane was a success.

Love from us both,
Patrick.

NEW YORK, 29.iv.71
TO JOHN McGRATH
Looking forward to seeing you again and to reading the script but I must say the prospect of meeting Russell alarms me somewhat: it isn't that he makes me nervous, but we may not agree over some of the essentials. Perhaps I should throw the fit you suggest: I can stage a pretty good one if necessary.

NEW YORK, 12.v.71
TO GEOFFREY DUTTON
I think all foreigners should be driven around this wonderful country, otherwise they tend to believe it consists only of New York and Washington. Mary McCarthy is sitting in Paris saying: 'Nature is dead' when there is plenty of evidence that it is alive and kicking if she would emerge from her own skull, but of course if she came back here she would bring that with her and probably camp down in a room in New York.[67]

The Adirondacks were looking fantastic this retarded spring: just a faint green here and there amongst the conifers, which allows those mauve-grey tones to show through. This is the moment I like best in deciduous country, when there is still an austerity of winter before that rather monotonous green takes over. Everybody has been lamenting the lateness

[65]Kawabata Yasunari (1899–1972) had won the Nobel Prize in 1968.
[66]Charles E. Tuttle Co., Inc. of Vermont and Tokyo, publishers in English of Japanese novelists.
[67]McCarthy (1912–89), who divided her time between Paris and Maine, declared nature dead in her novel *Birds of America* published at this time.

of the season for us, and it is useless trying to explain it is what one likes: they think we are being polite.

New York was looking staggeringly squalid when we returned, yet I can't say we ever feel frightened as you and so many other Australians claim to be when walking through the streets: it only makes us feel depressed; or perhaps in my case, I might feel frightened if I weren't protected by a certain *nostalgie de la boue*.[68]

18.v.71 I left off there to go to dinner with the Hambros.[69] He is Norwegian Ambassador to the U.N. and came to see me in Australia. They have an apartment overlooking the river in Gracie Square, and we spent a very pleasant family evening. Mrs H. is the daughter of Gwen Raverat.[70] She started off last night with quite a broken accent but would not have been recognised for anything but English as time wore on. Manoly said afterwards how easy it is to understand when everybody present is speaking English as opposed to American: some of the American sounds are so extraordinary one tends to close down on meanings, while wondering how they manage to achieve those distortions.

Today we are lunching with Maie Casey, and tomorrow, our last night, dining with Zoe and Robert Whitehead. I had had no reply to a letter and a message all this time, then suddenly they came to light yesterday after returning from the Bahamas. It would have been a great disappointment to have missed Zoe. Now we shall hear all.

Our final attempt at chasing satisfying theatre in New York ended in disaster at a production of The Long Day's Journey into Night, which is said to be the highlight of the season.[71] I don't know whether inferior acting made the play seem so bad, or whether such a lumbering bore of a play made the acting appear more mediocre than it was. Anyway, it was an intolerable evening as the characters repeated themselves over and over, and in the awful, superfluous last act started disgorging slabs of poetry. To me Albee is an infinitely superior playwright to O'Neill.

LONDON SEEMED CLEANER AND its people more cheerful now, but White wondered if this only seemed so in contrast with the squalor of New York. They took a room in the Basil Street Hotel and fell quickly into their usual rhythm: meeting friends, exploring the West End, making

---

[68]Longing for dirt.
[69]Edvard Hambro (1911–77), jurist and conservative politician.
[70](1885–1957), wood engraver, book illustrator and author.
[71]Directed by Arvin Brown at the Promenade Theatre with Robert Ryan, Geraldine Fitzgerald, Stacy Keach, James Naughton and Paddy Croft.

short trips into the country and complaining, as always, about London prices. White wrote to David Moore, 'Here our great find is a buffet at this hotel where you can eat till you burst for 52p.!'[72]

PARIS, 4.vii.71
TO THE DUTTONS
We had a most hectic six weeks in London which we hardly left during that time. We should have allowed longer, for we weren't able to get to the Orkneys as half-planned, or into Scotland at all. Apart from day trips to Oxford to my cousin Peggy Garland, and to Frances at her school near Newbury,[73] we only managed a week-end outside Dublin with Manoly's cousins the Biondi Morra. Ireland was as deadly as the time before, but we like the cousins, and the Italian Embassy is a beautifully restored 18th century house which was an experience in itself. There was also one of the inevitable Biondi Morra domestic crises: their Spanish maid who has been with them twenty years went off into hysterics and locked herself in her room most of the time we were there, out of jealousy over the Egyptian suffragi, who has been with them only ten years. The Egyptian, a normally dignified old man, spent most of our visit in tears. There is also an Egyptian cook, a cousin of the suffragis. I think it won't be long before this exotic situation must come apart, as the Egyptians are afraid to venture out of the house into the grisly Irish drizzle.

Talking of Egyptians we lunched with the Charles Johnstons[74] in London, and in addition to the Princess Bagratian had Princess Aly Khan[75] and Diana Duff Cooper![76] The latter still has a very blue stare, but by now is rather crippled and wafty: she told us a long and tangled story about a pair of gorillas having sex in a private zoo for the entertainment of a number of Bright Old Things.

I went down to Portsmouth one evening with John McGrath and we had dinner with Ken Russell and discussed the film. Russell was affable enough, but I don't think we shall ever agree over who should play the leading parts. It makes one feel that other people are completely incapable of visualising characters as the author saw them in the beginning. Russell

[72]23.v.71.
[73]Frances Peck had been sent to boarding school: Downe House.
[74]Charles Johnston (1912–86), diplomat, poet and translator, was just back from his last post as High Commissioner to Australia with his wife Natasha, Princess Bagratian – 'She is rather bizarre at first,' PW told Frances Peck, 3.xi.74, 'but nice.'
[75]Née Joan Barbara Yarde-Buller (1908–), mother of the Aga Khan and about to become, by her third marriage, Viscountess Camrose.
[76]Diana Cooper (1892–1986), hostess and legendary beauty, relict of Duff Cooper.

talks about coming to Australia after Christmas, wandering round for a bit, returning to direct the Peter Maxwell Davies opera at Covent Garden, then back to Australia to start shooting Voss in late July. (Please don't mention any of this, least of all to Max, as it would probably emerge completely distorted in the press.)

We saw quite a lot of the Nolans, going to plays and concerts together, and lunching on one of our few summer days in London at their house beside the river. I was amazed at the poems in the *Paradise Gardens* book, and not surprised at that bucket of slow vomit they brought forth from Max in *The Australian*[77] ...

Theatre in Paris is pathetic after London ...

We have also been to a magnificent exhibition of Rouault, and a display of Proustiana,[78] the latter strangely irritating, I think because all that *beau monde* which inspired his great book was essentially such trash. The portraits of them in the exhibition show them up in all their tastelessness and uselessness. But the Bed was most extraordinary: still full of life. I'm surprised at your attitude to Bonnard. Perhaps they haven't sent any of his important paintings to Australia. One certainly couldn't call him second-rate, though he has been cheapened, I admit, by the second-rate painters who have pinched ideas from him ...

Our house has been burgled, and we are not at all happy about the house-minders. Please no mention of that either, in case it gets blown up!

Love to everybody,
Patrick.

LASCARIS HAD BROKEN OUT in a rash which was diagnosed in Paris as diabetes. 'I suppose we shall get used to this new situation in time,' White told Graham C. Greene, 'But it is a strain to travel through Europe on a diet.'[79] Nevertheless they spent a happy fortnight exploring the Dordogne by taxi and then set out for Spain and Sicily. From the time they caught the train for Barcelona everything went wrong.

---

[77]*Paradise Gardens*, a book of poems and paintings by Nolan, published by his patron Alistair McAlpine, 1971; Max Harris' review, 22 May, p.18, began with gentle reminiscences of Sid and ended in damning judgment: 'This is art writing at its pretentious irrelevant worst, and would indeed win any parody competition anywhere.'
[78]'Centenaire de Rouault' at the Musée d'Art Moderne; 'En Son Temps', a display of Proustiana at the Musée Jacquemart-André.
[79]12.vii.71.

ROME, 11.viii.71

TO THE DUTTONS

I can only think somebody has put the Eye on us in spite of the fact that we are laden with holy medals to take to our Maltese ironing woman, and even splinters from Santa Teresa's staircase given us by a little nun in Salamanca.

ATHENS, 24.viii.71

TO ELIZABETH HARROWER

Apart from the Dordogne everywhere we have been was far too full. It looks to me as though the days of European travel are over: the human cattle trample all pleasure out of it.

At least in Madrid we put up at an excellent hotel, and some of the paintings we saw made the visit to Spain worthwhile. Now I have seen the Goyas; Toledo was so packed and sweltering I only really enjoyed the *Burial of Conde Orgas*, which we saw finally by pushing and craning. Then there was the architecture of Salamanca, a memory spoilt by a dreadful hotel, in which we looked out on a well full of fluff, grey dust, and cellophane. We escaped from there a day earlier, and went to Avila which melted us somewhat: it's the only place we saw in Spain which has charm as well as beauty.

Everywhere the food was dreary; they really only have three dishes: gazpacho (I think, I can make better than we got), paella (nowhere as good as one we ate at St Ives,[80] cooked in the garden by a Redfern Spaniard) and their rather heavy potato omelette. Otherwise chunks of toro or vaca, all very tough.

It was the meat which upset one of my key teeth, with the result that it was in full throb and my face ballooning by the time we reached Palermo. I think I must have cracked that aged tooth and the nerve proceeded to die. This made Palermo even more depressing than it would have been normally, with its plastic bags strewn along the waterfront, its stench of rotting mussels, bunches of intestines dripping from hooks outside doorways as the flies swarmed, and the inhabitants – almost everyone of them a Sicilian bandit.

But here again there were architectural splendours, like the Duomo and Cloister at Monreale, the Martorana church in Palermo itself, and the perfect little chapel in the Norman Palace. So I shouldn't complain too much about toothache and intestines.

And there was the drive through a magnificent landscape to Agrigento.

[80]Sydney suburbs: St Ives leafy, Redfern shabby.

Why I wonder, is the Sicilian landscape so full of interest and the Spanish so monotonous when they are both hot, dusty, and physically not unalike? I think perhaps it is the industry and skill of the Sicilian farmers which adds variety to theirs: each of their haystacks is a work of art, and there is something happening all the time, stubble burning, sheep and cattle grazing at dusk on shabby velvet.

We used my tooth as an excuse to escape a week early to Rome. I don't expect we shall go back to Sicily, and I shall always regret not having seen Erice, Taormina and Segesta sans toothache as originally intended.

We had a peaceful fortnight in Rome which we know so well we don't feel guilty about not embarking on a round of rigid sightseeing. We spent our time dropping into many cool and seductive churches, and confirmed that St Peters is just about the most vulgar important building on earth: it wouldn't look out of place in Manly. On the other hand, Santa Maria in Cosmedin, where we went to a Byzantine mass for the Assumption of the Virgin, and my favourite Santa Maria Sopra Minerva, next door to the hotel where we stay, could almost bring me over to Rome.

My cousin Eleanor Arrighi lives in Rome and that always adds to the pleasure of being there. She is the mother of Luciana, and the younger daughter Niké is also very attractive and talented: she's had small parts in several films, toured with an operetta (leading role) through Italy, and is now concentrating on her singing and drawing. I feel that all her various talents will somehow eventually coalesce, if she doesn't marry or else go quite haywire. She is about to be taken to court on a charge of obscenity having danced naked except for a coating of blue, in the opera house at Genoa.[81]

We slipped back into life in Athens with the greatest ease, in the rooftop flat M.'s sister Elly always lets us have. Good to make one's own tea and coffee again, and wash and dry one's smalls in comfort. Elly's husband Elias, a very good doctor, who has read the Paris specialist's report, says that M. can have only a very mild diabetes so he can now eat a few potatoes and have a drink before dinner. Tomorrow he is going for another sugar test.

When we have got over the first round of reunions, I hope we shall make for the northern frontiers and escape from the last of the heat, then back for another spell in Athens and some island-hopping.

[81] In Brecht's *Seven Deadly Sins*.

ATHENS, 8.ix.71

TO LUCIANA ARRIGHI

You should see Métsovo in the Pindos: that is one of my favourite places on earth. It's like one long opera. At five o'clock the men's chorus, all in black, starts taking up positions round the plane tree in the *plateia*. Mule trains begin to trickle across. Then the women stride down, a lot of them still in costume, though some have begun to expose their thighs. On our last night there was a procession of children carrying wedding presents from a bride's house to the groom's, accompanied by violin, clarinet, accordion, and drums. All very innocent. The milkwoman sits knitting beside her donkey in the morning, waiting for customers to wake and buy.

SANTORÍNI-PIRAEUS, 24.ix.71

TO GEOFFREY DUTTON

Dear Geoffrey,

Having just got soaked to the skin by an Aegean wave, it seems an appropriate moment to write to you. Your last was from K.I.[82] and full of sea matters. Sorry about the stingray, but if the doctor and his wife are good value it paid off.

Very rough this morning, but it's something to have got away from Santoríni at all. The boat we should have caught yesterday didn't leave Piraeus because of the weather, and this one was held up for a couple of days in Crete. This morning we were warned at 1 to be ready by 4 so we didn't have much of a night. We clambered down the famous staircase of 750 steps with a donkey carrying our baggage and were well on time (perhaps only enough for half *War and Peace*.) The wretched boat arrived at 6. One should be used to this kind of thing on Greek islands, but it never fails to irritate me, and I have vowed that this will be my last bout of island-hopping.

Santoríni we found most overrated and depressing. Since the earthquake a few years ago a lot of the houses haven't been re-built, in fact today there are more ruins than houses. But the view as one approaches is stupendous: one sails into what is almost a lake, the two 'Burnt Ones' in the middle (both thrown up by volcanic eruption), and the razorback of the main island, with its white villages apparently in the sky. After this, and the scramble up the *scala* on mule back, all is anti-climax. It's one of the most arid islands, growing little more than tomatoes and grapes, and supporting scarcely a sheep or goat. Unless one likes lying about on a beach, there is nothing to do and little to see: a few nice things in the

[82]Kangaroo Island.

museum, but all the most interesting finds have been taken to Athens. So I left Santoríni with no regrets.

On the way we spent some time on Páros, which I found most appealing, and Náxos, a no-hope town, but with the most magnificent scenery I have seen on any of the islands, and a lot of the soil apparently very fertile.

Our travels are rapidly petering out and we are both looking forward to getting back under our own roof; I shall be particularly glad to start cooking again, as we've had dismal eating experiences in Greece.

Earlier on we did a trip through the North starting at Salónika and finishing up at Iamina: lots of magnificence in the way of landscape, but most of the towns gave us the Balkan blues, particularly at dusk, as we sat, usually on a terrace, before a panorama almost totally obscured by black mist. Nor did the usual diarrhoea exactly improve one's frame of mind. At least Métsovo is as sympathetic as on our first visit some years ago. Its precarious position on a mountainside will prevent its being too easily spoilt, and besides that, the rich and powerful Averoff family keep good watch over the village from which they came.

Now when we get back to Athens there won't be much time for more than farewells, though I hope we shall be able to squeeze in a few days on Pélion, another of my favourite places. We leave for Sydney on October 15th.

This is rather a miserable letter – too much rolling and too many draughts – but the best I can do.

Love to everybody from us both,
Patrick.

ATHENS, 10.x.71

TO JOHN McGRATH

I haven't heard a word from Harry M.M., but it isn't surprising after the argument we had (through agents) about whether he should pay for renewing the option or get the option free. He climbed down in the end.

Still haven't seen *The Music Lovers*[83] and *The Devils* and probably shan't either. Somehow I think Ken Russell will feel in the end that *Voss* is too much off the track he has chosen. Certainly if I were choosing a director for *Voss* today, K.R. would not occur to me. Or perhaps he may

[83]Russell's 1970 film with Richard Chamberlain as Tchaikovsky.

suddenly decide he ought to alter direction and develop the country which lies between the earlier telly films and *Voss*[84] ...

I tell myself I shan't think about this film anymore, and on the whole I don't. Since we came to Greece I have been too busy getting down the first version of a novella which popped up out of our visit to Sicily.[85] Together with some other things I have, both published and unpublished, it will probably give me enough for a volume of short pieces.

However, this is unimportant beside getting back to the novel I left behind in its first version. A lot has been going on at the back of my mind in connexion with it while we have been travelling, so I think I was wise to get away from it for a bit.

Now we leave for home in less than a week. Very sad in some ways. I always enjoy being with Manoly's youngest sister and her husband, and this time have felt even closer as Elias has been recovering from a coronary ... Teeth have been my trouble during this trip ... But the other day, a different and very conspicuous tooth broke off while I was eating some fried eggs on Pélion. Soon I shall be faced with having everything out and wearing a rabbit-trap for the rest of my life.

I hardly know what to tell you about the Greek situation because it is so difficult to find out, even though some of the people we know are close friends of Amalia Fleming.[86] Most of our friends are pretty gloomy about the chances of a change. But the people we meet as we travel about the country are unwilling to give us any clue to what they think. Perhaps they don't. They may be preparing to turn into the apathetic cattle the Spaniards seem to have become.

20 MARTIN ROAD, 7.xi.71
TO MAIE CASEY
Dear Maie,
Since speaking the other day on the telephone, I have heard from someone who corresponds with Martin Boyd that he is having difficulties making ends meet, particularly since a major operation in Rome carried off a large

---

[84]Russell dropped out of the picture: 'I don't want to go to Australia,' he told McGrath. 'It's too far. I don't like long plane journeys.'
[85]'Sicilian Vespers'.
[86](1912–86), bacteriologist and Greek patriot, widow of the discoverer of penicillin Sir Alexander; imprisoned by the Colonels in September and deported to Britain from where she campaigned against the regime. After the restoration of democracy she became a deputy in the Greek parliament.

sum and left him with only partial use of his legs, at least at the time when he wrote to my friend.

I have taken this up with the CLF. They will probably give him a pension,[87] but this won't go far as things are today.

You know the Boyd family, I seem to remember. Could you perhaps stir them into doing something if the money is there which I'm sure it is (Arthur Boyd alone.)[88] On the other hand he may have quarrelled with his family, or he may be a sponger to whom they have already doled out, or they may be mean: if I were lying in the gutter, the Whites would step over me without doing anything, with the exception of one or two who haven't any money.

DISQUIETING REPORTS OF LIFE at Martin Road had followed the travellers for months, and they flew home in mid-October not knowing what to expect. At first White was delighted with the state of the house, scrubbed and filled with flowers, but his mood shifted and his correspondence began to boil with rage. Until the new year hardly a letter left his desk without some exaggerated complaint of wear and tear. He told James Stern in Wiltshire, 'None of the saucepan lids fit.[89]' Somewhere here White seemed to recognise fact and fiction might be enmeshed for he saw himself living the role of the violated homeowners of 'The Night The Prowler', the novella he had written three years before, 'about a girl drop-out of respectable family who revenges herself on society by violating houses!'[90] An elderly solicitor of distinction was wheeled out of retirement to calm White down. He meanwhile, stimulated by the row, was working steadily away at the second draft of The Eye of the Storm.

20 MARTIN ROAD, 21.xi.71
TO RONALD WATERS
Dear Ronald,

Thanks for your letter. It is good to know that a production of Lear will be coming; I've never seen a good one, and hope this will be it. I particularly want to see Lear now because the actor in my novel plays him. The actor is a ham of the Wolfit type, so the book on Wolfit has come out very opportunely;[91] I hurried to order it when I read the first review . . .

[87]They did.
[88]The painter (1920–   ) was sending money to his uncle.
[89]12.xii.71.
[90]To Stern, 12.xii.71.
[91]Wolfit (1902–68), actor-manager and tragedian; Ronald Harwood's biography was Sir Donald Wolfit, C.B.E.: His Life and Work in the Unfashionable Theatre, 1971.

Sad to hear about Glad Cooper.[92] I feel very close to her as the woman in my novel (not an actress) has always been for me the same kind of dazzling beauty as Glad in her heyday.

I am now writing the second version and am glad to have had that to take my mind off other things since we got back ... Well, that is that. I try not to think about it any more, but over and over again my rage boils up against that pretentious Bellevue Hill trash. Three times before we've had decent honest ordinary people looking after the house and nothing to complain about ...

Manoly had some more tests for the diabetes last week, and they showed that he still has traces of it. Nothing to worry about, however. He only has to keep off sugar (doesn't like sweets anyway) and watch his weight. My teeth have continued to behave abominably: a front one broke off just before we left Greece, and another beside it a couple of days after we got home. I now have two more moveable false as the roots were not good enough for capping. Shan't be long now before the whole rabbit trap is in.

20 MARTIN ROAD, 28.xi.71
TO FREDERICK GLOVER
Dear Frederick,
That Nobel Prize! I hope I never hear it mentioned again.[93] I certainly don't want it: the machinery behind it seems a bit dirty, when we thought that only applied to Australian awards. In my case to win the prize would upset my life far too much, and it would embarrass me to be held up to the world as an Australian writer when, apart from the accident of blood, I feel I am temperamentally a cosmopolitan Londoner.

We saw *Wake in Fright* while the Chetwynds (Luciana Arrighi and her husband) were staying here on their way back to Europe from Japan. I thought it a brilliant if revolting film. For the first time a film made in Australia can hold its own with all comers.[94] I also want to see *Walkabout*[95] which I am told is even better. And *The Conformist*,[96] an Italian film now running here.

[92]Gladys Cooper had died at the age of 83.
[93]Again the press had PW as a contender; he lost narrowly to Alexander Solzhenitsyn.
[94]Shot around Broken Hill, directed by Ted Kotcheff, starring Donald Pleasence and Gary Bond; the film was praised but unpopular in Australia, yet successful in Europe where it was released in 1971 as *Outback*.
[95]Director Nicholas Roeg's 1970 film was also shot in the Australian desert to a script by the playwright Edward Bond.
[96]1969, written and directed by Bernardo Bertolucci from the novel by Alberto Moravia.

We don't yet feel strong enough to face the Sydney theatre . . .

Don't think I'd care for Barry Oakley[97] from what I read about his books. Australian funny books never seem to me very funny.

Hope all well and no more possums.

P.

20 MARTIN ROAD, 28.xi.71

TO MAIE CASEY

Dear Maie,

The saint is Nicólaos[98] in Greek: the accent on the first 'o'.

Then, we have a new silent number: 663 7737. Hope you haven't been ringing the old one. I should have got in touch during the week but thought it would be easier to ask you this other thing by letter.

In the book I am writing there is a woman: born in Australia, but who has spent most of her life in France and become more French than Australian. She was married briefly to a French nobleman. She comes back to Australia to see her aged mother when she herself is about 60. She hasn't much money, but a few jewels and furs, and has remained elegant: a skin-and-bone type – the kind who buys a Chanel and makes it last for ever. She is rather rigid, 'frigid' the husband who left her, calls it; also a Catholic convert. There is one scene after she returns home where she sprawls on a fur rug and is surprised, and a bit shocked at the sensual pleasure it gives her through a dress – and what's underneath. Once women of that type used to wear a 'foundation garment.' But would an elegant Chanel-dressed woman of 60 still be wearing a foundation garment today? If not, what? It should, preferably be a bit rigid. Hope you can find the answer!

Yours,

Patrick.

20 MARTIN ROAD, 13.ii.72

TO GEOFFREY DUTTON

We have had a depressing week. Our friend Frederick Glover died unexpectedly on Thursday night. Haven't yet heard how, but imagine it was his heart: he had a heart attack a few years ago. We first met him a couple of years after we went to live at Castle Hill, and although we hadn't

---

[97](1931–) whose two comic novels *A Salute to the Great McCarthy* and *Let's Hear it for Prendergast* appeared in 1970.

[98]Bishop of Myra in Lycia in the 4th century, patron saint *inter alia* of children, sailors and pawnbrokers.

seen much of them since they moved to Melbourne, we kept up by letters. So his death will mean a gap. It was also due to him, when he was a manager of the Rural Bank, that I got the lowdown on the Australian (or N.S.W.) country town by going to stay with them at his various posts.

A curious ESP detail in connexion with Frederick's death: as you know I ask my friends on and off to burn any of my letters they may have lying around. About a fortnight before he died, Frederick wrote to say that, although he didn't like doing it, he had got round to burning all my letters! I hope others will take note.

Now I must come out with a pill and say I think it is rather shocking that you should be translating poets from the Russian without knowing the language. Even though you may have a crib, how good do you know it to be? How long is it since your Russian assistants lived in Russia? All our Hungarian and German friends who go back to their countries say the language has changed incredibly. So I just wonder how much justice you will do to Voznesensky.[99] I was never happy about those Yevtushenko translations: I could not make up mind whether he had gone off as a poet since the first collection I read, or whether he had suffered by the double-filter translation. And even if you knew the language, to whip off the poems of a complex poet like Voznesensky without a lot of searching and sifting could only amount to Oz slapdash. But the whole business of translation is usually dubious. I often wonder about the translations of my books into languages I can't read. Those in German, for instance, are mostly slapped together with an eye to the sale and nothing else.

I am now about two-thirds of the way through the second version of the novel: hating it at present; every word is a stone to be lifted painfully. I find it increasingly hard to convey ordinary objects (a telephone, say) or necessary moves (from one room to another) without being overwhelmed by the banality they have in everyday life – and particularly Australian everyday life. I suppose foreign writers are faced with all these difficulties, but one wonders. At least the telephone can't play such a part in the lives of Japanese or Russians.

20 MARTIN ROAD, 27.ii.72

TO THE NOLANS

The Caseys are worrying about a book of his which Collins is bringing out,[100] in which some photographs they themselves didn't censor, may give

[99]Andrey Voznesensky (1933–); *Little Woods*, the translation of his work by Dutton and Igor Mezhakoff-Koriakin, was published by Sun Books in 1972.
[100]*Australian Foreign Minister, the Diaries of R. G. Casey 1951–60*, edited by T. B. Millar, 1972.

somebody a laugh, or worse, outrage the public of today. The most controversial is one in which Dick is looking at an eagle he shot on the wing while they were up in the air. It happened at a time when there was a reward for a dead eagle, but that will not be taken into account. The other photograph is apparently of the Caseys in their kitchen with Maie wearing an apron. I am surprised at the Collinses publishing anything so hackneyed in theme, but of course the Collinses are corny publishers: something that people like the Caseys and the Duttons seem unable to see; they all go down like ninepins when Lush Billy and Pious Pierre appear on the scene.[101] I said to Maie it would have been a wonderful opportunity to use the title of the Fanny Brice song as a caption for the photograph: *Cookin' Breakfist for the One I Love*.

A Brett Whiteley exhibition is opening this week. I am most curious to see. It is called 'Portraits and Other Emergencies'. He is by now almost quite unintelligible in what he says to the press. From a photograph yesterday the portraits look like blown up photographs, Mao in particular. Whiteley is also writing a book about which he is very secretive – quite rightly; I can't help feeling it will be the most unintelligible book of all, or the hottest Bible for those who can't get on with the old one.[102]

I am plodding along through my book and at the moment hating it intensely. The only thing that keeps me going is to look back towards the beginning and finding bits I thought the most depressing mudholes now as clear as crystal springs. I shall be glad when I can put the whole thing in the bank, and go to sleep for a couple of months before starting the final version. (The bank is the only solution, I've found: otherwise, instead of staying clear, one keeps picking it up and having another look; although today is my letter-writing day, I've just picked it up and read pages in the middle of this, to make myself writhe.)

Had a letter yesterday from Charles Osborne (curse him) asking us to do something about the novelist Tuohy who is coming out to the Adelaide Festival.[103] I haven't read any of his books. I'm not even sure how you pronounce his name (is it like the beer?) Is he somebody you met recently? If so, he came at a point in Cynthia's letter where I could

---

[101]William (1900–76), chairman and managing director of William Collins, and his wife Priscilla known as Pierre.
[102]Probably The Big Orange Velvet Book, a notebook the artist sometimes exhibited but never published.
[103]Frank Tuohy (1925–   ), also a product of King's College, author of The Animal Game, 1957.

no longer make out whether you approved or disapproved. One comes to dread those streams of imported writers heading towards Adelaide, most of all the circuses of Russian poets. Some of them one would like to meet without knowing who they were, then discovering after one had started liking them, or creeping away if one didn't. But there is nothing more unnatural than to shove a couple of writers together in cold blood and expect them to be Writers Together.

20 MARTIN ROAD, 5.iii.72
TO BRETT WHITELEY
Dear Brett,
I arrived back in Australia on October 17th. Your exhibition the other day brought me alive again for the first time since then. If I didn't start gushing when you came up it was because it was too unexpected and I had only just stumbled on the roomful of heads. I used to know Francis[104] in my youth (he once designed a perfect desk for me) but I haven't seen him recently: any time I have been in London I have felt he was too taken up with other things to want to see anybody from the past.

I expect the scroll I am buying[105] is not the one you would have liked me to buy. (Painters are never really pleased with what other people choose.) But the head of Francis on that scroll has more of what I remember from the days before drink and drugs took over. If the series upstairs is split up (which I don't expect; in fact I hope it won't be)[106] I have reserved the Eye because of connexions with my own work.

That is why I bought the pink bird on a dark-blue sea[107] from the exhibition before: it is very closely connected with the book I have been working on over the last couple of years. I can see you have gone much farther with the pink and brown bird of the present exhibition: it is wonderfully subtle, fully achieved; but I am still very fond of my dark-blue sea, for reasons which I hope you will gather if you ever read the book.

There were lots of other things I should have liked to buy from this present show if I had space in my house and more money than I have at the moment for paintings.

[104]Bacon.
[105]'Head Studies'.
[106]It wasn't.
[107]'The Pink Heron', 1969.

The awful social and commercial rackets in Australia will try to kill your genius as they have picked off many lesser talents; I hope you will be strong enough to hold out against them.

Yours sincerely,

Patrick White

P.S. At one time I thought Francis B. would be your downfall as a painter; now I see you are making the right use of him.

20 MARTIN ROAD, 5.iii.72

TO GEOFFREY DUTTON

I went last week to look at the Whiteley exhibition. There are some extraordinary things in it. To me, Nolan and he are the creative geniuses of Australian painting. This exhibition brought me alive again, wanting to do things myself, as I only ever feel when in contact with a great artist in whatever medium.

AT BREAKFAST ON 16 March 1972, White opened the *Sydney Morning Herald* to discover that all the houses along the spine between Moore Park and Centennial Park, including his own, plus great slabs of both parks, were to be taken for a sports centre in which Sydney hoped to stage the Olympic Games in 1988. White had worked for political causes in the past – to reinstate Joern Utzon as architect of the Opera House, to bring Australian troops home from Vietnam – but in the battle for Centennial Park he discovered his strength as a campaigner. He found he had a taste for it.

20 MARTIN ROAD, 19.iii.72

TO ELIZABETH HARROWER

Dear Elizabeth,

Thanks for your letter, as lively as I feel dead at the moment. I had been meaning to write, but exhaustion set in some time before the Blow which fell lately. By that I mean the plan to bulldoze Martin and Robertson roads to make way for a stadium for the Olympic Games. It is quite probable this won't happen, and in any case the Games will not be held till 1988, when I hope I shall be dead. The silly city of Sydney may not even be given the Games, for which they will have to apply in 1982. But the fact that the plan is contemplated at all is pretty disturbing, and one doesn't know when the bulldozing will begin. Apart from the personal aspect, fancy contemplating running such a vast project in the centre of a large city, and spending such a fortune on SPORT (they say it would cost $76 million, but an architect tells us more likely $250) when we haven't enough hospitals, schools, poverty is increasing every month, we have done hardly anything for the Aborigines, and our art gallery and museum are miserable makeshift, patchwork affairs. The whole thing has been so upsetting I even got on the telly a couple of days ago for the first time in my life.[108] I thought it would be too gruesome to watch, but various people told me it came over all right. However, the *Herald* reported the interview leaving out certain key words, which made it look as though my concern is only for myself.[109] From now on I am afraid an awful lot of time and emotion will have to go into defeating this move . . .

There has been a very good Brett Whiteley exhibition, but the critics mostly tore into it. I bought one, possibly two, if the second is not sold as part of a series; don't know where I shall put them. Today he came here to lunch, and that is something of an experience: he speaks almost a whole new language. At times he becomes lucid and one agrees with a lot of what he is saying; but there are other moments when it is just a fizzing of fireworks. I expect he is used to most people looking blank. He brought me a book-rest for using in the bath, when I am hardly ever there for more than five minutes; there is so much to be done. Also a record by pop singer Van Morrison who, according to Brett, announced in an interview that I have been one of the greatest influences on his life. I find this sort of thing quite alarming. Also according to Brett, many of my followers belong to the acid world because I see things the way they do. He couldn't believe I had never been on acid; actually I have come across this before from people who are on it. Again mysterious and somewhat alarming, though I suppose it ought to be consoling to realise that they are no different from the very ordinary self one knows too well. Brett is all for pushing acid and grass on to us ('mescalin is a must') but I said if we took to that at our age we would show up like the parents in *Taking Off*.[110] Before he left he made us touch his hair, which is a mop of tight little corkscrew curls which look silky, but feel as though they have been rubbed with resin. Manoly thinks it was like touching some strange animal one had never touched before. His wife, who did not come, turns out to be the daughter of somebody I was at school with. This man became a respectable solicitor, but after years it was found that he was also practising as a burglar. He has been in Long Bay ever since. Funnily enough I based a character on him in a novel I began after coming to this house and then

---

[108]Interviewed by Mike Carlton, ABC *This Day Tonight*.
[109]18 March, p.1.
[110]Film by Milos Forman, 1971.

abandoned when I was almost at the end of a long first version.[111] I still have it, and may come back to it one day.

I wonder how you will get on this time with Christina Stead. I found her rather forbidding, and didn't feel she liked me. I always regret having given her two books which I was sure afterwards she would not have understood: a book of Berryman's poems and Cyril Connolly's *The Unquiet Grave*.

The first floats have arrived for the Show though it is still five days off: a warning to lay in provisions for the occupation. Perhaps it won't seem so bad this year since we are faced with being bulldozed for the Olympic Games.

Yours
Patrick.

20 MARTIN ROAD, 30.iv.72
TO MAIE CASEY

It is now 06.30. I got up four hours ago, unable to sleep because of the caterwauling outside, and being so close to the end of my book, I worked till 05.30, when I finished the second version of *The Eye of the Storm*. Finishing at that hour pleased me very much because that is when the story closes (as it opens also, towards dawn.) I already find myself wanting to go back to it, so I must put it in the bank tomorrow. Then I shan't look at it for two months, and perhaps it will read like something written by another person. (I can only really <u>see</u> what I have written if I pick it up years afterwards.)

Now I shall spend a couple of months campaigning for the neighbourhood. For a start I am planning a series of dinner parties with a newspaper editor at each (at least the three I know) with some of the more intelligent neighbours, and perhaps a dolly for those who dally. I might even come at a politician or two. We actually had a (civilised) one to dinner last Saturday, and he wrote an excellent letter to the *Herald* in return.[112]

---

[111]George Julius (1913–?), son of Sir George who gave the world the automatic totalisator, was at Tudor House with PW; George Jr became an engineer, a most charming and welcome guest in houses he later burgled. After admitting to 150 house robberies in 1959 Julius was sent to prison for eight years. 'You are not a member of the underworld,' remarked the judge. 'By day you live as a normal individual and are as respectable as you look . . . it would take a Shakespeare or a Zola to tell the tragedy of your life.' PW's attempt to tell the tale was his unfinished and unpublished novel, The Binoculars and Helen Nell.

[112]Jim and Freda McClelland; his letter was published 25 April, p.2.

I have also arranged (through Semmler) for Vincent Serventy to give a radio talk on the wild life of Centennial Park and how most of it will disappear if all these threatened projects are carried out. While at the ABC Serventy is going to try to work his way into television (*Four Corners*) and says I must come too.[113] So you may see me as an embarrassed stooge asking questions about waterfowl.

The Duttons have come and gone. The children are really the nicest I know, intelligent, attractive, and completely natural. When I think what a dreary speechless lump I was at the same ages![114]

Yrs,

Patrick.

20 Martin Road, 2.v.72

TO PEGGY GARLAND

If the worst happens, and we are bulldozed out, we shall bundle in just anywhere, provided there is a good back yard, and wait till the last of our aged dogs has died, then leave this country for ever. But I hope it won't come to that, much as I should like to spend the end of my life going to the theatre and listening to music in London. Better perhaps to live it up hectically till my bronchial tubes perish, than to eke out a careful, boring old age in some Australian backwater. What I should be sorry about is this house, which we love, and where the vibrations have been just right from the beginning.

20 Martin Road, 9.v.72

TO TOM MASCHLER

When I was reading Michael Howard's book on Jonathan Cape recently, I was interested to find that Hemingway had succeeded in preventing publication of his letters. How, I wonder? I should be glad if you could tell me as I should like to do the same. Yesterday I was at my solicitor's making a fresh will and he had no idea how to go about preventing the publication of letters.[115]

[113]Serventy (1925–   ), ornithologist, naturalist and president of the Wildlife Preservation Society of Australia; there was no *Four Corners* programme on the Centennial Park campaign.
[114]Francis was 14, Teresa (Tisi) 11 and Sam 9.
[115]Hemingway's *Selected Letters* edited by Carlos Baker were published in 1981.

20 MARTIN ROAD, 1.vi.72
TO ELIZABETH HARROWER

Dear Elizabeth,

I received *The Spoils of Poynton*, for which I thank you very much, though I may not be able to read it until my next fiction orgy. I am almost at the end of *Daniel Deronda*; then I think there will be just time for *L'Education sentimentale* (re-reading of) before I start the final version of my own. There are wonderful things in *Deronda* (the development of Gwendolen Harleth) but I also find a lot of it sadly stodgy (most of the Jewish bits, and Deronda himself; but of course all this has been said many times before.) I must try to work out how long before her death she wrote *Daniel Deronda*:[116] she does seem to be dragging herself on with a leaden weight round her neck, and it is rather painful to experience when one may not be so far off the end oneself!

All my energy nowadays goes into the campaign for the neighbourhood and Centennial Park. But it is very depressing. At times one feels that jealous and <u>mean</u> neighbours are more dangerous than the political and business interests which are trying to destroy us. Old ladies who are not well off will bring $50 out of a tin and promise another fifty next week, but to ask the well-laced industrialists and doctors for a miserable $100 is like asking them to cut off their right hand. I think far less of human beings since all this began, and not because of the enemy – though God knows they stink enough.

Anyway, on July 1st I am going to start reading through my novel before typing the final version. That must be finished before we become refugees – if we do.

I have had some telephone conversations with the Rodds, mainly in connexion with Martin Boyd.[117] Geoffrey Dutton says that Boyd is dying. They had some conversations after Geoffrey arrived, but he was very weak. Then after the Duttons had been away for a week-end, they found he had had a relapse and been taken back to hospital. Geoffrey doesn't think he will last long. A niece, Mary (I think Perceval)[118] has flown out from London to be with him. Apparently at the last CLF meeting they had been discussing an increase in the money they send him; he will certainly need it if he lingers on in a Roman hospital.[119]

[116]The novel appeared in 1876; George Eliot died in 1880.
[117]Kylie Tennant – Mrs Rodd – was on the advisory board of the Commonwealth Literary Fund.
[118]Née Boyd; future wife of Sidney Nolan.
[119]Boyd died, 3 June 1972.

The birthday honours are out, and A. D. Hope is an OBE (just about what he is worth.) I regret to say the jolly Dr Semmler has accepted the same bauble, and Rose Skinner is making a fool of herself over the MBE, which she thought was going to be an OBE. She is going to return what she considers 'an insult to W.A.' One could do a nice cartoon of that[120] . . .

I was approached the other day by Reuters wanting to do something for my 60th birthday for publication in London and New York. I agreed only because I thought I might work in something about the Proposal to catch the eye of our travelling politicians to show them we are not sitting here like a lot of turkeys waiting to be slaughtered for their political Christmas. God knows what will come out. The young man they sent was very nice, but rather *naif*. I expect I have said all the wrong things as usual, or else they will come out wrong. Anyway, I told him to make sure he says that if the Proposal goes through, I for one will leave Australia for ever and spend the rest of my life in London – not that the politicians and their business mates would worry one bit, I expect.[121]

Keneally's play *An Awful Rose* is said to be very good. We shall see if it transfers from Jane Street; I am not going to suffer any more Catholic conflicts on the Jane Street seats in the Jane Street draughts. The mixture sounds very familiar; anguished priest, rationalist mistress, blood on the altar cloths, priest loses mistress, leaves Church, taking with him the bloody cloths . . .

This is one of those unbelievable Sydney winter days, full of birds, sunlight, and barely stirring leaves. It is even hard to believe in the destroyer politicians who can't see these things.

What of the Nolans? Has there been a confrontation between Cynthia and Fox[122] over the mutilated rosetree? As usual I have had none of the letters Sid swears he is going to write every time we part.

Yours
Patrick.

---

[120]Rose Skinner (1901–1979), gallery owner, kept her MBE.

[121]The report by Brian Dale (1946–), journalist and spin doctor, never appeared in London and New York but surfaced in outlying Reuters territories. Under the name Ashley Owen, Dale wrote a longer version which appeared in the *Australian Financial Review*, 11 July 1972, p.2.

[122]Winifred Fox, the Nolans' Viennese housekeeper, had pruned one of the roses back to a stump; she disappeared until the storm blew over.

20 MARTIN ROAD, 19.vi.72
TO GEOFFREY DUTTON

Yesterday was the day of the great Rally and I now feel alive again after living in a peculiar kind of nightmare for the last couple of weeks. Now that I have addressed a multitude from the top of a lorry in Centennial Park, led a march, and made a second speech in the Town Hall, I feel I could face almost anything. People tell me my speeches came over all right, but you never know: they may have been speaking out of kindness. In the Park the other speakers were Harry Miller, Vincent Serventy the bird-man, and Jack Mundey.[123] I think the latter will probably be our saviour; he announced that the monster will not be built where proposed, and as he represents the Building Labourers Union he's in a pretty strong position. In the Town Hall the speakers were Neville Wran, Leader of the Opposition in the Legislative Council,[124] Kylie,[125] a girl called Anna Katzmann[126] who is Captain of the Girls' High School threatened by the Moore Park scheme, and Mundey and myself again. There were also four rather deadly (but most necessary) mayors, all of whom want the sport complex in their suburbs.

In the meantime the Government has appointed Walter Bunning to make an independent inquiry,[127] and have put off announcing their decision till December. I dare think we have won! But we shall have to continue throwing an occasional bomb during the next few months. I heard that bastard Lewis being interviewed the other day: he sounds the most shifty kind of thick-voiced politician, full of lies, and downright stupid.[128]

All this must sound comically parochial in London! I shall be glad to return to my book at the end of the month. It's going to be a long trudge, though; I'm almost too old for these long novels; yet I have a couple more I want to get off my chest.

---

[123](1932–   ), communist, and secretary of the NSW Builders' Labourers' Federation, a pioneer of Green Bans to protect Sydney communities, open space and old buildings.
[124](1926–   ), barrister, about to leave the Council to become leader of the Labor opposition in the NSW lower house and, in 1976, premier of the State. PW and Wran became friends after this meeting, for a time.
[125]Tennant.
[126]Later a Sydney barrister.
[127]Town-planner and architect (1912–77) whose mixed achievement included Sydney's first suburban shopping malls and the air-conditioned Parthenon of the National Library in Canberra; his study found Moore Park unsuitable and recommended Homebush Bay as the site for the Olympic Games.
[128]Tom Lewis (1922–   ) was minister responsible for the Olympic plans and later premier of NSW 1974–76.

Yesterday some of the strangest people came up and thanked me for my books: the usual intense ladies of course, but also some of the scruffiest young men, who seem to have liked *The Vivisector* in particular; Brett Whiteley must have been right when he said the acid people are all with me.

20 MARTIN ROAD, 28.vi.72
TO PETER BEATSON
Dear Peter,
Thank you for your two letters. In the first one, in spite of the break with your girl, you seemed to be getting more out of life than before, what with your house and garden, tenants' children, and meeting people in Oxford; so the second letter came as a disappointment. Simone Weil deals with 'affliction', if not always comprehensibly, far more subtly than I could ever hope to do, but then she herself was afflicted; if I have been, it was only in very superficial and transient ways. But I have always found in my own case that something positive, either creative or moral, has come out of anything I have experienced in the way of affliction.

What interests me in your second letter is that you in your deep-seated affliction share so many of my attitudes, and I suppose you would consider me a 'normal person'. There have been long periods when I have lived with what you refer to in yourself as 'the soul of a hunchbacked dwarf locked up in a reasonably presentable six-foot frame'; it has made me ashamed to go amongst people who have completely different and exalted ideas of what I am. You say that every time you walk it is an act of will because you are physically frightened. In only a slightly different way it is an act of will for me to sit down at my desk every day and start work: I am mentally very frightened indeed. You seem to think that the people who walk with you in a park are able to escape from themselves in nature. Perhaps some do. I find that half the time I remain locked up with my hunchbacked dwarf while appearing a different person to my companions.

Of course there are the other times, as you know, from sitting in the garden with your flute, the children playing round you; and it could be that you have had some very important effect on these children, even at that early age. I am continually amazed to hear the effect I am supposed to have had on people when I have felt at my most inadequate.

I think in your case waiting is most important. You may find that all kinds of new avenues will open up. In entirely different circumstances, I have found this happen to me during the campaign for the neighbourhood and the parks. Against my will I was forced to do things I should never have contemplated doing and which were quite out of keeping with my nature. Nobody would have persuaded me that I could address a crowd in the park from on top of a lorry, lead a march, and make another speech in Sydney Town Hall as I did the Sunday before last. I went through hell in the days leading up to all this, but now I can see that unexpected avenues have opened for me, and that I have found other ways of communicating with people.

I don't by any means want to suggest that you too might be a performing seal, but I do think you have to continue waiting for a lead: just as I sometimes sit for days at my desk, doodling and hoping, then suddenly I find that the clue has been given to me already in the blackest of the doodles.

Yours
Patrick

On quite a different level, you never told me what you did about the Mt Isa shares.

In your second letter you speak rather feelingly about the farm by the sea in New Zealand. Do you think perhaps you ought to go back there if there is nothing to keep you in Oxford. I hardly know you well enough to advise, and nothing about what sort of help you would have in living there. Manoly and I found it a hard life living in the country in Australia, though we were fairly young at the time, and with our full sight.

20 MARTIN ROAD, 9.vii.72
TO GEOFFREY DUTTON

We are having a very severe winter all of a sudden: freezing winds; cracks opening in one's fingertips. Hundreds of birds come to our garden to be fed. When Manoly takes the dogs round the block early, he is followed back from the corner by a cloud of firetails waiting for him to put out the seed.

MARTIN ROAD, 30.vii.72
TO CYNTHIA NOLAN

I am now typing the final version of *The Eye of the Storm*. I haven't got far enough to run into any <u>physical</u> difficulties (I've only done between one sixteenth and one eighth) but I have already grown fat and flabby from having sat so much. I am quite enjoying it at the moment, which may or may not be a good sign. But how different everything looks when one trans-fers it from longhand to typescript. I'm afraid my main character, who has to be a great beauty, bitch, charismatic figure, destroyer and affirmer all in one, may turn out to be no more than an impossibly selfish devouring female to the reader. It is still too early to tell, and she will change into something different again when she goes from typescript to print.

20 MARTIN ROAD, 13.viii.72
TO JEAN SCOTT ROGERS
Is Frank Burden conscious of what is happening to him?[129] If he is I don't understand why he doesn't put an end to it. I read a most interesting book recently by Alvarez the poet and critic called *The Savage God.* It has taught me what I think must be the ideal way of committing suicide: you simply put your head in a plastic bag; so clean, neat, and cheap. So if Frank Burden still has his wits about him, I think it would be kind of you to suggest the plastic bag.

MARTIN ROAD, 8.x.72.
TO CYNTHIA NOLAN
Dear Cynthia,
Your last letter was the most legible so far.[130] I think the secret lies in the spacing – in not squeezing it up on one of those air-letter forms. Sometimes I think as my typing deteriorates more and more while plodding through this present book, I shall have to write all my letters by hand. But one is less anxious in typing a letter. As I type a book my hand develops a dying fall which makes the fingers (or the two I use) linger on the wrong letters over and over again. Sometimes I have such a fit of drifting fingers I have to give up for that session.

I am almost three-quarters through *The Eye.* Can't see what it is really like, though at the moment I am liking the actual storm at which we have arrived, and at moments I believe I may be bringing off the destroyer-affirmer I mentioned. I have not come across the destroyer you say there is in Sid, but there is a kind of shadowiness in him at moments which could be hiding that. I am a destroyer, and feel that same shadowiness must descend (automatically) to prevent some people seeing it. I am also, alas, a self-destroyer. Time and time again I have not been able to resist ruining something just when I have got there. I try to turn this into a kind of 'retreat-to-advance' but it doesn't always work out that way . . .

Hope your chest is all right. I used to think my troubles came on when I was whatever you like to call it: exhausted, depressed, anxious,

[129]Having had both legs amputated after gangrene.
[130]Her handwriting was terrible; he had been urging her for years to type.

furious – anyway in the state of blackness. But that can't be the reason for I still have all of that.

Love to both,

Patrick

M.'s doctor is going to try the gold treatment on his arthritis. He must suffer a lot, judging by looks, but has been brought up not to admit.

20 MARTIN ROAD, 12.xi.72
TO THE DUTTONS
Dear Nin and Geoffrey,

Thank you for letters and the Asprey catalogue. It is really surprising that such expensive toys are made in present-day England; one wonders who would buy them: perhaps some of those faces one sees in the business section of the *Observer*. However, I must say some of the jewels appeal to me. I shall always be a sucker for jewels and furs; if I were a woman I expect I should have become the most rapacious kind of cocotte, and probably would have got stoned for wearing bird-of-paradise plumes on top of everything else . . .

With luck I may finish *The Eye of the Storm* this week. I've been forcing the pace a bit because Tom Maschler arrives early next month and has announced he would like to read it while here. Knowing all about the visits of English publishers to Australia I can't see him doing this. But perhaps what he really wants is to re-assure himself it is not unbearable. I still have no idea. After thinking of it under this title all the time I was upset the other day to read that a book has come out about the guerilla movement in Angola called *In the Eye of the Storm*. But perhaps as it is factual and probably won't be very widely read, a novel published a year later might get away with a title almost the same. What do you think? An alternative is *The Darker Purpose*, or better perhaps *Darker Purposes*. It comes from the opening of *Lear*:

> Attend the lords of France and Burgundy, Gloucester.– –
> Meantime we shall express our darker purpose.

I had a letter yesterday which took me by surprise: from a Queensland nun who wants to compose an opera to *Voss*! She says she composes in a modern idiom (whatever that may be) that she will go to England and Europe first to learn more about composition, and that she doesn't mind how long she takes or if it is the only opera she ever composes. Fancy if a simple nun should come up with the real thing. It is a remote possibility, but I think I shall let her try. Something might come out of it if not an opera. What I shan't let myself in for is writing the libretto as she suggests.[131]

Have you heard the big publishing scandal? that Keneally has gone over to Collins? I expect Reverend Mother Pierre[132] came good with an extra big Catholic handout. For once I feel sorry for A.&.R; they did so much for the little bastard. Poor Beatrice Davis, no Reverend Mother only a B.A., must be desolated to find that her 'dear humble little man' is a load of shit. And what about the CLF, unable to withhold that grant behind his sponsor's back?[133] It really pays to have been brought up in the Roman Catholic Church.

Last night we had dinner at the Donald Hornes',[134] a very good one too, when I had been expecting pineapple and banana cookery. I'm afraid I dropped a few Catholic bricks, not realising that a young man present was a priest in mufti.[135] His parish is Woolloomooloo and he has been trying to organise the people there to resist their destruction by developers and the civic sharks. I liked him very much and hope we shall be able to give them some help. Lately I'm afraid I have become rather anti-Catholic only because almost every lousy Australian writer seems to be a lapsed Catholic, and because there are times when you feel Australia is run only for Catholics . . .

The other day, at a price, I picked up at Rudy's a little Roy de Maistre which played a great part in my youth, influencing me, I feel, when I was starting to write. I never dared offer to buy it then because I thought Roy was too fond of it to sell. Then he sold it behind my back, to whom I never found out. Strange it should come home to roost thirty-six years later. But it's dreadful to think of his poverty and the prices his paintings are fetching now. According to Christies, the de Maistres are some of the most valuable I've got.

Patrick.

---

[131]Moya Henderson (1942–   ), Sacre Coeur nun who, having won PW's support, left the order to study in Germany. Her *Voss* opera was never written but she set PW's *Six Urban Songs*, first performed in 1986.

[132]Keneally moved to Collins after the death of John Abernethy (1930–72), his editor at A & R; his novels appeared not on the religious list established by the proprietor's wife Pierre Collins, but on the general fiction list.

[133]Unclear: PW appears to think the move to Collins should disqualify Keneally from taking up his grant because one of the advisers to the Commonwealth Literary Fund was on the board of A & R.

[134]Myfanwy and Donald; he (1921–   ), journalist, essayist, recent convert to the politics of Gough Whitlam's Labor party, author of the fine memoir *The Education of Young Donald*, 1967.

[135]Edmund Campion (1933–   ), critic and later author of *Rockchoppers: Growing up Catholic in Australia*, 1982.

20 Martin Road, 9.xii.72
TO JULIET O'HEA
Dear Juliet,

The Capes have come and gone. Tom read my new novel while they were here and seems very enthusiastic; in fact he says it is the one he likes best. They have carried it off and Graham will read it en route and let you have it when they return . . .

The big question, which you can help settle, is when I should be published in the States. For a long time I have felt I should be published first in England as the Americans aren't really interested: even the 'good' reviews are awful and the sales are miserable; nor do I feel the Viking particularly wants me except as a duty to Huebsch who liked my work and was my friend. But I don't want to offend Viking and have them drop me; I mightn't find another publisher in the States, and one still wants to be published there for the small flock of faithful. I don't know whom you should approach at Viking: Marshall, who is my friend of years, and who says he hopes he will be the first at Viking to read the new novel, has more or less dropped out, and grows vegetables in Connecticut; I never get the impression that young Tom Guinzberg[136] takes any interest in what I write, though Gwenda David[137] insists that he does; there is a man called Edwin Kennebeck who has recently become very attentive and sends me presents of books, I think because I told Marshall that the last time I was in New York the only friend I felt I had at Viking was the switchboard girl. This is the tangle you will have to unravel. I certainly don't want to hurt Marshall or go against the Huebsch tradition to which I owe so much. But I'd rather be published first by Cape. If there are some good reviews in London, it might give a lead to those incompetent Americans.

---

[136]Son of Harold Guinzberg, co-founder of the Viking Press with Huebsch.
[137]Viking's representative in London.

Laureate

December 1972 – November 1975

IN EARLY DECEMBER 1972 Australia voted out of office the conservative coalition that had ruled the nation for twenty-three years and the leader of the Labor Party, Gough Whitlam, became prime minister. This was the culmination of years of campaigning for profound change in Australia. White was at first sceptical about Whitlam: he was attractive, eloquent, protestant, bourgeois but could his Irish Catholic party drag the country out of its stagnation? 'Give them time enough,' White told John Sumner, 'and they will probably develop their own line of dishonesty.'[1] But in the last weeks of 1972 he became elated as the new government released the conscripts, brought the last troops home from Vietnam, recognised China and ratified international conventions on nuclear arms, racial discrimination and labour. Conservative Australia, appalled by this turn of events, vilified Whitlam. White began to break old friendships on behalf of the new prime minister.

At Martin Road a spirit of creative housework hovered over White's desk: there were proofs of *The Eye of the Storm* to correct, stories to finish for the new volume of short pieces, after which he planned to return to *A Fringe of Leaves*, the Mrs Fraser story abandoned years before.

20 MARTIN ROAD, 31.xii.72
TO TOM MASCHLER
Dear Tom,
Glad to get your letter and hear you were safely restored to your family.

The day we had lunch I mentioned the matter of a dedication for *The Eye of the Storm*. Maie Casey has since read the book, is very enthusiastic about it, and says she would like the dedication. (I wanted her to read it first because there are things in it which might start a certain kind of person saying, 'Fancy Lady Casey having anything to do with him and his dirty books!') So you might now get somebody to add to the typescript the attached sheet with the dedication.

We have had infernal heat on and off over the holidays. I was relieved

[1]4.xii.72.

I had asked nobody to meals this year. I have felt too exhausted without that. After the cold, windy Sydney you found, you would have been amazed at the furnace we turned on for Christmas.

The most pleasing recent development is that four white, sulphur-crested cockatoos have taken to visiting our garden several times a day. When the first one appeared Manoly started putting out sunflower seed. Now the relationship seems firmly established. They stride about the lawn, and look quite spectacular climbing amongst the white flowers of the big magnolia.

Best wishes from us both for 1973,
Yours
Patrick.

ANLABY, 13.i.73
TO MAIE CASEY
Dear Maie,
I came here last Monday, or rather, I left Sydney that night and left the bus at Nuriootpa at 5 the following afternoon. There were moments when I thought I should go mad, then finally settled down to the discomfort and endlessness. No one of interest on the bus, except a husband and wife who nearly came to blows over the lost cap of a Coke bottle. Instead they satisfied themselves by letting fly with a few 'bastards'.

Some of the landscapes looked as though they might have come out of what I imagine hell could be, but Mildura is a green and spanking town. I also liked the towns we whizzed through at night: fully illuminated and wholly deserted, they would have interested Magritte.

I found a lot of illness at Anlaby: Teresa Rose has returned from hospital where they drained an abscess in her ear; Nin has been having trouble with teeth; the maid is coughing her head off, and Geoffrey is in bed with pneumonia. I can't think why they didn't put me off, but they said they wanted to be cheered up, so I feel bound to give a virtuoso performance.

Actually I'm enjoying reading, writing letters, and doing nothing, all of which I intended to do at home after finishing *The Eye of the Storm*, but didn't succeed.

Have also been for one or two drives with Francis the eldest boy, through sheets of undulating gold with black trees appliquéd on them, and sturdy, German-built farmhouses. It's a neighbourhood which manages to look unperturbed even in times of drought.

The day after to-morrow I return to Sydney – by air! partly because I feel I have done my duty by the bus, and partly because my godson has given me three peacock feathers which I must contrive to take home intact.

Yrs

Patrick

P.S. I've bought a little Whiteley landscape, in ESP circumstances, of which I shall tell some other time.[2]

20 MARTIN ROAD, 21.i.73

TO INGMAR BJÖRKSTÉN

Dear Mr Björkstén,

Sorry not to have answered your letter sooner. 1972 was a bad year. Apart from the demolition threat, I had a book to finish, there was an election at the beginning of December (at least it went the way I wanted) my London publishers arrived soon after and insisted on reading the book there and then, which made a week of great tension; after that came the by now meaningless season of Christmas.

In any case your letter is very difficult to answer,[3] because how can one talk about anything so private as one's 'religion' and one's God? I suppose some people can, but I can't. You are fairly right in the line you seem to be taking, but I should play down the Jung part. I have great admiration for him and his findings, but I also have a belief in a supernatural power of which I have been given inklings from time to time: there have been incidents and coincidences which have shown me that there is a design behind the haphazardness. I suppose there is one line of thought which would say I see it because I want to, but from my teens till middle age I didn't want to: it was only when it was forced on me that I had to accept.

I don't know about influences: Joyce and Lawrence, yes, at the time when I began to write. I certainly began to read Dostoyevsky about the same time, and have read all his important novels, but it would not have occurred to me that I had been influenced by anybody so remote from myself, geographically and culturally, though I think I understand his temperament fairly well. Most certainly I shouldn't have made use of the stream of consciousness if it hadn't been for Joyce, but I also rely to a great extent on what you refer to as 'dream material'. By this time I find myself often wondering whether something has actually happened, whether I have dreamt it, whether it is an incident from one of those waking dreams, or

---

[2]Perhaps 'Preliminary sketch for large cream landscape', 1972.

[3]Björkstén was researching his book on White published in Stockholm later in 1973, *Patrick White: epikern från Australien*, translated as *Patrick White: a general introduction*, 1976.

perhaps some incident from one of my books. I have read the Bible from cover to cover, but wouldn't say I 'know it very well' (I may know it better than I think, however). I do think composers and musicians come closer to God, also some painters; it is the writer who deals in stubborn, colourless words who is always stumbling and falling. I can't talk about style. I only know I do what I do when I feel that has to be done; I tend to break up language trying to get past what is stubborn and unyielding, to convey the essence of meaning.

It's difficult to answer the paragraph about which novels are closest to myself. I tend to feel close to *The Aunt's Story* because in the beginning it was either ignored, or, in Australia, considered a freak. My feeling has been much as I imagine parents would feel towards a child who is not quite normal: they have to protect it. I also feel very close to *The Solid Mandala* because it conveys a certain nightmarish quality of life which I have experienced, though the incidents in the novel are hardly parallel to anything in my actual life. But at the moment I am obsessed by my latest book *The Eye of The Storm*, because in it I think I have come closer to giving the final answer.

I decided to write no more plays because I feel I can say more in a novel. Also, a novel depends on myself alone. Once I used to think it would be exhilarating to see one's work come alive on a stage, till I realised it never can, however good the actors and director may be. Then I find it distressing when an audience resents what I am saying, when you can hear them writhing and protesting audibly around you in the dark. At least you can't hear a reader rise in rage from your novel, and perhaps throw it on the fire. You've only got the critics to put up with. (Incidentally, I only turned <u>one</u> of my stories, A *Cheery Soul*, into a play, because I heard the character speaking with the voice of a certain actress, who afterwards played the part.)

I hope I have answered some of your questions adequately. Sometimes I think I shall have to write an autobiography and perhaps have peace after that.

Yours sincerely,
Patrick White.

20 MARTIN ROAD, 29.iv.73
TO TOM MASCHLER
The other day I started typing the stories for what I think will make my next book. I have finished the first . . . but had a lot of trouble as a new story started working in me. I am now getting it down on paper, which means I shall take longer than I calculated, but the book will now have

three new stories to balance the three already published. Four will be on the long side. The latest story is called 'The Cockatoos', from which I think the book should take its title, as I can see a beautiful jacket.

Our own cockatoos sometimes number fourteen, some of them growing very tame. I have been trying out gramophone records on them. They are very happy with Bach unaccompanied violin sonatas, and their movements go very well with Bach. Then I tried some *Così Fan Tutte*: they were a bit afraid of Ferrando, but flew back for Fiordiligi's big aria. Next time I want to try Elvira's *Mi tradì*.[4]

Last Sunday Barry Humphries was here to lunch, and mentioned meeting you and Fay[5] at Klosters. He brought his two beautiful little girls and it became rather an exhausting session: they skipped about all over the house and left chocolate fingerprints wherever they went. At one stage Manoly found them trying to get into my wardrobe, and one of them said, 'Haven't you got another door for us to go through?'

Yours,
Patrick.

20 MARTIN ROAD, 20.v.73
TO PEPE MAMBLAS[6]
Dear Pepe,
It was a surprise to hear from you, and on that attractive card (is it the Camargues?) I wonder who gave you my address. Possibly that collector of duchesses, Billy McCann.[7]

It's certainly a long time, and I wonder what you look like now. I am crumbling at the age of 61, but I expect you, as a diplomat, have had an easier life. Whatever one is in Australia (unless a millionaire) life is not very easy.

Fortunately Manoly Lascaris, the Greek friend I think I mentioned when I last wrote, has put up with me for 32 years. After we came out here we lived for 18 years outside Sydney, then when suburbia swallowed us up, we moved right into the centre, and have lived here almost 9 years,

---

[4]From *Don Giovanni*.
[5]His wife, the restaurant critic.
[6]The diplomatic career of Pepe Mamblas, now the Duke of Baena, had followed a low trajectory to end with a posting to the Hague 1957–63. Indiscretions in his memoir *The Dutch Puzzle*, published in retirement, lost him his intimacy with the Dutch royal family. He was now living in a suburban villa in Biarritz. Mamblas and PW had last corresponded in 1947.
[7]Cosmopolitan Australian (1912–   ), raised in Argentina, who fell in with Spanish aristocracy in the Civil War; worked later for Royal Dutch Shell in various Hispanic postings.

between two parks, which is very pleasant – if we are allowed to stay (we were threatened with demolition a year ago.)

Two years ago we were in Europe, but like it less and less. London, parts of the French provinces, and the mountains of Greece are all I want to see again. I am at heart a Londoner, only by fate an Australian; I imagine it's like being born with a hump or a clubfoot: one has to put up with it.

At least living in Australia drives me to work; that is my refuge. I have a new novel called *The Eye of the Storm* coming out in London in October or November, and am now working on some shorter novels which will come out in one vol. the following year.

It has suddenly occurred to me there is an Australian post-office ban on mail to France, until the French think better of holding their nuclear tests in the Pacific. So this will have to wait in a drawer. I hope I don't forget it.

Love,
Patrick.

20 MARTIN ROAD, 20.v.73
TO GEOFFREY DUTTON
Spent a pretty awful morning with my old nurse at Wentworth Falls. She can hardly put six words together by now, and sees people who aren't there. At one stage when I was trying to find out, unsuccessfully, which of her relations visit her, she said, 'I have Paddy White – he's very nice – he comes to see me.' I happen to know her saint of a brother-in-law drives over from Mount Wilson every Sunday.

20 MARTIN ROAD, 27.v.73.
TO INGMAR BJÖRKSTÉN
Dear Ingmar Björkstén,
As usual you ask a lot of difficult questions, and seem to be looking for a lot which isn't there. I hadn't thought of *The Eye of the Storm* as being 'mandalic', but I suppose it is. It is in one sense the still centre of the actual cyclone, and in another the state of peace and spiritual awareness which Mrs Hunter reaches on the island and again before her death. The fact that she is attended by four women doesn't have any particular significance.

A *propos* mandalas, I suppose symmetry appeals to me, and life I find symmetrical, when I used to think it haphazard, without design.

If my style and attitudes have changed in this book, I expect it is because I am growing old and one cares less about certain things, more about others. If I use the less punctuated stream of consciousness it is because Elizabeth Hunter spends most of her time dozing, dreaming, and in spite of her flashes of perception, is verging on senility.

My use of colour in any book has never been entirely conscious. Colour has always meant a lot to me, and it comes out spontaneously in my writing. If it is bluish silvery misty in *The Eye of the Storm* it is because Elizabeth Hunter is half-blind.

I think perhaps I am not so conscious of Australia as Australia in spite of all the chauvinistic ranting going on at present. I don't think I have learnt to accept Australia, but to endure it.

I can't see any connexion between the Jewish and homosexual minorities. It would not have entered my head, and I feel this connexion isn't in my unconscious mind. If I wanted to write a novel about homosexuals, I should have written it, but that is a theme which easily becomes sentimental and/or hysterical. It is anyway, rather worn.

I've read very little Nietzsche – some of *Also Sprach Zarathustra* when I was at Cambridge. He doesn't appeal to me.

The title *Return to Abyssinia* comes from Johnson's *Rasselas*: about the prince who set out to see the wonders of the world, and on seeing them, decides there is nothing for him but to return to Abyssinia. My play which was written before the War wasn't performed till after it. There isn't a copy in existence as far as I know. Anyway, it wasn't of anything but ephemeral, pre-War interest.

I can't really tell you what prompted me to write the books you name. If I ever knew, I've forgotten. The creative process can't be pinned down, as you seem to believe, and it is also far simpler. You ask about the 'mystery of ordinariness' – well, it is a mystery which one either sees and accepts, or doesn't. If you could carve it up like a lump of meat, then it wouldn't be a mystery.

Sorry to sound irritable, but I am asked so many of these questions which can't be answered.

I did go to Sweden very briefly with my parents when I was 16. Up from Malmö to Stockholm, then across to Oslo. After 45 years naturally I can't remember much. My impressions are only youthful and superficial ones: the lakes very dreamlike, in Stockholm the Town Hall and the Quays; I drank my first red wine while there. Nothing very significant, I'm afraid.

I do wish people wouldn't write these books. I'd write one myself if it wouldn't mean dropping everything else.

Yrs,

Patrick White.

20 Martin Road, 9.vi.73
TO GEOFFREY DUTTON
Most exhausting was *The Garden of the Finzi-Continis*,[8] which shattered me more than any film I have ever seen. Fortunately we were only able to get seats in the fourth row, so I was able to stay on when it was over and creep out into the back lane. There's not a false note in this marvellously acted, visually beautiful film. Everybody should see it to remind them of the anti-Semitism hidden in themselves. Such as I have in me had been boiling up lately owing to the activities of some of these unscrupulous Jewish developers we have in Sydney. I think that is largely why the film came as such a shock.

20 Martin Road, 5.viii.73
TO MARSHALL BEST
Dear Marshall,
Thanks for your letter. You sound pleasantly rural in your life, and I often wish I could do the same sort of thing but know I couldn't stand more than a fortnight of it. Perhaps in another ten years we shall be driven from this city as you have been from New York, although by then I don't imagine Manoly and I will have the strength to keep our chins above the weeds.

We don't envisage any long trips at this stage, only a few days on the Barrier Reef starting next week, and perhaps another short trip to Tasmania in November.[9] I hate the thought of it all, but it does have some connexion with the book I may write next.

I have now finished my book of shorter novels and stories in *The Cockatoos*, but think I shall wait till *The Eye of the Storm* is launched before sending it to the Viking.

Our local political squabbles never cease. I had to go to court last week over a ban by the Builders' Labourers' Union on a building development up the road after we had asked them for help. The situation is too complicated, corrupt, and for you, boring, so I shan't go into it. The secretary of the Builders' Labourers' is a most remarkable man, who has done a lot towards saving bits of Sydney we don't want destroyed. Because he is also a Communist there is a perpetual stream of screams from the Right, by whom I too, am labelled a Communist, though I think to the Left I am still a Fascist . . .

I don't know whether you've heard anything about our new Federal

[8]Directed by Vittorio de Sica, 1970.
[9]To explore the landscape of *A Fringe of Leaves*.

Government's assistance to the arts – all very lavish – salaries for creative artists on application. It will be interesting to see what happens; I suspect that nobody will write, paint, or compose any better than they have been doing already – but it's a good thing to try it out. Almost everybody is now on a committee of some kind deciding who shall have what. I was asked to be on the literary one, but felt I could contribute more by getting on with what I have to do. Any of my friends who are on this committee seem to spend so much time reading manuscripts I can't see how they will ever have time for their own work.

My typing doesn't get any better as you can see. In any case I ought to stop and get on with cooking a goose for Manoly's birthday feast.

Hope all is well with you and the vegetable garden,

Yours

Patrick

At last I've got hold of Edmund Wilson's *Upstate*. Haven't yet begun. His *Window on Russia* I thought a most illuminating book – but that is what he almost always was.[10]

HAPPY BAY, QUEENSLAND 17.viii.73

CARD TO ALICE HALMAGYI

This is the place we have liked best. Fortunately it doesn't seem to appeal to the average tourist because it has simplicity. I'd like to go back some time and spend a couple of weeks. The real nightmare is Daydream Island which has everything vulgar, including mature Hungarian whores stretched on banana-lounges. (One of them was having her thighs kissed as we passed.) Over everything hangs a stench of sewage. Swarms of tourists everywhere. Don't know how the parents manage to survive.

P.

---

[10] To the Duttons, 2.ix.73, he wrote: 'Did you read Edmund Wilson's *Upstate*? Have just finished it – to my loss. That and A *Window on Russia* make me feel I must set to and try to collect all the Edmund Wilsons, probably rather difficult at this stage. I've seldom wanted to meet writers I admire, only a few in whom I can see qualities which would have brought us together as friends. Edmund Wilson is one (too late) Stevie Smith (dead also) and Enid Bagnold (surely preparing to leave us soon). Do you know if there is a life of Edmund Wilson? After what I've said earlier in this letter I'd be most curious to know what made all those marriages break up. Somebody in *Upstate* refers to his four wives.' PW was reading Wilson in the weeks before he died; he told me, 'I never tire of him.'

20 Martin Road, 23.viii.73
TO TOM MASCHLER
Dear Tom,

I gather Tim Curnow[11] sent *The Cockatoos* to Juliet, so I expect you will have it before you go away.

I came across a most irritating mistake in *The Eye of the Storm*. On p.531 line 19 'stiff, grey, mushroom silk– – ' In my corrected proof copy I have written 'grainy' very distinctly in the margin, and here it has come out as that rather footling and unnecessary 'grey'. 'Mushroom' of course conveyed the colour, and 'grainy' was to have suggested texture. I imagine somebody was reading out the corrections and the printer mis-heard. Now I can't help wondering, without reading through the whole thing, what else has gone wrong!

I found this only because a woman called Patricia Brent of the BBC has asked me to read something from *The Eye of the Storm* for the Third Programme, and I thought I might do the last meeting between Mrs Hunter and Mrs Wyburd. It will not be taped until Sept 4th, and may not be even then. I am rehearsing to find out whether my false teeth will become fatally entangled with the words. I don't know whether you would approve anyway. I shall tell the woman that if I do make the tape, she must get in touch with you or Graham to see whether you want such a performance.

We arrived back earlier than we expected from our trip to the Barrier Reef because the air company said it wouldn't be worth their while to land two passengers at a place where they had agreed to put us down; we should have had to fly to Brisbane and then all the way back to Gladstone, so I said, 'home!' We did have a very good week before that, cruising round the Whitsunday Islands in a small boat. It's every bit as beautiful as the Aegean, though with no human life of any interest – none of those cubist villages and chapels and monasteries. Well, I suppose the human element is pretty uninteresting anywhere in Australia.

I've almost finished *The Golden Notebook*. To me *The Summer Before the Dark* says much more; it's much more a work of art. The *Notebook* becomes too much of a case-book. Perhaps I am too ignorant of the technicalities of psycho-analysis to appreciate it all. In any case, psycho-analysis is a dark cave into which I'd never venture for fear of leaving something important behind. I also get very bored with those tedious Communist stretches in Doris Lessing. But she is marvellous with her human beings when they are not being politically intense or becoming cases.

---

[11](1944–   ), manager of Curtis Brown's Sydney office.

I envy you the Dordogne. We spent a fortnight there last time we were in France (at Sarlat) and explored most of the region with the help of an amiable, though expensive taxi-driver. His name is Delpeyrrat if you are ever in need of a taxi. (When I say he was expensive, I should add that he and his wife gave us a nine course lunch of regional dishes the day before we left.)

Yours

THE EYE OF THE STORM was published in London in September. Cape had earlier rushed advance copies to Artur Lundkvist to distribute to members of the Swedish Academy. In Australia the book languished for weeks on strike-bound wharves.

20 MARTIN ROAD, 13.ix.73
TO GRAHAM C. GREENE
Dear Graham,
Thank you for remembering to send a cable. Everything has been held up this end owing to a strike by the lorry drivers who move the container cargo. They have gone back now, but God knows how long it will take to reach those books; hundreds of ships have queued up during the strike.

In the meantime I have read the review in the *Observer*. Well, what a lot of venom has been generating in the Bailey bosom![12] I think I can tot up the reasons for it, but am surprised at some of the misunderstanding. For instance, to propose Mitty Jacka for Pseuds' Corner when she was intended as a pseud: perhaps in this case my 'leaden satire' wasn't leaden enough for Bailey. And to accuse me of bashing up Mrs Cush of whom I am fond – the false teeth alone: my own life has been partly ruined by having to wear several sections of the wretched things. And to venture so coyly that I might be taking a swipe at somebody over that kermode? it's how the child would pronounce it.

I can't believe Bailey is as obtuse as he pretends to be. I've read two excellent novels by him (not yet the third) but as a critic, he gives the sad performance of a spiteful queen. I'm told there are good reviews in the *Statesman* and *Guardian*,[13] so it doesn't matter as much as it might to be spattered with Bailey's bile.

By now it looks as though the MS. of *The Cockatoos* is well and truly lost. I shall wait till Tom and Juliet get back from their holidays; if it hasn't turned up by then, I shall try to find somebody who is flying over and who is willing to take it to you.

Yours
Patrick.

20 MARTIN ROAD, 20.ix.73
TO TOM MASCHLER
There is one interesting point in Bailey's review you may not be aware of: his use of the word 'sludge' at the end.[14] That is the word used by A. D. Hope in his famous review of *The Tree of Man*. I think it more than coincidental that Bailey should have used it. I believe he got it from an Australian, and who more likely than Clive James of the *Observer*,[15] an admirer of A. D. Hope's, and who gave his *Collected Poems* an ecstatic review in the *Observer* when they appeared a couple of years ago. I think also that advertisement of yours in the *TLS* was a bit misguided and must have stirred some of them up: my 'Edwardian mansion' alone – which it

---

[12]Paul Bailey (1937–) dismissed the novel, 9 Sept., p.37, as PW's 'latest baggy monster' in which his saints and devils lack all independent life and the Hunter family is 'seen to be made of cardboard'. Bailey's novels include *At the Jerusalem*, 1967, *Trespasses*, 1970, and earlier in 1973 *A Distant Likeness*; all published by Cape.

[13]William Walsh in *Statesman*, 7 Sept., p.320; and William Trevor in the *Guardian*, 6 Sept., p.14.

[14]'Why this is sludge, nor is White often out of it.'

[15]James was the paper's television critic.

isn't; if it were, it would be physically impossible to live in it – keeping it clean and all that . . .

Yesterday we spent a pleasant day: the Ralph Richardsons[16] were here to lunch. Apparently he has been reading my books over the years; John Gielgud told me some time ago that R. was one of my fans, but we hadn't met until this time. All these old actors grow quite pop-eyed when they hear all the plays I have seen them in, because of course I was in London all through the Thirties, and not somewhere like Goondiwindi as is commonly thought. (One inaccuracy in your *TLS* advertisement is the reference to my being brought up in the outback till I was 13. We lived in Sydney, though there were visits to 'the country' – you could hardly call it the 'outback'. One critic of the *Eye of the Storm* refers to me as a 'naturalised' Australian, which I find irritating. My great-grandfather came here in 1825, and both my grandfather and father were born in Australia. If I was born in London, it was because my parents spent a couple of years travelling after they married. They returned here when I was six months old. Australia is not mine by naturalisation; it is in my blood – my fate – which is why I have to put up with the hateful place, when at heart I am a Londoner.

This letter has turned into far more than I expected when I set out. Must stop and get on with some of the more dismal jobs required by my 'Edwardian mansion'!

Yours

Patrick.

20 MARTIN ROAD, 7.x.73

TO BARRY HUMPHRIES

Dear Barry,

I had been wondering about you. You sound in the lowest spirits, and it's difficult to know what to tell you: one's spirits are so much one's own affair whether things are going good or bad. At least you are a performer and ought to be able to work some of it off that way, and being a performer you can also move about from here to there. You can't go on blaming yourself for ever about your marriage. Make yourself a new life, and see your children when you come out here. As they grow older they will probably decide to spend more time with you. All very trite, but I can't come up with more!

I don't see that the Lawrence Daws situation is similar to yours. Your marriage was really destroyed by something beyond your control. In his

---

[16]The actor (1902–83) and his wife Meriel.

case he left the boring, bedraggled sparrow he had married, for a dashing, sexy young woman who must be in every way more satisfactory. He chose to do what he has done, and so he doesn't have my sympathy. I like him well enough, but he irritates me when he starts spluttering his woolly aesthetic theories. I believe that all these painters and writers who leave their wives have an idea at the back of their minds that their painting or writing will be the better for it, whereas they only go from bad to worse. Of course this doesn't apply to the great; their art would have gone on tumbling out in what ever circumstances; but oh, the Daws.[17] . . .

Saw Harry M. and Wendy yesterday. They are preparing to move into the house they bought at the end of this street. I think you made a great mistake in taking up with that Packer,[18] but of course Harry has never had control over my life, which might make a difference. But <u>any</u> Packer!

The book has come out everywhere now (no, the States still to come) and there have been some good reviews and some hard knocks. In the *Observer* a jealous outpouring from another Cape novelist (whose work I admire) . . . I also had a blistering, but reasoned review from Tom Rosenthal in the *TLS*.[19] He sent it to me himself, which I appreciated, as there is nothing more wearing than wondering who an anonymous critic can be. The sad part is that he has been one of my great supporters in the past, but finds *The Eye of the Storm* a 'work of misanthropy at best, of hatred at worst'; it has none of the 'nobility' he finds in my other books. If one lives in a corrupt society, in a world which seems to grow blacker and blacker, I suppose some of it must rub off, and I don't see how one can go on turning out noble myths. In fact, I had a great affection for most of the flawed characters in this book, but this didn't come through to Rosenthal. I think the parent–children relationship is probably what shocked him: that it might turn out like this when he is hoping for something warm and idyllic in his own.

I sent over a book of shorter novels called *The Cockatoos* a couple of months ago, but it took six weeks to get there by air (bomb searches perhaps) and I haven't yet had the publishers' reactions.

---

[17]Dilys Daws, a child psychotherapist, told me, 4.vi.94, her family fell about laughing at her described as a 'boring, bedraggled sparrow'. She added: 'Although he had genius, this letter shows impoverished thinking about parents and children. At the time I knew Patrick I was a happy and intensely involved mother. But I sensed an antipathy to myself and to other women in pregnancy, as well as to our small children. This distaste coloured his attitude to the happy and unhappy marriages referred to here.'

[18]Clyde Packer (1935–), impresario son of PW's scourge Sir Frank, represented Humphries briefly and produced his show *At Least You Can Say You've Seen It*.

[19]'High Wind in Australia', 21 Sept., p.1072.

Now I'm sitting about, vegetating, reading and preparing for the next plunge. At the end of the winter, Manoly and I went to Queensland and cruised around the Whitsunday Islands. Unfortunately it was school-holiday time and we considered ourselves lucky when we found room for one buttock on the boat. The in-names, you might be interested to hear, are now Felicity, Melissa, Melanie, and Tiffany. Next month we are going to take a drive round Tasmania, where I haven't been since I was a child. All these places are so beautiful, if they weren't so empty of human interest.

So far we haven't been near the Opera House although there must have been quite fifteen openings. Now the great ladies of the town are preparing to compete against Our Lovely Queen's wattle-embroidered Hartnell on the 20th.[20] One hears hair-raising tales of what goes on behind the scenes: lighting controls too hot to handle (perhaps Old Moore will be right) lavatory bowls collapsing under leading actors, and actresses unable to force their costumes down the corridors. A possum appeared on stage at the dress rehearsal of *War and Peace*.[21] We'll have to go together when you are here at Christmas.

Hope the film will bring you a lot of success and smite the enemy.[22] Do see Bergman's *Cries and Whispers* if you haven't. I haven't always liked Bergman's films, but this was just about perfect.

Yrs

Patrick.

WHITE'S RIVAL FOR THE Nobel in 1973 was Saul Bellow. When the Academy found itself deadlocked, an ill academician was rung for his vote. He decided the contest for Patrick White: 'Why not award the prize to the new land of Australia?' In Canberra the Swedish ambassador was given advance warning in order to break the news to White early on 18 October, but none of the writer's friends would break the absolute rule against giving out his unlisted number. Chaos followed.

[20]Norman Hartnell (1901–79), dressmaker to the Queen, made a wattle yellow crinoline evening gown for her 1954 tour of Australia; she and the dress were immortalised in the 1955 portrait by William Dargie hung in the nation's classrooms and post offices.

[21]True. For years possums had come down from the Botanic Gardens to explore the building site but this was the last seen on stage. Prokofiev's *War and Peace*, first performed in Leningrad in 1946, was chosen in the absence of an Australian work to open the house.

[22]*The Adventures of Barry McKenzie*, 1972, written by Humphries and Bruce Beresford, directed by Beresford. From the *Private Eye* comic strip written by Humphries and drawn by PW's cousin Nick Garland, son of Peggy. The film's success was great in Australia, more mixed abroad.

20 MARTIN ROAD, 23.x.73
TO TOM MASCHLER
Dear Tom,

I was glad to get your reactions to *The Cockatoos*. I had begun to grow very despondent as the result of the typescript's taking six weeks to arrive, then the postal strike here, closing of the airport during the radar technicians strike, in fact every possible obstacle to receiving news of anything from anyone. At one stage it took letters six days to cross the Harbour ...

Thank you for your telegram on my receiving IT. I spent a very strenuous and alarming Thursday night and all day Friday. The press began pounding on the door about 9 p.m. and Manoly found out what it was about. I had gone to bed with a sleeping pill after cleaning the house all day and wasn't going to come down for anybody. They rampaged round the house, ringing bells, pounding doors, and making the dogs bark for at least an hour and a half. Once when I looked out there were about twenty people camped on the lawn, and others on the terrace at the back. I almost didn't dare grope my way downstairs in the dark to get at the whisky. Next morning at six o'clock they started coming back, and during the day I received six television teams, three radio interviewers, all the local newspapers, *Newsweek*, and a lady from Finland. Now things are calmer, but I have a drawerful of letters and telegrams to deal with, and am expected to judge a play competition, address political demonstrations, and hand over the prize-money to nuns who appear on my doorstep. (I have a plan for using the prize-money which is now being discussed with one or two people I am asking to help.)[23]

Well, that is that. I am amazed at the way Australians have reacted, in a way they usually behave only for swimmers and athletes. I am very touched, and have been feeling guilty for some of the things I have said about them in the past. On Sunday Manoly and I went to a concert given by the Moscow Chamber Orchestra and people kept coming up wanting me to sign their programmes.[24] One of my journalist friends says I am the only person ever to have upstaged the Queen.

---

[23]The prize was $81,862. PW explained to Marshall Best, 5.xi.73, 'I'm making the money into a trust fund to give something to ageing Australian writers who have been overlooked during their working lives. Because there is absolutely nothing I want for myself – except to write another book, or two.'

[24]PW's first visit to the completed Opera House: 'An extraordinary building,' he told O'Hea, 22.x.73, 'like some place of pagan pilgrimage.'

Shall be glad when the 4th November is here and we leave for a couple of weeks in Tasmania.

Yours,

Patrick

Yes, this war – I am torn between wanting it to stop and hoping to see the Israelis drive into Cairo and Damascus before that happens.[25]

20 MARTIN ROAD, 3.xi.73
TO TOM MASCHLER
Dear Tom,

I can't remember at what stage I wrote last, but have dug this letter TM: jm of 19th October out of the mass on my desk (I should add, the least part of the correspondence littering various parts of the house). I have also had a letter from Graham written after reading *The Cockatoos* so perhaps this letter from me can be regarded as thanking you both.

I should have liked to go to Stockholm with you both, and Juliet too, as you suggested in your letter, but there were various things against my going at all. I don't want to risk plunging into a northern winter when the flight to Europe from an Australian winter to European <u>summer</u> always upsets my chest badly. A few years ago my sister, who had much the same chest condition, flew over before Christmas to see her grandchildren in London, and died of the expedition. Apart from that, all the ceremony and speechmaking on this occasion would give me the horrors. I have had enough with the 'media' in Sydney and feel mentally and physically exhausted as a result. God knows how I am going to cope with all the mail, some of which can be torn up, but an awful lot I feel I shall have to answer with a few personal lines. The Swedes are determined to have an Australian, and a distinguished one. Mercifully, Sidney Nolan is prepared to go, and as he is a close friend as well as Australian and distinguished, nothing could be better.

Here the political scene is growing very tricky. I ought to become involved, but once you are, you are in it for ever, and I want to write another book.* Manoly and I are leaving tomorrow for twelve days in Tasmania, which will solve the matter temporarily. But before I go I shall have to write a letter which will probably let me in for further fireworks when I get back.[26] I can't go into the political situation in New South

[25]The papers that morning reported details of the ceasefire with Israeli forces 24 km short of Damascus and 72 km from Cairo.

[26]Rebuking both sides of NSW politics for offering only vague promises to protect Sydney, *SMH*, 5.xi.73: 'There is no real indication that historic buildings will not be capriciously destroyed, or that small communities of human beings will not be herded off like cattle . . .'

Wales – it would be too boring for anybody in the outer world – but the Premier we have is a crook, and some of those who are fighting him are rather far to the left. I'm afraid we shall have him till he dies, because the orthodox Labour party, which I shall support when it comes to the vote, is far too wet. (This needs a lot of elaboration, but you will understand.)[27]

One day I shall hope to meet you and hear about what has been going on in the *Observer*. First, Pearl Bailey's venomous outpouring (it amused me to read her ecstasies over Emlyn Williams's pick-ups in the park after that stern criticism of the 'couplings' in *The Eye of the Storm*) then the bitchy little piece from Stockholm about my candidacy for the Prize, after that– – nothing.[28] It saddens me when *The Observer* has played such a part in my life. Perhaps this embarrasses you, as it obviously embarrasses Graham. But I always have to find out the reason for this and that.

Yours

Patrick

* They can't understand you've got to save yourself for the kind of thing I do, but the dozens and dozens of letters I've had tell me that I'm right.

TASMANIA, 6.xi.73

TO JILL HELLYER[29]

Dear Jill,

Thanks for your letter of congratulations. I should have answered before, but life became overwhelming and only started settling down again after I escaped to Tasmania a couple of days ago.

You say, 'No doctor should try to stop anyone dying if they must die.' You should at least wait to hear Cape's reactions to your new book; perhaps you will find reason for not dying. Though I must say waiting for a publisher's reactions makes me feel pretty hopeless even now, and waiting

[27]The crooked premier was Askin; his most effective opponents were the leaders of the Builders' Labourers' Federation. The NSW Labor Party was still a month away from the rejuvenating appointment of Neville Wran as leader of the opposition in the House of Assembly.

[28]Reviewing Williams' *Emlyn An Early Autobiography*, 7 Oct., p.41, Bailey praised his 'very funny and very sharp' observations of life in the 'twilight world' including one rapid exchange after sex in a park: ' "Rent?" "Ten-and-six a week but no bathroom". He looked puzzled. "I meant d'you want money?" "Good God, no," I said. "Do you?" ' A week later the paper carried on page 2 a brief but accurate report that PW was favourite for the Prize.

[29]Poet (1925–   ) and driving force in the establishment of the Australian Society of Authors; from 1970–82 PW gave her advice about writing and other matters.

for press reviews is worse. Still, one hobbles on. And I'm sure if you really look into the matter thoroughly you'll find many quite simple reasons for living – like getting up early and watching the sun rise, or cooking a good meal, or making the furniture shine. Sometimes even now I feel that writing is the least satisfactory occupation: I'd rather have been a baker, or a carpenter, or a farmer, which I could have been if I hadn't taken another path. If you're younger, which I'm not, and which you are, you can retrace your steps and find what you might have been.

But perhaps Cape will take your book[30] I only throw out these hints in case they don't, to show that there are many other more consoling occupations than writing.

Yours
Patrick White.

HOBART, 9.xi.73
TO PEGGY GARLAND
I've brought with me three grocery bags full of letters and telegrams – PRIORITY, OFFICIAL and PERSONAL (there is a fourth NO HURRY, which I left at home) and these I try to deal with at the dressing tables of our motels, in the evening and the early morning, without making a dent on the mountain.

Quite apart from friends and acquaintances, I've had letters from the unknown from Saskatchewan to Bengal (floods from Bengal) mostly begging. They want me to buy them houses, farms, trucks, caravans, from having glaucoma, paralysed husbands (or wives) asthmatic children – it all comes from my having said that I wasn't going to keep the money. I'm surprised that so much is relayed to so many corners of the world, though certainly, on the day of the explosion, I spent twelve hours with television teams, radio reporters, and newspaper representatives. It was a nightmare. I wonder if I shall ever recover from that day, and whether the book I had been contemplating hasn't been killed.

I've gone through life resenting the spite of critics, and here I am thinking adulation is worse! Certainly it could be more destructive.

TASMANIA, 14.xi.73
TO CYNTHIA NOLAN
Brown's River where we spent the Summer when I was about five is now almost unrecognisable as Kingston Beach though I remembered the pines

[30]Cape didn't, but Hellyer continued to write and her novel *Not Enough Savages* was published in 1975 in Sydney.

along the front and the black stream they used to call a river. I can remember sitting on a bench underneath those pines with a number of other children being read to – one of the Pollyanna books – by a friend of my mother's. The other children were in ecstasies, but I thought it was awful, and said so when she asked me how I found it. To which she replied, 'I know what you are. You're a little changeling.' I had no idea what a changeling was, but felt horribly mortified to be told I was something different from the others.

We're leaving for Launceston on the last lap. Home to-morrow.
Love,
Patrick.

20 Martin Road, 16.xi.73
TO JULIET O'HEA
Our trip round Tasmania was exhausting though rewarding. It is one of the most beautiful countries, alternately lush and green, and wild and majestic. It has little connexion with mainland Australia, and I think Tasmanians feel they belong to another country. Much as I enjoyed the landscapes, and the sight of fat sheep and cattle, I think it would be deadly living there: the towns are as provincial as can be, with the arts just beginning to come to life in them. In one country town we were terribly taken with an old house. I could have worked in it, but I said, 'What else would we do?' Manoly replied, 'Sit by the fire and eat scones' which about sums it up. I'd rather risk bursting a blood vessel every week in Sydney.

20 Martin Road, 29.xi.73
TO THE SPEAKER
HOUSE OF REPRESENTATIVES[31]
Dear Mr Cope,
Thank you for your telegram inviting me to the House. Unfortunately, this is the kind of situation to which my nature does not easily adapt itself. I have received congratulations from the Prime Minister, from friends, and from hundreds of Australians unknown to me. It is gratifying and moving that so many people from such varied walks of life should have wanted to express their enthusiasm. So may we, please, leave it at that?
Yours sincerely,
Patrick White.

[31]Jim Cope (1907–   ) had, at Whitlam's instigation, invited PW to Canberra to receive Parliament's congratulations.

20 MARTIN ROAD, 13.xii.73
TO TOM MASCHLER
Dear Tom,
Thank you for the 'oblique' letter of 6th Dec. By the same mail I received
Juliet's explaining everything fully. I am very happy to think there will be
a uniform edition. I'm less happy about those suggested prefaces; I am no
Henry James with elaborate theories on the novel: I simply write a novel
when it can no longer be avoided. But I shall think about the possibility
of prefaces. Juliet suggests including the plays in the uniform edition, and
I would agree to that. There was no mention of *Happy Valley* and I still
don't feel I want it reprinted.

You should have had the jacket design for *The Cockatoos* by now. I
think it is the best Desmond has done. What is worrying me at present is
that there is no sign of proofs, when you said I should have them early in
December. I have begun to wonder whether they are lost. On the other
hand you probably would have warned me by letter if a parcel were on its
way. The correction shouldn't take me very long.

Yesterday we saw in the papers photographs of Sid Nolan at the
ceremony. How thankful I am that I was able to keep out of it! But I
think Sid enjoys that sort of thing. Last night he rang through from
Stockholm and we spoke to them both.

Hope you succeed in having a pleasant Christmas in spite of the
present awfulness. Our sole trial is that the garbage hasn't been collected
for a fortnight.

Yours
Patrick.

20 MARTIN ROAD, 18.xii.73
TO RONALD WATERS
There are great re-printings in all directions – paperbacks, and countries
which wouldn't touch me before are now falling over themselves to get
translation rights. Piracy in Japan and India, and mysterious goings-on in
Russia. I am becoming more cynical every day.

20 MARTIN ROAD, 23.xii.73
TO SUZANNE NÉTILLARD[32]
When I said that Tasmania was beautiful and dead, and you seemed
surprised that I wasn't sufficiently impressed by rural beauty, fresh air,

[32]Translator of *Le Char des élus*, 1965, for Gallimard; now working on *L'Oeil du Cyclone*
which appeared in 1978.

birdsong and so forth, it is because you don't realise the kind of double personality I am. Landscape unspoilt, tranquillity and so forth, is what I long for until I am plunged into it, then before very long I can't wait to plunge back into the city, because I must have that kind of turmoil and stimulus, go to plays, films, look at paintings, talk to people, or simply roam the streets, looking. I suppose the edge of this park where we live is as good a compromise as I shall ever find. It is peaceful, natural, a sea of trees, birds coming by hundreds to our garden, and yet I can rush off, and in ten minutes, be in the thick of awfulness.

20 Martin Road, 28.xii.73
TO THE DUTTONS
Dear Nin and Geoffrey,
I'm sorry I was not at home the other day when you rang up. I was trying to catch a taxi to take something to Beatrice Tildesley, but had to give up as all taxi drivers apparently were suffering from Christmas Eve, or perhaps they were engaged to drive the faithful to mass . . .

When the New Year comes I am going to throw everything connected with the Nobel Prize in the incinerator, forget about it, and start work on the novel which has been trying to squeeze its way out. There will be an awful lot of people offended, I'm afraid, by not getting answers to their letters. So many seem to think that theirs is the only letter I have received. I've had as many as three letters from some irate ladies saying, 'Didn't you receive my registered letter?' . . .

Have by now read most of Manning's Vol III,[33] which has given me even more than the others, perhaps because I am reading it at the right moment when I am about to plunge back into the Nineteenth Century. What is so amazing is that Australians have changed so little; we are the same arrogant plutocrats, larrikins, and Irish rabble as we were then. At least the graziers have been damped down. But the torturing of men like Gipps and Eardley-Wilmott might be taking place today.[34] And at the bottom of the dung heap lots of little black Harris cockroaches were scurrying about self-importantly then as now.

Did you read Max's last piece in the *Australian*[35] 'Only Martin Buber

[33] *A History of Australia III: the beginning of an Australian civilisation 1824–51*, 1973.
[34] George Gipps (1791–1847), governor of NSW whose liberal measures were bitterly opposed by the graziers of the early Legislative Council. John Eardley-Wilmot (1783–1847), lieutenant-governor of Van Diemen's Land, liberal but incompetent who was recalled for *inter alia* tolerating homosexuality among convicts.
[35] Max Harris, 27 Dec., p.7.

believes it is possible to enter into the otherness of other people to be aware of what it would be like to be their "thou" instead of your own "I".' Surely this is what any creative novelist, dramatist, or actor does incessantly? Max believes it would be a 'tough test of the imagination to contemplate what it would be like to be a female instead of a bloke.' I suspect this was coaxed out by Thelma Forshaw's statement that in *The Eye of the Storm* I join the ranks of those male writers who understand Woman better than women themselves.[36] The hopeless Max then goes on to say, 'How much of a woman's sex life is histrionic – acting out ecstasies, intensities, and orgasms in order to assure her threshing-machine of a partner that his grunting pleasures are biologically reciprocated? How much acting do how many women have to do?' This is rather reminiscent of p.27 of *The Eye of the Storm* '– –The Juggernaut of stifling nights under a mosquito net etc– –' . . .

Tonight we are going to a party Kylie is giving for the Comet,[37] at which there are going to be ninety guests, we are told, and where I expect I shall have to hide amongst the acalyphas.

Love to everybody,
Patrick.

WRITING *A FRINGE OF LEAVES* was a deliberate discipline, the only way White knew of returning to a normal life. As if to bind himself to the task, he announced the book to Tom Maschler on 2 January 1974. 'To-day I started on *A Fringe of Leaves* which I want to finish before I am finished.' The strategy of the novel had not changed: to turn to his own purposes the story of the wreck of the *Stirling Castle* and the ordeal of one survivor, Eliza Fraser. But where he once saw only horror and frustration in her ordeal with the Aborigines of Fraser Island and her escape with her convict rescuer, now White was willing to admit pleasure. Though he complained endlessly about the Prize, it was liberating him: here was heady vindication mixed with the fear of becoming a museum object. Both impelled him to show the world he was still alive, still a passionate artist. White's work from this point is saturated with a late, relaxed sensuality.

[36]Forshaw (1923–   ), critic and writer of short stories, commenting in the *Australian*, 22 Dec. 1973, p.18.
[37]Tennant, to celebrate the disappointing Kohoutek.

20 Martin Road, 6.i.74
TO INGMAR BJÖRKSTÉN

Dear Ingmar,

Thank you very much for your letter. If I haven't replied before, it's because I find it very difficult to cope as the letters continue to pour in with demands for this and that. Since the New Year I have started another novel, and mean to concentrate on that, turning my back on everything else, because I realise it is the only way to survive.

Your book has not arrived in any form or language! Perhaps it will eventually. Bonniers[38] pocket translation of *The Tree of Man* sent by my London agent did finally get here a few days before I received from Bonniers both *The Tree of Man* and *Riders in the Chariot*.

We certainly shan't attempt to travel in 1974 because I want to get on with my next novel, but I should like to visit Sweden and Norway eventually as I want to see Lapland and the fiords, and to meet my Swedish translator Magnus Lindberg, as well as you, again, and my schoolfriend Ragnar Christophersen at Oslo University.[39] All this must be fitted in some time in the future.

Between ourselves, the Nobel Prize is a terrifying and destructive experience though it mightn't be to somebody else. (I'm sure Heinrich Böll was able to take it in his stride, and it was a shot of life to the unfortunate Solzhenitsyn.) But the back-wash is too much, for me at least. I have sent an autobiographical sketch to Stockholm, to the man who has asked for it, at the strange address 'Fack'.[40] But I can't face an essay: everything I have of *Vernunft*[41] and *Poesie* goes into my novels.

At the moment I am disgusted by most of the world – great Western powers rushing independently to curry favour with the Arabs and sell out on Israel. We are keeping carefully aloof, or not altogether, as we speed up wheat consignments to Egypt. I may have blotted my copybook the other night at dinner with the Prime Minister by bringing this up. There is an excellent article by Dürrenmatt in the *Züriche Zeitung*,[42] which I took with me and urged him to consider with his Minister for Foreign Affairs. Otherwise we got on well. I think Whitlam is on the right side which is

[38]PW's publishers in Sweden.
[39]Christophersen, professor of English at Oslo University, was at Cheltenham with PW.
[40]Fack=post office box; the sketch was for a collection of brief lives of all the 1973 laureates, published in Sweden by Imprimerie Royale P. A. Norstedt & Soner, 1974; PW's essay was later republished in *Patrick White Speaks*, 1989, pp.39–44.
[41]Reason.
[42]'Ich stelle mich hinter Israel', *Neue Züricher Zeitung*, 22 Oct. 1973, p.31.

more than can be said for the Federal Liberals and the dreadful government of New South Wales.

The Nolans rang from Stockholm a couple of times. Haven't heard from them since, but Sidney is always pouring forth in paint, and can't write more than a few lines from time to time on a post-card, and Cynthia has to screw herself up above her ailments: some years ago she was suffering from TB and I don't think she has ever really recovered. I love them both and hope to see them out here in February or March when Sid has an exhibition at the Adelaide Festival. (Perhaps you will be in Australia too, I seem to remember you saying.)

If a film called O Lucky Man (director Lindsay Anderson) should turn up in Stockholm you must go and see it: we were both carried away.

Best wishes from us both,
Patrick.

20 MARTIN ROAD, 20.i.74
TO GEOFFREY DUTTON
Dear Geoffrey,
Thanks for the note about ABR. The copy didn't arrive, but James Allison, who had been promising to let me see it since before Christmas, came good the other day. The article is excellent, and will make several people gnash their teeth. That Lawson is the academics' great cover-up boy.[43] Recently somebody gave me a correspondence, or ding-dong, conducted by various intellectuals, for and against, in the Canberra Times. Funny up to a point, then disgusting, and finally a waste of time. All the same I feel like going down to the ANU to have a look at his thesis.[44] I was told he had dug up such a lot of 'valuable biographical information'. If it's as inaccurate as some of his other statements I really could refute him in public. But again, is it worth while?

[43]Alan Lawson, compiling his bibliography of PW's work for Oxford University Press in Melbourne, came to doubt PW's bitter claim to be a writer praised abroad while misunderstood at home. Lawson's letter to the Canberra Times, 27 Oct. 1973, expressing these doubts provoked several articles and letters over the next few weeks; he set out his argument in full in 'Unmerciful Dingoes?', Meanjin, December 1973, p.379: 'In general it needs to be insisted that White's Australian reception has been much better, the overseas reviews often less favourable, and the general critical standard of the response higher, than the accepted account would suggest.' Dutton's review of The Eye of the Storm in Australian Book Review, Nov. 1973, p.121, weighed into the argument on PW's side, attacking Australian critics for 'gagging' on PW's early novels.
[44]MA, Australian National University, Patrick White. An analysis of the structural use of imagery in the earlier novels – together with a comprehensive bibliography.

We spent a lovely evening at *The Magic Flute* with the Manning Clarks. Opera has come on a hundred miles since we last went, while the theatre, in spite of all the trumpet-blowing, remains at amateur level. And the minute you get inside that opera theatre, there is all the glamour and excitement I expect when I go to the theatre, which I get in London, whereas usually in Sydney one is battered into a state of moral and physical despair in some Nissen hut or church hall. Manning was very circumspect and sober on this occasion. I find her difficult to come to terms with, but I'm told she only blossoms when he isn't there. That must go for both of them! There was also a very tall son, Andrew, a journalist starting work with the *National Times*,[45] whom we hadn't met before, with a willowy young woman I gather he is shacked up with rather than married to, and a daughter,[46] the Russian expert, who doesn't look at all well. Also a funny little man from the Department of Slavonic Studies at Yale,[47] who knew Jinx Nolan at Bennington, and whom I finished liking very much.

Again I am in trouble, just when I thought I had reached calm waters and could get on with my work in peace: the other day a man arrived on my doorstep, rather a nice brigadier called James, who announced that I had been picked on by the Federal Australia Day Council as Australian of the Year, and was expected to go to Melbourne on the 25th to an official lunch with the Lord Mayor, Premier and other notables, to receive a plaque from the Governor. As you can imagine, I was horrified – and so was the brigadier to find he wasn't received with gladness and joy. I tried to fob them off, then to think of somebody who could do it for me, but everybody suitable is having holidays. So I shall have to go. At least I have thought of a number of things I want to say, and I shall be able to talk about the three other people from whom they might have chosen, and given me a rest. But I've spent sleepless nights with the speech revolving in my head, and foreseeing what might go wrong.

I am working as regularly as possible at the novel. I'm glad to have it, otherwise I should have gone mad by now. I think it's a good thing you are resigning from the Literary Board and that awful Adelaide Writer's Week Committee: you'd go mad too, in time.

It's weeks since I opened the *Observer* without reading about Athol Fugard: his plays are the rage of London, and again we have missed the bus, through no fault of mine.[48] One play is being done in Sydney towards

[45] Australian weekly of immense distinction, now defunct.
[46] Katerina.
[47] Katerina's husband Michael Holquist, then an associate professor at Yale.
[48] PW had been nagging the Adelaide Festival to import the company run by Fugard (1932–   ), the South African actor and playwright.

the end of the month, but at a theatre which has a worse amateurish stench than any other.⁴⁹ Even so, I shall have to venture along.

A few days ago a season-at-Sarsaparilla started up in Martin Road – a nice little kelpie bitch somebody had dumped, and who attracted the whole Paddo pack as well as inflaming all the neighbourhood males. There was a terrible slaughter next door on Thursday when a beagle fought with our neighbour's spaniel. She and her eldest child each got bitten on a leg, and Manoly, in trying to separate the dogs, through the most dangerous part of the hand. We rushed up to St Vincent's casualty where he spent about an hour and a half, waiting for the doctors to finish their lunch, and then having stitches and other treatment. The sister who knew the answers to all the ignorant young doctor's questions (he spent most of the time combing his moustache in the glass) had been given an anti-tetanus injection herself that morning after being bitten by a patient.

Hope you have a good season at KI⁵⁰ to make up for New Year with Bubbles.⁵¹ I never heard of her having anything to do with Yevtushenko while he was in Sydney, but I suppose even I don't hear everything. Can you, please, send me an address where I can write to Vosnezensky?

Love to all

Patrick

P.S. You can put any meat in that press provided it has been cooked and boned. It would be good for spiced beef for instance, which I haven't done because our press is smaller, and we're not a family, nor do we have such large gatherings. I have done things like boiled bacon, pickled pork, and chickens. A whole leg of pork should squeeze into the press you have. It would take a turkey, or goose, or several ducks and chickens. Then when the meat is pressed and cold, you can carve from the slab in professional slices using that EVA⁵² you've got, and serve with a glamorous sauce.

MARTIN ROAD, 27.i.74.

TO CYNTHIA NOLAN

Dear Cynthia,

I've now had two letters from you: the Full Account of What Happened in Stockholm and the later one in answer to mine. It was fortunate you

⁴⁹The Australian Theatre in Newtown, now defunct.
⁵⁰Kangaroo Island.
⁵¹The headmaster of Geelong Grammar Charles Fisher and his wife Anne had gathered family and friends to celebrate the New Year; present were his brother Humphrey, an ABC television executive, wife Diana (Bubbles) Fisher, a television personality somewhat in the Andrea mould, and their father, the Archbishop of Canterbury.
⁵²A brand of circular knife.

felt like going on that mission, because I should have found it agony
however good the food. I'm sorry that part of it didn't agree with you and
that you broke your crown before leaving (nothing compared with what
happened to me last week, as you will hear). A pity you felt like that
about the Lundkvists. I must say I felt they were very difficult when they
were here, and I couldn't understand a lot of what he was saying in English.
He is apparently my greatest supporter. Ingmar Björkstén, the young man
who came here to interview me for television, told me that Lundkvist had
worked his way up from the lowest social level and made himself the
greatest authority in Sweden on foreign literatures. Björkstén seems to see
them sometimes; he too, says they are complicated, but you get over that.
I haven't heard lately from my translator Lindberg. He must be worked to
death, poor man. The translation of *The Vivisector* reached me the other
day, and the publishers are driving him as hard as they can to finish *The
Eye of the Storm*. I told him to take his time otherwise it won't be any
good.

Last Friday I had one of the most awful experiences: the Australia
Day Committee which gives that annual lunch in Melbourne Town Hall
decided I was Australian of the Year (they've been through all the swimmers
and tennis players.) I felt I could hardly avoid going with Melbourne only
a bus ride away. I was met by Barry Jones, whom I found I liked.[53] We
had a walk round the Art Gallery before the Event. Hadn't been there for
years, but I wasn't able to concentrate very well in the circumstances.
Then we went to the Town Hall where the Notables had begun to gather.
Managed to have a few words with Maie. Dick is now so deaf one can
hardly get through even shouting at the top of one's voice; Maie must
have a most exhausting life. I rather liked the Vice-Chancellor of Melbourne
University,[54] but everyone else was pretty anonymous. One man made me
sign his Diary for 1974. He told me that last year he got Shane Gould,
and the year before Evonne Goolagong.[55] Then, suddenly, my lower false
teeth broke up on a savoury boat. The two halves of the structure continued
to lie in quite a well-behaved way on my gums, but I was afraid that when
I tried to eat the lunch I might swallow pieces of metal, or worse, spit out
a few teeth while making my speech. So I had to put them in my
handkerchief while seated between the Lady Mayoress, quite a jolly big

---

[53](1932–   ), author, energetic polymath and politician whom PW came to trust almost
alone among ministers in the Labor cabinets of the 1980s.
[54]David Derham (1920–85), lawyer.
[55]Previous Australians of the Year: Gould (1956–   ), record-breaking swimmer, and
Goolagong (1951–   ), the Aboriginal Wimbledon champion.

rinsed blonde called Whalley,[56] and the British High Commissioner Sir Morrice James, nothing special, but we had a few laughs.[57] The Lunch itself was not at all attractive, and the speeches were endlessly boring. Also there was a baritone who sang Dorothea Mackellar[58] and a few other items. Then I was presented with the plaque (not bad) by Jumbo Delacombe, who, I am told, likes to play with vinyl toys in his bath.[59] Then I made the speech, and offended quite a number I believe, because that I said Australia Day should be a day for self-searching not trumpet-blowing. I was able to bring in Manning Clark's History, the third volume of which I had just finished reading. What one does notice in this is that we are almost exactly like what we were then. I was able to point out a few things like the solitary confinement cells we are now building at Long Bay, and which are very reminiscent of those at Port Arthur and Norfolk Island, and that we are still wondering unsuccessfully how we can do the best by the Aborigines we dispossessed. I also said I thought Manning, Barry Humphries and Jack Mundey, had an equal right to be standing there as Australian of the Year, and that I might try sawing the plaque in four when I got home and sending a piece to each of them. I suppose the fact that I was hissing all this through the gaps in my teeth did make it sound a bit vindictive. Afterwards I found I had a few ecstatic supporters, but there were dirty looks from many directions, including the Army (the Navy and Air Force approved) and the organisers. Then I went with Barry Jones, Phillip Adams,[60] and a Professor McLeod, a Melbournian from Auckland University,[61] to have a drink at Parliament House. They took me to the airport where I found I had lost my ticket; I think it had probably disintegrated in all the sweat I had lost that day.

Well that will be my last public appearance . . .

Heard one very depressing thing while I was in Melbourne: Tim Burstall is preparing to make a film about Mrs Fraser with Diane Cilento. That beefy, insensitive boor will bugger it up properly, and I should have

[56]Patricia (Paddy) Whalley.

[57](1916–89), diplomat created Baron Saint Brides, 1977.

[58](1885–1968), author of the stanza that begins, 'I love a sunburnt country . . .' PW met her on the ship bringing him back to jackeroo in 1930: 'She was drifting about in veils, pissed.'

[59]Rohan Delacombe (1906–91), governor of Victoria.

[60](1939–   ), commentator, advertising executive, producer of The Adventures of Barry McKenzie, 1972, and other films. Adams and PW never hit it off.

[61]Bill McLeod (1933–   ), psychiatrist.

thought by now that Diane C. would make a very wrinkly nude when the Australian light plays on her skin.[62]

I have been working on A *Fringe of Leaves* all this month and am now on with it. (I wonder how many others are at present writing this novel?) I had hoped it might be a short book, but don't expect it will be: I keep seeing so many fresh aspects which will have to be dealt with if it is to have any depth.

20 MARTIN ROAD, 17.ii.74
TO MARY BENSON
Dear Mary,

DAVID MCNICOLL! One of the worst Australian reactionaries and philistines. For years he edited a dreadful paper the *Daily Telegraph* for another reactionary, philistine monster, Sir Frank Packer. I thought McNicoll had retired, but apparently he is still around. I am told he went to South Africa a few months ago and wrote a series of articles in support of the S.A. regime which were published here in *The Bulletin*, a Packer-owned magazine.[63] Packer also owns a TV channel, but has sold out of the *Telegraph* to Rupert Murdoch. For years McNicoll did everything to kill my novels and plays by getting 'funny' columnists to review them and send them up. When *Voss* came out, there was a large headline: 'Australia's Most Unreadable Novelist'.[64] Before my play *The Season at Sarsaparilla* came on, he personally wrote a piece which began, 'What does Patrick White know about suburbia? He was brought up in a mansion at X – –' I was forced to write and say you don't have to commit a murder to write about one, and in any case, I had lived in suburbia for twelve years, between sink and stove, and scrubbing

---

[62]Burstall (1929–) made *Eliza Fraser* with Susannah York in the title role; the success of the film seems, rather, to have boosted PW's sales when it appeared within weeks of the book in 1976. Cilento (1934–) so impressed PW in the 1979 ABC television version of *Big Toys* that he began to sketch a play for and about her called, The Lyrebird and the White Mountain. Unfinished; lost.

[63]Visiting Robben Island, this 'island of pleasant surprises', McNicoll enjoyed an hour's conversation with Nelson Mandela then employed gathering seaweed along the beaches. The visitor was impressed by the food (Mandela was not) and handsome stands of blue gums growing in that stony ground. As a keepsake he gave Mandela an Australian $5 note. *Bulletin*, 14 April 1973, p.28.

[64]In fact, the headline on this cruel and very funny review by Ross Campbell, 15 Feb. 1958, p.18, was 'Foggy weather over Leichhardt'.

my own floors, before writing that play.[65] McNicoll has a brother, an admiral, who I once met, and his 'trained mind' of a wife.[66] I was flattered to find out that I was on the admiral's list of unreadables – along with Tolstoy. If David McNicoll, the ex-editor, ever found out that I had recommended your play to the ABC, I'm afraid that would go against you . . .

Again I have hopes for the filming of *Voss*. I suddenly had the idea that Losey[67] might be the director for it, and the producer flew him out here last week for talks. We get on very well. I have hopes, though there are still lots of difficulties to surmount.

Yours
Patrick.

THE PRIZE PUT WHITE briefly back on top of the New York literary pile. His new editor at Viking Press, Alan Williams, more than doubled the planned print run of *The Eye of the Storm* to 18,000 copies; the paperback advance was the largest White ever had in North America. When the novel appeared in mid-January, Patrick White's reviews led the book pages once again as they had in the 1950s.

20 MARTIN ROAD, 17.ii.74
TO ALAN WILLIAMS
Some of the reviews you sent were very good, but there were also a few stinkers. The one in *Time Magazine* stank so high I have been forced to write to the lousy paper to correct a factual detail. I enclose a copy of the letter in case you get any repercussions . . .
P.S. Am in the middle of the Chekhov letters you sent: they are so wonderfully visual, and that is what appeals to me most in writing; but

[65]McNicoll's query, *Sunday Telegraph*, 26 May 1963, came with this preamble: 'How refreshing to see some of the critics summoning up enough courage to be critical of something written by Patrick White. This is long overdue. I haven't yet seen *The Season at Sarsaparilla* but I hear that if it were a film it would probably not have got past the censors. What I want to know is this: How would a rich bachelor . . .' etc. McNicoll sidestepped PW's reply published 7 July by protesting, 'he is well-to-do by average standards. And if he really does do all the cleaning and cooking then it's by choice not necessity.'
[66]See PW to Desmond Digby, 8.iii.63, page 220.
[67]Joseph Losey (1909–84), American director working since McCarthy days in Europe. PW was hoping for another of the Losey/Harold Pinter collaborations which had produced such successes as *The Go-Between*, 1970. PW discovered when the director came to Sydney in 1974 that they had much in common: asthma, anger, theatre, dogs, etc. Losey had admired *Voss* when first published and even considered filming it then. PW's work, he told the *Australian*, 23 Feb. 1974, p.23, 'is quite fantastic'.

really, to travel in Russia, or just to live there, was a form of torture long
before the Soviet.

20 MARTIN ROAD, 17.ii.74
TO THE EDITOR,
TIME MAGAZINE
Dear Sir,
It isn't my habit to write to papers after reading reviews of my books, but
after coming across Martha Duffy (whoever she is) on my novel *The Eye
of the Storm* where she refers to me as 'living in Sydney with several dogs
and a male housekeeper', I feel I must draw your attention to an incorrect,
and I should have thought gratuitous, biographical detail. The distinguished,
and universally respected man who has given me his friendship and moral
support over a period of thirty-four years, has never been a housekeeper. *I*
am that, and shall continue playing the role at least till I am paralysed: it
keeps me in touch with a reality often remote from those who dish up
their superficial, slovenly pieces for *Time Magazine*.[68]
    Yours Sincerely,
    P.W.
    (Patrick White)

20 MARTIN ROAD, 17.iii.74
TO RONALD WATERS
Dear Ronald,
I wrote saying we expect you in May, but Fred says you didn't receive it.
I certainly didn't receive the letter saying you had got the sweater, which
Fred says you wrote! The Sydney postal service gets worse and worse the
more we pay. Strikes all the time ...
    Last week also we had a function in the home: the Swedish Ambassador
brought the plaque and diploma which go with the Prize. I managed to
get round it this way, because otherwise they wanted me to go to a dinner
at the Embassy in Canberra with dinner jackets and speeches and the
Prime Minister, the lot. The Nolans turned up just in time for the occasion,
and Cynthia wore the dress and the jewels she wore when they represented
me in Stockholm. A couple of other friends also came, and we had a
pleasant evening, though I spent three days sweating over the dinner. (The
Sydney climate has never been so abominable as this summer.)
    Really very little news. I am working as much as possible on my new

---

[68]Published 25 March, p.2, omitting the barbs 'whoever she is' and 'often remote from
those who dish up their superficial, slovenly pieces for *Time Magazine*.'

novel, but am getting a lot of backwash from the Adelaide Festival as writers return from there to the outer world. This week we are seeing Nadine Gordimer. I am looking forward to that as she is one of the writers I admire most. She is one who ought to get the Nobel Prize, though I wouldn't wish it on to her having experienced it myself.[69]

Have been invited to fly to New York to address PEN International at a dinner in June. Imagine all those vultures of the media! They said in their cable that I should be 'protected' but that is no longer possible unless you stay at home and don't open the door.

Lots of dog dramas. Fanny had an enormous (benign) tumour taken off her belly. Fortunately her heart didn't give out, and she is now quite skittish on digitalis and an injection Manoly gives once a month. However, she now has difficulty in holding her water, so I have to get up in the middle of the night or have a piss-mopping session first thing in the morning. Ethel's cheek swelled up. They thought she had cancer at first, and for a couple of days we went round thinking we shouldn't see Ethel again. But it turned out to be no more than an infection of the salivary gland.

Must go and stuff some mushrooms for lunch. Looking forward to May.

P.

20 MARTIN ROAD, 31.iii.74
TO JOSEPH LOSEY
Dear Joe,
Thank you for your letter, and since then the Malcolm Lowry and Pinter's script[70] have arrived. I have just finished the latter, and am most impressed. I quailed at the thought of starting on it, and when I did there was rather a lot of Spot-the-Character about my reactions, but when I settled down it became a marvellous visual read. What surprised me most was the way Albertine, who is such a bore in the book, turns into perhaps the best acting part. This may be because so much about her is unrevealed, and what suits Pinter best is the unrevealed. The Guermantes and Charlus have wonderful moments of course. I was a little bit disappointed Madame Verdurin didn't come out more strongly, and that there was not more of Odette who impressed me most in my youth. Marcel himself will come through very well if he is not too American nor too English. I am surprised it will take as much as you say to make such a film, although the dresses will cost a lot if you don't skimp on them, and yes, I suppose all those

[69]Gordimer (1923–   ), South African writer and supporter of the banned African National Congress; she won the Prize in 1991.
[70]Published 1978 as The Proust Screenplay.

carriages – and everything. But I hope you make it, now that it is raising its head again. It only makes me sad to think that *Voss* will not be made for years, by which time we may all be dead or too decrepit. (One point, a very minor one, in connexion with *A la recherche*, couldn't 'syringa' be called 'lilac'. I know the first is botanically correct, but lilac is what it means to most people, including myself, though Ivor Novello almost withered the stuff for ever.)

Pinter is now the one I should like to write the script for *Voss* if it could possibly be fitted into his writing schedule – or perhaps he definitely wouldn't like to do it, as I can imagine there are many who wouldn't – but do try to persuade him . . .

Harry is rushing about in all directions – Senegal Ballet, just launched, *The Rocky Horror Show* next month. They still haven't moved into their house in this street where craftsmen come and go and a readymade garden has been potted out. (Two things I couldn't submit to are a landscape gardener and an interior decorator.) You never told me who your fellow guests were at the Lees' jacket-and-tie dinner,[71] and no doubt have forgotten by now. I no longer have any contact with Jack. I think he was offended when suddenly he heard that Losey might be directing *Voss*, though there had never been any indication that he aspired to do it.

I have had the first copy of *The Cockatoos*, jacket and all. The book won't be out till June, but I have asked Cape to send you one of the early copies. I am now well into another novel – don't know what it is like – it is giving me a lot of trouble, but for that matter, so have they all.

Shall return the Pinter script next week. Thank you for letting me read it.

Yours,
Patrick.

20 MARTIN ROAD, 31.iii.74
TO TOM MASCHLER
Dear Tom,
Thank you for your letter of March 22.

I am enclosing with this some additions to the list of complimentary copies for *The Cockatoos*, and I expect there will be some more before the book comes out.

We enjoyed meeting Nadine Gordimer. She had dinner one night on her way to Europe from Adelaide – very cool and self-possessed, like her writing in fact. I was sorry not to see more of her, but that is what

[71]The filmmaker Jack and his wife Isobel.

happens when one is divided between the hemispheres and communications are overdeveloped. It would have been far more satisfactory to have lived earlier in the century.

I forget whether I told you I was invited to fly to address the annual PEN International dinner in New York in June. Needless to say I declined. American reviews of the most bitchy kind continue to arrive. George Steiner's in the *New Yorker* is the prime example. If I had not taken the Nobel Prize away from the US I feel it would have been otherwise – or perhaps not. I think all the Jewish High intellectuals got a shock from *The Eye of the Storm*, because however intellectual and emancipated they may have become, the Sacred Jewish Momma is still lurking somewhere in the depths. George Steiner does understand what I am writing about, even though he suddenly pretends he doesn't, but most Americans don't, and I find it very disturbing.[72] They say of *The Eye of the Storm*, 'you will put this book away after 50 pages because there is no character you can like' etc. etc. Then they come out with the 'no compassion' crap just because I don't pour milk-bar syrups over human relationships. Anyway, I have had wonderful reactions to *The Eye of the Storm* from Australia and England (if Pearl Bailey reacted à l'Americaine it's because she is a jealous bitch under the influence of the expatriate Australian Clive James.)

Sorry this is such an appalling piece of typing; American critics have made me take to the bottle.

Yrs
Patrick.

20 MARTIN ROAD, 23.iv.74
TO JOSEPH LOSEY

I am glad there is perhaps a faint possibility of Pinter for *Voss*. Your other two candidates I shall have to take on trust. Reading what some of the critics have had to say about *Gatsby* and Mia Farrow's 'waif look' has made me recoil from her again.[73] She was rather like a waif in *Secret Ceremony*, which perhaps is why I did not care for her in it.[74] Laura Trevelyan certainly has nothing of the waif in her. She is rather cold and hard. If she is passionate in her relationship with Voss, it is something of a proud,

[72]Steiner praised him, 4 March, p.109, as 'one of the very few now active novelists capable of evoking transfiguration, the rush of light that passes through the human frame when men and women are possessed by great love, by philosophic conviction, by sacrificial courage'. But he had reservations about the prose and PW's grim view of the human race: 'Unrelieved blackness rings false. It celebrates itself.'
[73]*The Great Gatsby*, 1974, directed by Jack Clayton with Farrow as Daisy.
[74]Directed by Losey in 1969, with Farrow, Elizabeth Taylor, etc.

icy passion. She is the kind of girl who would not have gone down at all well in Eastern Suburbs society of that period, so I am glad you went to that dinner party at the Lees' which would have shown you something of today's version. I have an old aunt who is very discreet and who doesn't really like or understand any of my books; one of her few remarks on reading any of them was, 'That awful girl Laura Trevelyan– –!' (I see Diana Rigg is playing the lead in *Pygmalion*; perhaps she is on the way to real stardom – but that is only a casual hint. Rigg is far more Laura as I see her; so is Vanessa Redgrave, though I find that performance of Vanessa Redgrave-as-Revolutionary very hard to take.)

I must say I was most depressed by your seeing Donald Sutherland as Voss. He is somebody I have disliked intensely in the two films I have seen him in – less in *Don't Look Now*[75] than in *Klute*.[76] Before anything else, that flabby wet mouth is entirely wrong. Voss was dry and ascetic – he had a thin mouth like a piece of fence-wire. I do think a whole characterisation can go astray on a single physical feature like that. Both Laura Trevelyan and Voss are Will personified, and that rather goes against soft, appealing Mia Farrow and flabby-mouthed Donald Sutherland. But I shall have to wait and see them both in something else. (Mia would probably have been accepted in Sydney society as 'so sweet' or 'pretty' or 'charming'. They were frightened by Laura Trevelyan and Voss.)

AUSTRALIA'S CONSERVATIVE PARTIES MOUNTED a ruthless parliamentary counter-attack on Whitlam. For the first time since Federation, a threat was made to block Supply in the Senate. Whitlam decided to hold fresh elections and White was recruited to speak at a political rally in support of the government at the Opera House in May. He said: 'I was a friend and supporter of the architect who conceived this noble building, who was driven away by Those Who Know Better before he had a chance of finishing his work. Today I am here in support of a man with similar aims whom we must not *allow* to be sacrificed as Utzon was . . .'[77] This was White's debut on the national political stage.

[75]Nicholas Roeg's 1973 film of the du Maurier short story with Sutherland and Julie Christie.
[76]Directed by Alan Pakula, 1971, with Sutherland and Jane Fonda who won an Academy Award for her performance.
[77]*Patrick White Speaks*, p.51.

20 Martin Road, 2.vi.74
TO FRANCES PECK
Dear Frances,

I'm glad you are going to try Camden Art Centre, though you can't expect to get much out of a single term. Still, you will be able to find out, perhaps, which way you want to launch out, and then go to a proper art school. I can imagine you will be longing to leave boarding school; I couldn't wait to get away from mine – and of course one does feel comparatively free, but as one grows older one sees that real freedom is unattainable. That is what makes all those shrieking Women's Libbers seem so idiotic. A lot of people seem to think that anybody creative is free, whereas to be an artist of any kind, if you really practise your art, you are totally enslaved, worse even than a mother of six children.

I thought you might be interested to know that the jeweller Tony White,[78] who made the necklace I sent you, has been commissioned by Tiffany to make jewellery for them, so you are really 'in', and I feel pleased I chose the necklace.

The other day I had all the paintings revalued by Christies and was horrified to find what they are now worth by present artificial standards. They are all going to the Gallery of N.S.W. when I die, but now I have decided to give the most important paintings (the Fairweather, the de Maistres, and the Nolans) at once; it is too big a responsibility having them in the house. I shall miss them, but I shall also enjoy filling the gaps with younger painters I think may come good.

The Election is over and the Government safely returned. It has been a time of great strain. A few days before we went to the polls I was asked to speak for Whitlam in a rally at the Opera House, and I said I would because I felt I had to. It was quite alarming until, I think, the performer in me must have taken over – to be faced with 3,000 faces in the hall, and we were told 8,000 listening outside – anyway I got through it in rather a dazed fashion, and now feel I can face anything. I am even toying with the idea of taking a theatre, to give readings from novels, and raise money for some of my causes.

We had a shattering experience last week: Fanny's cancer flared up and we had to take her for her last needle. She was almost 13 and had led a much happier life than most dogs, but we miss her very much as she had the sweetest nature of any of the many dogs we have owned. I suppose we must expect this to happen now: all the animals are growing old and rather decrepit.

[78](1942–   ), Sydney jeweller, no relation.

I hope you do well in your exams, and of course I shan't expect you to write till they are over.

Love

Patrick.

20 Martin Road, 7.vii.74

TO RONALD WATERS

Went down to Grenfell to open the Henry Lawson Festival, and had to make a speech on a truck in the main street. It was all very rustic, except that Barry Humphries was there to receive the award for Artist of the Year. I had also to present the awards that evening at the bowling club; they wanted me to crown the Festival and Charity Queens, but I got out of that, and thankful I was when I saw somebody else struggling to get the glass tiaras over those hair-dos (one of the Queens was called Miss Diprose) . . .

11.vii   No time to finish this on my correspondence day as we had people to dinner that night. Since then I have had some good runs at the book I am writing, but today I had to put the MS. in the bank as we are leaving for Fraser Island at the week-end and there is a lot to tidy up before then. Feel very lost without the MS., though after receiving a lot of English reviews of The Cockatoos today I wonder why I go on writing. Apart from the one in the Observer, which stank as high as I expected,[79] they were mostly very favourable, yet there were stabs in most of them, which you mightn't see, but I do. It is all the result of that bloody Nobel Prize, which has let loose streams of venom all over the world. I wish I had never had won it, and been left in peace to get on with my work. Manoly said not long after it happened, 'You must realise life will never be the same again', and he was right . . .

The Harry M. Millers are moving into the mansion down the street while we are away. I think we are getting a bit closer, financially, to the making of Voss. I correspond regularly with Losey and have a very good relationship. Pinter doesn't want to write the screenplay, as I knew he wouldn't, but I thought I'd try.

Next year there is going to be a Festival of the Arts (yet another one) at Canberra, where I think The Season at Sarsaparilla may be done. I have announced that I want to do a reading of scenes from my novels if I can have the theatre for a Sunday night – because I think that I could

[79]Russell Davies, 16 June, p.33: 'those whose patience can survive the flaring of grandiose poeticisms in desert places are rewarded with that feeling of virtuousness which comes of having seen justice gravely done to a Great Continent.'

bring it off by now, if I practise a bit and have some production. I finally plucked up the courage to listen to the tape of my BBC reading from *The Eye of the Storm*. It wasn't bad, though the breathing was uncontrolled, chiefly because it was too close to the Nobel thing which had brought me to the verge of a nervous breakdown. On the occasion when I had to make the election speech in the Opera House, I suddenly realised I had got the feel of an audience, that I could move them and also make them laugh, and from then on, I knew I could do these readings.

Must go and get the dinner. I have invented a fennel sauce for fish which I think is going to be something.

Love to you both – and the tabby

Patrick

20 MARTIN ROAD, 18.viii.74
TO PEGGY GARLAND
Dear Peggy,
I think I must owe you a couple of letters, but nowadays there is so much correspondence, not only the letters which one drops automatically into the w.p.b., but a lot of boring stuff from translators, agents, universities etc. which has to be answered, and I realise I neglect the people I have always written and want to continue writing to.

I'm sorry you disliked *The Cockatoos* so much. At least you didn't like *The Eye of the Storm*, and then said you suddenly realised what it was about. I had a letter from Antony[80] in which he said you both felt battered by the 'words' in *The Eye*. This amazes me. If 'words' hurtle around me I can't avoid using them, just as I can't help reflecting a life which seems to me to be closing down into darkness. So perhaps you will come to *The Cockatoos* in time instead of telling me that what I need is a psychiatrist, which I am sure is what you meant. I think you have done too much crafty weaving in a village, drawing too much wool over your eyes, and stuffing it into your ears, so that you won't have to see and hear. Perhaps you are right – or again, perhaps I am wrong!

I am getting towards the end of a first version of another novel. It is set in the 19th Century and I began it years ago, then abandoned it because I thought I must deal with others. My taking it up this year may have been prompted by the desire to escape from the unpleasant present, but I have found it is linked inescapably with now and the recurring awfulness of human beings. As Dorothy Osborne's mother said, 'However awful you may think they are, you will always find them worse!' That, I

---

[80]Alpers.

think, is essentially true, though there are many human beings I love . . .

I have given the more important paintings to the Gallery of N.S.W. as we are always being broken into and as I was afraid something might happen to them. We now have lots of blank spaces, but no doubt they will fill up in time, as I don't think I shall ever overcome my vice for buying paintings. I must say, in all vanity, that my judgment has been vindicated, too: one that I bought for £100 years ago is now valued at $12,000 and a young Lithuanian[81] whose paintings (a series of six) I bought last year for the Gallery has been invited to exhibit at Sâo Paolo . . .

I can imagine the cantankerousness of the cantankerous Betty increasing. You might tell her that the paintings of Roy de Maistre are increasingly admired.

20 MARTIN ROAD, 22.ix.74
TO TOM MASCHLER
Dear Tom,
I have put off answering your letter about prefaces because I have been in the last throes of the first version of A Fringe of Leaves. Thank God it is down on paper. What it is like, I can't think; all sorts of things I hadn't dreamt of, or which perhaps I did dream in the course of writing, got into it. Now I hope to resist thinking about it for a couple of months, but always after a couple of weeks I start feeling perhaps I shall die before the whole thing is ready, and rush back into it. About those bloody prefaces: I just don't want to write them. If I were the kind of writer who likes to write about himself, I should be writing an autobiography. But I feel that would be unnecessary as all my fiction is in a sense about myself. If you must have prefaces why can't somebody else write them? It would be more discreet and less likely to put a weapon into the hands of the enemy. I see the William Gerhardie novels are being re-issued with prefaces by somebody else. Do please consider my suggestion. I think it is good advice.[82]

At present I am being driven mad by the woman who is translating The Eye of the Storm into French. She has sent me sixteen pages of questions through which I am wading. She is not only ignorant but insolent. She can't get any of the allusions to Lear of which the book is full, and says,

---

[81]Imants Tillers (1950–   ), Australian-born of Latvian parents.
[82]Cape continued to press and PW continued to refuse, so plans for a uniform edition at this time foundered.

'I have no time to read the play.' Yet, she can waste my time to the tune of sixteen pages of queries.[83]

Plans for the filming of *Voss* are boiling up again, but it will cost so much money I doubt it will ever get off the ground . . .

I'm having endless trouble trying to turn the Nobel prize-money into a trust fund, making sure that it will be tied up in perpetuity, and tax free. I wanted to give the first instalment away at the end of the year, but I doubt it will be arranged by then, and some of the aged writers who should be getting the money will die in the meantime. Adding some royalties on the original sum, I am making the capital up to $100,000.

Must go now and cook the dinner.

Yours,

Patrick.

20 Martin Road, 9.xi.74

TO GEOFFREY DUTTON

This week I start work again, which gives me cold shivers and pleasant anticipations. My eyes have improved with the rest, though an eye doctor tells me I am a borderline glaucoma case. I don't need treatment yet, but have to go back to him in nine months. My mother went blind, but not till she was 80. I think all these troubles recur in families. The asthma does, and now, it seems, this. However, if I can have another ten years of sight I shall probably tidy things up, and perhaps enjoy another ten as a composer of electronic music.

My Swedish translator[84] was in Sydney for a week, which meant a certain amount of running around, and a lot of cooking – though I don't think Swedes like what we eat, or else they are afraid of looking like eaters. Anyway, I never have much success with them in that department.

Will you and Nin be in Sydney at all in December? From 5th till 27th the Gallery is going to have an exhibition of the paintings I have given over the years. They must have 50 or more, most of which have remained in the basement. I shall be interested to see them all together,

---

[83]Suzanne Nétillard wrote to me, 27.xi.92: 'Pulling my hair because of the difficulty of rendering an expression of *The Eye* – as I too am extremely rigorous in my work – I wrote to him *humorously* – I insist – and in a kind of brotherly feeling (2 horses, as it were, pulling the same cart!), and asked him in mock fury whether he could not write more simply etc.' PW asked Gallimard to remove her from the project; the crisis was smoothed over. 'But this left me an unpleasant impression, as of from an unmanly person.'

[84]Magnus Lindberg.

and perhaps find out what makes me acquire paintings – as well as my mistakes[85] . . .

The other night we had dinner at the Lees', with Jack lying upstairs after the motor-bike incident. It was an awful evening all round as they always ask the people least likely to go together. We had the dreadful Humphrey, of course, and that creepy pair the Blackmans.[86] Humphrey turns out to be a fight perv; he had to drop out during dinner to watch Muhammed Ali on the telly. Charles B. started his usual cerebrations about painting, and tried to trap me into saying which I think is the best Australian painter. I can see there is a big grudge because I haven't fallen over myself to buy Blackmans. He told me he thought there was nothing of a painter in Hurtle Duffield, to which I replied there are different kinds of painter and he is a pretty shitty one. When we left he rushed out and started embracing me. (Incidentally, in the Drama theatre at the Opera House there is about the worst painting I have ever seen, a Blackman given by a Japanese.)[87] . . .

Had a card from Mick Stow[88] from the Azores. He had jumped ship out of boredom, and would like to settle there. The post-card, all wild hydrangeas and shaggy horses, made the Azores look as dank as the English countryside.

Hope all well – oh, one of the Cavafy brothers became secretary to a one-handed General Horsey de Horsey 'who played the piano very charmingly with his one hand'![89]

Love to all
P.

20 MARTIN ROAD, 24.xi.74
TO JAMES STERN
Dear Jimmy,
Manoly and I were terribly sorry to hear about the car smash. We have

---

[85]He wrote to Waters, 29.xii.74, 'The exhibition of the paintings I have given to the Gallery of New South Wales looked quite impressive although I say it. It took up the whole of the lower part of the Gallery (52 works). The de Maistres had a court to themselves, and when one saw them all together, properly spaced and lit, one could at last see the painter he is. So I feel I have vindicated Roy.' Almost all of the works were then returned to the basements.

[86]Humphrey Fisher, husband of Diana; the painter Charles Blackman and his wife Barbara.

[87]'Girl Listening to Music', 1972, a gift of Akio Morita, President of Sony.

[88]Mick=Randolph Stow.

[89]This episode in the career of the poet's destitute brother Paul (1860–1920) appears in Robert Liddell's Cavafy, 1976, pp.110–11.

been in several and know what it does to you even if you aren't hurt physically as poor Tania was. You're lucky to have that married couple; may they last. Our attempts have always ended in failure, but we have never had the right quarters for them.

You say why did I accept the Nobel Prize. I might not have if I had realised what a nightmare it would turn into: always somebody wanting something, either materially, or my moral support of a cause. Anyway, I could hardly refuse something like that when it had never been won by an Australian before, and I also saw how I might use the money. Ever since receiving it I have been trying to turn it into a watertight, tax-free trust fund to award something to Australian writers who haven't received the recognition they ought. I had the greatest difficulty persuading my legal advisers to get together over it, and they only produced a satisfactory document when I announced a few weeks ago that I was going to make the first award, with or without deed, on November 14th. The first has gone to Christina Stead the novelist.[90] Even so, we are not yet absolutely sure about the fate of the fund, and a bill may have to be introduced in Parliament. The Prime Minister has promised to do this if the Law doesn't find our terms acceptable. What I am working for at the same time is to make all awards for creative achievement tax-free.[91]

I realise your birthday is somewhere around (can never remember the exact date) and have sent a book which will arrive weeks late, but which I think you will appreciate if you can bring yourself to read it. (Not one of mine.)

I have started on a second version of my new novel in spite of all the hindrances. I've just finished reading it through; bits of it are very good, other bits quite awful: the only consolation is that everything I have ever written has proceeded like that. What I do find increasingly painful is the physical as well as the nervous strain of writing, and now I have developed glaucoma, only a very slight one, but I keep remembering that my mother went blind in her old age.

Manoly seems healthy, but suffers on and off from arthritic pains, which only acupuncture relieves. He does too much, however, is an obsessive gardener, never out of the garden, and when there is nothing left to do, sweeps up every fallen leaf. The bitches say that is the way he escapes from me.

Shan't comment on the world of human rats in which we live. It depresses me more every day. (Did you know there was an 18th Century

[90]She was awarded $6,000.
[91]He failed: of all the literary prizes in Australia, only the Patrick White Prize is untaxed.

didactic poet called Grainger who came up with the marvellous line, 'Come, Muse, let's sing of rats!')[92] At least for myself I want less and less: a bed, a table and chair, a few cooking pots; I know a lot of ways with haricot beans, and I'd like to have my dogs around me, and to be able to afford the two bottles of whisky I consume a week.

Hoping you are both recovered from the smash, I shall now go and start the *navarin*.

Love from us both
Patrick

20 MARTIN ROAD, 29.xii.74
TO RONALD WATERS
Christmas has never been such a nightmare; those commercial carols sounded more cynical than ever. Although the Australians are crying poverty the shops have never been so full. I went into DJ's the Monday before Christmas to buy a few things for children and geriatrics and it was interesting to see the bourgeois drop-outs in their carefully frayed denims and tangled hair snapping up all the luxury tins. I was cheated by a Polish Jewess (very like Lady Fairfax) over a goose I had ordered from her delicatessen; when I got it home, after my third trip to the shop, and unwrapped the parcel, I found what was not much more than a drake. I couldn't face a fourth trip and a row, so we made do with that. Fortunately we were only four at dinner on the night, and I made a good stuffing.

20 MARTIN ROAD, 13.i.75
TO GEOFFREY DUTTON
Every asthmatic we know has been having violent attacks, I suppose as the result of the terrible humidity, and there has also been more grass than I have ever seen in the Park this summer.

As always when I have asthma, work got hold of me and I have gone ahead well (I think.) Yesterday when I was feeling particularly awful I unravelled one of the most knotted passages in the first version. Of course on these occasions I think to myself, supposing I die? The publisher may get hold of it, and in spite of the clause in my will, give it to some hack who will turn it into something quite different from what I intended. So one has to push on. I've re-written about a third and would like to finish

---

[92]James Grainger (1721–66), physician and poet. 'Say, shall I sing of rats?' comes from a four-book poem on sugar cane, and when Samuel Johnson heard the line he shouted, 'No!'

the second version by the spring when we hope Elly will be here for a couple of months.

Have been reading C. Stead's *Letty Fox*, a kind of picaresque of sex American style. It's extraordinary to think of that quiet, sedate woman writing anything so hilarious. Nadine Gordimer's *The Conservationist* was difficult till I got my bearings, after that a magnificent book. Am now struggling with *A Glastonbury Romance* which Kylie's Rodd gave me for Christmas, perhaps I shall get my bearings in that too![93] Did you know Tass had been operated on for cancer of the bowel.[94] Apparently tidied up, though that is how Eleanor Arrighi's began.

    Love to all
    Patrick.

20 MARTIN ROAD, 8.ii.75
TO ALAN WILLIAMS
Half the trouble was going to a performance of Brecht/Weill's *Mahagonny*[95] while I was feeling ill. The Opera House is full of viruses as people who succeed in getting tickets rise from their deathbeds to use them. As it happened the production was not a very good one, without style, and suggesting none of the Berlin bitchery and bitterness it should have had, but I am glad to have collected it, if only after a fashion. I prefer it to that plugged-to-death *Threepenny Opera*. We have also had a grand *Aïda*,[96] staged in the Concert Hall, which should have been the Opera Theatre if the ABC hadn't seized it for their orchestral concerts. *Aïda* worked marvellously and was very well sung. An elderly American couple next to us, who rather fancied themselves as opera authorities started off very sniffy but gave way to raving enthusiasm. Afterwards the man said to me, 'I think that would compare with *Aïda* anywhere in the world.' Well now that I have seen the definitive *Aïda* I am going to leave it alone for ever; I think it's a great bore, and I only went the other night out of curiosity. It is amazing how Australian opera has come on since we had that opera house which everybody condemns non-stop. Whatever the practical

---

[93]'What do you think of J. C. Powys?' PW asked Losey, 26.i.75. 'He was a great novelist, I think, but an evil mind. He has something in common with Stanley Spencer and Delius. If I wrote factual books, and were younger, I might consider writing something about the three of them, with that emerald-green, scum-on-water kind of evil as the connecting thread.'
[94]Drysdale survived this bout with cancer.
[95]Directed by Sam Besekow with the Danish soprano Lone Koppel as Jenny Smith.
[96]Directed by Stephen Hall and designed by Tom Lingwood.

drawbacks there is something most inspiring about it as a building and Sydney is far more bearable than it used to be.

20 MARTIN ROAD, 16.ii.75
TO MARSHALL BEST
Christina Stead's two New York novels are *The People with the Dogs* (Little, Brown 1952) and *Letty Fox, Her Luck* (Harcourt Brace 1946). The latter caused a stir because it was considered an insult to American woman i.e. it was too truthful. I don't know whether you can get hold of copies over there. If not, I could at least send you a nasty cheap re-print of *Letty Fox* (A & R) They have also reprinted Christina's favourite *House of All Nations* (Simon and Schuster 1938) in a horrible hardback so fat that it is like holding Mrs Beeton. The Simon and Schuster, which she gave me is normal fat. I could send you the A & R *House of All Nations* if you are interested. I was put off partly by the A & R format, partly because it is all about finance. For the same reason I was never able to get along with Balzac's *César Birotteau*. But it is a subject which ought to go down well in the States. My own favourites are *Cotter's England* which was published in the States under (I think) *Dark Places of the Heart* and *The Little Hotel*, her most recent. I could send you the latter: it is witty, cosmopolitan, and not over long. Her best known book is *The Man Who Loved Children*, which Randall Jarrell's enthusiasm finally brought to the attention of the public.[97] I do hope the Viking will take up C.S.[98] The three novelists writing today who interest me most are all women! Christina Stead, Nadine Gordimer, and Doris Lessing.

20 MARTIN ROAD, 9.iii.75
TO JOSEPH LOSEY
I don't know how much you have been hearing from Harry M. of late. I ran into him in the street about three weeks ago, and he was full of the usual talk. I told him I had lost faith in him and did not think he would ever raise the money. Since then he has told me that the project has found favour at a very high level and that he should have the Prime Minister's signature by 1st April.[99] I told him I was too old to believe

[97] US critic (1914–65) who blessed the 1965 reissue with a long introduction: 'If all mankind had been reared in orphan asylums for a thousand years, it could learn to have families again by reading *The Man Who Loved Children*.'
[98] They didn't, but years later Viking Australia published Stead's posthumous collection *An Ocean of Story*.
[99] Miller says, July 1994, he was not referring to the PM but the Minister for the Media, Doug McClelland (1926–   ).

anything but what actually takes place. We shall see. It could be that it will happen this time. In any case, we are not supposed to talk about it, and I can see the point of that, because if the press got hold of the Prime Minister bit the whole thing could be fucked. Personally I never talk to the press, and I imagine you are pretty cagey.

FOR SOME TIME White had settled into a pattern of having one 'correspondence day' each week: on 30 March 1975 he wrote a long letter to Geoffrey Dutton discussing troubles at Anlaby, the horrors of the Sydney Show, and Glenda Jackson's visit to Sydney. Jackson and her idea of filming *The Aunt's Story* was the common thread running through all the day's letters. He ended the letter to Dutton:

20 MARTIN ROAD, 30.iii.75
TO GEOFFREY DUTTON
We're worried about Cynthia. She's ill and he was dragging her to the Congo on the way back. Now they are going to arrive in England in the snow. Cynthia is the kind of skeleton my sister was when she died of flying from steamy Sydney to London in winter. All very pessimistic but there are more and more reasons for pessimism.
    Love to all, and better stars.
    P.

OPERA WAS HIS VIKING publisher Alan Williams' passion, and White's letter to him that correspondence day ran through the latest productions at the Opera House. White refused the Melbourne writer Morris Lurie an interview for *Esquire*. To Moya Henderson, still planning to compose *Voss*, he sent congratulations for prizes won in her studies in Germany. And with Stephen Murray-Smith of *Overland* he raised the question of Herbert Dyce Murphy, gentleman transvestite, whose supposed portrait in the Melbourne gallery, a fragile figure in a white dress standing in an arbour, had set simmering the idea for his next novel.

20 MARTIN ROAD, 30.iii.75
TO STEPHEN MURRAY-SMITH[100]
Dear Stephen,
Thank you for your letter with that information. Francis Murphy seems to

[100](1922–88), communist until the late 1950s, journalist and literary figure. Against the tide of Left disapproval for PW's work, *Voss* was praised in *Overland* in 1958 and thereafter PW and Murray-Smith enjoyed a warm professional friendship. PW's last published piece, 'Credo', appeared in the magazine in June 1988.

have been an extraordinary man. I'm sorry the character in my novel, novella, or whatever, will be so little like him, but mine has developed out of the few snippets of information I was given in the beginning.

I think it might be embarrassing to meet Murphy's wife although he didn't hide his transvestite side. I doubt whether anybody would connect him with my book, except that I feel I must use that piece of dialogue between Murphy and his mother. ('No, but I am your daughter Edith.' 'I'm so glad. I always wanted a daughter.')

The book I am working on will take me till about this time next year. Then I want to go to London and Europe to revive one or two places I can use in the Murphy story.

Do you know a Melbourne painter called Clarice Beckett?[101] Some of those landscapes seem to belong to the Murphy thing.

If you do come across the file you mention I'll be glad if you can tell me more.

I hope the island continues to exercise its charm – and is safe from depredations.[102] At the moment we are very worried about the future of Fraser Island.

Yours,
Patrick.

20 MARTIN ROAD, 13.iv.75
TO NINETTE DUTTON
Dear Nin,
Very sorry to hear of the financial difficulties on top of everything else. I've always wondered about your financial affairs, because you always seem to be flying about all over the place, buying cars, boats, and houses while having these difficulties.[103] Now it is clear you must go carefully. I am fortunate in having not exactly mean, but cautious blood in my veins. That, and not feeling attracted to the kind of life one can live in Australia, has kept me anchored to my work. If I had been born to somewhere else in the world, my story would probably be quite a different one. At least you still have Anlaby, and I have always felt that if I had that, I'd be quite content to spend all my time there. It ought not be much hardship if you have to do pretty much that when you all love the place.

Last week we went to Lawson and spent a day with the Phelans.[104]

---

[101](1887–1935), painter of Melbourne bay scenes, a master of mist and wet roads.
[102]Erith in Bass Strait where the Murray-Smiths spent part of each summer.
[103]The pig-breeding venture at Anlaby was proving expensive and unprofitable.
[104]The writer Nancy (1913–   ) and her husband Peter.

It is the first time I have enjoyed being in the Blue Mountains since I was a youth. Then it seemed a kind of paradise, but since then I usually go there to see people who are old, crippled, senile, living in what approaches 'squalor' and tangled wildernesses. The other day we went to an attractive house, beautiful garden, pleasant company (Elizabeth Harrower and a very charming Russian young woman[105] were also there) yet the whole time I felt restless and boring, as always happens when I go away any distance from the book I am working on.

I am getting towards the end of my second version, and this gives me the increased shivers. If only I could rid myself of it in one lazy retch instead of jittering about for short and anguished spells.

Yesterday was rather an ordeal. I had promised James Fairfax in return for something I wanted him to do, to go to a lunch he was giving for the visiting American millionaires.[106] Some of these turned out to be quite nice, but there were some fearsome locals, including Dad Fairfax and his Presbyterian wife (in eyelashes)[107] and every social queen in Sydney. As there were eighty people in all it was comparatively easy to avoid the monsters. At lunch I sat between Mrs Rockefeller[108] and the widow of a diplomat called Simmons.[109] The latter started talking about Plimsoll[110] the ambassador who had introduced her to my books. He had spoken about me a lot, and professed to be a friend, but alas, I could not claim to have met him. Mrs Rockefeller was very straightforward and natural. I'm afraid these people made our own, with the exception of a few like James F. and Helen Blaxland,[111] seem very trashy. It is sad that poor James can't produce better on an occasion. Madam Du Val cooked the lunch. Most unwisely they chose to give us omelettes. I went into the kitchen afterward to see her and she said, 'I'm fucked!' She looked it too, after eighty omelettes. I said I was fucked after one; I find cooking an omelette a highly emotional experience. Some of the elderly maids standing around seemed rather shocked.

[105]An Australian of Russian parents, Paula Bannatyne.
[106]The International Council of the Museum of Modern Art, in Australia for the museum's exhibition 'Modern Masters – Manet to Matisse'.
[107]Warwick and Mary; Presbyterian=Jewish.
[108]Mrs John D. III, president of the Museum of Modern Art.
[109]Mrs John Farr Simmons of Washington.
[110]James Plimsoll (1917–87), Australia's ambassador to Washington 1970–74 and for a time a member of the council of the Australian National Gallery.
[111]Blaxland (1907–89) was a survivor of the society Ruth White knew in Sydney, and a pillar of the National Trust. She lisped. 'You know, Patrick, I find your books awfully hard to wead,' she said over dinner one night. He replied, 'And I find them awfully hard to wite.'

Am very concerned about the way Whitlam and Connor are disposing of Fraser Island.[112] I've had to write two letters to the PM, but I'm afraid he's very stubborn. I don't want to end our alliance, but it won't be what it was if he sells out on Fraser Island. I too, can see my way to being stubborn. But there is no alternative to Gough. That Lewis bastard[113] gives one another glimpse of thuggery almost every other day; if he and the head prefect Fraser[114] were in power together I feel one would have to leave the country.

Love,

Patrick

Am reading *Ottoline*.[115] She was so much more of a person than the Great surrounding her. Full of wisdom and remarkable insights.

20 MARTIN ROAD, 27.iv.75

TO GEOFFREY DUTTON

I was interested in what you have to tell about the sows not coming in. The pug world is in a state of chaos from bitches either missing their seasons or having too many. Ours have been having too many, and we put it down to the pill we give them to cut the season short. However, the breeders, who don't give the pill, have had the same experience and their breeding programme is wrecked. Vets can't give any reason for it. I must check up on women's periods through our doctor to see whether they are having the same trouble. Supernature must be at work.

20 MARTIN ROAD, 25.v.75

TO PEGGY GARLAND

Dear Peggy,

I'm glad the Christina Stead arrived at last. Why they should all have taken six months is something I can't explain. I think she is a very good writer. She is the first to win the award from the trust fund I have set up with the Nobel prizemoney. She has come back here to live in her old age, and is pretty hard up, and feeling lost since the death of her husband.

---

[112]Whitlam and his minister for minerals and energy, R. F. X. Connor (1907–77) were keen for the island to be mined; protests, which PW supported in person and with cash, compelled Whitlam to hold an inquiry into its impact on the island; but sand-mining was only halted in 1976; logging continued until 1992.

[113]Succeeded Askin as conservative premier of NSW in 1974.

[114]Malcolm Fraser (1930–   ), leader of the opposition in Canberra, a conservative figure hated all the more by PW for being from the White world of Oxbridge-educated graziers.

[115]Sandra Darroch's life of Ottoline Morrell, 1976.

She is not nearly well enough known, chiefly I think because she has lived and worked in too many countries . . .

That friend of yours whose name I can't remember (the Mystery of Eynsham) put in an appearance. One day when we were having our siesta somebody started ringing the bell and prowling round. We were rather annoyed and didn't go down. He prowled round to the back causing pandemonium in the dog world, possibly getting bitten on the ankle by Gloria, who has developed the habit of doing that, and I saw a man's head disappearing into the lane. Then at dusk, when I had started to cook dinner for some people we were expecting, the bell went again, and your friend was there. He caught me in not the best of tempers. (He must have been peering in at the bow-windows during his first visit, because we found a columbine squashed by a foot.) He said he had been sent by you, and that he should have brought a piece of pottery from you, but had forgotten. I can't say I took to him at all. He struck me as being a con man; in fact, he reminded me of Stonehouse.[116] I said I couldn't see him then, and where could I get in touch with him. He was going to Canberra and somewhere else. Couldn't he have my telephone number? I said he couldn't because it was a silent one. Well, couldn't he just knock on the door when he comes back? I said he couldn't, that I hate people turning up on the doorstep. And that was that. Unless he has a real rhinoceros hide I don't expect we'll see him again. I must say there was something very suspicious about him; nor did you sound particularly impressed except by his Stonehouse looks.

My youngest niece has come out here and will be staying with us on and off for the next three months. She is rising nineteen, but very shy and unworldly. Since Suzanne died she has been brought up by her two sisters and the boarding school in which they shoved her. The sisters each have two small children, and are preoccupied with those and their husbands. I think poor Frances spent most of the holidays child-minding. I find it very difficult dealing with somebody who only speaks when spoken to, and reveals nothing of her true self unless you winkle it out. It's almost impossible to know whether she's enjoying herself, or bored, or unhappy, or what. When she leaves here she's going back to an art school in Camberwell at which she enrolled herself. In the letters she wrote before coming here she could only talk about paintings, yet here she hardly raises her eyes to the dozens hanging on the walls, and never comments on the

---

[116]John Stonehouse, the former British cabinet minister who staged his own death in 1974, was discovered in Melbourne a few months later posing as Donald Clive Mildoon, a retired British businessman who loved sunbaking and Bach.

art books I give her to look at. She sits about drawing and dabbling in paint, but we haven't been shown anything, and I suppose we shan't. At least it's a relief to know that she has that desire.

I have to go back to the specialist about my glaucoma in July, when he will decide what has to be done. I must have it only very slightly, otherwise he would have got going on the first visit; and I've heard of a man who has kept it at bay for 25 years by using drops. Apart from eyes, I've been feeling very well, and Manoly's aches seem to be under control; anyway, he looks well, and doesn't complain. He gave up smoking, and I have given up drink, which I think has done us both good. It's certainly much cheaper. I don't know what we'd be paying if we were drinking as well as eating; M. only has some wine with his meals when we go out.[117]

I had a letter from Peter Beatson. It seems a strange existence at Aix when one is blind. I can't think why he doesn't go back to New Zealand, but perhaps he's not old enough yet. He never tells us who is living with him. Is it still the Indonesian?

I can understand your feeling gloomy in England as it is now. It's difficult to believe things have gone so far. I'm sure we're in for a much worse time here too, than Australians can imagine. The Government of which I expected so much has turned out disappointing in very many ways (not that the other would be any better – in fact, they'd be a disaster) and now they seem intent on digging out every dollar there is in the ground, destroying natural beauty which is the only thing we've got in any way distinguished. If we ever succeed in preventing any of this, it's through the unions, not the Government.

I haven't any news of interest, so I suppose the best thing I can do at this stage is get some food for my silent niece.

Love
Patrick.

20 MARTIN ROAD, 9.vi.75
TO THE YORKES[118]
Dear Ritchie and Annette Yorke,
Thank you for your letter of some time ago. I don't envy you in Toronto, though it may have improved since I passed through in 1932.[119] Then it had all that I disliked about Sydney and had to escape from, without any of Sydney's better features.

---

[117]Lascaris stuck to his resolution; PW did not.
[118]Ritchie (1944–   ), rock historian, and his wife Annette (1948–   ).
[119]On his way to Cambridge.

Australia has improved since you left[120] but like everywhere else we are going through a bad time. We shall have to be very careful or we might destroy the most distinctive part of us – by that I mean the landscape.

I hope I'll read the novel one day, though I must say rock doesn't mean much to me. I listen with pleasure to jazz – oh, and I did have a brief passion for Janis Joplin,[121] perhaps because I became so interested in her as a character. She would make a novel if I knew enough about the world she lived in.

Yours sincerely,
Patrick White.

20 MARTIN ROAD, 13.vii.75
TO XAVIER HERBERT[122]
Dear Xavier,
It was good to hear from you, if not so good in that particular connexion. Years ago I saw a couple of issues of *Australian Literary Studies* and found them full of the most futile kind of academic cerebrations. I can't see that its death would be a great loss. Look at *Meanjin*, kept alive artificially for years, and what point is there in that?

I must say I am astonished at your reverence for the Australian academics. With a few exceptions they are a sterile lot, remote from anything creative unless it has been a hundred years in the museum. But perhaps I am prejudiced by their misunderstanding and misinterpretation of what I write.

You are equally astonished that I should have accepted that gong.[123] I did it because this is a moment of crisis. Otherwise, it is only going to bring me a lot more trouble, just as that bloody Prize did. I didn't want that either, but took it because it might have done something for this country to which I belong by fate not choice.

If you are down here again and would like to meet, I hope you'll get in touch. I'm working all out at present to finish my novel before next Easter when I want to go to Europe about something else I have to write.

I hope your book is a great success.[124]
Yours
Patrick.

---

[120]In 1966.
[121]Singer (1943–70).
[122](1901–84), novelist.
[123]PW was persuaded by friends in the Labor government and the Governor-General Sir John Kerr to become a Companion – the highest rank – in the new Order of Australia.
[124]*Poor Fellow My Country.*

20 Martin Road, 31.viii.75
TO GEOFFREY DUTTON

Talking of copyright, I received a Japanese translation of *Voss* a couple of days ago. The day after there came a letter from the publisher to say that there had been no contract because according to Jap copyright law, a publisher can take anything after ten years. He hoped I understood! He then went on to say that our Dept of Foreign Affairs is bringing him here (from today) as a guest, and that he hoped to snap up more Aust writers to improve Australian-Japanese relations. The rest of the morning I shall have to spend writing letters to Gough and Foreign Affairs telling them what stupid, ignorant cunts they are. They seem to fall for any kind of foreign crook who comes along.[125]

20 Martin Road, 31.viii.75
TO TOM MASCHLER
Dear Tom,

Thank you for your letter of August 15 and the book of Ian McEwan stories.[126] I shall keep the latter to read when I am no longer tied to my own book.

I shall probably finish that some time during the next month. It will be a relief. My eyes are in ruins and I am looking forward to resting them, if that will ever be possible. I've no idea what the book is like. There are days when it excites me, then the same pages can look so awful I could throw the whole thing away. Writing it has been a discipline, and I shall be glad to go on to something which will leave me free to splash about more.

We are thinking about leaving for London and Europe soon after Easter, but I want to keep this dark as it would be intolerable to be pestered by the media wanting interviews and TV appearances. As usual we'd like to stay about a couple of months in London, but I have no idea how long money lasts nowadays. I have no desire to live on a daily sandwich, especially when we go to France. Joe Losey the film director has said his house will probably be empty after Easter and we could live there. That would be a great help of course. Otherwise there used to be some serviced

---

[125]After gathering a number of writers to join him in a protest to the government, PW discovered that Simul Press of Tokyo could, under the Berne Convention, publish translations of novels ten or more years old without paying royalties. Somewhat embarrassed, he wrote to Ninette Dutton, 17.xi.75: 'I don't feel so badly about it knowing that the Japanese were given their copyright concessions as a "developing" country. What were we in those days in the world of books? I shall not apologise to anybody.'
[126]*First Love, Last Rites*, published in 1975 by Cape.

flats off St James's which I investigated four years ago, but they might be too expensive by now. We want something within walking distance if we can't get taxis after the theatre. Losey's is in Royal Parade Chelsea, close enough, St James's would be ideal.

Sid Nolan has said he will do a jacket for *A Fringe of Leaves*, but that may mean going to his studio and carrying off something not connected with the book at the last moment. That is what happened in the past; sometimes the drawing suited the book, sometimes not at all. I'd be happier about Desmond doing it, but I had to ask Sid because he is the one who discovered Mrs Fraser. If he can produce the right thing at the right moment without interfering with his serious work, that will be perfect. I am dedicating the book to Desmond; the Nolans already have *The Vivisector* . . .

We have Manoly's sister arriving the day after tomorrow from Greece on a two-month's visit. They will go to Western Australia for a bit as the wildflowers will be out. I was hoping to go too, but I don't want to leave my book so close to the end. Frances is going to a cousin, and I shall live by myself on Tartarbeefsteak and peanut butter sandwiches, finish the book, and keep the garden alive.

André Deutsch when he was here told me you have a third child. I didn't know about that. In fact, I don't know about anything, you have been silent so long. I see in the catalogue that you are publishing something by the archturd Clive James,[127] and are re-issuing two of my books. I should have thought *The Living and the Dead* had been reprinted far too often and too recently, and that *The Solid Mandala* might have been a wiser choice, but that may be because the latter is my favourite and I have never cared for the other, written too soon and too hastily on the outbreak of war.

What happened to that life of Blake you were going to publish, and which I was looking forward to?

Yours
Patrick.

MARTIN ROAD, 15.ix.75
TO CYNTHIA NOLAN
Dear Cynthia,
Thank-you very much for the balletic photograph of some weeks ago. I like it except that you look even thinner than when we saw you last. You

---

[127]*Britannia Bright's Bewilderment in the Wilderness of Westminster*, a political poem in rhyming couplets.

are a dreadful warning against mortifying the stomach with diets. I hope you are all right in spite of the thinness.

I should have written sooner, but there has been so much going on – the drama of Frances getting ready for her interview with the art school, painting enough to replace the portfolio which wasn't sent from England, or anyway enough to be able to satisfy the people she saw (she won't know the result till Christmas) then Elly arriving, Frances moving on to a cousin's, Manoly and Elly leaving for W.A. and the wildflowers, and all the extra jobs I have been doing with M. away. The day before he left we had to take Gloria for her last needle; I don't think Lucy will be with us much longer either.

The big relief was finishing A Fringe of Leaves yesterday morning. It should mean the lifting of a load, but one now has to face people's reactions, and this morning going into town on the bus I had my next book burning up very forcibly. Tom Maschler is already thinking about a jacket, although I don't imagine he will publish till towards the end of 1976. He says he would go and talk to Sid about it. But is Sid still prepared to do it? As I never hear from him it is impossible to know, and even if I did hear it might not be possible to tell whether he really wants to do the jacket. He would have to read the book first to find out how different my Mrs Roxburgh is from his Mrs Fraser. Don't know whether to send a typescript, which would now cost a small fortune, or get Cape to send him a Xerox from theirs. I shall probably send a typescript anyway. But in the meantime I must re-read it for mistakes and suffer all the shock of finding quite a different book from that which one thought one was writing . . .

Xavier Herbert's Bible has burst upon us; it is about the size of the Gastronomic Larousse and costs $20. I am holding back, hoping that somebody will arrive with a copy under their arm.[128] I was most surprised when I got to know X. to find such a charming and witty man, but from what one reads about him in interviews one wouldn't want to read a word he writes. Charm and all, life isn't long enough for such a vast novel and so much else still to cram in.

I must fall into my unmade bed. The day after tomorrow I shall start a big house-cleaning for the return from Perth.

Love to both

Patrick.

[128]After dipping into Poor Fellow My Country's 850,000 words, PW told Dutton, 10.vii.77, 'Some beautiful landscapes but I couldn't take all that cartoon dialogue and the cartoon characters.'

20 Martin Road, 30.ix.75
TO TOM MASCHLER
Dear Tom,
I sent the typescript to Juliet about a week ago, so I imagine it will have
arrived by now. Yesterday I sent a copy to Sid Nolan. He rang a few days
ago from London, and said that he would like to do a jacket. I think you
could get in touch and talk . . .

I have not yet sent a copy of the book to New York, really because
I have been feeling exhausted after finishing the thing, and correcting two
copies. I no longer think it matters much which country it comes out in
first: in either, the trendy critics will send me up for having won the
wretched Prize, and the Australophobes and expatriates because it is their
policy to destroy anything Australian. One hopes there are still a few
honest and fairly objective critics about. (I realise that the wholly objective
critic does not exist.) . . .

I've been having teeth and eye troubles. It has taken me a month to
find a dentist who will go to work on me after my breaking a tooth on
which two false ones depended. Doctors and dentists in Sydney are usually
either away or about to leave for trips, or conferences, at Kuala Lumpur
or Acapulco. At least the eye-doctor was here, but we had a somewhat
depressing session: I've had to change my glasses after only a year with the
last pair, and he discovered a gathering of cholesterol on one eye-ball.
Now I have to have a blood test. If the cholesterol is more than local I
shall be threatened with a diet. But I don't propose to give up food or sex
for the pleasure of continuing to live in this stinking world. I gave up
smoking years ago, and haven't had a drink for nearly a year; that is
enough.

20 Martin Road, 1.x.75
TO MOYA HENDERSON
A couple of weeks ago I finished my book, and am feeling free, if also
depressed wondering how people will react to it. Manoly is reading it, but
always takes six months to get through one of my books, which he does
in almost total silence, commenting only at the end, which you can
understand is rather unnerving.

20 Martin Road, 8.x.75
TO PEGGY GARLAND
I've been re-reading Katherine M.'s letters lately. They do jump at one,
but at times become painfully fey and self-conscious. At their best they're
as perfect in their imagery as early morning. It is tragic to think that the

South of France of those days no longer exists. It didn't really by the time I went there, but there were still hints.

Since I started this I've been to the dentist and he told me all my surviving teeth are infected (abscesses on the roots of four) and although he could keep them going, it would cost a fortune, and they'd probably go on breaking singly as they've done in the recent past. So I've decided to have them out, and what a relief to be rid of the rotten things. They've probably been affecting my eyes too. Hope you are all well, and that we meet next year.

Love,

P.

20 Martin Road, 4.xi.75
TO BRETT WHITELEY
Dear Brett,

Thanks for your letter. If you but knew it is Everybody's Life Story (not the vegetables of course) with a different background and in a different frame.

Since I went to the exhibition,[129] toothless and in a post-'flu haze, I was haunted every night by that window with the necklace and the vase of flowers. I went back last Saturday, but alas, it had been sold a couple of days before. However, somebody had brought back 'Grief',[130] which I had hovered over when I first saw it, and I bought that. Perhaps the people who bought the window will decide against it in the end (I'm told the wife wants it, but the husband isn't so keen.)[131] I had begun to see it on the wall above my desk where I need such a window.

Today I am happy, momentarily: I've had a cable from my publisher very enthusiastic about the new book A *Fringe of Leaves*. There's also talk of *The Season at Sarsaparilla* being revived next year by the Old Tote with Sharman directing.

We must get together again soon.

Yrs

Patrick.

---

[129]'Thirty-Six Looks at Four Sights on Three Themes' at the Bonython.
[130]Actually, 'Crying Woman'.
[131]They kept it.

THIRTEEN

Applause

November 1975 – December 1978

DESPITE HIS MANY DISAPPOINTMENTS with Whitlam's government, White sided with Labor in the great political crisis of late 1975. He was shocked when the Governor-General John Kerr dismissed Whitlam on 11 November and commissioned the conservative opposition leader Malcolm Fraser to take the country to elections. The 'sacking' of Gough Whitlam was another decisive political event in Patrick White's life. Nineteen seventy-five made him a radical republican and his anger at the conservatives never left him. He campaigned for Labor in the elections that confirmed – by a landslide – Fraser and the conservatives in office.

20 MARTIN ROAD, 15.xi.75
TO MANNING CLARK
Bad as things are, I can't feel quite as pessimistic as you. I've had good reactions from unexpected people who would, I think, support us in an election if only the minions don't get carried away before then. Of course the Fraser Gang may still pull some foul punches. The whole thing is awful and extraordinary. When I was hesitating over taking that order because I don't think artists should be hung about with such jewellery, Kerr got me aside at a dinner at the James McClellands' and told me, 'You'll ruin everything if you don't!' It's ironic to think about that incident after <u>he</u> had ruined everything . . .

I am wondering what I can do to support the Government publicly (I have sent them money privately) as everything I would have said has been said over and over by everybody else, so that my statement would come as a banal after-bleat. No doubt the right moment will occur closer to the day and I shall hope to say the right thing.

20 MARTIN ROAD, 25.xi.75
TO JULIET O'HEA
Life has been rather chaotic since Whitlam's dismissal on Nov 11. Since then there have been political meetings every other day, and a vast one yesterday in the open air in support of Labor. I have never seen so many people gathered together. I have had to do something on telly, which

always makes me want the ground to swallow me up, and in a couple of days time I have to speak at a rally of writers, painters and performing artists in support of our legitimate government. The election is on Dec 13th – may it soon be here. Fortunately I am not working or perhaps unfortunately, for it is good to be able to burrow into one's created world if only for brief interrupted moments.

20 MARTIN ROAD, 22.xii.75
TO GEOFFREY DUTTON
Since I spoke for Labour I've come in for plenty of black looks and abusive letters. Worse still, some of my friends have been attacked. At the Museum party the former director John Evans rushed at David Moore and told him, 'Your friend Patrick White's made a fine fool of himself.' David said he shared my views. J.E.: 'Fancy falling for all that stuff Whitlam tells you.' D.M.: 'I've been considering migrating from Australia if the others get in.' J.E.: 'A good thing for Australia if you do!'

Harry Miller, who keeps carefully out of my way, collected a new car four days after the election. In fact I've noticed a number of the poor bankrupt rich[1] coming out in new cars since the 13th. Manoly says the Rolls and Jaguars infest the Double Bay shopping centre like snails after rain.

This rotten hypocritical country really deserves a revolution. But if Fraser makes his supporters suffer as I'm sure he will, perhaps that will be justice enough for the silly farting sheep who scampered after him.

I'm afraid this won't arrive before Christmas as I had hoped. There's been too much dentistry going on, and in between sessions, apathy on my part. The last of the old teeth were pulled out this morning, and the new ones went in. I think it will be a long time before I shall enjoy eating; even the softest stuff is painful.

20 MARTIN ROAD, 11.i.76
TO ALAN WILLIAMS
Dear Alan,
I'm glad the second typescript of A Fringe of Leaves arrived safely and that you liked it as a book. You refer to 'Victorian sensibilities' when Victoria only actually came to the throne the year after the wreck. Sensibilities, yes, but those are to be found also in the earlier part of the century. I like to think that the style old Mrs Roxburgh helped Ellen cultivate belonged to that earlier period.

[1] Poor bankrupt=the rich who cried poor in the Whitlam years.

If the American reader has to be told about Van Diemen's Land and Moreton Bay, can't you say something on the jacket about their being the Tasmania and Brisbane of today?

The story is based of course on the wreck of the *Stirling Castle* off the Queensland. The captain and his wife (the Frasers) and some of the crew were driven up the coast in the boats and finally landed on the island which is known as Fraser Island today. Mrs Fraser was a shrew from the Orkneys, her husband rather a feeble character after the style of Captain Purdue, though with some of the ailments real and imagined of Mr Roxburgh. I feel historical reconstructions are too limiting, so I did not stick to the original facts. I made Ellen Gluyas Cornish, because I know something of Cornwall and nothing of the Orkneys, and I married her to a gentleman so that I could make her function at more than one level, and turn something which would otherwise have been a mere adventure story into a novel of psychological interest. However, I don't consider it necessary to tell readers anything of this.

I assure you those masts were copied religiously from the accounts of the wreck of the <u>brig</u> *Stirling Castle*, the original of *Bristol Maid*!

I don't feel it is necessary to labour the time element in Mrs Roxburgh's ordeal. Actually it would have lasted about a year, I suppose, after the landing on the island but the period is a kind of elastic nightmare in which I set out to lose the compartments of time, just as the style loosens and coarsens, becomes more modern, during her life with Jack Chance the convict, and only constricts again after she returns to her corsets and life in so-called civilisation.

I feel very guilty not having done anything about your musical friend, but the year had such a bad end, with the defeat of the Government in which I believed and the loss of my teeth. I am only just beginning to get used to the false ones, but still feel exhausted and depressed as the result of these events.

Manoly and I will probably leave for London after Easter, and spend some time in France and Greece after that. Any chance of your being in any of those places during the year? We propose to be away about six months, unless the money runs out and we come shooting back sooner than that. (At least I shall be less greedy and cost less to feed now that I have a mouthful of false teeth.)

A summer opera season has just started, with revivals of *Aïda* and *The Magic Flute* which we are not bothering about, and a new *Salome, Cosi* and *Albert Herring*, all of which we want to go to. A new young Scottish singer called Isobel Buchanan, discovered by the Bonynge, is having a great success.[2]

Yours
Patrick.

25 MARTIN ROAD, 18.i.76
TO JOSEPH LOSEY
Dear Joe,
Thanks for your letter of December 19th – also the Christmas cable. I should have replied sooner but have been feeling very low, slightly less dispirited since my false teeth have settled down.

You and Mercer[3] will have to decide between you your attitude to the Voss story as the film will be yours. When I wrote the novel I was more involved with the journey than the preparations, but since recent weeks I'd like to see the 'arrogant and philistine bourgeoisie' get a full broadside. I'm only worried that you and Mercer should know so little about the look and feel of Australia, unless, like D. H. Lawrence, you can get it all from the drive between the station (airport) and hotel[4] . . .

Best wishes for a better year.
Patrick.

THOUGH WHITE TRIED TO give the impression he was finished with the theatre, his theatrical ambitions were only ever on ice. In the bleak months of the political crisis the director Jim Sharman appeared at Martin Road with a plan to revive *The Season at Sarsaparilla*. Sharman was young and famous. Theatres around the world were playing his productions of *The Rocky Horror Show*, *Jesus Christ Superstar* and *Hair*. But earlier in the year he had come home to Australia to seek a new theatrical career; what followed was a ten-year collaboration with Patrick White which the writer judged 'a perfect example of fruitful sublimation'.[5] Sharman immediately encouraged him to rework 'The Night the Prowler' as a filmscript. Greatly stimulated by this, White set to work researching the next novel, *The Twyborn Affair*, which he was to dedicate to Sharman. Research took him

[2]Buchanan (1954–   ) protégé of conductor Richard Bonynge (1930–   ), made her professional debut that month in Sydney; a career in Europe and North America followed.
[3]After failing to snare Pinter, Losey chose the Yorkshire playwright and scriptwriter David Mercer (1928–80), best-known for the television drama *A Suitable Case for Treatment*, 1962, and the film *Morgan*, 1965.
[4]PW boasted the same intuition and scorned his friends' reading histories and guides before they travelled.
[5]*Flaws in the Glass*, Jonathan Cape, 1981.

back to the Monaro to explore the landscape of his – and Eddie Twyborn's – jackarooing days.

20 MARTIN ROAD, 21.ii.76
TO GEOFFREY DUTTON
Dear Geoffrey,

What you let yourself in for! And you ought to know all about writers, particularly Russian ones, or their Soviet literary ringmasters, by now.[6] I was asked to open the Australian-American writers' seminar, but am not having any of that. I've also been asked to sign a document got up by some Australian writers to protest against American publishers' unkindness to Australian writers. I can't very well sign that as my own publishers have stuck to me since 1939, making very little out of me till I won that wretched prize. They even published two other Australian writers on my recommendation. I think the difficulty with Americans is that the public for the most part can't understand any version of the English language but their own, and they're not interested in any but their own problems. With the Fraser Government snuggling up so cosily to their American counter parts I'd like to show I wasn't with it, but I can't protest against the publishers.

We too, have had a wedding, a few doors down. The girl and her young man had been fucking for years, when suddenly she had to get married: bridesmaids appeared in pale blue with gardenia corsages and the Catholic bourgeoisie rolled up in hundreds. It seems so ridiculous to go through all that pantomime after sleeping together so long; perhaps that is how it struck Charlotte's young man.[7]

I am just back from four days in the Monaro. It turned out most rewarding thanks to a Cooma taxi-driver. I was afraid I might only come across foreign migrants, or Australians too young to know about the district's past. But Max Kaufline's great-grandfather came out from Bavaria not long after mine arrived from Somerset and since then four generations have been born in Cooma. The first day we drove to Adaminaby, Old and New, up to Kiandra, which has almost entirely disappeared, and out to Bolaro. I went to the cottage where I lived while a jackeroo, and saw

---

[6] As chairman of the Adelaide Festival Writers' Week, Dutton was having a difficult time with writers – Vonnegut, Baldwin, Moravia – dropping out at the last minute. 'And the Russians,' he told me, 'Instead of sending those I asked for, including (yet again) Akhmadulina, announced they were sending two Party hacks and a KGB-bureaucrat.'

[7] No; but Alistair Calder who was marrying Dutton's niece had protested that the simple ceremony they planned in the family church at Hamilton near Anlaby had turned into an immense country wedding.

the room where I wrote my first (mercifully unpublished) novel. The cottage is pretty tumble down by now, with overgrown hawthorns pressing up against it, and rabbits shooting out of the fat-hen[8] as one approaches.

Next day we drove down through Nimmitabel and Bibbenluke to Bombala, up to Dalgety and Jindabyne and back through Berridale. Jindabyne I found rather depressing, with its souvenir shops and fake alpine chalets. Nor is the lake very attractive, whereas Eucumbene, in spite of Adaminaby Old and New has something of the atmosphere of an Irish lake, perhaps from the souls of all the drunken Adaminabites who must be haunting it.

The third day we drove to Michelago, and back through Lanyon, Tharwa, and Naas down the road along which a half-witted stockman and I brought a mob of sheep to Bolaro. It amazed me to think that anyone should have had the idea of sending a half-wit and a boy of 18 on a journey through such country, though today the road is a hundred times better than the rutted track it was then.

I was tempted to go on to Queanbeyan while we were in those parts, but read in the *Herald* this morning that 'Mr & Mrs D. Campbell and Mr & Mrs J. B. Osborne' were at luncheon with the Governor General. I suppose it would have been those Campbells and Virginia's parents.[9] David and Virginia must have been laughing up their sleeves the night of the 11th Nov when they came to dinner and the rest of us were lamenting The Event.[10] (I'm told Virginia signed the Artists for Fraser thing.)[11] Well, well, my low opinion of human beings is never quite low enough.

We leave on April 23 and I shall be glad.

Love to all

P.

Have you read David Malouf's *Johnno*? I think it's one of the best books I've read by an Australian.

Another marvellous book is Sumner Locke Elliott's *Going*.

But I couldn't read Frank Hardy: unbearable stodge laced with cliché.[12]

---

[8]*Chenopodium album.*

[9]The poet David Campbell lived a few miles from Queanbeyan at Folly Run on the Molonglo; PW had held a dinner at Martin Road on 11 Nov. to award him the second Patrick White Prize; the Osbornes' daughter Virginia – at one time an actress and reader for Curtis Brown in Sydney – was also present. Now the Campbells and Osbornes were defying the total boycott of vice-regal events which PW was to try to enforce for the rest of his life. Despite these noises, Campbell never fell out of favour with PW.

[10]No.

[11]No.

[12]His novel *But The Dead are Many*, 1975.

20 MARTIN ROAD, 29.ii.76
TO MARSHALL BEST

Now to answer some of your criticism of A *Fringe of Leaves*– – I thought I'd made Mrs R.'s distress abundantly clear after Oswald Dignam was drowned. If I'd made it more emotional I'd have lost the English tone and the measure of that period. She was so pregnant and, I feel, would have restrained herself instinctively from giving way to great bursts of emotion. In the circumstances I don't think the loss of her husband's Virgil would have distressed her particularly; everything is being stripped away from her and then she herself was never bookish; she sat with a book to please her husband and mother-in-law. To hammer home such points, as you crave, is just what I didn't want to do.

Punctuation has never been my strength. I do it, to use your own words, 'according to the way we pause in reading it'. I expect Americans have a different way of pausing and reading – well, of course they do!

The typing seems to have upset everybody.[13] It happened by accident. I am always in a state of tension when starting the final version. My hand must have slipped and the spacing gadget shot up to single-spacing.[14] I did not notice this until I had typed about 25 pages. As it did not seem to me to look so bad, and because it would cost much less to send, I continued typing that way.

I suppose different people have different meannesses. Typing, apparently, is one of mine, and certainly postage, along with tooth-brushes and paste (probably the reason I lost my teeth) and underclothes (I can never bear to buy new ones till the old ones are in rags). Apart from anything else, to employ a typist would involve so much explaining, re-reading, and correcting, I couldn't face it. Another time I shall have to type my book in three volumes and everybody will be satisfied, though I doubt I shall run to parchment.

We are leaving here, God willing, on April 22nd, and shall fly straight to London. It would be good if we could go for another drive with you, but I doubt the money would run to the US as well as Europe and London, both of which I must see again for reasons connected with the book I hope to write next. Then, if we set foot in the US, we shall have to visit the frightful

[13]Best had written, 2.ii.76: 'After struggling an hour at a time – my maximum without eyestrain – with that ghastly flimsy typescript – single-spaced and with no margins at all for breathing – my eyes just managed to get to the end intact. I can't understand why, after all these years, you are still so cruel to your first readers! I'd gladly raise a Better Typing Fund for Nobel Prizemen for the extra paper and postage, be it three times as long. I'm really not joking now.'

[14]By this Best pencilled, 'Oh come off it!'

St Petersburg and Fort Lauderdale, and I don't think either of us can face venturing there again. Manoly's mother is now pretty old and presumably won't last for ever. Then we can say to the Fort Lauderdale sister, 'Either come to New York, or . . .' This may sound heartless, but the mother did abandon six of them when Manoly was six years old, and did not bother with him again until he forced himself on her a few years ago.

My nineteen-year old niece is still with us, but starts at her art school today, and is moving in a couple of weeks to share a house with a young man the Jesuits were training for the priesthood but who found he hadn't a vocation.[15] An interesting situation; I feel she won't be seduced, unless by the rattle of the rosary. I have found it a great strain having this brooding girl in the house for almost nine months. But I must do what I can for her as she was orphaned when thirteen, and had rather an awful time in an English boarding school just as I had. I think we are quite fond of each other too, again in a strained way.

The political situation in Australia remains as awful as could be, with Murdoch the monster of the press, doing everything possible to destroy Whitlam.[16] I shall be glad to breathe another air for a few months.

Patrick.

[15]Gerard Windsor (1944–   ) who became a writer and served, in the 1980s, as a judge for the Patrick White Award.
[16]So biased were the many papers of Rupert Murdoch (1931–   ) in the crisis of 1975 that his journalists struck in protest.

MARTIN ROAD, 20.iii.76
TO CYNTHIA NOLAN
Dear Cynthia,
Your letter depressed me infinitely – that exhibition at Johannesburg![17] I've made a point of never setting foot in that country. Years ago, after the Canal was closed, Manoly went back to Greece by sea and spent a day in Capetown and found what he saw of apartheid most disgusting. Perhaps I am 'naif', but Sid seems to take one step after another to show he is on the wrong side. You say you hope these subjects won't come up conversationally while we are in London, but I find the days when one could avoid politics are over: one must come out on one side or the other.

At least the Governor General was relentlessly booed all through his speech yesterday when he was opening a new college of adult education in Adelaide. If a few more such occasions occur I don't see how the Queen can avoid removing him ...

Adelaide Writers' Week seems to have been a shambles. The usual attacks on me led by Frank Hardy. I suppose I ask for it because I always refer to him as the Great Australian Bore. The Blackmans have now joined in since I had a crack at Charles at election time when he sawed a painting in half to give a piece to each side and some people saw that as 'integrity'. Now Barbara Blackmail has written a piece on Writers' Week for the SMH in which it says that the gathering affirmed 'an end to the Patrick White Australia Policy.'[18] Charles did a dreadful jacket for the latest dreadful Frank Hardy novel The Dead are Many, which would surely make a good title for a book on Australian writers.

Tom Maschler wrote about the jacket for A Fringe of Leaves and said they were using the Mrs Fraser painting.[19] Why they have to make a fuss about its not wrapping over when most jackets don't wrap over, is something I don't understand. A lot of them have extracts of the reviews of previous books printed on the back. Desmond has had trouble with that art director at Cape; amongst other things he always wants lettering which we don't feel goes with the designs. They sent me a dreadful blurb this time which I had to re-write entirely, but of course that won't prevent them sticking on some embarrassing bits of their own. Still, I have found Cape much more understanding and co-operative than other publishers.

[17]At the Pieter Wenning Gallery in April.
[18]Not quite: in a list of impressions she included, 'a lady interviewer privying poets behind the bushes, rumours ripening word-o'-mouth, statements taking shape, end of the Patrick White Australia Policy . . .', 20 March, p.14. The last phrase was Frank Hardy's.
[19]'Mrs Fraser and Convict', 1962–4.

I was speaking to Gough this morning on the phone. There is a Jugoslav sculptor who somehow also has Australian nationality and who did a bust of Solzhenitsyn after he escaped from Russia. The sculptor then came out here and did Gough. Now apparently he wants to do me and is using Gough as the go-between. I had to say I thought him a bad artist and a pushing man, and that was that.

Shall be seeing Gough on Monday when he will launch another book about the Events by Andrew Clark (one of Manning's sons) and another man.[20] I hate launchings, but feel I must be there as it will be an opportunity to show publicly that I am still with Gough.

It's going to be an exhausting day. We have the Steegmullers[21] and some others coming to dinner, which I shall have to get ready before and after the launching. Shall be in a fine sweat when the guests arrive. We like the Steegmullers very much. I wonder why you don't . . .

We arrive in London on 23rd April when I expect you will be in the disgusting Johannesburg. Shall go to the Wilbraham Hotel and hope Manoly won't complain as he did at the Basil. But I'm not going to waste money on hotels when we may not have enough to do all we have to do. If that spa with the mud baths is on Evvoia, it will fit in very well as it is one of the parts of Greece I feel will not be overrun with tourists. The other is the Mani in the south the Peloponnese. No more islands. I think if it weren't for Elly and Elias we wouldn't want to go to Greece again.

This letter started off very depressed but I have felt better as it progressed. I am depressed most of the time nowadays.

Love
Patrick.

BEARING THEIR SPLINTER OF Santa Teresa's staircase, the two men set out for Europe in late April. The Nolans were there to meet them at Heathrow and for the next two months the best times were those spent in the Nolans' company. Cynthia was skeletal.

WILBRAHAM HOTEL, LONDON, ABOUT 5.v.76
TO GEOFFREY DUTTON
We had a most exhausting direct flight, and worse arrival at Heathrow in a milling mob of Pakistanis, Arabs, and Malaysians. Not a trolley to be had and certainly not a porter. Fortunately we caught sight of Sid as soon

[20]*Kerr's King Hit!* by Clark and Clem Lloyd, 1976.
[21]Francis Steegmuller (1906–   ), the American biographer, editor and translator, and his wife, the Australian novelist, Shirley Hazzard (1931–   ).

as we reached the barrier, but were almost ruptured by then.

My first impression of London was a kind of suppressed hysteria in the Londoners of today. Later on, I put it down to hysteria in myself as the result of that nightmarish arrival. It has taken us about a fortnight to recover, and we are still constipated (we hear the hostesses have an enema at the end of the flight so that they are quickly restored.)

Our hotel is amiable and inefficient, the room too small – we bump bums if we both bend down at the same time, and one night we had water through the ceiling. The service is Spanish, with one Bolivian, and an Alexandrian Copt with whom Manoly exchanges Arabic.

Have seen a lot of the Nolans. Cynthia is looking very ill, thinner than ever; she has been suffering agonies from her back. They took us for a couple of marvellous drives, one to that inspired Sissinghurst (I'm sure her ghost haunts at night) and another to the horticultural experimental garden at Wisley – spring in full flower at both.

We should really make the effort to go more to the country while we are here, but London is in my bones and I can't tear myself away from it. London is something you and David Campbell will never understand! . . .

So far I've staved off the media and think the worst must be over. I'm keeping quiet and I'm sure they won't realise I'm here. We were offered the Kingsley Amises, Rebecca West, and Paul Theroux all at once, but I got out of that. Have seen Beckett twice, on one occasion coming out of the Minstrels' Bar, Sloane Square, at 11 a.m. We flickered at each other from a distance. I don't expect he knew who I was; he only suspected a possible predator.

ÖSTERVÅLE, SWEDEN. 22.vi.76
TO GWEN MOORE
We are at present somewhere in the middle of Sweden, where we were brought by Ingmar Björkstén, whom we met on his two visits to Australia. (His mother actually lived in Perth for a bit, with her second husband, a Norwegian.) Ingmar has a cottage on the edge of a forest, beside it a field full of dandelion-clocks, purple cranes-bill, buttercups, and blue campanula. The mists roll down from the north at night and the light remains white throughout.

Midsummer Eve there was singing, dancing round a green maypole, but none of the drunkenness one expected, and no Miss Julie letting down her hair. Stockholm is beautiful, clear, and serene after the squalor of present day London . . .

So far we have been able to remain anonymous, except at the end of our London visit, when the Australian press started battering, wanting to know why I had turned in my Order of Australia. I did make a statement through my agent, whether it was published or not. Orders and titles have been made seem more ridiculous than ever by the recent handout in England. But in our own context, I withdrew more than anything because Kerr is head of the Order, and it is impossible to respect such a man.

We really had a wonderfully full two months in London – theatre or opera every other night; meetings with a lot of interesting people; and the Nolans drove us to a number of wonderful gardens which I had not seen before.

I had a couple of days in Paris with Losey, where I met David Mercer and read his screenplay, which seems to me to keep the essence of the book. I think we are actually moving towards the filming. My last night we were taken to dinner by a German producer who is interested in putting up some of the money.[22] There is also an American, who was on the phone while I was in Paris. But all will depend on Harry Miller doing his part. Losey would like to start shooting in October, which I find worrying, as I can't see how an important film could be got together in such a short time. (Better not repeat any of that.)

OSLO, 1.vii.76
TO ELIZABETH HARROWER
The night at Igmar Björkstén's before we left, we had, in addition to the Lundkvists, a lady who has spent her life translating Proust into Swedish, and the [Australians]. It was a curious and rather nightmarish occasion as it would be difficult to introduce [her] into any society outside the . . . suburbs. She is huge, and was dressed on this occasion in opium poppies and green eye-shadow. After a quarter of an hour of her voice which holds forth above everyone else's, one feels battered into a state of desperation. Her husband is obviously aware of this, and suffers considerable mental anguish. It would be impossible to explain [her] to foreigners and the intellectual Swedes were reduced to a state of incredulous horror. She told me she was struggling with one of my books, but she never let a book beat her; even with Ngaio Marsh,[23] whom she loves, it takes six or seven chapters before she settles down. After dinner Ingmar pushed the Lundkvists, the Proust lady and myself into a corner, while he and Manoly carried off the [Australians] to the other end of the room. I was

[22]Klaus Hellwig.
[23](1899–1982) New Zealand-born writer of detective novels.

sorry, because I would have liked to ask [him] a lot of things in better circumstances.

So far we have not explored Oslo very thoroughly. Norway is more beautiful than Sweden, but far less civilised; The people are closer to the English, I'd say. They are scornful of the Swedes, who, they tell us, are really Germans disguised as human beings. I think the chief difference is that the Swedes have had it too good, whereas the Norwegians have suffered, through poverty, and a foreign occupation.

Last night we were given dinner by my school friend Ragnar Christophersen, whose wife, concert pianist who didn't make it, came from Grafton NSW. They live on a mountain outside the city with a vast northern landscape spread out around them. They also have their own fantasy world. She is addicted to *Jonathan Seagull*[24] and Mahler, and seldom comes down into the city. He is a professor at the university, gives a clown performance in several languages, and will talk endlessly about the school he hated. His chief hobbies are sailing (he has sailed the Atlantic several times in his own boat) skiing, and flying. If he dwells on any intellectual subject he is inclined to apologise like an old-style public schoolboy.

At dinner we also had my Norwegian publisher[25] and a man who directed a Norwegian radio version of *Willy Wagtails by Moonlight*.[26]

Today Christophersen is taking us to the Munch Museum (apologetically) and the yacht club, for which I am unable to show any enthusiasm. However I find him interesting because he is the kind of person with whom, normally, I don't have any connexion.

We shall go on that fantastic train journey over the mountains to Bergen while we are here, see the town briefly, and fly back to Oslo . . .

Thank you for all the cuttings. I don't know whether the press announced that I had withdrawn from the Order of Australia. I made a statement giving my reasons, and gave it to Peter Grose[27] before we left London. I don't imagine Government House would have published the reason as being my inability to respect the Queen's present representative.[28]

---

[24]*Jonathan Livingston Seagull*, a fable by Richard Bach with photographs by Russell Munson, published in 1970.

[25]Gordon Hølmebakk of Gyldendal Norsk Forlag.

[26]Gerhard Knoop, distinguished theatre director.

[27]Curtis Brown's former Sydney man, now in London.

[28]Press reports followed PW's own statement faithfully: emphasising his objection to knights appearing in the Order and adding his disrespect for Kerr almost as an afterthought.

Hope you are both well and getting on top of the house renovations.
Yrs
Patrick.

NICE, 19.vii.76
TO THE DUTTONS
(This top sheet turns out to be blotting paper.)
Dear Nin and Geoffrey,
This should reach you in time for the first of the two birthdays, the actual
dates of which I can never remember! There is no sign of anything suitable
by way of a present, so you will have to wait for that.

We have now forged our way across the South of France as far as
Nice. And when I say 'forge', I don't think it's an exaggeration. Did you
ever see Godard's film Weekend?[29] That's what's happening in France.
They're being destroyed by cars. How I've got to hate them!

We went to stay at Hyères, but found ourselves stuck for a week 17
km outside on a Florida-style highway, devoured by mosquitoes, plagued
by diarrhoea in my case, and surrounded by a most unsympathetic type of
French bourgeoisie. However, we did get one or two glimpses of what the
past must have looked like in Hyères (also the ruined Bandol and Cassis,
through which we trundled in a bus on our way from Marseilles.) Two
finds we made were the little town of Giens (not quite destroyed because
it is perched on a mountain by the sea) and the island of Porquerolles,
where we got away from the awfulness for a while in a pine forest deserted
by practically everything but cicadas.

While we were near Hyères we also had the pleasure of seeing Peter
Beatson who came over from Aix with his Indonesian girl friend Rana,[30]
without whom I can't imagine what he would do. The parents of Rana
are diplomats. She spent some of her childhood in Canberra. She also
turns out to be a goddaughter of Irene Worth, how we can't decide – Irene
Worth being a Jewess and Rana a Moslem, the parents so strict she has
had to pretend her relationship with Peter doesn't exist.

We also saw Jim Sharman the other day. He came down from London
to meet us at Marseilles, to talk about one or two things in connexion
with the production of Sarsaparilla and the film of The Night the Prowler,
for which he has a producer and hopes to do next year. (I hope we can
get it out before Voss, which looks as if it's hanging fire again.)

[29]1967 comedy involving an immense French traffic jam, rape, cannibalism, etc.
[30]Rana Helmi.

Now that we're in Nice, with plenty of buses and the chemist round the corner, I'd feel rejuvenated if it weren't for this wretched diarrhoea. The South of France really has aged me a lot. I thought I'd had it on one dreadful occasion, dragging too much luggage to catch a train at Toulon. After that the landscapes seemed to put things right, no sign of a dreadful freeway or the endless string of cars, but, real life going on as though nothing had happened.

Nice is bouncing and vulgar, but with a style. There are also some excellent restaurants and intriguing streets. We found the Palais Lascaris which is now a museum.[31] In the 17th Century Manoly's ancestress the Princess Eudoxia of Nicea married a Ventimille, and that's how Nice got its name.[32] The custodian of the museum became quite tremulous when I told him who Manoly was.

[31]In the Rue Droite: the home of the ruling Lascaris-Vintimille family until the revolution. Manoly Lascaris' uncle liked to tell how he was offered the Italianate palace but turned it down as impractical.

[32]Not so: Nice – from the Greek niké, victory – had its name for over a thousand years before the arrival of the Lascaris. The Arrighis' second daughter was named Niké because she was born there.

ATHENS, 6.viii.76
TO GEOFFREY DUTTON
Dear Geoffrey,
We reached Athens a couple of days ago and found your letters waiting. It is very distressing to hear you have accepted the AO at this stage. I took it in the first place against my better judgment, conned into it by that legal crook the G.-G., who said 'You will ruin everything if you don't.' As I had become enthusiastic about Australia for the first time in my life during the Whitlam regime, I agreed to accept. But of course artists should have nothing to do with such things. All such honours are bribes, and all honours are political. Everything is political unless you plump for indifference. I was indifferent until Whitlam appeared on the scene and injected life into Australia. But the last election showed that that was illusion. We shall never be anything of a nation because we are too bloody greedy and too bloody stupid. Thinking as I do, I shall get on with my dreadful fate of being an Australian but at least without the irrelevant baubles.

It is good to be in Athens in the flat Elly has lent us, though the electric drills are at work all around, and though the Parthenon is scarcely visible for smog (if we come here again we shan't see her for the wall of new apartment houses.)

I feel very feeble after our rugged journey across France and Italy, neither of which I shall want to return to. The fact that Norway and Sweden are not yet littered with filth and swarming with the human animal makes them such a delight. However, Genoa was worth seeing, in spite of being filthier even than Constantinople: magnificent palaces in the most squalid streets, and I've never seen such a display of whores as in the waterfront bars, sitting topless in their red-lit interiors; you could feel the clap and the crabs jumping through the doorways at you.

ATHENS, 1.ix.76
TO ELIZABETH HARROWER
We took a boat to Monemvasia, a vast, and rather sinister fortified rock, on which mainly foreigners seem to be living. We only spent one night there in a room without water, but at least a clean, flushing, communal lavatory, then took a crowded bus to Gythion, from which we drove out into the Maui, again by taxi. This is a comparatively sterile part of Greece, but very beautiful in its austere way. The villages are clumps of stone towers, fortified in the past, and the most powerful were those who had the highest towers. Most of the towers are now abandoned, or the owners live away and only come back occasionally.

Our stay at Gythion was spoilt by a bathroom which had a smell, and bad food in the restaurants. However, on one of our drives, the taximan took us to a village by the sea, where we ate a most memorable fish soup with a salad of courgette flowers . . .

There was also a trip to Mistra, which for dazzling grandeur, is difficult to beat. We found the remains of the Lascaris house and in the church the ancestor built, his mural, or what the Turks left of it, also the place where his bones are said to lie.

Now back to Athens, which is more than ever the picture of urban squalor and vulgarity. Still, we spent a very pleasant evening yesterday with Elly and her family. Both her sons are here, the American one with his lazy but pleasant Jewish wife, and their child (a bit too much the American Child)[33] and the one from Germany, with German attachment, a girl with mermaid hair who sits disconcertingly smoking a man's old pipe.[34] Both the sons are scientists, but you are not made aware of that.

ATHENS, 9.ix.76
TO CYNTHIA NOLAN
Dear Cynthia,
Thanks for your letter. It seemed a long time since we had heard from you and we had begun to wonder whether something had happened. So many dreadful things have happened lately . . .

Your letter should be discussed in detail. It is difficult, however, to do it on paper. I hope you continue well; you do sound so much better.[35]

ATHENS, 18.ix.76
TO PEGGY GARLAND
Dear Peggy,
I hope you have got rid of that incubus by now, at least as far as the other cottage, but I doubt you will have;[36] you are too passive, sentimental, I even detect signs of your hoping that you may turn into a Darby and Joan. God help you! Of course I blame your children, who have been thoroughly selfish about the whole thing, plonking him down at the other end of the

[33]Costa Polymeropoulos of Rutgers University, his wife Jill Waksman and their son Mark.
[34]Notis Polymeropoulos of Hamburg University and his wife Ulrike.
[35]His last letter to her.
[36]After Tom Garland's second marriage ended, he stayed for a time in Eynsham – while a broken leg mended, with Peggy herself. In early letters to Peggy PW admitted, 'I don't know Tom'; then when the Garland marriage was in difficulties in the 1950s, PW urged Peggy to 'endure everything' but once the split came he took sides vengefully, baffled that his distaste for Tom Garland was not shared by all who knew the man.

same village. They should have got him into a home. Nick alone must have tons of money.[37]

As for your grand-daughter, I should have told her to stuff the pill into her exposed navel, and take herself off until she had learnt more civilised manners. You say you can see her ending up as a callgirl; she must be throwing back to her grandfather.

(I know your habit of showing people letters. I hope you show him this.)

We leave here on the 28th and fly straight to Sydney. We shall both be most relieved to get back into our own house, though apart from that, the thought of the Australian situation makes me recoil. However, I must try to do something about it if I can, as Australia is my fate.

We did two marvellous trips in Greece, one to see Euboea, and the other to the Southern Peloponnese. Athens today is an inferno of petrol fumes, cement dust, chicanery and apathy. So I shan't be sorry to leave, except that it will mean leaving Elly and Elias who are two exceptional Greeks.

I wonder whether Cape sent you a copy of *A Fringe of Leaves*? It has had what pass for good reviews, though I wouldn't want to read the book on reading them. The *Sunday Times* describes it as 'the adventures of an English couple in Australia– –'[38] It makes me feel I shouldn't write another word, though I am already embroiled in a rather painful story which suggested itself while we were in Euboea.[39]

I read a good review of one of Sarah's books[40] while we were traipsing about Europe. She is a sympathetic young woman, and although I know neither of them would want Tom on their hands, I'd have thought Sarah might help protect you from him.

You will probably think this an awful letter. It is, rather, a call to arms. Otherwise you will end up a miserable drudge emptying the bed-pans of an increasingly smelly old man.

Love
Patrick.

THOUGH WHITE WAS BACK in time for the start of rehearsals, Sharman made him wait a fortnight before letting him see the cast of *The Season at*

[37]Nick Garland the cartoonist.
[38]But also called it a 'magnificent and colossal novel' that stood comparison with *Voss*; David Pryce-Jones, 12 Sept., p.40.
[39]'Fête Galante'.
[40]*Henry and Fowler*, 1976, by Peggy Garland's daughter-in-law Sarah.

Sarsaparilla at work. Unperturbed, he marked time unpacking, cooking and writing letters. *A Fringe of Leaves* sold well in Britain and Australia. In these weeks he began to correspond with an eccentric fan in Hamburg, Elizabeth Falkenberg. She had written several times before the gift of a brooch provoked White to reply. Her particular eccentricity was to send gifts: jewellery, blocks of cheese, jumpers, etc. Often she slipped several hundred-mark notes between the pages of her letters. White sent books. Falkenberg made several visits to Sydney in person and spirit. She told me: 'I often sit invisible on the roof . . . I was never in love with Patrick as a *man*, for me he was a wizard, who had touched me with his wand!'

20 MARTIN ROAD, 4.x.76
TO ELIZABETH FALKENBERG
Dear Frau Falkenberg,
Thank you indeed for your letter and for the very beautiful little brooch . . . Above my desk I have a frame with two drawings by my friend Sidney Nolan, one of Lear and one of the Fool. I have fastened the brooch to the corner of the frame so that I shall spend a lot of time looking at it. I too, believe in magic objects. Cynthia Nolan wife of the painter has given me one, a flat circlet of brown jade, which we call an open mandala. I carry it in my pocket wherever I go.

20 MARTIN ROAD, 6.x.76
TO JOSEPH LOSEY
Dear Joe,
Received your letter of Sept 6th. I'm sorry if I appeared unenthusiastic about the script, which I thought overcame all the difficulties quite marvellously. I must write to David. Actually when I read it I was feeling ill and depressed and would probably have sounded unenthusiastic about anything.[41] I am starting to feel better since we came home, but I have arranged to have a check-up all the same.

Good to think you will be here soon. I met Harry the other day in the street and the meeting went off amiably. You say I am too 'obsessive'

---

[41]After reading the script in Athens he had gracelessly written to Losey, 1.ix.76, making corrections: 'Laura makes several appearances in her riding habit off her horse. I've not seen pictures of Victorian women in riding habits except when mounted, but I have memories of women in habits as far back as 1917, and they looked quite grotesque when not mounted. I suspect Laura would look a rather unromantic sight when on the ground.' And so on.

where Harry M. is concerned but you have not been through all the publicity antics which so disgust me. I only hope he can raise the money, but I don't yet see any sign of his doing so.

My play is in rehearsal. Sharman and the actors are pleased with the way it is going. I shall stay away till they have a run-through. It opens, I believe, on Nov 3rd. Perhaps you will see it, anyway, some time during the run.

The pugs came back from their boarding-house – so overfed it's alarming. Apparently they spent their nights sitting on a sofa watching the telly. Pansy would not allow a bird or a horse on the screen, but would rush at the set, round and under, till she'd chased them off.

Lots of things I don't like about Australia. Prices have shot up alarmingly since we left. There is also a sinister move towards censorship. Our leading historian who is to give some lectures on the radio is to have them vetted by the ABC because he supported the Socialist Government.[42] Lots more but it can wait.

Yrs
Patrick.

20 MARTIN ROAD, 9.x.76
TO PEGGY GARLAND
Dear Peggy,
Your letter was here when we arrived back after a very prolonged flight. I'm glad *A Fringe of Leaves* appealed to you. It has had an astonishing reception, so much so, I'm beginning to wonder if something isn't wrong.

I was terribly sorry to hear about Joyce. Like her friends, I feel she must be got away from Betty by all means. Aren't there some nuns near Oxford who would look after B.?[43] She ought to like that, her being a lay one and all, and if she bitches the nuns they would have to put up with it since they are what they are. However, I remember somebody who was nursed by nuns telling me that there's no bitch like a bitch-nun. Which would be good for B. Let me have Joyce's address some time.

[42]Manning Clark, about to deliver the prestigious Boyer Lectures on ABC radio, was attacked by a Liberal senator for speaking – with PW – at a public forum in Sydney on 'Kerr and the Consequences'. ABC management then asked to read the Boyer scripts before they were recorded; this was unprecedented. Allan Ashbolt, head of Radio Special Projects, refused to hand them over and appealed to the ABC commissioners who decided on 11 October that the lectures would be broadcast, 'as Professor Manning Clark has written and recorded them. They will not be subject to review.'
[43]Joyce was ill; Betty was sharing her cottage and going blind; soon she left Joyce to move to a flat in Oxford.

I expect you didn't like my letter from Oxford,[44] but it was something I had to write, feeling as I did about various Garlands. At least you've got rid of him back to the other end of the village. But how long will it be before he imposes himself again?

After ten days at home we are beginning to re-learn what you do in a house. But I am still dizzy from the high-flying and full of aches from lugging luggage across airports.

Lots of awfulness in Australia. Must get down to work. *The Season at Sarsaparilla* is in rehearsal, opening at the Opera House on Nov 3rd.

Patrick.

20 MARTIN ROAD, 17.x.76
TELEGRAM TO JOHANNES VORSTER
PRIME MINISTER OF SOUTH AFRICA
Dear Mr. Vorster,
In a lifetime of theatre-going in London, Paris, New York, Berlin and Athens, I thought I had seen only three performances of the kind which become legendary, until recently in Sydney I was able to add to my short list those of John Kani and Winston Ntshona in *The Island* and *Sizwe Bansi is Dead*.[45] As a personal opinion, this might not carry much weight. But consider the critical acclaim these artists received in London and New York. May I point out the irreparable harm you will do your country in the eyes of the world if you condone the humiliating detention of these great South Africans.[46]

Yours sincerely,
Patrick White.

SHARMAN'S PRODUCTION OF *THE SEASON* at *Sarsaparilla* gave White the dazzling theatrical success he had craved most of his life. This was not Broadway nor the West End, but it was the Opera House and the theatre was packed. Sydney's critics celebrated White's return to the stage. He began to write *Big Toys*. At the centre of the new play stands a figure rather like Jack Mundey the hero of the Green Bans, and the plot grows out of attempts to

---

[44]Athens.
[45]Both by the South African playwright Athol Fugard whom PW admired with reservations: to Mary Benson (who had solicited this letter to Vorster) PW wrote, 8.x.76, to say Fugard's new play *Dimetos*, 'was so bad one couldn't believe it was by the same man. It even made Schofield seem a bad actor.'
[46]The actors were gaoled in the Transkei on 6 Oct. as they were about to perform *Sizwe Bansi*. PW's cable to Vorster was part of an international campaign to force the actors' release which came about on 25 Oct.

seduce such a man into joining the corrupt Sydney society around him. In these heady weeks came news of Cynthia Nolan's death.

20 Martin Road 28.xi.76
TO RONALD WATERS
Dear Ronald,
Well, *Sarsaparilla* has been accepted at last, thanks to Jim Sharman and very good casting.[47] We are doing so well we could move to another theatre if there was one, but there isn't: the Royal stage not wide enough, too vast an auditorium in Ireenland.[48] The main thing is that it has been proved that the play can entertain a large number of people.

We went to Gordon's piece and he is quite remarkable, but the play disappointed us a bit, brilliant though it is in parts.[49] After so much manic come-and-go in the first part, the tone alters, and I don't think the man in bed holds one's attention. However, Hammerstein has paid a large sum for a year's option – without Gordon, alas.[50]

I rang up this morning, and he had been broken into again a couple of nights before: TV, tape recorder, fur bedspread, and telephone money all taken, everything turned upside down. Of course an actor living alone is a gift to the burglar, who knows he will be shut up safely in a theate all evening: I think a burglar alarm is the best safeguard.

You will be surprised to hear that I have got the first version of a new play down on paper. I've had the germ of it in my head for some time, then the whole thing got together as the result of hearing actors one wants to write for and having a director in whom one has faith. It came pouring out – a rather black comedy.

The blackness increased somewhat by hearing of Cynthia Nolan's suicide. Sid rang up in the middle of the night. Don't know exactly how

[47]Kate Fitzpatrick and Max Cullen as Nola and Ernie Boyle, Bill Hunter as Digger Masson his mate and her seducer, Robyn Nevin as the sentimental harpie Girlie Pogson.
[48]Her Majesty's, an ugly brick auditorium where the musical *Irene*, directed by Freddie Carpenter, was performed in 1974 and 1975.
[49]Gordon Chater (1922–   ) playing a cross-dressing speech therapist driven to violence by respectable society in Steve J. Spears' *The Elocution of Benjamin Franklin*. PW had high ambitions for Chater, an English-born Australian comic who made his name in revue and on television. PW thought him very, very funny. He wrote to Waters, 6.x.74: 'There are so many classic parts for which he is made, but the stupid cunts who rule the theatre here can never see that because he has been on the telly and at the Chevron Hilton.'
[50]But Harold Prince persuaded Hammerstein to take Chater too; in New York the one-man show became the only piece ever given three OBIEs – awards for Off Broadway productions – for author, actor and the director Richard Wherrett.

it happened, but I do know that theirs was a very difficult marriage – so much good in it too, and it lasted so long, this is shattering. Feel I shall never want to go to London again; we had such happy times together on our last visit.

I lost five of my best friends this year: only two of normal old age, two from terrible cancer, and now this. Did you know Jonquil made an attempt?[51] In her case I can understand it: blind, ageing and living alone. I've told her she ought to go to the nuns. They look after one very well, and don't bother about one's not being R.C. Those Protestant fox-terriers would be unbearable.

Have had the working script of my screenplay *The Night the Prowler*. That begins in August.

But I must get on with my new play as there is so much that is topical in it. Although I say that, I think it will be able to go international if it is any good. Only three characters and one glamorous set. Lots of chic for the one lady.

20 MARTIN ROAD, 2.xii.76
TO CHARLES OSBORNE
The most shattering thing of all was Sid's call the other night to say Cynthia had done herself in. I was frozen. I'm always inhibited by long distance calls, and Sid probably won't write. What do you know? How did she do it?[52] Cynthia told us things from time to time, but one could never be sure if some of it might be fantasy; she was so distraught half the time, and suffering physically. It makes my relationship with Sid very difficult. There has always been a lot in him that I felt I didn't know about. In spite of appearances, I don't find him a candid character. So, please, if you can throw any light on this awful business, let us know.

20 MARTIN ROAD, 26.xii.76
TO ALAN WILLIAMS
Dear Alan!
Thank you for the copy of *A Fringe of Leaves*. The jacket– – Well, your letter prepared me for worse: I expected something of a boob show in the style of American airport paperbacks. What I don't like is the cluster of African huts and the ship standing practically on end on the back. Why won't you let me have plain lettering like any writer one respects? I don't believe many people buy books for awful jackets. They put me off . . .

---

[51]The scriptwriter Jonquil Antony.
[52]An overdose of barbiturates taken in a Piccadilly hotel.

When the festivities are over I expect to start the novel which has been in my head for over a year. It was working so hard in me this morning it got me out of bed at 4 o'clock. Thank God for the Demon Work to combat the other devils.

Best wishes,
Patrick.

WHITE BEGAN TO WRITE *The Twyborn Affair* in the first days of 1977. He confessed that this was the most autobiographical of all his novels, and for the first time a homosexual stood at its centre. The prose of this late masterpiece has the sensuality of a great romantic novel, but it was White's peculiar genius to turn this expectation on its head: purity, not love and happiness, is the goal of Eudoxia Vatsatses, the jackeroo Eddie Twyborn and the brothel keeper Eadith Trist. That quest left White free to explore without self-pity the difficulties of his life as a homosexual: a man who saw himself cursed with unreason and a rebellious body who lived in exile wherever he settled. White called himself and his triple hero: 'the stranger of all time'. Despite political rallies and the arrival of Joseph Losey's production team preparing to film *Voss*, White worked steadily at the manuscript.

20 MARTIN ROAD, 23.i.77
TO MANNING CLARK
What is the official colour of your eyes? That may seem an odd question, but the morning we sat on the bench in the Gardens they seemed to have a bit of everything, and I am trying to give them to one of my characters. I must have a good look next time we meet! The way I have described them sounds unconvincing.

20 MARTIN ROAD, 6.ii.77
TO RONALD WATERS
Dear Ronald,
As I haven't been able to think of anything to send from here, I am enclosing a draft for a delayed Christmas. You mentioned not having any plates that match. Perhaps you can put this and the draft I am sending to Fred into the one sum and buy a dinner service. Have no idea what a good one would cost nowadays.

I find I am asking people to meals only when absolutely necessary now. It is too exhausting as I grow older, and I must finish the novel I have started on before I drop dead.

You may read the play if Helen Montague will let you have it, but don't please show it around.[53] You may not like it anyway. I am told it will go into rehearsal at the Tote in June and open on July 27th, Jim Sharman directing, and with the actors for whom I wrote it. Jim is marvellous at getting things organised. It was a fortunate day when he was moved in my direction, because he also understands what I am going on about.

Losey has been here, with a German producer who is putting up money, Joe's production manager Richard Dalton, and David Mercer. It turned out that the German, Klaus Hellwig, paid for the whole team to come, when Harry ... Miller kept telling me, '<u>I</u> am bringing Joe on such and such a date ... ...'[54] ... ..., ... if the film comes together it will be through the efforts of Joe and Klaus. I must say there is considerable opposition in Australia to the foreigners, though I think they have now convinced people they are genuine, ... There was a terrible dinner party at Miller Villa in the ox-blood dining room with suits of armour from *Conduct Unbecoming*[55] and family portraits from the auction rooms. Everybody got a bit drunk, I shouted a little,[56] and Manoly fell down in the street on the way home.

They all went off to look for houses and deserts for the film, in the course of which Joe developed virus pneumonia and spent the last few days of his visit in hospital, then rushed back to Europe not fully well. I am very worried about him. He means to come back in July to start shooting, and it is now only up to the frightful Miller to raise his part of the money. One always heard about his rich friends. But where are they now?

David Mercer lapsed into a kind of alcoholic melancholy while here, and started ringing ex-wives on the other side of the world, who proceeded to heap shit on him. He came here to a couple of meals. We get on very well together.

I brought Losey together with Sharman, and Hellwig and Richard Dalton with Tony Buckley the Australian producer whom you met in London.[57] I think they all got something out of one another. I wish Harry Bull[58] had a competent co-producer in Australia. This week, we read, he has an equestrian function at his Property, at which three thousand are

[53]Nothing came of the producer Helen Montague's interest in *Big Toys*.

[54]Miller insists, July 1994, the Germans paid for themselves and he paid for Losey's party.

[55]Staged by Miller in Sydney in 1971.

[56]He *raged* at Miller; Losey considered this one of the most remarkable outbursts he had ever witnessed.

[57]Buckley (1937–) was producing *The Night the Prowler*.

[58]Miller bred Simmental bulls at his Manilla property.

expected to participate and Americans are being flown specially from the US. I'd like· to go up and collect a few buckets of manure.

Sorry to hear about Julie's throat. She must have been swallowing the sword too enthusiastically; I bet it's huge. I liked the *Ireen* card at Christmas.

Manoly is much better, but shingles is really a major ailment; he says he still feels at times that he has a stomachful of cats.

The garden is looking beautiful at the moment in spite of a couple of heatwaves and a violent storm which tore a couple of branches off the largest of the gumtrees and flung them almost on the front fence.

Must go and do a lot of boring jobs.

Love

Patrick

P.S. We're about to get D. Fairbanks, S. Holloway and that tapping girl of Fred's who is now publicised as 'the Australian actress.'[59]

20 MARTIN ROAD, 20.ii.77

TO ALAN WILLIAMS

Dear Alan,

Thank you for the reviews.[60] I only glanced very quickly and threw them away. I could see that most of them, although bad, were intended as flattering. Then there was the one from the jealous novelist, but that sort of thing no longer hurts. I do think, however, that American reviewing has sunk very low.

That jacket asks for a bad review. Why must you subject me to this indignity when others are allowed lettering? I detect a whiff of JACKIE, who could well be your downfall.[61]

However, let's depart from that. There's an Australian writer at last who I think has it. His name is David Malouf, his origins mostly Lebanese, part London-Jewish. He was born and grew up in Queensland. He is a poet, who wrote a kind of autobiographical novel called *Johnno*, which to me is one of the best books about Australia. He has now written another very imaginative novel based on Ovid in exile. It will not be the big money-spinner, but it is literature and perhaps Viking can still afford that.[62]

---

[59]Geriatrics Fairbanks (1910–   ) and Holloway (1891–1982) were touring with Carol Raye (1923–   ) in *The Pleasure of His Company*.

[60]*A Fringe of Leaves* had appeared in New York.

[61]Jacqueline Onassis (1929–94) when published was an editor at Viking.

[62]*A Letter from Pontus* was rejected by Viking but enjoyed a great success when published as *An Imaginary Life*.

Some of his recent poetry I find miraculous. For certain reasons it is privately printed, but for me it is doing something with words and sensations which hasn't been done before. Again, alas, literature!

Things are happening out here. You ought to come, but consult me before you do, for the right moments in opera.

Yours,
Patrick.

20 MARTIN ROAD, MARCH 77
TO JOSEPH LOSEY
Dear Joe,

Thank you for your letter about our sad film situation. I think Harry Miller is ... ..., trying to blame the unions ('Patrick's friends') for his own inability.[63] If he had been able to raise the money overseas, or from the private sector here, I'm pretty sure doors would have opened. ... ... I have not seen him since you were here. I think they must have a periscope, and avoid coming out from behind the palisade while I am passing. He is now trying to raise money for the Queen's Jubilee Youth Fund, which no doubt will help him join the other dubious Australian knights. Jim Sharman had lunch with the Millers the other day. He says both look battered! Harry is huge, and Wendy has not yet recovered from the famous dinner party. I'm sorry about that, but the poor thing will have to wake up sooner or later ...

I am well into the first draft of my novel. It is causing me plenty of despair. However, despair for a novel is nothing like the despair over a film or play with which one has rashly become involved ...

The Australian political situation is disgusting: both sides rushing towards uranium, which I try my best to discourage, as I try to discourage them from that minor issue, seduction by Elizabeth the Last.[64] She's been and gone, thank God. I was terrified somebody might snipe her and ruin our chances of getting away.

[63]PW never grasped the full difficulties. He realised the Australian film unions were hostile to public funds being invested in a foreign director and scriptwriter and star; but he never realised Losey himself was a liability – a great name in contemporary cinema, but everything he had made after *The Go-Between* in 1970 lost money. In the eyes of Australian funding bodies and film distributors, Losey was unbackable.

[64]In March, as the Queen was about to arrive in Australia, PW spoke at large rallies in Brisbane and Sydney: 'Let us receive the Monarch with the dignity she deserves, but let us keep our heads as she walks among us, the myth made flesh, wearing a democratic smile.' *Patrick White Speaks*, p.63.

Hope your health is better, and that we shall all meet again, though I can't think where.

    Love

    P.

20 MARTIN ROAD, 9.iv.77

TO DR GEORGE CHANDLER

DIRECTOR-GENERAL

NATIONAL LIBRARY OF AUSTRALIA

Dear Dr Chandler,

Thank you for your P 23/3/978 of 25th March.

    I can't let you have my 'papers' because I don't keep any. My MSS are destroyed as soon as the books are printed. I put very little into notebooks, don't keep my friends' letters as I urge them not to keep mine, and anything unfinished when I die is to be burnt. The final versions of my books are what I want people to see and if there is anything of importance in me, it will be in those.

    Yours sincerely,

    Patrick White.

20 MARTIN ROAD, 15.iv.77

TO GEOFFREY DUTTON

On Monday I too, set out for Canberra, my first visit for about 30 years. I must say I don't look forward to the Canberra bit, but think I shall enjoy being driven round the Monaro by David.[65] It's bound to be cold though. We froze here over Easter. However, it did not deter the Show. We are told (certainly by the *SMH*) that nearly a million people attended. It felt like it and looked like it. Every morning there was a pall of purple smog hanging over Sydney; on one spectacular morning it had a perfectly full, ghostly moon showing through.

    The final script of *The Night the Prowler* is being typed today. It will then be ready for the film bodies to decide whether they want to give us the money.

    The *Voss* film is definitely off . . . Losey will make a film in France this year[66] as Harry was unable to meet his deadline. It's all very sad; I had

---

[65]Campbell.

[66]*Don Giovanni* filmed in Italy as well as France, with Kiri Te Kanawa and Ruggero Raimondi.

very good relationships with all concerned, except the frightful Miller, who no doubt will soon have his knighthood . . .

I grow more embittered every day – such double values in every direction – and all the money that is being poured into the uranium-mining campaign.

A very strange incident yesterday: I was labouring at the house-cleaning when the telephone went, and it was Mary Fairfax. 'It's such years since we saw you, darling. I wonder whether you – and Manoly – would come to a little lunch on Friday. I have a woman from South Africa who's brought some 17th Century Dutch landscapes. Judy Cassab[67] is bringing her. And I thought as you're so generous to the Art Gallery– –' I said Fridays were always bad, and that the Dutch School didn't appeal to me. 'Not their genre perhaps, but don't you think some of those outdoor ones of people skating and enjoying themselves are rather fun?' I agreed but said, 'The Dutch just don't turn me on.' She went into a few murmurs about her children being Dutch,[68] to which I didn't respond. So she said, 'It's such years since we saw one another darling, why don't you – and Manoly – come and have a little dinner one night just with Warwick and me.' I said I was very bad at dinner parties. 'Oh, but darling – you can hardly call that a dinner party!' I agreed, and said I was working. 'Oh, I understand, and adore your books.' I thanked her. She thanked me. I rang off.

It's extraordinary when we haven't exchanged a word for the last ten years, when we have cut each other several times in between, and Warwick always jumps in the air and faces in the opposite direction when he catches sight of me. I believe that the Great Liberals are starting a big seduction campaign since the monarch was here scattering democratic smiles and baubles. The most extraordinary part, however, is that our telephone conversation could have come out of Big Toys.

The omens for that are good. A management is talking about taking it to Washington and London, but I'm not getting excited till I see what it's like. What looks good doesn't always cook good.

I'm about halfway through the first version of the novel, which is the point where X goes down to the Monaro. There could not be a more appropriate moment for a pause.

Have you ever heard of a Canadian novelist called Margaret Atwood? She is published in Canada by McLelland and Stewart and in the U.S. by

---

[67](1920–   ), reliable contemporary portrait painter.
[68]Charles Thomas and Anna Bella: adopted.

Simon & Schuster, but doesn't seem to have a British publisher.[69] The novel I have been lent, *Lady Oracle*, is a very funny and original book. I have sent for it and the two others, *The Edible Woman* and *Surfacing*. I'll lend her to you when they arrive.

How do I get in touch with Aggie Grey?[70] Unless the weather in December is impossible in Western Samoa I am thinking of going there to be out of the way while that PEN Conference is on in Sydney.[71] No need to repeat what I think of writers' gatherings, and PEN Australia seems to be a body of non-writers organised by Hungarians and Croats. I was asked to give an address on 'Literature the Link between South-East Asia and Australia.' Who knows what about literature in South-East Asia? I certainly know fuck all.

20 MARTIN ROAD, 24.iv.77
TO ALAN WILLIAMS
I'm just back from a whirl round the Monaro ... It was freezing already and I got a cold on my chest which has depressed me considerably. However, I got what I wanted – a charge for that section of my novel which is set in the Monaro. I went again to the place where I worked for a year of my youth (1930). It was always forbidding – now it is full of ghosts and vengeance. The cottage where I lived was deserted, unlocked, and beginning to collapse. The double-seated dunny, where fowls used to roost and fall down the holes, has already done so.
　　Yrs,
　　Patrick.

20 MARTIN ROAD, 24.v.77
TO CLEM SEMMLER
Dear Clem,
Thank you for *Quadrant*, which I don't see normally; I wonder why you write for it? Anyway, Keneally is a disgusting subject for a disgusting paper; he's come out at last as the bad egg I always suspected I could smell. No

---

[69]She did: André Deutsch.
[70]Legendary proprietress (1898–1988) of a hotel in Western Samoa, and raw material for Bloody Mary in James A. Michener's novel *South Pacific*.
[71]He stayed home.

doubt his Jesuitical training will help him put things right![72]

I have been in the grip of a chest infection for some weeks, the last couple in bed; don't seem able to throw it off – which is irritating as I am halfway through writing a novel for which I no longer find the strength or enthusiasm. I expect both will return in time; it takes longer with age.

I wonder what on earth you will do at Burradoo?[73] Petrify in boredom I should think. Every time I go to the country I feel this would be wonderful; then I realise I couldn't stand more than a fortnight. For me, the pavement and the crowd. You've got to have something to fight against. Otherwise you'll die of bush ballads.

Yours,

Patrick

The only possible reason I might drop out to some Burradoo is that I could keep a few fowls.

20 MARTIN ROAD, 12.vi.77

TO RONALD WATERS

Had a Tape from Jonquil which I dreaded playing, but we faced it this afternoon and it did us a lot of good. Her situation is so much worse than any one else's, yet she is coping. One brilliant remark, 'Jean's friend Louise – it's really rather funny – she had a stroke in Harrods– –' That's the kind of thing Australians can't understand about the English; if I wrote it into something they'd rend me limb from limb.

BIG TOYS, WHITE'S CORRUPTION play, opened in late July in Sydney. Many who knew something of the real players in that corrupt city found White's protagonists naive. In Sydney, and later when Sharman's production moved to Melbourne, White suffered a critical battering.

---

[72]In May, Quadrant listed, p.4, similarities in characters, events and dialogue between Keneally's 1976 Season in Purgatory and Bill Strutton's 1961 Island of Terrible Friends, both about British surgeons and Yugoslav partisans on an island off the Dalmatian Coast during the Second World War. Both books, countered Keneally, were based on the facts of the time which he gathered, in part, while living for six months in the house of George Lloyd-Roberts, one of the surgeons. There he read Strutton's book and discussed the events with Lloyd-Roberts' companion, a Mrs Broughton-Adderley. (Quadrant quoted the surgeon saying he 'never discussed' his war experience with the Australian.) Keneally denied plagiarising dialogue, and argued he and Strutton had 'fed at the same source' in gathering this; Strutton claimed the dialogue in Island of Terrible Friends, 'while true in spirit, is almost wholly mine'. To settle a later legal action, Keneally agreed to share a proportion of his royalties with Strutton.

[73]Damp village not far from PW's old school in the Southern Highlands.

20 MARTIN ROAD, 31.vii.77

TO RONALD WATERS

Dear Ronald,

The piece opened. Lots of stress – and good times. The peope who have seen it are divided, which is as it should be. I have not had many individual reactions because in Sydney they are so unsure of themselves they wait to read the reviews first. I am sending the main ones of these separately. The one who really gets it right is the woman in the *National Times*.[74] It is a play which should really be sent on the road first. The performances are not yet interlocking, but I'm sure they will be in three weeks time. I personally am very happy the way things are going.

I had some of them to dinner with Brian Thomson the designer when he arrived back, and on that occasion I showed them a letter I had written to Father Christmas when I was about five asking for at least fifteen presents. At the main preview they gave me a pillowslip filled with all these small toys, including a plastic violin, mouth organ, pistol, some marbles, a butterfly-net, *Robinson Crusoe*, a history of Australia, and a mechanical mouse. Most of these things, if I come to think, have played a part in my life and work, though I'm not sure where the mouse creeps in. The pillowslip even had 'Paddy' painted on it, very much like my signature of then. There was also a Christmas version of a laurel wreath in tinsel holly. Quite a brilliant idea, and I shall have to give the whole thing together with the original letter to the Library of NSW, which already has my Nobel plaque and diploma.[75]

After that preview we all had supper together *en famille*, and last week before Brian T. flew back to London I gave a dinner for him and the pals in a private room at *Le Café*, the in-place, with the cast coming on after the performance.

Senile delights no doubt, but none the less delightful. I hope to continue. Next year they are going to revive *A Cheery Soul*, Jim directing . . .

I have written about two-thirds of the first draft of my novel, which I expect will divide them far more than *Big Toys*. I also have an idea for an original film[76] which I shall try to get down on paper between drafts of

[74]The critic and publisher, Katharine Brisbane (1932–   ), wrote, 1 Aug., p.26: 'It is a bitter, grotesque and appalling indictment of the trivial motives that bring people to power in this country – and the more appalling because it is couched seductively as a comedy of artifice.'

[75]Only the letter reached the library, given by Lascaris after PW's death.

[76]Monkey Puzzle; never filmed.

the novel. We now have a grant for most of the money for the film from *The Night the Prowler*, which Jim will start directing in October or November, Tony Buckley of *Caddie* as producer.[77] Not a word from, or glimpse of that frightful Harry Bull Miller. I saw a photograph of him handing a medal to a Red Cross lady who had raised funds for Our Lovely Queen's Jubilee. Harry M. was wearing a new hair-do and a new smile, both cut on the cross. Also a tie, which one couldn't quite work out: it was either celebrating the Jubilee, or the Old Pantyhose-salesmen's Club.[78] . . .

We have seen Sutherland twice, giving dazzling performances in *Lucrezia Borgia* and *Suor Angelica*. Met her and Bonynge one night at Desmond Digby's (he designed the latter very beautifully). At supper she was giving rather a strange performance as a wound-up Ocker Olympia.[79] He is rather quiet, refined, and very handsome.

In the theatre *Boeing Boeing* is on, so you can't complain about poverty.[80] There is also your friend's[81] *Three Sisters*, which got very bad reviews, but I must go to find out for myself. His *Home* was good, and I haven't seen anything else. He sent me a wah and we shook hands at the preview of *Big Toys*. He has aged, as haven't we all. There was a publicity photograph of him in *The Australian* holding hands with the other sisters.

Manoly has been enjoying all the events, though his arthritis pains have been troubling him. He has started acupuncture again. He is also wearing the woollen cap you always ask about, and the garden is about to burst into Spring.

Oh dear, how one runs on. I must go and put on the boiled eggs for Sunday night.

Love to both.

Patrick.

WHITE HAD BROKEN HIS silence with Betty Withycombe to ask to see the letters he had written from Bolaro in the early 1930s. These he hoped

---

[77]Buckley's 1975 film, the life of a plucky Sydney barmaid starring Helen Morse, had been a great success in Australia.

[78]Miller was chairman of the Queen's Jubilee Committee.

[79]Sutherland stung PW by confessing cheerfully that she had never read a word he had written. Describing the night in *Flaws in the Glass*, PW remarked: 'The moral of this is an old one: divas should never meet.'

[80]Waters always cried poor; *Boeing Boeing* was another lucrative production in which his partner Freddie Carpenter had an interest.

[81]Bill Redmond (1928–   ), artistic director of the dying Old Tote; PW was scathing when this Australian director who had lived 25 years in England was appointed in 1974, but then admired many of his productions.

would help him work his way into the jackerooing section of *The Twyborn Affair*. In a great gesture of trust, Withycombe sent her cousin all the letters he had written her from 1928 on; there were about 400. White read a few, kept them stacked in the corner of the dining room for some months, then burnt them all.

20 MARTIN ROAD, AUG. 77
TO BETTY WITHYCOMBE
Dear Betty,
The box and the packet of letters arrived. I have not been able to bring myself to open them yet – and wonder whether I ever shall. There can't be more unattractive cold pudding than one's own old letters.

I don't suppose you will be able to read this. I should really send a tape, but don't think I'd be able to make one without drying up every few words. Jonquil Antony who is now totally blind sends us tapes, but she always had a wonderful flow of conversation and a voice full of comic inflections, unlike my monotonous unyielding one.

My own eyes seem to be going off. I have to visit the eye-doctor every three months and he is always increasing the drops I have to use, and changing my glasses. I hope I shall have my sight for a few more years as there are still a number of things I want to write. My play *Big Toys* was launched a few weeks ago. Some of the reviews were very pleasing, others poisonous, depending on the political complexion of the critic. There has been a lot of gnashing of teeth from the audiences, but at least the theatre is packed every night, sometimes chairs in the aisles . . .

We have had a vile winter, the coldest I can remember in Sydney, but things are beginning to flower again. It is gardening more than anything which gets Manoly through the arthritis. I used to join in at Castle Hill when we had so many acres, but now I leave it to him and get on with other things. Everything seems to take so much longer, especially cooking. At least that is something I enjoy, unlike writing; I am only driven at writing by some foul demon of self-justification. If I had another life I'd choose to be a cook. Although of course there might turn out to be a foul demon of self-justification in the kitchen.

20 MARTIN ROAD, 28.viii.77
TO JOSEPH LOSEY
Sharman will be shooting *The Night the Prowler* October/November. Casting
not entirely settled.[82] He wants me to play the naked old man in the
derelict house, which I think I could do very well (without teeth.) but
Manoly has got it into his head I'd make a fool of myself. Certainly there
are many enemies who would wade in with the axe.

MELBOURNE, 2.x.77
TO SHIRLEY HAZZARD
AND FRANCIS STEEGMULLER
I came down to Melbourne yesterday for the opening of *Big Toys*. I find
first nights unnatural occasions and bewildering when they are my own. I
never go to other people's and only to mine because I feel I must support
the actors. The theatre was full right up to the end of the Sydney run
although a lot of people hated the play. Down here we are in a much
larger theatre and Melbourne will not feel so involved with goings-on
which are far more Sydney; it is impossible to tell how it will go. I heard
a fair amount of teeth-sucking round me last night, even a few snores. At
least one can't hear the reader snoring over one's novels.

   Next month the filming of *The Night the Prowler* begins. Life will
become pretty chaotic I expect. I must finish the first draft of my novel
before I get drawn into all that.

   Sumner's novel[83] has lots of miraculous things in it. At the same time
it has some rather glossy stretches which let it down. I don't feel it is as
good as some of the others – as a whole I mean, and as writing. Still, it's
a gorgeous book, and I expect it will sell very well in Australia. Strange
how Sydney stays so wonderfully fresh in his mind.
   Yrs
   Patrick.

20 MARTIN ROAD, 17.x.77
TO MANNING CLARK
Dear Manning,
I was half-asleep when you rang and probably sounded rather strange It is

---

[82]But Sharman had cast Kerry Walker (1948–   ) as the 'raped' and liberated Felicity
Bannister; from this grew the intense, last theatrical passion of PW's life. He liked
'Kerro' from the moment they met, but friendship waited until the film was finished.
[83]Sumner Locke Elliott's *Water under the Bridge*.

a great honour, and I shall try to do my best by you.[84] The alarming thought is that of finding myself at a gathering of academics and personages, when I go down badly with most of those.

How far do you take us in this final volume?[85] (Perhaps it is not final.) Shall I be able to read it before the launching?

Some time ago you told me of a history which would give me the facts leading up to the outbreak of World War I. I wrote down the title and the author but I don't know where. I also want something which will give me the facts leading up to World War II, that first year of stalemate behind the Maginot and Siegfried Line and the first air raids on London. I believe the first major raid was at the end of summer or beginning of autumn 1940. I can remember coming out of the Café Royal and seeing the East End on fire. We walked back to where I was living in Ebury Street, and found ourselves having to lie on the pavement as bombs fell on Victoria Station.

Let me know what to read – and any more about the launching.
Love to you both,
Patrick.

20 MARTIN ROAD, 23.x.77
TO PETER BEATSON
Dear Peter,
Thank you for your interesting and pleasing letter. I don't think one can ever advise people in a situation like yours, only confirm what they want to hear. Anyway, I do think it important before anything that you and Rana should stay together. You have been together long enough to have found out about each other, and to an outsider Rana seems a very gentle, even noble creature. Personally, I wouldn't care about taking the Moslem faith. But in your situation I would, even down to sacrificing bulls; as you say, all this would only be a formality, and the important thing is to stay together. What I wouldn't care about is having to live in Indonesia, not that I have ever been there, so I'd go warily and not let myself be conned into that. After the War I wanted to live in Greece; Manoly didn't, so we settled here. Unpleasant though much of it has been I realise it was the right thing to do. Each time we return to Greece, even Europe, we find it more intolerable. I'd only have been a beachcomber in Greece, a curiosity, a freak. Here I'm often not much better, but it's what I come from and

---

[84]Clark had asked PW to launch Vol. IV of his *History of Australia: The Earth Abideth for Ever*.
[85]To 1888; two more volumes were to come.

what I can write about. From time to time I have to protest against various awful aspects of Australian life; even those serve a purpose, I think, providing the kind of irritant I need creatively. Indonesian exoticism is something which could only be of superficial use to you. You are going there as a mature man; the Durrells were at least brought up in Greece and around the Mediterranean.[86] You could only be a kind of journalist or sociologist in Indonesia. What Durrell says about language is most important. If you are writing in English you should hear it going on around you. I could not write about Australia satisfactorily even from another English-speaking country like England or the United States. Ireland has been the death of any writer who has not originated there. Another point to consider before you let yourself be swallowed up by Indonesia: there is a very strong totalitarian streak in those who run the country. I would not want them to run me. Why can't you go through the formalities you mention, return to New Zealand to live, and pay periodic visits to Indonesia? There may be endless complications I don't know about. I only have a feeling that, having swallowed you, the official and diplomatic Indonesians may try to use you for propaganda purposes. You've also got to think ahead to the possibility of international hostilities – war. I've known too many amiable foreigners who thought they had arranged everything for the best in the exotic landscapes of their choice, then to find themselves caught ...

Had a letter from Peggy the other day. The children seem to have woken up at last to the dreadful thing they did to her in introducing their father to the other house they owned in the village. I've had some amiable correspondence with Betty Withycombe, the eldest sister, to whom I hadn't spoken for years after a blow-up caused by gossips and Peggy's indiscriminate handing out of letters. Betty has now sent me boxes of letters from me to her written when I was a youth, which I shall never bring myself to read. I hope you will destroy all the letters I have written you. I shall only want to slip away decently and quietly, leaving my books for what they may be worth.

We have had to get rid of the Rover; it had started to cost us a fortune in repairs. Now we have a Fiat, which uses less petrol, and is easier to park. I wish we could dispense with a car altogether, but it just isn't possible, altogether.

I hope I may have given you some 'advice', though finally you will have to work it out for yourselves.

Patrick.

---

[86]The writer Lawrence (1912–90) and zoologist and writer Gerald (1925–94) settled in Greece with their mother in the 1930s – the brothers were then 23 and 10 – until driven from Corfú by the war.

20 MARTIN ROAD, 27.xi.77
TO MANNING CLARK
Dear Manning,

Thank you for the list of histories. They all sound a bit exalted, not the worm's eye view of events I hope to find somewhere. If I told you about my novel you'd get a better idea, but if I began I might not know where to end, and it's always better not to talk about work in progress.

The filming of *The Night the Prowler* is in full swing. I go there sometimes to watch, and to rushes which fill me with hope. I'm so glad I've dropped on to this medium for my old age; it's so much easier on the lungs than grinding away for a couple of years at a novel. I hope to have my new screen play The Monkey Puzzle ready by Christmas.[87] Then back to grinding away at the novel.

We have had to have a new sewer put down as the old one is full of roots. The garden is a shambles down one side. Mad excitement on the part of the dogs, who enjoy the smells and our . . . who comes out to inspect the rather handsome pair of plumbers. At any moment I think she will ask for a quote.

I feel the election is looking increasingly hopeful. Does it strike you how <u>common</u> the Liberal politicians sound on the radio? Or perhaps it's the absence of credibility which seems to make them sound like that.

Hope you are both well.

Yrs

Patrick.

[87]He wanted Barry Humphries to play Will Garlick, a writer allowing his life story to be taped by an over-awed archivist Henrietta Birdsell, who finally loses her regard for the Great Writer and leaves him in peace.

20 MARTIN ROAD, 11.i.78
CARD TO RONALD WATERS
Fred tells me you have pains in the chest. Why don't you see a doctor? Though I must say I'm always pretty loath to do so myself. The film is coming along, but has to be pruned to 1½ hours: at present 2 hrs. We're so sick of lumbering films in which the brilliant director can't bear to sacrifice 1 cm. of his genius. He wants this one to be dynamite all the way.

20 MARTIN ROAD, 26.i.78
TO FRANCES PECK
Dear Frances,
Of course I know that if you hadn't arrived we should have heard from your sisters, but to write to somebody after you've spent some time under their roof and then gone on a long journey is one of the small civilities which shore up civilisation against barbarism. I hope you'll remember that after you've been staying with Elly . . .
I have to go to Canberra on the Australia Day holiday to a party of thanks which is being arranged for the Whitlams. My still unwritten speech is hanging over my head.
Hope you find Greece interesting.
Love
Patrick.

FOR OVER A YEAR, White had been looking forward to Jim Sharman's revival of *A Cheery Soul*: this was to be the crucial test of his durability as a playwright. But in its dying days, the Old Tote cancelled Sharman's production. With his co-director Rex Cramphorn, Sharman now searched for a Sydney theatre in which to begin a new company. White promised cash. In South Australia the Duttons' attempts to make Anlaby pay through intensive pig-breeding failed. The house and the last paddocks were sold.

20 MARTIN ROAD, 12.ii.78
TO GEOFFREY DUTTON
Dear Geoffrey,
I hope this will reach you before you finally leave Anlaby. Getting out must be the worst of nightmares. Remembering the comparatively minor operation of leaving Dogwoods I hope I shall die in Martin Road. Couldn't

face another move, though I expect this house will grow larger every year. If only one could say bong and find oneself in a cottage with table, chair, bed, and a few pots and pans.

So much that is depressing in recent weeks I don't know what I'd do if I hadn't my novel to hand, like a piece of knitting.

Still no place in which to do the Sharman–Cramphorn season of plays. From time to time a flicker of hope, but the flicker never kindles properly. Jim has also been slapped down over the film he wants to make from Louis Nowra's novel.[88] At the same time he doesn't like my new screenplay because he says the final message is 'So what?' which is, as I see it, the message today.

There is a possibility that I may write a libretto for an opera. The composer (one I respect) wants me to. I have an idea and it is building up.[89] I'd like to get this down between the second and final versions of the novel.

I went down to Canberra to speak at the Whitlams' testimonial shivoo. Quite a stirring occasion about which the daily press said as little as possible. Yet they come out in their full hypocrisy lamenting the Kerr appointment, for which they paved the way.[90] One can only hope that guzzling pig will blow up on all the good things he will eat and drink in Paris ... But think of what we shall have to shell out in the meantime.

I had some good conversations with David Campbell while I was in Canberra.[91] Have to go there again next month to launch Manning's Volume 4. That is the last time I shall let myself in for any kind of public speaking.

I can't think that two such performers as Barry Humphries and Sumner Locke Elliott will be pleased to find themselves on the same platform. But the Adelaide Fest has always been lacking in Tact. (Last night the Blackmans were on the air, drunk, I am told, giving recipes.)

---

[88]Nowra (1950–   ), playwright and novelist, was a protégé of Jim Sharman who wanted to film The Misery of Beauty, 1976.

[89]Births, Deaths and Lotteries, a project PW pursued intermittently over the next seven years, describing it to Richard Meale, the composer he had in mind, 26.ii.78, as 'satirical, closer to Brecht–Weill and Stein–Thomson, though there would be opportunities for straight as well as cod Romantic music.' PW sketched it for Joseph Losey, 20.iii.84: 'a revolution, a fire in which Sydney is partly destroyed, a miracle after one of the leading characters leaps from a skyscraper, and a few moments of sprechstimme from portraits of the Queen of England and her Jolly Juke'. Meale prevaricated; PW was furious.

[90]Kerr was appointed ambassador to UNESCO headquarters in Paris, but such was the uproar that after three weeks he decided not to go through with the job.

[91]Campbell had lung cancer.

Let us know the Mount Lofty address. I hope you're not going to blow all the money from Anlaby building the new house at Piers Hill; it could easily happen today.

Love to all

Patrick

I've taken 100 *Years of Solitude* to Europe twice without being able to read it.[92] Don't think I can read long novels any more. And no one seems able to read mine. A man I met last night said he was so glad to <u>see</u> *Big Toys* because he hadn't been able to <u>read</u> what I've written.

20 MARTIN ROAD, 26.ii.78

TO GOUGH WHITLAM

Dear Gough,

I have been asked by Graham Greene, one of the partners of my publishers Jonathan Cape, whether you were writing your memoirs, and if so, would you consider letting Cape publish. They are a respectable firm and have always treated me well. They now have a branch in Australia. Graham Greene, who is of the Left, and a friend of Dr Owen,[93] is a nephew of the novelist. He comes here periodically.

Sorry I made the terrible blunder of suggesting you might go to the UN, when the Kerr appointment was sprung upon us so soon after.[94] At least my unfortunate remark was barely reported.

I was shown a piece in the *Bulletin* the other day, written by McNicoll a man I particularly dislike. However, I'm sure he was right about Fancy Nancy's influence; all through, she has probably been half the trouble.[95] I was only puzzled to see her referred to as a 'woman of infinite charm.' To me, as much charm as an elderly lizard in green eye-shadow . . .

Yrs

Patrick (White).

[92]*Cien Años de Soledad*, 1967, by Gabriel García Márquez, trans. 1970; PW disliked the South American blend of fantasy and realism despite (or perhaps because of) similarities to his own early work.

[93]David Owen (1938–   ), Labour foreign secretary 1977–79; PW ate with him at Greene's London house and found him cranky and self-obsessed.

[94]PW had said: 'Whitlam, more than anyone, has the stature, the intellect, the drive, the knowledge of world affairs to make himself heard at the United Nations as Australia has not been heard since the days of H. V. Evatt.' As it turned out, Whitlam took up in 1983 the UNESCO post Kerr was offered (and declined) in 1978.

[95]Fancy Nancy=Anne Kerr, known as Nancy Robson before her divorce; McNicoll, explaining why Kerr now wanted to 'bludge' in Paris, wrote in the *Bulletin*, 28 Feb., p.33: 'I feel the key lies in *cherchez la femme*. Lady Kerr is a woman of great charm and a most forceful personality . . . she has converted Sir John.'

20 MARTIN ROAD, 12.iii.78

TO GRAHAM C. GREENE

I am back peacefully, with *The Twyborn Affair*. Not that it won't be an abrasive novel, which will probably earn me complete social ostracism in Australia. But it doesn't drag me as far into schizophrenia as involvement in film and theatre does.

They are still tinkering with *The Night the Prowler* – the film is made, it is now a matter of sound. I think it will probably be released in London in September, though film plans change all the time.

I'm about a third of the way through the second version of *The Twyborn Affair*. After that I shall type and tinker some more before it is ready. So please don't expect it too soon. Probably another year. I can't be driven.

20 MARTIN ROAD, 19.iii.78

TO MANNING CLARK

I'm told Volume IV is selling fabulously in Sydney, and like to think I have had some small part in it. I enjoyed the launching. It is the brooding over what to say, and the initial jump, which drain me physically and morally.[96]

I know all about that 'How very peculiar!' you suffered in your childhood, because I encountered exactly the same. One of my worst moments was in a taxi in Oxford Street, London when I had refused to go to a cricket match with my father and my mother shouted at me 'I never thought I'd have a freak for a son!' It made me determined to go on being just that.

All my novels have been to some extent autobiographical, but the present one is more explicit than the others. There are still plenty of disguises of course, otherwise it would be the kind of humdrum documentary expected by Australians.

20 MARTIN ROAD, 9.iv.78

TO GEOFFREY DUTTON

Have you come across a Sikh in Adelaide, an authority on Aldous Huxley, who claims to be my spiritual friend? He is one of many pestiferous correspondents who think one has nothing to do but take them to one's

---

[96]Launching the book, PW said: 'Knowledge of his work has helped me to continue living in the country of my fate when, in recent years, it has become increasingly abhorrent to me as I believe it has to all men of goodwill and those who are engaged in something more than a material search.' *Australian*, 7 March, p.2.

bosom. There is also a Korean who says I was cold to him at Manning's launching (perhaps I was, considering the way he was slithering over Keneally) and a lady who tells me her mother died of *The Solid Mandala.*

The other night we had dinner at Elizabeth Riddell's[97] for David Malouf, who leaves in a couple of weeks. Last night a very trendy affair at Margaret Fink's. She is somebody I like very much, when I thought I didn't from listening to what people say about her.[98]

The Paris Theatre Company plan is coming good, it seems,[99] and the score for *The Night the Prowler* is said to be marvellous.[100] the film may be launched in Sydney in July.

Barry Humphries drifting about. He is a mad supporter of Bjelke![101] Sid too, is on with all the wrong people. I haven't seen him and shan't. Can't really forgive him for falling into the other one's arms five minutes after C. was dead – quite apart from his fascist associations. He is going to receive a pat on the head from Fraser in Canberra next week.[102]

Love to all.

Patrick.

20 MARTIN ROAD, 30.iv.78

TO THE SMITH FAMILY

I have no objection to your putting the money into home units for pensioners, though I'd prefer it to help Sydney pensioners. The Queanbeyan ones, no doubt equally deserving, are a far cry from here, where pensioners and the poor in general are so painfully in evidence against the ostentation

---

[97]Riddell (1907–   ), poet, critic and journalist was the shrewdest and most self-possessed of PW's circle of women. She interviewed him for *People*, 12 Dec 1956, p.47 and their friendship grew after her second interview, *Australian*, 1 Aug 1970, p.15. She mended fences. PW told Dutton 18.ii.73: 'She has judgment, taste and wordliness'.

[98]Fink (1933–   ), film producer and hostess, was preparing to shoot *My Brilliant Career* from Miles Franklin's 1901 novel set partly in the hills behind Bolaro. PW disapproved of the result – homestead life was never so *pretty* in his experience – but he admired Fink's later film of Stead's 1944 novel *For Love Alone*.

[99]Sharman and Cramphorn had persuaded the City Council to lease them this old cinema and the season was to open in July with *Pandora's Cross* by the poet Dorothy Hewett (1923–   ) who had a cameo role in *The Night the Prowler* as a drunk in Centennial Park.

[100]Score by Cameron Allan (1957–   ).

[101]Johannes Bjelke-Petersen (1911–   ), lay preacher who led the shabby and conservative government of Queensland 1968–87.

[102]The prime minister was opening an exhibition of Nolan's Gallipoli paintings at the National War Memorial.

of the rich. That is only a personal feeling. Sorry I can't give more at the moment.[103]

20 MARTIN ROAD, 4.vi.78
TO JANICE KENNY[104]
Dear Janice Kenny,
Reference to your 402/17/186 of 23 May, it astonishes me that after reading my letter to H. M. Pharabet you should think I want him to have a copy of *The Ploughman and Other Poems*. Perhaps you can't read my handwriting or we speak a different language. I return the letter so that you can have another look.[105] I want nobody to have a copy of what is best forgotten. Perhaps I shall contrive to steal and destroy the book you have next time I am in Canberra.

    Yours sincerely,
    Patrick White.

20 MARTIN ROAD, 8.vii.78
TO PEGGY GARLAND
Could you tell me when marsh marigolds are in flower? I seem to remember them in late spring to early summer. And would you or anybody know whether there were always railings round Battersea Park, particularly the strip along the river where there is now a pleasure garden? I can't remember railings in the Thirties, whereas a couple of years ago I could only get over early in the morning by climbing. I believe one could always get into Hyde Park – at a risk. Would it have been the same at Battersea in the Thirties?

20 MARTIN ROAD, 17.vii.78
TO DAVID MALOUF
Lots about you in the press here. I was sent *An Imaginary Life* by a bossy woman called Anne Summers[106] who wanted me to review it for the *Nat. Times*, but as I've never reviewed a book, and wouldn't like to start now, particularly with a friend's, I sent it back.

    The Night the Prowler got some good reviews on the fringe, but was slain by the Establishment critics, The SMH called it a 'savage piece of

---

[103]This winter he gave $10,000; for twenty years PW was the biggest private benefactor of this charity which clothes, feeds and shelters the poor in NSW.
[104]Principal Librarian, General Reference, National Library of Australia.
[105]PW had denounced the poems to Pharabet, a thesis writer in France, who gamely tried to persuade the library PW's letter amounted to permission to copy the book. The library, unconvinced, had checked with PW.
[106](1945–), journalist, feminist, author of *Damned Whores and God's Police*, 1975.

bourgeois-bashing.'[107] Of course if the bourgeoisie had been foreign they would have swallowed it without a murmur. It's going to be released before Christmas, probably earlier overseas.

We've been only twice to the opera this season ... Mitchell[108] now lifts *Butterfly* on to a noble tragic plane in spite of that fatal flaw Pinkerton. He was well sung by Furlan,[109] but for me Pinkerton will always remain one of the worst examples of the American Shit (Perhaps I'm unduly prejudiced because I've experienced a Pinkerton!) At the end of the week we shall go to *Don Giovanni* and soon after that *Norma*, which are two I really want to see.

I wonder whether you have come across Bertolucci's *1900?* In spite of a shaky start and some dreadful dubbing it builds up wonderfully. It should be seen by all the people who won't go near it.

I hear you've bought a house[110] which makes us sad as there is a ring of permanence about it, and we can't afford to lose you.

Yrs

Patrick.

20 MARTIN ROAD, 24.vii.78

TO THE MOORES

The Paris Theatre Company got of to a shaky start with Dorothy Hewett's *Pandora's Cross.* The play is certainly rather a muddle, but full of entertainment the way Jim has produced it and the actors have responded. People are going for that reason, but it won't run as long as we hoped. After that Louis Nowra's *Visions.* Then the revival of *A Cheery Soul.* We thought Ruth Cracknell[111] was going to be Miss Docker, but she has withdrawn in favour of a safe commercial run in an Alan Ayckbourn. Most actors are fly-by-nights. Now Miss Docker will be Robyn Nevin, a manic clockwork mouse instead of a large bully.[112] I think it will work very

---

[107]Bob Ellis wrote in *Nation Review*, 22 June, p.17: 'for almost the first time in our history we have an Australian film with levels of meaning, wit, irony, plot, complexity of characterisation and something to say.' Martha DuBose wrote in *SMH*, 5 June, p.7: 'White cooks up a furious piece of bourgeois bashing. But his recipe calls for an excess of ingredients, and the end product is overdone.'

[108]Leona Mitchell (1949–), black American diva.

[109]Lamberto Furlan (1935–), Italian tenor much used by the Australian Opera.

[110]Malouf now divided his time between Australia and Campagnatico, an unfashionable Tuscan village.

[111]Distinguished comic actress (1925–), the suburban mother in *The Night the Prowler.*

[112]Nevin (1942–) first came into PW's orbit as Girlie Pogson in Sharman's 1976 revival of *The Season at Sarsaparilla.*

well that way. (She's a marvellous actress who never gets enough to do. I'm brooding over a screenplay which I want to write for her when the novel is off my hands.)

DESPITE THE MONEY POURED into the Paris Theatre Company by White and the Australia Council, it never had the financial resources to match its high ambitions. The company folded before Sharman's production of *A Cheery Soul* could begin. White told Dutton, 'The public can only think of opera.'[113]

20 MARTIN ROAD, OCT. 78
TO PETER BEATSON
Dear Peter,
I had been wondering what had become of you. I was on the point of asking, then thought you had probably left Sumatra, and would turn up on the way to New Zealand. Now your letter has come with the disturbing news. Admittedly it would be difficult for you to live in Indonesia or Rana in New Zealand but surely there is some geographical meeting point on which you could agree. Of course I realise from what you haven't told me that there is something far deeper than that. I wonder whether you have tried hard enough. Any two people living together have to make endless sacrifices, as Manoly and I have found from living together nearly forty years. Your remark that 'Rana and I found we were not among those unique couples who get married and live happily ever after' is just childish. Living together means endless disagreements and patching up. I imagine only vegetables live happily ever after, and then only in a vague, vegetable way.

I can't ask you stay when you pass through Sydney, because Manoly's sister Elly arrives this week and will be with us for a couple of months, and I don't feel, at my age, and trying to finish a book, that I can cope with more than one house guest at once. But I hope to see you while you are in Sydney – Rana too.
Yours
Patrick.

20 MARTIN ROAD, 3.xii.78
TO PEGGY GARLAND
Dear Peggy,
I received your letter to-day. Had been thinking about you, while neglecting

[113]27.viii.78.

everybody in finishing my novel *The Twyborn Affair*. It is now done, and I have had an enthusiastic letter from one of the partners at Cape. Don't know how it will strike readers; probably they'll be shocked as they expect me to behave like a stuffed owl after winning that wretched prize . . .

A week to-day Jim Sharman starts rehearsing a revival of *A Cheery Soul* which will open at the Opera Theatre on Jan 17th.

You say you haven't enough energy. Mine comes and goes; I have periods of abject despair. I regret having wasted so much time in my life, and here I have so much I want to do at the tail end.

Manoly's youngest sister Elly has been staying with us a couple of months. They've just come back from a trip to Queensland.

Peter Beatson wrote me a disturbing letter some time ago to say that he and Rana found they were incompatible, that she was staying on at Aix, and he returning to N.Z. I told him the most compatible were incompatible from time to time and that they should try harder. Haven't heard from him since.

End of paper.

Love,

P.

Just read the bits over the fold in your letter about Peter and Rana. So you know. We don't know enough but I'm sure it's a mistake for both of them.

20 MARTIN ROAD, 17.xii.78

TO MANNING CLARK

I heard something fantastic the other day: Frank Hardy sold the chair on which he wrote *Power Without Glory* to ANU. Can it be true? Perhaps I should offer the bed on which most of my novels were begotten, with a few mattress stains thrown in for good value.

FOURTEEN

The Face in the Mirror

January 1979 – December 1981

THESE WERE WONDERFUL MONTHS for White. The new Sydney Theatre Company had offered Jim Sharman its first production at the Opera House and he chose *A Cheery Soul*. The terrible figure of Miss Docker, do-gooder and militant Christian, appeared at last on the Sydney stage as White was putting the last touches to *The Twyborn Affair*. Book and play were both triumphs. In letter after letter White confessed, 'I could not wish for better.'

20 MARTIN ROAD, 14.i.79
TO GEOFFREY DUTTON
I went last night to a pre-view of *A Cheery Soul*, which opens on Wednesday. It's a dazzling production, and Robyn Nevin is electrifying: I got the classic shivers down my spine. I dread the opening, however, when all the Divine People will flood in, bitching to High Heaven . . .

Cape seem to be charging ahead with *The Twyborn Affair*, but I'm afraid the strikes and the snow will hold everything up. England must be hellish at the moment.

My dream of Apia, Samoa, has been destroyed by a post-card sent by Ruth Cracknell in which Aggie Grey looks pure North Shore – in fact, another Doris Fitton. Oh dear, soon there will be nothing left. Fortunately, I shan't be either. At least I have a more functional set of teeth to sustain me in my last days as I eat, drink etc.

By the way, you mentioned a case of wine, which hasn't arrived, and I'm wondering whether it was stolen, or smashed and nothing said.

Our garden is looking lush in spite of the heat, and we've never had more birds. I don't know why I have the urge to go into the city, but I do.

Yrs
Patrick.

20 MARTIN ROAD, JAN. 79

CARD TO PEPE MAMBLAS

Though I dislike so much of what happens in this country, we hated Europe when we went there a couple of years ago, and I don't know that we shall ever go there again. I have a lot of work to finish anyway, and can't do that while travelling. I remember you with intense delight, but you also hurt me intensely in the end. Manoly and I have been together for almost forty years. Thanks to him I am as happy as one who is not made for happiness can be.

I wish you happiness. You have a jolly-looking cook! I spend half my life at the stove, but fortunately enjoy cooking. It goes with writing.[1]

Love,
Patrick.

20 MARTIN ROAD, 18.i.79

TO MANNING CLARK

Dear Manning,

Had your card – which distressed me. However, you can't be all that ill if you propose to wander about South America and visit the scene of Cook's murder. What puzzles me is the remark, 'Somewhere along the line I made the wrong turn.' I feel I do continually, but somehow manage to find my way back. My life is a series of blunders and recoveries and so it will be, I expect, till the end.

A *Cheery Soul* opened last night at the Opera House with an audience composed of all those who have to be seen – very careful of their reactions. But before that we had three previews, paying audiences, long queues and great enthusiasm. It is really quite a dazzling production, and Robyn Nevin gives what would be considered a great performance in any part of the world where there is a tradition of theatre.[2] Alas the final performance is on February 13th. Don't you think you could get back a little earlier? I'm sure you'd get more out of this play than the majority will.

I don't know how the snows and industrial chaos in England will affect the printing of *The Twyborn Affair*. I expect it will be held up like everything else.

Gough and Margaret were at the play last night, he looking rather pale and puffy, she still the Statue of Liberty. My next ordeal will be a dinner organised by the radical Greek community. I thought it would only

[1]Mamblas had sent a photograph of himself and his cook outside his house in Biarritz; this was PW's last communication with him; Mamblas died in 1985 at the age of 92.
[2]In gratitude PW gave her a spray of diamonds (later stolen).

be an intimate affair, then they announced that Gough will be there, which means I suppose, I shall have to make an awful speech. The Greeks are speech mad. Shall be relieved when you're back. Australia feels empty without you.

Love to both.
Patrick.

20 Martin Road, 11.ii.79
TO NINETTE DUTTON
Dear Nin,

Thanks for your letter. You must be feeling exhausted but relieved. Remembering our comparatively minor move of fifteen years ago, I can't imagine facing another one. If we ever have to get out of this house, I hope I'll drop dead in it before the operation begins.

I still haven't seen David Campbell, but we talked the other night on the 'phone. Perhaps I'll be able to see him after he's settled down to the radium treatment though other people have said the treatment is so painful they'd rather die of the cancer. Every second person we know seems to be developing the disease. I suppose it's not surprising in such horrendous times. Only two more performances of *A Cheery Soul*. It's developed into a stampede, with people fighting to stand; and I can remember going to a performance in Melbourne years ago when there were seven in the audience.

The next project is to try to get the money for the film I wrote last year, and which is at present being typed more professionally. I'm also well on with writing another screenplay.[3]

All this will help occupy me till I feel I'm ready to embark on my final novel. Would like to fly round Australia before I start, but where to find a reliable pilot? I'd also like to see more of the country from the ground. None of this is really necessary, as the book is by no means a documentary, but I'd like to do it.[4]

Love to all,
Patrick.

[3]*Monkey Puzzle* was being typed as *Last Words* was written. In the project he hoped Robyn Nevin would play Eureka Steel, a version of his childhood nurse Lizzie Clark. PW described the character to Nevin as 'a survivor'.

[4]The plot: a children's book writer and her husband, both fed up with the world of children's writing, decide to fly round Australia to see the reality of the country, then descend on Mount Wilson to disrupt a bunch of fellow children's writers holding a seminar. This project grew out of PW's twin disdain for seminars and writers of children's fiction.

20 MARTIN ROAD, 18.ii.79
TO GEOFFREY DUTTON

Dear Geoffrey,

Manning got back yesterday and we had some telephone conversation. He sounded quite cheerful, still under the influence of the rarefied life he led at Harvard.[5] He went yesterday to see David, who seems to be taking the radium treatment much better than many I have known. But there has been another tragedy, if you haven't heard of it: Raina electrocuted herself last week. No one has been told whether it was accidental or deliberate, so I suspect the latter.[6] (Manoly says that when he was a boy several Athenian ladies whose husbands were carrying on, stuck their scissors in the electric plughole.)

I was waiting to hear from David when he wanted to see me, but decided to give them a ring this morning. He sounded quite cheerful in spite of everything, but was coughing a lot, and says he has arthritis in the arm he lies on; he can't breathe in any other position. He obviously doesn't feel up to seeing people yet, so I left it like that.

But all these dreadful incidents one on top of the other – Don Dunstan too.[7] Everyone I admire in this country is driven into the ground before their time.

I read your piece in the *Nat Times*,[8] also the review of *Big Toys*.[9] Both were acceptable from my point of view, but I always feel your critical writings revolve round friendship. Nice and soothing for the friends, and one doesn't want knives; I only feel you could be more objective.

A Cheery Soul ended its run, alas, on the 13th. There were increasing numbers standing for the last performances. We broke the Box Office record for the Drama Theatre by averaging 85% full throughout the run. Apparently they're pleased if they get as much as 50%. I'm sorry you didn't like this production better; to me it was all I could have wished for, so much more life than the one in Melbourne.

I've had a 4-page scrawl from that old bore Xavier Herbert. In an

---

[5]Clark held the chair of Australian studies from Sept. 1978 to Jan. 1979.

[6]Campbell's daughter was killed accidentally by a faulty washing machine.

[7]The South Australian premier, forced out of politics, resigned from his hospital bed on 15 February 1979.

[8]'The Return to Confidence', a survey of Australian literature, 17 Feb., pp.24-8, in which he wrote, 'Patrick White's greatest achievement was to make Australia "a country of the mind" as, for instance, Marquez has made Colombia, or Olive Schreiner South Africa or Neruda Chile.'

[9]By Peter Corris, 10 Feb., p.29, after its publication by Currency Press: 'a biting criticism of our lives and lies'.

interview with a journalist from a Northern Territory paper he told the man that I didn't answer his letters, and that I was a lousy letter writer anyway.[10] The Sydney *Telegraph* got hold of this and wrote a send-up of Xavier. He is now trying to put himself right with me and explain his position. What an intolerable egoist the man is; if he could see the stuff that arrives in my letter-box he'd understand why I don't carry on a 'literary' correspondence with somebody I hardly know. In fact I gave away 'literary' correspondence years ago when I realised I didn't have all time before me, as one believes in youth.

We're enjoying a few overcast days after the most appalling heat and humidity; it's wonderful to use a blanket at night. I expect S.A. has been a furnace. Perhaps Tisi[11] organised a real Christmas dinner. She was lamenting the fact that you weren't having it hot enough at Christmas.

Love to all.

Patrick.

20 MARTIN ROAD, 25.ii.79
TO XAVIER HERBERT
Dear Xavier,
If you saw the stuff which arrives in my mailbox you would understand why I no longer write literary letters. Many of my correspondents are nuisances who can be ignored, but there are the causes I support, and many lesser genuine appeals which have to be answered, as well as people who want me to make speeches, lecture at the universities, attend conferences, seminars – all of it takes time even when you brush most of it off. I hardly have the time to write short factual notes to people I have known all my life and with whom I would like to keep in touch.

So much for that. Now for my working life. Last year I finished a novel which will come out in a few months' time. I was involved with a film which will soon be released. I wrote a second screenplay for which we are at present trying to raise the money. One of my plays has just finished a run at the Sydney Opera House. (As you haven't been into the performing arts you don't know what a nervous strain it is.) At present I am working on a third screenplay, while thinking about what I hope will be my final novel. I feel I shan't be ready for this before a couple more years and who knows whether I shall have the time or strength. I shall be

[10]Herbert complained in *Northern Territory Newsletter*, vol.1, no.5, p.17, that PW's letters were earnest and sometimes thoughtful but ungenerous. 'Patrick has never even mentioned that I am a writer in his letters to me . . . he has never complimented me on my work.'
[11]The Duttons' daughter Teresa.

67 this year. I should mention also that I cook and clean year in year out. You're probably not aware of that, very little of the foregoing in fact, when you tell the press about my lousy letter-writing.

You constantly amaze me. You call yourself a 'revolutionary' when here you are sucking up to the Establishment and accepting honorary doctorates. That is farcical; even Princess Margaret has a few Honorary Doctorates, and next month Charlie will receive an Honorary Fellowship from the Academy of Sciences in Canberra. That's the kind of club you've joined.

Then all this talk about 'greatness', yours and mine; only time will show who is great. The Nobel Prize is another farce to anybody but the innocent. Look down the list of the winners and you will see that half of them have lapsed into nonentity.

Well, you provoked me to write this letter. Now I must go to cook the dinner, and in between doing so, perhaps sit down to an hour of the work which matters to me.

Yrs

Patrick

P.S. My regards to Sadie[12] whom I liked very much on the occasion when we met.

20 MARTIN ROAD, 4.iii.79

TO DAVID MOORE

Last Australia Day was so awful, so much hypocrisy and unreality afloat as we tried to persuade ourselves we are a wonderful nation, I started writing another film and am now about two-thirds of the way through a first version. It's called tentatively Last Words because I've always been fascinated by those, and I see it as a vehicle for Robyn Nevin.

We're having difficulty getting a theatre for The Night the Prowler in Sydney, too much American money-making frightfulness around, but it should start very soon at the Rivoli in Melbourne, which I'm told is the right theatre.

I don't know how much you have heard of the Harry Miller scandal. His computer ticket business went bust, leaving him and his partners (Myer, Syme, and David Jones) owing thousands to theatres and entrepreneurs. The story is that Harry . . . put the money into a big concern called Associated Securities which went bust a few weeks ago in spite of having all the nicest people on the board of directors. The idea was for

---

[12]Herbert's wife.

Harry to make a few dollars for himself.[13] Now he's properly in the shit, the Home Beautiful in Martin Road (with butler's pantry and saddle room) is for sale at $700,000, and the farm at Manilla is also on the market. Haven't yet heard about the rights to Voss.[14] Worse still the Labor Party is calling for an enquiry into his Silver Jubilee activities because the figures don't add up. I'd love them to catch him on that one.[15]

Another big scandal has cropped up as the result of Tamie Fraser's family receiving $100,000 for damage done to their property by bushfires a couple of years ago, when the handout to most farmers averaged $4,000.[16]

Apart from the showing up of crooks, the only thing I am aware of at present in this deadly country is the increase of cancer amongst one's friends and neighbours . . .

To end on a slightly more positive note, I may fly round Australia when I've finished correcting my proof. I started wanting to do this in connexion with another novel I have in my head. Wasn't quite sure how to go about finding a plane and a pilot. Then Maie Casey offered to lend me her plane and her pilot – almost too good to be true! Of course there will still be a lot to go into – the cost of fuel, accommodation and so forth. I don't want to follow every bay and cape, but I'd like to get an idea of the shape of the whole from the air, then go over a bit of it by land later on.

We are going through awful days of humidity, and now two whole days of black rain as the result of a cyclone up north. My bronchial tubes feel all furred up, Manoly's aches are making him depressed, and we are going through a series of complicated and most expensive dog ailments.

I too, have come to an end too quickly. Must write again soon.

Love to both.

Patrick.

---

[13]Computicket Australia Pty Ltd was Miller's brightest idea: a computer network selling seats to concerts, sports events, etc. across Australia. He owned half the shares and took a profit of half a million dollars tax-free at the start. Soon after Computicket began operations in August 1978 the company found itself short of funds and it crashed in February 1979 after using ticket money – over $700,000 held on behalf of rock promoters and the Australian Opera – to try to stay afloat. (The collapse of Associated Securities Ltd at this time had no bearing on Miller's predicament.)

[14]The rights were sold in effect to Sidney Nolan; no progress was made on the film in the lifetime of either man but plans to make Voss remain alive in 1994.

[15]Labor senators complained of apparent overspending by organisers of the Queen's Silver Jubilee but no allegations of wrongdoing were made against Miller. No enquiry was held.

[16]No wrongdoing was established. The prime minister's wife Tamie Fraser at this time famously accused her family's critics of sinking, 'lower than a snake's duodenum.'

20 MARTIN ROAD, 25.iv.79
TO GEOFFREY DUTTON
Thank you for the offer of names and addresses if I fly round Australia, but I shall want to do it as anonymously as possible. The people you meet come up with more if they have no idea who you are. What I really want from this trip is the country's shape, more or less as an abstraction, and to worm in from there to its rotten core.

20 MARTIN ROAD, 13.vi.79
TO GRAHAM C. GREENE
I'd like the people on my list for advance copies of *The Twyborn Affair* to have them as the book becomes available. It may do some good if they enthuse or deplore a few weeks before publication. I think PR should seep rather than batter (though Penelope Mortimer's telling how she·was raped by her parson father a week before her autobiography popped out must have produced pretty good results.)[17]

I do very much wonder how the jacket will turn out. It has been an anxious time, for myself, and even more so, Luciana.[18] I see so many awful jackets nowadays. Here the bookshop windows all suggest American airports. But perhaps that is what sells books to telly watchers.

The Night the Prowler is released in Sydney commercially to-morrow night. It has been well received in Adelaide but I think it will die a speedy death in Melbourne, city of sodden rectitude ...

Jim Sharman is enthusiastic about my screenplay Last Words, which I finished recently and has plans for getting money for it from the US. Now that I'm free of film and play (one never really is) I'm looking forward to starting my next novel in a couple of months.

Yrs
Patrick.

20 MARTIN ROAD, 17.vi.79
TO MARY LORD[19]
Dear Mrs Lord,
I can't accept the Honorary Life Membership you offer, because I feel that in many ways ASAL is misguided in its aims. Australia seems to be suffering

[17]Attempted rape; interviews promoting *About Time* in the *Guardian, Sunday Telegraph,* etc.
[18]Arrighi, who had, at PW's instigation, designed the jacket.
[19](1929–   ), ex-academic, first president of the Association for the Study of Australian Literature founded in 1977, later the biographer of Hal Porter.

from a sickness called seminar. To me the literary seminar is a time-wasting and superfluous event; it may encourage a few lonely hearts and dabblers, but I don't believe anyone intended and determined to be a serious writer would get anything positive out of these occasions.[20]

Surely what the writer needs is orthography, grammar and syntax, which he learns at school; after that he must read and write, read and write, and forgetting all about being a writer, live, to perfect his art.

In my childhood and youth I groped my way through what I was supposed to read, and came across what I needed. When I went up to Cambridge I received a certain amount of guidance, but I can honestly say there was only one academic who kindled my imagination.[21] The others dispensed a course in desiccation, so I gave up lectures – and read, and read.

Since then I have been suspicious of the academic approach to literature and attempts to foster it through seminars. True writers emerge by their own impetus; to encourage those who haven't got much to contribute you are prolonging false hopes and helping destroy the forests of the world.

This must appear a churlish reply to your kind letter with its offer of an honour and literary conviviality. But it's what I believe, and much as I enjoy conviviality, I suspect that more literature plops from the solitary bottle than out of the convivial flagon.

Yours sincerely,
Patrick White.

20 MARTIN ROAD, 26.vi.79
TO GEOFFREY DUTTON
Dear Geoffrey,
A clam in the lung – what next.[22] I hope not a baby, but I expect one

---

[20]ASAL holds an annual conference to discuss Australian writing and now awards the Gold Medal which PW had won in 1941, 1955 and 1965; it was no recommendation for PW that A. D. Hope was one of the association's patrons.

[21]Jean Joseph Seznec (1905–83), distinguished critic of French thought and literature, and authority on the 19th century French novel, 'put his head up and didn't read from notes'. Seznec fuelled PW's life-long passion for Flaubert. *Madame Bovary*, first read at Cheltenham, was for PW the greatest novel ever written; before making a pilgrimage to Rouen, he wrote to Cynthia Nolan, 7.iv.68: 'I have never found another writer whose beliefs are so much my own. He took five years to write *Madame Bovary*. That, too, is a comfort to know, when agents and publishers are trying to whip one into writing something superficial and trashy every year.'

[22]Actually pleurisy: Dutton was very ill for a time.

has to be Japanese for that. (Did you hear about a young woman who had an ovarian tumour (benign) weighing 60 kg? Fancy lugging that round the supermarket.)

If I had a secretary and entourage of Victorian servants, I might emerge benignly to receive visiting celebrities. As it is today, I come out sweating from stove or sink, or in a bad temper from the paragraph or scene which has been torturing me. I just can't face any more of it. In any case, in spite of my great love for 19th Century Russian literature, and for Pushkin in spite of being unable to read him, I am allergic to Russians. It would be most embarrassing besides, to receive one whose work I haven't read, and who is a close friend of that bellowing bull Solzenhitsyn, who I can't endure.[23]

The chances of my flying round Australia are pretty slim considering the shortage of aviation fuel,[24] but I shall go on hoping. Things may improve by the end of July.

The Night the Prowler is dying a speedy death in Melbourne and Sydney. It was madness to put it on during film festivals. Those who venture are very enthusiastic, but they're not enough. On the good side, the Manchester Guardian film critic, Derek Malcolm, who is here for the Sydney Film Fest, saw The Prowler. He has said publicly that it is far subtler than most of the Australian films successes and he's going to recommend it for the London Film Festival.

I'd have hired an ambulance to go to Vanessa Redgrave in The Lady from the Sea after the wonderful photograph of her fresh from the fiord, with hair and droplets all over her face.[25]

Love to both,

P.

---

[23]Dutton was hoping to bring to Australia on a lecture tour (and introduce to PW) Vladimir Maksimov, editor of the exiles' magazine Kontinent founded by Solzhenitsyn. The tour fell through.

[24]Caused by a strike at the Caltex oil refinery in Sydney.

[25]She had played Ellida in New York and Manchester and now at the Round House in London.

20 MARTIN ROAD, 15.vii.79
TO DYMPHNA CLARK[26]
Dear Dymphna,

Sorry not to have answered your letter before. At least I sent something for the Aborigines.[27]

We have had a rather unpleasant winter: weeks of bronchitis on my part, a short but virulent 'flu, and Manoly throat infections twice.

Also a lot of work. Proof correcting. Screenplays. I've written another longer film, also quite a short one, for which we now have to get the money. *The Night the Prowler* has been driven into the ground temporarily, but I refuse to lie down. If I had obeyed *Those Who Know* I'd have written no more novels after *The Aunt's Story*, no more plays after *The Ham Funeral*. So it is now with films.

I am awaiting the appearance of my novel *The Twyborn Affair* with some trepidation. The long knives will be out, Dorothy Green probably have a stroke, and the Festival of Light demand a burning,[28] but it had to be written.

A pity we never see you. I'd like you to give warning and come to a proper meal, not those miserable afternoon-tea or morning-coffee appearances. I have a new stove. So you really ought to come.

Yrs
Patrick.

THE FAILURE OF THE film made it impossible for Sharman to raise the cash for Last Words and White's short career as a screenwriter ended. The new novel was dying, too, as the refinery strike forced him to postpone once again his circumnavigation of Australia. Now White's mind turned to another project: a self-portrait in which to make a public declaration of his sexuality. He knew once *The Twyborn Affair* appeared he must declare himself: 'say so before it was said'. Research for the memoir took him briefly back to Belltrees on his first visit since 1948. Straight afterwards he visited the Duttons for the first time at their new house in a beautiful stretch of country near the Barossa Valley. White was surprised by the scale of things at Piers Hill. Relations with the Dutton family, so happy for so long, began to sour. *The Twyborn Affair* appeared in Australia and the UK in September. Reviews and sales were good.

[26]Manning Clark's wife.
[27]PW had responded to her letter by contributing to the Aboriginal Treaty Committee promoting the idea of a formal compact between black and white Australia. The movement died.
[28]Wrong on all counts.

TO GEOFFREY DUTTON

Dear Geoffrey,

I haven't received the parcel you mentioned in your note of 18th Aug. But parcels now take as long as our great-grandparents did to arrive in Australia. On 24th Aug. I received some copies of the French translation of The Vivisector[29] posted on April 6th. I'm expecting a parcel of books from England posted 9th July.

I quite definitely couldn't accept any favours from Mobil.[30] It surprised and shocked me that you could take up with them, and years ago the Encyclopaedia Britannica – both of them trying to tidy themselves up in

[29]By Georges Magnane for Gallimard.
[30]The oil company had commissioned Dutton to write the text of a photographic book, Patterns of Australia.

Australia. I could not have remained with Macmillan Aust after their devious operations with Nixon and Kerr.[31] I find them dishonest too in promoting their books – that jacket for *Water Under the Bridge* being one instance.[32]

I've been re-reading the letters of J. B. Yeats, that marvellous man you told me about some years ago. I think you've reached a stage where you too, should re-read him.[33]

Yrs

Patrick.

20 MARTIN ROAD, 11.xi.79

CARD TO BRETT WHITELEY

When people stand me up and ask me who my favourite painter is, I go blank, as happened the day we had lunch at Kate's.[34] Thinking it over I realised next day that GOYA is the painter who gives me most.

To-day is the 11th Nov when you came to the dinner for David Campbell and news of the Fraser-Kerr Coup poured out of the radio. That night is still very vivid.

Yrs,

Patrick.

20 MARTIN ROAD, 9.xii.79

TO SHIRLEY HAZZARD

Dear Shirley,

I should have written you long ago, after reading *The Transit of Venus*, which was full of impressive insights and solid detail. Some of your other books I've found too dependent on atmospherics and décor. You are still inclined to strike attitudes and pirouette round yourself, but only here and

---

[31]Dutton remained editorial director of Sun Books when the imprint was bought by Macmillan which published in 1978 both *The Memoirs of Richard Nixon* and John Kerr's apologia *Matters for Judgment*.

[32]The jacket announced, 'Patrick White Literary Award Winner 1977' but the winner was Sumner Locke Elliott himself, not this particular book which PW rated below Elliott's best.

[33]PW told *New York Times*, 27 April 1980, p.32, that he valued father Yeats for his 'worldly wisdom and approach to people and affairs . . . far more contemporary than the mystic convolution of his genius son'.

[34]Kate Fitzpatrick (c. 1946–), intimate member of PW's theatrical family, actress in a line that stretched back to the glamorous stars he chased as a stage-struck schoolboy. PW had written the role of Mag Bosanquet in *Big Toys* for Fitzpatrick after her success as Nola Boyle in Sharman's revival of *The Season at Sarsaparilla*.

there. What I see as your chief lack is exposure to everyday vulgarity and squalor. You are lucky, but it is what is closing down on us.

I have always wondered about giving extracts from work in progress to magazines. When I have done it (chiefly to show I am still alive and working) readers have been slightly mystified. I first read that piece in which your less spectacular sister has her fantasy affair with the doctor when it was printed by the *New Yorker* and somehow it didn't work for me.[35] But in its place in the novel it's one of your more perfect achievements.

Recently I did exactly what I've been advising against: I gave some sketches for a self-portrait to the *Bulletin* centenary anthology.[36] This portrait began as a doodle, and grew and grew, so that I don't feel I shall be able to waste it. I've grown so tired of people showing me as someone I am not, that I thought I'd try to put the warts in the places where they belong. The past is easy enough, everybody dead, but as one approaches the present it becomes a walk across a quagmire.

I didn't see the Bird of Paradise[37] because I forgot the dates of her visit, and only realised towards the end, while I was in South Australia. Anyway, I'm sure she was kept busy during her stay, and we shouldn't have had all that much in common. In fact I've often wondered why you sent me that B. of P![38]

Love to you both,
Patrick.

20 MARTIN ROAD, 22.xii.79
TO RANDOLPH STOW
Dear Mick,
Thanks for your letter. I hope the cheque arrived;[39] it if <u>didn't</u> you must let me know. When Sumner won the award the cheque was sent to the wrong New York bank, and for a long time he was too discreet to tell us he hadn't received it[40] . . .

---

[35]'A Crush on Doctor Dance', 26 Sept. 1977, p.36.
[36]29 Jan. 1980, p.146, edited by Dutton.
[37]Marietta Tree (1917–91), a distinguished figure in New York society who served with Adlai Stevenson at the UN before becoming a company director; she visited Australia often as a director of Lend Lease Corporation Ltd from 1977–87.
[38]She was generous and charming, Hazzard explained to PW, 14.xii.79. 'Charm is uncommon here.'
[39]$11,000: the Patrick White Award for 1979.
[40]$9,500 in 1977; even after PW raised Cain with the bank in Sydney, Sumner Locke Elliott had to hire an accountant to run the cheque to ground on Manhattan. PW claimed that SLE never spoke to him again after winning the prize.

I no longer have any connexion with Sid, I realised when Cynthia died that it was she who was my friend. Sid had always been very nice to Manoly and me, but somehow we never got through to each other, and I couldn't forgive his falling on the bosom of the other one when Cynthia's ashes were hardly cold, that is why he has become such a dreadful painter. I have never met Mary. I am told 'she can be very charming when she wants to be.' I am sorry it is like this, but there it is; I don't feel broken friendships ever mend successfully.

I'm now working on a self-portrait which may explain my attitudes to those who misunderstand them. I hope we see you again one day.

Yrs,

Patrick.

20 Martin Road, 22.xii.79
TO JAMES STERN
Dear Jimmy,
This probably won't reach you before Christmas and you may feel offended, but this most detestable season has been the worst bulldozer yet. For the last two months half the Northern Hemisphere has been landing on our doorstep. Some of the invaders one loves to see but cooking meals for visitors in an Australian summer is very exhausting, and staving off the people one doesn't want, more exhausting still.

I'm glad you liked *The Twyborn Affair*.[41] Its reception in Australia has been extraordinary. In the beginning reviewers didn't know quite what they ought to say. Then some of them started coming out in the book's favour and it's a best-seller, only just below the latest Forsyth. There's probably some sort of trouble ahead, but at least I've shown that I'm not a stuffed owl in a museum, which is what they expect of somebody who has won the destructive Nobel Prize.

The other day I came across a good remark by Philip Larkin: 'I don't

---

[41] PW was gratified by the novel's reception in the UK and particularly pleased by Angus Wilson's shrewd review in the *Observer* – 'the first time in decades that I haven't been done dirt in the *Observer*,' PW told Alan Williams, 21.x.79. Wilson wrote, 30 Sept., p.37, 'Across his pages people of all nationalities and tastes and cultures and classes and incomes – his range is unsurpassed today – cross and recross one another's paths, seeking desperately some sign of human connexion that goes below the surface talk, the dead domestic round, the play-acting, the self-indulgent "affair" or the easy lay. Again and again they think they have found "it" – love, feeling, something more than the cherished self that now so bores them – in a sudden glance or word, a chance bodily contact. But "it" turns to dust. Yet the sad human play White puts on for us never turns to dust for the audience . . .'

want to go around pretending to be myself.'[42] That is exactly how I feel about those unnecessary people who want to come here and talk about my 'work and life'. I'm now working fitfully on a kind of self-portrait. It's far more difficult than fiction, for obvious reasons. Its virtue is that one can come and go adding a few strokes (which may be painted out later on) then get on with cooking the dinner without much sense of frustration or guilt.

Manoly is leaving on Jan 3rd to spend a month in Athens. He wants to see whether Greece is more bearable in mid-winter. We found all our European travels – France, Italy, Greece – quite intolerable a few years ago. But I had to get the background for the first part of *The Twyborn Affair*.

I am staying behind to look after the house and animals – nothing heroic about that; I can't say I have much desire to travel. I can't say I have much desire for anything but a peaceful death. If it weren't for Manoly I probably would have gone looking for it already.

Love to you both,
P.

20 MARTIN ROAD, 20.i.80
TO SHIRLEY HAZZARD
Dear Shirley,
I'm sorry if some of my remarks hurt, because I found your novel solid, serious, and impressive. But to me you do lead an unusually charmed life writing away in the N.Y. apartment and Capri villa,[43] while collecting your celebrities and charmers and pairing them off round the world. I do hope you get down to those grey office legions which you tell me I have left untouched.[44] I have, because in my own life I have had less experience of those than of the highly-coloured squalor (which, I felt, since my return to grey Australia, the inhabitants should have their noses rubbed in.)

At present I'm doodling away at a kind of self-portrait to try to show the person (I think) I am, because so few of my critics seem to know. My

[42](1922–85), poet, admired by PW who wished someone would spray-paint the famous line, 'They fuck you up your mum and dad' on David Jones' Sydney store for Mother's Day.
[43]Steegmuller replied to this, 4.v.80: 'two rented rooms in an ex-pensione, with discarded pensione fittings'.
[44]Hazzard had replied to PW's strictures by arguing, 14.xii.79, that *his* was the sheltered life: sheltered from the 'arid squalor' of office work to which millions are condemned in the West. 'This central and even dominant theme of modern life has yet to find its interpreter of genius . . . it is not for the squeamish however.'

life nowadays must look pretty conventional and protected, but in the 'Thirties and during the war in the Middle East I often reached the lowest depths. Did you ever see the film *Looking for Mr Goodbar?*[45] That was very much like my New York life before World War II – allowing for the difference in sex. For all I know, you too may have done the streets of New York or wherever in your youth!

Elizabeth[46] was very pleased with the two friends you sent recently. No doubt they were my loss, but I can't cope with everybody who arrives during a steam-heated Sydney summer particularly when I am on my own.

I went to that party on the ferry, to which you hark back, because it was one way of seeing the B. of P., though really because I wanted to interest Dusseldorp in a theatrical venture which he wouldn't take on, and which failed rather miserably;[47] still, I am glad to have been associated with it and the most creative of our Sydney directors and actors.

I hope Francis is recovered. When Manoly returns I'd like to take to my bed in a good hotel – if there were one – and sleep for a week.

Yrs,

Patrick.

20 MARTIN ROAD, 22.iii.80
TO DAVID MOORE
Dear David,
Sorry to hear about the recurring ailment. Try to find out as much as you can while over there, though I think we are pretty good medically in Australia if you can discover the right doctor. Manoly was quite happy to be home. He now goes to the psoriasis clinic only once a month, but I'm afraid the arthritic pains will be with him always.

The political situation here is more and more distressing; at the moment there isn't much to be said for either side. Fraser has a new speech writer[48] who is trying to present him as a philosopher – with faces to match. I'm glad we don't have TV; I might break it.

Our Fran announced the other day that she is going to marry the lover with whom she's been living, a fellow art student of Pom origins, about 28, and seemingly as mousy as herself. I said I hoped she was

---

[45]Melodramatic 1977 sex drama written and directed by Richard Brooks from the 1975 novel by Judith Rossner. 'Not perfect,' he told Waters, 2.iv.78, after seeing the film, 'But a good perv for all those who have led double lives.'
[46]Harrower.
[47]PW hoped to get money from Gerardus (Dick) Dusseldorp (1918–   ), chairman of Lend Lease, for Sharman's Paris Company.
[48]Alan Jones (1943–   ), teacher and football coach, later a popular Sydney broadcaster.

absolutely sure, and she replied (about 24) she's as sure as she'll ever be about anything. Nothing one can do beyond help pick up the pieces when things fall apart.[49]

I went to Adelaide for the first night of Jim Sharman's *Death in Venice*[50] – a triumph, as well as a relief because he's been appointed the next artistic adviser for the Festival. *The Night the Prowler* was in a Film Festival in London, praised by the *Guardian*,[51] damned by the *Observer*.[52] They can't stop gushing over *My Brilliant Career* which to me is one of the phoniest ever.

Yesterday I finished <u>shaping</u> my self-portrait. Shall probably have to fiddle with it for years, but at least it is down on paper. At the same moment Brett Whiteley started getting his portrait of me on canvas. Neither of us knew the other had reached this stage. Surely a good omen.

20 MARTIN ROAD, 1.iv.80
TO THE EDITOR
SYDNEY MORNING HERALD
Sir,
In his letter in which he condemns me for speaking up about the state of the colony, Donald R. Palmer comes out with some wildly incorrect facts and refers to me as an 'English immigrant,' when my great-grandfather settled in Australia in 1825.[53]

Certainly I was born in London in 1912, only because my Australian parents happened to be there when I was ready. They returned to Australia bringing me with them when I was six months old. At least my bloodlines and history ought to make me acceptable to the likes of Mr Palmer.

If I was sent to school and university in England it was because my mother was convinced that what is English-made is best. The only thing English I can remember coming in for her disapproval was the butcher's shop with its meat exposed to flies off the street.

Up to the end, I disagreed with my mother on most counts, though whatever else, she was a woman of principle, and I sometimes wonder how she would react to the blowies fouling our own contemporary society.

---

[49]Again at this engagement to Patrick Richardson, PW expressed all the anger and disbelief he felt each time one of the women in his family married.
[50]Benjamin Britten, 1973.
[51]Derek Malcolm, *Guardian Weekly*, 22 July 1979, p.21: 'original and daring . . . mixing fantasy and reality in a manner that certainly does justice to its author'.
[52]Tom Milne, 18 Nov. 1979, p.14: 'Amateur talent night all round.'
[53]James White actually arrived in 1826.

No, Mr Palmer, as an Australian republican I can't pull in my head while watching this humiliating spectacle.

Patrick White.

20 MARTIN ROAD, 1.iv.80
TO FRANCIS STEEGMULLER
Dear Francis,

The elegant edition of the letters arrived.[54] Thank you very much. I am reading. It is just what I need at this stage. The introduction is particularly good. You and Flaubert between you tell so many idiot Australians what they don't, and perhaps can't understand that you mustn't expect 'answers' from works of literature and art. Alas, they will never read this book, but I'll stick it in front of the noses of some of the more pestilential who ask me to 'explain,' or develop the imagination of their unimaginative children.

Life in Australia becomes increasingly depressing, but I'm sure it does everywhere. It's just that what you're responsible for is always the worst: in our case that great philistine bullock Fraser asking to be pole-axed. After his performance in the States I've tried to say something about him in an interview I gave the N. Y. Times against my principles. Perhaps they won't print it.[55]

I hope Shirley's novel has been well received, and that she's not too offended by some of my remarks . . .

Have you read the letters of Flannery O'Connor? If not you must get hold of The Habit of Being.[56]

Yrs
Patrick.

20 MARTIN ROAD, 6.iv.80
TO ELIZABETH FALKENBERG

Just now I am reading the letters of Flaubert in a translation by the American scholar Francis Steegmuller. Anyone who reads those would never again accuse me of being a pessimist. In 1850 he wrote, 'We are going to drown in nineteen centuries of shit.'

---

[54] The Letters of Gustave Flaubert 1830–1857, selected, edited and translated by Steegmuller.
[55] Andrew Clark's interview appeared 27 April 1980, sect. VII, p.32, but there was nothing of PW's criticism of Malcolm Fraser. In Washington in February the prime minister had enthusiastically pledged Australian support for US efforts to dislodge the Soviets from Afghanistan and then set off on a hapless mission to persuade the leaders of Western Europe to join a boycott of the Soviet Union.
[56] A collection of her letters edited by Sally Fitzgerald.

In this neighbourhood we are threatened with drowning in horse manure after twelve days of the Royal Agricultural Show. The crowds grow worse every year, the dust, the traffic. The horses have never been so arrogant, the park churned like a battlefield.

I am not surprised your *Faust* was set in a railway-station lavatory. It reflects the times in which we live.

As for my *Big Toys*, it was performed in Saarbrücken, for God's sake, where it was received with polite applause: a *Boulevardstück* the critics considered it. So that is that.[57]

Our pug Daisy died of a heart attack in the middle of the night a week ago. We dug her grave by torchlight. She was our most loveable dog character and we miss her very much.

20 MARTIN ROAD, 16.vi.80
TO THE EXECUTIVE DIRECTOR,
NATIONAL BOOK COUNCIL
Dear Mr Edwards,
I thought it generally known that I accept no invitations to functions where the Governor-General will be present. After the coup of 1975, engineered by the present Prime Minister and his puppet the Governor-General, I became an advocate of constitution reform, and am since then an increasingly convinced republican. So I can hardly recognise and meet the British Monarch's representative whoever he may be.[58]

Until we have the republic I look forward to, I shall continue in my way doing what I can for Australian writers and literature.

Thank you for inviting me to your dinner.

Yours sincerely,
P.W.
(Patrick White)

---

[57]The second and last production of a PW play in German. *Night on Bald Mountain*, trans. by Renate Völkner, had had a brief season at the Stadltheater Hildesheim. *Big Toys* was translated by Ursula Grüzmacher-Tabori for the Staatstheater Saarbrücken season opening on 7 Sept. Kiepenheuer of Berlin reported to me, 17.i.94: 'So it was not a flop but not something like an event.'

[58]Boycott was always PW's first political response. Kerr had been succeeded by the vice-chancellor of Queensland University, the lawyer and scholar Zelman Cowen (1919–) who provoked PW's rage all the more for also being, as PW told ABC TV's *Nationwide*, 7 March 1981, 'a model servant of the Crown who has done more than any body to undermine the republican movement . . .'

20 Martin Road, 16.vi.80
TO MANNING CLARK
Dear Manning,
Here is my answer to the NBC. You said on the 'phone that the invitation was nothing to do with you; it was your Council. On looking at the letter again I see the wording includes; 'Our President, Professor Manning Clark, has asked me to say that he hopes you will be able to accept. He will be presiding at the dinner– –'

I must say I am terribly disappointed in you. Where do we stand if everybody caves in, accepts gongs and honorary doctorates (the disgraceful example of 'Doctor' Herbert whose teeth have been so effectively drawn) and courtship from the Governor-General? Cowen's apologists try to see him as an exceptional Australian, but I cannot feel he is sincere: he is there because he was attracted to pomp and ceremony, money and power.

These two letters have been most distressing to write, but I had to: a good many Australians continue to believe as I do.

Yours
Patrick
I'd be a Rum Puff indeed if I accepted, and you're a stuffed turkey to submit!

20 Martin Road, 22.vi.80
TO SHIRLEY HAZZARD
AND FRANCIS STEEGMULLER
American critics don't seem able to concentrate, or else they are stoned or drunk when they write their reviews. Even the one in the N. Y. Review of Books which some would read as a 'good' review was so full of inaccuracies I gave up reading.[59]

Some of the trouble lies in the language, I feel. The gap is widening between the one I use and the one Americans speak. (The same thing is happening here as children spend their time watching television, the language of which is riddled with contemporary American cliché.) Then, most Americans seem to want to be shown what they conceive Australia to be. One critic said they expected me to write screenplays for John Wayne characters and are puzzled when an explorer or a farmer is something more than an explorer or a farmer. They want to think of Australia as a

---

[59]Of The Twyborn Affair, Rosemary Dinnage wrote, 17 April 1980, p.25: 'I quail myself at the task of conveying why I believe this turgid, crotchety, tortuous, racked, oblique writer is nevertheless great . . .'

folksy backwoods, and can't believe we have caught up with American pseudo-sophistication and decadence.

I hope I shall be able to finish the self-portrait I am working on, to try to show what I am and what I have been getting at in my work. It is also very necessary to admit to my own flaws if I am to go on criticising the Australians – which I shall have to do, as I grow more disgusted every day. There are masses of admirable, humbler Australians, but one can respect very few of those at the top. Even those I thought on the same side are starting to cave in.

Elizabeth keeps her principles. Whether she is also <u>writing</u>, I have given up asking in case I get the wrong answer.[60] Too many vampires make too many demands on her . . .

I hope you can read my writing. My typing is not much better.

Yours

Patrick

For the Americans to take notice, I'd really have to go there, show myself on TV, visit universities and speak at women's clubs. They are more interested in personalities than books, though no doubt they'd buy my latest and explore it for a bit after they'd seen and touched me. But I can't go in for any of that, or only very rarely and when absolutely necessary. Next September I am going to address the Library Association of Aust. – librarians as keepers of the written word, so important when the dreadful jargon and indoctrination of TV is taking over. Of course I shall be indoctrinating a bit myself as I expect there will be an election not long after.

20 Martin Road, 6.vii.80

TO BOB BRISSENDEN[61]

We'd like to accept your invitation to dinner in a restaurant, but one can be more indiscreet at home, and as I usually end up being indiscreet, why not dinner here – say August 14th? I'll mark that till you let me know.

As I turned down a professor from Venice a few weeks ago I don't think I can see yours from Barcelona. I've already had a letter from Veronica Brady offering her, and no doubt I shall hear from the Department of Foreign Affairs. For some time now the Establishment has tried to set me up as an entertainment for visiting celebrities. They don't seem to realise

---

[60]Harrower's last novel was *The Watch Tower*, 1966.

[61](1928–91), poet and critic, author of the 1966 and 1969 studies of PW's work in the Longmans, Green 'Writers and their Work' series; chairman of the Literature Board of the Australia Council 1978–81.

I am ageing, slowing up, and still have work to finish. If they want to kill me off as a writer, they are on their way to doing it. But I do not intend to be killed off until I have finished *Flaws in the Glass*. After that, at least they may be too embarrassed to introduce me to their celebrities, or they may even want to run me out of the country. Either way, I shall then be left in peace to write one or two other things if I don't lapse into senility.

Quite apart from writing, nobody has any idea of all the correspondence I have to deal with (if I employed a secretary I'd spend endless time explaining and have less money to give the various causes I support) or that I am cook and bottle-washer, or that I have to read endless stuff, mostly during my insomniac nights, in connexion with the award I set up. I have very little time to see my friends or read for pleasure or keep up with interests like theatre, film and music, which are what keep one alive.

Hope the date I chose will be all right and that we can meet here then, when I shall get a bit more off my chest.

Yrs
Patrick.

20 Martin Road, 13.vii.80
TO GEOFFREY DUTTON

Did you know Angus Wilson has been knighted? I had a letter from him the other day, and shall have to reply to that. The knighthood may help advance the homosexual cause, but as an Australian, a republican and a socialist, I shall find it difficult to congratulate him.

20 Martin Road, 10.viii.80
TO MANNING CLARK

I wish we could talk. But you never will. You say repeatedly you are coming to see me. You never do, or if you do, you bring one of your children to act, I feel, as a shield. I am one who believes in seeing children and parents apart, otherwise you have an unnatural and inhibiting situation.

I feel you are a most unworldly man, and for that reason you are thoroughly frightened now that Australia has become as corrupt as the rest of the world. I feel if we saw each other occasionally and I had the opportunity to talk to you I might be able to help you.

I was horribly shocked and depressed when I read the guest list at that dinner party at Yarralumla. You are unable to see what a very foxy number that Zelman Cohen is. If as you say, he is a friend from Uni days, you could surely have gone and had a private cup of tea instead of confusing many people who are your admirers. But it was distressing to see you and the Brissendens rubbing shoulders with Phillip Blow-with-the Wind Adams (who made messy copy out of the occasion)[62] my creepy lawyer cousin Roddy Meagher[63] and one of Askin's knights, a Greek ... who was on with the colonels when they were in power. Since your dinner party, there has been another one of the same kind, including, I think, some cousins of mine, but she would lick the arse of anyone standing in for royalty ...

I could go on for pages, but it is pointless. I must get on with my self-portrait. After that I don't mind what. At least I shall feel at liberty to say what I think about others. If I have lost everybody's respect, as so many of them have lost mine, *tant pis* as they say in Fancy Nancy's language.[64]

Love,
Patrick.

20 MARTIN ROAD, 24.viii.80
TO RANDOLPH STOW
I'm nearing the end of a second version of my self-portrait *Flaws in the Glass*, and so am pretty edgy at the moment. God knows what they will think of it ... Manoly and I have been together nearly forty years, which is one of the reasons I wanted to do this self-portrait – show those censorious heteros that some homosexuals can beat them at their own game.

20 MARTIN ROAD, 11.ix.80
TO JEAN LAMBERT[65]
Dear Jean Lambert,
Your letter was a pleasant surprise. I had been wondering what had happened to *Ceinture de feuilles*, but didn't imagine you would be starting so soon on *The Twyborn Affair*. I can see the pronouns will offer great difficulties. I had tried to keep the sex of Eudoxia a secret till the end of Part 1, only dropping a few hints through hands, feet, gait etc. Eudoxia/ Eddy would be thinking of himself as a boy while writing the diary. But

---

[62]*Bulletin*, 5 Aug., p.68: '... the royal toast. I could feel the eyes and the mocking smiles of the bemedalled staff on me as I muttered the hypocritical words. But when in Rome– – and all that sort of thing. It was a case of closing one's eyes and thinking of England. Anyway, when Sir Z. said "The Queen" I thought of Oscar Wilde.'

[63](1932–), Tory barrister and art collector, of a medical and country-store dynasty, the Lipscombs, which provided PW with a grandmother.

[64]Anne Kerr's vocation was simultaneous translation from the French.

[65](1914–), novelist, translator from English and German (Hermann Hesse and Thomas Mann) into French; Lambert translated PW's late novels for Gallimard. PW was intrigued by Lambert being the son-in-law of his youthful enthusiasm André Gide.

you know how English homosexuals in talking about one another switch sometimes from the masculine to the feminine, satirically – I don't know whether you could make use of this habit – whether it would help disguise the situation, or merely confuse the reader, before the deathbed dénouement. I'm afraid these are difficulties, you as a Frenchman will have to resolve for yourself . . .

I don't feel we shall ever go to Europe again. Neither of us want to. Manoly went to Greece for a month after Christmas, to see his family and find out whether the country is more bearable during winter. It did not cure his disillusion. However, I recently finished reading a one volume compression of George Sand's *Ma Vie*, and am now well into Maurois' biography[66] and these have made me long to see those inland provinces of France where I have never been. I have always nibbled at the edges and I find those impossible now. What about Berry? Would it be rewarding today? I fell in love with George as described by herself. Maurois is beginning to make her look a bit of a monster. Perhaps this is why I am doing my *Flaws in the Glass* – to display my own monster and save others the trouble of doing it for me. Or will it reverse proceedings and make them come up with a rose-tinted version?

It always amazes me that anything arrives at some of those skeletal French addresses. I must write yours down now that I have it again.

Sincerely,

Patrick White.

20 MARTIN ROAD, 17.ix.80
TO GEOFFREY DUTTON
Dear Geoffrey,
I thought when I'd finished the latest version of *Flaws in the Glass* I'd have a month of peace before looking at it again, but there are so many other things cropping up. Writing a speech is always a nightmare, then delivering it; the one to the Librarians is this Friday.

Now I have to start on my Income Tax return, which is overdue, write the speech for the Book Council, and try to clean up the mountain of letters on my desk – all of which makes me long to succumb to a stroke.

We enjoyed our evening with the boys. They are very civilised, and I feel both are more aware than their parents of what is going on today and what is ahead of them.

---

[66]André Maurois (1885–1967), *Lélia; ou, La Vie de George Sand*, 1952, trans. 1953.

I found the photographs in the Mobil epic very beautiful and original.[67] I've only flipped through the text because I've had so little time for reading, and anyway some of your statements froze me and made me realise how far apart we are in our beliefs, and how little of me you understand. (This of course is why I am writing *Flaws in the Glass*; even those I have known for years know very little about me.)

That bit about the 'aristocrat' was particularly blood-curdling.[68] You can't have met many of my family – Somerset farmers who came here early in the piece, got hold of a lot of land, made money by hard work, but have remained most of them pretty crude. We were the new-rich of the turn of the century. Hardly aristocracy. If I am anything of a writer it is through my homosexuality, which has given me additional insights, and through a very strong vein of vulgarity. All of this I hope to bring out in *Flaws in the Glass*.

The first letter you wrote me after the publication of *Voss* froze my blood in the same way as the statement in this book. I have tried to shove the memory away, but it pops up again in moments like these. You complimented me on *Voss* and said you were so glad Australia had another writer who was also a gentleman. I found this remark so vulgar, in the colonial social sense, as opposed to the vulgarity which strengthens creativity.

I'm sorry to dredge this up, but now that I am losing faith in almost everybody in this two-faced jingleland I might as well try to explain a few other things which have contributed to what must have seemed like churlishness, or at least coldness, after years of friendship.

When you had to leave Anlaby you had all our sympathy. We were glad to hear you had found somewhere else which pleased you and were building a house. However, we were rather surprised by accounts of the Altman-style house-warming[69] you gave to the Adelaide establishment and your remark 'the children have to show the flag'. Then when I went to stay with you in what is certainly the most beautiful house in the most idyllic landscape, I was even more surprised considering the times and what we understood had happened to you. But what really shocked me

---

[67]*Patterns of Australia*, with photographs by Harri Peccinotti, published by Macmillan and Mobil Oil.

[68]Dutton had written, p.63: 'White himself is an aristocrat, if such a being is allowed in a land of compulsory democracy, and he has the aristocrat's ability to talk to and understand anyone in any level of society . . . He is the only Australian writer, with the exception of Martin Boyd, who can understand the manners and customs and pretensions of an upper class which has no confidence in being upper and no certainty of class.'

[69]The chaotic and pretentious celebrations in Robert Altman's *A Wedding*, 1978.

was to arrive back in Sydney and read the day after that you had been given that enormous grant by the Literature Board,[70] particularly when you had been jetting round the world with Mobil, helping them tidy up their Australian image, and living it up in the old Dutton funster fashion. Australia disgusts me more and more, but what really shatters me is when those I have loved and respected shed their principles along with the others.

No doubt you'll think this is all fatuous and humourless, and carry on as before. But for some time I've been screwing myself up to say it. Now it's said, and you can destroy the letter.

Yours
Patrick.

20 Martin Road, 22.ix.80
TO RONALD WATERS
Last night I had to deliver the first of my two speeches – this one to the Librarians of Australia.[71] It seemed to go off very well. I am getting better at it. Although I continue to read, I have found out how to make it sound as though I am making the speech. I've also found out that the best place to rehearse is in front of the bathroom mirror: the tiles amplify and help one project, and the mirror teaches one how to use one's face. All this must sound childish to professionals.

20 Martin Road, 20.x.80
TO THE DUTTONS
Dear Geoffrey and Nin,
I'm sorry you were so upset by my letter. I imagined you would be but I had to say it, otherwise our relationship would have trundled along in the unnatural way it has been going for some time. If I'm a moral megalomaniac it's from living in this increasingly corrupt colony over the last few years. It wouldn't be so bad if we weren't still supposed to be so pure, and if we weren't expected to turn to and be patriotic about a stink. All very humourless, no doubt, on my part but I've noticed that when one comes up with something others would rather not face, one is accused of humourlessness. I don't know what Humphrey McQueen told you. I've

---

[70]A two-year senior fellowship at $10,000 a year.
[71]'To me, having gone through it all, real education is self-education, though of course you've got to get the nudge from somebody. I got very few nudges at the schools I went to . . . wide and independent reading – self-education – is what matters.' 'The Reading Sickness', *Patrick White Speaks*, p.73.

never met him. I only heard him speaking on the radio during Writers' Week. What he said seemed to hit the nail on the head every time, and with wit.[72]

The reason I'm writing *Flaws in the Glass* is to try to show others what I think I am like, including those who have known me for years without really understanding me.

It's relevant to drag in a man called David Tacey who has spent some years writing a book about my work in spite of my attempts to deter him. I had a letter from him about the same time as your reply to mine. On Ash Wednesday when the fires swept through the Adelaide Hills he lost his house and all his possessions, including the book he had been working on, which was to go to the publishers in January.[73] In his letter he quotes a remark made by Lieselotte, a character, figment or facet of my self in *The Aunt's Story*: 'We must destroy everything, everything, even ourselves. Then at last when there is nothing, perhaps we shall live.' I wrote that in 1947, before you knew me, yet the remark shows that the 'humourlessness' of which you complain was already there. I had lived in London through the Thirties, through the Spanish Civil War (certainly only at a distance), I discovered Spengler, and became fairly intimately involved with Hitler's War. All those experiences contributed to Lieselotte's remark. After quoting it in his letter, Tacey says, perhaps Lieselotte is right, he has started work again on the book and is writing much better.

To come to the house at Piers Hill which you say cost no more than a small house in Paddington, that may well be. But when you imply that we are living in splendour in Martin Road, let me point out that when we came here 18 years ago, this was a rundown neighbourhood. We bought the house for £17,000 and the Nice People of the Eastern Suburbs exclaimed, 'But you can't possibly live there!' It was only much later that doctors, barristers, and a few less orthodox crooks started falling over one another to acquire 'property' in Martin Road. I hope we weren't to blame for the rot which set in.

I admit it appears pretentious today. If I could press a button so that we could find ourselves in a couple of rooms with a back yard, I'd do it at once. But the upheaval at our age is more than we could face. So we're hanging on here: we shall let the dust gather when it is no longer possible

[72]McQueen (1942–   ), historian, commentator and revolutionary socialist and later a trustee of White's prize. Dutton believed PW was echoing McQueen in his criticism of Mobil.
[73]David Tacey (1953–   ), psycho-analytic critic; PW helped him after the fires to secure a scholarship to America.

to do anything about it, and hope to die before too long. Certainly it would be welcome after Saturday's election.[74]

You don't quite say in your letter, but seem to imply there's no give and take in a homosexual marriage. My God – if you knew! And as for missing the give and take provided by children and their friends, I have a whole clutch of younger friends, middle-aged today but young enough to be my children, and whom I consider as such (people like Jim Sharman, Luci Arrighi, Penny Coleing and others whose names wouldn't convey anything) – endless give and take – as with their friends who snowball on. I think these children are what keeps me going. The wonderful part is they understand me much better than most of my contemporaries.

As for my private income, we did have enough to live on during the years at Castle Hill, by carefully counting every penny. Since there was an income of any size, I've been giving it away. By now I give most of it – not a noble gesture when one no longer has much desire for anything beyond a roof, a bed, a table, and a few pots and pans.

Yrs
Patrick.

20 MARTIN ROAD, 28.xii.80
TO THE STERNS
Dear Jimmy and Tania,
Thank you for your card. I was brought up to see the potato as a mortal sin because my mother was a figure fanatic, but in my false-toothy old age it has become one of my great joys. We eat masses of them.

This year I have neglected everybody as the result of a bad chest infection in early Dec. It kept me in bed for ten days except when my G.P. had me dashing for X-rays (twice) and blood tests (two.) Feeling like death I imagined I had lung cancer, galloping leukaemia, TB – the lot. Then my specialist of years sorted things out, and it seemed to have been only my recurring chest complaint with a virus thrown in. I now feel full of life on prednisone.

What made me particularly depressed was not having finished my self-portrait and perhaps no time to do it. I am now bashing away again and hope to finish in a couple of weeks. I even have another novel coming along hot and strong in my head.

Manoly's arthritis has been bad, his feet are now terribly misshapen, but the garden keeps him going.

We are seeing very few people as I must finish the book as soon as

---

[74] The conservatives under Malcolm Fraser had won another term in Canberra.

poss. Had a felafel and tsatziki Christmas on our own. Perfect peace on this suburban island. Everyone seems to have gone away, poor poverty-stricken things.

Love
P.

MORE THAN EVER NOW, White's health was a common thread running through all his correspondence. Once the cancer scare was past, he sent full reports to Maschler at Cape, Peter Beatson in New Zealand, Peggy Garland, Cynthia Nolan's daughter Jinx, Kylie Tennant, Elizabeth Falken-berg in Hamburg, Jean Scott Rogers, Professor Gerry Wilkes at Sydney University, the Jungian David Tacey, the Sydney writer Jean Bedford, Juliet O'Hea now retired from Curtis Brown, the translator Jean Lambert, David Malouf, Dorothy Green and his niece Alexandra.

20 MARTIN ROAD, 2.i.81
TO ALEXANDRA BISHOP
Dear Alexandra,
I'm late for Christmas this year. I started preparing a bad chest infection towards the end of Nov and went down with it early in Dec. I felt like death . . .

I was also afraid I mightn't be well enough to go to Fran's wedding and that it would look as though I didn't approve, or that I was chickening out. But my temperature was down in time, and I was able to perform as a witness. The ceremony was quite short and satisfactory. Fran looked very pretty, spoke up loud and clear, and marshalled the guests afterwards at the breakfast. She has actually grown up at last. Patrick too, has improved. The awful punk phase in sloppy army-disposal clothes is fortunately over for both of them. The in-laws were better than I expected. Manoly and I found we had plenty to talk about with the father-in-law as he was with the British Merchant navy in the Eastern Med during the War in much the same parts as we were.

I shan't start on the state of the world, or this piffling reactionary colony in particular. I grow more disgusted every day. The crooks are rewarded one after the other, the only thing you can't get away with is honesty. Bombs have started going off but never under the right people.

Hope you are all well,
Love
Patrick.

20 MARTIN ROAD, 2.i.81

TO TOM MASCHLER

As soon as I felt well again I started bashing away at *Flaws in the Glass* and finished yesterday – New Year's Day. Now I must wait a couple of weeks before looking through for the last time. After that there will be some notes to write and photographs to sort out, but those can wait; I shall send the typescript as soon as I have been over it. I even have another novel churning in my head, and must get on with it as soon as possible. These illnesses are good warnings that time is short . . .

I hope you are not going to say that *Flaws in the Glass* will destroy my literary reputation. Any literary reputation that can't stand up to the truth isn't worth having.

20 MARTIN ROAD, 18.i.81

TO JEAN BEDFORD[75]

Enjoyed two days euphoria after being told I didn't have the plague, then yesterday read about the rehabilitation of the Kerrs[76] by that foxy little lickspittle Zelly Cohen who, of course owes them a very lucrative position. Somebody also told me they had read in the *Bulletin* that Harry Miller is becoming Gough's literary agent.[77] I haven't yet checked on this through somebody reliable, but if it is accurate I feel I might as well have floated out of this cancerous society on my own cancer. Peter wrote a good letter.[78] I no longer trust any politician. We amount to nothing but votes and a means to their career.

I expect I shall now be flung into gaol for *Flaws in the Glass* for what I have written about the canonised Kerrs and a few more of the sainted mighty, but I don't intend to retract a word.

Hope to see you eventually.

Yrs

Patrick.

[75](1946–   ), writer and journalist whose *Country Girls Again* was published in 1979; at this time she was working, with her partner, the crime-writer Peter Corris, on the *National Times*.

[76]The Kerrs had returned from exile in Surrey, made cautious appearances in Sydney society over Christmas and revisited Admiralty House as the Cowens' guests for lunch on 17 January.

[77]No, not at this stage.

[78]Corris urged Neville Wran, *SMH*, 20 Dec., to begin fundamental reforms in NSW.

20 Martin Road, 29.i.81
TO JEAN LAMBERT

I have another novel churning round in my head, and must get on with that after this recent warning, but I shall also be ready to answer any of the questions you may have to ask about *The Twyborn Affair*. I can understand the difficulties you are having over 'tu' and 'vous'. Never having had a French lover, and finding the French in France rather standoffish, I have always kept cautiously to 'vous'. I feel you will have to follow your own instincts in most cases in the translation. I think Curly Golson would use 'tu' to his wife; she would vary with him, according to the mood she was in. The same with the Lushingtons when addressing each other. Or don't the French behave like this? I think you are right in what you plan for the Twyborns. Marcia, I feel, would use 'tu' with Eddie when he becomes her lover, returning to 'vous' when he annoys her. I am less sure about Prowse until he becomes Eddie's passive lover. That swimming episode – would he use 'tu'? There are moments when Prowse is full of self-pity and drink earlier on when he might use 'tu', don't you think? and the reader would put it down to paternal feelings for the younger man. But a lot of this you will have to decide for yourself. I don't understand how rigidly the French are governed by formality and how much swayed by sentiments of the moment in their relationships. If Manoly and I used French in conversation I know there are moments when I would switch from 'tu' to 'vous'!

Glad you contemplate coming again to Australia.[79]

Yours sincerely,

Patrick White

Wish we could do that trip to Berry. I am sure there is still a lot I could enjoy inside France, but the edges have appalled me on recent visits.

P.W.

20 Martin Road, 1.iv.81
TO DEBORAH SHEPHERD[80]

Dear Deborah Shepherd,

Sorry about those asterisks. Glaucoma must be to blame. There are moments when my eyes seem to suffer a blackout. I hope all the answers are here . . .

Pp.225–231. This is one of the most important sections in the book and vital to my 'self-portrait'. The Kerrs' behaviour had a great influence

[79]Lambert had visited PW the previous year on his way to Tasmania where his daughter was married to a farmer.
[80]Copy editor at Jonathan Cape.

on me. It moved me farther to the left and made me a convinced republican. I could have said far more about Lady Kerr's activities, and I did not know at the time of writing the extent of Kerr's connexion with the CIA.[81] I discussed the section 'Sir and Lady' with an Australian judge who does not consider I could be sued. He says Whitlam was always being warned by the Attorney-General that he could be caught for seditious libel, but nothing ever happened. (I'd happily go to prison for what I say about the Kerrs because I think it would advance the republican cause.) All Australia knows that Kerr is a drunk. He was photographed lying on the ground at the Tamworth Agricultural Show, and on national television staggering forward to present the Melbourne Cup. The drinking habits of politicians are referred to regularly in the Australian press. However, in the light of what has been happening recently I must add a postscript (?) to this section.

Postscript. In 1981 the Kerrs returned on a visit to Australia where it seems that those who used him in their rise to power are now at pains to rehabilitate him. Kerr may even be canonised. One hears that he aspires to the House of Lords[82] . . .

P.162[83] Don't you know the Maupassant story 'Boule-de-Suif'? During the Franco-Prussian War a coachload of virtuous French bourgeoisie and a prostitute Boule-de-Suif are crossing enemy-held territory on their way from Paris to Rouen. The others deplore and ignore the prostitute, but as they all, including a couple of nuns, grow increasingly hungry, they accept the delicious food Boule-de-Suif offers them from the hamper she has brought along. When they are stopped by a Prussian detachment and taken to the C.O. at the inn which he has made his headquarters, all the virtuous beg Boule-de-Suif to sleep with the Prussian officer, who has taken a fancy to her, and persuade him to release them. Boule-de-Suif does this most unwillingly. The virtuous are overjoyed, but finally settle down to ignoring and deploring again, and forget all about her on arrival. It is a situation I have seen recurring over and over.

20 MARTIN ROAD, 4.iv.81
TO JOSEPH LOSEY
Sid has developed into the great commercial traveller and gravy-train artist. He has an exhibition of large paintings done after a visit to China which

---

[81]The CIA was very unhappy with Whitlam and there are reports that Kerr knew of this, but it has not been established that he acted on 11 Nov. at the agency's behest.
[82]'Sir and Lady' was eventually published uncut with PW's postscript, pp.227–33 in the Johnathan Cape edition.
[83]P.164 as published.

those I go by say are awful. Snippets of gossip appear in the newspapers about the film of *Voss*. The most recent of these said that the film would be made through the South Australian Film Corporation with private money, and Maximilian Schell, Judy Davis, and Lee Marvin in the leading parts, designed by Sidney Nolan – no mention of a director. My agent spoke to the head of the South Australian film body, who says that it is all nonsense . . .

A couple of weeks ago I felt I must speak out about the Australian awfulness or blow up. So I went on the telly and had my say.[84] It didn't come naturally to me, as you might imagine, and was a nerve-racking experience, but since then I have been inundated with letters from people all over Australia who say they think exactly as I do. However, they now seem to hope I may lead them out of the wilderness which, at my age, state of health, and with my rather introspective temperament, I am not capable of doing. My aim was to draw attention to the rot, and if there was any response, perhaps spur on the younger ones to do something about it. I expect, when my book comes out, and they realise they have been spurred on by a homosexual (aren't they usually spies?) a lot of them will think they have been duped. So this is a risk which had to be run.

How I wish I had been born later. I'd have become a film director, one can do so much more about today in a film – or I'd have taken up criminology. As it is, I'm a dated novelist, whom hardly anybody reads, or if they do, most of them don't understand what I am on about. Certainly I wish I had never written *Voss*, which is going to be everybody's albatross. You would have died of him, somewhere in an Australian desert, so it's fortunate you were frustrated.

Do you still have Tyger? We are reduced to one pug, a Jack Russell, and a large mongrel bitch, possibly a cross between a Rhodesian ridgeback and a Labrador, who was dumped in the park across from our house a couple of years ago. We call her Eureka. She has been a great trial, but is coming good.

Yrs
Patrick.

---

[84]'At every level of the power structure we are missing our chances to create a great independent democracy of the South. Everything is done to distract our attention from reality . . . the rape of this country for its mineral wealth regardless of the shambles we'll be left in when foreign interests are appeased and the dollars blown . . .' An interview with Paul Murphy of ABC-TV's *Nationwide*, filmed in Centennial Park and broadcast on 7 March; text, *Patrick White Speaks*, pp.91-2.

20 Martin Road, 12.iv.81
TO PEGGY GARLAND
Dear Peggy,

Your letter about Joyce came a few days ago. It must have been a great shock to you and Betty, although at our age I am more or less prepared for these events, so perhaps you are too in your heart of hearts. With me, I think, death is not the shock, but the loss of a person. It was certainly the most proper way Joyce could have died and I like to think of her soul at peace in the fields.[85] I am going to have my ashes scattered on one of the lakes in Centennial Park because, in the end, the park is the place which means most to me. I hope I shall haunt it, and protect it from tree-vandals and all those who want to build car parks there and turn it into football fields . . .

Lots of correspondence with Cape about *Flaws in the Glass*. There are bits which worry them, but I have said those bits must stay if it is to be published at all. Somebody else will, anyway.

With all these distractions, the novel and the play I am working on flicker only fitfully.[86] Again my chest is mucky, but I don't expect it is in danger while I am taking cortisone – unless it is indeed the plague.

Love from us both –
Patrick.

JIM SHARMAN HAD BEEN appointed artistic director of the 1982 Adelaide Festival and asked White for a play. The result was *Signal Driver*, an essay in White's grim philosophy of marriage: endure everything. There are only four characters: a couple who spend their lives 'just failing to signal the driver and escape from each other and their responsibilities',[87] and two invisible spirits, music-hall clowns who act as White's chorus. Sharman chose as director the young Neil Armfield whose work had a clarity and passion that was rare on the Australian stage. The courage to tackle difficult texts without flinching made him an ideal interpreter of White's writing. Armfield joined Kerry Walker, star of *The Night the Prowler*, in the extended theatrical family of Martin Road. 'Kerro' was the closest to White in his last years: his protégé, a deadpan clown onstage and off, the funniest gossip in his life; a daughter to fret over, to help, to boast to the world. They spoke every few days on the telephone.

---

[85]She walked out into the fields early in the morning and was found dead later in the day beside the stream at Combe.
[86]The novel died in the hubbub at publication of *Flaws in the Glass*.
[87]PW to Falkenberg, 31.iii.82.

20 MARTIN ROAD, 27.v.81
TO KERRY WALKER
Dear Kerry,
When anybody rings from a distance I forget half of what I have to tell . . .

I know it is early days to hear about the play, but I feel depressed and always expect the worst in any situation of this kind. What I fear is that somebody of 26 will not get many of the allusions. Of course I can go over it with him line by line, but that will not be the same.

I read *Prick Up Your Ears*[88] when it came out, and made it one of my books of the year in the *Nat. Times*, to the surprise, I expect, of some of those who follow my advice . . .

I do like Neil immensely, and I'm sure if we go over the play together and we get to know each other better, all will be well.

Sorry the telephoning has been so one-sided. But I don't know when you are not being fêted. Glad you liked *Maria Braun*. Fassbinder is one of my favourite directors; we have the same birthday.

Love
Patrick.

20 MARTIN ROAD, AUG. 81
TO TOM MASCHLER
The novel is coming along by fits and starts. I hope I have the strength to finish it. You don't know about old age until you're into it yourself – the dreadful slowing up process, and always more to do, the letters to answer, the people to stave off. Every other day I'm expected to wave a wand and save somebody or something.

20 MARTIN ROAD, 20.ix.81
TO GRAHAM JAMES[89]
Dear Graham,
Thanks for your letter. *Flaws in the Glass* should appear (strikes permitting) the middle of next month. The thought is a daunting one. I may be torn to shreds, and lose the respect of many I have been supporting. But I feel that unless I wrote the book I could not go on criticising other people, and I want to go out as my true self.

---

[88]John Lahr's 1978 biography of the playwright Joe Orton.
[89](1945–   ), sculptor who began as a designer of furniture and fabrics. PW wished him, 28.xii.69, 'overwhelming success' and over the next eighteen years they exchanged visits and books, and James sent samples of designs, wood sculpture, seedlings, essays and letters.

The red gum you gave us flowered and showed us it is truly red. It is struggling up through surrounding shrubs and will be happier when it reaches the light. The sarsaparilla continues to flower in season, above the vine which covers the trellis, and can be seen best from my bedroom window.

Manoly's arthritic hands and feet are giving him a lot of pain. I have a bad chest, bad eyes, and shrivelling gums! We are all slowing up, but try to keep going. I have a play which will be produced next year at the Adelaide Festival, and am writing another novel.

I've never been to the Victoria Market. If I come to Melbourne again I'll get you to show it to me.

Yrs
Patrick.

20 MARTIN ROAD, 4.x.81
TO TOM MASCHLER
As the publication date hurtles towards me I feel really disturbed. This is nothing like having a novel come out. It opens up a whole new range of dreadful possibilities. I may have a pack of furies on my back. Or on the other hand the enemy may simply encourage it to go off like a squib. At the moment everyone in Australia seems to be writing autobiographies or offering themselves as the subject for a biography. It's become far too fashionable. As for novels I don't think Australians will be reading them by the end of the century, so I have wasted my life and would have done better learning to cook properly in the beginning. Whatever happens, people will always need to be cooked for.

20 MARTIN ROAD, 5.x.81
TO BRETT WHITELEY
Dear Brett,
Thanks for your card.[90] It isn't so much monarchy as that vein of dishonesty from which so many of your acts and attitudes stem. When you asked me to write down my likes and dislikes for <u>you alone</u> before you painted the portrait, and then I found them pasted on the thing itself, that really rocked me, but I swallowed my feelings at the time. However, one sees that this kind of dishonesty is behind everything you do – whether running

---

[90]Inviting PW to a private view of his new exhibition 'Recent Nudes'.

after politicians, Capon,[91] John Laws,[92] Sandra McGrath,[93] or the trendy social world in general. If you go along once to a Royal event, for the experience, you don't go along twice in the light of what is happening in Australia today.[94] In our last conversation you sounded upset because you hadn't been 'honoured', as though it isn't more distinguished to be without honours when half the Australian knights and establishment 'personages' are crooks. At your best you are a genius, but at your worst it shows up too plainly that you are as bad as they.

I find this very distressing in one I wanted to accept as a friend. I'd like to see the new paintings, but shall wait till the novelty has worn off and the trendy scum recedes – unless you have been offended by what I had to tell you.[95]

Yrs
Patrick.

WHITE'S ORDERS TO CAPE were: 'No films, no interviews. If the book can't speak for itself that's just too bad.'[96] *Flaws in the Glass* spoke with a roar when the first extracts appeared in the London *Observer*. White's acerbic comments were quoted in newspapers throughout the English-speaking world. Victims went to ground. Sidney Nolan, forewarned of the book's harsh verdict, tried to have it stopped. But hard as White was on others, he was also brutal on himself. Reviews were good and *Flaws in the Glass* became the best-seller of White's career.

20 MARTIN ROAD, 28.x.81
TO GEOFFREY DUTTON
Dear Geoffrey,
Thanks for your letter about the book. I have been through a time of great tension, and the way some of the press has behaved (particularly the *Bulletin*)[97] has piled it on. Still, I have had wonderful reactions from people

[91]Edmund Capon (1940–   ), director of the Art Gallery of NSW and authority on oriental art whose taste PW did not admire.
[92](1935–   ), poet and broadcaster.
[93](c.1940–   ), author of *Brett Whiteley*, 1979.
[94]The Whiteleys had been for the second time to dinner on the Royal Yacht *Britannia*.
[95]Whiteley defended himself, 9.x.81: 'You make me feel wicked as though I've ripped you off, like Chinese think when you photograph them . . . your fidelity of accuracy is so deeply moving why would you deny another man's attempt to show some truth . . . so you think I'm dishonest I'll just have to reset the computer, and press forget.'
[96]PW to Maschler, some time in Aug. 1981.
[97]Which 'reviewed' the book by quoting thousands of (unpaid) words, 20 Oct., pp.26–30.

who have read it from beginning to end, without picking out the 'scandalous' bits, or looking to see whether <u>they</u> are mentioned. Silly old Donald Horne seems put out that I haven't mentioned him.[98] If the book were an autobiography he would have been, but the Hornes came into our lives late in the piece, and Donald can't be said to have had any influences on my character.

I did say early on in the book that my inability to forgive is probably inherited from my Uncle James, who never came near us again after my mother received him in a sleeveless dress when they returned to Australia after my birth. This inability to forgive is one of my worst flaws, and every time I come to the bit about forgiveness of trespasses in the Lord's Prayer I know I can't pretend to be a Christian – as I admit in the book.

You take me to task about the Nolan passage. Maie Casey rang me up after reading the book and said, 'I'm glad you wrote that about Cynthia. I knew her so well.' Because I felt so close to Cynthia I couldn't ignore what happened. It was the speed with which Sid threw himself on the other one that made it indecent. Nobody expected him to remain unmarried forever. But he is a weak and devious man, and the rot continues. I'm sorry I wasn't able to include the rush to call on Zelly Cohen and then to scratch Charlie's arm at the banquet, leading up to the creation of Sir Ned Kelly Nolan of Hereford U.K.[99]

As for Joan Sutherland, I pay tribute to the voice while depressed by the Ocker in her. Just as Melba was a prime vulgarian with a miraculous voice. (Did you ever hear how an interested admirer asked her what she thought of her fellow artist Caruso, and she replied, 'the best semen I've ever gargled with.')

My life has been additionally complicated by that nuclear disarmament rally I spoke at in Melbourne last week.[100] Letters have been pouring in from people asking what they can do. Somebody said 'if you go down there after *Flaws in the Glass* you won't have any credibility left.' It seems to have had the reverse effect. Some of them came to the meeting bringing *Flaws in the Glass* to be autographed . . .

[98]Asked by the *National Times* why he was not mentioned in the book, Horne replied: 'Maybe he doesn't dislike me enough.' 25 Oct., p.25.

[99]Nolan had been knighted in the Queen's Birthday list; one of his many addresses was a farm in Herefordshire.

[100]Speaking to the inaugural meeting of People for Nuclear Disarmament: 'Today when science has perfected the techniques of destruction, nuclear warfare could mean the immediate annihilation of what we know as civilisation, followed by a slow infection of those who inhabit the less directly involved surface of this globe – as it revolves in space – swathed in its contaminated shroud.' *Patrick White Speaks*, p.102.

Yesterday I did something I really enjoyed. I went to the Art Gallery to choose the paintings for an exhibition they are putting on during the Festival of Sydney in January. I expect it will meet with a lot of disapproval as I am setting out to avoid on the whole the paintings of over-exposed, established painters. It will probably be dismissed as a ratbag's choice. But I was glad to be given the opportunity after Olly Polly's[101] spreading it abroad that I have no taste.

Must go now and cook the tea.

Yrs

Patrick.

20 MARTIN ROAD, 14.xi.81

TO RONALD WATERS

Dear Ronald,

We had your letter, as much of it as we could understand. M. says if only you would type your letters you might reach immortality under your own steam.

The book has been a great strain, but I felt it had to be written. At least Angus Wilson understood what it's about.[102] The dreadful Terry Coleman in *The Guardian* is what you would expect of an Oz expatriate journalist and . . . historical novelist.[103]

Do you remember Boycott at Southwood?[104] He wrote to me hoping he wasn't the Borzoi who had bullied me! Now living in Queensland. A Brigadier. I wrote back telling him he wasn't. Actually Crewe-Read was the Borzoi.[105] I twisted Boycott's tail a bit by asking what had become of his friend Parselle (a Wing-Co, later AVM when I was in the ME.) There

[101]Family nickname for John Olsen.

[102]*Observer*, 1 Nov., p.32: 'But more than anything this short and very original autobiography gives the kind of insight into the significance of a creative artist of an enduring companionship that only a writer of White's stature could offer.'

[103]*Guardian Weekly*, 8 Nov., p.22: 'Mr White admits to bitterness, and it is there – a peculiarly sharp queenly bitterness . . . This is a disagreeable and very disappointing book.' Coleman's 1979 novel *Southern Cross* was praised at the time as 'an Australian *Gone with the Wind*'.

[104]G. P. H. Boycott (1909–   ) left the British Army and came to Australia where he supervised the building of Monash University.

[105]John Crewe-Read (c.1909–79). In *Flaws in the Glass* PW wrote of him: 'I believe he became a general. I wonder whether that narrow, almost fleshless, borzoi skull is above ground, or whether it lies whitening, snapped shut on the last of its vicious intentions.'

used to be a lot of giggling behind Boycott's study door.[106]

We are having a terrible time with Manoly's arthritis. On top of the osteo, he has developed rheumatoid and is in constant pain. Next week he must undergo a complicated blood test. I dread the consequences. Can't go on if anything happens to him.

We now have all the cast (only four), composer and designer for my play which will be done at Adelaide Festival.[107] A young director in whom I have faith. All this would excite me in other circumstances, but I find it difficult to think of anything but Manoly.

What's become of the Brown Cow?[108] Not a word from her since I sent the recipe she was on about. Well, I read she has an earthquake coming to her, as well as Reagan's 'contained' nuclear war.

Hope Fred is not suffering too much,[109]

P.

20 Martin Road, 17.xii.81

TO JAMES STERN

So we stagger on. M. still manages to do a lot in the way of shopping and gardening, but he's no longer able to accept invitations for lunches and dinners, because the pains come on if he sits too long at table, and he can't sit through a play or film.

This is very sad as we always enjoyed doing those things together. I find it difficult to relax, wondering what may have happened, or what may happen next.[110] On top of all this, I seem to have more than ever to do. Every other day I have meetings with theatre people about my new play which will be done at the Adelaide Festival in March. I find this reviving, to be with all these intelligent and enthusiastic young people, but it also leads to a lot of cooking . . .

I doubt I shall write another novel. Have written about half of one, then began to feel the physical effort was going to be too much. Anyway,

[106]T. A. B. Parselle (1911–79), Boycott's fag. 'He was a very good lad,' recalled Boycott. 'We must have had some good laughs in my study, interpreted by PW as "giggling" . . . but we were being looked at by somewhat unusual eyes.' Parselle did not reach the heights of Air Vice-Marshal until 1958 and was later Deputy Air Secretary.

[107]The cast for *Signal Driver* was Kerry Walker and John Wood as the Beings, Melissa Jaffer and Peter Cummins as Ivy and Theo Vokes; with music by Carl Vine and design by Stephen Curtis.

[108]Actress Coral Browne, living in Los Angeles with her second husband Vincent Price.

[109]He had had a stroke.

[110]The intensity of pain abated after a few weeks and the two men were able to resume their old routine.

people will be reading fiction less and less, <u>even if we are not wiped out by a nuclear war</u>. I can't see that anything else matters beside this great issue, and I shall do all I can to rouse people to awareness. The way to do this, I feel, is through plays, films, and public appearances. So I shall carry on like this while I have the strength and if I can develop the right techniques.

I don't think there will be any more travel. The jets and airports were strain enough even while Manoly was comparatively mobile, and I wouldn't want to go without him. There will be plenty to do here while I can be actively involved. I only regret the friends I shan't see again in other parts of the world. In some ways it would be wonderful to have spent one's life in the house in which one was born and avoid so much painful fragmentation.

Love to you both,
Patrick.

20 Martin Road, 30.xii.81
TO TOM MASCHLER AND GRAHAM C. GREENE
One of my doctors had a good idea I should have thought of: to include an x-ray of my chest among the photographs.

FIFTEEN

An Angry Man

February 1982 – December 1984

OFFICIAL ADELAIDE HAD SNUBBED White twice but now he found himself the totem of Jim Sharman's 1982 Festival. *Signal Driver* had its première on the opening night of the celebrations and a few days later two scenes from the opera *Voss* were performed in concert. David Malouf had adapted the novel and Richard Meale was writing the music. White admired the collaborators but after the humiliations of the *Voss* film he feared his 'albatross' of a book would bring disaster on them all. Only very reluctantly did he give permission for these scenes from the unfinished work to be performed.

20 MARTIN ROAD, 28.ii.82
CARD TO ELIZABETH HARROWER
Very hectic. The play is developing well, but I have no idea how it would strike an audience. It tears me to bits, so much of our life in it, and I cry all through Act III, which becomes embarrassing. Melissa Jaffer would be considered a great actress anywhere else. I'm also involved in some film-making in connexion with the Festival.[1] See hardly anyone from the outside world.
    Love
    P.

ADELAIDE, 9.iii.82
TO RICHARD MEALE
Dear Richard,
I went to the concert but did not go round to see you afterwards because I was still sorting out my feelings and was also exhausted after the days of preparation for my play.
    Your music for the garden scene is very beautiful, but more than ever I am convinced you shouldn't have released that fragment on its own. You should have waited till you can present the whole opera, because the excerpt could create a wrong impression. Perhaps I am too close to *Voss*;

[1]*The Hall of Mirrors*, 1982, a documentary on the Festival directed by Scott Hicks.

in any case I am hostile to a novel which has become distasteful to me. The book is austere and gritty, even in that gentler scene – as I remember it. Then the singers were wrong, the man downright bad, the woman too mellifluously perfect.[2] They were like two giant waxworks standing there on the platform. I couldn't imagine them ever developing human passions. No doubt these bad impressions will be corrected when the whole work is heard as opera and not a static concert piece.

You are a composer I admire, so I hope you will bring it off. My disappointment is that you haven't composed a contemporary opera instead of a romantic work based on the hateful *Voss*.

Do you remember those ideas for a contemporary opera I gave you?[3] If you still have those notes could you please send them back to me at 20 Martin Road, Centennial Park, NSW 2021, where I'm returning tomorrow. I want to tinker with, and possibly use those ideas in some form or other.

Good luck with your work.

Always

Patrick.

SPOONER

---

[2]Gregory Yurisich as Voss and Marilyn Richardson as Laura, both praised by the critics in Adelaide – as were the excerpts themselves: 'more beautiful, more grateful for the voices and more genuinely operatic than most people would have dared to hope,' wrote Covell, *SMH*, 8 March, p.8.

[3]Births, Deaths and Lotteries.

20 MARTIN ROAD, 13.iii.82
TO HU WENZHONG[4]
Dear Wenzhong,
Received your letter of 26th Feb – about motivation. Oh dear! I don't know what 'motivated' me to write any fiction short or long; it simply popped out because it had to. (On the other hand I wrote my self-portrait *Flaws in the Glass* to try to show people what I am.) I suppose most of my stories were written while travelling when I couldn't settle down to anything longer.

On looking up *The Burnt Ones* I see that 'The Letters' was published in *Quadrant*. This was in the days of my innocence before I realised that this magazine is the organ of the Australian intellectual fascists. (Needless to say Professor Kramer is devoted to it.)[5] 'Dead Roses' doesn't appear to have been published in any magazine. That is quite in order: if you don't give readers something fresh, they may not buy a volume they see as being full of stuff they have come across already.

If I haven't written any short stories since the two collections, I expect it's because the desire left me – or I stopped travelling.[6]

I don't know whether the structure and scope of my novels is found in my stories as you suggest. A lot of Australian 'experts' have decided I can't write short stories. It depends what you see as a short story. O. Henry is a short story writer. So is Chekhov. For me, two of C.'s greatest stories, 'Peasants' and 'In the Ravine' might be seen as short novels. If *I* had written a story like C.'s 'The Darling' Australian critics would have condemned it as schematic.

The English writer V. S. Pritchett, whom many consider the doyen of short-story writers, recently published an anthology of short stories in which he included my 'Five-Twenty'.[7] Some of the Australian 'experts' were surprised, not to say put out by Pritchett's choice, as I don't belong to the select company of Australian short story writers.

Just back from Adelaide and the production of my new play *Signal Driver*. An exciting but exhausting few weeks.

---

[4](1935–) of the English department of the Beijing Institute of Foreign Languages, translator of *The Tree of Man*.

[5]PW's distaste for Leonie Kramer (1924–) grew out of her friendship with A. D. Hope in the 1950s and her priggish response to PW's novels in the years since. From 1968–89 she was professor of Australian literature at Sydney University and sat for many years on the editorial board of *Quadrant*. The magazine's politics were Cold War – it was at one time financed covertly by the CIA – but its literary taste was merely conservative.

[6]One story had been written since: 'Fête-Galante' begun on Euboea in 1976.

[7]*Oxford Book of Short Stories*, 1981.

Best wishes to you both.
Sincerely,
Patrick.

20 MARTIN ROAD, 21.iii.82
CARD TO CHRISTINA STEAD
Sorry you have had so much illness,[8] but hope things will improve.
Elizabeth[9] says you ask whether I'm happy. Working on my play *Signal
Driver* in Adelaide made me happy, but I can't feel really happy with
Manoly crippled by arthritis and so much nuclear madness around in the
world. I have to speak about nuclear disarmament at the end of a march
on April 4th, and this is hanging over me at the moment, whether I shall
survive the march from Circular Quay to Hyde Park South, then the
speech.[10] By now I've spoken often but each new occasion appals me.
When all this is over perhaps I could pay you a visit if you feel like it.
    Patrick.

JIM SHARMAN STAYED ON in Adelaide to direct the State Theatre Company
which he renamed Lighthouse. He recruited Kerry Walker, Neil Armfield
and others of White's theatrical children. In the weeks after the Festival,
Lighthouse staged a second season of *Signal Driver* and White and
Lascaris flew to Adelaide together for the occasion.

20 MARTIN ROAD, 26.iv.82
CARD TO NEIL ARMFIELD
Thank you for the dinner which all the alarums and excursions prevented
us enjoying in peace.[11] Anyway, thank you now. Back at the Gateway Inn
Manoly just had time to flop down on the dunny before the explosion. I
wondered what had caused it. He said, 'Emotion, I expect.' Quite apart
from the Trucks' display of vindictiveness, *Signal Driver* must have been
an emotional event for him – so much of our life together in it. The
Anzac ceremonies have been less deadly than in the past. Some nice
photographs of old men in their plumes. The anachronism of the British
Empire has never been so plain in spite of the efforts of Governors and

[8]Heart and drink.
[9]Harrower.
[10]The march was 1.5 km; the speech, delivered to an audience of 30,000, was one of the
great performances of these years. In this 'Letter to Humanity' he said, 'Our work will not
be done until we have eradicated the *habit* of war.' *Patrick White Speaks*, p.105.
[11]A difficult occasion from the start: PW and Lascaris left when one of two women, 'the
Trucks', began to fight about a miscalled sound cue.

Generals to revive it. I read that in England girls are wearing the names of battleships on their knickers. And did you see the last word on Australia – the Oz peacekeeping force in Israel upset because the lavatories in their absolution block won't work. Meeting with Le Moignan soon to discuss casting of the soapie – 42 episodes.[12] My new play[13] jerks into action on odd occasions – not this morning, after spilling pork fat all over the kitchen last night. Hope the spellbind goes well for you.[14]

Love

P.

20 MARTIN ROAD, 10.v.82

CARD TO KERRY WALKER

Missed sending the wah for fairies night[15] because my eye doctor, after telling me my eyes had never been better at the last few check-ups, announced last Wednesday that I ought to have the glaucoma op. So now I have to get opinions from other doctors, the whole business disrupting life considerably. That same day my niece Fran came to tell us why she was thinking of separating from her husband of less than two years. Too long and silly to tell you here, but it is another unwanted discussion. Wonder what the Dwarf said about the fairies.[16] You ought to drag him in for a romp-interview onstage, full costume, and he'll be climbing up the Lighthouse for ever after. Have been recommended a housekeeper Mrs Sylvia Cummins.

Love

P.

20 MARTIN ROAD, 20.v.82

TO INGMAR BJÖRKSTÉN

Dear Ingmar,

Thanks for your p.c. and more recent letter. How you flip around the world, I wonder you manage to edit your paper. Frankly I don't much care

---

[12]Michael le Moignan (1947–   ), co-writer of ABC radio's *The Tree of Man*.

[13]*Netherwood* which grew out of PW's rage at the 'fabulously disastrous' idea of emptying lunatic asylums and sending the mad out to live in the community.

[14]Armfield was rehearsing Louis Nowra's *Spellbound.*

[15]Sharman's production of *Midsummer Night's Dream.*

[16]Alan Roberts (1913–   ), theatre critic for the Adelaide *Advertiser*, was frankly unsympathetic to PW's plays and the work of his theatrical family in Adelaide, but he thought Sharman's *Midsummer Night's Dream, Advertiser*, 10 May 1982, p.26, 'a huge success'.

for that interview in the *Advertiser*. The best one was in the Melbourne *Age*[17] . . .

I am faced with an operation for glaucoma which will take place at the end of June. I don't worry about the operation, only the period of inactivity after it. Now I am trying to clear up various bits of work, business affairs and so forth, in preparation. We also have to find a suitable housekeeper.

In speaking about your novel, you say, 'When does one know that something is what one wants it to be?' My answer is, 'Never.'

I shan't listen to your speculations on the next Nobel Prize winner. The winner is usually unexpected. Certainly Canetti was the most unexpected of all – that most unreadable of unreadable *Auto da Fé*.[18] I am amazed that Nad. Gordimer has never been given it, both for her writing and her political stance.

My eyes have never been pale blue – grey green, now going off like the eyes of a stale fish.

Yrs
Patrick.

WHITE TURNED SEVENTY ON 28 May 1982 but was at pains to discourage any public celebrations: there were to be no interviews, no official tributes, no volumes of essays. Despite the edict from Martin Road, Geoffrey Dutton published a chatty, self-promoting essay in the *Bulletin* which ended: 'All of those, not only in Australia, who rejoice in true creativity, in the poetry of the imagination, will be wishing Patrick White well on his birthday.'[19]

[17]Though he had not for years given interviews to promote his novels, PW used them to promote the plays: first, because plays, unlike novels, had no time to find their own audience and, second, because many livelihoods other than his own were at stake. For *Signal Driver* PW spoke to Alan Roberts, Adelaide *Advertiser*, 13 Feb. 1982, p.21, and Melbourne critic Len Radic in the *Age*, 13 March, 'Saturday Extra', p.1.
[18]Elias Canetti, *Die Blendung*, 1935, translated as *Auto da Fé*; he won the Prize in 1981.
[19]1 June, pp.62–6.

20 Martin Road, 30.v.82
TO DOROTHY GREEN[20]
Dear Dorothy,
Thank you for the beautiful card . . . I hadn't expected or wanted people to write about me on my birthday. That is something you leave for Sir Ned Kelly Nolan and Peter Tabu[21] Sculthorpe. The birthday had its pleasing moments, but was ruined by my being told about Geoffrey Dutton's nauseating effusion in the *Bulletin*. That, I'm afraid, will be the end of an increasingly uneasy relationship. I suppose he was piqued by my not writing at length about the Duttons in *Flaws in the Glass*. I often enjoyed their company, but they played no part in my <u>development</u>, except that in recent years they have contributed to my disillusionment in human beings – by their remorseless pursuit of the rich and important, and their inability to see that the Edwardian values of the Dutton tribe don't belong anywhere today. Well, that is that.

20 Martin Road, 30.v.82
TO THE KRIEGERS
Dear Fritz and Ile,
Thank you for your letter.[22] My birthday was rather a chaotic one . . .

Poor Fritz, we often wonder about him living in Melbourne, which he always hated so much – as indeed I do too. At least, we read, you are going to have orange trams to lighten the Liverpudlian gloom.

Today is actually one of light and colour in our garden and looking out across the Park, so I ought to be in a better mood.
Yrs
Patrick.

20 Martin Road, 31.v.82
TO NEIL ARMFIELD
Dear Niely,
Thanks for your letter full of shrieks, tears and other alarums. I don't think you need worry about the evening we spent in Adelaide. As Manoly says,

[20](1915–91), critic and biographer whom PW had mocked with her rival Leonie Kramer as 'the Goneril and Regan of Australian letters'. But from the late 1970s Green became an eloquent exponent of PW's work and after her review of *The Twyborn Affair* he told her, 28.vi.81: 'To my knowledge no one else in Australia has understood it so well.' The friendship that began then deepened when they found themselves working together in the anti-nuclear cause.
[21]*Tabuh Tabuhan*, 1968, for wind quintet and percussion.
[22]After many years' silence.

even the things which went wrong were interesting. I've had a sad letter from Louis about *Spellbound*. I'd be interested to see it.[23] Had thought to come over to that and *The Dream*, but the eye op has put paid to such plans; everything is now geared to that.

Why I am writing so precipitately is to ask whether you would write an introduction to *Signal Driver* explaining the visual changes to the original, so that when it goes out to other theatre companies and for publication by the Currency Press,[24] people can make up their own minds. Tim Curnow[25] says he now has the final version of the script, in which I gather my original visual conception still stands. I now have to look at the script to make sure all our changes to the dialogue in the course of the rehearsal are there, those I feel are most important, because we improved a lot on the original.

Various theatres are interested. I would hold off if there were any chance of our original four playing it. Perhaps, even if they're not in a position to, you might be able to direct the play somewhere on your return.[26]

My birthday went off rather hectically, marred only by that nauseating effusion by Geoffrey Dutton . . .

I was interested to hear Terry Martin[27] and I share a birthday; that must be why I felt drawn to him after the first suspicions. Now I have Terry Martin, Tom Uren,[28] Bea Lillie, Gertrude Lawrence, Fischer-Dieskau, Fassbinder and a woman down the street – don't know what I have in common with her except that her aunt is a Mother Superior.

Look forward to seeing you around the 14th June. That will be during the Film Fest.

You are right about Sylvia Cummins and the Tagliatelle etc. only

[23]PW was an early supporter of Louis Nowra's work. As the crowds stayed away from the Paris Theatre, PW told Dutton, 27.viii.78, 'Louis Nowra's *Visions* is about the most imaginative and wittiest play by an Australian, also very relevant to our national mess though set in Paraguay.' A 1980 letter defending *Inside the Island* from a harsh *SMH* review was not published by the editor, so PW allowed it to be used in advertisements for the production, 6.ix.80: 'I must take up the cudgels again for a play I believe has been mistakenly dismissed . . .' His enthusiasm for Nowra cooled towards the end.

[24]From this time, Currency Press of Sydney published all PW's plays.

[25]Manager of Curtis Brown's Sydney office which handled his affairs after the retirement of Juliet O'Hea.

[26]From a Churchill Scholarship tour of European theatres; on his return Armfield did two further productions of the play – in Brisbane touring to Melbourne, and in Sydney.

[27]Stage manager for *Signal Driver*.

[28](1921–), ex-boxer, POW on the Burma railway and leader of the Labor Left, he organised peace rallies which PW addressed.

she's not cummin; she pulled out to look after a former patient who needs her. Now (we think) we have Ruby Stock, a spry widow from Clovelly. No tagliatelle there either, but perhaps I can give a few cooking lessons. Actually she has a nephew who's a chef in a restaurant. I like Ruby, and she likes dogs, so perhaps it will work out. Don't think she'll want to talk literary, which is an advantage.

Does Sandy[29] know Terry and I have a birthday in common? Tell her if she doesn't.

Must go and look at one of my last experimental dishes. It may be disintegrating. Day after tomorrow I shall be lunching with Michael Le Moignan, the producer, and the director of *Tree of Man* on radio. It could be good if I get the voices I want. Nearly wrecked my eyes reading it. I hadn't read it since it went to the printer, and lots of emotion was engendered by becoming involved with it again.

Love to you and others –
Patrick.

20 MARTIN ROAD, 1.vi.82
TO GEOFFREY DUTTON
Dear Geoffrey,
I was amazed by your effusion in the *Bulletin*, as were any of our friends who have read it. I am told you wanted to organise a *Festschrift* and were choked off by those who knew I would dislike any such carry-on. But the unexpected alternatives – – Manoly and I both squirmed all the way through it, not only for the inaccuracies, but for its silliness and vulgarity. Perhaps you did it out of pique because there weren't references enough to the Duttons in *Flaws in the Glass*, when the book really only dealt with those who were of influence in my development. If I had been writing an autobiography I expect I should have made more of the rich and famous I have met on social occasions around the world. But *Flaws in the Glass* is not an autobiography, and you I should have thought would never have sunk to the level of Andrea and Nola Dekyvere. No doubt the *Bulletin* was thrilled: those dames were pillars of the Packer press, and here is Geoffrey Dutton upholding the tradition.

I'm sorry, but I've had enough of Duttonry, and ask you not to ring me when you fly from capital to capital for what I can't see as any good

[29]Sandy McKenzie, Lighthouse production assistant.

reason. And please let there be no correspondence.[30] As you know, I don't keep letters, but this one will be an exception – to show the curious why our relationship ended.

Patrick.

20 MARTIN ROAD, 19.vi.82
TO RICHARD MEALE
Dear Richard,
I didn't expect you to dash off a letter the minute you received mine. I know you must hate writing them. I have to write more and more letters as time goes on. It grows no easier, and I always have to consult dictionaries.

I'm sure you'll get *Voss* into shape as you're so obsessed with the undertaking. I'm only sorry it had to be *Voss*, which I've grown to dislike so much. I think opera today should perhaps be composed round original ideas, just as it is a mistake to try to film novels; a film should grow out of an original idea. There are many who won't agree with me, and I used to think otherwise.

Anyway, *Voss* is yours to do what you will with it. I hope you have a tremendous success – a success I shall enjoy, even when the members of the establishment, the company directors and their vacant women are madly clapping something they don't understand.

I'm going into hospital for a glaucoma operation at the end of the month. In the meantime, they discovered a wrong rhythm in my heart, and I had to go into the Prince Henry in a hurry to be treated. Drugs didn't work, so they gave me three electric shocks, the last of which threw my heart back on to the right beat. Now it is hoped I shall be able to stand the two-hour anaesthesia for the eye operation. If all goes well, I shall only be bandaged for a few days, but must take it easy for a few weeks after the bandages are off. Even so, they say I shall be able to read and write during that time – and I hope I have wits enough left to think; there's still a lot I want to do.

That piece of Geoffrey Dutton's made us both squirm. It has ended a relationship, and he now says I am swollen with vanity from winning

---

[30]Dutton replied *inter alia*: 'My sole aim in writing that article was to try to show that you were once a humane, generous and even good man as well as a complex artist. I realise now that unconsciously I was writing an elegy . . .' PW also rebuffed Nin Dutton on the telephone. Geoffrey Dutton wrote once more to PW after reading *Patrick White Speaks*, 1989, 'The book brought back a lot of memories. I am thinking in particular of the letter you wrote me which resulted in the end of communication between us. I was enraged at the time. Now I think you were quite right. My life was all wrong, and you had been trying to tell me so for some time.' He did not expect a reply; there was none.

the Nobel Prize – anti-semitic into the bargain. For a long time the Dutton pretensions and two-faced carry-on have been getting me down. The *Bulletin* effusion only brought things to a head, and it's a relief to be free of Duttonry.

Your rain forest sounds wonderful.[31] I wish we could envisage some such paradise for ourselves, but it would be foolishness for two old men to let themselves be lured by the forests and waterfalls.

Yrs
Patrick.

20 MARTIN ROAD, 19.vi.82
CARD TO CHRISTINA STEAD
Thanks for card. Am home again from hospital where my heart was given electric shocks so that it can stand up to the big anaesthetic I must have for the glaucoma op at end of month. Never imagined I had a heart. Hope they don't turn *For Love Alone* into a pretty romance as they did with *My Brilliant Career* – a film phoney in every aspect as I know from working in the Monaro and coming from that kind of family. Of course *MBC* was a nothing of a book, and *For Love Alone* is good, which will make it worse if they muck it up. Don't let them give you a theme song! I still feel rather ghostly after the week in hospital. Trying to keep off alcohol till after the eye operation, which makes life v. bleak indeed.

Love
Patrick.

20 MARTIN ROAD, 21.vi.82
TO PEGGY GARLAND
All this has prevented me concentrating on work. At one stage I wrote about a third of a novel, at another I wrote about half a play. I am toying with a libretto for an opera for the composer who did the music for *Signal Driver*.[32] The opera idea was for another composer originally, but he wanted something romantic, got hooked on the wretched *Voss*, and has now practically finished. The other opera, which pleases me and the other composer, is ribald, satirical, and contemporary. That may make for difficulties with the kind of establishment audience which patronises opera in Australia . . .

---

[31]The composer was building a house in the forest behind Mullumbimby.
[32]Carl Vine (1954–   ), composer and conductor, had written scores for Armfield's productions of *Signal Driver*, 1982–5; like Meale he prevaricated in the face of Births, Deaths and Lotteries.

None of this is of much importance beside the nuclear issue. It is what I have on my mind most of the time. Even the apathetic Australians are starting to take notice. But what with the Falklands and the Middle East I'm afraid we shall have started blowing up the world before we realise.

I doubt I shall travel any more, unless it is suggested that I might in some way contribute something to nuclear disarmament. Otherwise, jet flights and the airports of today are not something to contemplate. Last time we went to Europe we were disillusioned on the whole almost everywhere. I'd like to have explored China and India, but they're too large for one's old age, and I'd like to have been to Russia anonymously. If I went there as myself I'd have to look up some of the writers I've met, and that would mean being dragged to the Soviet Writers' Union for a lot of boozing and hugging.

20 MARTIN ROAD, 23.vi.82

TO RONALD WATERS

We've found a housekeeper we like who came in while I was in the Prince Henry (a stone's throw from Harry Miller)[33] and who will do the same when I am in the Prince of Wales and for a few weeks after I come out. Apparently you can upset the eyes if you do too much too soon.

Harry Miller was guilty all right. Like many others who haven't been caught. Australian society is increasingly corrupt. Manoly was saying today he is sure the only people who haven't accepted bribes are those who haven't been offered them.[34]

We were very shocked to hear that Fred was collaborating with the South Africans. Doesn't he know about apartheid? You old actors of the musical comedy era seem to live in a trance. Your own reaction to Thatcher's war seemed to centre on the lamentable fact that people were no longer going to the theatre. Well, the British have the Thatcher Gang, every bit as Fascist as the Argentinians, they have their temporary false patriotism, and they have the BABY.[35] Soon they'll wake up to the dreadful

[33]In Long Bay gaol.
[34]Miller had faced two trials after the Computicket crash. He was charged first with defrauding his fellow shareholders, the jury failed to reach a verdict and these charges were dropped. At the second trial, Miller faced several charges of aiding and abetting the fraudulent misappropriation by Computicket of its clients' cash. He was sentenced on 30 April 1982 to three years in prison. Miller was never accused of offering or taking bribes.
[35]William, heir to the throne.

truth, I only hope before a full-scale nuclear war is launched. (No doubt all this is as boring as Miriam Karlin.)[36]

That BABY! It's even being sent booties from deepest Australia. There seemed something definitely peculiar about the way the birth was reported. Everyone went in smiling and came out glum. Perhaps Our Lovely Queen just didn't like the other grandparents. Or is it that they've produced the Monster of Glamis . . . ?[37]

My cousin Betty Withycombe turned 80 the other day. Her sister Peggy Garland wrote to me the other day, 'Betty has mellowed, she no longer snaps and snarls at me.' When I told Manoly, he sighed and said, 'Ah, well, we shall have to wait till 80.'

20 MARTIN ROAD, 24.vi.82
TO KERRY WALKER
The Butterley piece we enjoyed,[38] except that before it began an eye doctor I went to years ago, and who went blind, was led past us, and a man in the row in front of us had a heart attack towards the end of *Golden Grove* . . .

Didn't tell you that Tacey the Jungian sent me his essay on my work. Like all such obsessed characters, he tries to tie his subject down in the strait jacket of his system and finds I don't fit. Of course I'm no expert on Jung, only picked a few bits which suited my purpose, just as I've picked a few bits from Christian theology and the Jewish mystics.[39] In the end I

---

[36]The comic actress (1925–   ), an odd obsession of PW.

[37]Glamis Castle, a gloomy house even before the witches bestowed it on Macbeth; seat of the earls of Strathmore, childhood home of Queen Elizabeth the Queen Mother, birthplace of Princess Margaret. The castle administrator reassured me, 29.iii.94, 'There is absolutely no truth in the story that there was once a Glamis monster. The story dates back to the Victorian times . . .'

[38]Nigel Butterley's (1935–   ) *Golden Grove* performed by the Australian Chamber Orchestra was dedicated to PW and Lascaris. At times PW subsidised performances of Butterley's work.

[39]The essay was 'Patrick White: The Great Mother and her Son' which argued 'a classic mother-complex was to be found in the deep archetypal structure of his fiction. There were symbolic incestuous drives and patterns, and there was a longing for ecstatic self-dissolution, a desire to plunge the conscious self into the maternal matrix, in each of the novels . . .' etc. *Meanjin*, Autumn 1990, pp.123-33. This emphasis on his mother's influence PW thought 'radically wrong' and told Tacey, 12.i.81: 'I came to the conclusion some years ago that it was the male parent who had the deeper influence on me. Certainly my mother influenced me in many ways, but after childhood, I admired rather than loved her, and often did not even admire. We were too much alike. That is why we couldn't spend more than a couple of hours in each other's company without fighting, and why I chose to live in another hemisphere.'

shall have seen nothing of the Film Fest. In between hospitals I have been too busy seeing more doctors, and tidying up my affairs. Nearly had a real heart attack on receiving my Income Tax with only two days in which to pay. My cousin-accountant[40] dropped dead two days before my birthday, leaving his partner with everything to unravel. An afternoon of wild telephoning, then a courier called Safe Hands, and nobody will be able to accuse me of tax avoidance . . .

Am told your latest hair do makes you look as if you're being treated for lice.[41] Must try to find a snap of myself taken after I was shorn while on the Sudanese-Eritrean frontier, purely for comfort in the heat and dust storms. Of course the day after I had it done we were posted to Alexandria.

Domestic duties call. Don't yet know how private I shall be at the Prince of Wales, but hope for a telephone somewhere close.

Love

P.

PRINCE OF WALES, RANDWICK, 2.vii.82
TO NEVILLE WRAN
PRESIDENT OF THE ALP.

Dear Neville,

I am writing on the eve of the Conference[42] to express some opinions which I find after some of the other public statements I have made are shared by many of my fellow Australians. We are not necessarily Party members but have supported it loyally over the years, seeing a strong Labor Party as the only hope for this country in the late 20th century. It has seemed more than ever desirable during prolonged inflation and unemployment and the existing government's two-faced, naive, and sycophantic conduct of foreign affairs. Yet from time to time our faith in those we hope will replace the Fraser Government is shattered and we ask ourselves whether the Labor Party is once more preparing to destroy itself even before it is re-instated, when we are in need of unity as never before to face a perilous future.[43] Only unity can produce the kind of strength which is desirable – strength which comes from within, not from powerful allies

---

[40]Bruce Minell of W. Percival, Minell & Co.

[41]Shaved to play Mother Courage.

[42]The ALP's national conference to begin in Canberra on 5 July.

[43]After only twenty months in parliament, the former trade union leader Bob Hawke (1929–) was moving to depose Bill Hayden (1933–) from the party leadership. In this brawl, PW preferred the moderate left Hayden – once a Queensland policeman and later treasurer in Whitlam's government – to the populist, conservative Hawke. Hayden survived as leader of the party and the Opposition until early 1983.

who will butter us up, use us for their own ends, and not be all that helpful when we come to pick ourselves up out of our country's ruins.

Since World War II, we have been set up as a series of military targets. In World War III, Australians cannot hope that time and distance will protect them from advanced nuclear technology. So that we cannot afford to 'soften' the terms on which we treat with allies.[44] There is every reason for hardening them. Nor should we delude ourselves into thinking that a softer policy at home and abroad will attract desirable votes at a forthcoming election or that by ditching one leader for another we shall appeal to more than the odd trendy swinger, impressed by a public figure's 'image', the hair-do and the well-cut suit rather than basic integrity. If we don't search our conscience in the months to come and realise there is more to life than money, minerals, and missiles, we run the risk of offering ourselves for destruction as well as helping to destroy the world. We must remember that the most important issue today is the PREVENTION OF NUCLEAR WAR. It is not that we are greedier than many other nations; it is not that we are blinder to the events of history. Those who are most intent on promoting the nuclear arms race were also responsible for the horrors of Hiroshima. One image in particular from the Hiroshima holocaust seems to me to sum up and warn against what today would be a far more horrific and widespread nuclear situation: that is the figure of a naked man reported standing on a dark plain which had been his city, holding his eye on the palm of his hand. In the light of this symbol of humankind reduced to disbelieving despair, let us not succumb to our own blindness. Let us not 'soften' to gain votes or appease allies. Moral steel could be our most effective armament against political dishonesty at home and the ultimate physical violence which will annihilate the world.

Sincerely

Patrick White.[45]

20 MARTIN ROAD, 27.vii.82

TO DOROTHY GREEN

The eye is making good progress. But I feel rotten as the result of all the things I have to take in connexion with my chest and heart. I imagine

---

[44]The conference was to consider softening the party's radical opposition to the mining and export of uranium. Labor had pledged on coming to government to shut down the mines, repudiate all mining deals and ban the export of yellowcake.

[45]Copies of this letter were circulated at the conference but PW's argument did not prevail: it was decided that on coming to power Labor would allow mining and export to continue but no new uranium mines would be permitted. They called this a policy of 'phasing it out'.

that if only I could get hold of some ancient brew I might dispense with all but the eye doctor.

20 MARTIN ROAD, 5.viii.82
TO NEIL ARMFIELD
Dear Neil,
Thanks for the letter from Avignon which we both enjoyed very much. It made me feel slightly envious though I found Avignon pretty depressing when I went there before World War II (the real meridional horror was Montpellier; I kept awake all night in case I missed the train in the morning.)

I'm still taking pills by the handful and putting in eyedrops every couple of hours. I went again to the heart man last week, and believe it or not, he wanted me to rush straight to the Prince Henry and have some more electric shocks. I refused because I'd planned to make a strudel stuffed with vegetables and a *grüne Sosse*[46] at the week-end. I told him I had to have some little frivolity in my life, and this seemed the only way. I think he thought me completely nuts, though I promised to go for the shocks after my visit to the chest expert and my next to the eye surgeon, if I'm still around.

I still feel pretty feeble at times, but perhaps I'm on the mend as I've gone back to tinkering with *Netherwood*, the play I began someway back. There are moments when I feel it's good, but wonder whether anybody else will. My chief trouble is not to give all the best lines to the Kerro character,[47] when it is a play of equal parts.

We dispensed finally with the worthy Ruby. She was driving us steadily towards an ugly scene. As she chirped away at lunch, M and I sat glooming at each other across the lunch table. We aren't yet ready for being 'looked after' and perhaps never shall be.

There is a big scandal in the Aust. Lit. world – Hal Porter was caught shop lifting! He had bought himself an old house in Ballarat to which he was supposed to retire, but is in fact living with a Sicilian, with whom he is having an affair in spite of a signora and numerous children. The lifted goods were two pieces of fillet steak for himself and the lover.[48] Apparently the Sicilian has a very disapproving brother, so the silly idiot of a randy Porter is probably going to get himself bumped off by the Ballarat Mafia.

---

[46]Green sauce.
[47]Mog, the child-murderer.
[48]Plus two lavender plants and a handful of gladioli bulbs to a total value of $13.50, for which he was placed on a good behaviour bond for six months.

We had a visit from Willy Young[49] the other day and I'm getting some of the Festival photos. He's also taken some of Eureka and one of the icons which Athens has been asking for, to add to the record of Kontoglou who is considered the most important of 20th Century iconographers.[50] Willy is really the most patient creature ever . . .

Today is Manoly's seventieth birthday. Not a very happy one in that he has had to spend the morning in the ultra-violet oven and will have to keep out of natural light for several more hours. Tonight I'm going to try to make a *timballo* of ravioli with a cream and chicken-liver sauce. This sort of thing is my only recreation nowadays . . .

Must begin the last phase of the birthday dish. Wish you were here to try it.

Love,

P.

Did you know the Italians have an annual screaming competition? We've seen a photograph of a 90-year old peasant doing his scream. Manoly thinks I'd stand a chance of winning if I left out my teeth.

20 MARTIN ROAD, 15.x.82

TO ELIZABETH FALKENBERG

The play I started before my hospital antics began dribbling out again. Jim Sharman told me he would like to see it as a possibility for the next season at the Adelaide State Theatre instead of reviving *The Ham Funeral* as planned. So I have been typing away as hard as I could. If there hadn't been this matter of haste I would have written it once more, slowly, by hand, then typed the final version. At least I know the company, and Jim has directed several of my plays. I finished last week, sent it off, and a few days later he rang me to say it had left him feeling rather stunned. If I can stun somebody like that in my seventies, there must be some life left in me. They will do it next June with himself directing. The play is called *Netherwood* and is about the sanity in insanity and insanity in sanity. *Netherwood* is the name of an old house or 'sanatorium' somewhere outside Sydney.

[49]William Yang (1943–   ) had abandoned architecture studies and acting to photograph Sydney. Sharman had made Yang official photographer for the Adelaide Festival; PW was one of Yang's great subjects.

[50]PW and Lascaris had commissioned from Fotis Kontoglou (1896–1965) an icon of 'Manoly's sainted ancestor, Christodoulos' who founded the 11th century monastery on Pátmos. PW added to Dutton, 30.xi.64: 'We are told he had it blessed by the Church when finished, so now we shall have to get Ezekiel [Orthodox Archbishop of Sydney] to decontaminate the house when the icon arrives.'

The man Claasen engaged to translate the remainder of my <u>fiction</u> lives in Hamburg. Can't remember his name offhand.[51] Needless to say he is a Doktor and somewhat *ernst*. They say they don't want *Flaws in the Glass* because it is difficult enough to sell my fiction. That could be. Though it sold well in Australia and Great Britain, it hasn't in the U.S. where the German psyche abounds.

Thank you for the two film books. I shall probably pass them on to Jim Sharman who is an admirer of both those film-makers. I can remember him raving about Fassbinder's *Chinese Roulette* when he saw it at the Sydney Film Festival some years ago. I missed it then, and ever since have been waiting for it to come back commercially, but it hasn't. Perhaps now that F. is famous and dead they will have a festival of his films.

This pure Australia is suddenly riddled with corruption and the reputation of many important characters in jeopardy. They have been getting away with millions in all quarters of the country. Unfortunately the rich and powerful never seem to land in gaol. At the same time there is one of the worst droughts in a hundred years, stock dying, farmers ruined. It rains only on the coast, where there are even floods. We get it every other day in Sydney, almost a heat wave for twenty-four hours, then a freezing gale and lashing rain. A few days ago thousands of shorn, starving ewes and their lambs died of the cold between Armidale and Walcha.

I must say our garden is looking exceptionally beautiful. Manoly is much better and all his energy goes into the garden. His deformed feet, however, are terrible to see. I wonder he gets around.

20 MARTIN ROAD, 8.xi.82
TO DAVID MALOUF
Dear David,
Work of my own kept me from your two new books till recently. Also, I have to confess, some of the reviews and PR deterred me a little. When finally I got down to the books themselves, I was carried away. *Fly Away Peter* is quite devastating. The effect it had on me was so emotional it took my waning eyes twenty-four hours to recover from the explosions. *Child's Play* appealed less, but after the first fifty pages, it got me in. I re-lived many of those Italian landscapes, and found myself becoming both the assassin and the victim. I found myself hating the writer for his ordered

---

[51]Kurt Heinrich Hansen whose translation of *The Twyborn Affair* appeared in 1986. Claasen had already published *Der Maler*, 1970, trans. Wilhelm Borgers and Erwin Bootz, and two translations by Matthias Büttner: *Im Auge des Sturms*, 1974, and *Die ungleichen Brüder*, 1978.

life – daughter, typist, food, peace, quiet etc – when my own life will be a shambles to the end, led between stove and desk, burnt food, and chaotic foolscap.

Are you much influenced by films? I am nowadays in my writing, and I kept on recognising film landscapes in *Child's Play*.

I am much more decrepit than when you were here last. So much of my time is spent putting in eye-drops and taking pills for heart and chest that I don't get about much. Films and plays pass me by. Towards Christmas I shall probably have my second eye op.

At least I managed to finish the play I was working on when the troubles began to accumulate. Jim is enthusiastic, and will direct it himself in June. I hope I shall be able to go over and work with them at rehearsals, but don't know whether I shall escape from the doctors' clutches. Working with the actors on *Signal Driver* I learnt a lot more about theatre, and was able to explain a lot to them. In the past my presence wasn't exactly encouraged.

Looking forward to seeing you when you are next here.

Yrs

Patrick.

20 MARTIN ROAD, 13.xi.82
TO INGMAR BJÖRKSTÉN
Dear Ingmar,
Your Swedes unfortunately arrived on our doorstep during the siesta. I saw them only briefly, toothless and glaring in my underclothes, from a balcony. Manoly got down to the door in time to speak and we hope to see them when they return to Sydney in December. They left a book of wonderful paintings which I feel I know all about though I'm unable to read the text.

Somebody (probably you) once told me that any Nobel Laureate can nominate a writer they consider worthy of the Prize. Now I am nominating David Malouf and sending his best works to date. They include:

Johnno (novel) 1975
An Imaginary Life (novel) 1978
Child's Play (novel) 1982
Fly Away Peter (novel) 1982
Neighbours in a Thicket (poems) 1974
Selected Poems 1981

I am sending the books to you because I don't know whether Artur[52]

---

[52]Lundkvist.

would be up to dealing with such matters since his illness. Perhaps the Nobel people will not find me acceptable since I said one or two things about the Prize in *Flaws in the Glass*, but I am convinced that Malouf is of great literary worth.

My Award for 1982 will be announced next week (someone you may not have heard of).[53]

Hope your own work is progressing.

Yours

Patrick.

20 MARTIN ROAD, 18.xi.82

TO JILL HELLYER

Dear Jill,

This question of 'papers'! I always tell my friends I hope they will destroy any letters I may have written them. I never keep letters (apart from two which I feel should be seen.)[54] I also have it in my will that all unfinished MSS be destroyed at my death, though knowing what people are, I hope I shall have time to destroy them myself.

All this is a personal matter and I leave it to you to decide what you want to do. I'm sure those letters I wrote you are quite piffling and of no interest to posterity.

Yours sincerely,

Patrick.

20 MARTIN ROAD, 20.xi.82

TO DAVID TACEY

You hope I don't feel it is vain of you to ask my advice. I only hope nobody would think me vain enough to encourage someone to publish a book about me. In my youth, when I was ignored, yes. The way things have gone I want nothing of that till after I am dead. Only after a hundred years shall we know whether I am worth writing about.

Yours sincerely,

Patrick White

I find John Barnes' references to your tact in dealing with my 'personal life' unnecessarily coy. I wrote *Flaws in the Glass* to make sure people know

[53]The poet Bruce Beaver (1928–   ).
[54]Final blasts: one of the two was to Dutton, but later PW kept copies of letters to Harry Miller, Tom Uren, Curtis Brown and others.

I am homosexual. Better to come out with it oneself before others have a go.[55]

20 MARTIN ROAD, 21.xii.82
TO RONALD WATERS
Dear Ron,
Happy Chris. if poss. Haven't yet thought what to send you or anybody else. Recently spent a week in bed with a vile chest virus which drove all thought from my head and energy from my body. Am starting to come together again, but the geriatric ailments are climbing up and down in both of us; at least we don't yet wet the chairs . . .

Had a letter from Harry Miller from gaol, saying a lot of what I said to and about him is true, but not all. He is setting himself up as a repentant sinner. Wants to have lunch with us when he comes out i.e. be seen in public with us. I shall have to say I want to see him prove his honesty, and what about paying back the money he embezzled?[56]

Love to both from both
P.

20 MARTIN ROAD, LATE DEC. 1982
TO HARRY MILLER[57]
Dear Harry,
Your letter surprised me. I suppose if I were a Christian I'd take you to my bosom here and now. But I don't profess to be one. The forgiveness bit has always been the stumbling block. I must have very good reason before I can forgive. When you come out, after your favoured treatment the other side of the wall, I shall want to see proof of your reformation. I shall wait for you to pay back the money you embezzled.[58] Nobody apparently expects

---

[55]Tacey was pressing PW for a response to his work, and asking advice about publication. Barnes was an academic whose assessment Tacey included. On failing to get any comment from PW, Tacey wrote in 'The Politics of Analysis', *Meanjin*, Autumn 1990, pp.123-33: 'White's way of responding to my work tells us a lot about his psychic situation.'

[56]Not embezzling, but aiding and abetting the fraudulent misappropriation of more than $700,000 belonging to Computicket's clients. Some of Miller's fellow shareholders had made – in proportion to their shareholding – voluntary repayments to out-of-pocket clients. The law did not compel this. Whether Miller made any voluntary repayments is not clear; certainly he paid nothing to the Australian Opera which had lost $257,812 in the crash.

[57]Draft, found among PW's papers after his death.

[58]Not embezzled: see footnote 56.

you to make material amends. After all, you are still amongst the rich and powerful. Could a man who produces those sumptuous leather-and-gold Dunmore Manilla diaries for 1983 be amongst the bankrupt and repentant?[59] The inner council of the RAS may be prepared to accept you, but I could not until I see you are of a different world.

20 Martin Road, 25.xii.82
TO JEAN SCOTT ROGERS
Dear Jean,

Late this year I was struck down by a chest virus . . .

No more novels – they are too wearing, physically, and I think by now I know how to machine-gun more accurately in the theatre. It's what Australia needs; we've become so rotten – catching up with the rest of the world. Just heard that abominable woman QEII exalting Britain's part in the Falklands War. It seemed from here that Thatcher's Fascist gang was every bit as bad as the Argentinian one.

If you send me your size in gloves I'll try again.[60] Have found a shop that specialises in such things and might even have them at this season in Australia.

Hope the year doesn't turn out as bad as it promises to be.

Best wishes from us both,
Patrick.

20 Martin Road, 26.xii.82
CARD TO SHIRLEY HAZZARD
AND FRANCIS STEEGMULLER
Elizabeth[61] tells me you kindly sent Flaubert's *Letters* Vol II months ago. Not a sign of it here, but we have an abominable postman and a postmaster who seems to have no control over his staff. I hope the book may still turn up, but anything could have happened to it. M. and I have had a year of geriatric ailments, which I expect will increase now that they have started. Best wishes to you and Shirley in a stinking world.

P.W.

IN THE NEW YEAR a fresh complaint appeared in the lexicon of his medical grumbling. No one paid particular attention – a bad back was

---

[59]The diary was a Christmas gift; Dunmore was Miller's cattle property; Miller was never bankrupted.
[60]A long-term project to buy her Australian woollen gloves.
[61]Harrower.

more Lascaris' territory – but back, chest and eyes between them sapped much of White's pleasure in Sharman's production of *Netherwood* in Adelaide and the political transformation in Canberra. Bob Hawke had deposed Bill Hayden and led the Labor Party back into government.

20 MARTIN ROAD, 8.i.83
TO RONALD WATERS
Dear Ronald,
Have you read Louise Brooks's *Lulu in Hollywood*? If not, I shall send it to you as your Christmas present. But I fear you will have read it. To me it's one of the best books, also very disturbing because so truthful. You should also read Tynan's interview with her, but I couldn't send that as I only have the one copy of it. I suppose I could send a photostat of the photostat I was given, but I'm bad at organising such things.

Thank God the holidays are (officially) over, and the fucking Ashes lost or won. Feeling very depressed. Had a bad chest bout before Christmas, and since then have strained my back. There is nothing like a bad back for draining one of energy and willpower. I look like a skeleton probably hiding a cancer ... Will you come here again before we all die? Don't think I could face any more jetting, and those airports, even though we're promised a flat in Albany for our London stay.[62] Have to climb up to the flat. We've been trying to remember why you left that flat with the big rooms and melancholy garden.

Love to both.
P.

20 MARTIN ROAD, 30.i.83
TO JEAN LAMBERT
Dear Jean,
I enclose answers to your queries.[63] I hope my explanations are adequate.

I find it strange that you should think *Flaws in the Glass* more tightly written than anything of mine you have translated. I am always receiving letters from Australians saying the book is so easy to read they must try my novels again.

I haven't allowed them to re-issue *Happy Valley* for two reasons. One I can't tell you,[64] the other is because there are too many influences, too

[62]Graham C. Greene had met PW's near-impossible challenge of finding one of these discreet and opulent apartments off Piccadilly to rent for a few weeks.
[63]About *Flaws in the Glass*; earlier Lambert proposed culling the book; PW decreed, 11.ii.82, 'It is all or nothing.'
[64]He still feared a libel suit from a Chinese-Australian family whose scandals he had drawn on in the novel; but any who might have sued were long dead.

many styles as I cast about trying to find a style of my own.

It is sad the tragedy in Tasmania prevents you coming back to Australia, but perfectly understandable.[65] Your daughter's hope deserves to be rewarded and I hope it will. In spite of the evidence against them, I too believe in miracles.

Manoly and I have had a bad year healthwise ...

How you buzz about – the US, where I never want to go again, and now Egypt, which I must say I'd be curious to see after all these years and the expulsion of the Europeans. My only foreseeable trip is to Adelaide for rehearsals of a new play, Netherwood. I shall go there at the end of April for the first week of rehearsals, and again for the last week and the opening in mid-June. Sharman is directing.

I have also been asked to speak at a gathering of experts on the effects of nuclear war in Canberra in May. Of course I am not an expert, but I shall hope to make a few points as a human being. Nuclear disarmament is to me the only issue of real importance today.

Sincerely,
Patrick

Your suggested title sounds all right.[66] If you want to translate the dedication simply 'à Manoly', so be it. I put 'again' in the original because my first book to succeed (The Tree of Man) was also dedicated to M.

p.1.[67]   women bleeding. Their mouths.
2.   larries=larrikins (Aust. hooligans)
5.   green boy=green-complexioned
8.   [Upper Hunter] The upper reaches of the Hunter River.
27.   Butcherbird=scient. Cracticus torquatus.
35.   boudie caps=boudoir caps
36.   fire in the kitchen. fire breaking out in the kitchen, as it did on one occasion.
57.   The Ham Funeral. The landlady serves ham at her husband's funeral to suggest affluence.
79.   [That exploratory fingernail.] The first glimpse of Betty Field is a long red fingernail reaching out to explore the rim of a piecrust.[68]
91.   [woozy kindness] The English doesn't quite convey what I intended. You might translate it as 'heavily-accented kindness'.

[65]Lambert's grandson had been left brain-damaged by encephalitis, but in 1984 Lambert did make a second trip to Tasmania.
[66]Défauts dans le Miroir.
[67]Page numbers from Jonathan Cape's 1981 edition.
[68]In Of Mice and Men, 1939.

95.   a precinct of rum, bum etc. Bum=arse, implying sodomy.

104.   [hot stuff in the] filter room. Attached to an airforce operations room of any importance there was a 'filter room' which received information on air activity for miles around from radar and observation posts. This was 'filtered' or analysed and passed on to the operations staff to take necessary action. Stockbrokers were often posted to filter rooms because they were quick off the mark sorting out the activities of the stockmarket.

110.   bully=bully beef; the canned variety of corned beef was a great wartime luxury and object of barter.

114.   AOC=Air Officer Commanding.

115.   UNRRA=United Nations Relief and Rehabilitation Administration.

117.   chemical physics. Nobody has ever been able to explain this abstruse subject to my unscientific mind. I only know it has something to do with engineering in its higher reaches.

121.   Pongo officers=Army officers.

130.   Paspalum=ergot-bearing pasture grass, native of South America. There is a theory that pregnant women who drink the milk of cows grazed on paspalum are prone to miscarriages.

Patterson's curse=scient. *Echium plantagineum*. Has a pretty purple flower, but is inclined to take over vast stretches of country if allowed to have its way.

wax-infested: a soft, reddish, sap-sucking insect lives and lays its eggs beneath the sticky white, wax-coated covering.

NB 136.   Some mistakes have been pointed out to me on this page. l 6. *Sleeping Cypriot* should read *Sleeping Greek*, and *Billy Budd* should read *Billy Boy*. Likewise l 7. should read *Sleeping Greek* instead of *Cypriot*.[69]

148.   minpin=miniature pinscher.

159.   Agatha Christie had gone missing. A police search had been laid on, until she turned up at that Harrogate hotel suffering from amnesia. I believe the explanation (not to be mentioned here) was that her husband was leaving her for someone else and that at some time or other he had stayed at this same hotel with the other woman.[70]

179.   glam'rous Turkey. Can't find it on this page, but know I use it somewhere.[71] During the Thirties there was an American who did very banal screen travelogues which always ended with, '– –and so we bid farewell to glam'rous Wherever.' His name was James Fitzpatrick.

[69]Both paintings by Dobell.
[70]PW believed he and his family were in the hotel at this bizarre moment in early Dec. 1926. Perhaps, but the winter term had not ended at Cheltenham.
[71]On p.170.

173. *donner kebab*: Turkish origin. Rounds of boneless lamb interspersed with fat from the tail are loaded on to a vertical spit which revolves before a charcoal fire or electrically heated elements. As the lamb cooks, slices are carved off for customers.

181. key pattern=the Greek key pattern which one sees on urns and on the garments in ancient friezes.

203. *mezé*=hors d'oeuvre.

221. [We saw some of her.] We saw some paintings of her.[72]

223. Giant mushrooms: the blurred faces of an audience looking like huge mushrooms.

232. Balmain: a Sydney suburb inhabited by workers in the days of Kerr's father, but now become very trendy.

237. [Alice from Bootle had rootled with a safety pin.] Betjeman's poem *The Flight from Bootle* begins:

> Lonely in the Regent Palace,[73]
> Sipping her 'Banana Blush',
> Lilian lost sight of Alice
> In the honey-coloured rush.
>
> Settled down at last from Bootle,
> Alice whispered, 'Just a min,
> While I pop upstairs and rootle
> For another safety pin.'

The implication is that she will have another try at getting herself an abortion.

[incompatible guardians] incompatible=disapproving.

238. Ocker=aggressively Australian.

240. [not taken one in months] When upset he used to rush and take another valium.

248. [drorings] Australian pronunciation of 'drawings'.

254. Pansy has a pronounced vulva, hooded in shape, which might look as though she has balls.

255. the exotics=Jews, Lebanese, negroes, a Japanese lady, and a Portuguese from Macao.[74]

dashi=stock basic to Japanese cooking.

---

[72]The Queen, of Eliza Fraser: 'The Naked *Lady*!'
[73]The London hotel where Cynthia Nolan committed suicide.
[74]Neighbours in Martin Road.

20 MARTIN ROAD, 12.iii.83

TO PEGGY GARLAND

Dear Peggy,

We received your letter about David not long before he was due to arrive, and his own the day before his arrival. I'm afraid we can't ask people to stay and look after them as we used to. Nobody seems to realise that we have aged since they saw us last though they should from their own ageing. David spent an evening with us and we much enjoyed seeing him. I always thought him the best of your children and his recent visit confirmed this (I remember you saying rather pettishly when he was a boy, 'My silly old David, he'll probably become a farmer.' How much better than a genius, and now, best of all, he's a mature, responsible human being. I hope his trip to N.Z. is rewarding and that he and Sarah will be able to find peace there for a few years.)[75]

Half the people we know in the Northern Hemisphere have been turning up here – two unconnected octogenarians since David. It has been a great strain, wondering whether they are going to fall down, have strokes, or die. You can't tell them nobody should come to Sydney between Jan and April because of the vile weather. This year has been exceptionally vile, what with the drought, bushfires, and dust storms. A few days ago we had 40°, followed by a cold change and gale in the evening when the temperature dropped to 24°.

You would be crazy to sail up the Nile at your age, or set out on a long trip anywhere at any season. You can't imagine what the crowded planes or the airports are like. I have no desire to travel again – and where? Certainly nowhere I have known to contemplate the awfulness of 'progress'.

At least our election has gone the way we wanted. We are rid of that lying bastard Fraser, but the Libs have left us with such an enormous deficit (concealed before the election) life is going to be very difficult for the ALP. Hawke is flash, but right for Australia.[76] Hayden is the one I have always admired and supported. He will now become Foreign Affairs, and won't shame us when he goes into the world.[77]

---

[75]But Garland decided not to move to New Zealand after this exploratory visit and his career in Britain then flourished with his first one-man exhibitions of pottery in the Crafts Council Sideshow at the Institute of Contemporary Arts in 1983, and of paintings at the Oxford Gallery, Oxford, in 1984.

[76]PW's approval did not last; Hawke was prime minister 1983–92.

[77]After a successful stint as foreign minister, Hayden became governor-general in 1988 despite PW's public plea: 'Bill, don't do it!'

Although I preach non-violence I wish somebody would shoot that Thatcher monster.

Shall answer Betty's letter in time. Amazing that she can still write.

Love,

P.

ADELAIDE, 3.v.83

CARD TO ELIZABETH HARROWER

First reading yesterday – a nightmare, but expect it will come right . . . A deluge last night. Fortunately able to stay at home and pull the blankets over my head.

Love

P.

20 MARTIN ROAD, 28.vii.83

TO JOSEPH LOSEY

Dear Joe,

It's a long time since your letter (perhaps two) and birthday wishes were received, but I've had a busy few months ending with a vile bout of bronchial 'flu. I don't know how far up to date you are with the *Voss* news. When Harry M. sold the rights they were bought, supposedly, by a mediocre director of Canadian or American origin called Stuart Cooper. I have never been allowed to see his films.[78] It finally turned out that Cooper was only a front for Sir Ned Kelly Nolan, the Irish Ascendancy peasant knighted by the Queen of England. Neddy Nolan has it in for me for what I said quite truthfully and in a dignified manner in *Flaws in the Glass*. He began braying intolerably throughout the Australian press, exhibiting caricatures of Manoly and me, including drawings in which we are consigned to Dante's circle of purgatory reserved for sodomites.[79] None of these

[78]Cooper (1942–   ) had done the deal with Nolan's backing making the painter, in effect, producer of the *Voss* project. PW's contempt for the American was misplaced: Cooper had a number of films to his credit including *Little Malcolm and His Struggle Against the Eunuchs*, 1974; a semi-documentary on D-Day called *Overlord*; and *The Disappearance*, 1977, starring Donald Sutherland and David Hemmings. All plans for *Voss* have, as at 1994, come to nothing.

[79]'Nightmare', a diptych depicting Lascaris as a dog/pig pointing his arse at PW was exhibited at the Perth Festival in 1982; the drawings based on the *Divine Comedy* were shown in May 1982 at the Rex Irwin gallery in Sydney; about a quarter of the Rimbaud series at this time were related to PW – the whole series was recorded in Malcolm Otton's 1983 film, *It is of Eden I was Dreaming*.

travesties sold, and he has done far more harm to himself than to us. His talent has left him, he is permanently drunk, and full of delusions. One of these is that my veto on the director of the *Voss* film is not valid if the film is made outside Australia, and he has announced that it will go into production next year, probably in Libya, with a German actor playing Voss and Italian financial backing. Nobody in the film world has heard about this project, and probably it won't advance beyond the fantasies in Sir Bonkers' mind. I certainly continue to hold the veto wherever the film is made.

I made trips to Adelaide in May and again in June for a new play, *Netherwood*, which Jim Sharman directed at the State Theatre.[80] In between there was a session in Canberra where I read a paper at a conference organised by the National University on nuclear war and disarmament. It was an alarming experience, myself the innocent amongst a lot of scientists from America, Britain, Russia, a Greenie from West Germany, and a very impressive American ex-Army officer called Hackworth, who went through Vietnam, renounced the States and came to live in Australia. He is a contemporary of the Army officers now advising Reagan, and is said to be the inspiration for *Apocalypse Now*[81] . . .

Neither *Signal Driver* nor *Netherwood* stands much chance of being seen in my native city as I am bad at doing the right thing by the wrong people.[82]

My novel *The Tree of Man* has been adapted as a radio serial; the first of forty-two episodes will be broadcast this evening. So I haven't been altogether idle, though I have to confess it is all pretty wearing and I shan't mind when the time comes for the journey to the crematorium if we haven't already gone to ash in a holocaust.

I wonder how you find Thatcher's England. I have no desire to go

---

[80]Reviews were mixed. Though an evangelist for PW's early plays, Harry Kippax wrote of *Netherwood*, *SMH*, 14 June, p.8: 'There is potential conflict in plenty . . . but in the upshot it is asserted, illustrated and dissected, not dramatised.'

[81]This speech, 'Australians in Nuclear War', had the greatest impact in White's public-speaking career: 'I feel it all starts with the question of identity . . . Australia will never acquire a national identity until enough *individual* Australians acquire identities of their own. It is a question of spiritual values and must come from within . . .' *Patrick White Speaks*, p.113.

[82]The Sydney Theatre Company, unimpressed by *Signal Driver* and *Netherwood*, did not take up the plays. PW thereafter vilified the company, its artistic director Richard Wherrett and the Sydney critic Harry Kippax. PW wrote to Meale, 3.vii.83: 'I can make no headway in my native city, at least for the moment.' As it turned out both plays *were* later seen in Sydney.

there again or to any place we knew in the past. Our last trip was too disillusioning. In any case, I couldn't stand those jet flights, even more, the hellish airports.

Love to Patricia, Tyger, and yourself, in which Manoly joins me.
Patrick.

20 MARTIN ROAD, 7.viii.83
TO JULIET O'HEA
I suppose I've had worse attacks in the past, but this one seemed particularly vile, perhaps because I'm that much older. Now I'm feeling alive again, doodling fitfully at another play . . .

Don't think I'll write another novel. I read reviews of brilliant <u>sounding</u> novels in the *Observer*, so your remarks on the state of fiction surprise me. However, most of these reviews of brilliant novels leave me thinking So what? Actually the only thing of importance today is the nuclear issue and how we can stop the war which is threatening . . .

Before World War II I explored Annecy, Chambery, and those parts, finding them rather chaste and chilly. I used to prefer the Southern parts of France, but from what I've seen of them in recent years they haven't much of their charm left. If one must travel today, never go back to places one has known.
Yrs,
Patrick.

20 MARTIN ROAD, 27.viii.83
TO RONALD WATERS
Dear Ronald,
Your last letter was almost the most undecipherable so far. As it gave me particularly interesting glimpses here and there, it was more than maddening. Why do you persist in pursuing this affectation? Fred, Mrs Browne Price[83] – everybody deplores it.

Expect Desmond will have been in touch with you by this about the Oz Opera's abysmal plan to produce *Fiddler on the Roof*. Now that they have sunk so low as that, it won't be long before the Dame[84] is doing *The Maid of the Mountains*.

I am planning to send you a tape of a speech I made on Nuclear war a few months ago at the national University in Canberra. Hope you will have something which can release it. I share the tape with a doctor who

---

[83]Coral Browne.
[84]Joan Sutherland.

carries on about sex education. I haven't heard it, but he may steal the show.

Went to Brisbane for the opening of my play *Signal Driver*. The same production now goes to Melbourne. Same director as in Adelaide, but the set and some performances much better. My last play *Netherwood* crashes into Sydney despite great opposition during the Festival of Sydney in January. At present I'm writing another one.[85]

Had a terrible bronchial 'flu earlier this month, thought I was going to die, and now Manoly is going through bad gastro troubles. You two seem very healthy compared with us.

Love,

P.

Let Jean share the tape.

ANDREAS PAPANDREOU, PRIME MINISTER of Greece, invited White to celebrations marking the tenth anniversary of the student occupation of the Athens Polytechnic, an heroic episode in the fall of the Colonels. White went despite the risk of bronchial complications, flying from a Sydney summer into an Athens winter. The European journey he refused to make to collect the Nobel, he was willing to risk on behalf of Greece, his 'other country'.

20 MARTIN ROAD, 25.xi.83

TO DOROTHY GREEN

The expedition to Greece could well be my last Great Experience. I wouldn't knowingly undertake anything like it again, though I wouldn't have missed it. My fellow traveller from Australia was a representative of the Waterside Workers from Melbourne called Ted Bull, an exceptional man of 70. I'd say completely honest – intelligent, simple, yet in some ways surprisingly sophisticated. It was a relief to find oneself going on a long journey with somebody one could like and admire, and whose views are mostly shared.

The nine days in Athens were pretty well filled with official functions, though there was enough free time for me to spend with Manoly's two sisters and brothers-in-law, also an old friend Robert Liddell, whom we knew as far back as Egypt. It will probably be the last time I see Robert, now 80, and one of the brothers-in-law, Dimitri Photiades, the historian, well into his eighties, and writing twelve hours a day to finish his memoirs. Over the years D. was banished several times to rocks in the Aegean.

[85] Abandoned.

Gough arrived from Paris for one night of the recent celebrations. Usually too many people have been making a fuss of him and it hasn't been possible to talk, but on this occasion my only rival for his attention (a pretty considerable one) was the excellent food of the Grande Bretagne, and we had quite a lot of interesting conversation. Then Papandreou began advancing through the guests preceded by a moving wall of photographers, backing on to one's corns if one didn't step aside. Of course P. was able to spot Gough above everybody else, motioned to the photographers to make way, and the meeting of the two great men took place. Then, to our surprise, Papandreou beckoned to Ted Bull and myself. We joined them, and the four of us were photographed together. I must get hold of a print of this and force it on the odious Fairfax Press.

The last night there was a march of a million Athenians through the city, all ages, sexes, banners high, lots of red flags, voices chanting. Not only were they commemorating the original appropriation of half Cyprus by the Turks and the uprising of the Athenian students, but they were protesting against the latest Turkish outrage in Cyprus. That morning there had been the murder of an American naval commander near one of the American bases on the outskirts of Athens (the assassin unknown) to add to what was already quite an inflammable situation. It was a bit of an anticlimax to look out the window next morning and see the black figures of normal human beings trotting to work through the drizzle under their umbrellas.

Later that day the wet season began in earnest: steep streets became torrents, and on level ground, the potholes turned into a series of dangerous lakes. I spent the afternoon in bed, to be ready for departure at 2 a.m. I expect all this, and floundering to Elly's through rivers, lakes and dark, for a last supper (no chance of a taxi) brought the bronchial troubles on.

I should really sit down and try to sort out all that happened during those nine days – write about them and the people I met – Hugh Greene of the BBC,[86] the Abatielos,[87] an Italian Communist leader imprisoned for 12 years under Mussolini,[88] Alexandra Fleming,[89] Mercouri,[90] the wife of a minister in the present Government who told the Junta she would rather

---

[86]Greene (1910–87), father of PW's publisher Graham, was director-general of the BBC 1960–69 and engaged by Papandreou's government to write a report on broadcasting in Greece.
[87]Immensely rich Greek shipowners.
[88]Giancarlo Pajetta (1911–86).
[89]Amalia Fleming, Greek political figure and widow of Alexander.
[90](1925–94), actress, deputy for Piraeus in the Greek parliament and minister for culture and sciences.

be locked up with the prostitutes than with the women Communists.[91] All
sorts!

How much we deserve, who haven't yet had anything but the
Depression. Hawke seems to change his coat on alternate days. I wonder
how many of those he is trying to charm and impress in Delhi are taken
in one bit.[92] Would give anything to have watched and listened to his
session with Thatcher and Our Lovely Queen; the snob might have been
less crushing than the kind lady, but perhaps his skin would have been
too thick to realise.

After the nightmare city Athens, the traffic noise, cars driving straight
at pedestrians, polluted skies, strained, desperate faces, the peace and beauty
of our garden is hardly credible. Instead of screeching metal, the sound of
cicadas and crickets, birdcalls, nesting doves and bulbuls, a brilliance of
sky and flowers, and one of my favourite sights, bark shredding from
angophoras and the lemon-scented gum.

I hope you will soon be back in your own garden and well enough
to look after yourself. Manoly and I both find it very trying to be 'cared
for'.

Yrs
Patrick.

20 Martin Road, 17.xii.83
TO FRITZ KRIEGER
Dear Fritz,
Manoly and I were most upset to hear about your ailment[93] from Maurice
Joseph when I went to him for a check-up on returning from Greece last
month. Having to go to a hospital must be the worst part of it, as I know
from being in so many. However, I hope they are looking after you well
wherever you are. I am very bad at being looked after: when I came home
from an eye operation some time ago, I had to have a cheery soul to look
after me, and found it very painful in my own home. So it is better,
perhaps, to be looked after in a hospital.

Mollie Glover is at the Mowll Village.[94] She fell and broke a bone
in a hip. She had to spend some time in hospital, but is now back in the
room she normally inhabits. We ought to pay her a visit, but I find it

[91]Unidentified.
[92]Hawke was in Delhi for the meeting of heads of state of the British Commonwealth.
[93]Alzheimer's disease.
[94]An Anglican retirement village of great respectability which became the Sundown
Home for Old People in A Cheery Soul.

painful to return to Castle Hill. Passing through it on the way to somewhere else is bad enough. The Josephs try to coax us to visit them, and I think can't understand why we are unwilling to accept; they themselves are so free from complications. Anyway, Manoly's arthritic feet won't allow him to undertake long drives, and he never drives at night now that his eyesight is deteriorating.

We are cracking up at a great rate, when here I should be writing you a horribly cheery letter! But I'm sure you would prefer reality to pretence.

Sooner or later I expect I shall be in Melbourne for something unavoidable. I shall get in touch with Ile and hope to see you if you feel like it.

Regards from us both

Patrick

Years ago when Manoly returned to Greece briefly to exorcise his homesickness I had come home from seeing him off. I was desperately miserable on finding myself alone, in the evening. I ran down out of the house where the Cecile Brunner rosebush grew against the veranda. I saw through my tears that you were standing at the front gate. You melted away on seeing what the situation was. Whenever I remember this incident I feel most grateful for your kindness and consideration.

AUSTRALIA'S ANTI-NUCLEAR MOVEMENT grew as Labor's resolve to end the export of uranium collapsed. The radical policy of shutting down the mines had given way in 1982 to the softer policy of 'phasing it out' which would allow the export of yellowcake from Australia to continue almost indefinitely. But an incoming Labor government was pledged never to permit new mines. Soon after taking office in 1983, Hawke's government gave permission for an immense new uranium mine at Roxby Downs.

White's faith in Labor's leaders never recovered from this blow. He accused the government of turning its back 'on the most important moral issue in history';[95] he lobbied Australian politicians and admonished the leaders of the West; he was drawn into discussions that led to the formation of the Nuclear Disarmament Party; to this fledgling he contributed $10,000 and valuable public support. Busy as he was this winter with these political chores, White began to draft his last novel *The Memoirs of Many in One*.

[95]'In this World of Hypocrisy and Cynicism', *Patrick White Speaks*, pp.152–8 at p.157.

My Day by Patrick White  Victoria Roberts

I RISE WITH THE BIRDS...
AND THE DOGS.

MIND YOU,
I'M LESS
VAIN SINCE
LOSING MY
TEETH.

I LOOK OLD — THE
PRICE A NOVELIST PAYS
FOR LIVING SO MANY
LIVES IN ONE BODY.

EXOTICE!

NOT MUESLI
AGAIN!'
I WANTED
BOUREKAKIA.

A SOLID BREAKFAST FOR
MY SOLID MANDALA.

SO THAT, IN
THE END,
THERE IS
NO END.

I WAS DRAWN TO GREECE
FROM A DISTANCE AND
ONE GREEK IN PARTICU-
LAR. THE GREEK FATALI-
TY IS ALSO MY OWN. I
DO THE DISHES.

THERE WOULD
BE NO LIFE
OR WORK IF
I SAT AROUND
DISCUSSING
THESE!
SHOOO!

MISOGYNIST!

AN INTRUDER— WORSE! A
JOURNALIST! IT WANTS TO
DISCUSS MY LIFE AND
WORK. THAT'S WHAT I
GET FOR WINNING THE
NOBEL PRIZE.

32½ INVITATIONS
TO LUNCH, AND
HOLIDAY ON ICE'
WANT TO DO
VOSS!

EXTRAORDINARY MAIL. IF
I HAVE NOT LOST MY MIND
I CAN SOMETIMES HEAR
IT PREPARING TO
DEFECT.

NUNS FART. WHY,
EVEN
STRAVINSKY...

I FINISH THE VACUUM-
ING AND CONCENTRATE
ON MY FAVOURITE
SUBJECT—
DECAY.

SEE YOU UNDER
THE PERGOLA-
SOON!

BLAH

SLAM

BLAH

THE PURITAN IN ME WRES-
TLES WITH THE SENSUA-
LIST. THEN THE PHONE
RINGS. I LOVE THE
PHONE ALMOST AS MUCH
AS I LOVE MY PRE-LUNCH
VODKA.

HE'S PAINTED YOU AS
HALF-PIG, HALF-FLEA,
AND NEVER MIND
WHAT HE'S DONE TO
ME!

NASTY SIR NED KELLY NOLAN
OF HEREFORD, U.K., HAS
BEEN BEHAVING IN THE
MOST EXTRAORDINARY
WAY. MUST BE A SIDE EF-
FECT OF HIS IRISH CHARM.

HOW COULD SID BEHAVE
SO ABOMINABLY! AND
HOW COULD I NOT IN-
CLUDE THIS IN MY
AUTOBIOGRAPHY?

BUT I RECOVER, AS FROM
ALL THE CUPS OF VINEGAR
I HAVE BEEN FORCED TO
DRINK IN LATER LIFE...
EARLIER LIFE... MIDDLE
LIFE.

I LOVED YOUR CHARIOTS
OF FIRE'

I RATION MYSELF SOCIALLY—
ONE GALLERY OPENING FULL
OF OUT-OF-THE-CUPBOARD
QUEENS AND PEOPLE TO
WHOM ONE SAYS "HELLO"
AND "GOODBYE"!

GOD GAVE US MEAT. WE
HAVE TO GO TO THE
DEVIL FOR SAUCE!

SPAGHETTI ON A STEAMY
SYDNEY SUMMER'S EVE.
I REMEMBER MY MOTHER
RUTH AND HOW AFTER
TEN YEARS OF CULTIVA-
TING HER FIGURE, SHE
FINALLY TOOK TO TUCKING
IN.

20 Martin Road, 1.v.84
TO DOROTHY GREEN
Dear Dorothy,

I thanked you for sending *The Music of Love*,[96] but am ashamed not to have written since reading it, to express my admiration for your scholarship, and far more important, the sensitivity which makes you, as far as I know, the only creative Australian critic. I particularly liked the article on Louis Stone – I discovered *Jonah*[97] just after World War II, and it became one of the reasons for my returning to live in Australia – Grant Watson, of whom I had never heard,[98] and the background to *On Our Selection*. Oh, and lots of other things! Martin Boyd, I must confess, I've always found a bit watercolour . . .

There is so much I would like to write you. I have bought copies of Allan McKnight's *The Forgotten Treaties*[99] to send Australian politicians as well as Reagan and Thatcher. I thought I should start with Hawkie, but keep tearing up the letters I scribble. It is so difficult to write to somebody one can no longer respect, but cannot dismiss, because the alternative would probably be as bad or worse. One cannot let him see this, however – only suggest he is in danger of losing support from those who elected, not necessarily the panjandrum he has become, but the ALP.

I received yesterday from the Party an invitation to a fund-raising dinner – $150 a head with an additional $150 for a partner of any kind – to meet Hawke and Keating.[100] That morning I had sent my winter contribution to the Smith Family.[101] Perhaps I was feeling smug. I longed to reply that I felt it more important to see that the needy were clothed and fed than to spend evenings guzzling with a lot of cockahoop politicians and their sycophants . . .

As we were going out last night, Michael Denborough rang and we

---

[96]A 1984 collection of her essays and literary criticism.

[97]Stone's 1911 novel about a Sydney larrikin's unhappy rise to success.

[98]English biologist, writer and mystic (1885–1970) who wrote several novels set in Australia; Green championed his claim for recognition as a pioneer in Australian literature for recognising the creative possibilities of the continent's desert emptiness.

[99]A draft treaty and commentary by McKnight (1918–   ), an Australian lawyer, prepared for the UN Association of the UK as a possible basis, 'for negotiation between the super-powers on the practical level of how to dismantle the horrendous war machines which threaten our continuation as a species, and how the dismantlement might be verified to the satisfaction of both parties'.

[100]Paul Keating (1944–   ), Treasurer, sophisticated machine politician and later prime minister.

[101]$20,000.

had a short conversation about his Plan, which he says you support.[102] I agree that an alternative is needed, but it must be given a lot of thought. Who would lead a new party? I was given no real clue, and unless we can unearth a skilful, and <u>selfless</u> ringmaster we shall end up with another circus in which a clown has grabbed the spotlight for himself.

I'd welcome a government with a firm, honest anti-nuclear policy, but if we can't be sure, it's better to work on the present one with every threat and any kind of blackmail we can think of.

P.

IN LATE MAY, 1984 White wrote open letters to the presidents of the United States and France, and to the prime minister of Great Britain pleading the cause of nuclear disarmament. Each letter was addressed to a major newspaper; none was published.

SYDNEY, 29.v.84
AN OPEN LETTER TO PRESIDENT REAGAN
Dear President Reagan,
In case you have not come across *The Forgotten Treaties* by the Australian lawyer Allan McKnight I am sending you a copy. It is a book which should be known to yourself and those other supercreatures who in their desire to dominate the world could be racing it towards extinction. Friends who are unwilling to bestir themselves or think about the consequences of nuclear war say to me: what can a single individual do to stop the arms race? Yet they and you must be aware of the increasing numbers of single individuals in both hemispheres clustering together in masses to oppose their leaders' recklessly aggressive policies.

I followed your visit to China with interest. Your progress was charmingly superficial, but no doubt your Chinese hosts have noticed your taste for the trivial. Sumptuous banquets, dancing, and a few squirts of milk from a baby panda's bottle do not exorcise suspicion, while your promises of technological assistance could help in furthering global war. The baby panda's milk, however, could be a form of purification ritual, and for the world's sake I hope it is.

When will you visit Russia, Mr. President? Surely that should be your first priority, not the trip to Ireland, a nostalgic but comparatively trivial junket. Incidentally, I am told your great-grandfather's birthplace was

---

[102](1929–), director of the ANU's Centre for Resource and Environmental Studies; he organised 'The Consequences of Nuclear War' conference and was now taking the first steps to establish the Nuclear Disarmament Party.

Ballyporeen – in English 'Home of the Small Potato'. But Russia– – Why not face up to that vast land where the fear and suspicion of its leaders matches your own? Initiate a confrontation between the celluloid hero and the jittery bear. You might start something constructive. Though I believe nothing much can be achieved till there is a free flow of ordinary people between the two countries and you discover that most of you are human beings after all. Come on, cowboy! Get it going! Or are you afraid the ordinary Russian people who have suffered the agonies of war on their own soil might indoctrinate Americans with a reality too bitter for them to take? Personally I feel the greatest danger is that ordinary Russians might be seduced by the appliances, the junk food, the cars, and drugs which have softened up Americans since the tough days of their founding fathers, and later, when men like Emerson and Thoreau offered their brand of moral guidance.

I know something of your country from before World War II, and have visited there several times since the takeover by celluloid, plastic, and decadence. I got to know it the railroad way, from Maine to New York City, down to the South, across Texas to the promised land of California. I remember the patient negro car attendants, conversations into the night with naive middle-aged, middle-class citizens. I gather the railroads don't count for much any more – unless when the Long White Train rides, carrying its load of nuclear warheads across the continent to the Trident submarines at Seattle. Some of those concerned with the continuance of life, ordinary Americans, and a handful of Buddhist monks, lay down in front of the death train.

Money is the poison which infects and destroys all advanced societies. The money which dazzles those who manufacture armaments, deluded scientists, and politicians. Humility could be the antidote, such as I remember in the soft voices, soft palms of the pullman-car attendants, old black washerwomen, farmers, characters I spoke with along the road when I was a feckless youth doing the United States. But there is a greater humility than that which simple souls are born with: the humility which evolves after sophisticated intellects have wrestled with their passions, self-hatred, and despair in their search for truth.

After following your China journey through the media, Mr. President, I went back to the writings of Thomas Merton,[103] a monk in the Trappist Order of the Cistercians at the Abbey of Gethsemane, Kentucky, who did much to reconcile Christian faith with the beliefs of Taoism, Buddhism, Hinduism, and the intuitions of Zen.

---

[103](1915–68) died by electrocution in Bangkok.

The tragedy of the lives of those in high places is that they have little opportunity to read and think. Make a point, Mr. Reagan, of dropping out from time to time to contemplate problems which seem insoluble. Probably they will remain so. But you may be changed, as Thoreau was in solitude by Walden Pond, and Tom Merton in his hermitage beyond the Abbey within sight of the Kentucky Knobs. As Merton found deep similarities in Eastern and Western thought, you may even discover affinities which could bring Americans and Russians together in peace and amity. You will not achieve it through futile Olympic Games. It has been proved over and over that athletics, sports of any kind end in ill-feeling and strife. Peace and amity are engendered through peaceful non-competitive pursuits. Throughout the world, thoughtful people of all ages are sick of living with the threat of extinction – death brought about by those nations competing in the arms race. Bread and games is an old cliché. Athletes, as self-centred performers, many of them open to commercial offers, may still go along with the games bit. The hungry will find it harder to swallow. Full bellies are more important than a games programme costing millions. Give us bread before games, Mr. President. And life rather than death.

How your attendant scientists, old enough to recall the horrors of Hiroshima and Nagasaki, can run the risk of inflicting on the world a holocaust on a far more grandiose scale, I fail to grasp. Ordinary Russians and Americans are human beings. Love and compassion, not bombs, are what we must create through discovering one another's similarities. Merton and Chekhov, Pushkin and that diamond-sharp poet Emily Dickinson were all inspired by the same spirit, and suffered torments from which they emerged triumphant, Merton from the struggle with selfhood, Chekhov with tuberculosis, Pushkin from persecution by his fellow Russians, Dickinson from the conflict between her own private Heaven and Hell.

Recently in a moment of despair, I tried to work out from my own experiences, what I see as American culture, from the rarefied to the rorty vulgar level. What stimulates me, will of course appear valueless to others. But here is my capsule of American culture, for what it is worth; the writings of Emerson and Thoreau, Tom (Father Louis) Merton, Charles Ives[104] that most American composer, Edward Hopper[105] the painter who conveys through landscapes and interiors the great American loneliness, the jazz wizards of the South, Edmund Wilson the intellect from Upstate New York, wisecracking Fanny Brice[106] ('– –cure a cold? Get a good hot

[104](1875–1954).
[105](1882–1967); PW had seen the Whitney Museum's travelling show of Hoppers at the 1982 Adelaide Festival.
[106](1891–1951); PW saw her in New York in 1940.

Jew on your chest.') Miss Dickinson, the genteel new England spinster, yet
remote from the plush gentlewomen of her poem, Robert Lowell and his
forebears, the orgiastic dancers of the Harlem Ballroom, Ethel Merman the
human trumpet– –[107] I have no breath or space for more. Yet I must evoke
that crock of beans on Saturday night, when the washing is over, the scent
of baking and freshly laundered linen in the air. This for me embodies the
American virtues, of greater value than the proverbial crock of gold.

My hope is that the women of America, traditional guardians of the
crock of beans, will compel you to face reality. Their army is growing. I
hear them on the air. Women have to bear the brunt of things. They are
far more intuitive. In one sense at least they are more creative: they bear
the children who will be sacrificed in the holocaust of a man-made nuclear
war.

You, Mr. Reagan, hold the future in trust, the children born and
unborn of these increasingly purposeful women. You and I, we are both
old, Mr. President, I have not been a satisfactory human being, if not quite
a monster. You have played celluloid heroes. Would you not rather play a
real one in the time remaining to you by throwing in your lot with the
men and women of all ages, faiths, every social level, and colour, who are
trying to avert the destruction of life on earth?

Yours sincerely,
Patrick White
Nobel Prize Literature 1973.

20 MARTIN ROAD, 13.vi.84
TO DOROTHY GREEN
I was disgusted on Monday while dawdling through the Birthday Honours
to read that they had given Dorothy Green an OAM! Why did you accept
such an insult?[108] Or perhaps you needed to humble yourself. Seeing you
in the same category as a Queensland phoney ... almost made me vomit.
Oh God, this piddling awful country!

The uranium business has been getting worse and worse ...

I don't know whether I told you the Soviet Embassy invited me to
Moscow a few weeks ago to speak to the Writers' Union. The snag is they
want me to pay my own fare which, I told them, I can't – I have too
many commitments here. The embassy is now consulting its superiors in

---

[107](1909–84).
[108]To PW it made matters worse that the OAM is the lowest rank of the Order of
Australia.

Moscow. I do very much want to go, after thinking it over – to speak about them, us, and the others.[109]

Quite apart from politics and uranium, life becomes increasingly depressing – so many of our friends are falling down and breaking limbs, starting senility, or dying. Dying is best, and I shall plan the pills if I feel death approaching. Of course, until then, I shall do all I can to avert the horrors of the mass death our leaders are threatening us with.

A wonderful vista of leaves and light outside the front windows makes me feel we <u>must</u> live. On the other hand, our beautiful innocent tortoiseshell cat had to be put down last week with mouth cancer.

Love from us both
Patrick.

20 MARTIN ROAD, 20.vi.84
TO INGMAR BJÖRKSTÉN
If you are not careful you'll find yourself an old thing with nobody to love or depend on. Personally I find sex without love so boring.

20 MARTIN ROAD, 8.vii.84
TO KERRY WALKER
Dear Kerro,
I can't help feeling you will need some money[110] for your trip, that it would boost you a bit if you sweep back into the dreadful Mell-bourne in some New Yorky clothes.

Love,
Patrick
I don't want to have to argue about this.

20 MARTIN ROAD, 16.viii.84
TO RONALD WATERS
I am feeling exhausted after weeks of supporting the anti-nuclear movement. Recently I spoke at a Melbourne university and a week after in Sydney Town Hall for Hiroshima Day. Packed houses – and good coverage in each case. Never thought I could manage this sort of thing. It must be the

---

[109]He added a second condition: that he have an audience with the foreign minister Andrei Gromyko. But the plan foundered on the Soviet insistence that he pay his own way.
[110]A cheque for $1,000.

frustrated actor in me added to the despair of life today.[111] I have become involved with a Nuclear Disarmament Party which is being formed as a result of our Labor Party's turning into a sycophantic follower of Reagan's – or at any rate, that is what our P.M. and his Right Wing supporters are up to.

None of this will interest you, alas. I only wish I could get back to my own work – a fiction I started some weeks ago, about a senile character who is myself in my various roles and sexes. It gives me great scope.

Manoly is bearing up under all this. He is wonderful. Don't know what would have happened if I hadn't found him. We still have screaming rows, but not so many.

20 MARTIN ROAD, 19.viii.84
TO PEGGY GARLAND
I am trying to get back to some work of my own – something I started a few weeks ago – the memoirs of a senile woman, whose family have asked me to edit them after her death. A fiction, I should add. By now I have known a number of senile geriatrics and am well on the way myself. So it gives me a lot of scope. It will be bliss after having to check on every fact before opening my mouth.

It has been a horrible winter – driving rain, then dry gales penetrating one's body. I developed an agonising back which has been put right at last by a chiropractor-osteopath. Manoly has his ups and down, but is amazingly active, and has the garden looking wonderful.

I'm so glad I made it up with Betty. She's a remarkable character. I suppose it is her religion, as you say, though religion doesn't do much for the majority of the religious.

Love from us both
Patrick.

THE NEW ZEALAND FOUNDATION for Peace Studies invited White to Auckland in November to present its first Peace Media Prizes. He knew the journey would be difficult but he decided to go as a private gesture of thanks to the prime minister David Lange who had banned from New Zealand ports all warships that were nuclear-powered or might be armed

---

[111]These were the occasions on which he unofficially launched the new party. At La Trobe he spoke on 'The Search for an Alternative to Futility': 'We can no longer depend on our leaders anywhere on this threatened planet. This wonderful earth . . . !' At the Sydney Town Hall he commemorated Hiroshima Day: 'Alas, the habit of war will not let go. Our leaders are hooked on it . . .' *Patrick White Speaks*, pp.151, 161.

with nuclear weapons. The ban had brought grim trade reprisals from the US.

TO ELIZABETH HARROWER

We are off to N.Z. the day after tomorrow. My back is still bad and blood pressure high. Yesterday I thought I was going to fall in the streets on my way from acupuncture to fetch the tickets and travellers' cheques. Vile weather day after day.

The NDP is looking up – a number of impressive, <u>active</u> people are taking part. We could give the Hawke government quite a kick in the pants. That is all I live for now.

Betty Roland has been launched.[112] At the Mitchell Library. There was doubt about whether Manning could manage it. He had taken drink instead of the cuppa. But I think he got away with it . . .

Some of David's short stories are amongst the Great Short Stories of the World (at least two.)[113] I hope he isn't destroyed by adulation.

SOON AFTER HIS RETURN from a painful few days in Auckland, White was forced into hospital and, as he lay recuperating there for weeks, elections were called and held for the Federal Parliament. With high hopes the Nuclear Disarmament Party fielded Senate candidates in all States promising to shut down uranium mines, close the American military bases and keep nuclear-armed ships from Australian waters.

ST VINCENT'S HOSPITAL, SYDNEY
6.xii.84

TO DOROTHY GREEN

I should have written before, about a variety of things, but have been in trouble myself. The pain in my back increased. I felt like putting off the visit to New Zealand, then decided I must say what I had thought of saying. The few days there were agonising, as I had to move about a lot and give radio and TV interviews as well as speak at the peace rally and presentation of awards. The day after we returned, I had an X-ray; it showed that several of my lower vertebrae had crumbled. It happened probably because my bones are thin and aged, and has been helped on by all the cortisone I have taken for my chest. I've been in hospital ever since this discovery, and am much better. (Shall go home probably in three days

[112]Her memoirs, *The Eye of the Beholder*.
[113]PW had read an early copy of David Malouf's collected stories, *Antipodes*, 1985.

time.) I'm supposed to take lots of calcium, vitamin D, and do certain exercises to strengthen back muscles. I hobble about with a stick, but tire easily.

I don't know how useful I shall be from now on. I suppose I must resign myself to a fresh phase and doing a lot less than before. We are trying to find someone to do some cooking, as Manoly can't cope with everything. He has been wonderful. I don't know what I should have done without him.

Naturally I haven't been able to do much about the NDP, beyond distributing literature to the hospital staff and selling badges to raise funds. I don't expect we'll hear final results of the election till the end of the month.

Last week a friend went to a party given by Murdoch. I expressed surprise but she defended herself by saying one sometimes learns something on such occasions. As she was about to go up to the rooms where the party was being held, she noticed two little conspiratorial figures at the foot of the stairs. They turned out to be Hawkie and Sir Neddy Nolan!

I'll write again when I'm more settled and perhaps able to work out what my future will be.

Love,
Patrick.

SIXTEEN

Autumn to Winter

December 1984 – September 1990

AS SOON AS HE was able, White returned to work on *The Memoirs of Many in One*. The conceit was that he, Patrick White, had been asked to edit the memoirs of the late Alex Xenophon Demirjian Gray of Alexandria and Sydney. All his writing life he had written about old age and dying; now he knew what it was about. To his great surprise he did not feel old despite his crumpled body. Alex Gray was ancient, rather mad and very alive. 'It is religious in a sense,' he explained. 'And it's bawdy; the ones who like the bawdiness will be offended by the religion.'[1] He was having a lot of fun writing. His mastery of the first person was now so complete, he made himself a figure in the book, and the self-portrait was true: Patrick the old sod, the performer, the prim disapprover, the occasional bore, the born Mother Superior. Though he could sit for only a couple of hours a day at his desk, he wrote swiftly. 'I should really spend years on it,' he told Kerry Walker. 'But my own senility might overtake me.'[2]

20 MARTIN ROAD, 14.xii.84

TO RONALD WATERS

I came home a couple of days ago. The pain for a long time was agonising, now it is much less and I can hobble about but have to lie down a lot. At least we know it isn't cancer. The worry is that I shall have to lead, probably, a very limited life. If only I can sit long enough at desk or table to finish a few bits and pieces– – Who knows? There is so much to tidy up. M. has been wonderful, and fortunately is in pretty good health for the moment. We are trying to find somebody to do some of the cooking. We are also trying to find a home for Eureka, who is too energetic for us to manage as things are. Pansy the surviving pug, has an infection of the womb, which from our experience means the first stage of cancer. So everything happens at once.

My plays – three of them – are being revived in various parts of

[1] To Lyndall Crisp, *National Times*, 17 May 1985, p.20.
[2] 17.viii.84.

Australia. There has even been an enquiry for one of them from Broadway. Of course nothing will come of that.

I hope you are both well. You must be, or you wouldn't be facing the hells of New York. Who is Lady Isabel – dog? cat? or perhaps your aunt's mummy. Had a card from Mrs Brown-Price. Must write and thank her for that wonderful film.[3]

Love to both from both.

P.

20 MARTIN ROAD, 28.xii.84

TO BETTY WITHYCOMBE

Dear Betty,

Thanks for your Christmas letter. You say you would like nothing better than for us to sit in a couple of comfortable armchairs and talk. But a comfortable armchair is something I don't think I shall ever be able to manage again. You will have heard from Peggy, I expect, about the drama of my crumbled lumbar vertebrae. I am now hobbling about at home, still in a certain amount of pain, and tiring quickly . . .

I wish I felt less inhibited when faced with a tape-recorder. Perhaps when forced to accept it I shall shed my inhibitions – as I did when forced to speak to crowds.

My greatest luxury is a cordless telephone which I can carry about in my pocket and answer or make calls in comfort, instead of scurrying through the house like a maimed cockroach to answer the conventional phone before the caller gives up. I can make myself heard on the cordless as far north as the Queensland border and as far South as Melbourne. I am about to try it out on Perth where one of my plays will be revived in the Festival.[4]

Sorry about your gout . . . David Garland's lung condition sounds rather alarming as referred to only briefly by Peggy on a postcard.

Love and best wishes

Patrick.

---

[3] *An Englishman Abroad*, 1983, in which she played herself.
[4] *Signal Driver*.

20 MARTIN ROAD, 28.xii.84
TO JIM JENKINS[5]
Dear Jim Jenkins,
I received your letter of Dec 4. As a homosexual I have always detested the Gay Mardi Gras nonsense, particularly since so many non-gay trendies seem to have jumped on the wagon.

The homosexual issue is an increasingly serious one. We shall be persecuted more and more since AIDS came to stay. A lot of screaming queens in Oxford Street will not help the cause for which we shall have to fight.

I can't give you any message beyond: Come to your senses and call off the piffling Gay Mardi Gras.
   Yours
   Patrick White.

20 MARTIN ROAD, 28.i.85
TO LUCIANA ARRIGHI
I hobble about on sticks, can manage to cook, and have returned to working on something I began in 1984. But the prospect isn't good. I can't get around and do and see the things which stimulated me. No films, plays, restaurants, because my back couldn't last out. I am trapped in this house. Manoly has been wonderful in spite of his own arthritic pains, and our friends are very good. Still, this is a new and depressing phase of life.

The telephone (I have a cordless one which I carry about) newspapers, and radio are my links with what goes on. I refuse to have the telly till I am paralysed and senile.

I gave a radio interview for Straylier Day in which I had to let fly at Hawke, the Reagans, Thatcher et al.

I supported Labor for years, but Hawke's behaviour has put a stop to that. Not that there are alternatives in a country like this. I support the NDP but we did not do as well as we had hoped in the Elections. Still, we gave Hawke a fight and a reduced majority.[6]

[5]As promotions co-ordinator of the 1985 Mardi Gras, Jenkins was gathering messages of support for the official guide to the celebrations; PW's response was published.
[6]Nearly 700,000 votes were cast for the NDP and one senator was elected – Jo Vallentine from Western Australia – but she and many other NDP leaders left the party almost immediately in protest over the strong presence there of the Trotskyist Socialist Workers Party. PW took no further part in the NDP's affairs. Another senator was elected in 1987 but the NDP, its funds exhausted, expired in 1993.

20 Martin Road, 14.iii.85
TO MOYA HENDERSON
Yesterday I finished the first version of a thing I have been writing fitfully
and literally painfully for months. Shall now pull down a shutter for a
little. I'm afraid I may find chaos when I go back to it. It <u>should</u> be chaotic
but not to the extent that it won't be intelligible to reasonably intelligent
readers. There are lots of mad nuns in it!
> Yrs
> Patrick.

As White was toying with last changes to the novel, rehearsals began for
Armfield's Sydney production of *Signal Driver*. Kerry Walker was playing
Ivy Vokes. As always, rehearsals and the prospect of an opening night
drove White back to his desk, this time to begin sketching *Shepherd on
the Rocks*, a kind of miracle play based on the pathetic life of the vicar of
Stiffkey who ministered to prostitutes and died in a lion's cage. White was
ill again by the time *Signal Driver* opened at the Belvoir Street Theatre.

20 Martin Road, 25.v.85
CARD TO KERRY WALKER
Kerry –
Age beautifully –
> Love Patrick.[7]

20 Martin Road, 1.vi.85
TO ELIZABETH FALKENBERG
I got up from my bed for the first night. Manoly couldn't come because
his cough would have drowned the performers. It is a great success in spite
of the review from the *SMH* critic with whom I have a long-standing
feud[8] . . .
> I was a fan of Gide's in my youth, then went right off him. We both
did. The worst kind of desiccated intellectual . . . Did I ever tell you that
the man who has been translating my more recent novels into French is
a son-in-law of Gide?
> The composer who is interested in my opera libretto, Births,

---

[7]This came with first-night flowers.
[8]Harry Kippax liked the play less on second viewing. In *SMH*, 27 May, p.10, he declared the
vaudeville 'beings' who deliver PW's commentary, 'The unfunniest clowns I have ever seen'.
Signal Driver had done good business elsewhere, but in Sydney the crowds stayed away.

Deaths, and Lotteries[9] was preparing to start work, then, a couple of days ago I had an idea for another play drop into my head from the past – a Thirties scandal which I shall have to set in Australia to avoid trouble. The possibility of a film from *The Tree of Man* is also being discussed again.

So I am keeping busy, in spite of the political horrors. Perhaps I may even start marching again and making speeches. One of the worst political horror spots in Australia today is Queensland – a real nest of Fascism.

20 MARTIN ROAD, BEFORE 9.viii.85
TO TOM UREN[10]
Dear Tom,
I received your appeal for contribution to the Hiroshima Rally. I enclose $10. I don't send more as I spend my life dishing out money for causes, including a recent appeal by a team of important Labour politicians who intend to approach the UN over nuclear disarmament. (I haven't heard whether these politicians received my contribution.) . . .

In my decrepit state I felt I could not take part in the last Peace March. Then when I saw a photograph of the front row of politicians, I was sorry I hadn't hired a wheelchair, asked somebody to push me in the second row, and stuck the ferrule of my walking stick from time to time up Neville Wran's hypocritical arse – he who had changed his mind from day to day on whether US ships should or should not be allowed to enter Sydney Harbour.[11]

I don't know how I shall vote next time in the Federal election . . .

As for Hawke, the little big man, the Americans' . . . (oh shades of Curtin and Chifley) with his cigar, his ring, and his expensive wristwatch – worst of all his ignorance of history – Ataturk Park, indeed,

---

[9]Had *Shepherd on the Rocks* not cropped up at this point – Vine composed the music and songs for PW – he would still not have gone further with Births, Deaths and Lotteries which he had decided was unfeasible. He set only one passage, *Aria*, for soprano and chamber players in 1984. Vine also composed the music for Armfield's 1989 Sydney revival of *The Ham Funeral*.
[10]Uren, now minister for local government, was architect of the party's abandoned 'keep it in the ground' uranium policy. PW had expected him to leave the government once its promise to open no new uranium mines was broken at Roxby Downs: boycott was PW's first political instinct.
[11]No. Wran continued to ban all nuclear-*powered* ships from Sydney Harbour as hazards to public safety—he never changed his mind about this—but political developments in early 1985 made it more widely known that the ban had never extended to the nuclear-*armed* ships of the US navy.

in Canberra[12] – when the Turks occupied Greece for over four centuries, did their best to exterminate the Armenians, and when today Turkish gaols are crammed with political prisoners with the approval of Bob's buddies the Yanks.

You, Tom, used to be one of my heroes. Then recently I see you announcing in the *SMH* that you are dedicated to people.[13] That is an attitude which should speak for itself. Once upon a time you espoused the anti-uranium cause. But this seems to have gone by the board. Are you coming out against the Oz Government's plan to sell uranium to Egypt?[14] When I read of this proposal I saw it as yet another example of our politicians' pitiful ignorance. I spent several years in the Middle East during World War II. Manoly Lascaris, my Greek friend of 45 years, was born in Cairo, and spent years working in Egypt before joining me in Australia. We know the Egyptians, their apathy (particularly during the bemusing feast of Ramadan) and treachery – though possibly not all that different from the treachery of Oz politicians . . .

As we head towards the Bi-Centenary I am glad of my age. I probably shan't be here. If I am, I shall take no part in celebrating the history of a country which tries to ignore so much that is shameful. I know a distinguished Australian who says he will leave the country during the celebrations. As a lesser being, I shall show the Eureka and Aboriginal flags, and sit out the shenanigans on my own veranda.[15]

Yours sincerely,
P.W.

20 MARTIN ROAD, 15.viii.85
TO MICHAEL GIFFIN[16]
Dear Michael Giffin,
I am ashamed not to have answered your message before, but I have had a lot more illness since returning from hospital. Thank you for offering to

---

[12]On Anzac Day a memorial to Kemal Atatürk – whose troops had sacked Smyrna in 1922 and *inter alia* confiscated the Lascaris estates – was unveiled near the Australian War Memorial; the Turks in return gave the landing beach on Gallipoli the name Anzac Cove.

[13]Uren said, 27 July, p.43: 'I have been a servant of the Left all my life. I have a commitment to people.'

[14]Uren was not a member of the inner cabinet that decided to sell uranium to Egypt.

[15]PW held to this resolve: in 1988 he tacked the republicans' blue and white Eureka flag to a front window and the red, black and gold flag of the Aborigines flew in the garden. It was stolen.

[16](1953–   ) parishioner and later assisting priest at Christ Church St Laurence.

bring us Communion to the house. If I refuse the offer it is because I cannot see myself as a true Christian. My faith is put together out of bits and pieces. I am a <u>believer</u>, but not the kind most 'Christians' would accept.

Yours sincerely,
Patrick White.

20 MARTIN ROAD, 4.ix.85
TO PEGGY GARLAND
Dear Peggy,
I am sending you a young Oz lawyer/journalist, David Marr, who is arriving in London on the 23rd gathering material for a biography he is writing. I am putting him in touch with you (if you want) as you saw a lot of me in the past. Betty too, if she likes. <u>We only want the truth.</u>

Love,
Patrick.

ST VINCENT'S HOSPITAL, 11.ix.85
TO GRAHAM C. GREENE
Dear Graham,
You will have heard from Barbara[17] that I am back at St Vincent's – went out to dinner on the 7th and was struck down in the night with curiously persistent lapses of memory, Manoly with the vomits. We got a doctor in the morning who said I only had a hangover – a pity because we had eaten such an excellent lamb biriani.[18] I had drunk too much local vodka with mine, but Manoly only a little white wine to his food.

Next night M. fetched a neighbour-doctor who is also one of the heads of this hospital. He had me admitted through the casualty (which I now call the Russian Dungeons) was moved up to a ward in the Thoracic that morning and finally accepted as an inmate attended by our neighbour.

The annoying part of this is that William Yang should have come the day before yesterday to take the frontispiece and author's photograph. I have some ideas for getting round this in a hospital and shall make my

[17]Barbara Mobbs who now handled his affairs in the Sydney office of Curtis Brown.
[18]Cooked by Neil Armfield, cf. *The Complete Asian Cookbook*, Charmaine Solomon, 1976, p.28.

way to a public phone as soon as a physio leaves me alone.[19] It's maddening that this should have happened but I doubt it will last more than three more days.

Barbara is about to leave for Queensland and I shall be left to the mercies of Dim Tim[20] for a fortnight. Last night the Premiers' Gongs were awarded: to screams of rage, a speech by Morris West, and elderly ladies bursting into tears. Tim's favourite playwright David Williamson got the sulks when his screenplay didn't win; He is refusing to go to W.A. to start a new one which has been set up for him.[21]

I have a wonderful view from my hospital window. It is one I am only starting to disentangle at the end of my life: nuts to all that is minimal.

An old man of 80 called Tom Heapes has been my room-mate part of the time. He has told me how to cook an octopus in a pressure cooker so that the skin peels off like a glove: that will be my first mission in the outside world.

20 MARTIN ROAD, 8.x.85
TO GRAHAM C. GREENE
Dear Graham,

I don't know whether it has reached you that we have abandoned the idea of a frontispiece, with Alex as nun against a background of icons. The idea is a good one, and witty as William Yang has done it.[22] I now think we should have no more than the photograph of myself as myself (also a good one) at the back of the book. Various people feel that having the nun as frontispiece could backfire. So, I am retreating, regretfully. I have nothing to lose at the end of my life; and only look forward to leaving a diabolical world and a piddling country.

It is sad we meet so seldom because I feel very close to you. At least

---

[19]He had Yang photograph him a few days later in his hospital bed as the dead Alex Gray of *The Memoirs*.

[20]Dim Tim=Tim Curnow.

[21]A celebrated débâcle: Neville Wran, then premier of NSW, had instituted annual literary awards some years before. At this ceremony, venom from Wran and waffle from Morris West left the crowd restive. Tears and rage were general that night, but Williamson had no film project awaiting him in Western Australia.

[22]These photographs have never been published.

I have Manoly, a few very devoted friends, and in Barbara Mobbs an efficient agent with whom I can laugh. In the last couple of days I have even got back to quite long walks in the Park, which can look miraculously exotic in spring. See you next time – a pity it couldn't be October – amongst all this gum blossom and birdcall.

Patrick.

20 MARTIN ROAD, 20.xi.85

TO DAVID TACEY

Dear David Tacey,

Thank you for your letter. A Life Sentence doesn't seem too bad a title.[23] A Death Sentence might be better. I've been in hospital twice in the last twelve months since my lumbar vertebrae crumbled, and my chest is in permanently bad shape. For some time I was more or less housebound, but have become a bit more active lately.

I don't like the title *Laden Choirs* one bit,[24] it sounds like Mahler having an acute attack of constipation. Haven't read the book but can imagine.

Memoirs of Many in One comes out on April 1, or that is what is planned. You who write books about me may find you have been deceived. You should wait.[25]

I am tired of myself. I wish I had never written a word. (A Wasted Life could be a title). It would have been more to the point if I had run a soup kitchen to feed the hungry.

Yrs

Patrick White.

[23]Tacey chose, instead, *Patrick White: Fiction and the Unconscious*; the title 'A Life Sentence Here on Earth' was PW's first choice for *The Tree of Man*.

[24]Peter Wolfe's 1983 study of PW's work.

[25]Reviewing the novel in the *Age*, 'Saturday Extra', 19 July 1986, p.13 Tacey wrote: 'The ideology to which White makes his appeal is that of homosexuality and gayness. White can do virtually anything, write the most ordinary work, and somehow it is all justified under the wondrous banner of gayness.'

20 MARTIN ROAD, 3.xii.85

TO INGMAR BJÖRKSTÉN

As soon as I can lay hands on both the vols. of Janet Frame's autobiography[26] I am sending them to you. They are amongst the wonders of the world. Taking into account her novels as well, she seems to me more eligible than most people for the Prize – and she's experienced such harrowing events in her life she wouldn't suffer unduly from being given it.

Best wishes from us both.

Patrick.

20 MARTIN ROAD, 1.i.86

TO THE STERNS

Dear Sterns,

Thanks for your card. As I grow more decrepit, and slower, I neglect a lot of niceties . . .

We shan't be travelling any more. My publishers have been trying to persuade me to go to London for a novel I have coming out around Easter. Bad enough to face the event out here. It's a novel in the form of memoirs (*Memoirs of Many in One.*) I don't think I'll inflict it on you as I sense you no longer like reading my novels.

I'm also stroking another play, a few lines a day, in between cooking our meals and trying to deal with correspondence. I could employ at least four slaves, but shouldn't have anything left to give away. The only solution

[26]*To the Is-Land*, 1983, and *An Angel at my Table*, 1984; a third volume *Envoy from the Mirror City* was published in New Zealand in 1984 and reached Australia in 1985. Jane Campion's film, *Angel at My Table*, 1990, covered the span of all three.

is death, which I hope will carry me off at least before 1988 when this piffling country celebrates its Bicentenary. I shan't have anything to do with that. There's too much to be ashamed about.

Nowadays we are never without members of the Royal Family. If it isn't Princess Gigglequick and her Monkey Prince, it is the Queen of England herself and her Bully Boy. Or various Lascelles. Or Fog, promoting Jaguars in Central Australia.[27]

Sorry we shan't meet again on earth. Perhaps we shall collide somewhere after the powerful send us whirling through space.

Yrs
Patrick.

20 MARTIN ROAD, 7.i.86
TO ZOE CALDWELL
Australia stinks. The world stinks. If it weren't for Manoly I'd probably take the pills. My best bit of work was discovering M. He has feet horribly crippled by arthritis, but gets around on will-power and a sweet nature. I who am black and sour am in a worse condition.

20 MARTIN ROAD, 30.i.86
TO MAY-BRIT AKERHOLT[28]
I'm sick of people writing about me. I'm sick of me. However, Jim says you understand my plays, so I suppose you'd better finish writing the book you've begun. But I don't want to be asked questions. I have so much to cope with nowadays. I am crumbling. I am slow. I crawl from my desk to stove and sink. And there are still things I want to say before I finally get carted off to the crematorium.

After *Signal Driver* at the Belvoir was destroyed by the Critic, I started another play for some of the actors in that production, and Neil Armfield. I've got about 3/4 of the new play down on paper, but shall still have to put in a lot of work, and research some of the themes.

[27]Diana and Charles arrived in October for the traditional royal photo-opportunity at Uluru; the Duke of Edinburgh came in the same month as President of the Royal Agricultural Society; George Lascelles, 7th Earl of Harewood, was flying in and out as artistic director of the 1988 Adelaide Festival; and Captain Mark Phillips, then husband to the Princess Royal, came to give equestrian clinics and demonstrate Range Rovers.
[28](1948–   ), lecturer in drama at NIDA and later a dramaturg at the Sydney Theatre Co.; her study of PW's plays, *Patrick White*, was published in 1988.

20 Martin Road, 14.ii.86
TO GRAHAM C. GREENE
Dear Graham,

The novel is almost upon us. I am full of the usual alarm. The media started up weeks ago, but I'm not having any of that. I hope for reviews, good or bad, and we shall go from there.

I enclose a list of people I'd like to have copies on your side of the world. The local ones can be sent from here. As usual far more than my entitlement, but my royalties will look after the excess copies.

Last night Manoly and I went to a run through of Richard Meale's *Voss* opera, direction Jim Sharman, libretto David Malouf, and a number of other talented people in charge of other departments. I had been dreading this, because the meddling of ... Harry Miller and Sir Ned Kelly Nolan had got me hating everything to do with *Voss*. We spent a thrilling evening, with the minimum of props and characters, and only piano music. The complete thing will open at Adelaide Festival on March 1st. Adelaide will supply the minor roles and orchestra. I shall not be there as I can't appear at a Festival which invites the Queen of England. However, I shall see the complete version when it comes to Sydney later in the year.

I see your uncle has been given the OM. Perhaps that will make him happier. It is a legitimate gong as he is one of hers, unlike that devious little renegade Irish-Oz peasant Sir Ned Kelly Nolan OM.

There is so much that stinks in this country ...

I have almost got my new play down on paper. So much happening or threatened. I am stuck in the last scene. It will come with a rush eventually.

Hope your life is more bearable.
As always
Patrick.

20 Martin Road, 26.ii.86
TO BETTY WITHYCOMBE

I don't know what I'd do without Manoly ... I expect having a sweet nature has helped him, while I have been destroyed by irritability and Withycombe rages.

We see David Marr from time to time. I don't know how far he has got with the book, but he never stops working at it, and has dug up people and incidents I had completely forgotten. I try to steer him towards people who dislike me, as well as those who may be on my side, or who may in fact turn out not to be.
Patrick.

VOSS PROVOKED A STORM of applause in Adelaide. White wrote to Greene after hearing the news, 'I dare say it may move eventually into the outer world.' *Memoirs of Many in One* appeared on April Fool's Day provoking anger and delight. Critics mourned the passing of his talent or discovered a master writing at the height of his powers. The debate the novel sparked left White almost indifferent. He was working on the new play. More than ever he was caught up in his own fears for the world; the disaster at the Chernobyl reactor in the Ukraine seemed a vindication of all the bleak predictions of the anti-nuclear movement.

20 MARTIN ROAD, 6.v.86.

TO ELIZABETH FALKENBERG

And now the radiation storm. Has fresh *Kaninchenfutter*[29] been banned from Hamburg? Australians continue to take off into the world, regardless of hijacking, terrorists, bombs. That's what comes of having so little imagination.

20 MARTIN ROAD, 25.vi.86

TO GRAHAM C. GREENE

Dear Graham,

Thank you for the reviews of *Memoirs*. Some of them were rather quaint. Particularly the lady who says: 'Alex is presumably based on Mr Lascouras– –' Poor Manoly! I felt like writing and telling her Alex is 100% P.W.

Somebody gave me John Mortimer's interview with Graham Greene.[30] I hadn't realised your uncle and I have so much in common e.g. dreams are my greatest source, names can be the first step towards a novel. I wonder if your uncle ever read *The Tree of Man* in which Quigleys abound.[31]

Memoirs has been selling very well in Australia though Cody probably wouldn't admit it.[32] He is sour because I wouldn't let him lead me round on a publicity spree.

The *Voss* opera is a tremendous success – full houses and enthusiastic

[29]Rabbit food.

[30]Later published in Mortimer's collection *In Character*, 1983.

[31]Greene *met* a Quigley in Washington in the 1970s, the name haunted him and he used the form 'Quigly' in *Getting to Know the General*, 1984, and again in *The Captain and the Enemy*, 1988.

[32]John Cody, urbane director of Jonathan Cape's Australasian subsidiary.

audiences, lots of people going to opera for the first time. The novel should start selling again if Cody pulls his finger out. Manoly and I went to the first Sydney performance. It was a stupendous occasion, but it took me several days to recover physically and emotionally.

So glad you will be here in October. That is usually a good month in Sydney. I have various ventures coming up (only performing arts I'm afraid) but shall wait to tell you when you are here.

Yrs
Patrick.

20 MARTIN ROAD, 14.viii.86

TO CORAL BROWNE

I've asked the Viking to send you the American edition of *Memoirs*. Perhaps you've already found you didn't like the Anglo-Oz version I sent. But I want the Viking to see I still know a few Americans . . .

The other day I came across an article on the saints of Lyons with reference to the Pope's coming visit. Among the saints is the Curé d'Ars.[33] Do you remember, you used to get around London in a costume Ronald called the Curé d'Arse?

Since *Dreamchild* came off in the city it bobs up here and there in the more likely suburbs.[34] I hope lots of people are enjoying it. I'd like to see it again. I wonder if one can get the script.

Our country, particularly NSW, is in a terrible economic mess. Sydney is as full of crims as Chicago, and some of the police and politicians amongst them. There is a murder a minute in Straylia which does at least take one's mind off the political situation to some extent. 40,000 people at a time watching football on our doorstep, and jogging in all directions. Last Sunday there was Siddytersurf,[35] a race when thousands charged from the Town Hall to Bondi. We've also just had the worst floods for a century, fortunately only blackouts on this hill . . .

Perhaps I've written most of this before when I wrote about *Dreamchild*. Senility will be next on my list.

Love to you both
Patrick.

[33] Jean-Baptise Vianney (1786–1859), unlearned and austere priest whose confessional attracted tens of thousands; the Devil set his bed alight; canonised 1925.
[34] Dennis Potter's 1985 film about the old age of Lewis Carroll; Alice played by Browne.
[35] City to Surf.

IN SPRING WHITE WROTE the prose poems *Three Uneasy Pieces* and was again out in the streets campaigning: this time against a clumsy monorail being built through the city. He joined sixty writers at a peace conference in Canberra and made a personal armistice with Thea Astley. Upheaval came to his professional life towards the end of the year when Barbara Mobbs left Curtis Brown. He went with her.

20 MARTIN ROAD, 24.xii.86
TO LUCIANA ARRIGHI
Dear Luci,
A real Straylian Christmas card to cheer you up.[36] I wonder if your hubby got Lady Miriam's latest, in which one sees 'Mary with help from Nina Ricci'[37] She was dressed just like that at the first performance of *Voss* in Sydney.

This is a chaotic Christmas. I have been having pleurisy and worse pains in my bones as a result of the laborious coughing. I hobble around in the home, but don't get out much, except to have my corns and hair cut. Poor Manoly has to take on more than ever, in spite of his own arthritic pains.

We hear that Barry Humphries and the awful Diane have split up. Barry is preparing to get together with . . . who is divorcing her husband for that purpose.[38] I suppose the more wives and houses you have, the bigger star you are.

Jim Sharman has run away from Christmas to Paris and Barcelona, bombs going off in both places, but perhaps he will enjoy that.

Shepherd on the Rocks goes into rehearsal in Adelaide in April. Hope I shall be able to get over there for some of the preliminaries, but I seem to grow increasingly decrepit.

The script of *Twyborn* is excellent.[39] Now we have to find the right person to play the lead – very difficult.

Mateland is going to end up with casinos all round its coasts. We shall be wrecked by the time we reach 1988 and the fucking Bi. If I am

---

[36]The Christmas aerogram showed a cute child, crook and lamb.

[37]Miriam was the name under which he burlesqued Mary Fairfax in *Memoirs of Many in One*; her Christmas cards were famous, odd little booklets with family snaps and uplifting quotes taken from her recent reading; the 1986 card showed her posed in a tiny and vivid red dress by Nina Ricci.

[38]PW's wildly libellous guess at the next wife was wide of the mark; instead in 1990 Humphries married Lizzie Spender, writer of plays and cookbooks.

[39]Filmscript by David Malouf for Jim Sharman to direct; not made.

still alive I shall take no part in anything so shameful. I shall sit on the front veranda under the Aboriginal and Eureka flags.

Our Spanish treasure[40] of many years has left us for work in Spain, but we have a wonderful replacement except that we can only speak through the dictionary.

Like the photographs of Bomarzo which is one of the places we have missed seeing. Read an article the other day by Edmund Wilson on its history and legends.[41] Flavia must be rather a pain – and not all that pretty judging by the photos.[42]

The Pope was here. And Sam Neill.[43]

Love

Patrick.

PLEURISY LAID HIM LOW for a few weeks but he recovered and gathered his strength for Adelaide and the opening of *Shepherd on the Rocks*.

20 MARTIN ROAD, 14.v.87

TO JEAN LAMBERT

Dear Jean,

The death of your son[44] must be a terrible blow, particularly as you hoped he might carry on your name. At least the name bit is something I have never had to worry about, and having children of any sex would have worried me intensely. I would have made an awful father.

The title for *Memoirs of Many in One* – –*Triples Mémoires* doesn't seem to me to convey the book. How would you translate *Splinters of the Ego* into French? Or would it be possible to suggest a company of actors which make up the central character? Would *Comédiens du Moi* sound just silly?[45] . . .

My new play opened in Adelaide a few days ago. I was there for a lot of the rehearsals and the opening. Thanks to the director, designer,

---

[40]Cleaner.

[41]The Italian ducal park with grotesque statues discussed in Wilson's 'The Monsters of Bomarzo', republished in the 1973 collection of essays, *The Devils and Canon Barham*.

[42]Arrighi's niece Flavia Borghese: in time, a beauty.

[43]PW was a great fan of the New Zealand actor, star of *My Brilliant Career*, etc.

[44]In a car accident.

[45]Finally published by Gallimard as *Mémoires éclatés d'Alex Xenophon Demirjian Gray*.

composer, and a wonderful company of actors, *Shepherd on the Rocks* was enthralling.[46] I wish you could have been there.

    Patrick.

20 MARTIN ROAD, 8.vi.87
TO ELIZABETH FALKENBERG
You complain that you only have 34 letters from me in 11 years. That is far more than many of my longer established and more intimate friends could count up. This isn't the age of letter-writing. I always telephone to those within reach but can't come at international calls; I dry up if faced with long distance.

20 MARTIN ROAD, 10.vi.87
TO MOYA HENDERSON
Dear Moya,
Thanks for your wishes. I spent half my birthday being interviewed by the surgeon who is going to operate on me in a couple of weeks. Something very minor,[47] only I am afraid they may dig up something nastier while they're at it.

    Shepherd on the Rocks brought in the public. As far as I'm concerned, it was a great success: design, music, acting, direction all that I could have wished. Perth, Brisbane, and the Sydney Festival want it for next year, but I won't have anything of mine performed during the nauseating Bi.

AT HOME AGAIN, HE began working on four little theatre pieces for Kerry Walker. From time to time he rescued them from the mess on his desk, but never finished them to his satisfaction. He was offered and refused doctorates from Cambridge, Melbourne and Sydney universities.

20 MARTIN ROAD, 1.ix.87
TO ELIZABETH FALKENBERG
You were right about the novel. I did begin one, but left off when I realised it would take a lifetime when there is so little of that left to me. I switched to some short plays, three so far, possibly four, very black, which are called *Four Love Songs*.

---

[46]Directed by Neil Armfield, set designed by Brian Thomson, music by Carl Vine, and cast including John Gaden, Kerry Walker, Geoffrey Rush.
[47]Hernia.

20 Martin Road, 30.xii.87
TO RONALD WATERS
Dear Ronald,
Your card came today. I didn't realise you had a breakdown, though there
had been references to something mysterious by Coral and Luci. At least
you are better. You mustn't give in. Easy to say that, of course! Cooking
can be quite simple. You can surely stick a roast in the oven, or chop on
the grill without the hate rising in you. Nowadays we eat a lot of things
like pasta with good sauces, and dried things like beans, lentils, and chick
peas . . .

Manoly is suffering a lot from his arthritic, and by now terribly
deformed feet. My success in life is my discovery of Manoly. Nothing is of
importance beside that. Books – shit!

Did you see David Marr this time?[48] I hope I am still alive when the
book comes out. I expect I shall turn out to be a monster, otherwise I
can't think why he should want to do me. Sitting at a desk doesn't make
an interesting life. Very few of the big names. Only an occasional flutter
with Nounou, and Nada and Nell– –[49]

Patrick.

HE BOYCOTTED THE BICENTENNIAL: nothing of his was to be published or
performed in 1988. *Three Uneasy Pieces* had appeared just in time to beat
the ban in late 1987. White campaigned angrily against the celebrations.
Television crews were welcome once again to gather on the lawn. In
March he suffered a bad spell that took him to hospital for a few days.
He recuperated very slowly.

20 Martin Road, 30.v.88
TO PEGGY GARLAND
Dear Peggy,
Thanks for your birthday letter.[50] It arrived almost on the day. I find
birthdays particularly gloomy events the way Australia is going. The Labor
Party is now run by a mafia of millionaires. Labor lost out in the last State
election as the result of their corruption, but I don't think the Liberals

---

[48]I had been back in England interviewing and collecting letters.
[49]From Noel Coward's song – 'I've been to a marvellous party/With Nounou and Nada and
Nell . . . People's behaviour/Away from Belgravia/Would make you aghast,/So much
variety/Watching Society/Scampering Past . . .'
[50]He was 76.

will make much difference. The same broken promises. I voted for an assortment of independents.

At least we are almost halfway through the year of the abominable Bi. We are hardly ever without a member of the British Royal Family. Busloads of school-children waving flags try to make them look popular, but the people in general are apathetic. Betty England opened our new Parliament House, which cost billions and looks like a vast hotel for new rich.

Our Jack Russell, Nellie, rising 12, was run over a few weeks ago and killed. A great shock. We now have a replacement, Milly, 5 months, which I am giving M. for his birthday. She is going to be very intelligent, but is going through a hyperactive stage. I don't know that starting a new dog when we are both 76 is a wise move. We shall see. Eureka is still with us, and fortunately accepts the pup.

Had an interesting visitor yesterday, Sister Angela Solling, an Anglican nun,[51] whom I met when we were both young, and she was a protegée of one of my Armidale cousins. She is an interesting woman, a sculptress, and politically radical. A sister of hers in England is known to Betty.

Extraordinary that Betty could recognise small flowers in your garden. This blindness thing is something I can't understand. My eyes seem to be holding out, but my chest is a mess, and my crumbling bones a worry.

20 MARTIN ROAD, 31.v.88

TO KATE GRENVILLE[52]

Dear Kate,

Thanks for sending me your Joan book.[53] I had been put off by various things: the ABA connexion,[54] the girl on the jacket looking so like Aurora the non-character in *1841*,[55] and the launch with that philistine adwoman, Margaret Whitlam. But when I read it I was carried away. I liked it even better than *Lilian*.[56] When I finished I even had a cry. After finishing writing something of my own I never feel it's any good if I don't have a cry.

---

[51]Of the Franciscan community of St Clare at Stroud in the Hunter Valley; she gave PW a 'holding cross' which he wore round his neck for the rest of his life.
[52](1950–   ), Sydney writer whose work PW admired and promoted.
[53]The novel *Joan Makes History*.
[54]The Australian Bicentennial Authority which gave Grenville a fellowship to work on the novel.
[55]A play by Michael Gow commissioned for the celebrations.
[56]Her novel *Lilian's Story*, 1985.

I hope you'll get on with your writing now, instead of giving way to the performing virus which seems to have infected so many writers.

Yrs

Patrick.

20 Martin Road, 5.vi.88
TO ELIZABETH FALKENBERG
Dear Elizabeth,

Thanks for the 'present'. We were horrified by the way it floated in so casually.[57] But it will come in most useful, making two of our gates safer for dogs. Also our sheets are wearing out, and we shall probably spend much more time in bed if we are able to see things out at home . . .

It is the shit that rises to the surface and gains power. I have been keeping out of things, but I shall have to go to La Trobe University in mid-July whatever the state of weather and chest. I have been asked to speak on 'A Sense of Integrity'. I have a lot building up in me, and it must come out if it is the last thing I do. I spoke at La Trobe once before and it was a success. However, this time will be at night, there will be a dinner afterwards, and I shall have to spend the night in the Vice-chancellor's house. Don't know what the Vice-chancellor and his house are like. I hate farting about in anybody's house at night . . .

It is true when i say I can't find things. The dining room is full of unanswered letters and unread books.

I read a hair-raising biography of Giacometti recently by James Lord, published in New York.[58] His last days, illnesses, hospitals etc. too close to home. Certainly he was smoking 80 cigarettes a day, drinking endless cups of coffee, and up all night in bars and restaurants putting away the alcohol.

David Marr is writing away. I hope I live to read the result. For my birthday he brought a piece of fantastic Gippsland blue cheese, better than authentic Italian Gorgonzola. Now when the Australians are skiting like the worst loud-mouthed American of having the greatest cricketer, tallest tower, biggest casino in the world, I can truthfully say, what we do have is a humble cheese.

Love

Patrick

I hope this is legible.

---

[57] Hundreds of Deutschmark folded into an envelope.
[58] A *Giacometti Portrait*, 1980.

20 Martin Road, 6.vi.88
TO HUMPHREY McQUEEN
Dear Humphrey,

Thanks for your interesting letter, I can see that Japan is not for me.[59] Perhaps I should get to know more Japanese. Two of my friends have Japanese wives – both admirable women – and there is a professor-fan who came here once, and grunted at me like something from *Planet of the Apes*.

About the Award panel: your being in Japan for two years makes your participation very difficult. I'd like you to stand down, at least while you are away. I am not in favour of Jack Davis getting the Award. He gets endless acclaim.[60] I hear all his plays will soon be done in Sydney, a Jack Davis Festival to show how they develop out of one another.

I have been reading the poems of Roland Robinson.[61] Years ago I didn't like him as a human being, didn't pay much attention to his work, now I find some of his poetry very appealing.

I am asking Gerard Windsor to stand down. As a writer of fiction, he could become eligible eventually for the Award, though I hear he is going round saying there soon won't be anyone left to give it to[62] . . .

Archbishop Manning Clark rang up yesterday, rather mournful; he can't understand why I've lost my respect for him. I wish I hadn't, but I can't continue to respect someone whose vanity causes him to flaunt himself so shamelessly at his age.[63]

I must go and get our tea. Domesticity is really what keeps me going. Shall recommend it to the Archbishop.

Yrs
Patrick.

---

[59]McQueen was a temporary professor in the department of international and social relations at Tokyo University; one product of his time there was *Tokyo World, an Australian Diary*, 1991.
[60](1918–), Aboriginal poet, playwright and activist, whose *No Sugar* Armfield directed in Sydney in 1985; the play was later seen in the World Theatre Festival in Vancouver.
[61](1912–92), bushman, critic and Jindyworobak poet, PW's choice for his prize this year.
[62]Windsor had just published his third novel, *That Fierce Virgin*. He had no doubt there were many old writers about, but argued they were no longer as neglected as they had been when PW established the prize.
[63]PW disliked the historian – 73 to PW's 76 – becoming a star of the Bicentennial celebrations which included an unfortunate musical based on Clark's *History of Australia*. Clark refused to take these attacks seriously and continued to call at Martin Road to the end.

20 MARTIN ROAD, 12.vii.88
TO JEAN SCOTT ROGERS
I am trying to quell a bacillary infection, as I have promised to speak at
La Trobe University outside Melbourne in a week's time. I wish I could
wake up and find it is all behind me.

VERY FRAIL, HE FLEW to Melbourne to make his last public address; the
night was a great success: 'I pray regularly (prayer does rub off on
someone somewhere) . . . I pray that we may comfort the failed, the
humiliated, the deranged; remove fear from the threatened, the
frightened; eliminate torture; see that the poor and blacks receive the
justice so often denied them . . . follow the path of humility and
humanity, and Australia might develop a civilisation worthy of the
name.'[64]
    Another bout of asthma and bronchitis took him to hospital for
three weeks and when he came home he needed a nurse to help
with his food and pills. Each week he grew a little stronger. He
began to sort through his cupboards and drawers. Now only a few
letters written in a spidery hand left Martin Road. The flow ended
much as it began at Lulworth seventy years before in politenesses:
thanks, refusals and barbed condolences.

20 MARTIN ROAD, 12.iii.89
TO RONALD WATERS
Dear Ronald,
I heard about Fred in a roundabout way from Elizabeth Riddell.[65] How
terrible for you. Gordon has been a wonderful friend to you and Fred, but
for some extraordinary reason he won't have anything to do with me.[66] I
should have thought in a case like this he might have shed his dislike and
let me know the details of what has been happening. I wish I could do
something for you, but I can't in our own circumstances. Last year I was
in and out of hospital most of the time with chest, eye, and other ailments.
I finally escaped from hospital and am now at home with a nurse for most

[64]*Patrick White Speaks*, pp.194-5.
[65]Carpenter had died in January.
[66]In 1984, after touring the world in the show, Chater had returned to Australia for a
revival of *The Elocution of Benjamin Franklin*; he rang PW who abused the show and its
director Richard Wherrett; Chater defended both and his friendship with PW ended.

of the week.[67] She is excellent, and is interested in the things which interest me. Manoly has also been wonderful in helping look after me, but has his own troubles. I wish I could say come and we shall look after you, but as you see, we can't look after ourselves. At least Fred can't have left you penniless as I know from the days when Gordon was still on speaking terms.

David Marr's book should be out before the end of the year. There is also a book of my political speeches. I shall see you get copies. My play *The Ham Funeral* is being revived towards the end of the year. There is also a radio version of *The Aunt's Story*, and telly versions of some of the novels are being discussed. Perhaps Gordon will stop being shitty and take part in some of these events. I was always fond of him and his attitude in recent years has been hard to take.

Let me know your plans if there is anything I can do to help.

Love,

Patrick.

20 MARTIN ROAD, 28.ix.89

TO BARRY O. JONES

Dear Barry O.,

Some time when you are in Sydney I'd like to show you a small Rapotec which has turned up under our stairs. If it appeals to you, I'd like you to have it as you still seem under his spell.

From the same hiding place I've unearthed a very interesting object: a target map of GONDAR drawn by Abyssinian patriots during World War II. I must have got hold of this when I was in the Air Force in the Middle East. It ought to be in a museum. Would it be suitable for the War Museum in Canberra? If you think it would, perhaps you would give it to them.[68]

I was pleased to read somewhere that you aren't interested in sport. I am sick to death of football and cricket. Sport could be our downfall.

Yrs,

Patrick

WHEN *PATRICK WHITE SPEAKS* appeared, he bought a hundred copies of the book to send to friends, family and writers – most with this pithy inscription: 'Last Words'. In October rehearsals began for Neil Armfield's revival of *The Ham Funeral* and on the opening night White allowed

---

[67]Jill Bailey.

[68]Now in the museum, ref. no.: PR 89/170.

himself to be filmed for television. This was the last public sight of him: a parcel of bones delighted by this success.

20 MARTIN ROAD, 16.xii.89
TO ELIZABETH FALKENBERG
Dear Elizabeth,
Yes, I am a grumbler, but must thank you for your generosity. I am sending you a book by the person who won my Literary Award this year.[69] Of course it will arrive long after Christmas.

The revival of the *Ham Funeral* was a smash hit. The public paid to stand towards the end of the run, which proves that my plays can draw big audiences, given the right director and cast.[70] Neil Armfield, the director, is going to make a film of *The Tree of Man* some way hence.[71]

David Marr is still writing away at the biography. I'm afraid he will overdo it, and a lot will have to be ripped out. Biographers become, unfortunately, obsessed by their subject. All biographies are too long.

Love,
Patrick.

20 MARTIN ROAD, NEW YEAR'S DAY
TO CORAL BROWNE
Dear Coral,
I was shocked to hear of Ron Waters' behaviour, all considered. He must have gone a bit nutty with Fred's death. But of course he was always crying workhouse – kicking you under the table if one ordered any but the cheapest dish for supper. (I think he learnt that from Cyril and Madge, two other members of the workhouse fraternity.)[72]

I've just had a terrific success with a revival of my play *The Ham Funeral* by Neil Armfield, who is about our best director. Later on he is going to make a film of *The Tree of Man*.

My next cause for alarm will be David Marr's biography if he finishes it before I die. I am also doing an updated version of *The Master Builder* with a Norwegian dramaturg.[73]

[69]Thea Astley's *It's Raining in Mango*.
[70]Robyn Nevin (Miss Docker in Sharman's *Cheery Soul*) was one of the music hall gals; Max Cullen (Terry Legge the union man in the first *Big Toys*) played the landlord. The music was by Carl Vine.
[71]The producer Margaret Fink later dropped the project.
[72]The actor Cyril Ritchard (1897–1977) who gave the first professional performance of PW's skit 'Peter Plover's Party' and his wife Madge Elliott (1898–1955).
[73]May-Brit Akerholt; but this was not begun.

Your fantastic last films will remain with me till I die. You are indeed one of the actresses. Love from us both to you both. Happy New Year if that is possible.

Patrick.

THE LAST MONTHS OF summer were always the worst time for White. Somehow he managed to survive them again, hanging on, he said, to see the biography. The last letter of his I have was to Juliet O'Hea on 19 May offering condolences on the death of her sister and complaining about the endless delay with the book. 'I doubt if I shall be here to get the reactions of friends and enemies.'

He read the typescript in July. In August a mild bout of pleurisy led slowly to a complete bronchial collapse. He died at dawn on 30 September 1990. In accordance with his will, his body was cremated without ceremony and his ashes scattered on a lake in Centennial Park.

Notes

WHITE AND HIS LETTERS

PATRICK WHITE'S LETTERS ARE the work of a master of English prose. His seventy-year correspondence from childhood in the First World War until his death in 1990 is earthy, shrewd, camp, savage, dramatic, very funny and free. White wrote novels to impress a hostile world, but most of his correspondence was written to amuse, inform and at times upbraid his friends. He was an old man before he wrote fiction as easy and direct as the best of his letters.

White kept no copies of his correspondence and all the letters he received were thrown away. As friends and relations died and bundles of his own letters came back to him, White destroyed them all. He spoke of his perpetual shedding as a way of keeping free of the past's stale entanglements. All he needed of the past lived in his imagination; an artist with his formidable memory did not need souvenirs.

White was urging his correspondents to burn his letters as early as the 1950s but his requests became more urgent after he was shown Katherine Mansfield's papers in Wellington in 1961. 'Letters are the devil,' he told Marshall Best afterwards. 'I always hope that any I have written have been destroyed.' A few of White's correspondents did what they were told; some lied that they had; most carefully stored White's letters away.

By the early 1970s White knew there was a mass of his correspondence loose in the world. He knew he could not make it disappear, but pestering people to put letters to the torch was a holding operation that made friends and colleagues at least keep the letters to themselves. So while his privacy mattered most to him, White was able to hold the line for years.

Occasionally fragments from his letters appeared in print. Ben Huebsch writing in the July 1957 issue of *Book of the Month Magazine* used half-a-dozen paragraphs from letters over the years to promote *Voss*. White thanked Huebsch, 19.viii.57, for a copy of the article, 'which gets away with quoting from letters without making the writer of them writhe. That is, indeed, a triumph of discretion.' But he added, as if putting a shot across the publisher's bows, 'It is dreadful to think, however, that one's letters still exist. I am always burning and burning.' Years later White helped Peter Beatson, Ingmar Björkstén and David Tacey write books about his work by sending them letters designed to be quoted in their texts. In Tacey's case, White helped reconstruct the originals after these were lost in the Ash Wednesday bushfires.

Because White knew the ways of the literary world, he realised his letters must some day end up in public collections. Indeed he was a great enthusiast for the correspondence of Chekhov, Lamb, Katherine Mansfield, Jack Yeats, Pushkin and Hugo von Hofmannsthal whose letters had reached a safe, if public, haven in libraries. But White seemed unaware that this process had been under way since the 1960s. The Library of Congress received most, but for some inexplicable reason not all, of White's letters to Huebsch after the publisher's death in 1964. A few years later Spud Johnson's papers were hoovered into that great repository of literary remains, the Harry Ransom Centre for Humanities Research in Austin, Texas. Neither White nor White academic scholars seemed aware of these remarkable public holdings.

In Australia no great collection of White's correspondence came into public hands until Cynthia Nolan gave her papers to the National Library in 1976. Even if White was aware of her gift, the papers seemed safely buried under a 45-year embargo. Other smaller donations of his letters were made to Australian libraries in the 1970s and early 1980s but libraries had a deliberate policy of making no fuss about these acquisitions. This was partly out of respect for a great artist's privacy, partly to keep White on side in the hope of hauling in the big fish curators believed was lurking at Martin Road: Patrick White's own papers.

Well into the 1980s White could believe he was still in control of the situation: only a little had ever been published from the letters; many hundreds had been destroyed; most of the survivors were still in private hands; and libraries were sitting quietly on their holdings. Then in 1986 Geoffrey Dutton sold his immense White correspondence to the National Library of Australia. Around this core has accrued the finest collection of White's letters in the world: his letters to Peggy Garland, James Stern, Ronald Waters, Pepe Mamblas, Gwen and David Moore, Jean Scott Rogers, Juliet O'Hea, Alice Halmagyi and Mollie McKie.

By this time I was working on White's biography and he was no longer urging the destruction of his letters. In Peggy Garland's cottage in Oxfordshire in 1985, I had seen the first wonderful cache of White's letters: forty years' correspondence in a fat manilla folder. From that day I concentrated on hunting his letters down and discovered they were everywhere, but closely guarded, in public and private hands. After six months I raised the matter of letters with White and at my request he wrote a general direction to friends, family and libraries to give me access to all that had survived. I spent the next two years, this authority in hand, copying his letters in Australia, New Zealand, France, the USA, Germany, Scandinavia and Britain. When I finished writing the biography I had 2,000.

White's change of heart puzzled many of his friends but its cause was simple: privacy was not now the issue; the biography was; and White knew biographies fed on letters. He also gave me some of the very few scraps he *had* kept in his desk: the childhood letters to 'Father Xmas' and 'The Fairies', a 1939 note of encouragement from his London maid Hilda Richardson, and drafts of several grand remonstrances filed away as evidence of his reasons for breaking off bitterly with Geoffrey Dutton in 1982 (p.562), Tom Uren in 1985 (p.602) and his agents of 50 years Curtis Brown in 1986. Found in his desk after his death was another of these remarkable farewells – to Harry Miller in 1982 (p.574) – plus a fan letter from Salman Rushdie written after coming late to *Voss*, the wartime diary, part of which is published here, and a quantity of hand-painted cards from Sidney Nolan.

I warned White that once the biography was finished I would be asking to edit the letters. He gave his permission the day we finished working through the typescript together. He had greatly enjoyed rereading letters in the biography that had left his desk thirty, forty and sometimes fifty years before. Still he insisted he was glad many had been destroyed, 'But the best of them here are terrific.'

Three major collections have come into my hands since I finished the biography. I had seen – and was able to use at the last minute – a couple of early letters White wrote to Jean Scott Rogers, but the full correspondence from 1931 to 1988 arrived too late for the biography. A year further on the poet Peter Skrzynecki alerted me to the survival of Frederick Glover's collection despite White's boast that Glover had, a few days before he died, burnt them all. Finally, as this book was on its way to press, Jinx Nolan generously gave me access to over a hundred of White's letters written to her parents Cynthia and Sidney Nolan.

In all, since the biography appeared, I have had access to about 1,000 more letters. Of the smaller collections I particularly value White's correspondence with his niece Frances Richardson, the director Joseph Losey, the novelist Shirley Hazzard, her husband Francis Steegmuller, and the writers Edna O'Brien, Xavier Herbert and Randolph Stow.

None of these new finds would, beyond a little fine-tuning, have made any difference to what I wrote in the biography. Instead they confirm the verdict I reached then: Patrick White's life and writing continue to take our imaginations by surprise, and to illuminate our experience of living in this savage and beautiful world.

ABBREVIATIONS

ABC Australian Broadcasting Commission (later Corporation)
A & R Angus & Robertson, publishing house and bookseller
ABR Australian Book Review
ALP Australian Labor Party
ANU Australian National University
BBC British Broadcasting Corporation
C of E Church of England
DJs The Sydney store, David Jones
E & S Eyre & Spottiswoode, publisher
GP Doctor in general practice
Herald Sydney Morning Herald
MP member of parliament
NIDA National Institute of Dramatic Art, Sydney
NDP Nuclear Disarmament Party
NSW New South Wales
PMG Post Master General, the Australian Post Office
P & O Peninsula & Orient, shipping line
RAS Royal Agricultural Society Show and Showgrounds
SA South Australia
SMH Sydney Morning Herald
TLS Times Literary Supplement
WA Western Australia

ACKNOWLEDGEMENTS

I HAVE PATRICK WHITE to thank above all: he gave me permission to collect and publish these letters and I finish the task with only one regret, that he is not here laughing and gnashing his teeth over the result. The advice and forbearance of Manoly Lascaris continues to be indispensable to my work. White's literary executor Barbara Mobbs has been both a great supporter and stimulating critic of my efforts. Her decision to volunteer the fragment of White's wartime diary gave this collection an unhoped for, fresh dimension.

Forbearance has shaped this book. I owe a particular debt to those who are bearing with good humour and understanding the publication here of very painful remarks White made about them. This impressive company includes Sir Zelman Cowen, Robert Hughes, Geoffrey Dutton, Patricia Pearl, Frances Richardson, Tom Lewis, David McNicoll, Paul Bailey, Peter Sculthorpe, Dilys Daws, Charles Blackman, Barbara Blackman-Veldhoven, Barry Humphries and Tom Keneally. Only a handful refused my request to be among this company.

The *Letters* are built on the foundations of the *Life*. My thanks again go to all White's correspondents who generously helped me with the biography and to those correspondents and others who have led me to another thousand of White's letters since the *Life* appeared. I'm particularly grateful to the friends of Jean Scott Rogers who persuaded her not to burn 60 years of White's letters but give them instead to the National Library of Australia; to Peter Skrzynecki for alerting me to the existence of the Glover letters and to Alan Young who gave me access to these annals of Sarsaparilla; and to Jinx Nolan for lifting the embargo under which lay buried White's correspondence with her parents Cynthia and Sidney Nolan.

All White's correspondents are listed in 'The Cast of Correspondents'. To those who survive, their heirs, or the libraries that now hold the letters they once received from Patrick White—my thanks.

Some correspondents who gave me great help will not find their letters in the collection. Nevertheless, I want to thank them for their assistance and reassure them if I can that their efforts were not wasted. My aim was to produce a living book of White's prose not a fat monument. So I had to cut and cut. Many fine letters disappeared in the final months and many hundreds of ingeniously researched footnotes.

The research task was enormous. The burden of research lay on the brothers Kirton: first Andrew, a colleague from my years at the *National Times*, and then the laconic James. The Kirtons were exactly what was needed: persistent, careful and astonishingly tolerant of both my indecision and unreasonable demands. I had great help also in the early days from my friend Kath Vallentine.

I spent the last three years begging everyone for information. Of the hundreds I turned to I want particularly to thank Peggy Garland and Geoffrey Dutton. They had the worst of it but month after month I hounded Ronald Waters, Ingmar Björkstén, Jean Scott Rogers, Nick Enright, Heather Johnston the biographer of Roy de Maistre, White's physician Maurice Joseph, Ann Lewis who advised me on the arcana of Sydney society, Ray Stanley who found answers to impossibly difficult questions about show-business, Dr Urasidas Karalis who explained modern Greece until his patience was exhausted, and my friends who could never escape the subject.

I came to rely particularly on seven libraries: the National Library of Australia, the NSW State and Mitchell Libraries, the Dennis Wolanski Performing Arts Library at the Sydney Opera House – my thanks to Evelyn Kopfler and her colleagues – and the libraries of the National Institute of Dramatic Art, the Art Gallery of NSW and the Film Television and Radio School.

Two books became indispensable to my research: Alan Lawson's 1974 bibliography *Patrick White* – if only its text came up to the present day! – and the 1985 *Oxford Companion to Australian Literature* compiled by William Wilde, Joy Hooton and Barry Andrews. Both are published by Oxford University Press.

Grateful acknowledgement is made to Judith Wright for permission to quote the opening lines of 'Turning Fifty' on p.310, and to the estate of John Betjemen and John Murray (Publishers) Ltd. for permission to use lines from 'The Flight from Bootle' on p.579.

In April 1993, when I thought I had collected all the letters I wanted to publish, and with the footnoting still incomplete, I turned the material over to two friends: Nick Enright who was my sounding-board as I wrote the *Life* and Liz McDonald, publishing director of Lothian Books in Melbourne, who edited my spy book *The Ivanov Trail* in 1984. After weeks of sifting through the typescript they suggested cuts which were essential to me finding the final shape of the collection a year later.

When the decision was made to edit the book in Australia instead of London, I asked Liz McDonald to recommend me an editor. She took the *Letters* on herself and through the summer of 1993–94 somehow managed to add these to her responsibilities and maintain her vigilance, patience, rigour and good humor as we worked through this immense text. I can't thank her enough.

Responsible, finally, for bringing this ramshackle enterprise to order was Matthew Kelly, a gentle man of almost infinite patience who knows when to show the whip. I came to hold him in very high regard: few books in Australia, I think, can have had such a devoted publisher.

I also want to thank Di Adams, Alliance Francaise in Sydney, Don Anderson, the Angles, Angus & Robertson, Franca Arena, Neil Armfield, J. Wray Armstrong, Christopher Arnott, Melanie Aspey of News International, Thea Astley, the Australian Archives, the Australian War Memorial Research Library, Paul Bailey, Bruce Beresford, Tim Bestelink of Perpetual Trustee,

Michael Bott of Reading University, Yolande Bird of the National Theatre, John Brack, Veronica Brady, Jo Bramble of Penguin Books, Katharine Brisbane and Currency Press, Paul Brunton, Tony Buckley, Peter Burch, Elizabeth Butcher and John Clark of NIDA, Nigel Butterley, John Byrne, Geoffrey Cains, Charlotte and Alistair Calder, Margaret Cameron, Kathleen Cann of Cambridge University Library, Gordon Chater, Rosalind Chatto, Anne Chisholm, Dymphna Clark, Tony Clune, Tony Colwell, the consulates in Sydney of Sweden and Greece, Penny Coleing, Jeremy Coleman, Peter Coleman, Fred Colins, Patrick Cook, Alison Corfield, Roger Covell, Zelman Cowen, the Crafts Council (UK), Tim Curnow, David Dale and Brian Dale (no relation), Jenny Darling, Michael Davie, Dilys Daws, Michael Denborough, Francis de Groen, Ethel de Keyser, Jane de Teliga and (Mrs) Rae de Teliga, Rosemary Dobson, Espie Dods, Sue Douglas, Alan Drury of the BBC, David Dryden, Sue Du Val, Ken Dutton of St Paul's and Newcastle University, Chuck Elliott, the embassies to Australia of France, Spain, Turkey and Italy, Warren Fahey, the Fairfax Library, Julie Fallowfield of McIntosh & Otis, Penelope Feltham of the Alexander Turnbull Library, Andrew Fisher, Fisher Library, Michael Fitzjames, Kate Fitzpatrick, Sandra Forbes, Thelma Forshaw, Lindsay Foyle, Ian Frazer of Melbourne City Council, Gwen Frolich, Tom Gaffney, Lyn Garton, Nicholas Garland, David Garrett, Ron Geering, Sally Gell, Fay Gervasoni, Mary Gibson, David Godwin, Elise Goodman, Sue and Sandy Gordon, Tony and Liz Gregory, Kate Grenville, Hannah and Ferry Grunseit, Ian Gunn of the Watters Gallery, Guy Halliday, Janet Hawley, Douglas Hedge, Jill Hickson, the Hobart *Mercury*, Boris Hoffman, Christopher Hogwood, Gordon Hølmebakk, Donald Horne, Robert Hughes, the Imperial War Museum, Ivor Indyk, International Casting Services, Alan Jones, Anna Katzman, Tom Kirk, Lou Klepac, Christopher Kuhn, Diana Langmore, Alan Lawson, Ward Lee, Angela Liddy, Hilary Linstead, Tim Lloyd, Andy Lloyd-James, Mary Lord, Patricia Losey, Robin Lucas, Michael Ludgrove of Christies, Caroline Lurie, Billy McCann, Jim McClelland, Donald McDonald, Jane Macgowan, Jeannette McHugh, Mary McKie, Bill McLeod, David McNicoll, Paul Maloney, Pam and Ewan Marr, Rosemary Meares, Harry Medlin, Patricia Methven of King's College London, Janet Moat of the British Film Institute, Anthea Morton-Saner, Jack Mundey, Rafael Martinez Nadal, the National Gallery of Victoria, Robyn Nevin, the NSW State Archives, the New York Historical Society, John Nieuwenhuizen, Patrick O'Donovan of King's College Cambridge, Margaret O'Hagan of the Fryer Library, Ward O'Neill, Jenya Osborne, Andy Palmer of Forbes in NSW, Eileen Parbury, Ted Pask, Tim Pearce, the Performing Arts Collection of Adelaide, Peter Pierce, R., Nicholas Pounder and Simon Taafe, Graeme Powell, the Power Institute Library, Maria Prerauer, Vincent Price, Angie Quick, Helen Railton, Carol Raye, Barrett Reid, Bronwyn Renni, Elizabeth Riddell, Andrew Riemer, Alan Roberts, Mark Robertson, Colin Roderick, Patricia Rolfe, Hazel Rowley, the Royal Agricultural Society, the RAF Museum, the Royal Botanic Gardens of Sydney, Robin Rue, Janne Ryan for particular forbearance, Patricia Seales, Andrew Sayers of the

Australian National Gallery, Paul Schnee, Leo Schofield, Maurice Shadbolt, Tom Shapcott, Jim Sharman, Pam Short, Vivian Smith, Margaret Spira, Des Stammers and John Shillinglaw of Wattyl Victoria, Maria Müller Sommer, the state libraries of Western Australia, South Australia, Victoria and Queensland, Ross Steele, Anne Straton, David Stratton, Sun Books/Pan Macmillan, Sydney Girls High, Les Tanner, the Tasmanian State Library, John Thompson, Peter Thompson, Tiny Tim, the *Times Literary Supplement*, Glen Tomasetti, Brian Toohey, Guy Tranter, John Tranter, Lyn Tranter, Andrew Traucki, the University of NSW Library, Mary Vallentine, Carl Vine, Jenny and Steven Vogel, Thea Waddell, John Walsh of the Wollongong Art Gallery, Dennis Watkins personal trainer, Liz Watts of the Australian Film Commission, Elizabeth Webby, the Weed Society of NSW, Michael and Judy White, Gough Whitlam, Alan Wilson of Shanahans Management, Gerard Windsor, Marian Wilkinson, Robyn Williams, Ruth Williams and her inner-city team of transcribers, Arkie Whiteley, Wendy Whiteley, Mary Young, and all the others who helped me find, compile, research and publish Patrick White's letters.

ILLUSTRATIONS

Illustrations: Credits and Sources (by page number)

Frontispiece	John Spooner, 1980
p.7	Adrian Feint, Patrick White's bookplate, 1931, reprinted with permission of the Estate of Adrian Feint
p.48	Jenny Coopes, 1994
p.73	Cyril Dubois, *Bulletin*, 10 April 1957
p.96	*Bulletin*, 25 January 1961
p.121	Sidney Nolan, *Voss*, 1957
p.166	Nado Milat, Sydney *Observer*, 21 March 1959
p.194	George Ferke, *Sydney Morning Herald*, 28 October 1961
p.239	George Ferke, *Sydney Morning Herald*, 24 October 1964
p.277	Nicolas Bentley, London *Sunday Telegraph*, 15 May 1968
p.316	Maie Casey, 1968
p.359	Anthony Ladd-Hudson, *Sydney Morning Herald*, 17 October
p.417	John Spooner, *National Times*, 11 October 1976
p.472	Ward O'Neill, *Sydney Morning Herald*, 23 July 1977
p.479	Jenny Coopes, *National Times*, 27 March 1978
p.502	Emeric Vrbancich, *Sydney Morning Herald*, 13 October 1979
p.523	David Levine, *New York Review of Books*, 17 April 1980, reprinted with permission from *The New York Review of Books*, © 1980 Nyrev, Inc.
p.555	John Spooner, *Age Monthly Review*, February 1982
p.588	Victoria Roberts, *Sydney Morning Herald*, 16 July 1983
p.607	Brett Whiteley, 1980

THE CAST OF CORRESPONDENTS

AGENTS, LITERARY: In London PW's agent from 1941 until her retirement in 1975 was the forthright **Juliet O'Hea** of Curtis Brown. 'He is temperamental, prickly and I fear you will find his letters far from cosy,' she warned her New York counterpart in a 1966 memo. 'He is full of inhibitions of all sorts but he is brilliantly clever.' PW's correspondence with O'Hea was destroyed in 1965 when Curtis Brown moved to new offices in Regent Street – some duplicates survived in his agent's files in New York – but his business letters to O'Hea after 1965 are in the agency's London records, and twenty personal letters to O'Hea written after her retirement in 1975 are in the National Library of Australia. In all, eleven letters to O'Hea appear here.

In New York PW dealt at first with **Naomi Burton** of Curtis Brown; two of his letters to her appears here. In the same office **Edith Haggard** tried to place his short stories; and one letter to her appears here. Both correspondences are now in the Curtis Brown Archive at Columbia University. In 1965 Curtis Brown in London switched its clients to the **John Cushman** agency in New York. Cushman represented PW from 1965 to 1978. After meeting PW in 1968, Cushman wrote to O'Hea, 25.x.68, 'He does have very fixed if vague ideas about all his affairs.' One card from the Cushman papers at Columbia University appears in this collection. After 1978 Curtis Brown New York took the London list back again and PW was represented thereafter by Perry Knowlton.

In Australia the Curtis Brown office in Sydney handled PW's affairs once O'Hea had retired in London in 1975. He worked most closely with **Barbara Mobbs** to whom he dedicated *The Memoirs of Many In One*, 1986: 'To the flying nun'. When Mobbs was dismissed from the agency in 1986, PW went with her and angrily broke all his links with Curtis Brown. Mobbs was named in his will as sole literary executor.

AKERHOLT, MAY-BRIT: (1948–   ), academic and dramaturg, author of *Patrick White*, 1988, a study of the plays. She has four letters from PW; one appears here.

ARMFIELD, NEIL: (1955–   ), director whose work PW admired in Sydney from the late 1970s. Armfield's first PW production was *Signal Driver* at the 1982 Adelaide Festival; he directed two further productions of the play; PW dedicated the published text to him. *Shepherd on the Rocks*, 1987, was written for Armfield to direct; he also directed PW's last theatrical triumph, a revival of *The Ham Funeral* in Sydney in late 1989. Three of PW's letters to Armfield are published here.

THE ARRIGHIS: **Eleanor** (c.1910–73), and her daughters **Luciana** (c.1941–) and **Niké** (1944–), did not meet their cousin PW until 1961 and most of his letters to Eleanor (Nellie) were not written until she left Sydney to live in Europe in 1965. Niké Borghese has eight of PW's letters to her mother; two are published here. Luciana designed *The Night the Prowler*, 1978, for PW and then the jacket of *The Twyborn Affair*, 1979, and the opera *Voss*, 1986. She has a dozen letters from PW; four appear here.

BARNARD, MARJORIE: (1897–1987), novelist and historian. One letter to Barnard surviving in the *Meanjin* Archive of the Baillieu Library of the University of Melbourne is published here.

BEATSON, PETER: (1942–), scholar. PW's surviving correspondence with the New Zealander begins in 1970 (the first letter is lost); that year he stayed at Martin Road for a few days and they met again in Hyères in 1976. Much of the correspondence concerns PW's religious ideas and Beatson's study of these, *The Eye in the Mandala*, was published in 1976. Thereafter contact was slight. Beatson has 26 letters from PW; four appear here.

BEDFORD, JEAN: (1946–), writer and journalist. Bedford and her partner Peter Corris have four letters from PW; one is published here.

BENSON, MARY: (1919–), South African writer who contacted PW in 1968 when recruiting famous names to campaign against apartheid. PW became an advocate for her work, especially among local and foreign politicians. She has sixteen letters from PW; two appear here.

BEST, MARSHALL: (1901–82), **Ben Huebsch**'s protégé and successor at Viking. Best's correspondence with PW began in 1947 but concentrated on chores – proofs, libel, jackets, etc. – until the old man retired from day-to-day publishing in the late 1950s. Thereafter a rich correspondence continued even after Best's own retirement in 1973. Though remembered by his colleagues as the most decorous man in the history of publishing, Best fought a long and fruitless campaign to edit PW's prose. The letters to Best survive in the Viking files; eleven appear here.

BISHOP, ALEXANDRA: see **The Family**.

BJÖRKSTÉN, INGMAR: (1936–), Swedish critic, journalist and novelist who corresponded with PW from the time of his first visit to Australia in 1962. Björkstén's *Patrick White: epikern från Australien* was published as PW won the 1973 Nobel Prize and appeared in English as *Patrick White: a General Introduction* in 1976. Twenty-three of Björkstén's letters are now in the Australian National Library; eight are published here.

BRISSENDEN, BOB: (1928–91), poet, critic and academic; author of *Patrick White*, 1966, in the Longmans, Green series 'Writers and their Work'. Thirty-six letters from PW to Brissenden are in the National Library of Australia; one appears here.

BROWNE, CORAL: (1913–91), actress. She destroyed a large correspondence from PW. Only two survive, now in the National Library of Australia, and both are published here.

BURTON, NAOMI: see **Agents, literary**.

ZOE CALDWELL: (1933–   ), actress and one of the 'loves' of PW's life, was also a terrible correspondent. From Greece, 15.v.63, PW raged: 'Dear Zoe you old cow I wonder if you will ever write.' Caldwell has five letters from PW; two appear here.

THE CAPES: **Tom Maschler** (1933–   ) was chairman and **Graham C. Greene** (1936–   ) managing director of Jonathan Cape when the firm accepted *The Vivisector*, the first of the PW novels it published. PW corresponded mainly with Maschler in the early years but Greene later became a friend, PW's principal contact and chairman of Cape's holding company. Among the Jonathan Cape papers at Reading University are letters from PW to members of the editorial staff, blurb writer **Juliet Page** and copy editor **Deborah Shepherd**. In all, 28 of PW's letters to 'the Capes' are published here.

CARPENTER, FREDDIE: see **Waters, Ronald**.

CASEY, MAIE: (1892–1983), writer and hostess, wife of Dick Casey, Governor-General 1965–69. Her fine correspondence with PW began in 1966 but declined in later years as they settled into a routine of long telephone calls on Sunday mornings. Fifty-one letters by PW have been found in Maie Casey's papers; eleven are published here.

CHANDLER, GEORGE: (1915–92), director-general of the National Library of Australia from 1974–80 who had great hopes of landing PW's papers. One letter by PW to Chandler held by the National Library is published here.

CHRISTESEN, CLEM: (1911–   ), poet and editor of *Meanjin* who was remarkably reluctant to meet PW but they corresponded regularly for a decade from 1956. A subject frequently canvassed was asthma cures. Thirty-four letters from PW are in the *Meanjin* Archive of the Baillieu Library at the University of Melbourne; four appear here.

CLARK, MANNING: (1915–93), historian. He began to correspond with PW in 1961, some years after their first meeting. PW greatly admired the early volumes of Clark's *History of Australia*. They continued to correspond until PW grew enraged with Clark's prominent role in the Bicentennial celebrations of 1988. Thirty-eight of PW's letters to Manning and Dymphna Clark are in the National Library of Australia; nine appear here.

COLLINSON, LAURIE: (1925–   ), poet and playwright. Eleven of PW's letters to Collinson are in the National Library of Australia; one is published here.

CUSHMAN, JOHN: see **Agents, literary**.

DAWS, LAWRENCE: (1927–   ), painter and enthusiast for the writings of Carl Jung. Eight letters from PW to Daws survive; one is published here.

DICKSON, WENDY: (c.1939–   ), designer of the Sydney *Ham Funeral*, 1962, *Night on Bald Mountain*, 1964, and Sharman's revival of *The Season at Sarsaparilla*, 1976. She has nine letters from PW; one appears here.

DIGBY, DESMOND: (1933–   ), painter and designer who met PW in 1961; their friendship was sealed the following year when Digby designed the set for the Adelaide première of *The Season at Sarsaparilla*. He went on to design the Sydney *Sarsaparilla* and the Melbourne *Cheery Soul*, both 1963; and the jackets for *Four Plays*, 1965, *The Solid Mandala*, 1966, *The Eye of the Storm*, 1973, and *The Cockatoos*, 1974. Theirs was the great telephone friendship – he is D in *Flaws in the Glass* – but PW also wrote when Digby and his partner James Allison were on holidays and when the pair moved to the north coast of NSW in the late 1970s. Digby made available only two letters from PW; both are published here.

THE DUTTONS: **Geoffrey** (1922–   ) and **Ninette Dutton** (1923–   ), to whom PW wrote 277 letters from 1957 until he broke off with them shortly after his 70th birthday in 1982. These letters – written mostly to Geoffrey Dutton – with news of books, cooking, people, paintings, dogs, films and illness are the backbone of this collection. By the early 1980s the correspondence was only a ghost of its former self as PW's disapproval of Dutton's life and career mounted. Two hundred and sixty-one of the letters are in the National Library of Australia; a further sixteen remain with Ninette Dutton. A total of 96 appear here; all are from the National Library collection except for those to Ninette Dutton 21.ix.68, 10.v.70, 24.viii.70 and 11.ii.79.

FALKENBERG, ELIZABETH: (1903–   ), an eccentric fan in Hamburg. PW began to reply to her letters in 1976 and continued to write until shortly before his death. Lascaris reports that PW regarded writing to Falkenberg as a particular chore, but his letters to her are quirky and revealing. She gave 33 of them to the National Library of Australia; nine are published here.

THE FAMILY: Nothing survives of PW's correspondence with his father Victor Martindale (Dick) White (1867–1937), his mother Ruth (1877–1963), or his sister Suzanne (1915–69). At the outbreak of war Suzanne married Geoffrey Peck (1908–56), and, as always at the marriage of women in his family, PW expressed rage and disappointment. The Pecks had two children in these years: **Gillian** (1941–   ) and **Alexandra** (1944–   ). Soon after Geoffrey Peck's sudden death in 1955, Suzanne discovered she was pregnant with **Frances** (1956–   ). Suzanne tried to move her family to Australia in the mid-1960s but Alexandra never left London where she married Christopher Bishop, the EMI recording producer, later managing director of the Philharmonia Orchestra. Thirteen of PW's letters to her survive; all pre-date her divorce in 1987 and remarriage to an English company director, Guy Dawson; two of those letters are published here. Gillian stayed briefly and unhappily at Martin Road – a great melodrama in PW's correspondence – before returning to London to marry. PW was enraged by the match but came later to accept this man in the family. Suzanne and Frances settled in Sydney in a house not very far from Martin Road. When Suzanne died in early 1969, Frances was sent to boarding school in England, an ordeal that engaged all PW's sympathy. His correspondence with her began at this time. After she left school, Frances lived for a while at Martin Road. Their close relationship was shattered – characteristically – by her marriage to a fellow-art student Patrick Richardson. She broke off contact with her uncle. Frances Richardson has 29 letters from PW; two are published here.

GARLAND, PEGGY: (1903–   ), sculptor, one of the three Withycombe cousins PW met in the late 1920s who became his English family. Though **Betty Withycombe** made the most immediate impact and the youngest, Joyce, was a lifelong friend, Peggy had the most intimate and lasting friendship with PW. His letters to her in the early years at Dogwoods are among his finest: he confided in Peggy Garland and argued with her. From him she provoked the frankest accounts of his inner life – especially the shifting religious beliefs that underpin his writing from the early 1950s – and to her he wrote the most vivid accounts of life on the farm. After the break-up of her marriage, she returned to London and in 1962 moved to a village north of Oxford where she still lives. PW's letters to Peggy Garland remained always engaged and never routine to the end of his life. One hundred and eleven of them are now in the National Library of Australia; 50 are published here.

GARLAND, PHILIP: (1947–86), son of **Peggy Garland**. PW's one letter to the boy, now in the National Library of Australia, is published here.

GIFFIN, MICHAEL: (1953–   ), Anglican priest and academic commentator on PW's religious thought. His one letter from PW is published here.

GLOVER, FREDERICK: (1913–72), bank manager, Christian and thespian of Castle Hill. He wrote plays including *The Inward Part*, 1947, contrasting the pleasures of wartime comradeship with later civilian life; and he acted and directed in amateur theatricals first in Sarsaparilla and then the bush to which the Rural Bank posted him in 1957. PW's correspondence with Glover never faltered for the next fifteen years. Glover advised PW on investments and encouraged him to disinter *The Ham Funeral*; in gratitude PW dedicated *Four Plays*, 1965, to him. Though Glover appears to have claimed shortly before his death to have destroyed all PW's letters, 221 survive in the hands of his family. Thirty-six appear here.

GREEN, DOROTHY: (1915–91), critic and biographer who championed PW's work from the 1970s. Their friendship and correspondence which began then intensified through a shared interest in preventing nuclear war. Eighteen letters from PW to Green are in the library of the Australian Defence Forces Academy in Canberra; six are published here.

GREENE, GRAHAM C.: see **The Capes.**

GRENVILLE, KATE: (1950–), writer whose work PW admired. She has one letter from PW which is published here.

GROLIER CLUB: New York publishers' club. One letter, written to mark the death of **Ben Huebsch**, is published here.

HAGGARD, EDITH: see **Agents, literary.**

HALMAGYI, ALICE: (1922–), PW's GP and friend for twenty years from 1957. He consulted her most weeks and wrote only when travelling. The unhappiness she suffered after her divorce came to irritate PW who chose to break with her when her name appeared on a public statement about nuclear medicine in 1977. Fifteen letters to Halmagyi are in the National Library of Australia; two appear here.

HARROWER, ELIZABETH: (1928–), novelist and friend who met PW through **John Sumner** in the early 1960s. There are few PW letters to Harrower for they lived in the same city and spoke for an hour each Sunday on the telephone, 'about life and death and recipes and human nature'. One intense burst of correspondence came in 1971 when Harrower spent seven months living with **Cynthia Nolan** in Putney. In all Harrower has 26 letters from PW; nine are published here.

HAZZARD, SHIRLEY: (1931–), novelist born in Australia who has lived abroad since 1947. PW corresponded with her and her husband the American biographer and translator **Francis Steegmuller** (1906–) from 1973 for a decade. They have fifteen letters from PW; six appear here.

HELLYER, JILL: (1925–), poet and one of the founders of the Australian Society of Authors. Thirteen of PW's letters to her are in the National Library of Australia; two are published here.

HENDERSON, MOYA: (1941–), composer who set out, in 1972, to write an opera based on *Voss*. She left the Sacre Coeur Order to study composition in Germany; no opera was written but she set PW's *Six Urban Songs* first performed 1986. She has fifteen letters from PW, three are published here.

HERBERT, XAVIER: (1901–84), novelist whom PW met in the mid-1970s and corresponded with occasionally from 1975 to 1979. This ended with a blistering letter after Herbert told the press PW was a bad correspondent. Eight letters to Herbert are in the University of Queensland's Fryer Memorial Library; two appear here.

HOLT, HAROLD: (1908–67), conservative prime minister of Australia from 1966 until he disappeared in the surf a few days before Christmas 1967. One letter to Holt surviving in the Australian Archives is published here.

HU WENZHONG: (1935–), scholar of PW's work in Beijing, translator of *The Tree of Man*. The National Library of Australia has fourteen letters from PW to Hu; one is published here.

HUEBSCH, BEN: (1876–1964), publisher, the rock on which PW's career was built. Theirs was one of PW's few consciously literary correspondences and one of the best, for PW could not strike easy attitudes with this worldly old man. Apart from a few letters about *Happy Valley* now somewhere lost in private hands, there are 73 letters to Huebsch surviving in three collections. Of the 36 quoted here, those of 11.i.47, 4.ii.48, 29.iii.50, 3.iv.52, 8.xii.52, 24.xi.54, 15.ii.55, 25.x.55, 29.xii.55, 8.ii.57, 25.ii.57 and 11.ii.58 remain in the files at the Viking Press; those of 18.iii.64 and 12.vi.64 are in the Ben Huebsch Collection at Columbia University; all the rest are in the Library of Congress.

HUMPHRIES, BARRY: (1934–), collector, writer and comedian whom PW declared on Australia Day 1974, 'One of the most original scintillating minds we have produced'. For Humphries PW wrote the screenplays Clay, 1963, and Monkey Puzzle, 1977, but neither was filmed. Drunkenness, divorce and mockery of Gough Whitlam's supporters took their toll on PW's affection, but crucial to their drifting apart in the late 1970s was PW's notion that Humphries' creation Edna Everage was exhausted. Humphries made nine letters from PW available to me; two are published here.

JAMES, BRIAN: (1918–), actor whose presence has contributed to much of the best film, television and theatre in Australia since the 1960s. PW met and courted James when he was cast as the clergyman in the 1963 Melbourne production of *A Cheery Soul*. James has thirteen letters from PW; three are quoted here.

JAMES, GRAHAM: (1945–), sculptor and designer. James has 21 letters from PW; one appears here.

JENKINS, JIM: 1985 Sydney Mardi Gras promotions co-ordinator. One letter from PW condemning the event is published here.

JOHNSON, SPUD: (1897–1968), poet, journalist and lover. PW began their correspondence in 1939 as the train took him east from Santa Fe after their first weeks together. These early letters to Johnson are the only love letters of PW to come into my hands. Though discreet, they are among the finest letters PW wrote. He and Johnson continued to correspond through the war but PW stopped writing in 1945 about the time he decided to head to Australia. PW never told Lascaris of Johnson's existence. At the Harry Ransom Humanities Research Centre of the University of Texas at Austin are 27 letters and cards PW wrote to Johnson; fifteen are quoted here.

JONES, BARRY O.: (1932–), thinker, politician and author; the only Labor figure with whom PW never broke. Jones has about half a dozen letters from PW; one is published here.

KENNY, JANICE: (1936–), principal librarian, general reference, National Library of Australia. One official letter to Kenny held by the library is published here.

THE KRIEGERS: Fritz (1904–86) and Ile (1907–89), neighbours in Castle Hill and a lifeline to civilisation for PW and Lascaris. Because they spoke to one another every few days, their intense friendship only generated a handful of fine travel letters. PW's quarrels with Fritz began in the early 1960s – these are recorded in PW's letters to **Frederick Glover** – and correspondence ceased for nearly twenty years until PW heard in the early 1980s that Fritz was ill in Melbourne. PW's letters and cards to the Kriegers are with Ile's brother Andrew Fisher. There are 33 in all, including PW's letters to the Fishers and their children. Seven letters to the Kriegers are published here.

LAMBERT, JEAN: (1914–), novelist and distinguished translator who translated five of PW's books for Gallimard: *Une ceinture de Feuilles*, 1981, *Les Incarnations d'Eddie Twyborn*, 1983, *Défauts dans le Miroir*, 1985, *Mémoires éclatés d'Alex Xenophon Demirjian Gray*, 1988, and *Des Morts et des Vivants*, 1990. Lambert has fifteen letters from PW; four are published here.

LORD, MARY: (1929–), academic and biographer of Hal Porter. One letter by PW to Lord held in the National Library of Australia is published here.

LOSEY, JOSEPH: (1909–84), director chosen by PW to film *Voss*. The project collapsed but it provoked a fine correspondence that continued until Losey's death. The British Film Institute has 43 letters from PW to Losey; nine appear here.

McGRATH, JOHN: (1935–), playwright, scriptwriter and collaborator with Ken Russell on an early proposal to film *Voss*. McGrath corresponded with PW until Russell dropped out of the picture. McGrath has eight letters from PW; three are published here.

MacKENZIE, MANFRED: (1944–), Sydney literary academic, one of many academics whom PW helped unobtrusively over the years. MacKenzie has seven letters from PW written in the 1960s; one is published here.

McKIE, MOLLIE: (1904–90), WAF Intelligence officer in PW's unit in Alexandria and later a teacher in the UK and Australia. 'A hearty Australian schoolmistress,' PW described her in a letter to Nolan, 7.ix.64. PW and McKie corresponded until they fell out over Gough Whitlam. Seventy-one letters to McKie are in the National Library of Australia; nine appear here.

McQUEEN, HUMPHREY: (1942–), historian, commentator and Revolutionary Socialist, author of the influential history, *A New Britannia*, 1970. PW appointed

McQueen a trustee of the Patrick White Prize. One letter from PW to McQueen is published here.

MALOUF, DAVID: (1934–   ), writer whose work PW greatly admired. Malouf wrote the libretto for **Richard Meale**'s opera *Voss*, 1986, and an unfilmed screenplay of *The Twyborn Affair*. PW wrote only a handful of letters to Malouf; two are published here.

MAMBLAS, PEPE: José Ruiz de Arana y Bauer, Viscount Mamblas and later the Duke of Baena (1893–1985), Spanish diplomat and PW's lover in the summer and winter of 1937. An intense correspondence continued until the spring of 1938 when the affair ended. Towards the ends of their lives, after many years' silence, they exchanged a couple of letters and photographs. Twenty-seven letters and cards to Mamblas are now in the National Library of Australia; nine are published here.

MASCHLER, TOM: see **The Capes**.

MEALE, RICHARD: (1932–   ), composer for whom PW sketched the libretto Births, Deaths and Lotteries in 1978. That Meale turned this satirical project down in favour of *Voss* aggravated PW's early hostility to the explorer opera. Meale ignored the novelist's directions not to write beautiful music and the result was a success PW himself acknowledged. Meale has seven letters from PW; two are published here.

MEDLIN, HARRY: (1920–   ), scientist of Adelaide University and chairman of the Adelaide University Theatre Guild in the years in which PW's plays were premièred by the guild. Medlin has 22 letters and telegrams from PW; one is published here.

MICHELL, KEITH: (1928–   ), actor and director who left his birthplace South Australia to become a leading figure in the West End and at Chichester. Correspondence began when Michell asked PW for a play in 1956. As a result PW exhumed and reworked *The Ham Funeral* which Michell rejected. He has a handful of letters from PW; two are published here.

MILLER, HARRY: (1934–   ), promoter of genius who tried and failed to produce a film of *Voss*. Miller was on the board of Qantas, chairman of the Queen's Silver Jubilee Committee and a consultant to the Australian Opera before the 1979 crash of his ticketing agency, Computicket. The only fragment of PW's correspondence with Miller published here is the draft of a letter sent to Miller in prison in 1982.

THE MOORES: Gwen (1910–   ), a teacher, and David (1918–   ), screenwriter and anthropologist, whose untroubled friendship with PW and Lascaris began in 1956 and lasted for life. PW dedicated *The Solid Mandala* to the Moores in 1966. Though PW wrote only when he or they were travelling, his letters to the Moores are among his best. Sixty-three are in the National Library of Australia; 21 are published here.

MURRAY-SMITH, STEPHEN: (1922–88), editor of *Overland*. He wrote in 1962 asking PW to comment on a review of *Riders in the Chariot* about to appear in the magazine; PW declined but that exchange set the ambit of their correspondence for the next 25 years: letters much concerned with critical reaction to PW's work. Thirty of PW's letters to Murray-Smith are in the La Trobe Library in Melbourne; one appears here.

NÉTILLARD, SUZANNE: (c.1920–   ), translator for Gallimard of *Le Char des Élus*, 1965, and *L'Oeil du Cyclone*, 1978. She exasperated PW and made the tactical error of joking that he should write more simply. She provided PW when visiting her in France with names for *The Eye of the Storm* from the 1950 telephone book for the Department of Lot. Only three of his letters to her survive; one is published here.

THE NOLANS: the painter Sidney (1917–93), and writer Cynthia (née Reed, c.1913–76). Correspondence began in 1957 when PW asked the painter for a jacket for *Voss*. Characteristically, it was Cynthia Nolan who replied. From the evidence of the letters, PW's friendship with the Nolans was at its most intense from the early 1970s by which time PW was corresponding almost entirely with Cynthia Nolan. Shortly before her suicide, Cynthia Nolan deposited PW's letters – among a mass of papers – in the National Library of Australia under an unprecedented 45-year embargo. During his lifetime, Sidney Nolan declined to lift the embargo to allow me access. In early 1994, the Nolans' daughter Jinx gave me access to her mother's papers for the purpose of this book. The National Library of Australia has 136 letters, cards and telegrams from PW to the Nolans, 21 are published here.

O'BRIEN, EDNA: (1932–   ), Irish novelist who sent PW a copy of *The Country Girls* in 1960 and declared herself a fan. They lost touch. 'Not through ill-will,' O'Brien told me, 'but the usual old weary reason – time and pressures.' She has six letters from PW; one is published here.

O'HEA, JULIET: see **Agents, literary**.

OSBORNE, CHARLES: (1927–   ), London literary figure and editor for many years of the *London Magazine*. Osborne opened the correspondence in 1961 asking PW to write about painting for the magazine; he refused but a professional friendship followed and PW's stories appeared in the magazine in the 1960s. Osborne sided with Nolan in the great feud, by which time PW was calling him, to Stern, 17.xii.81, 'that pushy little Charles Osborne'. PW's letters to Osborne 1961–65 are in the Harry Ransom Humanities Research Centre of the University of Texas at Austin; letters from 1968–76 are in the Cambridge University Library. Three in all are published here.

PAGE, JULIET: see **The Capes**.

PEARCE, BERYL: (1936–   ), secretary of the Adelaide University Theatre Guild in the years it premièred PW's plays. One of PW's letters to Pearce is published here.

PECK, ALEXANDRA (later Bishop, then Dawson): see **The Family.**

PECK, FRANCES (later Richardson): see *The Family.*

REAGAN, RONALD: (1911–   ), actor and president of the United States, 1980–88. An open letter to Reagan, intended for publication in the *New York Times*, is published here. PW addressed three such letters to world leaders via newspapers. Those to François Mitterrand and Margaret Thatcher also went unpublished. Copies were found among PW's papers after his death.

SCOTT ROGERS, JEAN: (1908–   ), screenwriter recruited by **Ronald Waters** in 1931 as a pen friend for PW in Australia. They met later in London. From the late 1940s Scott Rogers worked for the Rank Organisation at Pinewood and switched to television as a scriptwriter in 1957. She wrote over a hundred episodes of *Emergency – Ward Ten* and her films include the Boris Karloff horror *Corridors of Blood*, 1962. Early in their friendship, after a dinner in Ebury Street, she wrote in her diary, 15 September 1936, 'I felt myself giving off that slight glitter which his company always provokes from me.' Theirs is the longest-surviving correspondence: from 1931 to 1988. In 1991 she gave 98 letters to the National Library of Australia; 23 are published here.

SCULTHORPE, PETER: (1929–   ), composer. A brief but fertile correspondence accompanied their doomed collaboration on the 'Mrs Fraser Opera'. From its collapse in late 1964, PW vilified Sculthorpe. The composer has seven letters from PW; two are published here.

SEMMLER, CLEM: (1914–   ), critic and deputy general manager of the ABC 1965–77. Their friendship developed at **Maie Casey**'s literary parties at Admiralty House; PW felt Semmler on the 'right side' of various literary issues and found his ABC position useful in promoting his causes. After Semmler retired to the Southern Highlands their friendship faded. Thirteen letters from PW to Semmler are in the Mitchell Library; two are published here.

SHEPHERD, DEBORAH: see **The Capes.**

SMITH, RALPH: (1900–93), bachelor collector of books and paintings. 'What an anachronism Ralph is,' PW told Glover, 7.iii.59. 'He is still doing all those things that people did in the 'thirties . . . I suppose there must be other pockets of the same kind of dilettante behaviour still left here and there.' Their friendship ended in 1966 after an argument over Greece. Two of PW's letters to Smith have surfaced in the library of the Australian Defence Forces Academy; one is published here.

STEAD, CHRISTINA: (1902–83), novelist whose work PW championed after reading *The Man Who Loved Children* in 1966. She thought his writing, 'hardwon bilge' but kept this opinion to herself. PW awarded her the first Patrick White Prize. She destroyed a number of letters from him; only a few cards survive in the possession of her estate; two are published here.

STEEGMULLER, FRANCIS: see **Hazzard, Shirley.**

STEPHENSEN, P. R. (INKY): (1901–65), publisher, polemicist and hack, author of *The Foundations of Culture in Australia*, 1936. **Ruth** and **Dick White** were the most generous shareholders in his Sydney publishing venture which failed in 1935 before he could issue PW's *The Ploughman*. The money had been spent by Stephensen attempting to publish **Xavier Herbert**'s *Capricornia*, 1938. PW's correspondence with Stephensen about the poetry and the jackaroo novels is in the Mitchell Library. One letter is published here.

STERN, JAMES: (1904–93), eminent critic and writer whose 1955 *New York Times* notice for *The Tree of Man* made PW a major literary figure in North America, Britain and, by osmosis, Australia. Stern took the initiative and wrote first to PW in 1958; they met that year in England and there began a fruitful friendship and correspondence. His role as a public critic of PW's novels ended after reviewing *Riders in the Chariot* for the *New York Times* but his assessments – at times quite hostile – continued by letter. PW's replies contain insights into his work of an order once revealed to **Huebsch**. Stern gave 60 letters and cards to the National Library of Australia before his death; fourteen are published here.

STOW, RANDOLPH (MICK): (1935–   ), novelist and poet. PW admired Stow's work but was baffled by the man: he told Glover, 13.xi.59, that apart from some 'novelettish minor characters' *To the Islands*, 1958, was 'magnificently done'. Stow was awarded the Patrick White Prize in 1979. He has ten letters from PW; two are published here.

SUMNER, JOHN: (1924–   ), left the British Merchant Marine for the theatre and established in Melbourne in 1953 the first professional repertory theatre in Australia. For PW he directed *The Season at Sarsaparilla*, 1962, and *A Cheery Soul*, 1964. There were no rows with Sumner. PW told Glover, 26.x.62: 'Sumner is a sincere producer, with greater depth and mellowness than the Tasker.' Sumner and his second wife **Margaret** have 16 letters from PW; one fragment of a letter to her is published here.

SYDNEY MORNING HERALD: broadsheet published by the Fairfaxes, 1841–1990. The Fairfaxes were among the small group of families – including the Whites – who once dominated Sydney. PW's letters report the tangled romance of old Sir Warwick and his young bride Mary, but PW's contact with the family was through Warwick's elder son James (1933–   ). PW told **Dutton**, 1.v.67. 'He grows on one. There is much more in him than he cares to admit, but I expect he gets so outrageously flattered because he is a millionaire and a Fairfax, he has withdrawn into himself in embarrassment.' From the time of PW's return to Sydney in 1946, the *SMH* published nineteen letters from PW about immigration, painting, music, literature, the Olympic Games, Green Bans, etc. Three are published here.

TACEY, DAVID: (1953–   ), psycho-analytic critic who wrote *Patrick White: Fiction and the Unconscious*, 1988, and tore into PW's late writing for being camp. Tacey has six letters from PW; two are published here.

TASKER, JOHN: (1933–88), the young director to whom PW entrusted the first productions of *The Ham Funeral*, 1961, *The Season at Sarsaparilla*, 1962, and *Night on Bald Mountain*, 1964. After their final brawl, PW missed few opportunities to vilify 'Tilly'. Tasker's contribution to PW's career went unacknowledged in *Flaws in the Glass*. The National Institute of Dramatic Art in Sydney has fifteen of PW's letters to Tasker; three are published here.

UREN, TOM: (1921–   ), Left-wing Labor MP, minister in the **Whitlam** and Hawke governments. Uren and PW shared a birthday. PW lost faith in Uren when the Hawke government continued to sell Australian yellowcake to the uranium industry of the world. One letter from PW to Uren is published here.

VORSTER, JOHANNES: (1915–83), prime minister and later state president of South Africa from 1966–78, to whom PW wrote protesting the imprisonment of black actors. One letter to Vorster is published here.

WALKER, KERRY: (1948–   ), actress who became an intimate after being cast by Jim Sharman in 1977 to play the lead in *The Night The Prowler*. From that time, each of PW's plays contained a role for Walker. Few letters but many telegrams and greeting cards survive in her hands; five appear here.

WATERS, RONALD (formerly Waterall): (1909–   ), actor and actors' agent. Waters met PW at Cheltenham College in the 1920s and they corresponded for life. The letters to Waters are the most personal and least discreet of PW's correspondences to come to light: the letters are camp, splenetic and often mistyped in drink. Before the war Waters met Freddie Carpenter (1908–89), dancer and heir to an Australian pub fortune who later directed musicals and the drag artist Danny La Rue. In 1974 PW dedicated *The Cockatoos*, 'To Ronald Waters for having survived forty-eight years of friendship'. Waters, a gloomy man, found fresh cause for gloom in the book: 'Everyone died.' He is unable to lay his hands on any of PW's letters before 1960, but has given 56 later letters to the National Library of Australia; 23 are published here.

WHITE, PATRICIA: (1907–   ), cousin and friend whom in later years PW described as the only White he trusted. She worked most of her life for the Royal Sydney Golf Club and was a familiar figure to generations of Eastern Suburbs golfers. A dozen letters from PW to his cousin are in the Mitchell Library; one is published here.

WHITELEY, BRETT: (1939–92), painter whom PW named with **Sidney Nolan** as a genius of Australian painting. PW began buying the work and corresponding with the painter after Whiteley's 1972 Sydney exhibition but by the end of that decade PW had become wary of the man partly from seeing his face so often in the social pages of the Sydney press, partly from suspecting Whiteley was pressing work on him to raise cash to buy heroin. PW detonated their tentative friendship in 1981. Whiteley's family has seven letters from PW; four are published here.

WHITLAM, GOUGH: (1916–   ), politician and prime minister from 1972 until his dismissal in 1975. PW was at first wary of Whitlam, became a passionate supporter, addressed rallies on behalf of the man and his party, spoke of his 'alliance' with the prime minister yet challenged him on a number of issues. Letters to Whitlam were written protesting concessions to Japanese publishers, export of wheat to Egypt after the 1973 Arab-Israel war and Labor's support for sandmining on Fraser Island. Despite this the sacking of Whitlam by the Governor-General was the decisive political event of PW's life: he became a radical republican and his anger at the conservatives never left him. Whitlam has kept only a few letters from PW, one is published here.

WILLIAMS, ALAN: (1925–   ), editorial director at Viking Press. Williams supervised North American publication of PW's work from *The Eye of the Storm* to *Flaws in the Glass* but their correspondence was as much about opera – then a mutual passion – as writing and publishing. PW's letters to Williams remain in the Viking files; six are published here.

WILLIAMS, MARGERY: (1906–88), literary hostess in Sydney and other British Council postings on the globe. In her time, Williams was foremost of the women Lascaris called, 'Patrick's lady disciples'. Politics eventually wrecked her friendship with PW who accepted Williams' enthusiasm for the war in Vietnam but argued with her bitterly over Gough Whitlam. Their happy correspondence that began in 1960 simply stops in 1973. Thirty-three of PW's letters to Williams remain in family hands; six are published here.

WITHYCOMBE, BETTY: (1902–93), cousin and early mentor. She had the most immediate impact when PW met his three Withycombe cousins in 1928, though he was wary from the start of the strong possessive streak in her character. Withycombe's *Dictionary of Christian Names* published in 1945 by Oxford University Press remained a standard reference for 40 years. To her PW dedicated *The Aunt's Story*, 1948. Distaste for PW's sexuality sparked the 1959 row that ended their intimacy and there was little contact between them until 1976 when PW asked to see some of his early letters. She returned them all – about 400 neatly packed waiting to be deposited in the Bodleian Library – and he burnt them. He never told her this. From 1976, they corresponded occasionally and cordially for another ten years. Seven letters from this time and two early survivors are in the National Library of Australia; three are published here.

WRAN, NEVILLE: (1926–   ), barrister and politician, Labor premier of NSW

1976–86, and his wife, the literary agent Jill Hickson, were for a time close to PW. The two men spoke on the same platforms. But PW broke with Wran over uranium mining and so bitter was the breach that he took to haranguing Wran in the streets during peace marches. Published here is one public letter addressed to Wran as president of the Labor Party.

YORKE, RITCHIE: (1944–   ), rock historian, and his then wife Annette (1948–   ) had a brief correspondence as a fan of PW's in the late 1970s. He has two letters from PW; one is published here.

Index